Tests

Tests

A Comprehensive Reference for Assessments in Psychology, Education, and Business

Fifth Edition

Edited by

Taddy Maddox

pro·ed
An International Publisher

8700 Shoal Creek Boulevard
Austin, Texas 78757-6897
800/897-3202   Fax 800/397-7633
www.proedinc.com

© 1983, 1984, 1986, 1991, 1997, 2003 by PRO-ED, Inc.
8700 Shoal Creek Boulevard
Austin, Texas 78757-6897
800/897-3202   Fax 800/397-7633
www.proedinc.com

Library of Congress Cataloging-in-Publication Data

Tests : a comprehensive reference for assessment in psychology, education, and business / [edited by] Taddy Maddox. — 5th ed.
   p. cm.
   Includes bibliographical references and indexes.
   ISBN 0-89079-908-3 — ISBN 0-89079-897-4 (case bound)
   1. Psychological tests.   2. Educational tests and measurements.
3. Occupational aptitude tests.   I. Maddox, Taddy.

BF176 .T43   2003
150'.28'7—dc21

2002069865

This book is designed in Lucida Sans.

Printed in the United States of America

1   2   3   4   5   6   7   8   9   10   06   05   04   03   02

Contents

Preface

As this fifth edition of *Tests* is published, it is appropriate to comment on the project's development and background and to recognize the contributions of people who made the task possible. Richard C. Sweetland and Daniel J. Keyser prepared *Tests: First Edition* in response to the need for a resource containing consistent codified information describing and cataloging tests available for use by psychologists, educators, and human resources personnel. The professional community received *Tests,* published in 1983, enthusiastically. Within one year of publication, the first edition was in its third printing, indicating to the editors that thousands of professionals had come to rely on its quick-scanning, easy-to-read format. Committed to providing readers with the most current information possible on assessment instruments, Sweetland and Keyser launched a "search and find" effort that resulted in the 1984 publication of *Tests: Supplement,* a complement to the first edition that contained information on more than 500 new tests. The supplement was followed by *Tests: Second Edition* in 1986.

Sweetland and Keyser's ongoing search and find efforts, which uncovered information on hundreds of new tests; rapid developments in areas such as substance abuse, eating disorders, and chronic illness; the increasing role of technology in assessment; and Sweetland and Keyser's continued firm commitment to providing users with quick access to current test information resulted in the third edition, published in 1991. In the fourth edition, PRO-ED continued this commitment to providing a reference that can be used by professionals in the fields of psychology, education, and business to obtain information about testing instruments.

In this fifth edition, I have attempted to improve the usability of the reference guide. I have added Web site addresses for those publishers who have active Web sites, as well as a new subsection in the Psychology Instruments to identify those test instruments that measure a pathology (e.g., depression, anxiety). Tests and publishers (69) that were in the fourth edition but are not included in the fifth are again listed in indexes.

I thank the readers for the numerous suggestions they have offered, particularly for providing the names of assessment instruments not referenced in the previous edition. Special thanks are extended to the many test publishers and authors who generously and graciously contributed their staff time, information, and support for this book. Particular recognition must be given to Gwenda Zabor for her tireless entering of the data necessary to prepare this text.

How To Use This Book

Tests, a reference guide containing information on thousands of assessment instruments, is designed especially for psychologists, educators, and human resources personnel who search for tests to satisfy their assessment needs. In addition, students, librarians, and other nonspecialists who need to familiarize themselves with the broad range of available tests will find the contents and format helpful. *Tests* does not attempt to review or evaluate tests; its purpose is to present concise descriptions in a quick-scanning, easy-to-read format. This fifth edition, which presents the tests of 219 publishers, updates the information contained in the fourth edition and presents descriptions of new and revised tests.

How *Tests* Is Organized

The assessments described herein are organized according to a system of primary classification intended to make information as accessible to the reader as possible. Each of the book's three main sections—Psychology, Education, and Business—is divided into subsections. Psychology contains 21 subsections; Education, 49 subsections; and Business, 20 subsections. Each test has been given a primary classification in one of the Psychology, Education, or Business subsections and is described in detail in that subsection. The tests within each subsection are listed alphabetically by title.

To establish subsections that would be practical and functional for the reader, the editor sought considerable consultation from professionals who use tests on a daily basis. Based on feedback from these sources, the editor reorganized the subsections in this fifth edition both to facilitate the reader's search for assessments and to reflect contemporary terminology.

Format and Content of Descriptions

The format and content of each test entry are designed to provide the basic information necessary to decide whether a particular test is appropriate to consider for a given assessment need. Each test entry is structured as follows: test title and author(s), copyright date, population for which the test is intended, a purpose statement, a brief description highlighting the test's major features, format information, scoring method, relevant cost and availability information, and primary publisher. Each of these components is explained in greater detail.

The **title** of each test is presented exactly as it appears in the test publisher's materials, but without any articles (e.g., *the, a, an*). For example, one would find the description of The Wonderlic Personnel Test listed as Wonderlic Personnel Test. Readers who are familiar with a test's common or popular name rather than its published title may find the Index of Authors helpful in finding the test.

The test **author** names appear below the test title. Corporate authors are not listed; only specific individuals are.

The **copyright date** is the next entry. This date reflects the date the instrument or its revision was published.

A description of the intended consumers of the test is listed in the **population** entry. For children, the target age or grade of the examinee may be provided.

The **purpose** statement offers a succinct overview of the test's intended application and what it purports to measure, assess, diagnose, evaluate, or identify.

The **description** presents the number of test items, test format (paper–pencil, true-false, projective, oral, observational, etc.), factors or variables measured, materials used, manner in which the test is administered, foreign language availability, and special features.

The **format** section describes how the test is administered (individual, group, or both), estimated time of administration, and whether the instrument is timed (when the information has been provided by the publisher).

The **scoring** description provides information about the method used to score the test: hand key, examiner evaluated, machine scored, or computer scored. Hand key indicates that the test is scored using an answer key or template provided by the test publisher. An examiner-evaluated test is scored using an examiner's opinion, skills, and knowledge. A computer- or machine-scored test uses answer sheets that are scored by machine or computer. When a combination of these terms appears in the scoring section, the first listed is the primary method employed.

The **cost** section contains price information that is as accurate as the editor could establish at the time of the book's publication. Because the pricing structure for some tests (covering the various forms, kits, options, etc.) is extensive, only representative costs are included here. The editor encourages readers to contact the publisher for complete cost information.

The **publisher** lines identify the test's primary publisher. The Index of Publishers contains complete address, telephone, fax, and Web site information. The editor attempted to confirm the accuracy of every test entry through direct correspondence with the test publisher. Despite repeated contact attempts, however, some publishers did not respond to queries. Those publishers who did not respond are listed in the Index of Publishers Not in the Fifth Edition.

Indexes

Tests: Fifth Edition contains five indexes. The indexes were compiled to make this reference book user friendly. The following listing does not list the Indexes in the order in which they appear at the end of this book. The Index of Test Titles is used most frequently by many users, so that index is the last (and most accessible) in the book. The others have also been rearranged based on anticipated use.

The **Index of Test Titles** lists each test described in this book. As explained previously, the title of each test is presented exactly as it appears in the test publisher's materials, but without any articles (e.g., *the, a, an*) to allow for true alphabetical listing. British spelling has been retained in proper titles.

The **Index of Authors** lists all test authors except corporate and institutional staffs. This listing is in alphabetical order and includes all authors of each instrument, not only the first author.

The **Index of Publishers** provides addresses, telephone numbers, fax numbers, and Web site addresses for publishers whose tests are listed in this book.

The **Index of Tests Not in the Fifth Edition** lists those instruments that were in the fourth edition but are not included in this fifth edition. There are a variety of reasons for the exclusion of an instrument, including lack of response from the publisher, the publisher's going out of business, or the test's going out of print.

The **Index of Publishers Not in the Fifth Edition** lists those publishers who had tests listed in the fourth edition but not in this edition. For example, this listing includes those publishers who did not reply to the initial request for information and those publishers for whom current address and phone information is available but who did not return information on their instruments.

The purpose of *Tests* from the outset has been to provide a quick reference for tests available in the English language. When the first edition of this volume was published, the editors decided to omit detailed reliability, validity, and normative data—aspects considered too complex to reduce to the quick-scanning desk-reference format. The current editor has continued to leave out this information.

Use of the Book

The system of classification used in *Tests* and the inclusion of the indexes just described accommodate readers who need information about a particular test, as well as those conducting a general search for appropriate assessment instruments. The following suggestions for using *Tests* are intended to minimize the reader's efforts to locate information.

- Readers who are unable to locate a test using the Index of Test Titles should consult the Index of Authors or the Index of Publishers if either of these elements is known.

- Tests that cannot be located in the previously mentioned sections may be found in the Index of Tests Not in the Fifth Edition. Be aware that these instruments may not be out of print, but the editor was unable to determine current information about availability, price, or revisions.

PRO-ED fully supports the ethical and professional standards established by national and state professional organizations. The inclusion of specific restrictions on test accessibility noted in some descriptions in this book usually has been requested by the publisher or author; the fact that a test description does not list restrictions does not imply that such restrictions do not exist. When ordering tests, ask each publisher for the standards or requirements for purchasing.

Order forms, catalogs, and further information regarding tests may be obtained from each publisher. Anyone interested in ordering a specific test should contact the publisher, which can be facilitated by using the Index of Publishers, which provides mailing addresses, telephone and fax numbers, and Web site addresses.

Although the information in this book was obtained from primary sources, the editor is aware of possibilities for error. Each test entry has been researched, screened, written, edited, and read by professional test administrators; however, the editor emphasizes that the job of checking and ensuring the accuracy of a book such as this is a process that will continue throughout the publication of subsequent editions. The editor welcomes on an ongoing basis the submission of information about new tests and encourages test publishers and authors to apprise the PRO-ED staff of errors in the test descriptions or of test revisions made available since publication of this edition.

Psychology Instruments

The tests presented and described in the Psychology Instruments section have been selected on the basis of their appropriate usage in a clinical or counseling setting. In general, tests found in this section might be used by a mental health professional, rather than by an educator or human resources specialist. The classification of tests on the basis of typical usage or function is, of course, arbitrary, and the reader is encouraged to review the Education and Business sections for additional assessment instruments.

Attention Deficit

ACTeRS Self-Report

1998	MetriTech, Inc.

Population: Ages 12 years and up

Purpose: Diagnoses attention-deficit/hyperactivity disorder

Description: Total of 35 items in three categories: Attention (10), Hyperactivity/Impulsivity (15), and Social Adjustment (10). Scores for all three categories.

Format: Examiner required; can be administered to groups or individually; untimed: 10 to 15 minutes

Scoring: Hand key; examiner evaluated

Cost: Examiner Kit (50 rating/profile forms, manual) $51.00

ACTeRS Parent Form
Rina K. Ullmann, Esther K. Sleator, Robert L. Sprague

1996	MetriTech, Inc.

Population: Grades PreK to 12

Purpose: Aids in diagnosis of attention-deficit disorder with or without hyperactivity; used as a screening device to differentiate between children with ADD and those who may have other learning disabilities; useful for monitoring medication levels

Description: Paper–pencil or computer-administered 25-item multiple-choice test assessing behavior relevant to attention-deficit disorder. Pro-

vides separate scores for five factors: Attention, Hyperactivity, Social Skills, Oppositional Behavior, and Early Childhood. The computer version for IBM PC and compatible systems supports both the ACTeRS: Parent Form and the ADD-H: Comprehensive Teacher's Rating Scale (ACTeRS).

Format: Examiner required; individual administration; untimed: 10 minutes

Scoring: Computer scoring available; hand key; examiner evaluated

Cost: Examiner Kit (50 rating/profile forms, manual) $47.00

ADD-H Comprehensive Teacher's Rating Scale (ACTeRS)
Rina K. Ullmann, Esther K. Sleator, Robert L. Sprague

1987	MetriTech, Inc.

Population: Grades K through 8

Purpose: Aids in diagnosis of attention-deficit disorder with or without hyperactivity; used as a screening device to differentiate between children with ADD and those who may have other learning disabilities; useful in monitoring ADD medication levels

Description: Paper–pencil or computer-administered 24-item multiple-choice test assessing behavior relevant to the diagnosis of attention-deficit disorder. Provides separate scores for four factors: Attention, Hyperactivity, Social Skills, and Oppositional Behavior. The classroom teacher rates items on a 5-point scale ranging from *almost never* to *almost always*. An ACTeRS Profile (Boys' and Girls' forms) is generated. The computer version for IBM PC and compatible systems supports both the teacher's form and the ACTeRS: Parent Form. APA purchase restrictions apply.

Format: Examiner required; individual administration; untimed: 10 minutes

Scoring: Computer scoring available; hand key; examiner evaluated

Cost: Examiner Kit (50 rating/profile forms, manual) $42.00

ADHD Rating Scale-IV

George J. DuPaul, Thomas J. Power, Arthur D. Anastopoulos, Robert Reid

1998   Guilford Publications, Inc.

Population: Ages 5 to 17 years

Purpose: Used for diagnosing ADHD and assessing treatment response

Description: The test contains 18 items and is linked to DSM-IV diagnostic criteria. There are three versions of the scale: parent questionnaires on home behaviors, one in English and one in Spanish, and a teacher questionnaire on classroom behaviors. Permission to reproduce the scale is provided. Scoring profiles are provided for boys and girls.

Format: Rating scale; untimed

Scoring: Examiner evaluated

Cost: $36.00

ADHD School Observation Code (ADHD-SOC)

Kenneth D. Gadow, Joyce Sprafkin, Edith E. Nolan

1996   Checkmate Plus, Ltd.

Population: Grades K through 6

Purpose: Assesses behavioral symptoms of ADHD, oppositional defiant disorder, and conduct problems; used in treatment planning and for monitoring response to intervention

Description: Five classroom behavior categories and five lunchroom/playground behavior categories: Interference, Motor Movement, Noncompliance (in classroom and in lunchroom), Nonphysical Aggression, Offtask, Appropriate Social Behavior, Physical Aggression, and Verbal Aggression. Measures percentage of (15-second) intervals during which behavior occurs. Classroom code sheet, and lunchroom/playground code sheet.

Format: Examiner required; individual or group administration; untimed

Scoring: Examiner evaluated

Cost: Complete Kit $25.00

ADHD Symptom Checklist-4 (ADHD-SC4)

Kenneth D. Gadow, Joyce Sprafkin

1997   Checkmate Plus, Ltd.

Population: Ages 3 to 18 years

Purpose: Screens for attention-deficit and obsessive-compulsive disorders and monitors response to treatment

Description: Total of 50 items in four categories: ADHD (18), Oppositional Defiant Disorder (8), Peer Conflict Scale (10), and Stimulant Side Effects Checklist (14). Symptom count scores (DSM-IV criteria) and symptom severity scores (norms-based) are provided. Same form for parent and teacher.

Format: Rating scale; untimed: 5 minutes

Scoring: Examiner evaluated

Cost: Deluxe Kit (manual, 50 each of checklists and profiles) $52.00

Adult Attention Deficit Disorders Evaluation Scale (A-ADDES)

Stephen B. McCarney, Paul D. Anderson

1996   Hawthorne Educational Services, Inc.

Population: Ages 18 to 65+ years

Purpose: Aids in the diagnosis of ADHD

Description: Self-Report Version: 58 items (31 inattentive and 27 hyperactive-impulsive); Home Version: 46 items (24 inattentive and 22 hyperactive-impulsive); Work Version: 54 items (28 inattentive and 26 hyperactive-impulsive). Individual raw scores are converted to subscale standard scores, and then subscale standard scores are converted to percentile scores. Self-Report rating form is completed by the patient; Home Version rating form is completed by a spouse, parent, roommate, or someone who knows the person well; Work Version rating form is completed by a coworker or supervisor.

Format: Rating scale; untimed: 20 minutes

Scoring: Examiner evaluated

Cost: Complete Kit (all three versions) $158.00

Attention Deficit Disorders Evaluation Scale–Second Edition (ADDES–2)

Stephen B. McCarney

1995   Hawthorne Educational Services, Inc.

Population: Grades K through 12

Purpose: Aids in the diagnosis of ADHD

Description: The scale includes two subscales: Inattention and Hyperactivity/Impulsivity. The results provided by the scale are commensurate with criteria used by educational, psychiatric, and pediatric personnel to identify attention-deficit/hyperactivity disorder in children and youth. The scale comes in both a School Version (completed by an educator) and a Home Version (completed by the parent or guardian). Available in Spanish. A Windows Quick Score is available.

Format: Rating scale; untimed: 20 minutes

Scoring: Examiner evaluated; computer scoring available

Cost: Complete Kit $220.00

Attention Deficit Disorders Evaluation Scale: Secondary-Age Student (ADDES–S)

Stephen B. McCarney

1996   Hawthorne Educational Services, Inc.

Population: Ages 11.5 through 18 years

Purpose: Aids in the diagnosis of ADHD

Description: School Version: 60 items in two subscales: Inattentive and Hyperactive–Impulsive. Home Version: 46 items in two subscales: Inattentive and Hyperactive–Impulsive. Individual raw scores are converted to subscale standard scores, and then subscale standard scores are converted to percentile scores. The School form is completed by an educator; the Home Form is completed by a parent or guardian. A Windows Quick Score is available.

Format: Rating scale; untimed: 20 minutes

Scoring: Examiner evaluated; computer scoring available

Cost: Complete Kit $171.00

Attention-Deficit/Hyperactivity Disorder Test (ADHDT)

James E. Gilliam

1995   PRO-ED, Inc.

Population: Ages 3 through 23 years

Purpose: Identification and evaluation of attention-deficit disorders

Description: Multiple-item checklist that is completed by teachers, parents, or others who are knowledgeable about a referred individual. Based on the diagnostic criteria for attention-deficit/hyperactivity disorder of the DSM-IV, the instrument contains 36 items that describe characteristic behaviors of persons with ADHD. These items comprise three subtests representing the core symptoms necessary for the diagnosis of ADHD: hyperactivity, impulsivity, and inattention. Results are reported in standard scores and percentiles that are interpreted related to degree of severity and probability for males and females.

Format: Rating scale; untimed: 10 minutes

Scoring: Examiner evaluated

Cost: Complete Kit (manual, 50 protocols, storage box) $86.00

Auditory Continuous Performance Test (ACPT)

Robert W. Keith

1994   The Psychological Corporation

Population: Ages 6 through 11 years

Purpose: Screens for auditory attention deficits

Description: Pass-fail criterion scores for each age help the examiner identify whether a child's performance matches that of children identified as having ADD or ADHD. The child listens to single words and raises his or her thumb when hearing the targeted word.

Format: Examiner required; individual administration; untimed: 10 minutes

Scoring: Examiner evaluated

Cost: Complete Kit (manual, cassette, 12 record forms) $105.00

Behavioural Inattention Test (BIT)

Barbara A. Wilson, Janet Cockburn, Peter Halligan

1987   Thames Valley Test Company, Ltd.

Population: Adults

Purpose: Measures unilateral visual neglect

Description: The BIT is an objective behavioral test of everyday skills relevant to visual neglect, aimed at increasing our understanding of specific difficulties patients experience. There are two parallel versions with six conventional subtests and nine behavioral subtests.

Format: Examiner required; individual administration; untimed: 25 minutes

Scoring: Examiner evaluated

Cost: $272.00

Brief Test of Attention (BTA)
David Schretlen

1997	Psychological Assessment Resources, Inc.

Population: Ages 17 to 84 years

Purpose: Assesses severity of attentional impairment in hearing individuals without aphasia

Description: Two parallel forms, Numbers and Letters, presented via audiocassette. Respondent must count the numbers or letters read aloud and disregard the other.

Format: Examiner required; individual administration; untimed: 10 minutes

Scoring: Hand key

Cost: $58.00

Brown Attention-Deficit Disorder Scales
Thomas A. Brown

1996	The Psychological Corporation

Population: Ages 12 years through adult

Purpose: Evaluates cognitive and affective indications of ADD in adolescents and adults

Description: Self-report instrument that enables screening of ADD by examining a wide variety of factors believed to be associated with ADD. An adolescent form (for ages 12 to 18) and an adult form are available. Ready Score form gives an immediate summary score indicating overall impairment. Diagnostic Form includes guidelines and worksheets for conducting a clinical interview, scoring summary, multirater evaluation form, analysis of IQ subtest data relevant to ADD, screener for comorbid disorders, and overall diagnostic summary form.

Format: Examiner required; individual administration; untimed: 20 to 40 minutes

Scoring: Examiner evaluated

Cost: Starter Kit (manual, treatment monitoring worksheet, answer documents) $94.50

Children's Attention and Adjustment Survey (CAAS)
Nadine Lambert, Carolyn Hartsough, Jonathan Sandoval

1990	American Guidance Service

Population: Ages 5 to 13 years

Purpose: Evaluates behaviors related to hyperactivity and attention deficit in children

Description: A survey that identifies behavior problems associated with ADD and ADHD. Four scales are provided to enable more precise intervention planning: Inattentiveness, Impulsivity, Hyperactivity, and Conduct Problems/Aggressiveness. Because children's behavior often varies with their environment, CAAS uses an interactive systems model. The survey assesses behaviors observed both at home and at school through two 31-item forms: the Home Form (completed by the parent or primary caregiver) and the School Form (completed by the teacher or other school professional). Behaviors are classified according to criteria determined by DSM.

Format: Survey format; 5 to 10 minutes

Scoring: Examiner evaluated

Cost: Starter Set (manual, Home and School Forms, and Scoring Profile) $119.95

Conners' Adult ADHD Diagnostic Interview for DSM–IV (CAADID)
Jeff Epstein, Diane Johnson, C. Keith Conners

2001	Multi-Health Systems, Inc.

Population: Adults

Purpose: Aids the process of diagnosing adult ADHD

Description: Empirically based structured interview in two parts that are administered separately. Part I, Patient History, is a self-report questionnaire or may be administered as a clinical interview. It contains questions about the client's demographic history, developmental course of attention problems, and associated risk factors and comorbidity screen. Part II, Diagnostic Criteria Interview, assesses the client against DSM–IV criteria for ADHD, including age of onset, pervasiveness, and level of impairment.

Format: Examiner required; individual administration; untimed: 90 minutes each part

Scoring: QuikScore™ forms

Cost: Complete Kit (manual, 10 of each part) $85.00

Conners' Adult ADHD Rating Scales (CAARS)
C. Keith Conners, Drew Erhardt, Elizabeth Sparrow

1998	Multi-Health Systems, Inc.

Population: Ages 18 years and older

Purpose: Assists in the diagnosis of attention deficit disorder in adults

Description: A set of comprehensive instruments for use as an extensive part of a multimodal assessment of symptoms and behaviors associated with ADHD in adults. The CAARS elicits self-report and observer ratings. Both self-report and observer forms are available in long (66 items), short (26 items), and screening (30 items) versions. A 4-point Likert format is used and is written at a sixth-grade reading level. The long and short versions contain factor-derived subscales, symptom subscales, and an ADHD Index. Also available in Spanish, French, Portuguese, Hebrew, German, and more languages.

Format: Self-administered; untimed: 10 to 15 minutes

Scoring: QuikScore™ forms; may be computer scored

Cost: Varies per form and method of scoring

Conners' Continuous Performance Test for Windows: Kiddie Version (K–CPT)
C. Keith Conners

| 2001 | Multi-Health Systems, Inc. |

Population: Ages 4 to 5 years

Purpose: Identification of attention problems and monitoring of treatment effectiveness

Description: Assesses response and inhibition to stimuli (objects) that appear on a computer screen. The test measures response times and errors. The instrument yields raw scores, *T*-scores, percentiles, confidence index, and timing verification in single- and multi-administration reports.

Format: Computer self-administered; timed: $7\frac{1}{2}$ minutes

Scoring: Computer scored

Cost: $200.00 (unlimited use)

Conners' Continuous Performance Test II (CPT II)
C. Keith Conners

| 2000 | Multi-Health Systems, Inc. |

Population: Ages 6 years and older

Purpose: Identification of attention problems and monitoring of treatment effectiveness

Description: Computer-administered test requiring subject responses and inhibition to stimuli (letters) that appear on a computer screen. The test measures error rates, reaction time, and variability of reaction time. Statistics measure aspects of attention. Six blocks with three subblocks, each containing 20 trials. Compared with the CPT, the CPT II program contains larger normative samples, new ADHD clinical data and data on neurologically impaired adults, better psychometric properties, newly designed reports, an easier to use interface, a more comprehensive software manual, and timing verification to confirm the validity of the administration.

Format: Self-administered; timed: $14\frac{1}{2}$ minutes

Scoring: Computer scored

Cost: $495.00 (unlimited use)

Conners' Rating Scales–Revised (CRS–R)
C. Keith Conners

| 1997 | Multi-Health Systems, Inc. |

Population: Ages 3 to 17 years

Purpose: Assesses psychopathology and problem behavior

Description: This revision adds a number of enhancements to a set of measures that have long been the standard instruments for the measurement of ADHD in children and adolescents. The language has been updated with items that are simpler and clearer. Items have also been added that match the DSM-IV. The CRS-R evaluates problem behaviors as reported by the teacher or parents (or alternative caregivers). Norms are based on more than 11,000 ratings. Separate norms available for boys and girls. Available in a short or long version, as a self-report for ages 12 to 17 years, and in other languages (French and Spanish).

Format: Self-administered; untimed: 15 minutes (long), 5 minutes (short)

Scoring: QuikScore™ forms; may be computer scored

Cost: Contact publisher

Conners–Wells' Adolescent Self-Report Scale (CASS)
C. Keith Conners, Karen Wells

| 1997 | Multi-Health Systems, Inc. |

Population: Ages 12 to 17 years

Purpose: Measures psychopathology and problem behavior

Description: Paper–pencil or computer-administered instrument used to evaluate problem behaviors. The short 27-item version includes the following subscales: Conduct Problems, Cognitive Problems/Inattention, Hyperactivity, and ADHD Index. The 87-item long version includes the following subscales: Family Problems, Emotional Problems, Conduct Problems, Cognitive Problems/Inattention, Anger Control Problems, Hyperactivity, DSM–IV Symptom Subscales, and ADHD Index.

Format: Self-administered; untimed: 5 to 10 minutes (short), 10 to 15 minutes (long)

Scoring: QuikScore™ forms; may be computer scored

Cost: Contact publisher

Early Childhood Attention Deficit Disorders Evaluation Scale (ECADDES)
Stephen B. McCarney

1995	Hawthorne Educational Services, Inc.

Population: Ages 24 to 83 months for females; Ages 24 to 78 months for males

Purpose: Aids in the diagnosis of ADHD

Description: The School Version of the scale includes 56 items easily observed and documented by educational personnel. The Home Version includes 50 items representing behavior exhibited in and around the home environment and is completed by the parent or guardian. Available in Spanish. A DOS Quick Score is available.

Format: Rating scale; untimed: 20 minutes

Scoring: Examiner evaluated; computer scoring available

Cost: Complete Kit $154.00

Gordon Diagnostic System (GDS)
Michael Gordon

1984	Gordon Systems, Inc.

Population: Ages 4 years to geriatric

Purpose: The assessment of attention and impulse control used in evaluation of ADHD, and illnesses and injuries associated with attentional problems

Description: The device has three subtests: Delay, Vigilance, and Distractibility. Measures ability to control impulses with immediate feedback and ability to attend with or without distractions. Attention is measured with both visual and auditory stimuli. This is a self-contained microprocessor unit; no software is required. The device weighs 9 pounds and is portable.

Format: Examiner required; individual administration; timed: total 30 minutes

Scoring: Machine scored

Cost: $1,595.00; introductory rental trial available

Integrated Visual & Auditory Continuous Performance Test
Joseph A. Sandford, Ann Turner

2001	Brain Train

Population: Ages 6 years through adult

Purpose: Assesses problems in visual and auditory attention and response control, and small motor hyperactivity; diagnostic tool for ADHD, ADD, and mild brain injury

Description: Measures in seven stages: Enter Data, Visual RT Subtest, Auditory RT Subtest, Practice Period, Main Test Task, Visual Cool-Down, and Auditory Cool-Down. Test has 500 stimuli. Norms are gender based, although the test form is the same for both genders. Visual and Auditory scales are provided for each category: Full Scale Response Control, Full Scale Attention, and Fine Motor Regulation. Level B qualifications for examiner. Computer requires Pentium 166 or higher, Windows 98 or higher. Stimuli are available in Spanish, Japanese, Hebrew, Russian, Mandarin, and German. May be used with persons with mental impairment.

Format: Examiner required; individual computer administration; untimed: 20 minutes

Scoring: Computer scored

Cost: Ranges from $295.00 to $1,495.00

Scales for Diagnosing Attention Deficit/Hyperactivity Disorder (SCALES)
Gail Ryser, Kathleen McConnell

2002	PRO-ED, Inc.

Population: Ages 5 through 18 years

Purpose: Identifies and evaluates attention-deficit/hyperactivity disorder

Description: The SCALES has two separate forms: one for the home environment and one for the school setting. In-depth information is gathered from both parents and teachers rather than behavioral data from isolated clinical examinations. The instrument was standardized using more than 3,000 children and is designed with two sets of norms: persons not identified with or suspected of having ADHD and individuals already diagnosed with ADHD. The SCALES employs a 4-point Likert scale to measure the extent to which the child's behavior interferes with his or her functioning.

Format: Rating scale; untimed: 15 to 20 minutes

Scoring: Examiner evaluated

Cost: Complete Kit (manual, 25 each of school and home forms, storage box) $84.00

Spadafore ADHD Rating Scale
Gerald J. Spadafore, Sharon J. Spadafore

1997　Academic Therapy Publications

Population: Ages 6 through 18 years

Purpose: Indicates both presence and severity of ADHD symptoms

Description: A 50-item questionnaire assesses three behavioral clusters in the classroom setting: impulsivity/hyperactivity, attention, and social adjustment. A separate Likert-type scale is used to quantify the behavioral observations and to derive an overall ADHD Index. Observations and ratings are completed by the classroom teacher. Age- and gender-based norms are provided. Appropriate intervention strategies are included in the manual. Raw scores are converted to percentiles and severity levels.

Format: Observation and rating scale; untimed: 20 minutes

Scoring: Examiner evaluated

Cost: Test Kit (manual, test plates, 25 scoring protocols, 25 observational tracking forms, 25 medication tracking forms, in vinyl folder) $80.00

Test of Everyday Attention (TEA)
Ian H. Robertson, Tony Ward,
Valerie Ridgeway, Ian Nimmo-Smith

1994　Thames Valley Test Company, Ltd.

Population: Adults

Purpose: Measures selective, sustained, and switching attention

Description: The TEA gives a broad-based measure of the most important clinical and theoretical aspects of attention. It can be used analytically to identify different patterns of attentional breakdown with a wide range of applications, ranging from patients with Alzheimer's disease to young normal individuals. There are eight subtests: Map Search, Elevator Counting, Elevator Counting with Distraction, Visual Elevator, Auditory Elevator with Reversal, Telephone Search, Telephone Search Dual Task, and Lottery.

Format: Examiner required; individual administration; untimed: 35 minutes

Scoring: Examiner evaluated

Cost: $314.00

Test of Everyday Attention for Children (TEA-Ch)
Tom Manly, Ian H. Robertson,
Vicki Anderson, Ian Nimmo-Smith

1998　Thames Valley Test Company, Ltd.

Population: Ages 6 to 16 years

Purpose: Measures abilities to selectively attend, sustain attention, divide attention between two tasks, switch attention from one to another, and inhibit verbal and motor responses

Description: Using attractive graphics and sound, the subtests are designed to be appealing. The nine subtests are Sky Search; Score; Sky Search DT; Creature Counting; Map Mission; Score DT; Opposite Worlds; Walk, Don't Walk; and Code Transmission. The subtests have been designed to be as conceptually simple as possible so children with a wide range of abilities may be tested. The test package is light and portable and can be easily used in many different settings. Two parallel forms of the test are provided that allow for confidence in retesting of the same child.

Format: Examiner required; individual or group administration; untimed: 35 minutes

Scoring: Examiner evaluated

Cost: $428.00

Test of Variables of Attention (TOVA®)

2000　Universal Attention Disorders, Inc.

Population: All ages

Purpose: Used for diagnosing and monitoring treatment of children and adults with attention disorders

Description: The TOVA is a computerized continuous performance test for use with IBM compatibles and Macintosh computers. Highly reliable, cost-effective, and easy-to-administer tests provide relevant screening and diagnostic information about attention and impulsivity that is not otherwise available. Both tests (visual and auditory) have non-language-based stimuli that discriminate ADD from learning disabilities and minimize cultural differences. The visual test has two simple geometric stimuli, and the auditory test has two simple audible tones. The TOVA tests are deliberately long, simple, and boring to effectively test attentional variables. Each TOVA kit includes software, hardware, manuals, and five administrations.

Format: Computer administered; untimed

Scoring: Immediate computer-generated interpretations

Cost: Contact publisher

Vigil Continuous Performance Test

1996	The Psychological Corporation

Population: Ages 6 through 90 years

Purpose: Explores attention, concentration, sustained attention, and complex sequential stimulus tracking

Description: A computer-administered and scored measure with each test consisting of several modules, including the on-screen presentation of verbal and nonverbal targets. The built-in database manager allows examination of previous test results or presentation of a test with previously defined display characteristics. Because specific test combinations are prepackaged, clinicians and researchers can modify over 52 parameters or construct their own test combinations.

Format: Computer administered; untimed: 8 minutes

Scoring: Computer scored

Cost: Complete Kit (Windows® disks and binder) $515.00

Family

Ackerman–Schoendorf Scales for Parent Evaluation of Custody (ASPECT)

Marc J. Ackerman, Kathleen Schoendorf

1992	Western Psychological Services

Population: Adults

Purpose: Used to evaluate parent effectiveness in child custody evaluations

Description: ASPECT offers a practical, standardized, and defensible approach to child custody evaluations. It draws information from a variety of sources, reducing the likelihood of examiner bias. It yields three scale scores: Observational (a measure of the parent's appearance and presentation), Social (a measure of the parent's interaction with others, including the child), and Cognitive-Emotional (a measure of the parent's psychological and mental functioning). Research has shown 90% agreement between ASPECT recommendations and custody decisions made by judges. It has also proven effective in identifying those parents who will need supervision during child visitations. The clinician must answer 56 yes–no questions, based on information drawn from the parent questionnaire, interviews with and observations of each parent with and without the child, and test data.

Format: Examiner required; individual administration; untimed

Scoring: Examiner evaluated; hand key; scoring service available

Cost: Kit (includes 20 parent questionnaires, 10 AutoScore™ answer forms, 5 AutoScore Forms, manual, manual supplement, 2 test report prepaid mail-in answer sheets for computer scoring and interpretation) $120.00

American Home Scale

W. A. Kerr, H. H. Remmers

1982	Psychometric Affiliates

Population: Grades 8 and above

Purpose: Evaluates the cultural, aesthetic, and economic factors of an individual's home environment; used for counseling students and other individuals who may be experiencing problems due to their home environment

Description: Multiple-item paper–pencil inventory assessing an individual's home environment. Construction of the test is based on profile and factor analyses. The test discriminates between sociological areas. The norms are based on over 16,000 eighth-grade students in over 42 American cities.

Format: Examiner required; suitable for group use; timed: 40 minutes

Scoring: Examiner evaluated

Cost: Specimen Set $4.00; 25 Surveys $5.00

Assessment of Parenting Skills: Infant and Preschooler (APSIP)
Barry Bricklin, Gail Elliot

Date not provided	Village Publishing

Population: Parents

Purpose: Evaluates a parent's genuine interest in a child

Description: Assesses the mother's or father's knowledge of the details of the child's development, routines, special needs, fears, health history, school history, and personal hygiene. A special section of 26 items is used to compare one parent with the other or to assess one parent alone with respect to parental attunement to the child, strengths in parenting skills, and weaknesses in parenting skills.

Format: Examiner required; individual administration; untimed: 30 to 35 minutes

Scoring: Hand key

Cost: Kit (manual, 8 booklets, 8 summaries, updates) $169.00

Borromean Family Index: For Married Persons
Panos D. Bardis

1988	Donna Bardis

Population: Adolescents, adults

Purpose: Measures a married person's attitudes and feelings toward his or her immediate family; used for clinical assessment, family and marriage counseling, family attitude research, and discussions in family education

Description: Paper–pencil assessment in which the subject rates nine statements about "forces that attract you to your family" on a scale from 0 (*absent*) to 4 (*very strong*) and nine statements about "forces that pull you away from your family" on a scale from 0 (*does not pull you away at all*) to 4 (*very strong*). Suitable for individuals with physical and hearing disabilities.

Format: Examiner/self-administered; suitable for group use; untimed: 10 minutes

Scoring: Examiner evaluated

Cost: $1.00

Borromean Family Index: For Single Persons
Panos D. Bardis

1988	Donna Bardis

Population: Adolescents, adults

Purpose: Measures an individual's attitudes and feelings toward his or her family; used for clinical assessment, family counseling, family attitude research, and discussions in family education

Description: Paper–pencil test in which the subject rates nine statements about "forces that attract you to your family" from 0 (*absent*) to 4 (*very strong*) and nine statements about "forces that pull you away from your family" from 0 (*does not pull you away at all*) to 4 (*very strong*). Suitable for use with individuals with physical and hearing disabilities.

Format: Examiner/self-administered; suitable for group use; untimed: 10 minutes

Scoring: Examiner evaluated

Cost: $1.00

Bricklin Perceptual Scales (BPS)
Barry Bricklin

1984	Village Publishing

Population: Children

Purpose: Measures the child's perception of parents

Description: The BPS has been used successfully with children as young as 4, but was designed primarily for children who are at least 6 years old. Perception is measured in four major areas: Competence, Follow-up Consistency, Supportiveness, and Possession of Admirable Personality Traits. The BPS is made up of 64 cards.

Format: Examiner required; individual administration; untimed: 30 to 35 minutes

Scoring: Hand key; computer scoring available

Cost: Kit (manual, 8 sets of cards, 8 scoring summaries, stylus pen, placement dots, test box with foam insert, updates) $199.00

Checklist for Child Abuse Evaluation (CCAE)
Joseph Petty

1990	Psychological Assessment Resources, Inc.

Population: Children, adolescents

Purpose: Used for investigating and evaluating subjects who may have been abused or neglected

Description: Multiple-choice evaluation with 264 items in the following categories: Sexual Abuse, Physical Abuse, Neglect, Child's Psychological Status, Credibility/Competence of Child, and

Conclusions of Six Categories. Treatment recommendations are yielded. A manual and checklist are used. Examiner must be trained in the evaluation of child abuse.

Format: Examiner required; individual administration; untimed

Scoring: Hand key

Cost: Introductory Kit $112.00

Child Sexual Behavior Inventory (CSBI)
William N. Friedrich

| 1997 | Psychological Assessment Resources, Inc. |

Population: Ages 2 to 12 years

Purpose: Evaluates children who have been or may have been sexually abused

Description: Total of 38 items in nine major content domains are completed by mothers or primary female caregivers. Items are written on a fifth-grade reading level. Scores are reported in *T*-scores by gender and age.

Format: Self-administered; untimed: 10 minutes

Scoring: Examiner evaluated

Cost: $120.00

Clinical Rating Scale (CRS)
David H. Olson

| 1993 | Life Innovations, Inc. |

Population: All ages, families and couples

Purpose: Assesses communication, cohesion, and flexibility within couples and families; used in clinical work and research

Description: Includes 21 interview questions: 13 assessing cohesion and 8 assessing flexibility. Yields scores on cohesion, flexibility, communication, and family type. One form for therapist. Paper–pencil format.

Format: Ratings completed through interviews or observing the couple and family

Scoring: Examiner evaluated

Cost: $20.00

Coping and Stress Profile
David H. Olson

| 1995 | Life Innovations, Inc. |

Population: Adults (individuals, couples, and families)

Purpose: Assesses coping, stress, resources, and satisfaction

Description: Paper–pencil assessment with a total of 311 items to aide in counseling individuals, couples, and families. The items represent four categories: personal profile (97 items), work profile (74 items), couple profile (70 items), and family profile (70 items). Responses are given to a 5-point Likert scale. Scores are given for stress, problem solving, communication closeness, flexibility, and satisfaction.

Format: Self-administered; untimed

Scoring: Self-scored

Cost: $16.00

Cultural Diversity Test–Second Edition
Thomas J. Rundquist

| 1997 | Nova Media, Inc. |

Population: Adults

Purpose: Measures cultural diversity and social prejudices; used for training, affirmative action, and fair housing practices

Description: The Attributional Styles Questionnaire has 37 items; the Attitudes toward Diversity Scale has 24 items; the Discriminatory Response Questionnaire has 24 items; and the Racial Attitude Test has 74 items.

Format: Examiner required; can be administered in groups or individually; untimed

Scoring: Computer scored; also scoring service available from another company

Cost: Master Reproducible Booklet $29.95; NCS Answer Sheets $.15 each

Custody Evaluation Questionnaire Kit
Barry Bricklin, Gail Elliot

| Date not provided | Village Publishing |

Population: Children and parents

Purpose: Helps to gather information for custody evaluation

Description: Six questionnaires are available: Child Access to Parental Strength, Parent Self-Report Data, Child Data, "Would," Child Self-Report Data, and Child Sexual Abuse. The questionnaires are completed by the child or the parent. The manual describes how to integrate the questionnaires into the framework of the comprehensive custody evaluation.

Format: Examiner required; individual administration; untimed

Scoring: Hand key

Cost: Kit (manual, 8 of each questionnaire) $169.00

Discipline Index (DI)
Anita K. Lampel, Barry Bricklin, Gail Elliot

Date not provided   Village Publishing

Population: Children

Purpose: Obtains information from a child about overall perceptions of each parent's discipline style and practices

Description: Nonverbal responses spare the child both loyalty conflicts and the need to verbalize directly negative statements about either parent. This makes the instrument suitable for use in cases covering an exceptionally broad range of issues. The DI has 64 questions, 32 each about the mother and the father. The child has available a continuum of response choices because he or she responds by punching a hole somewhere along a horizontal black line anchored on the right end by the words *very often* (or *very well*) and on the left end by *not so often* (or *not so well*). The DI yields answers about parental disciplinary practices in six categories: clear expectations, effectively monitors, consistent enforcement, fairness, attunement, and moderates anger.

Format: Examiner required; individual administration; untimed: 35 minutes

Scoring: Hand key; examiner evaluated; computer scoring available

Cost: Kit (handbook, 8 sets of cards, 8 scoring summaries, stylus pen, placement dots, test box with foam insert, 3 years update service) $199.00

ENRICH-Enriching Relationship Issues, Communication and Happiness
David H. Olson, David G. Fournier, Joan M. Druckman

1996   Life Innovations, Inc.

Population: Adults, married couples and couples cohabiting 2 or more years

Purpose: Used in marital counseling and marriage enrichment

Description: Total of 195 items in 20 categories: Idealistic Distortion (7), Marriage Satisfaction (10), Personality Issues (10), Communication (10), Conflict Resolution (10), Financial Management (10), Leisure Activities (10), Sexual Expectations (10), Children & Parenting (10), Family & Friends (10), Role Relationship (10), Spiritual Beliefs (10), Couple Closeness (10), Couple Flexibility (10), Family Closeness (10), Family Flexibility (10), Self Confidence (8), Assertiveness (8), Avoidance (8), and Partner Dominance (8). Revised Individual Scores, Couple Type, Personality Assessment Idealistic Distortion Scores, and Positive Couple Agreement Scores. Test is available in Spanish. A separate version is available for married couples over 50.

Format: Self-administered; untimed

Scoring: Computer scored; test scoring service available

Cost: $30.00 for scoring; $125.00 for training

FACES II-Family Adaptability & Cohesion Evaluation Scales
David H. Olson, Richard Bell, Joyce Portner

1991   Life Innovations, Inc.

Population: Ages 12 years and up

Purpose: Used in research and family counseling to assess family adaptability and cohesion

Description: Paper-pencil Likert scale with 30 items on two scales: cohesion (16 items) and flexibility (14 items). Couple and family versions are used. Yields Cohesion score, Adaptability score, and Family type. FACES II is available in Spanish, Chinese, Dutch, German, Japanese, Korean, and Tongan.

Format: Self-administered; untimed

Scoring: Hand key

Cost: $30.00

FACES III-Family Adaptability & Cohesion Evaluation Scales
David H. Olson, Joyce Portner, Yoav Larce

1985   Life Innovations, Inc.

Population: Ages 12 years and up

Purpose: Measures family adaptability and cohesion

Description: Paper-pencil Likert scale with 20 items on two scales: cohesion (10 items), and adaptability (10 items). Uses include clinical work with couples and families. Family and couple versions are used. Yields Cohesion score, Adaptability score, and Family type. FACES III is available in other languages: Afrikaans, Chinese, French, Greek, Indonesian, Japanese, Korean, Norwegian, Portuguese, and Spanish.

Format: Self-administered; untimed

Scoring: Hand key

Cost: $30.00

Familism Scale
Panos D. Bardis

1988 Donna Bardis

Population: Adolescents, adults

Purpose: Assesses individual attitudes toward both nuclear and extended families; used for clinical evaluation, marriage and family counseling, research on the family, and discussion in family life education

Description: Paper-pencil test in which the subject reads 10 statements about nuclear family relationships and 6 statements about extended family relationships and rates them according to his or her personal beliefs on a scale from 0 (*strongly disagree*) to 4 (*strongly agree*). The Familism score equals the sum of the 16 numerical responses. The theoretical range of scores extends from 0 (*least familistic*) to 64 (*most familistic*). Separate scores may be obtained for nuclear family integration and extended family integration. Suitable for use with individuals with physical and hearing disabilities.

Format: Examiner/self-administered; suitable for group use; untimed: 10 minutes

Scoring: Examiner evaluated

Cost: $1.00

Familism Scale: Extended Family Integration
Panos D. Bardis

1988 Donna Bardis

Population: Adolescents, adults

Purpose: Measures attitudes toward the extended family (beyond the nuclear family, but within the kinship group); used for clinical assessment, marriage and family counseling, family attitude research, and discussions in family education

Description: Paper-pencil test in which the subject reads six statements concerning extended family relationships and rates them according to personal beliefs on a scale from 0 (*strongly disagree*) to 4 (*strongly agree*). The Familism score is the sum of the six numerical responses. The theoretical range of scores extends from 0 (*least familistic*) to 24 (*most familistic*). Suitable for use with individuals with physical and hearing disabilities.

Format: Examiner/self-administered; suitable for group use; untimed: 5 minutes

Scoring: Examiner evaluated; untimed: 5 minutes

Cost: $1.00

Familism Scale: Nuclear Family Integration
Panos D. Bardis

1988 Donna Bardis

Population: Adolescents, adults

Purpose: Measures attitudes toward the solidarity of the nuclear family; used for clinical assessment, marriage and family counseling, family attitude research, and discussion in family education

Description: Paper-pencil test in which the subject rates 10 statements about family relationships from 0 (*strongly disagree*) to 4 (*strongly agree*). The Familism score equals the sum of the 10 numerical responses. The theoretical range of scores extends from 0 (*least familistic*) to 40 (*most familistic*). Suitable for use with individuals with physical and hearing disabilities.

Format: Self-administered; untimed: 5 minutes

Scoring: Hand key

Cost: $1.00

Family Adjustment Test (Elias Family Opinion Survey)
Gabriel Elias, H. H. Remmers

1972 Psychometric Affiliates

Population: Adolescents, adults

Purpose: Measures intrafamily homeyness-homelessness (acceptance-rejection) while appearing to be concerned only with attitudes toward general community life; used for clinical evaluations and research

Description: Paper-pencil or oral-response projective test measuring adult and adolescent feelings of family acceptance. The test yields 10 subscores: attitudes toward mother, attitudes toward father, relatives preferences, oedipal, independence struggle, parent-child friction, interparental friction, family status feeling, child rejection, and parental quality. Subtest scores and clinical indicators of a number of adjustment trends, as well as an overall index of feelings of intrafamily homeyness-homelessness, are provided. Percentile norms are provided by gender for the following age groups: ages 12 to 13, 14 to 15, 16 to 18, and 19 and older. Interpretation is provided in terms of subtest profiles. Norms for specific parent-child relationships are provided also. No third party should be present if the test is administered orally.

Format: Examiner required; suitable for group use; timed: 45 minutes

Scoring: Hand key; scoring service available

Cost: Specimen Set (test, manual, key) $5.00; 25 Tests $8.50

Family Apperception Test
Alexander Julian III, Wayne M. Sotile, Susan E. Henry, Mary O. Sotile

1988	Western Psychological Services

Population: All ages

Purpose: Used by therapists to generate family systems hypotheses from the assessment of a single family member

Description: The instrument includes 21 stimulus cards that depict common family activities, constellations, and situations. These are shown to the client, one at a time, and responses are recorded. Following instructions provided in the manual, the examiner can score the test for Obvious Conflict, Conflict Resolution, Limit Setting, Quality of Relationships, Boundaries, Dysfunctional Circularity, Abuse, Unusual Responses, Refusals, and Emotional Tone. A Total Dysfunction Index can also be computed. The manual presents interpretive guidelines and evidence of the scoring system's reliability and validity.

Format: Examiner required; individual administration; untimed: 30 minutes

Scoring: Examiner evaluated

Cost: Kit (stimulus cards, 100 scoring sheets, manual) $125.00

Family Assessment Measure (FAM III)
Harvey A. Skinner, Paul D. Steinhauer, Jack Santa-Barbara

1992	Multi-Health Systems, Inc.

Population: Ages 10 years and older

Purpose: Assesses family functioning; used in family counseling

Description: Paper-pencil test with General, Dyadic, and Self-Report Scales. Categories include task accomplishment, communication, involvement, values and norms, role performance, affective expression, control, social desirability, and defensiveness control. Scores are yielded for each subscale and a total score. These scores can be converted to standard scores and plotted on a color-coded profile sheet. A fifth-grade reading level is required. The brief form consists of the same three categories, with 14 items each for screening and monitoring over time.

Format: Self-administered; untimed: 20 minutes per form

Scoring: QuikScore™ forms; may be computer scored

Cost: Kit (manual, 25 forms for each category, 15 profile forms) $135.00

Family Environment Scale (FES)
Rudolf H. Moos, Bernice S. Moos

Date not provided	Consulting Psychologists Press, Inc.

Population: Adolescents, adults

Purpose: Assesses characteristics of family environments; used for family therapy

Description: Paper-pencil 90-item test measuring 10 dimensions of family environments: cohesion, expressiveness, conflict, independence, achievement orientation, intellectual-cultural orientation, active-recreational orientation, moral-religious emphasis, organization, and control. These dimensions are further grouped into three categories: relationship, personal growth, and system maintenance. Materials include the Real Form (Form R), which measures perceptions of current family environments; the Ideal Form (Form I), which measures conceptions of ideal family environments; and the Expectancies Form (Form E), which measures expectations about family settings. The revised manual has been extensively updated and expanded with new normative data.

Format: Examiner required; suitable for group use; untimed

Scoring: Examiner evaluated

Cost: Self-Scorable Preview Kit (booklet, answer sheet, report form, manual) $56.80

Family Relationship Inventory (FRI)
Ruth B. Michaelson, Harry L. Bascom

1982	Psychological Publications, Inc.

Population: Ages 5 years to adult

Purpose: Evaluates family relationships along positive and negative lines; used as an aid in individual child-adult counseling, family therapy, youth groups, high school instruction, and marriage and family enrichment programs

Description: Paper-pencil test with 50 items measuring self-esteem, positive or negative perception of self and significant others, most and least esteemed family members, and closest and most distant relationships within the family. One numbered item is printed on each of 50 cards. Items 1 through 25 have positive valence, and Items 26 through 50 have negative valence. The subject lists "self" and "family members" across the top of a tabulating form and assigns each item to self, significant other, or the wastebasket column and tallies the data on scoring forms with the help of a counselor.

Format: Examiner required; suitable for group use; untimed: 30 to 45 minutes

Scoring: Examiner evaluated

Cost: Complete Kit (manual, 50 reusable item cards, 50 tabulating forms, 25 scoring forms, 50 individual relationship sheets, 25 Familygrams) $99.00

Family Satisfaction Scale
David H. Olson, Marc Wilson

1982	Life Innovations, Inc.

Population: Ages 12 years and up

Purpose: Measures level of satisfaction within families

Description: A paper–pencil instrument with a total of 14 items on two scales: family cohesion (8 items) and family adaptability (6 items). Items are rated on a 5-point Likert scale. The instrument, which is used in family counseling and research of families to determine levels of cohesion and adaptability, yields a total score, cohesion score, and adaptability score. One form is available for all family members.

Format: Self-administered; untimed

Scoring: Hand key

Cost: $30.00

Family Story Pictures
Morten Nissen

1984	Dansk psykologisk Forlag

Population: Ages 4 to 12 years

Purpose: Assesses a child's perception of and reaction to parents' divorce

Description: Thirteen-picture verbal test used in divorce counseling to assess the child's cognitive understanding, perception of the future, expectations of the future, and perception of the possibilities of influencing his or her own situation. Examiner must be a qualified psychologist. Also available in Danish.

Format: Examiner required; individual administration; untimed

Scoring: Examiner evaluated

Cost: $53.00

Family System Test (FAST)
Thomas M. Gehring

Date not provided	Hogrefe & Huber Publishers

Population: Ages 6 years and older

Purpose: Measures family structures to plan and evaluate preventive and therapeutic interventions

Description: The FAST is a figural technique that can be used quantitatively or qualitatively. It is based on the structural-systemic theory of families that provides for analysis of family structure, diagnosis of biopsychosocial problems, and planning and evaluation of preventive and therapeutic intervention. Test materials include a board and various schematic figures. The test is language independent and highly effective. Depending on the issue, the standard test procedure can be modified to include different phases of current conflicts as well as past and anticipated events.

Format: Examiner required; individual and group administration; untimed: 5 to 10 minutes for individuals, 10 to 30 minutes for groups

Scoring: Examiner evaluated

Cost: Complete Test (manual, 20 recording blanks, materials) $298.00

Family Violence Scale
Panos D. Bardis

1988	Donna Bardis

Population: Adolescents, adults

Purpose: Measures the degree of verbal and physical violence in an individual's family during childhood; used for clinical assessment, marriage and family counseling, research on attitudes toward family and violence, and classroom discussion

Description: Paper–pencil test in which the subject rates 25 statements about family violence on a scale from 0 (*never*) to 4 (*very often*). The Family Violence score equals the sum of the 25 numerical responses. The theoretical range of scores extends from 0 (*least violent*) to 100 (*most violent*). Suitable for use with individuals with physical and hearing disabilities.

Format: Self-administered; untimed: 10 minutes

Scoring: Examiner evaluated

Cost: $1.00

Grandparent Strengths and Needs Inventory (GSNI)
Robert D. Strom, Shirley K. Strom

1993	Scholastic Testing Service, Inc.

Population: Adults

Purpose: Identifies favorable qualities of grandparents

Description: Multiple-choice test with 60 items in six subscales: satisfaction, success, teaching, difficulty, frustration, and information needs. Scores yielded are *always* (4), *often* (3), *seldom* (2), and *never* (1). Three versions—grandparent, parent, and grandchild—are available. Booklets, profiles, and a pencil are used.

Format: Examiner required; individual/self-administered; suitable for group use; untimed

Scoring: Hand key

Cost: Specimen Set $22.05

Hilson Parent/Guardian Inventory (HPGI)
Robin E. Inwald

1992	Hilson Research, Inc.

Population: Ages 18 years and up

Purpose: Assesses custody determinations of parent or guardian of children

Description: A total of 156 items is administered to parents or guardians of children to determine custody, treatment, and child assessment. Test measures Parent Self-Worth, Family Patterns, and Coping Patterns.

Format: Examiner required; individual administration; untimed: 20 minutes

Scoring: Computer scored; scoring service available

Cost: Contact publisher

Home Screening Questionnaire (HSQ)
C. Cooms, E. Gay, A. Vandal,
C. Ker, William K. Frankenburg

1981	Denver Developmental Materials, Inc.

Population: Birth to 6 years

Purpose: Evaluates the quality of a child's home environment; used to indicate need for further evaluation

Description: Paper–pencil questionnaire filled out by the parents and scored by an examiner. Suspect results must be followed by an evaluation of the home by a trained professional to see if intervention is needed. A 30-item blue form is available for children up to age 3, and a 34-item white form is available for ages 3 through 6. Both forms have toy checklists. The questionnaires are written at third- and fourth-grade reading levels.

Format: Self-administered; untimed: 15 to 20 minutes

Scoring: Hand key

Cost: Manual $15.00; 25 Test Forms $15.00

Infant–Toddler and Family Instrument (ITFI)
Sally Provence, Nancy H. Apfel

2001	Paul H. Brookes Publishing Co.

Population: Ages 6 months to 3 years

Purpose: Measures family function and child development

Description: The caregiver/parent interview has 36 questions concerned with home and family life; child characteristics, daily activities, and health, growth, and development; family supports, issues, and concerns. The developmental map has 72 items in four categories: gross and fine motor development, social and emotional development, language development, and coping and self-help development. The checklist for evaluating concern has 38 items about home and family environment and child health, development and safety, and stressors. The ITFI may be used for persons with visual, physical, hearing, and mental impairments.

Format: Examiner required; individual interview; untimed

Scoring: Examiner evaluated

Cost: Manual and 15 Forms $45.00

Life Interpersonal History Enquiry (LIPHE)
Will Schutz

1989	Mind Garden, Inc.

Population: Adults

Purpose: Evaluates an individual's retrospective account of relationship to parents before age 6; used for counseling and therapy

Description: Paper–pencil report of an individual's early relationship with parents in areas of inclusion, control, and affection at both the behavioral and the feeling levels. Separate scores are obtained for the father, the mother, and the respondent's perception of the relationship between the parents.

Format: Examiner/self-administered; suitable for group use; untimed

Scoring: Hand key

Cost: Sampler Set $25.00; Permission for 200 Uses $125.00

Marital Communication Inventory
Millard J. Bienvenu

| 1969 | Northwest Publications |

Population: Ages 17 and above

Purpose: Assesses the level of communication of couples; used in marriage counseling, enrichment, research, and teaching

Description: The inventory has 46 items and requires a seventh-grade reading level. Examiner must have experience in couple counseling. Forms are available for female and male respondents.

Format: Self-administered; suitable for group use; untimed

Scoring: Hand key

Cost: Forms F and M $1.50; Guide $2.00 (Minimum order of $10.00)

Marital Satisfaction Inventory–Revised (MSI-R)
Douglas K. Snyder

| 1997 | Western Psychological Services |

Population: Adults

Purpose: Identifies the nature and extent of marital distress; used in marital and family counseling

Description: Multiple-item paper–pencil or computer-administered true–false test providing information concerning nine basic measured dimensions of marriage: affective communication, problem-solving communication, time together, disagreement about finances, sexual dissatisfaction, role orientation, family history of distress, dissatisfaction with children, and conflict over child rearing. In addition, a validity scale and a global distress scale measure each spouse's overall dissatisfaction with the marriage. The test is available in two forms: a 280-item version for couples with children and a 239-item version for childless couples. The results for both spouses are recorded on the same profile form, graphically identifying the areas of marital distress. Each spouse's scores can be individually evaluated as well as directly compared, thereby facilitating diagnostic and intervention procedures. Group mean profiles for each gender are provided for couples seeking general marital therapy.

Format: Examiner required; individual administration; untimed: 30 to 40 minutes

Scoring: Hand key; may be computer scored

Cost: Kit (20 AutoScore™ answer forms, manual, two-use disk, and 2 PC answer sheets) $99.50

Maryland Parent Attitude Survey (MPAS)
Donald K. Pumroy

| Date not provided | Donald K. Pumroy |

Population: Adults

Purpose: Assesses parents' attitudes toward the way they rear their children; particularly useful as a research instrument

Description: Paper–pencil 95-item test in which the parent chooses one of each pair of A or B forced-choice statements that best represent his or her attitudes toward child rearing: indulgent, disciplinarian, protective, and rejecting. The survey indicates child-rearing type or approach. Materials consist of a cover letter, a copy of the research articles, and scoring keys.

Format: Self-administered; untimed: 45 minutes

Scoring: Hand key

Cost: Complete Set $5.00

Michigan Screening Profile of Parenting (MSPP)
Ray E. Helfer, James K. Hoffmeister, Carol J. Schneider

| 1978 | Test Analysis and Development Corporation |

Population: Adults

Purpose: Evaluates an individual's perceptions in areas that are critically important for positive parent–child interactions; profiles segments of the individual's early childhood experiences and current relationships

Description: Multiple-item paper–pencil self-report questionnaire for parents and prospective parents. The questionnaire consists of four sections. Section A provides information about family characteristics, the respondent's health history, and relationships with employers, social agencies, and spouse. Section B provides information regarding the respondent's perceptions of childhood experiences and current interactions with family and friends. Section C (answered only by individuals having one or more children) provides information about the respondent's child (or children) and current parent–child interactions. Section D (answered only by individuals who do not have children) provides information with regard to the respondent's expectations for future interactions with prospective children. Section A requires various types of answers depending on the type of biographical information being requested. Sections, C, and D use 7-point

Likert scales to rate responses to individual test items.

Format: Self-administered; suitable for group use; untimed

Scoring: Computer scored

Cost: 25 Questionnaires (including scoring service) $50.00

Parent–Adolescent Communication Inventory
Millard J. Bienvenu

1969   Northwest Publications

Population: Ages 13 years and older

Purpose: Assesses communication in parent-adolescent relationships; used in family counseling, family life education, teaching, and research

Description: Forty-item yes–no–sometimes test. A seventh-grade reading level is required. Examiner must have family counseling experience.

Format: Self-administered; untimed: 15 minutes

Scoring: Hand key

Cost: $.50 per copy; Guide $1.00 (minimum order $10.00)

Parent–Adolescent Communication Scale
Howard Barnes, David H. Olson

1982   Life Innovations, Inc.

Population: Ages 12 years and older

Purpose: Used in family counseling, for parents and adolescents

Description: Paper–pencil test to aide in communication of families. Twenty 5-point Likert items on two scales: Open Family Communication (10 items) and Problems in Family Communication (10 items). Yields Open Family Communication score and Problems in Family Communication score, and totals three forms available: Adolescent and Mother form, Adolescent and Father form, and Parent form.

Format: Self-administered; untimed

Scoring: Hand key

Cost: $30.00

Parent as a Teacher Inventory (PAAT)
Robert D. Strom

1995   Scholastic Testing Service, Inc.

Population: Adults

Purpose: Assesses parents' attitudes toward their parent–child relationship; used with parents of children ages 3 to 9

Description: Multiple-choice inventory measuring parental attitudes in the following areas: feelings toward the parent–child interactive system, standards for assessing the importance of certain aspects of child behavior, and value preferences and frustrations concerning child behavior. Available in Spanish.

Format: Self-administered; untimed: 30 minutes

Scoring: Hand key

Cost: Starter Set (inventory manual, 20 inventory booklets/identification questionnaires, 20 profiles) $30.00

Parent Awareness Skills Survey (PASS)
Barry Bricklin

1990   Village Publishing

Population: Parents

Purpose: Reflects the sensitivity and effectiveness with which a parent responds to typical child care situations

Description: PASS targets skills that reflect a parent's awareness of what makes a given child unique, thus following the principle that the meaning of parental behavior is best understood in terms of a child's ability to be positively influenced by it. The scores pinpoint parental awareness of the critical issues in a given situation; adequate solutions; the need to communicate in terms understandable to a child; the desirablility of acknowledging a child's feelings; the importance of the child's own past history in the present circumstances; and the need to pay attention to how the child is responding in order to fine-tune one's own response. A completed PASS-BOOK provides a permanent record of each PASS that is administered.

Format: Examiner required; individual administration; untimed

Scoring: Hand key

Cost: Kit (manual, 8 PASS-BOOKS, 8 scoring summaries, answer pen, updates) $199.00

Parent–Child Relationship Inventory (PCRI)
Anthony B. Gerard

1994   Western Psychological Services

Population: Parents of 3- to 15-year-old children

Purpose: Used to evaluate parenting skills and

attitudes, child custody arrangements, family interaction, and physical or sexual abuse of children

Description: Self-report inventory with 78 items covering seven scales: parental support, involvement, limit setting, role orientation, satisfaction with parenting, communication, and autonomy. Includes two validity scales and separate norms for mothers and fathers.

Format: Self-administered; untimed: 15 minutes

Scoring: Examiner evaluated; computer scored

Cost: Kit (25 AutoScore™ answer sheets, manual, two-use disk, 2 PC answer sheets) $95.00

Parent Perception of Child Profile (PPCP)
Barry Bricklin, Gail Elliot

1991	Village Publishing

Population: Parents

Purpose: Elicits an extensive portrait of a parent's knowledge and understanding of a specific child

Description: Responses are gathered from the parent in a wide variety of important life areas to assess the degree to which a parent's perceptions are accurate, compare to other sources, and reflect genuine interest in a child. The PPCP also assesses the irritability potential of a parent.

Format: Examiner required; individual administration; untimed: less than 1 hour

Scoring: Hand key

Cost: Kit (manual, 8 Q-books, 8 recall worksheets, 8 summary sheets, pens, updates) $169.00

Parent Success Indicator (PSI)
Robert D. Strom, Shirley K. Strom

1998	Scholastic Testing Service, Inc.

Population: Ages 10 to 14 years and their parents

Purpose: Provides parents with self-reports of their perceptions of their children

Description: Family counseling applications. Total of 61 items, yielding PSI profile. Materials used: PSI manual, parent inventory booklets, child inventory booklets, and PSI profiles. Scales are available in Spanish. Enables parents to make better decisions about self-improvement.

Format: Self-administered; untimed: 15 to 20 minutes

Scoring: Self-scored

Cost: Starter Kit $71.40

Parental Acceptance–Rejection Questionnaire (PARQ)
Ronald P. Rohner

2000	Rohner Research

Population: Children to adults

Purpose: Assesses perceived parental acceptance and rejection

Description: Paper-pencil questionnaire measuring perceived parental acceptance and rejection in four scales: Warmth/Affection (20 items), Hostility/Aggression (15 items), Indifference/Neglect (15 items), and Undifferentiated Rejection (10 items). The test, designed to cut across social classes and available in 15 languages, can be combined with the formal interview (Parental Acceptance–Rejection Interview Schedule) and behavior observations. It is scored on a 4-point scale (*almost always* to *almost never*), with some items having reversed scoring to reduce response bias. Scores range from 60 (*maximum acceptance, minimum rejection*) to 240 (*maximum rejection, minimum acceptance*). Now 12 versions of instruments, including infant-toddler.

Format: Examiner/self-administered; suitable for group use; untimed

Scoring: Hand key; may be computer scored

Cost: Handbook $15.00

Parenting Alliance Measure (PAM)
Richard R. Abidin, Timothy R. Konold

1999	Psychological Assessment Resources, Inc.

Population: Adults

Purpose: Measures the strength of the child-rearing alliance between parents

Description: PAM is a 20-item measure. Materials include manual and 50 hand-scorable test forms. Requires third-grade reading level.

Format: Self-administered; untimed: 10 to 15 minutes

Scoring: Self-scored

Cost: $92.00

Parenting Satisfaction Scale (PSS)
John Guidubaldi, Helen K. Cleminshaw

1994	The Psychological Corporation

Population: Parents of elementary children

Purpose: Identifies troubled parent–child relationships

Description: A 45-item standardized assessment of parents' attitudes toward parenting. The instrument defines, compares, and communicates levels of parenting satisfaction in three domains: Satisfaction with the Spouse/Ex-Spouse Parenting Performance, Satisfaction with the Parent-Child Relationship, and Satisfaction with Parenting Performance. PSS can be useful in making child custody decisions and conducting family therapy.

Format: Self-administered; untimed: 30 minutes

Scoring: Examiner evaluated

Cost: Complete Kit (manual, 25 answer documents) $111.00

Parenting Stress Index–Third Edition (PSI)
Richard R. Abidin

| 1995 | Psychological Assessment Resources, Inc. |

Population: Parents of children ages 1 month to 12 years

Purpose: Used in family counseling, stress management, and forensic evaluation to identify parent-child problem areas

Description: Paper-pencil yes–no Likert scale index with four short form scales: Total Stress, Parental Distress, Parent-Child Dysfunctional Interaction, and Difficult Child. Long-form domains and subscales include Total Stress, Child Domain (distractibility/hyperactivity, attachment, reinforcement of parent, depression, mood, acceptability), and Parent Domain (competence, isolation, adaptability, health, role restriction, demandingness, spouse). A computer version using a PC is available.

Format: Examiner required; individual administration; untimed: long 20 to 30 minutes, short 10 minutes

Scoring: Hand key; computer scoring available

Cost: Short Form Kit $122.00; Long Form Kit $85.00

Perception-of-Relationships Test (PORT)
Barry Bricklin

| 1989 | Village Publishing |

Population: Children

Purpose: Measures how close a child feels to each parent

Description: The PORT is made up of seven tasks (mostly drawings) that measure the degree to which a child seems to be psychologically close to each parent, and the strengths and weaknesses developed as a result of interacting with each parent. One spiral-bound booklet contains everything necessary to administer, record, and score the test.

Format: Examiner required; individual administration; untimed: 30 minutes

Scoring: Hand key; computer scoring available

Cost: Kit (handbook, 8 booklets, pen, eraser, updates) $199.00

Physical Punishment Questionnaire (PPQ)
Ronald P. Rohner

| 1995 | Rohner Research |

Population: Grade 3 and above

Purpose: Assesses experiences of children and adults with physical punishment received; used for research on antecedents and consequences of physical punishment

Description: Paper-pencil oral-response test consisting of 59 items on child and adult forms and 29 items on parent form. Measures major variables: frequency, severity, consistency, predictability, incidence, deservedness, timing, and explanation of punishment; 13 specific forms of punishment; four write-in forms of punishment experienced; sum of different forms of punishment experienced from major caretaker; sum of different forms of punishment experienced from major disciplinarian; harshness of punishment received; justness of punishment received. Third-grade reading level is required. Soon available in Spanish, Arabic, and other languages.

Format: Examiner/self-administered; suitable for group use; untimed: 10 to 15 minutes

Scoring: Hand key

Cost: Test and Manual $15.00

Religion Scale
Panos D. Bardis

| 1961 | Donna Bardis |

Population: Adolescents, adults

Purpose: Measures attitudes toward religion; used for clinical assessment, family and marriage counseling, research on attitudes toward religion, and discussion in religion and social science classes

Description: Paper–pencil test in which the subject reads 25 statements about religious issues and rates them according to his or her beliefs on a scale from 0 (*strongly disagree*) to 4 (*strongly agree*). The score is the sum of the 25 numerical responses. The theoretical range of scores extends from 0 (*least religious*) to 100 (*most religious*). Suitable for individuals with physical and hearing disabilities.

Format: Examiner/self-administered; suitable for group use; 10 minutes

Scoring: Examiner evaluated

Cost: $1.00

Stress Index for Parents of Adolescents (SIPA)

Peter L. Sheras, Richard R. Abidin

1998	Psychological Assessment Resources, Inc.

Population: Parents of adolescents ages 11 to 19 years

Purpose: Identify stressful areas in parent-adolescent interactions

Description: The 112-item SIPA is an upward extension of the Parenting Stress Index with four subscales for Adolescent Characteristics and four subscales for Parent Characteristics. A fifth-grade reading level is required. Materials include the SIPA manual, 25 reusable item booklets, and 25 hand-scorable answer sheet/profile forms.

Format: Self-administered; untimed: 20 minutes

Scoring: Hand key

Cost: $95.00

Uniform Child Custody Evaluation System (UCCES)

Harry L. Munsinger, Kevin W. Karlson

1994	Psychological Assessment Resources, Inc.

Population: Individuals involved in child custody litigation

Purpose: Provides a comprehensive and uniform custody evaluation procedure

Description: Paper–pencil short-answer test. Twenty-five forms are organized into three categories: general data and administration forms, parent forms, and child forms. Materials include a manual and 25 different forms used to document and organize data for report writing and court testimony.

Format: Examiner required; individual administration; untimed

Scoring: Examiner evaluated

Cost: Intro Kit $159.00

Geropsychology

Arizona Battery for Communication Disorders of Dementia (ABCD)

Kathryn A. Bayles, Cheryl K. Tomeda

1993	PRO-ED, Inc.

Population: Adults

Purpose: Useful for the comprehensive assessment and screening of communication, memory, mental status, and visuospatial functioning of patients with Alzheimer's and other dementia

Description: Fourteen subtests evaluate functional linguistic expression, functional linguistic comprehension, verbal episodic memory, visuospatial functions, and cognitive status. The test provides raw scores, summary scores for intertask comparisons, construct scores, and an overall score. The Mental Status subtest is an efficient, valid, and reliable measure of cognitive status for all types of patients. Standardized on patients with Alzheimer's and Parkinson's disease and young and older normal individuals. Provides norms for patients with dementia of varying severity.

Format: Examiner required; individual administration; untimed: 45 to 90 minutes

Scoring: Examiner evaluated

Cost: Complete Kit (manual, scoring and interpretation card, 25 response/record forms, screening test, 2 stimulus books, storage box) $259.00

Clock Test
H. Tuokko, T. Hadjistavropoulos,
J. A. Miller, A. Horton, B. L. Beattie

| 1995 | Multi-Health Systems, Inc. |

Population: Ages 65 years and older

Purpose: Screens for dementia; used for neurology and geriatric counseling

Description: Paper-pencil test comprises three subtests: clock drawing (one clock must be drawn), clock setting (five clocks must be set), and clock reading (five times must be read). A score is obtained for each subtest, then the scores are plotted on a profile sheet and the pattern is used to screen for dementia.

Format: Examiner required; individual administration; untimed: 5 to 10 minutes per component

Scoring: QuikScore™ forms

Cost: Kit (manual, administration tent, forms, profile sheets) $165.00

Dementia Rating Scale–Second Edition (DRS-2)
Steven Mattis

| 2001 | Psychological Assessment Resources, Inc. |

Population: Ages 55 to 89+ years

Purpose: Provides a brief, comprehensive measure of cortical status in individuals with cognitive impairment, particularly of the degenerative type

Description: An extension of the original DRS, the DRS-2 can be used to track changes in behavioral, neuropathological, and cognitive status over time. The DRS-2 has improved user-friendliness, demographically corrected normative data for a wider age range, additional validity information, and a comprehensive review of the literature

Format: Examiner required; individual administration; untimed: 15 to 45 minutes

Scoring: Examiner evaluated

Cost: Kit $170.00

Fuld Object-Memory Evaluation
Paula Altman Fuld

| 1977 | Stoelting Company |

Population: Ages 70 to 90 years

Purpose: Measures memory and learning in adults regardless of vision, hearing, or language disabilities; cultural differences; or inattention problems

Description: Ten common objects in a bag are presented to the patient to determine whether he or she can identify them by touch. The patient names the item and then pulls it out of the bag to see if he or she was right. After being distracted, the patient is asked to recall the items from the bag. The patient is given four additional chances to learn and recall the objects. The test provides separate scores for long-term storage, retrieval, consistency of retrieval, and failure to recall items even after being reminded. The test also provides a chance to observe naming ability, left-right orientation, stereognosis, and verbal fluency. Separate norms are provided for total recall, storage, consistency of retrieval, ability to benefit from reminding, and ability to say words in categories.

Format: Examiner required; individual administration; timed: 60 seconds for each first trial, 30 seconds for each second trial

Scoring: Examiner evaluated

Cost: Complete Kit (testing materials, manual, 30 record forms) $75.00

Functional Linguistic Communication Inventory
Kathryn A. Bayles, Cheryl K. Tomeda

| 1994 | PRO-ED, Inc. |

Population: Adults

Purpose: Used for evaluating functional communication in patients with moderate and severe dementia

Description: Helps clinicians to determine status of greeting and naming, question answering, writing, sign comprehension and object-to-picture matching, word reading and comprehension, ability to reminisce, following commands, pantomime, gesture, and conversation. The examiner determines baseline level of function, dementia severity, and preserved functional skills. Comparison can be made of examinee's performance to performance profiles of other patients at different levels of severity. Information provided by test results is crucial for reports, treatment goals and functional management plans, discharge summaries, and counseling caregivers.

Format: Examiner required; individual administration; untimed: 30 minutes

Scoring: Examiner evaluated

Cost: Complete Kit (manual, 25 response/record forms, 25 score forms, stimulus book, objects, storage box) $169.00

Independent Living Scales™ (ILS™)
Patricia Anderten Loeb

1996	The Psychological Corporation

Population: Ages 65+ years

Purpose: Assesses competency in instrumental activities of daily living

Description: Provides a standardized approach for identifying areas of competence in forensic cases and for determining the most appropriate living setting for adults who are experiencing a decline in cognitive functioning. The ILS is composed of five scales: Memory/Orientation, Managing Money, Managing Home and Transportation, Health and Safety, and Social Adjustment. The performance-based results from the 68 items are more objective and reliable than third-party observations or examinees' self-reports. Performance data are also provided on samples of individuals, 17 years of age and older, who have a psychiatric diagnosis, dementia, mental retardation, or traumatic brain injury.

Format: Examiner required; individual administration; untimed: 45 minutes

Scoring: Examiner evaluated

Cost: Complete Kit (manual, 25 record forms, stimulus booklet, manipulatives) $240.00

Multiphasic Environmental Assessment Procedure
Rudolf H. Moos, Sonne Lemke

1996	SAGE Publications, Inc.

Population: Adults

Purpose: Measures the quality of residential facilities for older adults

Description: This comprehensive volume fully describes assessment procedures such as identifying the characteristics of the residents and staff, critiquing the physical and architectural features of a facility, determining residents' and staff members' appraisals of the social climate, and evaluating judgments from external observers. Throughout, the authors provide practical suggestions for administering and scoring all of the instruments and for giving feedback to program managers and staff. Case studies lead the user through patient assessment for a nursing home, a residential care facility, or a congregate apartment.

Format: Rating scale; untimed

Scoring: Examiner evaluated

Cost: $49.95

Older Persons Counseling Needs Survey (OPCNS)
Jane E. Myers

1993	Mind Garden, Inc.

Population: Ages 60 years and above

Purpose: Assesses an elderly person's needs and desires for counseling

Description: Likert-type scale with 56 items measuring personal, social, activity, and environment concerns. A fifth-grade reading level is required.

Format: Examiner required; individual administration; suitable for group use: untimed: 10 to 15 minutes

Scoring: Examiner evaluated

Cost: Sampler Set $25.00; Permission for 200 Uses $125.00

Recent Memory Screening Test (RMST)
Kathryn A. Bayles, Cheryl K. Tomeda

1998	PRO-ED, Inc.

Population: Adults

Purpose: Used for quick and reliable identification of individuals who may have Alzheimer's disease

Description: The RMST is a component of the Arizona Battery for Communication Disorders of Dementia. Examinees must tell a short story immediately after hearing it and again 10 minutes later. Individuals with Alzheimer's disease have severe difficulty recalling the story after this short delay. The story is printed in English, French, and Spanish. An accompanying videotape contains a discussion of the factors that can affect recent memory and how to interpret test performance.

Format: Examiner required; individual administration; untimed: 20 minutes

Scoring: Examiner evaluated

Cost: Complete Kit (manual, 25 scoring forms, videotape, storage box) $39.00

Ross Information Processing Assessment–Geriatric (RIPA–G)
Deborah G. Ross-Swain, Paul Fogle

1996	PRO-ED, Inc.

Population: Ages 55 years and over

Purpose: Assesses cognitive–linguistic deficits

in geriatric patients who are residents in skilled nursing facilities, hospitals, and clinics

Description: Multiple-item paper–pencil instrument that incorporates questions from the Minimum Data Set used by nursing staffs to provide correlational data with nursing staff's assessments of patients' cognitive–linguistic abilities. Enables examiner to quantify deficits, determine severity levels for the skills areas (Immediate Memory, Recent Memory, Temporal Orientation, Spatial Orientation, Orientation to Environment, Recall of General Information, Problem Solving and Abstract Reasoning, Organization of Information, Auditory Processing and Comprehension, and Problem Solving and Concrete Reasoning), and develop rehabilitation goals and objectives.

Format: Examiner required; individual administration; untimed: 45 to 60 minutes

Scoring: Examiner evaluated

Cost: Complete Kit (manual, 25 response forms, 25 profile/summary forms, picture book, storage box) $213.00

Illness

Battery for Health Improvement™ (BHI™)
J. Mark Disorbio, Daniel Bruns

Date not provided	NCS Pearson

Population: Adults

Purpose: Measures factors that would interfere with a patient's normal course of recovery from an injury; used for evaluation of patients in treatment or recovery from an injury

Description: Multiple-choice/oral response 202-item computer or paper–pencil test. Scales measure depression, anxiety, hostility, borderline dependency, failure to succeed, substance abuse, family dysfunction, job dissatisfaction, doctor dissatisfaction, and somatic and pain complaints. A sixth-grade reading level is required.

Format: Self-administered; untimed: 25 to 40 minutes

Scoring: Hand key; computer scored

Cost: Hand Score $1.50; Profile Reports $7.00 to $10.00

Coping with Health Injuries and Problems (CHIP)
Norman S. Endler, James D. A. Parker

2000	Multi-Health Systems, Inc.

Population: Ages 18 years and older

Purpose: Measures ability to cope with a broad range of health problems

Description: A 32-item multidimensional measure that examines four basic coping dimensions for responding to health problems: distraction, palliative, instrumental, and emotional preoccupation coping. Used with patients having chronic pain, sports injuries, cancer, asthma, diabetes, and other health problems, it is administered as a self-report over the course of the specific health problem to help determine the coping strategies used at different times in the development or treatment of the problem.

Format: Self-administered; untimed: 10 to 15 minutes

Scoring: QuikScore™ forms

Cost: Complete Kit (manual, 25 forms) $48.00

Health Attribution Test (HAT)
Jeanne Achterberg, G. Frank Lawlis

1990	Institute for Personality and Ability Testing, Inc.

Population: Adults

Purpose: Measures a patient's attitudes toward health responsibility regarding his or her own health maintenance or treatment program; used in rehabilitation therapy and for chronic illness treatments

Description: Paper–pencil test containing 22 items and three dimensions: Internal scale, Powerful Others scale, and Chance Dimension. A sixth-grade reading level is required.

Format: Self-administered; untimed

Scoring: Hand key

Cost: 25 Tests $30.00; Test User's Guide $15.00

Intelligence

Arlin Test of Formal Reasoning (ATFR)
Patricia Kennedy Arlin

1984	Slosson Educational Publications, Inc.

Population: Grades 6 to 12

Purpose: Assesses students' cognitive abilities; used by teachers to plan curriculum, modify teaching techniques, and identify gifted students

Description: Paper-pencil 32-item multiple-choice test assessing students' cognitive abilities at one of five levels: concrete, high concrete, transitional, low formal, and high formal reasoning in the application of Piaget's developmental theory. The interpretation of both the total test score and the subtest scores is based on Inhelder and Piaget's description of formal operational thought and the eight schemata associated with that thought (multiplicative compensation, probability, correlations, combinational reasoning, proportional reasoning, forms of conservation beyond direct verification, mechanical equilibrium, and coordination of two or more systems or frames of reference). A sixth-grade reading level is required.

Format: Examiner required; individual or group administration; untimed: 45 minutes

Scoring: Hand key; may be computer scored

Cost: Complete Kit (manual, 35 test booklets, 35 answer sheets, template, Teaching for Thinking) $69.00

Beta III
C. E. Kellogg, N. W. Morton

1999	The Psychological Corporation

Population: Ages 16 through 89 years

Purpose: Measures nonverbal intellectual abilities

Description: Beta III is easy to administer and score and is useful for screening large numbers of people for whom administering comprehensive test batteries would be time consuming and costly. It is the latest revision of an instrument with a long and distinguished history. The original version was developed by the U.S. Army during World War I to assess the intellectual ability of illiterate recruits. Four subtests have been retained from Beta II: Coding, Picture Completion, Clerical Checking, and Picture Absurdities. Matrix Reasoning is new to Beta III.

Format: Examiner required; individual or group administration; untimed: 30 minutes

Scoring: Examiner evaluated

Cost: Complete Kit (manual, 25 response booklets, scoring key) $139.00

Canadian Cognitive Abilities Test: Multilevel Edition (CCAT), Levels A–H, Form K
Robert L. Thorndike, Elizabeth P. Hagen

1998	Nelson Thomson Learning

Population: Grades 3 to 12

Purpose: Assesses students' abilities in three parallel batteries: verbal, nonverbal, and quantitative

Description: Series of multiple-choice paper-pencil subtests for three parallel batteries: Verbal, Nonverbal, and Quantitative. Materials include test booklets, examiner's manual, and answer sheets. A consumable booklet for Level A for younger children is also available. It is accompanied by a supplementary manual with a key insert. This test is a Canadian adaptation of the Cognitive Abilities Test published by Riverside Publishing Company. Examiner must have a teaching certificate.

Format: Examiner required; suitable for group use; timed: 90 minutes

Scoring: Test scoring service available from publisher; hand key

Cost: Contact publisher

Canadian Cognitive Abilities Test: Primary Battery (CCAT), Levels 1 & 2, Form K
Robert L. Thorndike, Elizabeth P. Hagen

1998	Nelson Thomson Learning

Population: Grades K.5 to 3

Purpose: Assesses students' verbal, nonverbal, and quantitative abilities

Description: Series of multiple-choice paper-pencil subtests in three areas: Verbal, Nonverbal, and Quantitative. Materials include test booklets, examiner's manual, and a score key for each level tested. Examiner must have a teaching certificate.

Canadian adaptation of Cognitive Abilities Test published by Riverside Publishing Company.

Format: Examiner required; suitable for group use; untimed

Scoring: Hand key

Cost: Contact publisher

CHIPS–Children's Problem Solving

Mogens Hansen, Svend Kreiner, Carsten Rosenberg Hanson

1995	Dansk psykologisk Forlag

Population: Ages 5 to 13 years

Purpose: Assesses the child's actual problem-solving strategies when faced with tasks of different cognitive complexity; used in the teacher's planning of classroom learning (global cognition, analytic/synthetic cognition, comprehensive cognition)

Description: Multiple-choice test requiring global cognition (11 items), analytic/synthetic cognition (14 items), and comprehensive cognition (15 items). Profiles depict the child's development through the stages of cognitive development. One group version and one individual version is used along with a test booklet with four items for the group version and a special test book with one item a page for individual use. Examiner must be a teacher or psychologist. Available in Danish and Slovakian, but not in English.

Format: Examiner required; individual administration; suitable for group use; untimed

Scoring: Hand key

Cost: Specimen Set $27.00

Cognitive (Intelligence) Test: Nonverbal [C(I)T:nv]

Morrison F. Gardner

Date not provided	Psychological and Educational Publications, Inc.

Population: Ages 4 to 15 years

Purpose: Measures nonverbal cognitive processing

Description: Uses discrimination and analogy to measure nonverbal reasoning of children who have poor or impaired linguistic skills. The test measures how well a child thinks, reasons, draws conclusions, deduces, and makes inferences.

Format: Examiner required; individual administration; untimed: 15 to 20 minutes

Scoring: Examiner evaluated

Cost: Complete Kit (manual, 25 record forms, test plates) $59.95

Columbia Mental Maturity Scale (CMMS)

Bessie B. Burgemeister, Lucille Hollander, Blum Irving Lorge

1972	The Psychological Corporation

Population: Ages 3 years 6 months through 10 years

Purpose: Assesses mental ability

Description: Test of general reasoning abilities, with 92 items arranged in a series of eight overlapping levels. The level administered is determined by the child's chronological age. Items are printed on 95 (6 × 9 inch) cards. The child responds by selecting from each series of drawings the one that does not belong. Guide for Administration and Interpretation includes directions in Spanish.

Format: Examiner required; not suitable for group use; untimed: 15 to 20 minutes

Scoring: Examiner evaluated

Cost: Complete Kit (95 item cards, guide for administering and interpreting, 35 record forms) $634.00

Comprehensive Test of Nonverbal Intelligence (CTONI)

Donald D. Hammill, Nils A. Pearson, J. Lee Wiederholt

1996	PRO-ED, Inc.

Population: Ages 6 years 0 months through 90 years 11 months

Purpose: Measures nonverbal reasoning abilities of individuals for whom most other mental ability tests are either inappropriate or biased

Description: Six subtests (Pictorial Analogies, Geometric Analogies, Pictorial Categories, Geometric Categories, Pictorial Sequences, and Geometric Sequences) require students to look at a group of pictures or designs to solve problems. Individuals indicate their answer by pointing to alternative choices. Three composite scores are computed: Nonverbal Intelligence Quotient, Pictorial Nonverbal Intelligence Quotient, and Geometric Nonverbal Intelligence Quotient. No oral responses, reading, writing, or object manipulation are required to take the test. Instructions for administration include pantomime and oral delivery.

Format: Individual administration; computer administration available; untimed: 60 minutes

Scoring: Examiner interpretation

Cost: Complete Kit (manual, picture books, 25 protocols, storage box) $314.00

Culture Fair Intelligence Tests
Raymond B. Cattell, A. Karen Cattell

| 1963 | Institute for Personality and Ability Testing, Inc. |

Population: Ages 4 years and older

Purpose: Measures individual intelligence for a wide range of ages without, as much as possible, the influence of verbal fluency, cultural climate, and educational level; aids in the identification of learning and emotional problems

Description: Nonverbal paper-pencil tests with three scales. Test items require only that the individual be able to perceive relationships in shapes and figures. Scale 1 contains one form with eight subtests. Scales 2 and 3 contain two forms each with four subtests. Scale 1 is designed for ages 4 to 8 years and individuals with developmental delays. Scale 2 is designed for ages 8 to 14 years and adults. Scale 3 is designed for adults.

Format: Examiner required; suitable for group use; timed: 22 minutes for Scale 1, 12½ minutes for Scales 2 and 3

Scoring: Hand key

Cost: Scale 1: Reusable Classification Test Cards $22.00, 25 Test Booklets $25.00, Scoring Keys $8.00, Handbook $6.00; Scales 2 and 3: 25 Reusable Test Booklets $25.00, 50 Answer Sheets $18.00, Scoring Keys $8.00

Das-Naglieri Cognitive Assessment System (CAS)
Jack A. Naglieri, J. P. Das

| 1997 | Riverside Publishing Company |

Population: Ages 5 years 0 months through 17 years 11 months

Purpose: Provides a cognitive processing measure of ability that is fair to minority children, effective for differential diagnosis, and related to intervention

Description: A norm-referenced measure of ability developed according to a well-researched and supported theory known as PASS. The Planning, Attention, Simultaneous, Successive theory is based on cognitive and neuropsychological research. The CAS is used to evaluate children's strengths and weaknesses in important areas of cognitive processing. The Standard Battery is composed of three subtests for each of the four PASS scales. The Basic Battery includes two subtests for each of the four scales.

Format: Examiner required; individual administration; time varies depending on battery administered

Scoring: Examiner evaluated

Cost: Complete Kit (stimulus book, manual, interpretive handbook, 10 record forms, 5 response books for 2 age groups, 10 figure memory response books, scoring templates, red pencil, case) $655.00

Differential Ability Scales™ (DAS™)
Colin D. Elliott

| 1990 | The Psychological Corporation |

Population: Ages 2 years 6 months through 17 years 11 months

Purpose: Measures overall cognitive ability and basic academic skills

Description: The DAS comprises 17 cognitive and 3 achievement subtests. In addition to obtaining a General Conceptual Ability score, cluster scores are obtained in Verbal, Nonverbal, and Spatial. Attractive and colorful manipulative materials enhance the testing experience for preschoolers, and interesting activities keep the attention of older children. The cognitive and achievement measures were developed and normed together so that ability-achievement differences can be interpreted with a single instrument.

Format: Examiner required; individual administration; full cognitive battery: 45 to 65 minutes; achievement tests: 15 to 25 minutes

Scoring: Examiner evaluated; computer scoring available

Cost: Complete Kit (manual, handbook, 10 of each record form, 5 of each school age form, manipulatives, briefcase) $698.00

Draw A Person: A Quantitative Scoring System (Draw A Person: QSS)
Jack A. Naglieri

| 1988 | The Psychological Corporation |

Population: Ages 5 through 17 years

Purpose: Provides a measure of intellectual ability through human figure drawing

Description: Used as part of a comprehensive assessment, as a screening device, or as a supplement to other intelligence tests. Clear scoring guidelines reflect the many possible ways a child can respond.

Format: Examiner required; individual or group administration; untimed: 15 minutes

Scoring: Examiner evaluated

Cost: Complete Kit (manual, scoring chart, 25 each of record forms and response forms) $136.00

General Ability Measure for Adults (GAMA)
Jack A. Naglieri, Achilles N. Bardos

1996	NCS Pearson

Population: Adults

Purpose: Measures intelligence

Description: A total of 65 nonverbal items measure matching, analogies, sequences, and construction.

Format: Self-administered; timed: 25 minutes

Scoring: Self-scored; machine scored; scoring service available

Cost: $260

Goodenough–Harris Drawing Test
Florence L. Goodenough, Dale B. Harris

1963	The Psychological Corporation

Population: Ages 3 to 15 years

Purpose: Assesses mental ability without requiring verbal skills

Description: Measures intelligence through three drawing tasks in three tests: Goodenough Draw-a-Man Test, Draw-a-Woman Test, and the experimental Self-Drawing Scale. The man and woman drawings may be scored for the presence of up to 73 characteristics. Materials include Quality Scale Cards, which are required for the short-scoring method. Separate norms are available for males and females.

Format: Examiner required; suitable for group use; untimed: 10 to 15 minutes

Scoring: Hand key

Cost: Complete Kit (test booklet, manual, quality scale cards) $122.00

Haptic Intelligence Scale
Harriet C. Shurrager, Phil S. Shurrager

1925	Stoelting Company

Population: Adults with visual impairments

Purpose: Measures the intelligence of adults who are blind or visually impaired; used as a substitute for or supplement to the Wechsler Adult Intelligence Scale

Description: Seven nonverbal (except for instructions) task assessments measuring the intelligence of adults who are blind or visually impaired. The subtests are Digit Symbol, Object Assembly, Block Design, Plan-of-Search, Object Completion, Pattern Board, and Bead Arithmetic. Wechsler's procedures were followed in establishing age categories and statistical treatment of the data.

Format: Examiner required; individual administration; timed: 1 hour, 30 minutes

Scoring: Examiner evaluated

Cost: Complete Kit (25 record blanks, testing materials, manual, case) $850.00

Kaplan Baycrest Neurocognitive Assessment™ (KBNA™)
Larry Leach, Edith Kaplan, Dmytro Rewilak, Brian Richards, Guy B. Proulx

2000	The Psychological Corporation

Population: Ages 20 through 89 years

Purpose: Assesses cognitive abilities

Description: Seven areas of cognition are measured: attention/concentration, immediate memory-recall, delayed memory-recall, delayed memory-recognition, verbal fluency, spatial processing, and reasoning/conceptual shifting. The KBNA allows examiners to choose among a general overview of cognition by calculating index scores only, a detailed analysis of neurocognitive functioning by also calculating process scores, or a combination of both.

Format: Examiner required; individual administration; untimed: 60 minutes

Scoring: Examiner evaluated

Cost: Complete Kit (manual, stimulus book, chips, cassette, 25 each of response booklets and record forms, response grid, box) $225.00

Kasanin–Hanfmann Concept Formation Test (Vygotsky Test) and Modified Vygotsky Concept Formation Test
Paul L. Wang

1983	Stoelting Company

Population: All ages

Purpose: Measures an individual's ability to think in

abstract concepts; used with uneducated adults, children, and special groups such as patients with mental retardation and cerebral organicity

Description: Task-assessment test consisting of 22 blocks that the subject analyzes and sorts. The blocks are of different colors, shapes, and sizes but are alike in some way. The subject must determine the common factor and sort the blocks according to that factor. The Modified Vygotsky Concept Formation Test provides a new method of administering and scoring. The modification standardizes and simplifies the observation of the subject and adds a divergent thinking test. The modification is particularly useful in the study of mental retardation, schizophrenia, and cerebral organicity (e.g., frontal lobe pathology).

Format: Examiner required; individual administration; untimed: 30 minutes

Scoring: Examiner evaluated

Cost: Test Materials $195.00; Modified Vygotsky Concept Formation Manual $35.00; 30 Record Forms $28.00

Kaufman Adolescent and Adult Intelligence Test (KAIT)
Alan S. Kaufman, Nadeen L. Kaufman

1993   American Guidance Service

Population: Ages 11 to 85+ years

Purpose: Comprehensive measure of intelligence

Description: The KAIT is a comprehensive measure of general intelligence. It includes separate Crystallized and Fluid Scales. Subtests are Auditory Comprehension, Double Meanings, Definitions, Rebus Learning, Mystery Codes, Logical Steps, Memory for Block Designs, Famous Faces, Rebus Delayed Recall, and Auditory Delayed Recall. Includes a well-standardized measure of Mental Status. KAIT's high-level, adult-oriented tasks require reasoning and planning ability. Because fine motor coordination and motor speed are not emphasized, the KAIT yields a more meaningful and pure measure of intelligence of older adults.

Format: Examiner required; individual administration; timed and untimed: 1 hour for Core Battery, $1\frac{1}{2}$ hours for Expanded Battery

Scoring: Examiner evaluated; DOS scoring available

Cost: Complete Kit (2 test easels, manual, 25 individual test records, 25 response booklets, audiocassette, blocks with holder, carrying case) $577.95

Kaufman Assessment Battery for Children (K-ABC)
Alan S. Kaufman, Nadeen L. Kaufman

1983   American Guidance Service

Population: Ages 2 years 6 months through 12 years 5 months

Purpose: Measures individual cognitive ability and academic achievement

Description: Individually administered intelligence battery based on the Luria–Das model of sequential versus simultaneous information processing. Subtests are Hand Movements, Number Recall, Word Order, Magic Window, Face Recognition, Gestalt Closure, Triangles, Matrix Analogies, Spatial Memory, and Photo Series. The Achievement Scale subtests are Expressive Vocabulary, Faces and Places, Arithmetic, Riddles, Reading/Decoding, and Reading/Understanding. Composite scores are Sequential Processing, Simultaneous Processing, Mental Processing Composite, Achievement, and Nonverbal.

Format: Examiner required; individual administration; timed and untimed: 35 minutes at age $2\frac{1}{2}$; 50 to 60 minutes at age 5; 75 to 85 minutes at ages 7 and above

Scoring: Examiner evaluated; computer scoring available

Cost: Complete Kit (test easels, 2 manuals, 25 individual test records, magic window, triangles, photos) $412.95

Kaufman Brief Intelligence Test (K-BIT)
Alan S. Kaufman, Nadeen L. Kaufman

1990   American Guidance Service

Population: Ages 4 through 90 years

Purpose: Used to obtain an estimate of intelligence

Description: A brief, two-subtest measure of verbal and nonverbal intelligence. Special features: it has a wide age range, has an excellent normative sample for such a brief test, and can be administered by nonpsychologists. Two subtests included: Vocabulary (Expressive Vocabulary and Definitions) and Matrices. Can be used to screen students who may benefit from enrichment or gifted programs.

Format: Examiner required; individual administration; untimed: 15 to 30 minutes

Scoring: Examiner evaluated

Cost: Complete Kit (easel, manual, 25 individual test records, carry bag) $136.95

Knox's Cube Test (KCT)
Mark Stone, Benjamin Wright

1983   Stoelting Company

Population: Ages 2 years to adult

Purpose: Measures short-term memory and attention span, which together constitute the most elementary stage of mental activity; used to evaluate individuals who are deaf, language impaired, and foreign speaking

Description: Multiple-task assessment of attention span and short-term memory measuring how accurately an individual can repeat simple rhythmic figures tapped out by the examiner. Test materials include four cubes attached to a wooden base and a separate tapping block. Directions can be delivered in pantomine. The manual provides procedures and rationale for administering, scoring, and interpreting a comprehensive version of the KCT, which incorporates all previous versions. This revision uses Rasch measurement procedures to develop an objective psychometric variable, along which both items and persons can be positioned. Two versions are available: KCT JR (ages 2 to 8) and KCT SR (ages 8 and above).

Format: Examiner required; individual administration; untimed: 10 to 15 minutes

Scoring: Examiner evaluated

Cost: Complete Kit (testing materials, manual, record forms) $95.00 each version

Kohs Block Design Test
S. C. Kohs

1919   Stoelting Company

Population: Ages 3 to 19 years

Purpose: Measures performance intelligence

Description: Multiple-item task-assessment test consisting of 17 cards containing colored designs and 16 colored blocks that the subject uses to duplicate the designs on the cards. Performance is evaluated for attention, adaptation, and autocriticism. This test also is included in the Merrill-Palmer V and Arthur Performance scales.

Format: Examiner required; individual administration; timed: 40 minutes or less

Scoring: Examiner evaluated

Cost: Complete Kit (manual, cubes, cards, 50 record blanks) $140.00

Leiter Adult Intelligence Scale (LAIS)
Russell G. Leiter

1972   Stoelting Company

Population: Adults

Purpose: Measures general intelligence in adults; used with individuals from the upper and lower levels of the socioeconomic hierarchy and with individuals with psychological disabilities

Description: Six oral-response and task-performance tests assessing verbal and nonverbal intelligence. The verbal tests are Similarities-Differences, Digits Forward and Backward, and Free Recall-Controlled Recall. The nonverbal tests are Pathways (following a prescribed sequence), Stencil Designs (reproduction of designs), and Painted Cube Test (duplication of designs). Test results identify deficits in cognitive, psychophysical, or social areas and provide a measure of functional efficiency for individuals with psychological disabilities and for individuals who are gifted.

Format: Examiner required; individual administration; untimed: 40 minutes

Scoring: Examiner evaluated

Cost: Test Kit (all test materials, manual, 100 record blanks) $225.00

Leiter International Performance Scale-Revised (Leiter-R)
Gale H. Roid, Lucy J. Miller

1997   Stoelting Company

Population: Ages 2 to 21 years

Purpose: Assesses intelligence in a totally nonverbal format

Description: This revision of the original Leiter consists of two nationally standardized batteries: a revision of the original Visualization and Reasoning domains for measuring intelligence and the new Attention and Memory domains. Included in both batteries are unique "growth" scores that measure small but important improvement in children with significant cognitive disabilities. The Leiter-R emphasizes fluid intelligence. Validity information is provided for psychometric studies with many groups to establish fairness for all cultural and ethnic backgrounds. The four social-emotional rating scales (Examiner, Parent, Self Rating, and Teacher) provide essential information about the child's activity level, attention, impulse control, and other emotional characteristics. There are 20 subtests standardized on 1,719 typical children and adolescents and 692 atypical children.

Format: Examiner required; individual administration; untimed: 25 to 40 minutes

Scoring: Examiner evaluated; scoring software available

Cost: Complete Kit (manual; 3 easels; response cards; manipulatives; 20 each VR and AM forms, attention and rating booklets, growth profile, case) $850.00

Matrix Analogies Test-Expanded Form (MAT-Expanded Form)
Jack A. Naglieri

| 1985 | The Psychological Corporation |

Population: Ages 5 to 17 years

Purpose: Measures nonverbal reasoning ability

Description: Paper-pencil multiple-choice 64-item test consisting of abstract designs or matrices from which an element in progression is missing. The child chooses the missing element from six alternatives. Items are organized in four groups: pattern completion, reasoning by analogy, serial reasoning, and spatial visualization. The test yields standard scores, percentile ranks, age equivalents for the total score, and item group scores. Because minimal verbal comprehension and response are required, the test can be used for assessment of individuals who are bilingual, gifted, learning disabled, mentally retarded, hearing or language impaired, or physically disabled with limited response capabilities. The test can be administered by psychologists, counselors, school psychologists and diagnosticians, rehabilitation psychologists, and other professionals with proper training and experience in testing.

Format: Examiner required; individual administration; untimed: 20 to 25 minutes

Scoring: Hand key

Cost: Complete Kit (manual, stimulus manual, 50 answer sheets, case) $210.00

McCarthy Scales of Children's Abilities
Dorothea McCarthy

| 1972 | The Psychological Corporation |

Population: Ages 2 years 6 months to 8 years 6 months

Purpose: Assesses cognitive and motor development of children

Description: Measure of five aspects of children's thinking, motor, and mental abilities. The subtests are Verbal Ability, Short-Term Memory,

Numerical Ability, Perceptual Performance, and Motor Coordination. The verbal, numerical, and perceptual performance scales are combined to yield the General Cognitive Index. Items involve puzzles, toylike materials, and gamelike tasks. Six of the 18 task components that predict the child's ability to cope with schoolwork in the early grades form the McCarthy Screening Test.

Format: Examiner required; individual administration; untimed: 45 to 60 minutes, 20 minutes for Screening Test

Scoring: Examiner evaluated

Cost: Complete Set (stimulus, manipulatives, manual, 25 record forms, 25 drawing booklets, case) $545.00; Screening Test Complete Set (manual, 25 record forms, 25 drawing booklets, case) $216.00

Mental Status Checklist™-Adolescent
Edward H. Dougherty, John A. Schinka

| 1988 | Psychological Assessment Resources, Inc. |

Population: Ages 13 to 17 years

Purpose: Surveys the mental status of adolescents; used to identify problems and establish rapport in order to prepare individuals for further diagnostic testing; also provides written documentation of presenting problems

Description: Paper-pencil or computer-administered 174-item checklist covering presenting problems, referral data, demographics, mental status, personality function and symptoms, diagnosis, and disposition. The computer version operates on PC.

Format: Self-administered; untimed: 10 to 20 minutes

Scoring: Examiner evaluated

Cost: 25 Checklists $42.00; Computer Version $305.00

Mental Status Checklist™-Adult
John A. Schinka

| 1988 | Psychological Assessment Resources, Inc. |

Population: Adults

Purpose: Surveys the mental status of adults; used to identify problems and establish rapport in order to prepare individuals for further diagnostic testing; also provides written documentation of presenting problems

Description: Paper-pencil or computer-administered 174-item checklist covering presenting problems, referral data, demographics, mental status, personality function and symptoms, diagnosis, and disposition. The computer version operates on PC.

Format: Self-administered; untimed: 10 to 20 minutes

Scoring: Examiner evaluated

Cost: 25 Checklists $42.00; Computer Version $305.00

Mental Status Checklist™-Children
Edward H. Dougherty, John A. Schinka

| 1988 | Psychological Assessment Resources, Inc. |

Population: Ages 5 to 12 years

Purpose: Surveys the mental status of children; used to identify problems and establish rapport in order to prepare individuals for further diagnostic testing; also provides written documentation of presenting problems

Description: Paper–pencil or computer-administered 153-item checklist covering presenting problems, referral data, demographics, mental status, personality function and symptoms, diagnosis, and disposition. The computer version operates on PC.

Format: Self-administered; untimed: 10 to 20 minutes

Scoring: Examiner evaluated

Cost: 25 Checklists $42.00; Computer Version $305.00

Merrill-Palmer Scale
Rachel Stutsman

| 1948 | Stoelting Company |

Population: Ages 18 months to 4 years

Purpose: Measures intelligence in children

Description: Task-assessment and oral-response subtests measuring language skills, motor skills, dexterity, and matching. The 19 subtests are Stutsman Color Matching Test; Wallin Pegboards A & B; Stutsman Buttoning Test; Stutsman Stick and String; Scissors; Stutsman Language Test; Stutsman Picture Formboards 1, 2, and 3; Mare-Foal Formboard; Seguin-Goddard Formboard; Pintner-Manikin Test; Decroly Matching Game; Stutsman Nested Cubes; Woodworth-Wells Association Test; Stutsman Copying Test; Stutsman Pyramid Test; Stutsman Little Pink Tower Test; and Kohs Blocks. The test deals directly with the problem of resistance in the testing situation and provides a comprehensive listing of the many factors influencing a child's willingness to cooperate. Refused and omitted items are considered when arriving at a total score, which may then be

converted into mental age, sigma value, or percentile rank.

Format: Examiner required; individual administration; untimed: 45 minutes

Scoring: Examiner evaluated

Cost: Complete Kit (tests, 50 record blanks, carrying case) $750.00

Multidimensional Aptitude Battery-II
Douglas N. Jackson

| 1998 | Sigma Assessment Systems, Inc. |

Population: Ages 16 to 74 years

Purpose: Assesses aptitudes and intelligence; used for clinical and research purposes with normal and deviant populations

Description: Multiple-item paper–pencil multiple-choice test consisting of two batteries of five subtests each. The Verbal Battery includes the following subtests: Information, Comprehension, Arithmetic, Similarities, and Vocabulary. The Performance Battery subtests are Digit Symbol, Picture Completion, Spatial, Picture Arrangement, and Object Assembly. Verbal, Performance, and Full Scale IQs and standard scores for the 10 subtests have been calibrated to those of another popular IQ test and permit appraisal of intellectual functioning at nine different age levels, ranging from ages 16 to 74. Separate test booklets and answer sheets are provided for the two batteries. One battery of five subtests (7 minutes per test) can be administered in one sitting. An optional tape recording of instruction and timing may be used to administer all subtests. Scoring templates are available for hand scoring. On-line software is available.

Format: Examiner required; suitable for group use; timed: 7 minutes per subtest

Scoring: Hand key; machine scored; computer scored; scoring service available

Cost: Machine Scoring Examination Kit (manual booklets, coupon for computerized scoring) $43.00; Hand Scoring Examination Kit (manual, test booklets, answer sheets, record form, scoring templates) $59.00

Naglieri Nonverbal Ability Test®-Individual Administration (NNAT®-Individual Administration)
Jack A. Naglieri

| 2000 | The Psychological Corporation |

Population: Ages 5 through 17 years

Purpose: Assesses general nonverbal ability

Description: The test uses progressive matrices that allow for a fair evaluation of nonverbal reasoning and general problem-solving ability. Four item types are used: pattern completion, reasoning by analogy, serial reasoning, and spatial visualization. Two parallel forms are available.

Format: Examiner required; individual administration; untimed: 20 to 30 minutes

Scoring: Examiner evaluated

Cost: Complete Kit (manual, stimulus booklet, 50 each of Form A and Form B) $220.00

Ohio Classification Test
DeWitt E. Sell, Robert W. Scollay

1977	Psychometric Affiliates

Population: Adults

Purpose: Assesses general mental ability; used for evaluation of penal populations, factory workers, general populations, management, and student populations

Description: Performance measure of general intellectual ability with four subtests: Block-Counting, Digit-Symbol, Number Series, and Memory Span for Objects. The directions are given by the examiner. Some number reading is required. The test may be used in any situation where a culture-fair measure of intelligence is needed.

Format: Examiner required; individual administration; timed: 20 minutes

Scoring: Hand key

Cost: Specimen Set $5.00; 25 Tests $8.75; 25 Answer Sheets $7.00

Pictorial Test of Intelligence–Second Edition (PTI-2)
Joseph L. French

2001	PRO-ED, Inc.

Population: Ages 3 through 8 years

Purpose: Measures general intelligence

Description: The PTI-2, a revision of the 1964 PTI, is an objectively scored, individually administered test of general intelligence for both normal children and children with disabilities. Administer three subtests and combine the scores to get the Pictorial Intelligence Quotient, a global index of performance to provide a multidimensional measure of *g*. The subtests are Verbal Abstractions, Form Discrimination, and Quantitative Concepts. The PTI-2 is helpful when used with

children who have difficulty with fine motor skills or a speech-language problem. Respondents do not need to use expressive language, but they do need to have near-normal vision and hearing.

Format: Examiner required; individual administration; untimed: 15 to 30 minutes

Scoring: Examiner evaluated

Cost: Complete Kit (manual, picture book, 25 protocols, storage box) $139.00

Porteus Mazes
S. D. Porteus

1965	The Psychological Corporation

Population: All ages

Purpose: Assesses mental ability

Description: Nonlanguage test of mental ability in which the items are mazes. Materials include the Vineland Revision, Porteus Maze Extension, and Porteus Maze Supplement. The Vineland Revision, consisting of 12 mazes, is the basic test. The Porteus Maze Extension is a series of eight mazes designed for retesting and is not intended for use as an initial test. The Porteus Maze Supplement is designed for a third testing in clinical and research settings.

Format: Examiner required; individual administration; untimed: 25 minutes per scale

Scoring: Examiner evaluated

Cost: Basic Set (mazes and 100 score sheets) $211.00, Manual $53.00

Quick-Test (QT)
R. B. Ammons, C. H. Ammons

1962	Psychological Test Specialists

Population: Ages 2 years to adult

Purpose: Assesses individual intelligence; may be used for evaluation of individuals with severe physical disability, individuals with short attention spans, or uncooperative subjects

Description: Fifty-item test of general intelligence. The subject looks at plates with four line drawings and indicates which picture best illustrates the meaning of a given word. The subject usually responds by pointing. The test requires no reading, writing, or speaking. Usual administration involves the presentation of 15 to 20 of the items. Materials include plates with stimulus pictures and three alternate forms.

Format: Examiner required; individual administration; untimed: 3 to 10 minutes

Scoring: Examiner evaluated

Cost: Complete Kit (manual, set of 3 plates, 100 record sheets) $50.00

Raven's Progressive Matrices
J. C. Raven

| 1998 | The Psychological Corporation |

Population: Ages 5 through 17+ years

Purpose: Assesses nonverbal abilities at three levels

Description: Three levels—Coloured Progressive Matrices (CPM), Standard Progressive Matrices (SPM), and Advanced Progressive Matrices (APM)—are designed to measure enductive ability, a component of Spearman's *g* related to the ability to enduce relationships. Many new features enhance assessment, including alternative forms of the CPM and SPM and an extended version of the SPM. The CPM is printed in several colors. It is considered an easy level test that spreads the scores of the bottom 20% of the population. The SPM is an average level test for the general population. The SPM consists of 5 sets of 12 problems each. The new extended version contains more difficult items while retaining the 60-item format. The APM is the difficult level test, spreading the scores of the top 20% of the population. It is divided into two tests: Set I with 12 problems and Set II with 36 problems.

Format: Examiner required; individual or group administration; untimed: 15 to 60 minutes

Scoring: Examiner evaluated

Cost: Complete Kit (manual, 2 booklets of each level, 50 answer documents for each level, supplement, case) $660.00

Ross Test of Higher Cognitive Processes
John D. Ross, Catherine M. Ross

| 1976 | Academic Therapy Publications |

Population: Ages 9 to 11 years

Purpose: Assesses abstract and critical thinking skills among gifted and nongifted intermediate-grade students; used to screen students for special programs and to evaluate program effectiveness

Description: Paper-pencil 105-item multiple-choice test in eight sections, each dealing with a specific level of higher cognitive processes within the areas of analysis, synthesis, and evaluation. Test is taken in two sittings. Responses may be recorded directly in the student test booklet or on an optional answer sheet.

Format: Examiner required; individual or group administration; untimed: first sitting 63 minutes, second sitting 58 minutes

Scoring: Examiner evaluated, hand key

Cost: Test Kit (manual, 10 student test booklets, 25 answer/profile forms, 2 overlays for quick scoring, in vinyl folder) $70.00

Schaie–Thurstone Adult Mental Abilities Test (STAMAT)
K. Warner Schaie

| 1985 | Penn State Gerontology Center |

Population: Ages 22 to 84 years

Purpose: Measures five separate factors of intelligence

Description: Multiple-item paper-pencil test in two forms measuring verbal, spatial, reasoning, number, and word fluency abilities of adults. Form A (adult) is the original Thurstone Primary Mental Abilities Test, Form 11-17, with new adult norms. Form OA (older adult) is a large-type version of the original test plus two additional scales relevant for adults ages 55 and older. The test was used by Schaie for assessing the development of adult intelligence longitudinally and cross-sectionally. New normative data are based on 4,500 people from ages 22 to 84. Instructions have been written to enhance performance by older adults.

Format: Examiner required; suitable for group use; timed: 45 minutes

Scoring: Hand key

Cost: Contact publisher

Schubert General Ability Battery (GAB)
Herman J. P. Schubert

| 1979 | Slosson Educational Publications, Inc. |

Population: Adolescents, adults

Purpose: Measures general mental abilities; used for scholastic and industrial placement and guidance in high school, college, and industry

Description: Multiple-item paper-pencil battery of tests assessing general mental abilities to predict educational and employment success. The battery yields scores for verbal skills, precise thinking, arithmetic reasoning, and logical analysis.

Format: Examiner required; individual or group administration; untimed: 45 minutes

Scoring: Examiner evaluated

Cost: Complete Kit (manual, 25 protocols) $57.00

Silver Drawing Test of Cognition and Emotion
Rawley A. Silver

1996	Ablin Press Distributors

Population: Ages 5 years to adult

Purpose: Assesses cognitive skills, screens for depression, provides access to fantasies and attitudes toward self and others

Description: Three multiple-item paper-pencil subtests with cognitive and emotional components. For Predictive Drawing, examinees are asked to add lines to outline drawings. Responses are scored for ability to show how objects would appear if filled, tilted, or moved. Drawing from Observation measures concept of space. Examinees are asked to draw an arrangement of cylinders. Responses are scored for ability to represent left-right, above-below, and front-back relationships. Drawing from Imagination measures cognitive skills, creative skills, and attitudes toward self and others. Examinees are asked to choose subjects from an array of 15 stimulus drawings and create narrative drawings with titles. Responses are scored for ability to select (content), ability to combine (form), ability to represent (creativity), and emotional content. Skill in drawing is not evaluated. Instruction may be pantomimed.

Format: Examiner required; individual or group administration; untimed: 12 to 20 minutes

Scoring: Examiner evaluated

Cost: $32.00

Slosson Full-Range Intelligence Test (S-FRIT)
Bob Algozzine, Ronald C. Eaves, Lester Mann, H. Robert Vance

1993	Slosson Educational Publications, Inc.

Population: Ages 5 to 21 years

Purpose: Provides a balanced measure of Verbal/Performance/Memory cognitive abilities

Description: The S-FRIT is intended to supplement the use of more extensive cognitive assessment instruments to facilitate screening in charting cognitive progress. The test can be given by regular or special education teachers, psychologists, counselors, or other personnel who have

taken basic courses in statistics and/or tests and measurements. Items are arranged according to levels of difficulty, and the examiner presents items at suggested starting points by chronological age. When the examinee fails 8 items in a row, testing is completed and the examiner very quickly gets a picture of the individual's mental abilities in the following areas: Verbal Skills, Quantitative, Recall Memory, and Abstract Performance Reasoning.

Format: Examiner required; individual administration; untimed: 25 to 45 minutes

Scoring: Examiner evaluated; computer scoring available

Cost: Complete Kit $98.00

Slosson Intelligence Test-Primary (SIT-P)
Bradley T. Erford, Gary J. Vitali, Steven W. Slosson

1999	Slosson Educational Publications, Inc.

Population: Ages 2 through 7 years

Purpose: Measures cognitive ability in verbal and performance areas

Description: Designed to facilitate the screening identification of children at risk of educational failure, to provide a quick estimate of mental ability, and to identify children who may be appropriate candidates for deeper testing services. Items are ordered with an approximate ascending degree of difficulty. The test yields Verbal and Performance subscale scores and a Total Standard Score. Scoring is simple; 1 point is awarded for each acceptable response. There are two separate scoring forms: Lower Level (ages 2 to 3 years 11 months) and Upper Level (ages 4 to 7 years 11 months).

Format: Examiner required; individual administration; untimed: 10 to 25 minutes

Scoring: Examiner evaluated

Cost: Complete Kit $98.00

Slosson Intelligence Test-Revised (SIT-R)
Richard L. Slosson, Charles L. Nicholson, Terry L. Hibpshman

1990	Slosson Educational Publications, Inc.

Population: Ages 4 to 65 years

Purpose: Measures mental age and intelligence

Description: Verbal screening instrument consisting of 187 questions arranged on a scale of chronological age. The administrator finds the basal, then adds the questions passed after the basal to find the raw score. Test scores range from 36 to 164. The national restandardization creates a Total Standard Score (TSS), establishes a 95% or 99% confidence interval, Mean Age Equivalent, T-score, stanine, Normal Curve Equivalent, and percentile, based on the TSS. Norms include regular and special populations, as well as individuals who are visually impaired or blind. Quantitative reasoning questions were designed to be administered to populations who use metric or standard references, using language common to both. Six cognitive areas of measurement include vocabulary, general information, similarities and differences, comprehension, quantitative, and auditory memory. New supplementary manual is available to assess the individuals with visual impairments.

Format: Examiner required; individual administration; untimed: 10 to 20 minutes

Scoring: Examiner evaluated

Cost: Complete Kit $85.00

Standard Progressive Matrices–
New Zealand Standardization (SPM)

1985	New Zealand Council for Educational Research

Population: Ages 8 to 15 years and adults

Purpose: Measures nonverbal reasoning skills; used in educational and psychological assessment

Description: Provides useful information complementary to verbal tests in a comprehensive assessment of children's abilities. The SPM is divided into five sets of 12 problems. Each of the 60 items is a design or "matrix" from which a part has been removed. The student examines the design and selects from a number of alternatives the pattern that correctly completes the matrix. In each set the first problem is as far as possible self-evident, and the following problems become progressively more difficult. The order in which the problems are presented provides experience in the method of working.

Format: Examiner required; group administration; untimed: 30 minutes

Scoring: Examiner evaluated

Cost: Norms $7.30; 20 Answer Sheets $6.30

Stanford-Binet Intelligence
Scale-Fourth Edition
Robert L. Thorndike, Elizabeth P. Hagen, Jerome M. Sattler

1986	Riverside Publishing Company

Population: Ages 2 years through adult

Purpose: Assesses intelligence and cognitive abilities

Description: Verbal and nonverbal performance test assessing mental abilities in four areas: verbal reasoning (vocabulary, comprehension, verbal relations, absurdities), abstract/visual reasoning (pattern analysis, matrices, paper folding and cutting, copying), quantitative reasoning (quantitative, number series, equation building), and short-term memory (memory for sentences, memory for digits, memory for objects, and bead memory). Items are arranged according to item type and order of difficulty. The following scores can be obtained: percentiles and scaled scores for each of the 15 subtests, four content area scores, a composite of the four area scores, a composite of any combination of the four area scores, and a profile on all 15 subtests. Results identify children and adults who would benefit from specialized learning environments.

Format: Examiner required; individual administration; timed and untimed: 45 to 90 minutes

Scoring: Examiner evaluated; computer scoring available

Cost: Examiner's Kit (4 item books, 2 manuals, record booklet, scissors, paper, manipulatives, briefcase) $744.00

Stoelting Brief Nonverbal
Intelligence Test (S-BIT)
Gale H. Roid, Lucy J. Miller

1999	Stoelting Company

Population: Ages 6 years through adult

Purpose: Measures nonverbal intelligence, memory, and attention

Description: Provides norm-referenced and criterion-referenced scores for IQ, Fluid Reasoning, and four subtests related to academic skills. The examiner pantomimes the instructions, and the individual responds by pointing or placing a card in the appropriate position. Test items include a variety of problem-solving tasks increasing in complexity and difficulty. The range of IQ scores is 30 to 170. The test is ideal for individuals who are cognitively impaired, disadvantaged, nonverbal, non-English speaking, or hearing or speech impaired, and for speakers of English as a second language. It is a good measure of fluid intelligence and is highly correlated with other intelligence tests.

Format: Examiner required; individual administration; timed: 15 to 20 minutes

Scoring: Examiner evaluated

Cost: Complete Kit (manual, easel, cards, 20 record forms, case) $295.00

Swanson Cognitive Processing Test (S-CPT)
H. Lee Swanson

1996 PRO-ED, Inc.

Population: Ages 4 years 5 months to 78 years 6 months

Purpose: Measures different aspects of intellectual abilities and information processing potential

Description: Battery of 11 subtests that can be administered in an abbreviated form (five subtests) or in a complete form under traditional, or interactive, testing conditions. Information is drawn from the work on information processing theory and dynamic assessment. Normative data for the S-CPT were gathered between 1987 and 1994. The test was individually administered to 1,611 children and adults in 10 U.S. states and two Canadian provinces. The sample closely matches the 1990 U.S. census figures. The S-CPT includes test-teach-test conditions that required measures of internal reliability. The total coefficient alpha score for the S-CPT is highly reliable. The results on composite and component scores indicate that the majority of scores range from .82 to .95, with 64% (16 of 25) of the reliabilities at .90 or greater. High construct and criterion-related validity coefficients are reported.

Format: Examiner required; individual administration; timed: 2 hours

Scoring: Examiner evaluated

Cost: Complete Kit (manual, 25 profile/examiner record booklets, picture book, card decks, strategy cards, storage box) $194.00

Test of Behavioral Rigidity (TBR)
K. Warner Schaie

1997 Penn State Gerontology Center

Population: Adults

Purpose: Measures cognitive flexibility and motor speed

Description: A paper-pencil short answer and true-false instrument that yields scores on Attitudinal Flexibility, Motor-Cognitive Flexibility, and Psycho-Motor Speed.

Format: Self-administered; timed: 30 minutes

Scoring: Examiner evaluated; computer scoring available

Cost: Contact publisher

Test of Nonverbal Intelligence-Third Edition (TONI-3)
Linda Brown, Rita J. Sherbenou, Susan K. Johnsen

1997 PRO-ED, Inc.

Population: Ages 6 through 89 years

Purpose: Measures intelligence, aptitude, abstract reasoning, and problem solving; requires no reading, writing, speaking, or listening on the part of the test participant

Description: A unique language-free format makes the TONI-3 ideal for evaluating subjects who have been difficult to test with any degree of confidence or precision. It is particularly well suited for individuals who are known or believed to have disorders of communication or thinking, such as aphasia, dyslexia, language disabilities, learning disabilities, speech problems, specific academic deficits, and similar conditions. The format also accommodates the needs of subjects who do not read or write English well, due to disability or lack of exposure to the English language and U.S. culture.

Format: Examiner required; individual administration; timed: 15 to 20 minutes

Scoring: Examiner evaluated

Cost: Complete Kit (manual, picture book, 50 each Form A and B record forms, storage box) $249.00

Universal Nonverbal Intelligence Test™ (UNIT™)
Bruce A. Bracken, R. Steve McCallum

1998 Riverside Publishing Company

Population: Ages 5 through 17 years

Purpose: Provides a fair assessment of general intelligence, measured nonverbally

Description: Unlike many nonverbal tests that include only matrices, the UNIT subtests require multiple response modes, including use of manipulatives, paper-pencil, and pointing. The materials and test stimuli are designed to be relatively universal and cross-cultural. The tasks are engaging to children across races, ethnicities, and cultures. A broad range of complex memory and reasoning abilities is measured. There are six subtests (symbolic memory, analogic reasoning, object memory, spatial memory, cube design, mazes) organized into four quotients (symbolic, nonsymbolic, memory, reasoning) and a full scale quotient. The UNIT may be administered in three forms: abbreviated, standard, or extended batteries.

Format: Examiner required; individual administration; time varies depending on battery administered

Scoring: Examiner evaluated; computer scoring available

Cost: Complete Test (manual, 2 stimulus books, manipulatives, 25 record forms, 25 mazes booklets, canvas case) $507.00

Visual Gestalt Test
Ruth Andersen

1989   Dansk psykologisk Forlag

Population: Adults

Purpose: Assesses cognitive dysfunction related to cerebral deficits applicable for research with patients with right hemisphere dysfunction

Description: Four-item paper–pencil test measuring quantitative and qualitative assessment of visual gestalts using these figures: circle, triangle, rectangle, and semi-circle. Materials include four stimulus cards, four pads with figure outlines, a scoring key, and a scoring sheet. Examiner must be a qualified neuropsychologist. Also available in Danish.

Format: Examiner required; individual administration; untimed

Scoring: Hand key

Cost: Specimen Set $38.00

Wechsler Abbreviated Scale of Intelligence™ (WASI™)

1999   The Psychological Corporation

Population: Ages 6 to 89 years

Purpose: Measures intelligence

Description: Consists of four subtests—Vocabulary, Similarities, Block Design, and Matrix Reasoning—resulting in Verbal, Performance, and Full Scale scores. All WASI items are new and parallel to their full Wechsler counterparts. Another new feature is the oral and visual presentation of words in the Vocabulary subtest.

Format: Examiner required; individual administration; timed and untimed: 30 minutes

Scoring: Examiner evaluated; may be computer scored

Cost: Complete Kit (manual, stimulus booklet, 25 record forms, blocks, bag) $212.00

Wechsler Adult Intelligence Scale®–Third Edition (WAIS-III®)
David Wechsler

1997   The Psychological Corporation

Population: Ages 16 to 89 years

Purpose: Measures intellectual ability

Description: One of the primary goals of the revision was to develop new norms on a contemporary sample. The focus was on improvements to the well-known features of this scale rather than on redesign. Item content, artwork, and materials have been improved and updated. Administration time was reduced and supplementary subtests were added to increase diagnostic utility. The Verbal subtests are Vocabulary, Similarities, Arithmetic, Digit Span, Information, Comprehension, and Letter–Number Sequencing. The Performance subtests are Picture Completion, Digit Symbol, Block Design, Matrix Reasoning, Picture Arrangement, Symbol Search, and Object Assembly. Four index scores are available.

Format: Examiner required; individual administration; timed and untimed: 75 minutes

Scoring: Examiner evaluated; computer scoring available

Cost: Complete Set (2 manuals, stimulus booklet, 25 each of record forms and response booklets, manipulatives, case) $750.00

Wechsler Intelligence Scale for Children®–Third Edition (WISC-III®)
David Wechsler

1991   The Psychological Corporation

Population: Ages 6 to 16 years

Purpose: Assesses intellectual ability in children

Description: A revision of the 1974 edition of the WISC-R. While retaining the basic structure and content of that instrument, this test offers updated normative data and improved items and design. Ten core subtests plus three supplementary subtests provide three composite scores: Verbal IQ, Performance IQ, and Full Scale IQ. Verbal subtests are Information, Similarities, Arithmetic, Vocabulary, and Comprehension, plus Digit Span. Performance subtests are Picture Completion, Coding, Picture Arrangement, Block Design, and Object Design, plus Symbol Search and Mazes. Both verbal responses and manipulation of test materials are required of the individual. Optional scoring and report writing software are available.

Format: Examiner required; individual administration; timed and untimed

Scoring: Examiner evaluated; may be computer scored

Cost: Complete Kit (manual, stimulus booklet, manipulatives, 25 record forms, case) $725.00

Wechsler Preschool and Primary Scale of Intelligence™-Revised (WPPSI-R®)
David Wechsler

1989   The Psychological Corporation

Population: Ages 3 years to 7 years 3 months

Purpose: Measures intellectual abilities in young children

Description: A revision of the original 1967 WPPSI. It retains the conceptual and technical foundations while incorporating new features and extending the age range. Contains the original 11 subtests, plus an additional performance subtest, Object Assembly. Pegs (formerly Animal House) and Sentences are now optional subtests. Provides norms for 17 age groups divided by 3-month intervals. Verbal, Performance, and Full Scale IQ scores are provided. Numerous validity studies were conducted. Optional scoring and reporting software are available.

Format: Examiner required; individual administration; requires about 75 minutes

Scoring: Examiner evaluated; computer scoring available

Cost: Complete Set (manual, manipulatives, 25 each of record forms and mazes booklets, 50 geometric design sheets, case) $711.00

Wide Range Intelligence Test (WRIT)
Joseph Glutting, Wayne Adams, David Sheslow

1999   Wide Range, Inc.

Population: Ages 4 to 80 years

Purpose: Measures cognitive abilities

Description: The WRIT yields a Verbal IQ and a Visual IQ, which generate a General IQ when combined. The Vocabulary and Verbal Analogies form the Verbal Scale, and the Matrices and Diamonds form the Visual Scale. Standardized on more than 2,500 individuals, WRIT IQs are highly correlated with those from traditional and much lengthier cognitive measures. The WRIT was co-normed with the Wide Range Achievement Test, allowing sound and efficient determination of an intelligence-achievement discrepancy.

Format: Examiner required; individual administration; untimed: 20 to 30 minutes

Scoring: Examiner evaluated

Cost: Kit (Diamonds/Matrices easel, Diamonds in case, manual, 25 forms, briefcase) $245.00

WISC-III® as a Process Instrument (WISC-III® PI)
Edith Kaplan, Deborah Fein, Joel Kramer, Dean C. Delis, Robin Morris

1999   The Psychological Corporation

Population: Ages 6 through 16 years

Purpose: Helps in better understanding a child's WISC-III performance

Description: The qualitative has been quantified in this instrument by permitting a finer analysis of the child's test behavior, strategies, and cognitive processing. Strengths and weaknesses are more accurately profiled. Additional scoring procedures for eight of the WISC-III subtests are provided. There are add-on procedures for Coding and Arithmetic subtests. Alternate administrations of seven subtests are given. New subtests, developed in the WISC-III tradition, assess different content. A WISC-III kit is required.

Format: Examiner required; individual administration; untimed: varies

Scoring: Examiner evaluated

Cost: Complete Kit (manual, 2 stimulus booklets, 25 of each record form and response booklet, manipulatives, case) $482.00

Woodcock-Johnson® III (WJ III®) Tests of Cognitive Abilities
Richard W. Woodcock, Kevin S. McGrew, Nancy Mather

2001   Riverside Publishing Company

Population: Ages 2 through 90+ years

Purpose: Assesses general intellectual ability, cognitive abilities, and scholastic aptitudes

Description: Based on the Cattell-Horn-Carroll theory of cognitive abilities. Two batteries—the Standard Battery and the Extended Battery—each consist of 10 tests. New features of the third edition are eight new tests that measure information-processing abilities; five new cognitive clusters; modified organization and interpretation plan that increases depth and breadth of coverage; expanded cognitive factor structure so that two to three tests clearly measure different narrow aspects of a broader ability; three broad cognitive areas—verbal, thinking, and cognitive efficiency; and expanded procedures for evaluating ability-achievement discrepancies. Co-normed with the WJ III Tests of Achievement to provide ability-achievement discrepancies and an intra-individual discrepancy.

Format: Examiner required; individual administration; timed and untimed: 5 minutes per subtest

Scoring: Computer scored; examiner evaluated

Cost: Complete battery (standard and extended test books, 2 manuals, cassette, 25 each of test records and response booklets, 5 Brief Intellectual Ability test records, scoring software, scoring guides, leather case) $650.00

Woodcock-Johnson®-Revised Tests of Cognitive Ability (WJ-R®)
Richard W. Woodcock, M. Bonner Johnson

1989	Riverside Publishing Company

Population: Ages 2 through 90+ years

Purpose: Assesses cognitive abilities, aptitudes, and oral language

Description: Seven cognitive factors are measured: long-term retrieval, short-term memory, processing speed, auditory processing, visual processing, comprehension-knowledge, and fluid reasoning. There are two to four tests for each cognitive factor, a measure of oral language, and five differential aptitude clusters. There are 21 tests in the complete cognitive battery. The first seven tests are the Standard Battery. The remaining 14 tests are supplemental and can be used selectively to obtain information on cognitive factors, intracognitive discrepancies, oral language, or differential aptitudes.

Format: Examiner required; individual administration; timed and untimed: 5 minutes per subtest

Scoring: Examiner evaluated; computer software available

Cost: Complete Battery (standard and supplemental test books, examiner's manual, norm tables, audiocassettes, 25 test records, case) $623.00

Neuropsychology

Auditory Verbal Learning Test (AVLT)
Gina Geffen, Laurie Geffen

2000	Australian Council for Educational Research Limited

Population: Ages 7 to 70 years

Purpose: Measures several indices of learning and memory

Description: Originally developed in France by Andre Rey, the test has been adapted for use with English-speaking clients. The primary appeal of this test is that it is brief and easy to administer and score. The test is administered on a computer. There are 15 items across 5 consecutive trials, then 4 additional trials. The program produces a summary of the client's test performance and compares it with a relevant normative group matched on the basis of age and sex. The manual is included in electronic format on the CD-ROM and can be printed if desired.

Format: Examiner required; computer administered; timed and untimed

Scoring: Computer scored

Cost: Contact publisher

Autobiographical Memory Interview (AMI)
Michael Kopelman, Barbara A. Wilson, Alan Baddeley

1990	Thames Valley Test Company, Ltd.

Population: Adults

Purpose: Designed to investigate retrograde amnesia

Description: Retrograde amnesia often leads to an impairment of autobiographical memory, the capacity to recollect the facts and incidents of one's earlier life. Although this is not measured by standard memory tests, it is valuable to asses autobiographical memory for at least three reasons: to understand the nature of any memory deficit observed, to allow more adequate counseling, and to provide an individual focus for subsequent treatment. An assessment of personal remote memory is provided.

Format: Examiner required; individual administration; untimed: 25 minutes

Scoring: Examiner evaluated

Cost: $102.00

Balloons Test
Jennifer Edgeworth, Ian Robertson,
Tom McMillan

1998	Thames Valley Test Company, Ltd.

Population: Adolescents, adults

Purpose: Measures visual inattention in individuals with neurological impairments

Description: The test has been designed as a screening test and has a number of potential advantages over existing screening tests. It is quick and simple to administer, can be used as a bedside test, and detects a higher proportion of visual inattention in patients with right brain injury than other commonly used tests. The test consists of two sheets, each containing 202 items. In Subtest A, the control test, 22 of the 202 items are targets to be cancelled. Targets are circles with a line adjoining (balloons); other items in the array are circles without lines. Patients are required to locate and put a line through each balloon in a fixed time limit. In Subtest B, the number and position of balloons and circles are exactly the reverse of those in Subtest A.

Format: Examiner required; individual administration; timed: 6 minutes

Scoring: Examiner evaluated

Cost: $149.00

Barry Rehabilitation Inpatient Screening of Cognition (BRISC)
Phillip Barry

1995	Valpar International Corporation

Population: All ages

Purpose: Assesses eight categories of cognitive function for patients with severe brain injuries

Description: Paper–pencil oral-response short-answer verbal test. Scores on the individual subtests may be compared to norms provided for adults and for children in separately normed Grades 2 through 12. The total score provides a reliable index of the relative severity of dysfunction and progress in the early stages of recovery. The subtests are Reading, Design Copy, Verbal Concepts, Orientation, Mental Imagery, Mental Control, Initiation, and Memory. A total score of under 120 points is indicative of impaired function in persons between the ages of 12 and 39. Scores between 110 and 120 should be interpreted cautiously in older adults. Results provide information on the patient's status and weekly changes, suggest methods of treatment, and predict what kinds of cognitive problems the patient may experience.

Format: Examiner required; individual administration; untimed

Scoring: Examiner evaluated

Cost: Set (1 manual, pad of 5 protocols) $74.95

Bayley Infant Neurodevelopmental Screener® (BINS™)
Glen P. Aylward

1995	The Psychological Corporation

Population: Ages 3 through 24 months

Purpose: Screens infants at risk for neurological impairment or developmental delay

Description: Reliably assesses basic neurological functions, auditory and visual receptive functions, verbal and motor expressive functions, and cognitive processes. Item sets contain 11 to 13 items selected from the Bayley Scales of Infant Development–Second Edition and neurological assessment. Three classifications of risk status (low, moderate, and high) are delimited by two cutoff scores, allowing selection of the cut score according to criteria for detecting impairment. A training video covers item administration and scoring for all item sets.

Format: Examiner required; individual administration; untimed: 10 to 15 minutes

Scoring: Examiner evaluated

Cost: Complete Kit (manual, 25 record forms, stimulus card, manipulatives, case) $264.00

Behavior Rating Inventory of Executive Function (BRIEF)
Gerald A. Gioia, Peter K. Isquith,
Steven C. Guy, Lauren Kenworthy

2000	Psychological Assessment Resources, Inc.

Population: Ages 5 to 18 years

Purpose: Assesses impairment of executive function

Description: Total of 86 items within eight non-overlapping theoretically and empirically clinical scales, as well as two validity scales. These scales form two broader indexes: Behavioral Regulation (three scales) and Metacognition (five scales), as well as a Global Executive Composite. Materials used: Professional Manual, Parent Form, Teacher Form, two-sided Scoring Summary/Profile Form.

Format: Self-administered; untimed: 10 to 15 minutes

Scoring: Examiner evaluated

Cost: $130.00

Behavioural Assessment of the Dysexecutive Syndrome (BADS)
Barbara A. Wilson, Nick Alderman, Paul Burgess, Hazel Emslie, Jonathan J. Evans

1996	Thames Valley Test Company, Ltd.

Population: Ages 16 to 87 years

Purpose: Measures executive functioning

Description: The test battery includes items sensitive to those skills involved in problem solving, planning, and organizing behavior over an extended period of time. There are six tests in the BADS: Temporal Judgment, Rule Shift Cards, Action Program, Key Search, Zoo Map, and Modified Six Elements. The battery also includes a 20-item Dysexecutive Questionnaire with items that sample the range of problems commonly associated with the syndrome in four broad areas of likely changes: personality, motivation, behavior, and cognition.

Format: Examiner required; individual administration; untimed: 35 minutes

Scoring: Examiner evaluated

Cost: $375.00

Bender Visual Motor Gestalt Test
Lauretta Bender

Date not provided	Western Psychological Services

Population: Ages 3 years to adult

Purpose: Assesses visual-motor functions; also used to evaluate perceptual maturity, possible neurological impairment, and emotional adjustment

Description: The test consists of nine figures that are presented, one at a time, to the person being tested, who copies them on a blank piece of paper. Responses are scored according to the development of the concepts of form, shape, and pattern and orientation in space.

Format: Examiner required; individual administration; untimed: 15 to 20 minutes

Scoring: Examiner evaluated

Cost: Complete Kit $255.00

Birmingham Object Recognition Battery (BORB)
Jane M. Riddoch, Glyn W. Humphreys

1993	Psychology Press

Population: Adults

Purpose: Assesses neuropsychological disorders of visual object recognition

Description: The tests assess low-level aspects of visual perception (using same–different matching of basic perceptual features, such as orientation, length, position, and object size), intermediate visual processes (e.g., matching objects different in viewpoint), access to stored perceptual knowledge about objects (object decision), access to semantic knowledge (function and associative matches), and access to names of objects (picture naming). The BORB serves as a companion test battery to the Psycholinguistic Assessments of Language Processing in Aphasia.

Format: Examiner required; individual administration; untimed

Scoring: Examiner evaluated

Cost: $250.00

Bloomer Blocks
H. Harlan Bloomer, Shelly Weaverdyck

2000	Western Psychological Services

Population: Adults

Purpose: Identifies factors responsible for language deficits in order to devise an appropriate treatment plan

Description: This flexible interview allows the examiner to describe language impairments and their possible neuropsychological substrates, and then track subsequent changes in the patient's adaptive status. Because the interview identifies both retained abilities and functional deficiencies, it is useful in treating a wide range of conditions that result in communication impairments, including head injury, Alzheimer's dementia, and Parkinson's disease. Simple tasks elicit both reactive and proactive, verbal and nonverbal communication. The interview enables the examiner to analyze all four principal modes of linguistic communication: speech, listening, reading, and writing. Bloomer Blocks scores are not interpreted in relation to the performance of a norm group; instead they indicate what an individual can and cannot do, thereby reflecting the nature and extent of his or her impairment.

Format: Examiner required; individual administration; untimed

Scoring: Examiner evaluated

Cost: Complete Kit (manual, 10 protocols, task cards, spatial grid, form board, blocks, wooden case) $299.00

Booklet Category Test (BCT)
Nick A. DeFilippis, Elizabeth McCampbell

1997	Psychological Assessment Resources, Inc.

Population: Ages 15 years and older

Purpose: Diagnoses brain dysfunction; used for clinical assessment of brain damage

Description: Test with 208 items that assess concept formation and abstract reasoning. Figures are presented one at a time to the subject, who responds with a number between 1 and 4. This is the booklet version of the Halstead Category Test. The first four subtests may be used to predict total error scores if time limitations do not allow administration of the entire BCT. Cutoff scores are used.

Format: Examiner required; individual administration; untimed: 30 to 60 minutes

Scoring: Examiner evaluated

Cost: Complete Set (two-volume set of stimulus materials, manual, 50 scoring forms) $390.00

Boston Qualitative Scoring System for the Rey-Osterrieth Complex Figure (BQSS)
Robert A. Stern, Debbie J. Javorsky, Elizabeth A. Singer, Naomi C. Singer-Harris, Jessica A. Somerville, Lisa M. Duke, Jodi A. Thompson, Edith Kaplan

1999	Psychological Assessment Resources, Inc.

Population: Ages 18 to 94 years

Purpose: Provides quantitative approach to rating the qualitative features of ROCF productions

Description: Evaluates Copy Condition, Immediate Recall, and Delayed Recall. Scoring criteria: presence, accuracy, and fragmentation.

Format: Examiner required; individual administration; untimed: 45 minutes

Scoring: Examiner evaluated

Cost: Kit (manual, 50 scoring booklets, 50 response sheets, stimulus card, reference guide, 1 set of scoring templates, metric ruler) $155.00

Brief Neuropsychological Cognitive Examination (BNCE)
Joseph M. Tonkonogy

1997	Western Psychological Services

Population: Ages 18 years and older

Purpose: Assesses the cognitive functions targeted in a typical neuropsychological exam

Description: A general cognitive profile is provided that can be used for screening, diagnosis, or follow-up. More efficient than a neuropsychological battery and more thorough than a screener, the BNCE is an ideal way to evaluate the cognitive status of patients with psychiatric disorders or psychiatric manifestations of neurological diseases. Composed of 10 subtests, it assesses working memory, gnosis, praxis, language, orientation, attention, and executive functions. The test focuses on processing skills needed for everyday functioning and is sensitive to mild impairment often missed by other brief cognitive screeners. The BNCE manual provides extensive guidance in interpreting the test results.

Format: Examiner required; individual administration; untimed: 30 minutes

Scoring: Examiner evaluated

Cost: Complete Kit (manual, stimulus booklet, 20 response booklets, 20 forms) $112.00

Brief Test of Head Injury (BTHI)
Nancy Helm-Estabrooks, Gillian Hotz

1991	PRO-ED, Inc.

Population: Adolescents, adults

Purpose: Used to quickly probe cognitive, linguistic, and communicative abilities of patients with severe head trauma

Description: The BTHI can be given to an individual in one or more short sessions. Results can be used in advising other team members on the best approaches for communicating with a patient and structuring individualized treatment. Item clusters include Orientation and Attention, Following Commands, Linguistic Organization, Reading Comprehension, Naming, Memory, and Visual-Spatial Skills. The test yields cluster raw and standard scores and a total. The total raw score can be converted to a percentile rank, standard score, or normative severity score.

Format: Examiner required; individual administration; untimed: 25 to 30 minutes

Scoring: Examiner evaluated

Cost: Complete Kit (manual, 25 record forms, stimulus cards, manipulatives) $229.00

Brief Visuospatial Memory Test-Revised (BVMT-R)
Ralph H. B. Benedict

| 1997 | Psychological Assessment Resources, Inc. |

Population: Ages 18 to 79 years

Purpose: Measures visuospatial memory

Description: The BVMT-R has six alternate, equivalent forms. Each form consists of 6 geometric figures and 12 recognition items.

Format: Examiner required; individual administration; timed: 45 minutes

Scoring: Examiner evaluated

Cost: $195.00

Burns Brief Inventory of Communication and Cognition (Burns Inventory)
Martha S. Burns

| 1997 | The Psychological Corporation |

Population: Ages 18 through 80 years

Purpose: Evaluates clients who have communication or cognitive deficits as a result of a neurological injury

Description: Three inventories (Right Hemisphere, Left Hemisphere, and Complex Neuropathology) are included to help determine which skills are impaired and may be appropriate for intervention. Results are plotted on the record form's treatment grid to determine a starting point and set goals for intervention. A goal bank is provided to develop treatment plans.

Format: Examiner required; individual administration; untimed: 30 minutes

Scoring: Examiner evaluated

Cost: Complete Kit (manual, 15 record forms for each inventory, stimulus plates, audiocassette) $149.00

California Computerized Assessment Package (CalCAP)
Eric N. Miller

| 2001 | Norland Software |

Population: Ages 13 years and older

Purpose: Measures reaction time, working memory, and selective attention

Description: Total of 10 subtests in standard battery; four subtests in abbreviated battery. The CalCAP assesses simple reaction time, one-back reaction time, visual scanning, sequential reaction time, lexical discrimination, and form discrimination. The test yields reaction times, true positive and false positive responses, signal detection parameters, and graphs. Also available in Spanish, French, Norwegian, Danish, and Flemish.

Format: Self-administered on computer; timed: 10 to 20 minutes

Scoring: Computer scored

Cost: $495.00

California Verbal Learning Test®- Children's Version (CVLT®-C)
Dean C. Delis, Joel H. Kramer, Edith Kaplan, Beth A. Ober

| 1994 | The Psychological Corporation |

Population: Ages 5 through 16 years

Purpose: Measures verbal learning and memory within the context of an everyday memory task

Description: Multitrial verbal learning task consisting of a 15-word shopping list used in immediate and delayed free-recall, cued-recall, and recognition trials. Aged-based norms are available on 27 key indexes.

Format: Examiner required; individual administration; untimed: 15 to 20 minutes, plus a 20-minute delay period

Scoring: Examiner evaluated; may be computer scored

Cost: Set (manual, 25 record forms) $129.00

California Verbal Learning Test®- Second Edition (CVLT®-II)
Dean C. Delis, Joel H. Kramer, Edith Kaplan, Beth A. Ober

| 2000 | The Psychological Corporation |

Population: Ages 16 to 89 years

Purpose: Measures verbal learning and memory

Description: A revision of the classic test that includes more comprehensive information provided by new items, flexible administration with new short and alternate forms, expanded age range, correlation with the Wechsler Abbreviated Scale of Intelligence, and technologically advanced scoring system. The CVLT-II measures encoding strategies, learning rates, error types, and other process data. The test includes forced-choice items useful for detecting malingering, thereby helping to reduce false results.

Format: Examiner required; individual administration; untimed: standard and alternate forms 30 minutes plus a 30-minute delay period; short form 15 minutes plus 15-minute delay period

Scoring: Examiner evaluated; may be computer scored

Cost: Complete Kit (manual, 25 record forms, 1 alternate record form, 25 short record forms, scoring software) $450.00

Canter Background Interference Procedure (BIP) for the Bender Gestalt Test
Arthur Canter

1975   Western Psychological Services

Population: Ages 15 years and older

Purpose: Assesses the probability of organic brain damage; used for diagnosis and to plan rehabilitation programs

Description: Paper–pencil 10-item test comparing the subject's results on the standard Bender Gestalt Test (in which the subject is presented with stimulus cards and asked to copy the designs on a blank sheet of paper) with the results of a Bender Gestalt Test in which the subject reproduces the designs on a special sheet with intersecting sinusoidal lines that provide background noise or interference during the copying task. The difference between the standard and the BIP results provides the basis for defining the subject's level of impairment. Specific ranges of adequacy and inadequacy of performance are defined to permit a measure of impairment having a high probability of association with organic brain damage or disease. Scoring is a modification of the standard Pascal-Suttell system.

Format: Examiner required; individual administration; untimed: 20 to 30 minutes

Scoring: Examiner evaluated

Cost: Kit (manual, 25 tests) $72.00

Category Test Computer Program
*James Choca, Linda Laatsch,
Dan Garside, Carl Arnemann*

1994   Multi-Health Systems, Inc.

Population: Ages 9 years and older

Purpose: Screens for neuropsychological functioning

Description: Halstead Category Test items appear on screen while accepting patient responses from the keyboard. The Category Test Computer Program provides the patient's answers, time to complete each subtest, Perseveration Index, and a narrative interpretation of the results. MS DOS compatible.

Format: Self-administered; untimed: 30 to 40 minutes

Scoring: Computer scored

Cost: $360.00 (unlimited use)

Category Test: Computer Version
Nick A. DeFilippis

1993   Psychological Assessment Resources, Inc.

Population: Ages 15 years and older

Purpose: Measures concept formation and abstract thinking; distinguishes individuals with and without brain damage

Description: Computer-administered version of the Halstead Category Test. Examiner must be a qualified neuropsychologist.

Format: Self-administered; untimed

Scoring: Computer scored

Cost: $450.00

Children's Auditory Verbal Learning Test-2 (CAVLT-2)
Jack L. Talley

1993   Psychological Assessment Resources, Inc.

Population: Ages 6 years 6 months to 17 years 11 months

Purpose: Measures auditory verbal learning and memory abilities; used for psychoeducational or neuropsychological assessment

Description: Oral-response verbal test with the following seven scales: Immediate Memory Span, Level of Learning, Interference Trial, Immediate Recall, Delayed Recall, Recognition Accuracy, and Total Intrusions.

Format: Examiner required; individual administration; untimed

Scoring: Examiner evaluated

Cost: Introduction Kit $89.00

Children's Category Test® (CCT®)
Thomas Boll

1993   The Psychological Corporation

Population: Ages 5 through 16 years

Purpose: Measures higher-order cognitive abilities nonverbally

Description: Appropriate for use in combination with intellectual and academic achievement tests to identify traumatic brain injury. The test accommodates the needs of children with color acuity problems. Two levels are available: colors for ages 5 to 8 and numbers for ages 9 to 16. The CCT was co-normed with the California Verbal Learning Test.

Format: Examiner required; individual administration; untimed: 15 to 20 minutes

Scoring: Examiner evaluated

Cost: Complete Kit (manual, 25 record forms of each level, 2 stimulus booklets, response cards) $329.00

Children's Memory Scale™ (CMS)
Morris Cohen

1997	The Psychological Corporation

Population: Ages 5 to 16 years

Purpose: Assesses children's memory abilities

Description: Provides comparison between memory and learning to ability, attention, and achievement. The CMS identifies deficits in learning and memory, deficient recall strategies, and underlying processing disorders. The results can be used to design remedial programs based on the child's strengths and compensatory strategies. The CMS can be used as a screening or diagnostic instrument in the following dimensions: attention and working memory, verbal and visual memory, short-delay and long-delay memory, recall and recognition, and learning characteristics. Two forms are available: ages 5 through 8 and ages 9 through 16.

Format: Examiner required; individual administration; untimed: 30 minutes

Scoring: Examiner evaluated; computer scoring available

Cost: Complete Kit (manual, 2 stimulus booklets, 25 record forms for each level, manipulatives, case) $449.00

Clinical Assessment Scales for the Elderly (CASE)
Cecil R. Reynolds, Erin D. Bigler

2001	Psychological Assessment Resources, Inc.

Population: Ages 55 to 90 years

Purpose: Assesses acute psychopathology

Description: Designed to assist the clinician in the diagnosis of selected DSM-IV Axis I clinical disorders, the CASE has 199 items on Form S and 190 items on Form R. These categories are included: Anxiety, Cognitive Competence, Depression, Fear of Aging, Obsessive-Compulsive, Paranoia, Psychoticism, Somatization, Mania, and Substance Abuse. The CASE yields 10 Clinical Scale Scores and three Validity Scales. A fourth-grade reading level is required. A Fear of Aging scale assesses an individual's level of apprehension about the aging process.

Format: Self-administered; untimed: 20 to 40 minutes

Scoring: Examiner evaluated

Cost: $150.00

Clinical Assessment Scales for the Elderly-Short Form (CASE-SF)
Cecil R. Reynolds, Erin D. Bigler

2001	Psychological Assessment Resources, Inc.

Population: Ages 55 to 90 years

Purpose: Assesses acute psychopathology

Description: The CASE-SF has 100 items on Form S and 88 items on Form R. These categories are included: Anxiety, Cognitive Competence, Depression, Fear of Aging, Obsessive-Compulsive, Paranoia, Psychoticism, Somatization, Mania, and Substance Abuse. The CASE-SF yields 10 clinical scale scores and three validity scales. A fourth-grade reading level is required.

Format: Self-administered; untimed: 10 to 20 minutes

Scoring: Examiner evaluated

Cost: $110.00

Closed Head Injury Screener (CHIS)
Michael Ivan Friedman

1994	Mind Garden, Inc.

Population: Patients with head injuries

Purpose: Determines a basis for evaluation and rehabilitation; used by clinicians evaluating post-concussion syndrome

Description: Oral-response yes-no test reporting the day-to-day manifestations of cortical functions. The CHIS is a systematic interview procedure based on neurobehavioral symptoms.

Format: Examiner required; individual administration; untimed: 30 minutes

Scoring: Examiner evaluated

Cost: Sampler Set $25.00; Permission Set $125.00

Cognitive Assessment of Minnesota
Ruth A. Rustad, Terry L. DeGroot,
Margaret L. Jungkunz, Daren S. Freeberg,
Laureen G. Borowick, Ann M. Wanttie

1993	The Psychological Corporation

Population: Adults

Purpose: Measures the cognitive abilities of adults with neurological impairments

Description: General problem areas are identified and presented in a concise hierarchical approach. Subtests measure attention span, memory orientation, visual neglect, temporal awareness, safety and judgment, recall/recognition, auditory memory and sequencing, and simple math skills.

Format: Examiner required; individual administration; untimed: less than 1 hour

Scoring: Examiner evaluated

Cost: Complete Kit (manual, test cards, 25 scoring booklets, case) $104.00

Cognitive Behavior Rating Scales (CBRS), Research Edition
J. Michael Williams

1987	Psychological Assessment Resources, Inc.

Population: Adults

Purpose: Determines the presence and assesses the severity of cognitive impairment, behavioral deficits, and observable neurological signs in individuals with possible brain impairment; also used to assess dementia

Description: Paper–pencil instrument consisting of 116 items on nine scales intended to elicit information about the examinee's daily behaviors: Language Deficit, Agitation, Need for Routine, Depression, High Cognitive Deficits, Memory Disorder, Dementia, Apraxia, and Disorientation. The items on the scales are rated by the examinee's family or significant other. *T*-scores and percentiles are reported for each of the nine scale scores.

Format: Examiner required; individual administration; untimed: 15 to 20 minutes

Scoring: Examiner evaluated

Cost: Kit (manual, 25 reusable item booklets, 50 rating booklets) $99.00

Cognitive Linguistic Quick Test (CLQT)
Nancy Helm-Estabrooks

2001	The Psychological Corporation

Population: Ages 18 to 89 years

Purpose: Measures cognitive strengths and weaknesses

Description: Tests in five cognitive domains (attention, memory, executive functions, language, and visuospatial skills) of individuals with neurological impairment due to strokes, head injury, or dementia. The CLQT can be administered at a table or bedside, as long as the patient can sit up and use a pen. It is available in Spanish.

Format: Examiner required; individual administration; untimed: 15 to 30 minutes

Scoring: Examiner evaluated

Cost: Complete Kit (manual, stimulus manual, 15 each of record forms and response forms) $150.00

Cognitive Symptom Checklist (CSC)
Christine O'Hara, Minnie Harrell,
Eileen Bellingrath, Katherine Lisicia

1993	Psychological Assessment Resources, Inc.

Population: Ages 16 years and older

Purpose: Evaluates areas of impaired cognitive functioning; used in rehabilitation counseling and occupational therapy

Description: Paper–pencil short-answer checklists in five cognitive areas: visual processes, attention/concentration, memory, language, and executive functions. A clinician guide for each of the five checklists is used. A seventh-grade reading level is required. The examiner must be trained in therapeutic approaches to rehabilitation of cognition.

Format: Self-administered; untimed: 10 to 20 minutes each

Scoring: Examiner evaluated

Cost: Introductory Kit $69.00

Color Trail Test (CTT)
Louis F. D'Elia, Paul Satz,
Craig Lyons Uchiyama, Travis White

1996	Psychological Assessment Resources, Inc.

Population: Ages 18 years and older

Purpose: Measures sustained attention and sequencing

Description: On Color Trails 1, the examinee connects circles numbered 1 through 25. On Color Trails 2, the examinee connects circles numbered 1 through 25, but alternates between pink and yellow circles.

Format: Examiner required; individual administration; timed: 3 to 8 minutes

Scoring: Examiner evaluated

Cost: Kit (manual, 25 record forms, 25 administrations) $87.00

Comprehensive Norms for an Expanded Halstead–Reitan Battery with a Supplement for the WAIS–R
Robert K. Heaton, Igor Grant, Charles G. Matthews

1992   Psychological Assessment Resources, Inc.

Population: Ages 20 to 80 years

Purpose: Provides normative data for 54 measures based on age, education, and gender

Description: A comprehensive norms book is used. Computer version is available. The authors analyze the influence of demographic variables on raw and corrected scores for all test measures. The distributional properties of the corrected scores are examined, and the performance of the correction system is checked at different age and education levels. Issues related to using corrected scores in clinical interpretation and research applications are addressed. Case studies illustrate using scaled and standard scores in interpretation.

Format: Examiner required

Scoring: Examiner evaluated

Cost: $89.00

Contextual Memory Test (CMT)
Joan P. Toglia

1993   The Psychological Corporation

Population: Adults

Purpose: Assesses awareness of memory capacity, strategy of memory use, and recall

Description: Effective treatment plans can be designed by using the CMT at bedside or in clinical settings. Used with a variety of diagnoses, including head trauma, cerebral vascular disorders, multiple sclerosis, depression, schizophrenia, and chronic alcohol abuse.

Format: Examiner required; individual administration; untimed: 10 to 20 minutes

Scoring: Examiner evaluated

Cost: Complete Kit (manual, 2 test cards, picture cards, 25 score sheets, case) $99.00

Continuous Visual Memory Test (CVMT)
Donald E. Trahan, Glenn J. Larrabee

1997   Psychological Assessment Resources, Inc.

Population: Ages 7 to 80+ years

Purpose: Assesses the visual memory of individuals with neurological impairments

Description: Multiple-item verbally administered oral-response visual memory test in three parts. The Acquisition Task (recognition memory) requires the individual to discriminate between new and old repeated stimuli from among 112 designs presented at 2-second intervals. The Delayed Recognition Task measures retrieval from long-term storage and is administered after a 30-minute delay. The Visual Discrimination Task assesses the individual's ability to perceive and discriminate stimuli, thus distinguishing visual discrimination deficits from visual memory problems.

Format: Examiner required; individual administration; untimed: 45 to 50 minutes (includes 30-minute delay)

Scoring: Examiner evaluated

Cost: $139.00

Cortical Vision Screening Test (CORVIST)
Merle J. James, Gordon T. Plant, Elizabeth K. Warrington

2001   Thames Valley Test Company, Ltd.

Population: Adults

Purpose: Measures visual loss due to neurological disease

Description: The test is designed to allow vision specialists without any detailed knowledge of neuropsychology to probe the higher visual areas of the brain. Cerebral lesions affecting the occipital or parietal lobes result in problems with the perception of faces, pictures, colors, and the ability to read fluently. Each of the 10 tests focuses on a different aspect of early visual processing by cortical centers. They are simple to administer and make minimal demands on the examinee. An individual who has any difficulty with any of these tests should undergo appropriate neurological and neuropsychological testing.

Format: Examiner required; individual administration; untimed: 15 minutes

Scoring: Examiner evaluated

Cost: $147.00

DCS-A Visual Learning and Memory Test for Neuropsychological Assessment
Georg Lamberti, Sigrid Weidlich

Date not provided	Hogrefe & Huber Publishers

Population: Ages 6 to 70 years

Purpose: Detects memory deficits resulting from acquired brain damage

Description: This third edition contains nine symmetrical geometric drawings shown in succession. After being removed, all have to be reproduced with five short sticks. Six trials are allowed, although the goal of reproducing all drawings in one trial can be reached well before then by some patients. Test performance is dependent upon several factors, such as directing one's attention and perceiving, storing, and reproducing forms. The results of the test give an immediate indication of the probability that brain damage has or has not occurred and also how extensive it may be.

Format: Examiner required; individual administration; timed: 20 to 60 minutes

Scoring: Examiner evaluated

Cost: Complete Test (manual, 50 sheets, cards, sticks, folder) $89.00

Delis-Kaplan Executive Function System (D-KEFS)
Dean C. Delis, Edith Kaplan, Joel H. Kramer

2000	The Psychological Corporation

Population: Ages 8 through 89 years

Purpose: Assesses key components of executive functions within verbal and spatial modalities

Description: This unique instrument incorporates principles from cognitive science to evaluate the component processes of tasks thought to be especially sensitive to frontal lobe dysfunction. The gamelike format is designed to be interesting and engaging for examinees, encouraging optimal performance without providing right-wrong feedback that can create frustration. There are nine stand-alone tests: Card Sorting, Train Making, Verbal Fluency, Design Fluency, Color-Word Interference, Tower, 20 Questions, Word Context, and Proverb.

Format: Examiner required; individual administration; untimed: 90 minutes

Scoring: Examiner evaluated

Cost: Complete Kit (manual, stimulus booklet, cards, tower and disks, 25 each of record forms and 2 response booklets, case) $450.00

Differential Diagnostic Technique (DDT)
S. L. North, H. Breen, O. Weininger

1995	Otto Weininger

Population: Ages 6 years and older

Purpose: Measures personality for gross brain function diagnosis, forensic psychology, marital counseling, and others

Description: The DDT has 12 items with a series of figures on cards to measure various aspects of ego strength and functions. Total scores are provided for ego strength, differential personality, hostility, interpersonal relationships, stress reactions, emotional energy available, and others. Two forms are available, one for children to age 12 and one for adolescents and adults. This is a projective technique.

Format: Examiner required; individual administration; untimed

Scoring: Examiner evaluated

Cost: Complete Kit (manual, cards) $150.00

Digit Vigilance Test (DVT)
Ronald F. Lewis

1995	Psychological Assessment Resources, Inc.

Population: Ages 20 to 80 years

Purpose: Assesses attention during rapid visual tracking

Description: The DVT has 59 rows of digits printed in red on the first stimulus page and blue on the second page. Respondents are asked to find and cross out either 6's or 9's to measure vigilance and accurate selection of target stimuli.

Format: Self-administered; timed: 10 minutes

Scoring: Examiner evaluated

Cost: Kit (user guide, 50 test booklets, set of 4 scoring templates) $99.00

Doors and People
Alan Baddeley, Hazel Emslie, Ian Nimmo-Smith

1994	Thames Valley Test Company, Ltd.

Population: Adults

Purpose: Measures visual and verbal recall and recognition

Description: The test is a broad-based instrument of long-term memory. It yields a single age-scaled overall score, as well as separate measures of visual and verbal memory, recall and recognition, and forgetting. It is designed for use as both a clinical tool and a research instrument. It provides a more analytic overview of long-term explicit memory. There are four subcomponents: Visual Recognition, Visual Recall, Verbal Recognition, and Verbal Recall.

Format: Examiner required; individual administration; untimed: 25 minutes

Scoring: Examiner evaluated

Cost: $296.00

Halstead Russell Neuropsychological Evaluation System, Revised (HRNES–R)
Elbert W. Russell, Regina I. Starkey

2001	Western Psychological Services

Population: All ages

Purpose: Provides a complete neuropsychological evaluation

Description: Uses a scaling system based on 10 index tests. The program takes raw scores from the tests administered, corrects them for age and education, and converts them to scaled scores. The HRNES–R generates three overall indexes of brain function: Percent Score, Average Index Score, and Lateralization Key. Tests are chosen from both the Halstead-Reitan Neuropsychological Battery and clinical practice.

Format: Examiner required; individual administration; untimed

Scoring: Computer scored

Cost: Kit (manual, 10 recording booklets, unlimited-use disk) $450.00

Hayling and Brixton Tests
Paul W. Burgess, Tim Shallice

1997	Thames Valley Test Company, Ltd.

Population: Adolescents, adults

Purpose: Measures deficits in executive functions

Description: People with deficits in executive functions present special difficulties for the clinician because the problems are often quite difficult to detect even though their effects on everyday life are devastating. The Hayling Sentence Completion Test yields three different measures that can be considered separately or combined into an overall score. The test consists of two sets of 15 sentences, each missing the last word. In the first section the examiner reads each sentence aloud and the examinee completes the sentence. In the second section the examinee is asked to provide a word that does not fit. The Brixton Spatial Anticipation Test is perceptually simple and does not require a verbal response.

Format: Examiner required; individual administration; timed: 15 minutes

Scoring: Examiner evaluated

Cost: $149.00

Hooper Visual Organization Test (VOT)
H. Elston Hooper

1985	Western Psychological Services

Population: Adolescents, adults

Purpose: Assesses organic brain pathology of both hemispheres; used for clinical diagnosis

Description: Thirty-item pictorial test differentiating between functional and motivational disorders. The subject is presented with drawings of simple objects cut into several parts and rearranged and is asked to name the objects.

Format: Examiner required; suitable for group use; untimed: 15 minutes

Scoring: Examiner evaluated

Cost: Kit (manual, 4 picture booklets, 25 test booklets, 100 answer sheets, scoring key) $180.00

Human Figure Drawing Test (HFDT): An Illustrated Handbook for Clinical Interpretation and Standardized Assessment of Cognitive Impairment
Jerry Mitchell, Richard Trent, Roland McArthur

1993	Western Psychological Services

Population: Ages 15 years to adults

Purpose: Used to evaluate cognitive deterioration in adults

Description: A complete scoring and interpretation system for human figure drawings that provides adult norms for cognitive impairment. Using the handbook and the AutoScore™ form, examiners can make a complete qualitative evaluation. The HFDT provides four measures of cognitive status: Impairment Score, Distortion Score, Simplification Score, and Organic Factors Index.

These scores are helpful in discriminating cognitive impairment caused by thought disorders from that caused by organic conditions. Norms are based on a sample of 800 individuals (over age 15), including the following groups: nonclinical, depressed, antisocial, manic, paranoid, schizophrenic, organic, and mentally retarded.

Format: Examiner required; individual administration; untimed: 15 minutes

Scoring: Examiner evaluated

Cost: Kit (handbook, 25 AutoScore™ forms, 25 drawing forms) $87.50

Human Information Processing Survey (HIP Survey)
E. Paul Torrance, William Taggart, Barbara Taggart-Hausladen

1984	Scholastic Testing Service, Inc.

Population: Adults

Purpose: Used in human resource development to assess learning styles and brain hemisphere dominance

Description: Paper-pencil 40-item survey with left-brain, right-brain, or integrated categories. Raw scores, standard scores, and percentiles are yielded. Research and Professional Forms are available. Booklets, profiles, and pencils are used. Examiner must be certified for assessment.

Format: Self-administered; untimed: 20 to 30 minutes

Scoring: Self-scored

Cost: Specimen Set $23.10

Infant/Toddler Sensory Profile™ (Clinical Edition)
Winnie Dunn

2000	The Psychological Corporation

Population: Birth to 36 months

Purpose: Evaluates sensory information processing

Description: Caregivers complete a questionnaire to provide a profile of how well a child with sensory processing issues functions in daily life. The six sections are general processing, auditory processing, visual processing, tactile processing, vestibular processing, and oral sensory processing. Results help to provide a method for linking performance strengths and barriers with sensory processing patterns, but must be combined with other evaluation data to create a complete picture of a child's status for intervention planning.

Format: Examiner required; individual administration; untimed: 15 minutes

Scoring: Examiner evaluated

Cost: Complete Kit (manual, 25 questionnaires) $39.00

Intermediate Booklet Category Test (IBCT)
Paul A. Byrd

1987	Psychological Assessment Resources, Inc.

Population: Ages 9 to 14 years

Purpose: Assesses concept formation and abstract reasoning; used by clinicians to detect brain dysfunction

Description: The test replicates in booklet format the slides used in the Halstead Category Test. Figures are presented one at a time to the subject, who responds with a number between 1 and 4. The test consists of a total of 168 items on six subtests. A cutoff score is derived.

Format: Examiner required; individual administration; untimed: 30 to 60 minutes

Scoring: Examiner evaluated

Cost: Intro Kit (manual, 2 volumes of stimuli, 50 scoring forms) $259.00

Kaufman Short Neuropsychological Assessment Procedure (K-SNAP)
Alan S. Kaufman, Nadeen L. Kaufman

1994	American Guidance Service

Population: Ages 11 through 85+ years

Purpose: Measures cognitive functioning

Description: Four subtests are organized in three levels of cognitive complexity: attention-orientation (Mental Status), simple memory and perceptual skills (Number Recall and Gestalt Closure), and complex intellectual functioning and planning ability (Four-Letter Words). An 8-point Impairment Index can be used to identify examinees who are likely to need further diagnostic testing.

Format: Examiner required; individual administration; untimed: 20 to 30 minutes

Scoring: Examiner evaluated

Cost: Complete Kit (manual, easel, 25 record forms) $173.95

Learning and Memory Battery (LAMB)
James P. Schmidt, Tom N. Tombaugh

1995	Multi-Health Systems, Inc.

Population: Ages 20 to 80 years

Purpose: Assesses specificity of and sensitivity to diverse memory problems

Description: Paper-pencil oral-response test with seven subtests: Paragraph Learning, Word List Learning, Word Pair Learning, Digit Span, Supraspan, Simple Figure, and Complex Figure. All subtests contribute to an overall assessment of learning and memory abilities. All components of memory are considered, including storage and retrieval. Scores are yielded for each of the subtests. These scores are plotted on a profile sheet for easy comparison to norms. A Windows-based computer version is available.

Format: Examiner required; individual administration; untimed: 1 hour or less

Scoring: Examiner evaluated; computer scored

Cost: Complete Kit $315.00

Luria-Nebraska Neuropsychological Battery (LNNB)
Charles J. Golden, Arnold D. Purisch, Thomas A. Hammeke

1984	Western Psychological Services

Population: Ages 15 years and older

Purpose: Assesses a broad range of neuropsychological functions for individuals ages 15 and older; used to diagnose specific cerebral dysfunction and to select and assess rehabilitation programs

Description: Multiple-item verbal, observational test available in two forms: Form I (269 items) and Form II (279 items). The discrete, scored items produce a profile for the following scales: Motor, Rhythm, Tactile, Visual, Receptive Speech, Expressive Speech, Writing, Reading, Arithmetic, Memory, Intellectual, Pathognomonic, Left Hemisphere, Right Hemisphere, Impairment, and Profile Evaluation. Form II also assesses intermediate memory. The battery diagnoses the presence of cerebral dysfunction and determines lateralization and localization. Test materials include six stimulus cards, an audiocassette, comb, quarter, and stopwatch. The Administration and Scoring Booklet includes the Profile Form and Computation of Critical Level Tables. It is used to record all scores during administration.

Format: Examiner required; individual administration; untimed: 90 to 150 minutes

Scoring: Examiner evaluated; Form I may be computer scored, Form II is only computer scored

Cost: Complete Kit Form I (set of test materials, 10 administration/scoring booklets, 10 patient response booklets, manual, 2-use disk) $499.00; Complete Kit Form II $430.00

Luria-Nebraska Neuropsychological Battery: Children's Revision (LNNB-C)
Charles J. Golden

1987	Western Psychological Services

Population: Ages 8 to 12 years

Purpose: Measures cognitive strengths and weaknesses; used to diagnose cerebral dysfunction and to select and assess rehabilitation programs

Description: Verbal, observational adaptation of the Luria-Nebraska Neuropsychological Battery with 149 items assessing cognitive functioning. The clinical scales are Motor Functions, Tactile Functions, Receptive Speech, Writing, Arithmetic, Intellectual Processes, Rhythm, Visual Functions, Expressive Speech, Reading, and Memory. The summary scales are Pathognomonic, Left Sensorimotor, and Right Sensorimotor. Two optional scales, Spelling and Motor Writing, are available.

Format: Examiner required; individual administration; untimed: 150 minutes

Scoring: Examiner evaluated; computer scored

Cost: Kit (manual, set of test materials, 10 administration/scoring booklets, 10 patient response booklets, 2-use disk, carrying case) $455.00

Memory Assessment Scales (MAS)
J. Michael Williams

1991	Psychological Assessment Resources, Inc.

Population: Ages 18 to 90 years

Purpose: Used in clinical rehabilitation and neuropsychology to assess memory functioning

Description: Contains the following subtests: List Learning, Prose Memory, List Recall, Verbal Span, Visual Span, Visual Recognition, Visual Reproduction, Names-Faces, Delayed List Recall, Delayed Prose Memory, Delayed Visual Recognition, and Delayed Names-Faces Recall. Examiner must be Level C qualified.

Format: Examiner required; individual administration; untimed: 40 to 45 minutes

Scoring: Examiner evaluated

Cost: Intro Kit (manual, stimulus card set, 25 record forms, attache case) $215.00

MicroCog2: Assessment of Cognitive Functioning Version 2.4 (MicroCog™)

Douglas Powell, Edith Kaplan, Dean Whitla, Sandra Weintaub, Randolph Catlin, Harris Funkenstein

1996   The Psychological Corporation

Population: Ages 18 through 89 years

Purpose: Assesses adults with cognitive impairment

Description: The user-friendly software allows most examinees to complete the test with minimal assistance; computer literacy is not required. The instrument covers a broad range of cognitive functioning, including both accuracy and speed of cognitive processing. The updated version allows the examiner to choose only those subtests wanted. Nine interrelated areas are measured: attention/mental control, memory, reasoning/calculation, spatial processing, reaction time, information processing accuracy, information processing speed, cognitive functioning, and cognitive proficiency. Standard scores are automatically computed for all indexes and subtests.

Format: Computer administered; untimed: 30 to 60 minutes

Scoring: Computer scored

Cost: Complete Kit (user's guide, manual, disks, 10 report credits—5 for each form) $179.00

Middlesex Elderly Assessment of Mental State (MEAMS)

Evelyn Golding

1989   Thames Valley Test Company, Ltd.

Population: Adults

Purpose: Used to detect gross impairment of specific cognitive skills in elderly individuals

Description: The test is designed to assist examiners in differentiating between functional illnesses and organically based cognitive impairments. The test items are sensitive to the functioning of different areas of the brain. The test will determine if parts of the brain are working less efficiently than they should and, consequently, whether it is necessary to recommend more investigation. The subtests cover the following areas: orientation, memory, new learning, naming, comprehension, arithmetic, visuospatial skills, perception, fluency, and motor perseveration.

Format: Examiner required; individual administration; untimed: 20 minutes

Scoring: Examiner evaluated

Cost: $146.00

Mini Inventory of Right Brain Injury–Second Edition (MIRBI-2)

Patricia A. Pimental, Jeffrey A. Knight

2000   PRO-ED, Inc.

Population: Ages 20 through 80 years

Purpose: Identifies severity of right-brain injury

Description: The examiner can quickly screen clients for neurocognitive deficits associated with right-hemisphere lesions. The inventory meets the need for a brief, standardized, right-brain injury screening instrument that yields severity levels for deficit areas. New features include more data collected on an increased number of cases. Many new validity studies have been conducted with particular emphasis on the relationships of MIRBI-2 scores to other measures of neurocognitive impairment. Principal components factor analysis was performed. Each item was reevaluated. A revised Right–Left Differential Scale was created. A table was added for converting raw scores. The rationale was updated to reflect current trends. The test booklet was revised to include more user-friendly areas for recording patient information, as well as revised criteria for scoring patient responses.

Format: Examiner required; individual administration; untimed: 25 to 30 minutes

Scoring: Examiner evaluated

Cost: Complete Kit (manual, 25 examiner record booklets, 25 report forms, 25 response sheets, caliper, storage box) $134.00

Mini-Mental™ State Examination (MMSE)

Marshal F. Folstein, Susan E. Folstein, Paul R. McHugh

1975   Psychological Assessment Resources, Inc.

Population: Adults

Purpose: Screens for cognitive impairment and estimates the severity of cognitive impairment at a given point in time; is ideal for routine and serial assessment of cognitive function

Description: The MMSE is one of the most widely used clinical instruments for quickly detecting and assessing the severity of cognitive impairment and for monitoring cognitive changes over time. Standard form has demonstrated validity and reliability in psychiatric, neurological, geriatric, and other medical populations. The convenient all-in-one test form includes a detachable sheet with stimuli for the Comprehension, Reading, Writing, and Drawing tasks. The form also includes alternative item substitutions for administrations in special circumstances. The pocket-size User's Guide provides valuable clinical information (population-based norms) and detailed instructions for standard administration and scoring.

Format: Examiner required; individual administration; untimed: 5 to 10 minutes

Scoring: Examiner evaluated

Cost: Introductory Kit $35.00

NEPSY®
Marit Korkman, Ursula Kirk, Sally Kemp

1997   The Psychological Corporation

Population: Ages 3 through 12 years

Purpose: Assesses neuropsychological development

Description: A child-friendly test that provides a wealth of clinical data useful for planning treatment. Strengths and subtle deficiencies are detected in five functional domains that facilitate or interfere with learning. The test provides a thorough means of assessing the neuropsychological status of children with congenital or acquired brain dysfunction, damage, or disease and is invaluable as a basis for planning treatment, special education, and long-term care. The domains measured are Attention and Executive Functions, Language, Sensorimotor Functions, Visuospatial Processing, and Memory and Learning. Each domain has a core set of subtests.

Format: Examiner required; individual administration; 45 to 65 minutes depending on age

Scoring: Examiner evaluated; computer scoring available

Cost: Complete Set (manual, stimulus booklet, 10 each of record forms for ages 3 to 4 and ages 5 to 12, 10 each of both response booklets, scoring templates, manipulatives, case) $524.00

Neurobehavioral Functioning Inventory (NFI™)
Jeffrey S. Kreutzer, Ronald T. Seel, Jennifer H. Marwitz

1999   The Psychological Corporation

Population: Ages 17 to 80 years

Purpose: Allows the development of an effec-

tive treatment plan and measures change for patients with traumatic brain injury

Description: The NFI is a brief self-report inventory that is completed by the patient or family member. There are 76 items organized into six independent scales reflecting symptoms and problems commonly encountered following the onset of neurological disability. The two forms (Patient Record Form and Family Record Form) allow comparison between two perspectives. The behaviors and symptoms are written at a sixth-grade reading level. Both scales use a 5-point Likert scale.

Format: Rating scale; untimed: 30 minutes

Scoring: Examiner evaluated

Cost: Complete Kit (manual, 25 each of family and patient record forms) $132.00

Neuropsychological Status Examination (NSE)
John A. Schinka

1983   Psychological Assessment Resources, Inc.

Population: Adults

Purpose: Evaluates and collects data pertaining to an individual's neuropsychological functioning; used for a variety of neuropsychological assessments ranging from screening procedures to extensive workups and preparation for expert-witness testimony

Description: Paper–pencil 10-page multiple-item assessment evaluating neuropsychological information, such as patient data, observational findings, test administration parameters, neuroanatomical correlates, reports of test findings, clinical impressions, and recommendations for treatment. The instrument consists of 13 sections, including patient and referral data; neuropsychological symptom checklist (NSC); premorbid status; physical, emotional, and cognitive status; results of neuropsychological testing; diagnostic comments; and follow-up and treatment recommendations. The NSC is a two-page screening instrument used to assess the status of potential neurological and neuropsychological signs and symptoms. Each section was designed with consideration of base rate data for common findings in neuropsychological evaluations. The manual includes a discussion of the rationale of the logic underlying the structure of the instrument and provides suggestions for its most efficient use.

Format: Examiner required; individual administration; untimed

Scoring: Examiner evaluated

Cost: Examination Kit $45.00

NeuroPsychology Behavior and Affect Profile (NBAP)
Linda Nelson, Paul Satz, Louis F. D'Elia

| 1994 | Mind Garden, Inc. |

Population: Individuals with brain injuries

Purpose: Assesses affective change used for clinical evaluation; intended for stroke patients, outpatients with dementia, and individuals with closed head injury

Description: Agree–disagree test with 106 items measuring reliability and validity data for indifference, inappropriateness, pragnosia, depression, and mania.

Format: Self-administered; untimed: 20 to 30 minutes

Scoring: Examiner evaluated

Cost: Sampler Set $25.00; Permission for 200 Uses $125.00

Older Americans' Resources and Services Multidimensional Functional Assessment Questionnaire (OARS–MFAQ)

| 1988 | Center for the Study of Aging and Human Development |

Population: Adults

Purpose: Assesses the functional status of adults, particularly elderly individuals

Description: Criterion-referenced 101-item paper–pencil and oral-response test assessing five areas of functioning: social, economic, mental health, physical health, and activities of daily living (ADL). The test also contains a 24-item services section, demographic information, and interviewer sections. The test yields both subscore ratings and summary ratings on 6-point scales for social, economic, mental health, physical health, and ADL. A videocassette is available for training purposes. Norms for ages 60+ are provided. Available also in Spanish, Portuguese, French, Chinese, and Italian. Suitable for individuals with physical, hearing, and visual disabilities.

Format: Examiner/self-administered; individual administration; untimed: 40 minutes

Scoring: Examiner evaluated; may be computer scored

Cost: Manual $40.00; Questionnaire $3.50

Pediatric Early Elementary Examination (PEEX2)
Melvin D. Levine

| 1995 | Educators Publishing Service, Inc. |

Population: Ages 6 to 9 years

Purpose: Assesses neurological development, behaviors, and health of children; used by clinicians in health care and other settings for educational planning, counseling, use of medication, and general programming

Description: Multiple-item response test providing standardized observation procedures for characterizing children's functional health and its relationship to neurodevelopmental and physical status. The test enables clinicians to integrate medical, developmental, and neurological findings while making observations of behavioral adjustment and style.

Format: Examiner required; individual administration; untimed: 45 to 60 minutes

Scoring: Examiner evaluated

Cost: Complete Set $62.00; Specimen Set (record form, manual) $9.70; Record Forms and Response Booklets $40.90; Stimulus Booklet $12.00; Examiner's Manual $10.25; Training Video $30.00

Pediatric Examination of Educational Readiness at Middle Childhood (PEERAMID2)
Melvin D. Levine

| 1995 | Educators Publishing Service, Inc. |

Population: Ages 9 to 15 years

Purpose: Assesses children's and adolescents' neurological development, behaviors, and health; used by clinicians in health care and other settings

Description: Multiple-item response test providing standardized observation procedures for characterizing children's and adolescents' functional health and its relationship to neurodevelopmental and physical status. The test assesses a wide range of functions, including neuromaturation, attention, many aspects of memory, motor efficiency, language, and other areas critical to the academic and social adjustment of older children. It is particularly sensitive to the often subtle developmental dysfunctions of junior high school students.

Format: Examiner required; individual administration; untimed: 45 to 60 minutes

Scoring: Examiner evaluated

Cost: Complete Set $72.90; Specimen Set (manual, form) $10.85; Record Forms and Response Booklets $47.75; Stimulus Booklet $12.00; Examiner's Manual $10.25; Training Video $30.00

Pediatric Extended Examination at Three (PEET)
Melvin D. Levine

| 1986 | Educators Publishing Service, Inc. |

Population: Ages 3 and 4 years

Purpose: Enables clinicians to integrate medical, developmental, and neurological findings and make observations of behavioral adjustment and style to assist them in identifying specific interventions

Description: Verbal paper–pencil, show-and-tell performance measure of five developmental areas: gross motor, language, visual–fine motor, memory, and intersensory integration. The child is asked to perform gross motor tasks (jumping, throwing and kicking a small ball), identify pictures, name objects, follow directions, and copy figures with a pencil. Tasks are presented using numerous miscellaneous items (sticks, crayon, doll) contained in the kit. Words and sentences are provided for language assessment. The examination produces an empirically derived profile of the child in the developmental areas, based on his or her performance of age-appropriate tasks, which can be used to clarify concerns, determine need for further evaluation in specific areas, and initiate services or continued surveillance.

Format: Examiner required; individual administration; untimed: 45 to 60 minutes

Scoring: Examiner evaluated

Cost: Complete Set $71.00; Specimen Set (manual, record form) $9.70; Record Forms $18.20; Examiner's Manual $9.15; Stimulus Book $12.00; Kit $31.85

Philadelphia Head Injury Questionnaire
Lucille M. Curry, Richard G. Ivins, Thomas L. Gowen

| Date not provided | Western Psychological Services |

Population: Adolescents, adults

Purpose: Used as a history-gathering instrument specifically for individuals who have sustained head injuries

Description: The questionnaire is composed of six sections: identifying information, accident description, persistent symptoms, cognitive aspects, personality changes, and pertinent personal/medical history. Each section includes 8 to 16 questions; virtually all questions can be answered yes or no. The questionnaire provides organized information about head trauma.

Format: Examiner not required, but recommended; individual administration or self-administered; untimed: 20 minutes

Scoring: Hand key

Cost: Pad of 100 with Manual $25.00

Portable Tactual Performance Test (P-TPT)

| 1984 | Psychological Assessment Resources, Inc. |

Population: Ages 5 years to adult

Purpose: Measures tactile perception and problem-solving ability

Description: Multiple-task examination measuring spatial perception, discrimination of forms, manual or construction ability, motor coordination, and the ability to meet new situations. This portable version features a wooden carrying case, which can be set up for standardized administration.

Format: Examiner required; untimed: 10 to 15 minutes per trial

Scoring: Examiner evaluated

Cost: Kit (manual, 50 record forms, case) $369.00

Quick Neurological Screening Test-II (QNST-II)
Margaret Mutti, Harold M. Sterling, Nancy Martin, Norma V. Spalding

| 1998 | Academic Therapy Publications |

Population: Ages 5 to 18 years

Purpose: Assesses neurological integration as it relates to learning disabilities

Description: A nonverbal test of 15 functions, each involving a motor task similar to those observed in neurological pediatric examinations. The areas measured include maturity of motor development, skill in controlling large and small muscles, motor planning and sequencing, sense of rate and rhythm, spatial organization, visual and auditory perceptual skills, balance and cerebellarvestibular function, and disorders of attention. Materials include geometric form reproduction sheets and flipcards printed with directions for administration and scoring. Scoring occurs simultaneously, and neurodevelopmental difficulties result in increasingly larger numerical scores. The test is interpreted in terms of three functional categories.

Format: Examiner required; individual administration; untimed: 20 minutes

Scoring: Examiner evaluated

Cost: Test Kit (manual, 25 scoring forms, 25 geometric form reproduction sheets, 25 remedial guideline forms, flipcards, in vinyl folder) $95.00

Repeatable Battery for the Assessment of Neuropsychological Status (RBANS™)
Christopher Randolph

1998	The Psychological Corporation

Population: Ages 20 through 89 years

Purpose: Measures cognitive decline in adults who have neurological injury or disease such as dementia, head injury, or stroke

Description: A quick sampling of five cognitive areas (immediate memory, visuospatial/constructional, attention, language, and delayed memory) is obtained. Two parallel forms are available to measure status over time. There are 12 subtests.

Format: Examiner required; individual administration; untimed: 30 minutes

Scoring: Examiner evaluated

Cost: Primary Form Kit (manual, 25 record forms, stimulus book, coding scoring template) $141.00

Rey Complex Figure Test and Recognition Trail (RCFT)
John E. Meyers, Kelly R. Meyers

1996	Psychological Assessment Resources, Inc.

Population: Ages 6 through 89 years

Purpose: Measures visuospatial ability and visuospatial memory

Description: The RCFT consists of four separate tasks that measure Visuospatial Constructional Ability (Copy Trial) and Visuospatial Memory (Immediate Recall Trial, Delayed Recall Trial, and Recognition Trial).

Format: Examiner required; individual administration; untimed: 45 minutes including 30-minute delay interval

Scoring: Examiner evaluated

Cost: Kit (manual, manual supplement, 50 test booklets, stimulus card) $195.00

Rivermead Assessment of Somatosensory Performance (RASP)
Charlotte E. Winward, Peter W. Halligan, Derick T. Wade

2000	Thames Valley Test Company, Ltd.

Population: Adults

Purpose: Measures somatosensory functioning after stroke or other neurological disorders

Description: The RASP consists of seven subtests covering a wide and representative range of clinical assessments traditionally considered important for somatosensory assessment. The battery is short, easy to administer, and simple to score. The seven quantifiable tests are divided into primary (surface pressure touch, surface localization, temperature discrimination, proprioception, sharp/dull discrimination) and secondary tests (extinction and two-point discrimination).

Format: Examiner required; individual administration; untimed: 30 minutes

Scoring: Examiner evaluated

Cost: $233.00

Rivermead Behavioural Memory Test (RBMT)
Barbara A. Wilson, Janet Cockburn, Alan Baddeley

1985	Thames Valley Test Company, Ltd.

Population: Ages 6 to 95 years

Purpose: Measures memory impairment

Description: The RBMT has eight subtests, each attempting to provide an objective measure of one of a range of everyday memory problems reported and observed in patients with memory difficulties. Two scores are available: a screening score based on a pass–fail grading of each item and a more detailed profile score. There are four parallel versions so practice effects due to repeated testing can be avoided.

Format: Examiner required; individual administration; untimed: 25 minutes

Scoring: Examiner evaluated

Cost: $216.00

Rivermead Behavioural Memory Test–Extended Version (RBMT-E)
Barbara A. Wilson, Linda Clare, Alan Baddeley, Janet Cockburn, Peter Watson, Robyn Tate

1998	Thames Valley Test Company, Ltd.

Population: Ages 5 to 96 years

Purpose: Designed to predict everyday memory problems in people with acquired, nonprogressive brain injury, and to monitor change over time

Description: The RBMT-E comprises tasks analogous to situations found in daily living that often appear troublesome for people with memory impairments. The intention of the authors was to design a set of simple subtests that could be passed by the majority of normal control subjects. Two parallel versions have been developed.

Format: Examiner required; individual administration; untimed: 35 minutes

Scoring: Examiner evaluated

Cost: $345.00

Rivermead Behavioural Memory Test for Children (RBMT-C)
Barbara A. Wilson, Rebecca Ivani-Chalian, Frances Aldrich

1991	Thames Valley Test Company, Ltd.

Population: Ages 5 to 10 years

Purpose: Measures memory impairment

Description: Applications include neuropsychology. There are a number of subtests, each attempting to provide an objective measure of one of a range of everyday memory problems reported and observed in subjects with memory difficulties. The RBMT-C has been validated using the observations of houseparents of children with severe epilepsy. Each of nine subtests yields screening and profile scores.

Format: Examiner required; individual administration; untimed: 25 minutes

Scoring: Examiner evaluated

Cost: $216.00

Ross Information Processing Assessment-Primary (RIPA-P)
Deborah Ross-Swain

1999	PRO-ED, Inc.

Population: Ages 5 through 12 years

Purpose: Identifies information processing skill impairments

Description: Eight subtests (Immediate Memory, Recent Memory, Recall of General Information, Spatial Orientation, Temporal Orientation, Organization, Problem Solving, Abstract Reasoning) allow assessment of a wide range of information processing skills in children who have had a traumatic brain injury, have experienced other neuropathologies such as seizure disorders and anoxia, or exhibit learning disabilities.

Format: Examiner required; individual administration; untimed: 30 minutes

Scoring: Examiner evaluated

Cost: Complete Kit (manual, 25 record forms, 25 profile/summary forms, storage box) $114.00

Ross Information Processing Assessment-Second Edition (RIPA-2)
Deborah G. Ross-Swain

1996	PRO-ED, Inc.

Population: Ages 15 to 90 years

Purpose: Enables the examiner to quantify cognitive-linguistic deficits, determine severity levels for each skill area, and develop rehabilitation goals and objectives

Description: The RIPA-2 provides quantifiable data for profiling 10 key areas basic to communicative and cognitive functioning: Intermediate Memory, Recent Memory, Temporal Orientation (Recent Memory), Temporal Orientation (Remote Memory), Spatial Orientation, Orientation to Environment, Recall of General Information, Problem Solving and Abstract Reasoning, Organization, and Auditory Processing and Retention. The study sample included 126 individuals with traumatic brain injury (TBI) in 17 states. The sample was representative of TBI demographics for gender, ethnicity, and socioeconomic status. Internal consistency reliability was investigated, and the mean reliability coefficient for the RIPA-2 subtests was .85, with a range from .67 to .91.

Format: Examiner required; individual administration; untimed: 45 to 60 minutes

Scoring: Examiner evaluated

Cost: Complete Kit (examiner's manual, 25 record forms, 25 profile/summary forms, storage box) $119.00

Ruff Figural Fluency Test (RFFT)
Ronald M. Ruff

1997	Psychological Assessment Resources, Inc.

Population: Ages 16 to 70 years

Purpose: Provides information about nonverbal capacity for initiation, planning, and divergent reasoning

Description: Test consists of 36 identical stimulus items containing five dots. Respondent is asked to connect two or more dots to make as many different patterns as possible. Test is given in five parts timed at 60 seconds each.

Format: Examiner required; individual administration; timed: 5 minutes total

Scoring: Examiner evaluated

Cost: $90.00

Ruff-Light Trail Learning Test (RULIT)
Ronald M. Ruff, C. Christopher Allen

1999   Psychological Assessment Resources, Inc.

Population: Ages 16 to 70 years

Purpose: Assesses visuospatial learning and memory

Description: Two stimulus cards provide alternate versions of the 15-step trail. Successive trials are administered until the trail is recalled without error on two consecutive trials.

Format: Examiner required; individual administration; untimed: 5 to 15 minutes, with 60-minute delay

Scoring: Examiner evaluated

Cost: Kit (manual, 50 test booklets, 2 stimulus cards) $99.00

Ruff 2 & 7 Selective Attention Test
Ronald M. Ruff, C. Christopher Allen

1996   Psychological Assessment Resources, Inc.

Population: Ages 16 to 70 years

Purpose: Measures sustained attention and selective attention

Description: Consists of 20 trials of a visual search and cancellation task, with 10 automatic detection trials and 10 controlled search trials.

Format: Examiner required; individual administration; untimed: 5 minutes

Scoring: Hand key; no scoring service available

Cost: Kit (manual and 50 test booklets) $124.00

Scales of Cognitive Ability for Traumatic Brain Injury (SCATBI)
Brenda B. Adamovich, Jennifer Henderson

1992   PRO-ED, Inc.

Population: Adolescents, adults

Purpose: Assesses cognitive and linguistic abilities of patients with head injuries

Description: The SCATBI consists of five subtests: Perception/Discrimination, Orientation, Organization, Recall, and Reasoning. Unlike other tests for this population, the SCATBI progresses

in difficulty to levels that even some noninjured adults do not typically master. This permits patients who functioned at very high levels prior to injury to be measured with the same instrument as they regain the use of higher level abilities. The results can be used to establish the severity of head injuries and can be charted to show progress during recovery. Administer only those scales that are useful for evaluating a particular patient. The test was standardized on a sample of patients with head injuries and a sample of matched adults with no history of head injury.

Format: Examiner required; individual administration; untimed: 30 minutes to 2 hours

Scoring: Examiner evaluated

Cost: Complete Kit (manual, stimulus book, 25 record forms, audiocassette, card set, storage box) $269.00

Screening Test for the Luria–Nebraska Neuropsychological Battery: Adult and Children's Forms (ST–LNNB)
Charles J. Golden

1987   Western Psychological Services

Population: Ages 8 years to adult

Purpose: Assesses cognitive functioning; used to identify individuals who will show a significant degree of impairment when administered the complete battery; also used for neuropsychological screening in schools and alcohol abuse programs

Description: Fifteen-item screening test predicting overall performance on the Luria–Nebraska Neuropsychological Battery. Testing is discontinued when the client reaches the critical score. Materials include an administration and scoring booklet, spiral-bound stimulus cards, easel. Forms are available for children ages 8 to 12 and adolescents and adults ages 13 and older.

Format: Examiner required; individual administration; untimed: 20 minutes

Scoring: Examiner evaluated

Cost: Kit (manual, stimulus cards, 25 adult administration and scoring booklets, 25 child administration and scoring booklets) $139.50

Seguin–Goddard Formboards (Tactual Performance Test)

Date not provided   Stoelting Company

Population: Ages 5 to 14 years

Purpose: Measures spatial perception in

children; used in a variety of neuropsychological applications

Description: Multiple-task examination of spatial perception, discrimination of forms, manual or construction ability, motor coordination, and the ability to meet new situations. The test materials consist of 10 sturdy blocks cut in the geometric forms of semicircle, triangle, cross, elongated hexagon, oblong, circle, square, flatted oval, star and lozenge, and a base with corresponding shapes cut into it. The child must place the blocks in the appropriate spaces on the formboard base. Two types of bases are available: one with raised geometric figures and one with flush geometric figures.

Format: Examiner required; individual administration; untimed: not available

Scoring: Examiner evaluated

Cost: Raised Formboard $340.00; Flush Formboard $185.00

Sensory Profile
Winnie Dunn

1999	The Psychological Corporation

Population: Ages 3 to 10 years

Purpose: Evaluates sensory information processing

Description: Helps to determine how well children process sensory information in everyday situations. The examiner can combine the information with other evaluation data to create a complete picture of the child's status for diagnostic and intervention planning. Caregivers complete the 125-question profile. The summary score sheet provides a profile of the child's sensory responses. The Short Sensory Profile is a 38-item caregiver questionnaire and score sheet designed for screening. The items are grouped into three major sections: sensory processing, modulation, and behavioral and emotional.

Format: Examiner required; individual administration; untimed: 30 minutes

Scoring: Examiner evaluated

Cost: Complete Kit (manual, 25 caregiver questionnaires, 25 short profiles, 25 summary score sheets) $99.00

Severe Cognitive Impairment Profile (SCIP)
Guerry M. Peavy

1998	Psychological Assessment Resources, Inc.

Population: Ages 42 to 90+ years

Purpose: Measures and tracks impairment of cognitive abilities in adults with primary progressive dementia

Description: Total of eight subtests: Comportment, Language, Motor Functioning, Conceptual Reasoning Abilities, Attention, Memory, Arithmetic, and Visuospatial. Identifies four levels of impairment: moderately severe, severe, very severe, and profound.

Format: Examiner required; individual administration; untimed: 30 to 45 minutes

Scoring: Examiner evaluated

Cost: $429.00

Severe Impairment Battery (SIB)
*Judith Saxton, K. L. McGonigle,
A. A. Swihart, F. Boller*

1993	Thames Valley Test Company, Ltd.

Population: Adults

Purpose: Assesses a range of cognitive functioning in individuals too impaired to complete standard neuropsychological tests

Description: The instrument is designed to assist therapists in the assessment of elderly individuals with severe dementia. Direct performance-based data are gathered on a wide variety of low-level tasks that take into account the specific behavioral and cognitive deficits associated with severe dementia. The test enhances understanding of the disease process and provides clinical information regarding the later stages of dementia. It is composed of very simple one-step commands that are presented in conjunction with gestural cues, and it allows for nonverbal and partially correct responses as well as for simpler response modes such as matching. The six major subscales are attention, orientation, language, memory, visuospatial ability, and construction.

Format: Examiner required; individual administration; untimed: 30 minutes

Scoring: Examiner evaluated

Cost: $191.00

Shipley Institute of Living Scale
Walter C. Shipley

1991	Western Psychological Services

Population: Ages 14 years to adult

Purpose: Used as a measure of intellectual ability and impairment

Description: The Shipley scale measures cognitive impairment and is composed of two brief subtests: a 40-item vocabulary test and a 20-item abstract thinking test. The scale produces six summary scores: vocabulary, abstraction, total, conceptual quotient (an index of impairment), abstraction quotient (the conceptual quotient adjusted for age), and estimated full scale IQ scores on the Wechsler Adult Intelligence Scale or Wechsler Adult Intelligence Scale-Revised.

Format: Self-administered; timed: 20 minutes

Scoring: Hand key; computer scored

Cost: Kit (manual, 100 test forms, hand scoring key, 2 AutoScore™ test forms) $105.00; 25-use PC disk $235.00

Short Category Test, Booklet Format
Linda C. Wetzel, Thomas J. Boll

1987	Western Psychological Services

Population: Ages 15 years and older

Purpose: Assesses brain dysfunction; used for clinical diagnosis of brain damage

Description: Multiple-item paper–pencil test assessing adaptability, abstract concept formation, capacity to learn from experience, and cognitive flexibility. This booklet format reduces the length and complexity of the Category Test of the Halstead–Reitan Neuropsychological Battery by using only half the items of the original and eliminating the equipment necessary for administering it. The test may be administered at bedside.

Format: Examiner required; individual administration; timed: 20 minutes

Scoring: Examiner evaluated

Cost: Kit (manual, 1 set of stimulus cards, 100 answer sheets) $175.00

Speed and Capacity of Language Processing Test (SCOLP)
Alan Baddeley, Hazel Emslie,
Ian Nimmo-Smith

1992	Thames Valley Test Company, Ltd.

Population: Adults

Purpose: Measures the rate of information processing

Description: The test enables differentiation between a subject who has always been slow and a subject whose performance has been impaired as a result of brain damage or some other stressor. The Speed of Comprehension Test requires the subject to verify as many sentences as possible in 2 minutes. The sentences are all obviously true or false. In the Spot-the-Word Vocabulary Test, the subject is given pairs of items, each comprising one real word and one nonword, and is required to indicate the real word. Words range from common to very obscure.

Format: Examiner required; individual administration; timed and untimed: 6 minutes

Scoring: Examiner evaluated

Cost: $105.00

Stroop Color and Word Test
Charles J. Golden

2002	Stoelting Company

Population: Grade 2 through adult

Purpose: Evaluates personality, cognition, stress response, psychiatric disorders, and other psychological phenomena

Description: Multiple-item response test of an individual's ability to separate word and color stimuli and react to them independently. The test consists of three pages: a Word Page containing color words printed in black ink; a Color Page with a series of X's printed in colored inks; and a Word-Color page on which the words on the first page are printed in the colors of the second page except that the word and color do not match. The subject is given all three pages and asked to read the Word Page; then name the colors of the X's on the Color Page; and finally name the color of the ink in which the words on the Word-Color Page are printed, ignoring the semantic meaning of the words. The test requires a second-grade reading level. Also available in Spanish.

Format: Examiner required; individual administration; timed: 5 minutes

Scoring: Examiner evaluated

Cost: Complete Kit (manual, 25 sets of 3 sheets, mail-in form for technical manual) $85.00

Stroop Neuropsychological Screening Test (SNST)
Max. R. Trenerry, Bruce Crosson,
James DeBoe, William R. Leber

1989	Psychological Assessment Resources, Inc.

Population: Ages 18 to 79 years

Purpose: Screens neuropsychological functioning

Description: A two-part (Color Task, Color-Word Task) oral-response short-answer test measuring neuropsychological functioning. Scores yield percentile and probability values for Color Score and Color-Word Score.

Format: Examiner required; individual administration; timed: 4 minutes

Scoring: Hand scored

Cost: Kit (manual, Form C stimulus sheets, Form C-W stimulus sheets, record form) $99.00

Survey of Teenage Readiness and Neurodevelopmental Status (STRANDS)

Date not provided	Educators Publishing Service, Inc.

Population: Ages 13 to 19 years

Purpose: Provides evaluation of ability to process information and function in school

Description: The questions are designed to elicit responses based on eight key neurocognitive constructs: attention, memory, sequencing ability, language, visual-perceptual ability, motor ability, organization and strategy, and higher-order cognition. Written in adolescent-friendly language, the STRANDS comprises two parts: a structured Student Interview and a Student Questionnaire. This survey is one of only a few measurement tools that directly asks adolescents how they perceive their own performance.

Format: Examiner required; individual administration; untimed: 45 to 60 minutes

Scoring: Examiner evaluated

Cost: Complete Set $78.00

Symbol Digit Modalities Test (SDMT)
Aaron Smith

1982	Western Psychological Services

Population: Ages 8 to 75 years

Purpose: Measures brain damage; used to screen and predict learning disorders and to identify children with potential reading problems

Description: Multiple-item test in which the subject is given 90 seconds to convert as many meaningless geometric designs as possible into their appropriate numbers according to the key provided. When group administered, the test may be used as a screening device. The test may be administered orally to individuals who cannot take written tests. Because geometric figures and numbers are nearly universal, the test is virtually culture free.

Format: Examiner required; individual or group administration; untimed: 90 seconds

Scoring: Hand key

Cost: Complete Kit (25 AutoScore™ test forms, manual) $68.00

Test of Memory and Learning (TOMAL)
Cecil R. Reynolds, Erin D. Bigler

1994	PRO-ED, Inc.

Population: Ages 5 through 19 years

Purpose: Measures various aspects of memory and their impact on learning

Description: The TOMAL includes 10 regular subtests and four supplementary subtests that evaluate general and specific memory functions. It features scores for Verbal Memory, Nonverbal Memory, Delayed Recall, and a Composite Memory Index and has supplementary composite scores that include a Learning Index, Attention and Concentration Index, Sequential Memory Index, Free Recall Index, and Associate Recall Index. The test includes highly interpretable and relevant scores, scaled to a familiar metric. TOMAL scores include standardized or scaled scores and percentiles.

Format: Examiner required; individual administration; timed: 45 minutes

Scoring: Examiner evaluated

Cost: Complete Kit (manual, 2 picture books, 25 record forms, 25 supplementary analysis forms, facial memory chips, visual selective reminding test board, delayed recall cue cards, storage box) $214.00

Test of Memory Malingering (TOMM)
Tom N. Tombaugh

1996	Multi-Health Systems, Inc.

Population: Ages 16 to 84 years

Purpose: Helps to distinguish between malingerers and true memory impairment in cognitively intact normal individuals and clinical samples that include no cognitive impairment, cognitive impairment, aphasia, traumatic brain injury, and dementia

Description: The TOMM consists of two learning trials and an optional retention trial. On each learning trial, 50 pictures (line drawings) are presented at the rate of one every 4 seconds. The same 50 pictures are used on each trial. Then 50 two-choice recognition panels are presented individually. Each panel contains one of the previously presented pictures and a picture not previously shown. From each panel, the examinee is required to select the correct picture. Designed to appear more difficult than they actually are, some TOMM tasks are mistaken as difficult when in fact they are quite easy. Almost everyone who takes the TOMM does well except patients who are malingering. Research has found the TOMM to be insensitive to a wide variety of neurological impairments. Two cutoff scores are included: below chance and criteria based on patients with head injuries and cognitive impairments. Also available in computer-administered format.

Format: Examiner required; individual administration; untimed: 30 to 40 minutes

Scoring: Examiner evaluated, computer scored

Cost: Kit (manual, stimulus booklets, 25 forms) $100.00

300 Series Valpar Dexterity Modules
1995   Valpar International Corporation

Population: All ages

Purpose: Used in cognitive assessment and psychomotor functioning to assess motor, manual, and finger coordination; intended for individuals with brain injuries and industrial rehabilitation

Description: The criterion-referenced performance test includes five 6-inch square plates (numbered 301 to 305) that fasten, one at a time, onto a lightweight plastic box (the Basic Unit). Each plate has several unique exercises of short duration that assess various aspects of hand function and upper extremity range of motion. The exercises may be administered to the client either horizontally or at a 45-degree angle of presentation. The exercises focus primarily on tasks that require fine finger and manual dexterity, and eye–hand coordination. The exercises assess upper body range of motion, strength, flexibility, ability to follow instructions, memory, and many secondary work-related characteristics. All of the exercises have Methods–Time Measurement industrial work rate standards to aid in the interpretation of scores.

Format: Examiner required; individual administration; untimed

Scoring: Examiner evaluated

Cost: Contact publisher

Tower of Londondx (TOLdx)
William C. Culbertson, Eric A. Zillmer
1999   Multi-Health Systems, Inc.

Population: Ages 7 years and older

Purpose: Assesses higher-order problem solving, specifically executive planning abilities

Description: Although similar to the original Tower of London, developed for assessing adult patients with frontal lobe damage, the TOLdx

presents a number of modifications in administration and scoring, including elimination of repeated trials for failed problems; introduction of six- and seven-move test problem configurations, which increase the sensitivity of the measure to executive functioning across age levels; and an empirical selection of test problem configurations. Uses of the test include diagnosis of attention-deficit/hyperactivity disorder.

Format: Examiner required; individual administration; untimed: 10 to 15 minutes

Scoring: Examiner evaluated

Cost: Complete Kit (manual, 25 adult forms, 25 child forms, 2 pegboards) $225.00

Verbal and Spatial Reasoning Test (VESPAR)
Dawn W. Langdon, Elizabeth K. Warrington
1995   Psychology Press

Population: Adults

Purpose: Measures fluid intelligence in neurological patients

Description: The VESPAR comprises three matched sets of verbal and spatial reasoning problems, each dedicated to one of three forms of inductive reasoning: odd one out, analogy, and series completion. A multiple-choice format has been adopted to reduce both short-term memory load and output demands on the patient. The reasoning items are all novel; thus the contribution of stored knowledge and procedures are reduced to a minimum.

Format: Examiner required; individual administration; untimed

Scoring: Examiner evaluated

Cost: Kit (manual, stimulus materials, 20 scoring sheets) $198.00

Victoria Symptom Validity Test (VSVT)
Daniel Slick, Grace Hopp, Esther Strauss, Garrie B. Thompson
1997   Psychological Assessment Resources, Inc.

Population: Ages 18 years and older

Purpose: Assesses possible exaggeration or feigning of cognitive impairments

Description: The VSVT is presented on-screen in three blocks of 16 items. A single five-digit study number is presented on the screen for 5 seconds, followed by the Recognition Trial in which the study number (the correct choice) and a five-digit foil are displayed. The respondent is then asked to choose the correct response.

Format: Computer-administered; untimed: 18 to 25 minutes

Scoring: Computer scored

Cost: $429.00

Visual Analog Mood Scales (VAMS)
Robert A. Stern

| 1997 | Psychological Assessment Resources, Inc. |

Population: Ages 18 to 94 years

Purpose: Assesses internal mood states in adults with neurological impairments and in patients in medical and psychiatric settings

Description: Eight individual scales with minimal cognitive or linguistic demands on the patient measure these mood states: Afraid, Sad, Energetic, Happy, Confused, Angry, Tired, and Tense.

Format: Self-administered; untimed: 5 minutes

Scoring: Examiner evaluated

Cost: Intro Kit (manual, 25 response booklets, metric ruler) $99.00

Visual Object and Space Perception Battery (VOSP)
Elizabeth Warrington, Merle James

| 1991 | Thames Valley Test Company, Ltd. |

Population: Adults

Purpose: Assesses object or space perception while minimizing the involvement of other cognitive skills

Description: The VOSP consists of eight tests that enable an examiner to compare the scores of an individual with those of a normal control sample and those obtained by patients with right- and left-cerebral lesions.

Format: Examiner required; individual or group administration; untimed: 20 minutes

Scoring: Examiner evaluated

Cost: $112.00

Visual Search and Attention Test (VSAT)
Max R. Trenerry, Bruce Crosson, James DeBoe, William R. Leber

| 1990 | Psychological Assessment Resources, Inc. |

Population: Adults

Purpose: Measures attentional processes in individuals with neuropsychological impairments

Description: Four paper-pencil visual cancellation tasks yield the following scores: overall attention score, and left- and right-side performance.

Format: Examiner required; individual administration; timed: 6 minutes

Scoring: Examiner evaluated

Cost: Intro Kit (manual, test booklet) $126.00

Wechsler Memory Scale®– Third Edition (WMS®–III)
David Wechsler

| 1997 | The Psychological Corporation |

Population: Ages 16 through 89 years

Purpose: Assesses adult memory abilities

Description: A primary purpose for developing the WMS-III was to expand its clinical utility. The revision includes five subtests from the WMS-R and four new subtests. Subtests are organized into summary index scores. The Primary Indexes are Auditory Immediate, Visual Immediate, Immediate Memory, Auditory Delayed, Visual Delayed, Auditory Recognition Delayed, General Memory, and Working Memory. In addition, four Auditory Process Composites have been added to help evaluate clinically meaningful aspects of memory functioning. The WMS-III and the Wechsler Adult Intelligence Scale-Third Edition can be used together to evaluate the discrepancy between IQ and memory.

Format: Examiner required; individual administration; untimed: 30 to 35 minutes

Scoring: Examiner evaluated; computer scoring available

Cost: Complete Kit (manual, 25 each of record forms and visual reproduction response booklets, 2 stimulus booklets, board, case) $427.00

Wechsler Test of Adult Reading™ (WTAR™)

| 2001 | The Psychological Corporation |

Population: Ages 16 to 89 years

Purpose: Estimates premorbid intellectual functioning

Description: This assessment tool was normed with the Wechsler Adult Intelligence Scale-Third Edition and the Wechsler Memory Scale-Third Edition. The test comprises a list of 50 words with atypical grapheme-phoneme translations. The intent in using words with irregular pronunciations is to minimize the current ability of the client to apply standard pronunciation rules and assess previous learning of the word. Reading recognition is relatively stable in the presence of cognitive declines associated with normal aging or brain injury. United Kingdom norms are also available.

Format: Examiner required; individual administration; untimed: 5 to 10 minutes

Scoring: Examiner evaluated

Cost: Complete Kit (manual, 25 record forms, word card, audiocassette) $115.00

Wessex Head Injury Matrix (WHIM)
Agnes Shiel, Barbara A. Wilson, Lindsay McLellan, Sandra Horn, Martin Watson

2000	Thames Valley Test Company, Ltd.

Population: All ages

Purpose: Assess and monitors recovery of cognitive function

Description: The 62-item observational matrix can be used by a multidisciplinary team to assess the patient and set goals for rehabilitation from the outset of coma. With a patient who is slow to recover, it is not unusual to believe mistakenly that no recovery is occurring even though subtle progress is being made over weeks and months. The WHIM has been designed to pick up minute indexes demonstrating recovery and provide objective evidence so that prediction is neither too optimistic nor too pessimistic.

Format: Examiner required; individual administration; untimed

Scoring: Examiner evaluated

Cost: $74.00

Wide Range Assessment of Memory and Learning (WRAML)
Wayne Adams, David Sheslow

1990	Wide Range, Inc.

Population: Ages 5 to 17 years

Purpose: Measures an individual's verbal and visual memory ability; helpful in measuring memory-related learning ability and problems within the psychological, educational, and medical disciplines

Description: The WRAML has nine subtests, some with repetitive trials and recall administrations. Subtests include Picture Memory, Design Memory, Verbal Learning, Story Memory, Finger Windows, Sound Symbol Learning, Sentence Memory, Visual Learning, and Number/Letter Memory. National stratified norms include over 2,300 individuals controlled for age, gender, race, region, and residence.

Format: Examiner required; individual administration; untimed: 45 minutes

Scoring: Examiner evaluated

Cost: Kit (manual, 25 each of examiner and response forms, briefcase, materials) $355.00

Wisconsin Card Sorting Test (WCST)
David A. Grant, Esta A. Berg

1993	Psychological Assessment Resources, Inc.

Population: Ages 6 years 6 months to 89 years

Purpose: Assesses perseveration and abstract thinking; used for neuropsychological assessment of individuals suspected of having brain lesions involving the frontal lobes; can help discriminate frontal from non-frontal lobe dysfunction

Description: Multiple-task nonverbal test in which the respondent matches cards in two response decks to one of four stimulus cards for color, form, or number. Responses are recorded on a form for later scoring. The test provides measures of overall success and particular sources of difficulty. A CD-ROM version for on-screen administration and scoring and a scoring program are available.

Format: Examiner required; computer or individual administration; untimed

Scoring: Examiner evaluated; may be computer scored

Cost: Intro Kit $250.00; Computer Kit $595.00

Pain

Behavioral Assessment of Pain Questionnaire (BAP)

Michael J. Lewandowski, Blake H. Tearnan

1989	Pain Assessment Resources

Population: Adults, patients with pain

Purpose: Pain management; diagnoses factors maintaining and exacerbating pain

Description: Paper–pencil or computer-administered test has 10 subscales with a total of 312 items: Pain Behavior (10 items), Activity Interference (34 items), Avoidance (34 items), Spouse/Partner Influence (27 items), Physician Influence (25 items), Physician Qualities (13 items), Pain Beliefs (52 items), Perceived Consequences (24 items), Coping (57 items), and Mood (36 items). Works with Windows 95, 98, 2000, and NT. Also available in Spanish and French.

Format: Self-administered; untimed: 45 minutes

Scoring: Computer scored or machine scored; test scoring service available from publisher

Cost: $18.50 per test

Behavioral Assessment of Pain-Medical Stability Quick Screen (BAP-MSQS)

Michael J. Lewandowski

2000	Pain Assessment Resources

Population: Adults, patients with subacute and chronic pain

Purpose: Screens pain beliefs, mood, and perception of pain

Description: This paper–pencil or computer-administered multiple-choice test was developed to provide a brief screening of information relevant to persons suffering from subacute and chronic pain-related problems. The BAP-MSQS can be useful in identifying patient assets and potential obstacles for recovery in terms of behavioral, cognitive, and psychosocial areas frequently seen in pain patients. In addition, the BAP-MSQS can be used to identify problem areas where more comprehensive assessment might be needed and to assess patient progress in functional restorations, pain, and work hardening programs. The clinical report is intended to be used by professionals who are trained or supervised in the appropriate uses and limitations of self-report

questionnaires and who have experience working with patients with subacute and chronic benign pain. Also available in Spanish. Used with Windows 95, 98, 2000, and NT.

Format: Individually self-administered; untimed: 5 minutes

Scoring: Computer scored; scoring service available from publisher

Cost: $5.00 per test

Chronic Pain Battery™ (CPB)

Stephen R. Levitt

1983	Pain Resource Center

Population: Ages 13 years and older

Purpose: Collects medical, psychological, behavioral, and social data and assesses correlates of chronic pain; used by health professionals to suggest treatment and management approaches of individuals suffering from chronic malignant or nonmalignant pain

Description: Paper–pencil or computer-administered 215-item multiple-choice and true–false test including the Symptom Checklist-90 Revised with a 10-page narrative. The results are used to coordinate therapeutic strategies in multidisciplinary health care settings and to aid the private practitioner's specific evaluation. The report topics include demographic and social history, past and current pain history, pain intensity ratings, medication and treatment history, medical history, personality and pain coping style, psychosocial factors (stress, psychological dysfunction, and support system), behavioral-learning factors (prior models, illness-behavior reinforcement, litigation–compensation, activity assessment), patient expectations and goals, and patient problem ratings. Two scoring options are available: mail-in and computer scoring. The examiner must meet APA guidelines. An eighth-grade reading level is required. Also available in Spanish.

Format: Self-administered; untimed: 60 minutes

Scoring: Machine scored; computer scored; test scoring service available from publisher

Cost: Examination Kit (question booklet, answer sheet, information sheet, patient record care, sample report) $13.95

Illness Behavior Questionnaire (IBQ)
Issy Pilowsky, Neil Spence

1994	I. Pilowsky

Population: Ages 19 to 94 years

Purpose: Used with the DSM-IV to categorize individuals who complain of pain with no somatic disorder; used in clinical settings

Description: The IBQ has seven scales with a total of 62 items. Both in-patient and nonpatient forms are available. The seven scales are General Hypochrondriasis, Disease Conviction, Psychological versus Somatic Concerns, Affective Inhibition, Dysphoria, Denial, and Irritability. Computer version is available.

Format: Self-administered; untimed

Scoring: Examiner evaluated

Cost: Contact publisher

Pain Patient Profile™ (P-3™)
C. David Tollison, Jerry C. Langley

1996	NCS Pearson

Population: Ages 17 to 76 years

Purpose: Assesses psychological factors that can influence the severity and persistence of pain

Description: Multiple-choice 44-item computer or paper–pencil test measuring psychological factors that influence patient pain. Scales include depression, anxiety, and somatization. Includes a validity index. Eighth-grade reading level is required.

Format: Self-administered; untimed: 15 minutes

Scoring: Hand key; computer scored; test scoring service available from publisher

Cost: Narrative Report $7.50 to $10.00; Hand Score Answer sheet (includes profile form) $1.50; quantity discounts available

Psychosocial Pain Inventory (PSPI)
Robert K. Heaton, Ralph A. W. Lehman, Carl J. Getto

1985	Psychological Assessment Resources, Inc.

Population: Adults

Purpose: Evaluates psychosocial factors related to chronic pain problems; used in the treatment of patients with chronic pain

Description: Eight-page multiple-item paper–pencil inventory assessing the following psychosocial factors considered important in maintaining and exacerbating chronic pain problems: several forms of secondary gain, the effects of pain behavior on interpersonal relationships, the existence of stressful life events that may contribute to subjective distress or promote avoidance learning, and components of past history that familiarize the patient with the chronic invalid role and with its personal and social consequences. Ratings take into account that patients differ in the degree to which they are likely to be influenced by potential sources of secondary gain. The inventory yields a total score. High scores predict poor response to medical treatment for pain.

Format: Examiner required; individual administration; untimed: 1 to 2 hours

Scoring: Examiner evaluated

Cost: Test Kit (manual, 25 forms) $32.00

TMJ Scale™
Stephen R. Levitt, Tom F. Lundeen, Michael W. McKinney

1985	Pain Resource Center

Population: Ages 11 years and older

Purpose: Screens for temporomandibular joint disorders, craniofacial pain, and dysfunction; used by dental practitioners; physicians; ear, eyes, nose, and throat specialists; and psychologists

Description: Multiple-item paper–pencil self-report tool measuring physical and psychosocial factors contributing to craniomuscular dysfunction. The report yields 10 scored scales in three domains: Physical (Pain Report, Palpation Pain, Perceived Malocclusion, Joint Dysfunction, Range of Motion Limitation, and Non–TM Disorder), Psychosocial (Psychological Factors, Stress, Chronicity), and Global. Patients may complete the report at home or in the office. A narrative report and a printout of the patient's scores and responses are generated. Also available in Spanish.

Format: Self-administered; untimed: 15 minutes

Scoring: Computer scored

Cost: Contact publisher

Pathology

General

ACDI–Corrections Version II
1989   Risk & Needs Assessment, Inc.

Population: Ages 12 to 17 years

Purpose: Measures six areas of concern for troubled juveniles

Description: Designed to assess troubled youth for juvenile courts and probation, the test contains six scales: Truthfulness, Alcohol, Drugs, Violence, Distress, and Adjustment. Each scale provides specific recommendations for intervention, supervision, and treatment. There are 143 multiple-choice and true-false items assessing juvenile's truthfulness, overall adjustment, and anxiety and depression level, as well as violence proneness. Provides truth-corrected scores. Computer-generated report summarizes risk range and recommendations. Standardized and normed on the juvenile population. Available in English or Spanish.

Format: Self-administered; untimed: 20 to 25 minutes

Scoring: Computer scored

Cost: Contact publisher

Adolescent Psychopathology Scale (APS)
William M. Reynolds
1998   Psychological Assessment Resources, Inc.

Population: Ages 12 to 19 years

Purpose: Evaluates the presence and severity of symptoms of psychological disorders

Description: The APS has 346 items, 20 Clinical Disorder Scales, 5 Personality Disorder Scales, 11 Psychosocial Problem Content Scales, and 4 Response Style Indicator Scales.

Format: Self-administered; untimed: 45 to 60 minutes

Scoring: Computer scored

Cost: Kit (APS scoring program with on-screen user's guide, two manuals, 25 test booklets, 25-use key disk) $189.00

Adolescent Psychopathology Scale–Short Form (APS–SF)
William M. Reynolds
2000   Psychological Assessment Resources, Inc.

Population: Ages 12 to 19 years

Purpose: Quickly evaluates psychopathology and a spectrum of common adjustment problems

Description: The APS–SF has 115 items with 12 Clinical Scales and 2 Validity Scales. Items are derived from Adolescent Psychopathology Scale.

Format: Self-administered; untimed: 15 to 20 minutes

Scoring: Computer scored

Cost: $125.00

Adolescent Symptom Inventory–4 (ASI–4)
Kenneth D. Gadow, Joyce Sprafkin
1995   Checkmate Plus, Ltd.

Population: Ages 12 to 18 years

Purpose: Screens for DSM-IV emotional and behavioral disorders

Description: The ASI-4 has 120 items that screen for emotional and behavioral disorders, including attention-deficit/hyperactivity disorder, oppositional defiant disorder, conduct disorder, depressive disorders, bipolar disorder, anxiety disorders, and eating disorders. Provides symptom count scores (DSM-IV criteria) and symptom severity profiles (norms based). Parent and Teacher checklists are included.

Format: Rating scale; can be computer administered; untimed: 10 to 15 minutes

Scoring: Examiner evaluated; computer scored

Cost: Deluxe Kit $102.00

Attitudes Toward Guns and Violence Questionnaire (AGVQ)
Jeremy P. Shapiro
2000   Western Psychological Services

Population: Ages 6 through 29 years

Purpose: Measures attitudes of young people

toward guns, physical aggression, and inter-personal conflict

Description: Composed of 26 items, this is a unique self-report inventory. AGVQ items focus on violence-related issues relevant to young people, with an emphasis on guns. The test form asks individuals to choose one of three response options to indicate the extent of agreement with each item. The test yields a total score, plus scores for the following subscales: Aggressive Response to Shame, Comfort with Aggression, Excitement, and Power/Safety. Norms are based on a nation-ally representative, age-stratified sample of 1,745 individuals in school and community settings. The AGVQ kit includes the Aggressive Behavior Checklist, which provides student and teacher ratings of violent behavior. By assessing atti-tudes, the examiner can determine what kind of cognitive and behavioral training should be im-plemented.

Format: Self-administered; untimed: 5 to 10 minutes

Scoring: Computer scored; test scoring service available

Cost: Complete Kit $82.50

Beck Youth Inventories™ of Emotional & Social Impairment
Judith S. Beck, Aaron T. Beck, John Jolly

2001	The Psychological Corporation

Population: Ages 7 through 14 years

Purpose: Evaluates children's emotional and social impairment

Description: Five self-report inventories with 20 statements each can be used separately or in combination to assess symptoms of depression, anxiety, anger, disruptive behavior, and self-con-cept. Children describe how frequently the state-ment has been true for them during the past 2 weeks, including the test day. Items are written at a second-grade reading level, with language that is easy to understand for self-reporting. The items may also be administered orally.

Format: Self-report; untimed: 5 to 10 minutes per inventory

Scoring: Examiner evaluated

Cost: Starter Kit (manual, 25 combination book-lets) $105.00

Brief Symptom Inventory (BSI)
Leonard R. Derogatis

1975	NCS Pearson

Population: Ages 13 years and older

Purpose: Used to screen for psychological problems and measure progress

Description: Multiple-choice computer-adminis-tered or paper–pencil test with 53 items rated on a 5-point scale. The nine primary dimensions are somatization, obsessive–compulsive, interper-sonal sensitivity, depression, anxiety, hostility, phobic anxiety, paranoid ideation, and psychoti-cism. A sixth-grade reading level is required. Ex-aminer must be M-level qualified. A computer ver-sion using an IBM-compatible 486 PC or higher is available. The test is available on audiocassette and in 23 foreign languages. Thirteen additional languages are available for research purposes only.

Format: Self-administered; untimed: 8 to 10 minutes

Scoring: Hand key; computer scored

Cost: Contact publisher

Butcher Treatment Planning Inventory™ (BTPI™)
James N. Butcher

1998	The Psychological Corporation

Population: Ages 18 years and older

Purpose: Assesses client characteristics that facilitate or interfere with treatment progress

Description: The BTPI Full Form consists of 210 items on 14 scales that fall within three clusters. It is useful early in the treatment process and serves as a baseline for evaluating symptom re-duction during treatment using the Symptom Monitoring Form. The 80 items on that form are from Cluster 3 scales (Assessment of Symptoms). The Treatment Issues Form has 174 items from Clusters 1 (Assessment of Validity of Self-Report) and 2 (Assessment of Treatment Issues). This form was created as an alternative to the Full Form for appraising treatment accessibility, not symptomatology. The Treatment Process/Symp-tom Form has 171 items from Clusters 2 and 3.

Format: Self-administered; untimed: 12 to 30 minutes

Scoring: Examiner evaluated

Cost: Hand Scoring Starter Kit (manual, 10 Full Form question booklets, 25 answer/profile sheets, scoring templates, 1 Symptom Monitor-ing Form booklet and scoring document) $139.00

Child Symptom Inventory–4 (CSI–4)
Kenneth D. Gadow, Joyce Sprafkin

1994	Checkmate Plus, Ltd.

Population: Ages 5 to 12 years

Purpose: Screens for DSM-IV emotional and behavioral disorders; provides behavioral ratings of child psychopathology

Description: A total of 97 items screen for emotional and behavioral disorders, including attention-deficit/hyperactivity disorder, oppositional defiant disorder, conduct disorder, depressive disorders, anxiety disorders, and pervasive developmental disorders. Provides symptom count scores (DSM-IV criteria) and symptom severity profiles (norm based). Parent and teacher checklists are included.

Format: Rating scale; can be computer administered; untimed: 10 to 15 minutes

Scoring: Examiner evaluated; computer scored

Cost: Deluxe Kit $98.00

Childhood Trauma Questionnaire: A Retrospective Self-Report (CTQ)
David P. Bernstein, Laura Fink

1997	The Psychological Corporation

Population: Ages 12 years and older

Purpose: Identifies clients with histories of trauma

Description: This 28-item self-report is useful with individuals referred for a broad range of psychiatric symptoms and problems. The examiner can determine whether traumatic childhood conditions are a factor to determine appropriate treatment. The CTQ has five scales: physical, sexual, and emotional abuse, and physical and emotional neglect. A minimization/denial scale is included.

Format: Self-report; untimed: 5 minutes

Scoring: Examiner evaluated

Cost: Complete Kit (manual and 25 answer documents) $93.00

Clinical Analysis Questionnaire
Raymond B. Cattell, Samuel Krug

1978	Institute for Personality and Ability Testing, Inc.

Population: Ages 16 years and older

Purpose: Evaluates personality and psychiatric or psychological difficulties; used as a measure of primary behavioral dimensions; used for clinical diagnosis, evaluation of therapeutic progress, and vocational and rehabilitation guidance

Description: Multiple-choice test with 331 items measuring 16 personality factors (the 16PF factors), as well as hypochondriasis, agitation, suicidal depression, anxious depression, guilt and resentment, low energy depression, boredom, paranoia, psychopathic deviation, schizophrenia, psychasthenia, and psychological inadequacy. General population adult norms are provided. A seventh-grade reading level is required. Completed using computer or paper–pencil. The test and interpretive reports are being updated to be available in 2002.

Format: Self-administered; untimed: 2 hours

Scoring: Hand key; may be computer scored

Cost: Manual $25.00; 25 Answer Sheets $15.00; Computer Profile and Interpretation $19.00 to $30.00; 25 Reusable Test Booklets $40.00

Coddington Life Events Scales (CLES)
R. Dean Coddington

1999	Multi-Health Systems, Inc.

Population: Ages 5 to 19 years

Purpose: Measures the impact of life events and change in development

Description: The three scales (primary, child, adolescent) measure significant events in terms of Life Change Units. The scale can be completed easily in the waiting room prior to client consultation and then quickly scored. The scales are written at a fourth-grade reading level. The importance of evaluating life change is demonstrated by a large body of research indicating that a high degree of change is associated with increased susceptibility to medical and emotional problems.

Format: Self-administered; untimed: 10 to 15 minutes

Scoring: QuikScore™

Cost: Complete Kit (manual and 25 of each form) $114.00

Cognitive Distortion Scales (CDS)
John Briere

2000	Psychological Assessment Resources, Inc.

Population: Ages 18 years and older

Purpose: Assesses negative thinking patterns that interfere with optimal functioning

Description: The CDS scales reflect five types of cognitive distortion: Self-Criticism, Self-Blame, Helplessness, Hopelessness, and Preoccupation with Danger. Requires fifth-grade reading level.

Format: Self-administered; untimed: 10 to 15 minutes

Scoring: Hand key

Cost: $99.00

Computer-Assisted SCID II Expert System (CAS II ES)
Michael B. First, Miriam Gibbon, Janet B. W. Williams, Robert L. Spitzer, Lorna Smith Benjamin

| 1997 | Multi-Health Systems, Inc. |

Population: Ages 18 years and older

Purpose: Guides the clinician through the Axis II personality disorders

Description: Depends on branching mechanism DSM-IV Axis II disorders. Yields Categorical Summary Report, Dimensional Score Report, Overview Questions Report, and Unknown/Missing Items Report.

Format: Examiner required; individual administration; untimed: 30 to 45 minutes

Scoring: Computer scored

Cost: $200.00 (unlimited use)

Computerized Assessment of Response Bias (CARB)
Lyle M. Allen III

| 1999 | CogniSyst, Inc. |

Population: Adults, those evaluated for compensation-related claims

Purpose: Used in detecting "incomplete effort" symptom exaggeration, response bias, feigning and malingering of cognitive deficits, often co-occurring with somatic complaints

Description: The CARB has been used effectively in detecting veritable and claimed head injury, chronic fatigue syndrome, musculoskeletal injuries, DSM-IV pain disorder, and psychiatric or emotional disturbances (mostly depression). The CARB was completely revised in 1997 and updated again in 1999. It rules out symptom exaggeration in as little as 5 minutes, references a database of 1,752 clinical compensation claimants, and provides multiple performance comparisons to various reference groups. It provides population-based risk assessment for symptom exaggeration, pattern analyses for detection of unusual response sequences, and full analysis of response-time data. Supports basic and clinical research with numerous options. Comes with both English and Spanish instructions.

Format: Self-administered on computer; timed: 12 minutes

Scoring: Computer scored

Cost: $300.00

Conners' Global Index
C. Keith Conners

| 1997 | Multi-Health Systems, Inc. |

Population: Ages 3 to 17 years

Purpose: Screens for general psychopathology and monitors treatment effectiveness and change

Description: Ten-item instrument comprises two empirically derived factors: Restless-Impulsive and Emotional Lability. Available in paper-pencil or computer-administered format.

Format: Self-administered; untimed: 5 minutes

Scoring: QuikScore™, computer scored

Cost: Contact publisher

Depression and Anxiety in Youth Scale (DAYS)
Phyllis L. Newcomer, Edna M. Barenbaum, Brian R. Bryant

| 1994 | PRO-ED, Inc. |

Population: Ages 6 through 18 years

Purpose: Useful in identifying major depressive and overanxious disorders in children and adolescents

Description: A battery of three norm-referenced scales: Student Rating Scale, Teacher Rating Scale, and Parent Rating Scale. The primary theoretical frame of reference for the scales is the DSM-III-R.

Format: Rating scales completed by student, teacher, or parent; untimed: 10 minutes

Scoring: Examiner evaluated

Cost: Complete Kit (manual; 50 each of student, teacher, and parent scales; 50 profile/record forms; scoring keys; storage box) $139.00

Derogatis Psychiatric Rating Scale™ (DPRS®)
Leonard R. Derogatis

| 1978 | NCS Pearson |

Population: Adolescents, adults

Purpose: Screens for psychological problems and measures progress; used in adolescent and adult personality assessment

Description: Computer or paper-pencil test using a clinician rating scale. The DPRS enables the clinician to rate observations of a patient's psychological symptomatic distress on the same nine primary dimensional scales as measured by the Symptom Checklist-90 Revised or Brief Symptom Inventory. The nine primary scales are somatization, obsessive-compulsive, interpersonal sensitivity, depression, anxiety, hostility, phobic anxiety, paranoid ideation, and psychoticism. The eight additional scales are sleep disturbance, psychomotor retardation, hysterical behavior, abjection-disinterest, conceptual dysfunction, disorientation, excitement, and euphoria. The examiner must have A-level qualifications. A computer version is available using an IBM-compatible 486 PC or higher.

Format: Examiner required; individual administration; untimed: 2 to 5 minutes

Scoring: Examiner evaluated; computer or hand scored

Cost: Contact publisher

Devereux Scales of Mental Disorders (DSMD™)
Jack A. Naglieri, Paul A. LeBuffe, Steven I. Pfeiffer

1994	The Psychological Corporation

Population: Ages 5 through 18 years

Purpose: Identifies behavioral or emotional problems

Description: Indicates whether an individual is experiencing or is at risk for an emotional or behavioral disorder. The instrument is designed for treatment planning and outcome evaluation. The 111-item child form and the 110-item adolescent form cover a full range of psychopathology and are based on DSM-IV categories. Behavior is evaluated in a variety of settings. Any adult who has known the child for 4 weeks may serve as a rater. The same form is used for parent and teacher raters, with separate norms provided for each.

Format: Rating scale; untimed: 15 minutes

Scoring: Examiner evaluated; computer scoring available

Cost: Complete Kit (manual, 25 each of child and adolescent answer documents) $195.00

Diagnostic Interview for Children and Adolescents IV (DICA IV)
Zila Welner, Wendy Reich, Barbara Herjanic

1997	Multi-Health Systems, Inc.

Population: Ages 6 through 17 years

Purpose: A computerized diagnostic interview based on DSM-IV for identifying a broad range of behavioral problems

Description: Covers 28 categories, each of which can take about 5 to 20 minutes to complete due to automatic branching of questions. Both the

Child/Adolescent and Parent versions yield three reports: Concise Report of Possible Diagnoses, Summary of Responses Report, and Possible Diagnoses and Criteria Report.

Format: Examiner required; individual administration; untimed

Scoring: Computer scored

Cost: $495.00 each for either Child/Adolescent or Parent Version; $795.00 for both

Domestic Violence Inventory (DVI)

1991	Behavior Data Systems, Ltd.

Population: Adult domestic violence offenders

Purpose: Used for evaluating domestic violence offenders

Description: Designed for domestic violence risk and needs assessment, the test contains six scales: Truthfulness, Violence, Alcohol, Drugs, Aggressivity, and Stress Coping Ability. Each scale provides specific recommendations for intervention, supervision, and treatment. There are 157 multiple-choice and true-false items. Truth-corrected scores are yielded. Computer-generated report summarizes risk range and recommendations; on-site reports are provided within 4 minutes of test completion. Designed specifically for assessing domestic violence. Available in English or Spanish.

Format: Self-administered; untimed: 30 minutes

Scoring: Computer scored

Cost: Contact publisher

Domestic Violence Inventory–Juvenile

Date not provided	Behavior Data Systems, Ltd.

Population: Ages 12 to 18 years

Purpose: Designed for evaluating juveniles accused or convicted of domestic violence

Description: The inventory has 156 items with six scales: Truthfulness, Violence, Control, Alcohol, Drugs, and Stress Coping Abilities.

Format: Self-administered; untimed: 30 minutes

Scoring: Computer scored

Cost: Contact publisher

DTREE: The DSM-IV Expert Computer Program
Michael B. First, Janet B. W. Williams, Robert L. Spitzer

1997	Multi-Health Systems, Inc.

Population: Ages 18 years and older

Purpose: Assists in diagnosing DSM-IV adult Axis I disorders

Description: Uses SCID Screen Patient Questionnaire or Screen PQ Extended results, or the DTREE Screener can be used to identify decision trees to explore. It rules out diagnoses to produce a differential diagnosis. Provides Case Summary Report and Positive Diagnosis Report.

Format: Clinician completed; untimed

Scoring: Computer scored

Cost: $295.00 (unlimited use)

DVI Pre-Post

Date not provided	Behavior Data Systems, Ltd.

Population: Adults

Purpose: Designed for measuring domestic violence treatment outcome

Description: The same test is given before and after treatment; upon posttest, results are compared. There are 147 items with six scales: Truthfulness, Violence, Control, Alcohol, Drugs, and Stress Coping Abilities. Although this test evolved from the Domestic Violence Inventory, it objectively compares pretest and posttest scores.

Format: Self-administered; untimed: 30 minutes

Scoring: Computer scored

Cost: Contact publisher

Early Childhood Inventory-4 (ECI-4)
Kenneth D. Gadow, Joyce Sprafkin

1996	Checkmate Plus, Ltd.

Population: Ages 3 to 5 years

Purpose: Screens for DSM-IV emotional and behavioral disorders; provides behavioral ratings of child psychopathology

Description: Total of 195 items that screen for emotional and behavioral disorders, including attention-deficit/hyperactivity disorder, oppositional defiant disorder, conduct disorder, depressive disorders, anxiety disorders, and pervasive developmental disorders. Scores yield Symptom Count scores (DSM-IV criteria) and Symptom Severity Profiles (norms based). Contains parent and teacher checklists.

Format: Rating scale; can be computer administered; untimed: 10 to 15 minutes

Scoring: Examiner evaluated; computer scored

Cost: Deluxe Kit $102.00

Feelings, Attitudes, and Behaviors Scale for Children (FAB-C)
Joseph H. Beitchman

1996	Multi-Health Systems, Inc.

Population: Ages 6 to 13 years

Purpose: Assesses emotional and behavior problems

Description: Self-report scale comprising 48 yes-no items that produces five factors that assess the following areas: Self-Image, Negative Peer Relations, Conduct Problems, Antisocial Behavior, and Worry. Also includes a Problem Index and a Lie Scale.

Format: Examiner required; individual or group administration; untimed: 10 minutes

Scoring: QuikScore™ forms

Cost: Complete Kit (manual, 25 forms) $60.00

Firestone Assessment of Self-Destructive Thoughts (FAST™)
Robert W. Firestone, Lisa A. Firestone

1996	The Psychological Corporation

Population: Ages 16 years and older

Purpose: Investigates a client's self-destructive thoughts

Description: Used as a preliminary screening device and as a measure of pre- and posttreatment progress. Consists of 84 items drawn from 11 levels of progressively self-destructive thoughts, including Social Isolation, Eating Disorders, Substance Abuse, Self-Mutilation, and Suicide. Clients endorse items on a 5-point Likert scale.

Format: Self-report; untimed: 20 minutes

Scoring: Examiner evaluated

Cost: Complete Kit (manual and 25 answer documents) $142.00

Gambler Addiction Index

Date not provided	Behavior Data Systems, Ltd.

Population: Adults

Purpose: Designed for gambler assessment

Description: The instrument has 166 items with seven scales: Truthfulness, Gambling, Suicide, Attitude, Alcohol, Drugs, and Stress Coping Abilities. The instrument assesses important gambler attitudes and behaviors.

Format: Self-administered; untimed: 35 minutes

Scoring: Computer scored

Cost: Contact publisher

Global Assessment Functioning Scale (GAF Report)
Michael B. First

| 2000 | Multi-Health Systems, Inc. |

Population: Ages 18 years and older
Purpose: Helps to assess patients on the DSM-IV GAF Scale
Description: Provide a GAF Rating (100-point scale) and a GAF report with 10 point ranges. Report decision tree is designed to guide clinicians through a methodical and comprehensive consideration of all aspects of a patient's symptoms and functioning. Windows-based with PsychManager™ Program.
Format: Completed by clinician; untimed: 3 minutes
Scoring: Computer scored
Cost: $95.00 (unlimited use)

G-MAP: The Maroondah Assessment Profile for Problem Gambling
Tim Loughnan, Mark Pierce, Anastasia Sagris-Desmond

| 1998 | Australian Council for Educational Research Limited |

Population: Adults
Purpose: Provides an individualized profile for problem gamblers
Description: An 85-item questionnaire gathers information on 17 different factors associated with problem gambling. The manual contains analysis and interpretation information and individual Action Sheets for clients, with information about each of the 17 factors. A reproducible Response Report is provided showing the 17 factors divided into five broad groups. This grouping allows the counselor to pinpoint more accurately why someone gambles and can assist with finding the best way to work toward resolving problems. A computer-administered format is available.
Format: Examiner required; individual administration; untimed: 25 minutes
Scoring: Examiner evaluated; computer scoring available
Cost: Contact publisher

Hare P-Scan Research Version
Robert D. Hare, Hugues F. Hervé

| 1998 | Multi-Health Systems, Inc. |

Population: Ages 13 years and older

Purpose: Assesses risk for antisocial, criminal, and violent behavior
Description: Has forensic applications with a total of 90 items: Lifestyle (30 items), Affective (30 items), and Interpersonal (30 items).
Format: Evaluator rated; untimed: 10 to 15 minutes
Scoring: QuikScore™ forms
Cost: Kit (manual and 25 forms) $42.00

Hare Psychopathy Checklist–Revised (PCL-R)
Robert D. Hare

| 1991 | Multi-Health Systems, Inc. |

Population: Ages 18 years and older
Purpose: Assesses psychopathic (antisocial) personality disorders
Description: Used in forensic assessment with a total of 20 items. Two major facets of psychopathy: callous, selfish, remorseless use of others (Factor 1), and a chronically unstable and antisocial lifestyle (Factor 2). Yields a total score indicating the degree to which the individual matches a prototypical individual with psychopathic personality disorder.
Format: Examiner required; structured interview and expert rating; untimed: 90 to 120 minutes, 60 minutes for collateral review
Scoring: QuikScore™ forms
Cost: Softcover Kit $215.00

Hare Psychopathy Checklist: Screening Version (PCL:SV)
Stephen Hart, David N. Cox, Robert D. Hare

| 1995 | Multi-Health Systems, Inc. |

Population: Ages 18 years and older
Purpose: Screens for psychopathic (antisocial) personality disorders
Description: Consist of 12 items yielding a total score and two factor scores. These factor scores are analogous to the two factors of the Hare Psychopathy Checklist-Revised.
Format: Examiner required; structured interview and expert rating; untimed: 45 minutes, 30 minutes for collateral review
Scoring: QuikScore™ forms
Cost: Kit (manual, 25 each interview guide and forms) $120.00

Hilson Career Satisfaction Index (HCSI)
Robin E. Inwald

1988   Hilson Research, Inc.

Population: Adults

Purpose: Identifies and predicts stress-related behavior patterns and career satisfaction

Description: Paper–pencil 161-item true–false instrument consisting of four scales: Stress Patterns, Anger/Hostility, Dissatisfaction with Career, and Defensiveness. Designed for individuals on the job who have been referred for evaluation. Total score measures overall level of stress and dissatisfaction related to current work-oriented activities. This score should be used only as a general indicator, and individual scale elevations should be reviewed whenever conclusions are drawn about test results. The teleprocessing software allows input of test responses.

Format: Self-administered; untimed: 25 to 35 minutes

Scoring: Computer scored

Cost: Contact publisher

Holden Psychological Screening Inventory (HPSI)
Ronald R. Holden

1996   Multi-Health Systems, Inc.

Population: Ages 14 years and older

Purpose: Assesses psychiatric and social symptomatology and depression

Description: Provides an efficient, concise, and practical method of exploring psychopathology, and is a valuable screening tool for assessing the need for lengthier clinical measures. Comprises 36 items, each of which is rated on a 5-point Likert scale. The HPSI is designed to be a component of a comprehensive psychological assessment procedure to be used with nonclinical, psychiatric, and forensic populations.

Format: Self-administered; untimed: 5 to 7 minutes

Scoring: QuikScore™ forms

Cost: Kit (manual, forms) $53.00

House Tree Person and Draw a Person (HTP/DAP)
Valerie Van Hutton

1994   Psychological Assessment Resources, Inc.

Population: Ages 7 to 11 years

Purpose: Used in outpatient counseling and school psychology to screen for sexual abuse

Description: Paper–pencil projective four-drawing test with the following categories: Preoccupation with Sexually Relevant Concepts, Aggression and Hostility, Withdrawal and Guarded Accessibility, Alertness for Danger, Suspiciousness, and Lack of Trust.

Format: Examiner required; individual administration; untimed

Scoring: Examiner evaluated

Cost: Kit (book, 25 scoring booklets) $85.00

Internalized Shame Scale (ISS)
David R. Cook

2001   Multi-Health Systems, Inc

Population: Ages 17 years and older

Purpose: Measures individual's feeling of shame

Description: Focuses on evaluating the extent to which the negative affect of shame becomes magnified and internalized. The ISS items reflect feelings of inferiority, worthlessness, inadequacy, and alienation, and help the practitioner isolate a client's specific feelings of shame that are involved in the presenting problem. Lends itself to repeated administration, which can be helpful in monitoring treatment progress.

Format: Self-administered; untimed: 15 minutes

Scoring: QuikScore™ forms

Cost: Kit (manual, 15 forms, 25 handouts) $73.00

Internalizing Symptoms Scale for Children (ISSC)
Kenneth W. Merrell, Amy S. Walters

1998   PRO-ED, Inc.

Population: Ages 8 to 13 years

Purpose: Measures internalizing symptomology (i.e., depression, anxiety, somatic problems, social withdrawal)

Description: The ISSC is a screening tool that helps determine relative risk that a serious internalizing disorder may exist or is developing in a child. It does not focus exclusively on a particular syndrome but allows the examiner to identify and measure symptoms that are common across internalizing syndromes. The ISSC has strong psychometric properties. It was standardized on a national sample of 2,149 students in Grades 3 through 6. The child completes the ratings on a 4-point Likert scale.

Format: Rating scale; untimed: 20 minutes

Scoring: Examiner evaluated

Cost: Complete Kit (manual, 25 response forms, 25 summary forms, storage box) $74.00

Interpersonal Behavior Survey (IBS)
Paul A. Mauger, David R. Adkinson, Suzanne K. Zoss, Gregory Firestone, J. David Hook

1980	Western Psychological Services

Population: Grades 9 and above

Purpose: Measures and distinguishes assertive and aggressive behaviors among adolescents and adults; used for assertiveness training, for marriage counseling, and in a variety of clinical settings

Description: Paper-pencil test in which the subject responds to 272 statements written in the present tense to provide sensitivity to ongoing changes. The test yields eight aggressiveness scales (including one that measures general aggressiveness over a broad range of item content, including aggressive behaviors, feelings, and attitudes), nine assertiveness scales (including one that measures general assertiveness over a broad range of behaviors), three validity scales, and three relationship scales (Conflict Avoidance, Dependency, and Shyness). Two shorter forms are available: a 38-item form providing a general sampling of behaviors and a 133-item form providing information on all scales. The Profile Form provides a display of raw scores, *T*-scores, and percentiles. Norms are provided for adult males, adult females, high school students, college students, and blacks. The manual presents validity and reliability data, interpretive guidelines, and a number of illustrated cases.

Format: Self-administered; untimed: 10 to 45 minutes depending on form

Scoring: Examiner evaluated

Cost: Kit (manual, 5 booklets, 50 profile forms, 50 answer sheets, key) $65.00

Inventory of Suicide Orientation–30 (ISO–30™)
John D. King, Brian Kowalchuk

Date not provided	NCS Pearson

Population: Ages 13 to 18 years

Purpose: Provides an overall suicide risk classification based on measurements of both hopelessness and suicide ideation

Description: This brief screening tool helps to identify adolescents at risk for suicide. It is appropriate for use by psychologists, social workers, and counselors in school settings, juvenile justice evaluations, and inpatient and outpatient mental health facilities. The test's brevity helps minimize test-taking resistance. Results help alert psychologists and counselors to the early signs of an adolescent's suicidal tendencies. Clinical data were collected on 366 adolescents. The test is written at a sixth-grade reading level.

Format: Self-administered; untimed:10 minutes

Scoring: Hand key; software scoring available

Cost: Hand-Scoring Starter Kit (manual, 10 carbonless answer sheets) $47.00

Inwald Survey 2–Adolescent Version (IS2–A)
Robin E. Inwald

1995	Hilson Research, Inc.

Population: Ages 9 to 19 years

Purpose: Measures risk-taking, temper control, and violence/antisocial behavior patterns

Description: Contains total of 119 items.

Format: Examiner required; suitable for group; untimed: 20 minutes

Scoring: Computer scored; scoring service available

Cost: Contact publisher

Jail Inmate Inventory (JII)

Date not provided	Risk & Needs Assessment, Inc.

Population: Adults

Purpose: Designed specifically for jail inmate risk and needs assessment

Description: The JII has 109 items with six scales: Truthfulness, Adjustment, Violence, Antisocial, Alcohol, and Drugs. The JII was designed to be compatible with overcrowded facilities, overworked staff, and very tight schedules.

Format: Self-administered; untimed: 15 to 20 minutes

Scoring: Computer scored

Cost: Contact publisher

Jesness Behavior Checklist (JBC)
Carl F. Jesness

1996	Multi-Health Systems, Inc.

Population: Ages 13 to 20 years

Purpose: Measures risk for antisocial behavior

Description: An 80-item scale measuring 14 bipolar behavioral tendencies and consisting of two parallel forms: an Observer Form and a Self-Appraisal Form. The scales measured are Unobtrusiveness, Friendliness, Responsibility, Consideration, Independence, Rapport, Enthusiasm, Sociability, Conformity, Calmness, Communication, Insight, Social Control, and Anger Control.

Format: Self-administered; untimed: 20 minutes

Scoring: QuikScore™ forms; computer scored

Cost: Complete Kit (manual, 10 each observer and self booklets, 25 each observer and self forms) $110.00

Jesness Inventory (JI)
Carl F. Jesness

1996	Multi-Health Systems, Inc.

Population: Ages 8 years to adult

Purpose: Provides a personality classification system for youths who are delinquent or who have conduct disorders

Description: True-false questionnaire with 155 easy-to-understand items yielding 10 trait scores, an index of asocial tendencies, and nine personality subtype scales.

Format: Self-administered; untimed: 20 to 30 minutes

Scoring: QuikScore™ forms; computer scored; scoring service

Cost: Kit (manual, 10 booklets, 25 forms) $75.00

Juvenile Profile (JP)

Date not provided	Behavior Data Systems, Ltd.

Population: Adolescents

Purpose: Designed for school systems, juvenile screening programs, and troubled youth treatment agencies

Description: The JP has 116 items with five scales: Truthfulness, Aggressiveness, Alcohol, Drugs, and Stress Coping Abilities. This is a fast way to screen juveniles in a nonintroversive manner. Identifies impaired stress coping abilities and existing emotional and mental health problems. This is a brief, yet comprehensive and standardized self-report test.

Format: Self-administered; untimed: 20 minutes

Scoring: Computer scored

Cost: Contact publisher

Level of Service Inventory–Revised (LSI-R)
Don A. Andrews, James L. Bonta

1995	Multi-Health Systems, Inc.

Population: Ages 16 years and older

Purpose: Assesses risk and needs in criminal offenders; used for criminal corrections and probation decisions

Description: Test with 54 items in these categories: criminal history (10 items), education/employment (12 items), family/marital (4 items), accumulation (3 items), leisure/recreation (2 items), companions (5 items), alcohol/drug problem (9 items), emotional/personal (5 items), and attitudes/orientation (4 items). The total score indicates the level of risk/needs.

Format: Examiner required; individual administration; untimed: 30 to 45 minutes

Scoring: QuikScore™ forms; computer scored

Cost: Kit (manual; 25 each of interview guides, forms, profiles) $130.00

Louisville Behavior Checklist
Lovick C. Miller

1984	Western Psychological Services

Population: Ages 4 to 17 years

Purpose: Measures the entire range of social and emotional behaviors indicative of psychopathological disorders in children and adolescents; used as an intake screening device

Description: Paper-pencil or computer-administered true-false inventory in which parents record their child's behavior by answering 164 questions that provide relevant information on a number of interpretive scales. The inventory is available in three forms for three different age groups: Form E1 (ages 4 to 6), Form E2 (ages 7 to 12), and Form E3 (ages 13 to 17). For example, the scales measured in Form E1 are Infantile Aggression, Hyperactivity, Antisocial Behavior, Aggression, Social Withdrawal, Sensitivity, Fear, Inhibition, Intellectual Deficit, Immaturity, Cognitive Disability, Normal Irritability, Prosocial Deficit, Rare Deviance, Neurotic Behavior, Psychotic Behavior, Somatic Behavior, Sexual Behavior, School Disturbance Predictor, and Severity Level.

Format: Examiner required; individual administration; untimed: 20 to 30 minutes

Scoring: Examiner evaluated; may be computer scored

Cost: Kit (30 reusable questionnaires, manual,

100 answer-profile sheets, scoring keys, 2 pre-paid mail-in answer sheets) $125.00

MacArthur Competence Assessment Tool-Criminal Adjudication (MacCAT-CA)
Steven K. Hoge, Richard J. Bonnie, Norman G. Poythress, John Monahan

| 1999 | Psychological Assessment Resources, Inc. |

Population: Ages 18 years and older

Purpose: Evaluates adult's capacity to proceed to adjudication

Description: Structured interview with 22 items measures three competence-related abilities: Understanding (8 items), Reasoning (8 items), and Appreciation (6 items).

Format: Examiner required; individual administration; untimed: 25 to 55 minutes

Scoring: Hand key, examiner evaluated

Cost: Intro Kit (manual, 20 interview booklets) $125.00

MCMI-III™ Report
Giles Rainwater

| 2000 | Psychometric Software, Inc. |

Population: Adults

Purpose: Assesses personality of persons with emotional and interpersonal difficulties

Description: With 175 Million Clinical Multiaxial Inventory items to interpret, the MCMI-III report is much shorter than comparable instruments. This inventory is almost self-administrating. The MCMI-III uses actuarial base rate data to determine the percentages of patients who are actually found to be disordered across diagnostic settings. The MCMI-III contains DSM-IV diagnostic codes and covers personality type, clinical syndrome, diagnosis, treatment, and narrative report.

Format: Self-administered on computer; untimed: 20 to 30 minutes

Scoring: Computer scoring

Cost: Contact publisher

Miller Forensic Assessment of Symptoms Test (MFAST)
Holly A. Miller

| 2001 | Psychological Assessment Resources, Inc. |

Population: Ages 18 to 80 years

Purpose: Provides a screening assessment of malingered psychiatric illness

Description: Used for inpatient and outpatient, forensic, and correctional evaluations. The MFAST has 25 items with seven scales that assess response styles and interview strategies useful for detecting malingerers.

Format: Examiner required; individual administration; untimed: 5 to 10 minutes

Scoring: Examiner evaluated

Cost: Intro Kit $105.00

Millon Behavioral Medicine Diagnostic (MBMD™)
Theodore Millon, Michael Antoni, Carrie Millon, Sarah Meagher, Seth Grossman

| 2001 | NCS Pearson |

Population: Adults

Purpose: Measures psychosocial assets and liabilities that may support or interfere with a patient's course of medical treatment

Description: The test was designed to help increase the probability of positive health-care treatment outcomes that may reduce medical utilization and overall costs of care. Results of the MBMD can be used in a number of medical settings to help identify patients who may have significant psychiatric problems and recommend specific interventions, pinpoint personal and social assets that may facilitate adjustment to physical limitations or lifestyle changes, identify individuals who may need more communication and support in order to comply with prescribed medical regimens, and structure posttreatment plans and self-care responsibilities in the context of the patient's social network. Written at a sixth-grade reading level. Also available in Spanish.

Format: Examiner required; individual administration; untimed: 20 to 25 minutes

Scoring: Hand key; scoring service available; software available

Cost: Starter Kit (manual; user's guide; 10 test booklets; 50 each of answer sheets, worksheets, profile forms, and keys) $298.00

Millon Clinical Multiaxial Inventory-II (MCMI-II™)
Theodore Millon

| 1987 | NCS Pearson |

Population: Adults

Purpose: Diagnoses adults with personality disorders; used in private or group practice, mental health centers, outpatient clinics, and general and psychiatric hospitals and clinics with individuals in assessment or treatment programs

Description: True-false test evaluating adults with emotional or interpersonal problems. The inventory has 175 items that form scales measuring both the state and the trait features of personality. The Clinical Personality Pattern scales are Schizoid, Avoidant, Dependent, Histrionic, Narcissistic, Antisocial, Aggressive/Sadistic, Compulsive, Passive/Aggressive, and Self-Defeating. There are three Modifier Indices—Disclosure, Desirability, and Debasement—and three Severe Pathology scales—Schizotypal, Borderline, and Paranoid. The Clinical Syndrome scales are Anxiety Disorder, Somatoform Disorder, Hypomanic Disorder, Dysthymic Disorder, Alcohol Dependence, and Drug Dependence. There are three Severe Syndrome Scales: Thought Disorder, Major Depression, and Delusional Disorder. A validity index is included also. The MCMI-II is intended to reflect DSM-III-R diagnoses.

Format: Self-administered; untimed: 20 to 30 minutes

Scoring: Computer scored

Cost: Manual $21.00; Interpretive Report $21.25 to $28.35 depending on quantity and scoring method; Profile Report $5.75 to $8.00 depending on quantity and scoring method

Multiphasic Sex Inventory I (MSI I)
H. R. Nichols, Ilene Molinder

1984	Nichols and Molinder Assessments

Population: Adolescent and adult male sex offenders

Purpose: Measures the sexual characteristics of adolescent and adult male sexual offenders; used to evaluate sexual deviance and assess progress in the treatment of sexual deviance

Description: Paper-pencil 300-item true-false test of psychosexual characteristics from which 20 scales and a 50-item sexual history are derived. Six of the 20 scales are validity scales. The inventory also contains a Treatment Attitudes Scale. The sexual deviance scales include the Child Molest Scale, Rape Scale, and Exhibitionism Scale. There are five atypical sexual outlet scales: Fetish, Voyeurism, Obscene Call, Bondage and Discipline, and Sado-Masochism. The four sexual dysfunction scales include Sexual Inadequacy,

Premature Ejaculation, Impotence, and Physical Disabilities. There is also a Sexual Knowledge and Beliefs Scale. The 50-item Sexual History includes a sex deviance development section, marriage development section, gender identity section, gender orientation development section, and sexual assault behavior section. Scores are yielded for all 20 scales and are recorded on the profile form.

Format: Examiner/self-administered; untimed: 45 minutes

Scoring: Hand key

Cost: Contact publisher

Multiphasic Sex Inventory II (MSI II)
H. R. Nichols, Ilene Molinder

2000	Nichols and Molinder Assessments

Population: Adult and adolescent sex offenders

Purpose: Evaluates clients who allegedly have engaged in sexual misconduct but who deny any such behavior

Description: The MSI II is an expanded version of the MSI I. The core scales remain basically intact but the wording of some questions has been revised for the sake of clarity. This is a paper-pencil test with true-false questions. It requires approximately a seventh-grade reading level; however, audiocassettes of the questions are available. The scoring information is placed on a profile form designed for ease in interpretation.

Format: Self-administered; untimed: 90 minutes

Scoring: Examiner evaluated; scoring service available

Cost: Contact publisher

Panic and Somatization Scales
Albert Mehrabian

1994	Albert Mehrabian, PhD

Population: Ages 14 years and older

Purpose: Assesses panic disorder and somatization or hypochondria; used for research and counseling

Description: Paper-pencil test with 18 items on two subtests: Panic and Somatization. A 10th-grade reading level is required.

Format: Self-administered; suitable for group use; untimed: 10 minutes

Scoring: Hand key; test scoring service available from publisher

Cost: Test Kit $33.00

Parolee Inventory (PI)

Date not provided	Risk & Needs Assessment, Inc.

Population: Adults on parole

Purpose: Designed specifically for parole department use

Description: The PI has 155 items and seven scales: Truthfulness, Violence, Antisocial, Resistance, Alcohol, Drugs, and Stress Coping Abilities. The PI is an objective, comprehensive, and standardized screening instrument that examines important attitudes and behaviors. The PI provides an on-site, objective second opinion, in a timely manner.

Format: Self-administered; 30 to 35 minutes

Scoring: Computer scored

Cost: Contact publisher

Paulhus Deception Scales (PDS)
Delroy L. Paulhus

1998	Multi-Health Systems, Inc.

Population: Ages 16 years and older

Purpose: Measures one's tendency to give socially desirable responses

Description: Total of 40 items with two subscales: Self Deceptive Enhancement and Impression Management.

Format: Self-administered; untimed: 5 to 7 minutes

Scoring: QuikScore™ forms, computer scored

Cost: Kit (manual, 25 forms) $50.00

Personal Problems Checklist–Adolescent
John A. Schinka

1985	Psychological Assessment Resources, Inc.

Population: Ages 13 to 17 years

Purpose: Assesses personal problems of adolescents; used as a survey instrument in clinical and counseling settings to initiate the consultation process and introduce the client to formal diagnostic testing

Description: Paper–pencil or computer-administered 240-item test identifying common problems cited by adolescents in 13 areas: social, appearance, job, family, home, school, money, religion, emotions, dating, health, attitude, and crises.

Format: Self-administered; untimed: 10 to 20 minutes

Scoring: Examiner evaluated

Cost: 50 Checklists $42.00

Personal Problems Checklist–Adult
John A. Schinka

1985	Psychological Assessment Resources, Inc.

Population: Adults

Purpose: Assesses the personal problems of adults; used as a survey instrument in clinical and counseling settings to initiate the consultation process and introduce the client to formal diagnostic testing

Description: Paper–pencil 211-item test identifying problems in 13 areas: social, appearance, vocational, family and home, school, finances, religion, emotions, sex, legal, health and habits, attitude, and crises.

Format: Self-administered; untimed: 10 to 20 minutes

Scoring: Examiner evaluated

Cost: 50 Checklists $42.00

Personality Assessment Screener (PAS)
Leslie C. Morey

1997	Psychological Assessment Resources, Inc.

Population: Ages 18 years and older

Purpose: Screens for a broad range of emotional and behavioral problems

Description: The PAS is a 22-item screener with 10 distinct clinical problem domains represented: Negative Affect, Hostile Control, Acting Out, Suicidal Thinking, Health Problems, Alienation, Psychotic Features, Alcohol Problems, Social Withdrawal, and Anger Control.

Format: Self-administered; untimed: 5 minutes

Scoring: Hand key; computer scoring available

Cost: Kit (manual, 25 response forms) $70.00

Personality Disorder Interview–IV (PDI-IV)
Thomas A. Widiger, Steve Mangine, Elizabeth M. Corbitt, Cynthia G. Ellis, Glenn V. Thomas

1994	Psychological Assessment Resources, Inc.

Population: Ages 18 years and older

Purpose: Assists in the diagnosis of DSM-IV personality disorders

Description: Oral-response semistructured interview with the following booklets: Thematic

Content Areas Interview Booklet (attitudes toward self, attitudes toward others, security of comfort of others, friendships and relationships, conflicts and disagreements, work and leisure, social norms, mood, appearance and perception) and Personality Disorders Interview Booklet (antisocial personality disorder, avoidant personality disorder, borderline personality disorder, dependent personality disorder, histrionic personality disorder, narcissistic personality disorder, obsessive–compulsive personality disorder, paranoid personality disorder, schizoid personality disorder, schizotypal personality disorder, depressive personality disorder, passive–aggressive personality disorder).

Format: Examiner required; individual administration; untimed: 2 hours

Scoring: Examiner evaluated

Cost: Intro Kit (PDI-IV book, 2 each of thematic content booklet and personality disorders booklet, 10 each of summary and profile booklets) $115.00

Positive and Negative Syndrome Scale (PANSS)
Stanley R. Kay, Lewis A. Opler, Abraham Fiszbein

1992	Multi-Health Systems, Inc.

Population: Ages 18 years and older

Purpose: Assesses positive and negative symptomology in people with schizophrenia

Description: The 30-item test is broken up into eight scales and one composite score. The scales are positive symptoms, negative symptoms, general, anergia, thought disturbance, activation, paranoid, and depression. Scores for all subscales are obtained, plus a composite and General Psychopathology score. A profile form is used to convert raw scores into standard scores.

Format: Examiner required; individual administration; untimed: 30 to 40 minutes

Scoring: QuikScore™ forms

Cost: Kit (manual, 25 scoring and response forms) $95.00

Pre-Post Inventory

Date not provided	Behavior Data Systems, Ltd.

Population: Adults

Purpose: Designed for objective pretest-posttest outcome comparison

Description: This is a counseling or treatment outcome measure. It has 148 items with seven scales: Truthfulness, Self-Esteem, Resistance, Distress, Alcohol, Drugs, and Stress Coping Abilities. It is suitable for evaluating intervention, counseling, or treatment effectiveness.

Format: Self-administered; untimed: 30 minutes

Scoring: Computer scored

Cost: Contact publisher

Prison Inmate Inventory (PII)

1991	Risk & Needs Assessment, Inc.

Population: Adult prison inmates

Purpose: Designed for inmate risk assessment and needs identification; helps determine risk and establish supervision levels and readiness for classification or status changes

Description: Designed for prison inmate risk and needs assessment, the test contains 10 scales: Validity, Violence, Antisocial, Risk, Self Esteem, Alcohol, Drugs, Judgment, Distress, and Stress Coping Abilities. There are 157 multiple-choice and true-false items. Truth-corrected scores are provided. Computer-generated report summarizes risk range and recommendations for each scale; on-site reports are available within 4 minutes of test completion. Available in English or Spanish.

Format: Self-administered; untimed: 45 minutes

Scoring: Computer scored

Cost: Contact publisher

Psychiatric Diagnostic Interview–Revised (PDI-R)
Ekkehard Othmer, Elizabeth C. Penick, Barbara J. Powell, Marsha Read, Sigliende Othmer

1981	Western Psychological Services

Population: Adults

Purpose: Identifies frequently encountered psychiatric disorders; used in all phases of diagnostic screening, intake, and follow-up

Description: Multiple-item verbally administered oral-response or computer-administered test consisting of questions usually requiring yes–no answers. The test offers diagnostic summaries evaluating the following basic syndromes: organic brain syndrome, alcoholism, drug abuse, mania, depression, schizophrenia, antisocial personality, somatization disorder, anorexia nervosa, obsessive-compulsive neurosis, phobic neurosis, anxiety neurosis, mental retardation, bulimia, posttraumatic stress disorder, generalized anxiety, and adjustment disorder. In addition, four derived syndromes are evaluated: polydrug abuse, schizoaffective disorder, manic-depressive disorder, and bulimarexia.The questions for each of the basic syndromes are divided into four sections. If simple response criteria are not met, the interviewer omits the remainder of the questions for that syndrome and proceeds to the next syndrome. All positive syndromes are recorded on the Time Profile.

Format: Self-administered; untimed: 10 to 15 minutes

Scoring: Examiner evaluated; may be computer scored

Cost: Kit (manual, administration booklet, 25 recording booklets) $99.50

Psychosexual Life History (PSLH)
H. R. Nichols, Ilene Molinder

1995, 2000	Nichols and Molinder Assessments

Population: Adult and adolescent sex offenders

Purpose: Used for clinical interview and assessment of behavior patterns, emotional states, attitudes, and personal history of sex offenders

Description: Short-answer 16-page questionnaire detailing experiences, thoughts, and feelings from childhood through adult life. Categories are Sexual History, Health, Parental and Family, Childhood and Adolescent Development and Behaviors, Education, Work, Substance Abuse, Marital, Adult Behaviors, and Treatment. A sixth-grade reading level is required.

Format: Interview; can be self-administered; untimed

Scoring: Examiner evaluated

Cost: Contact publisher

Psychotic Inpatient Profile
Maurice Lorr, Norris D. Vestre

1968	Western Psychological Services

Population: Adults

Purpose: Measures the behavior patterns of adult psychiatric patients; used with difficult patients and to evaluate treatment progress

Description: Paper-pencil inventory consisting of 96 questions about the subject's behavior, which a nurse or psychiatric aide answers by indicating frequency of observation. Analysis of

the responses provides objective and quantitative measures of 12 syndromes of observable psychotic behavior: excitement, hostile belligerence, paranoid projection, anxious depression, retardation, seclusiveness, care needed, psychotic disorganization, grandiosity, perceptual distortion, depressive mood, and disorientation. The six-page test booklet is a revised and expanded version of the Psychotic Reaction Profile. Norms are provided for men and women, both drug free and drug treated.

Format: Examiner required; individual administration; untimed: 10 to 15 minutes

Scoring: Hand key

Cost: Kit (manual, 25 forms) $45.00

RAND-36 Health Status Inventory (RAND-36 HSI)
Ron D. Hays

1998	The Psychological Corporation

Population: Ages 18 years and older

Purpose: Assesses physical, mental, and global health status

Description: Measures perceived health status, focusing on degree of limitation of functioning. The instrument takes into account both physical and mental aspects of health. Eight scales and three composite domains identify specific areas of limitation. There are 36 questions on the long form and 12 items on the short form.

Format: Examiner required; individual administration; untimed: 2 to 5 minutes

Scoring: Examiner evaluated

Cost: Complete Kit (manual, 25 each of question/answer sheets and scoring worksheets) $57.00

Reynolds Adolescent Adjustment Screening Inventory (RAASI)
William M. Reynolds

2001	Psychological Assessment Resources, Inc.

Population: Ages 12 to 19 years

Purpose: Screens psychological adjustment

Description: The RAASI has 32 self-report items with four scales: Antisocial Behavior, Anger Control Problems, Emotional Distress, and Positive Self. A third-grade reading level is required.

Format: Self administered; untimed: 5 minutes

Scoring: Hand key

Cost: Kit (manual, 50 test booklets) $99.00

Roberts Apperception Test for Children
Glen E. Roberts, Dorothea S. McArthur

1982	Western Psychological Services

Population: Ages 6 to 15 years

Purpose: Identifies children with emotional disturbance; used for clinical diagnosis, particularly with children just entering counseling or therapy

Description: Oral-response 16-item test in which the child is shown cards containing realistic line illustrations and is asked to make up stories about each. The illustrations depict adults and children in up-to-date clothing and emphasize the everyday, interpersonal events of contemporary life, including (in addition to the standard situations of the Thematic Apperception Test and Children's Apperception Test) such situations as parental disagreement, parental affection, observation of nudity, and school and peer interpersonal events. Stimuli are chosen to elicit psychologically meaningful responses. The clinical areas measured and reported on the Interpersonal Chart are conflict, anxiety, aggression, depression, rejection, punishment, dependency, support, closure, resolution, unresolved indicator, maladaptive outcome, and deviation response. Other measures include the Ego Functioning Index, the Aggression Index, and the Levels of Projection Scale. The manual includes a number of case studies and examples.

Format: Examiner required; individual administration; untimed: 20 to 30 minutes

Scoring: Examiner evaluated

Cost: Kit (manual, set of test pictures, 25 record booklets) $115.00; test pictures for black children $59.50

Rogers Criminal Responsibility Assessment Scales (R-CRAS)
Richard Rogers

1984	Psychological Assessment Resources, Inc.

Population: Adults

Purpose: Evaluates the criminal responsibility of individuals who may or may not, depending on their sanity or insanity at the time they committed a crime, be held legally accountable for their actions

Description: Paper–pencil inventory evaluating criminal responsibility. The instrument quantifies essential psychological and situational variables at the time of the person's crime that are to be used in a criterion-based decision model. This allows the clinician to quantify the impairment at the time of the crime, conceptualize the impairment with respect to the appropriate legal standards, and render an expert opinion with respect to those standards. Descriptive criteria are provided on scales measuring the individual's reliability, organicity, psychopathology, cognitive control, and behavioral control at the time of the alleged crime. Part I establishes the degree of impairment on psychological variables significant to the determination of insanity. Part II articulates the decision process toward rendering an accurate opinion on criminal responsibility with the ALI standard and includes experimental criteria and decision models for guilty but mentally ill and M'Naughten standards.

Format: Examiner required; individual administration; untimed

Scoring: Examiner evaluated

Cost: Intro Kit $85.00

SAQ-Adult Probation II

Updated yearly	Risk & Needs Assessment, Inc.

Population: Adults on probation

Purpose: Measures eight areas of concern

Description: Version II contains eight scales: Truthfulness, Alcohol, Drugs, Resistance, Aggressivity, Violence, Antisocial, and Stress Coping Abilities. The instrument has 181 multiple-choice and true-false items and is computer or paper–pencil administered. Computer-generated results are available within 4 minutes of test completion. Truth-corrected scores are provided. Computer-generated report includes summary reports on each scale. The instrument was standardized and normed on probationers and parolees. Available in English or Spanish.

Format: Self-administered; 35 minutes

Scoring: Computer scored

Cost: Contact publisher

SCID II Patient Questionnaire Computer Program (SCID II PQ)
Miriam Gibbon, Janet B. W. Williams, Robert L. Spitzer, Lorna Smith Benjamin

1997	Multi-Health Systems, Inc.

Population: Ages 18 years and older

Purpose: Provides information for diagnosing DSM-IV Axis II disorders

Description: Total of 119 items for diagnosing DSM-IV Axis II disorders. Provides Dimensional Score Report and Question-by-Question Report.

Format: Self-administered; untimed: 30 to 45 minutes

Scoring: Computer scored

Cost: $295.00 (unlimited use)

SCID Screen Patient Questionnaire Computer Program (SSPQ)
Michael B. First, Miriam Gibbon, Janet B. W. Williams, Robert L. Spitzer

2001	Multi-Health Systems, Inc.

Population: Ages 18 years and older

Purpose: A brief self-report version of the SCID for Axis I disorders

Description: Screens patients using approximately 76 questions dealing with mood, anxiety, somatoform, psychotic, substance use, eating disorders, and psychotic symptoms. Yields Complete Summary of Patient Responses, Concise Summary of Possible Diagnoses, and Long Summary of Diagnoses Reports.

Format: Self-administered: untimed: 20 minutes

Scoring: Computer scored

Cost: $395.00 (unlimited use)

SCID Screen Patient Questionnaire-Extended (SSPQ-X)
Michael B. First, Miriam Gibbon, Janet B. W. Williams, Robert L. Spitzer

2001	Multi-Health Systems, Inc.

Population: Ages 18 years and older

Purpose: A comprehensive self-report version of the SCID for Axis I disorders

Description: Approximately 589 items measure mood, anxiety, substance use, somatoform, eating disorders, and psychotic symptoms. Yields Summary of Responses Report and Diagnostic Report.

Format: Self-administered; untimed: 30 to 45 minutes

Scoring: Computer scored

Cost: $495.00 (unlimited use)

SCL-90 Analogue
Leonard R. Derogatis

1976	NCS Pearson

Population: Adolescents, adults

Purpose: Screens for psychological problems

Description: Paper-pencil test with an observer rating scale. The nine primary dimensions are somatization, obsessive-compulsive, interpersonal sensitivity, depression, anxiety, hostility, phobic anxiety, paranoid ideation, and psychoticism. Can be used with the Symptom Checklist-90 Revised or Brief Symptom Inventory. Examiner must be level-B qualified.

Format: Examiner required; individual administration; untimed: 1 to 3 minutes

Scoring: Examiner evaluated

Cost: Contact publisher

Severity and Acuity of Psychiatric Illness Scales
John Lyons

1998	The Psychological Corporation

Population: Ages 5 years to adult

Purpose: Assesses the need for admission for psychiatric care; used to monitor treatment outcomes

Description: The Severity Scale can be used at admission and provides validated cutoff scores that reduce the probability of inappropriate admissions. The Acuity Scale can be used during treatment to monitor patient progress and to document and justify decisions for discharge, step-down, or continued care. Two versions are available: adult and child/adolescent.

Format: Examiner required; individual administration; untimed: 5 minutes

Scoring: Examiner evaluated

Cost: Adult Starter Kit (manual, 10 each of Severity and Acuity booklets, 25 each of rating sheets) $74.00; Child/Adolescent Starter Kit (manual, 10 each of Severity and Acuity booklets, 25 each of rating sheets) $82.00

Sex Adjustment Inventory (SAI)

1991	Risk & Needs Assessment, Inc.

Population: Sex offenders

Purpose: Designed to identify sexually deviant and paraphiliac behavior in people accused or convicted of sexual offenses

Description: Screens sexual offenders and measures degree of severity of sexually deviant and paraphiliac behavior. The test contains 13 scales: Test Item Truthfulness, Sex Item Truthfulness, Sexual Adjustment, Child Molest, Sexual Assault, Exhibitionism, Incest, Alcohol, Drugs, Violence, Antisocial, Distress, and Judgment. There are 214 multiple-choice and true-false items. Computer-generated report summarizes risk range and recommendations for each scale;

on-site reports are created within 4 minutes of test completion. Two separate truthfulness scales permit comparison of client's test-taking attitude to sex-related and non-sex-related questions, which provides insight into client's attitude, motivation, and assessment-related behavior. Truth-corrected scores.

Format: Self-administered; 35 minutes

Scoring: Computer scored

Cost: Contact publisher

Sexual Adjustment Inventory–Juvenile

Date not provided   **Behavior Data Systems, Ltd.**

Population: Ages 12 to 18 years

Purpose: Designed for evaluating juveniles accused or convicted of sexual offenses

Description: The SAI-Juvenile has 195 items with 13 scales: Test Item Truthfulness, Sex Item Truthfulness, Child Molest, Sexual (Rape) Assault, Incest, Exhibitionism, Sexual Adjustment, Violence, Antisocial, Distress, Alcohol, Drugs, and Judgment.

Format: Self-administered; untimed: 30 to 35 minutes

Scoring: Computer scored

Cost: Contact publisher

Shoplifting Inventory

1995   **Risk & Needs Assessment, Inc.**

Population: Adolescent and adult shoplifters

Purpose: Designed for shoplifter evaluation

Description: This assessment inventory contains nine scales—Truthfulness, Entitlement, Shoplifting, Antisocial, Peer Pressure, Self-Esteem, Impulsiveness, Alcohol, and Drugs—and evaluates people charged or convicted of shoplifting. There are 185 multiple-choice and true–false items. The computer-generated report summarizes risk range and recommendations for each scale and includes truth-corrected scores. On-site reports are available within 4 minutes of test completion. Available in English or Spanish.

Format: Self-administered; 45 minutes

Scoring: Computer scored

Cost: Contact publisher

Structured Clinical Interview for Axis I Disorders–Clinician Version (SCID–CV)
Michael B. First, Miriam Gibbon,
Robert L. Spitzer, Janet B. W. Williams

1998   **Multi-Health Systems, Inc.**

Population: Ages 18 years and older

Purpose: Provides diagnostic interview for DSM-IV diagnoses

Description: Thirty-seven DSM-IV Axis I diagnoses are included: Mood Disorders, Substance Use Disorders, Anxiety Disorders, Somatoform Disorders, Eating Disorders, Adjustment Disorders, and Schizophrenic and other Psychotic Disorders. Yields Diagnostic Summary Report, Detailed Diagnostic Report, Unknown Items Report, and Overview Report. Also available in a computer-assisted version.

Format: Examiner required; individual administration; untimed: 45 to 90 minutes

Scoring: Computer scored

Cost: Starter Kit (user's guide, administration booklet, 5 score sheets) $88.00; Computer Preview $45.00

Structured Interview of Reported Symptoms (SIRS)
Richard Rogers, R. Michael Bagby,
Susan E. Dickens

1992   **Psychological Assessment Resources, Inc.**

Population: Adults

Purpose: Used for forensic assessment to detect malingering and feigning of psychiatric symptoms

Description: Oral-response short-answer interview with 172 items and the following scales: Rare Symptoms, Symptom Combinations, Improbable and Absurd Symptoms, Blatant Symptoms, Subtle Symptoms, Severity of Symptoms, Selectivity of Symptoms, and Reported versus Observed Symptoms. Supplementary Scales include Direct Appraisal of Honesty, Defensive Symptoms, Symptom Onset and Resolution, Overly Specified Symptoms, and Inconsistency of Symptoms. Materials used are a manual and interview booklets.

Format: Examiner required; individual administration; untimed: under 1 hour

Scoring: Examiner evaluated

Cost: Intro Kit $209.00

Symptom Assessment-45 Questionnaire (SA-45)

2000   **Multi-Health Systems, Inc.**

Population: Ages 13 years and older

Purpose: A brief assessment of symptomatology across nine psychiatric domains

Description: Contains a total of 45 items to assess Anxiety, Interpersonal Sensitivity, Paranoid Ideation, Hostility, Obsessive-Compulsivity, Phobic Anxiety, Somatization, Depression, and Psychotism.

Format: Self-administered; untimed: 10 minutes

Scoring: QuikScore™ forms

Cost: Kit (manual, 25 forms) $53.00

Symptom Checklist-90 Revised (SCL-90-R)
Leonard R. Derogatis

1975	NCS Pearson

Population: Ages 13 years and older

Purpose: Screens for psychological problems and measures progress

Description: Computer-administered or paper-pencil 90-item multiple-choice test with a 5-point rating scale from 0 to 4. The nine primary dimensions are somatization, obsessive-compulsive, interpersonal sensitivity, depression, anxiety, hostility, phobic anxiety, paranoid ideation, and psychoticism. A sixth-grade reading level is required. Examiner must be M-level qualified. A computer version using an IBM-compatible 486 PC or higher is available. The test is available on audiocassette and in 23 foreign languages; 24 additional languages are available for research purposes only.

Format: Self-administered; untimed: 12 to 15 minutes

Scoring: Hand key; computer scored

Cost: Contact publisher

Temperament and Atypical Behavior Scale (TABS)
Stephen J. Bagnato, John T. Neisworth, John Saivia, Frances M. Hunt

1999	Paul H. Brookes Publishing Co.

Population: Ages 11 to 71 months

Purpose: Measures critical temperament and self-regulation problems that may indicate a child's risk for atypical development, including attention and activity, social behavior, sleeping, play, senses, movement, and vocal and oral behavior.

Description: The TABS is an assessment tool with four categories (55 items): Detached (20 items) measures aloof, withdrawn behavior that may be indicative of autism; Hyper-sensitive/active (17 items) measures impulsive, nightly active, defiant behavior; Underreactive (11 items) measures passivity and lethargy that may be indicative of a variety of severe neurodevelopmental problems; and Dysregulated (7 items) measures sleeping, crying, self-comforting, and jitteriness. May be used for persons with visual, hearing, physical, and mental impairments. TABS screener yields raw score, and assessment yields raw score, percentile, and standard score for each of the four categories, plus overall score.

Format: Examiner required; individual administration; untimed

Scoring: Examiner evaluated

Cost: Specimen Kit (screener, assessment tools, manual) $85.00

Trauma Symptom Inventory (TSI)
John Briere

1995	Psychological Assessment Resources, Inc.

Population: Adults

Purpose: Evaluates acute and chronic posttraumatic symptomology

Description: Paper-pencil 4-point scale with 100 items assessing the following: anxious arousal, dissociation, depression, sexual concerns, anger/irritability, dysfunctional sexual behavior, intrusive experiences, impaired self-reference, defensive avoidance, and tension reduction behavior. A fifth- to seventh-grade reading level is required. Alternate 86-item version (TSI-A) contains no sexual content.

Format: Examiner required; individual or group administration; untimed: 20 minutes

Scoring: Hand key; computer scoring available

Cost: TSI Intro Kit (manual, item booklet, answer sheet, male/female profile forms) $159.00; TSI-A Intro Kit $159.00

Treatment Intervention Inventory (TII)

Date not provided	Behavior Data Systems, Ltd.

Population: Adults

Purpose: Designed for treatment intake assessment

Description: The TII has 162 items with nine scales: Truthfulness, Anxiety, Depression, Distress, Self-Esteem, Family Issues, Alcohol, Drugs, and Stress Coping Abilities. The TII is appropriate for HMOs' Employee Assistance Programs and chemical dependency treatment settings. The scales identify problems that warrant referral, intervention, or treatment.

Format: Self-administered; untimed: 25 minutes

Scoring: Computer scored

Cost: Contact publisher

Treatment Intervention Inventory–Juvenile (TII–Juvenile)

| Date not provided | Behavior Data Systems, Ltd. |

Population: Adolescents

Purpose: Designed for juvenile inpatient or outpatient and counseling intake screening

Description: The TII-Juvenile has 143 items with nine scales: Truthfulness, Self-Esteem, Family Issues, Anxiety, Depression, Distress, Alcohol, Drugs, and Stress Coping Abilities.

Format: Self-administered; untimed: 25 to 30 minutes

Scoring: Computer scored

Cost: Contact publisher

Violence Scale
Panos D. Bardis

| 1973 | Donna Bardis |

Population: Adolescents, adults

Purpose: Measures attitudes toward violence (words and actions aimed at property damage and personal injury); used for clinical assessment, marriage and family counseling, research on violence, and discussions in social science classes

Description: Paper–pencil test in which the subject rates 25 statements concerning various aspects of violence on a scale from 0 (*strongly disagree*) to 4 (*strongly agree*). The violence score equals the sum of the 25 numerical responses. The theoretical range of scores extends from 0 (*lowest approval of violence*) to 100 (*highest approval*). Suitable for use with individuals with physical and hearing disabilities.

Format: Examiner/self-administered; suitable for group use; 10 minutes

Scoring: Examiner evaluated

Cost: $1.00

Wahler Physical Symptoms Inventory
H. J. Wahler

| 1973 | Western Psychological Services |

Population: Adults

Purpose: Discriminates between patients with medical ailments and those with psychogenic complaints; used to screen new patients

Description: Paper–pencil test consisting of 42 physical problems on which the subjects must rate themselves using a 6-point frequency scale ranging from *almost never* to *nearly every day*. The test helps identify conversion hysteria, hypochondriases, and psychophysiological reactions, as well as physically determined disorders.

Format: Self-administered; untimed:15 to 20 minutes

Scoring: Hand key

Cost: Kit (manual, 100 inventory sheets) $49.50

Ways of Coping Questionnaire
Susan Folkman, Richard S. Lazarus

| 1988 | Mind Garden, Inc. |

Population: Adults

Purpose: Helps counselors work with clients to develop practical coping skills

Description: The Ways of Coping Questionnaire measures the style of the respondent's coping. Counselors evaluate clients' styles, strengths, and weaknesses, and provide models of alternative coping mechanisms. The instrument is excellent for research on coping. Scales include Confrontive Coping, Distancing, Self-Controlling, Seeking Social Support, Accepting Responsibility, Escape-Avoidance, Planful Problem Solving, and Positive Reappraisal.

Format: Self-administered; untimed: 10 minutes

Scoring: Examiner evaluated

Cost: Sampler Set $25.00; Review Set $20.00; Permission Set $125.00; Scoring Instructions $10.00

Whitaker Index of Schizophrenic Thinking (WIST)
Leighton C. Whitaker

| 1980 | Western Psychological Services |

Population: Grades 8 and above

Purpose: Provides an index of schizophrenic thinking; used for intake screening

Description: Paper–pencil 25-item multiple-choice test discriminating between schizophrenic and nonschizophrenic thinking. The test can be completed by anyone with an eighth-grade education. The test is available in two equivalent forms. The manual provides a discussion of relevant diagnostic issues and the development of the test, directions for administration and scoring, standardization and validity data, a discussion of diagnostic and clinical uses, case illustrations, references, and specimen copies of the test forms.

Format: Self-administered; suitable for group use; untimed: 15 minutes
Scoring: Hand key
Cost: Kit (manual, 50 tests, scoring key) $78.00

Youth Inventory–4 (YI-4)
Kenneth D. Gadow, Joyce Sprafkin

| 1997 | Checkmate Plus, Ltd. |

Population: Ages 12 to 18 years

Purpose: Screens for DSM-IV emotional and behavioral disorders and applies behavioral ratings of child psychopathology

Description: In 120 items, symptoms of multiple disorders are measured, including attention-deficit/hyperactivity disorder, oppositional defiant disorder, conduct disorders, depressive disorders, anxiety disorders, and bipolar disorder. Symptom Count scores (DSM-IV criteria) and Symptom Severity Profiles (norms based) are provided.

Format: Rating scale; can be computer-administered; untimed: 10 to 15 minutes

Scoring: Examiner evaluated; computer scored

Cost: Deluxe Kit $75.00

Anger

Aggression Questionnaire (AQ)
Arnold H. Buss, W. L. Warren

| 2000 | Western Psychological Services |

Population: Ages 9 through 88 years

Purpose: Measures aggressive responses

Description: The AQ measures an individual's aggressive responses and his or her ability to channel those responses in a safe, constructive manner. Because it takes only 10 minutes to complete, the AQ can be administered quickly to large numbers of people. The AQ is a full revision of the Buss-Durkee Hostility Inventory, a longtime standard for assessing anger and aggression. It consists of 34 items, scored on the following scales: Physical Aggression, Hostility, Verbal Aggression, Indirect Aggression, and Anger. A total score is also provided, along with an Inconsistent Responding Index. Standardization is based on a sample of 2,138 individuals, and norms are presented in three age sets: 9 to18, 19 to 39, and 40 to 88.

Format: Self-administered; untimed
Scoring: Hand key; computer scored; scoring service available
Cost: Complete Kit $82.50

Children's Inventory of Anger (ChIA)
W. M. Nelson III, A. J. Finch

| 2000 | Western Psychological Services |

Population: Ages 6 to 16 years

Purpose: Identifies situations that provoke anger and anger intensity in children

Description: This self-report inventory identifies the kinds of situations that provoke anger in particular children, as well as the intensity of their anger response. The ChIA contains 39 items and produces a Total Score, an Inconsistent Responding Index, and four subscale scores: Frustration, Physical Aggression, Peer Relationships, and Authority Relations. Response options are keyed to drawings of four faces, with expressions ranging from happy to furious. The child simply marks the option that shows how angry he or she would be in the circumstances described. The ChIA is ideal for a quick assessment of children's anger. The instrument is helpful in treatment planning and program evaluation.

Format: Examiner required; individual and group administration; untimed

Scoring: Examiner evaluated; computer scored; test scoring service available

Cost: Complete Kit $75.00

Inventory of Anger Communication
Millard J. Bienvenu

| 1974 | Northwest Publications |

Population: Ages 13 years and older

Purpose: Assesses subjective and interactional aspects of anger communication; used in individual, marriage, and group counseling and human relations training

Description: Yes-no-sometimes test with 30 items. A seventh-grade reading level is required. Examiner must have experience in anger management.

Format: Self-administered; suitable for group use; untimed: 15 minutes

Scoring: Hand key

Cost: $.75 per copy; Guide $2.00 (Minimum order $10.00)

State-Trait Anger Expression Inventory-2 (STAXI-2)
Charles D. Spielberger

1999   Psychological Assessment Resources, Inc.

Population: Ages 16 years and older

Purpose: Measures type and expression of anger; used as a screening and outcome measure in psychotherapy and stress management programs, with particular application in behavioral medicine

Description: Paper-pencil 44-item Likert-type test assessing anger along six scales: State Anger, Trait Anger, Anger Expression (In and Out), Anger Control (In and Out), and an Anger Expression Index.

Format: Self-administered; untimed: 5 to 10 minutes

Scoring: Hand key; computer scoring available

Cost: Kit (manual, 50 item booklets, 50 rating sheets) $69.00

Tiffany Control Scales (TCS)
Donald W. Tiffany, Phyllis G. Tiffany

2001   Psychological Growth Associates, Inc.

Population: Ages 11 to 99 years

Purpose: Assesses control problems anywhere anger and loss of control are involved

Description: The standard scales include eight situations: work, school (or learning), opposite sex, same sex, community, home, other people (other than peers), and self-in-general. Questionnaire items ask four questions for each of the eight situations, making up the 32-item instrument. All variables are measured in terms of standard situations, and all variable and situation interactions are normed. The TCS is written on a sixth-grade reading level.

Format: Self-administered; untimed

Scoring: Examiner evaluated; computer, machine, and scoring service available

Cost: Contact publisher

Anxiety

Beck Anxiety Inventory® (BAI®)
Aaron T. Beck

1993   The Psychological Corporation

Population: Ages 17 through 80 years

Purpose: Measures anxiety levels

Description: Patients respond to 21 items rated on a scale from 0 to 3. Each item is descriptive of subjective, somatic, or panic-related symptoms of anxiety.

Format: Self-administered; untimed: 5 to 10 minutes

Scoring: Examiner evaluated; can be computer scored

Cost: Complete Kit (manual, 25 record forms) $64.00

Endler Multidimensional Anxiety Scales (EMAS)
Norman S. Endler, Jean M. Edwards, Romeo Vitelli

1991   Western Psychological Services

Population: Adolescents, adults

Purpose: Used to evaluate phobias, panic attacks, generalized anxiety disorder, test anxiety, post-traumatic stress disorder, and treatment outcome

Description: Three related self-report measures assess and predict anxiety across situations and measure treatment response. The first scale measures state anxiety (the individual's actual transitory anxiety response). It assess both physiological and cognitive responses. The second scale measures the individual's predisposition to experience anxiety in four different types of situations. The third scale evaluates the individual's perception of the type and intensity of threat in the immediate situation. The scales can be given separately or as a set.

Format: Examiner required; individual and group administration; untimed: 25 minutes

Scoring: Examiner evaluated; computer scoring available

Cost: Kit (manual, 10 AutoScore™ test forms for each scale, 2-use disk, 2 PC answer booklets) $82.50

Multidimensional Anxiety Questionnaire (MAQ)
William M. Reynolds

1999   Psychological Assessment Resources, Inc.

Population: Ages 18 to 89 years

Purpose: Quickly screens for symptoms of anxiety

Description: The MAQ has 40 items to screen for the presence and severity of anxiety symptoms.

Format: Self-administered; untimed: 10 minutes

Scoring: Examiner evaluated

Cost: Kit (manual, 25 hand-scorable booklets, 50 profile forms) $95.00

Multidimensional Anxiety Scale for Children (MASC)
John. S. March

| 1997 | Multi-Health Systems, Inc. |

Population: Ages 8 to 19 years

Purpose: Assesses the major dimensions of anxiety

Description: The MASC consists of 39 items; a 10-item screener is also available. Scales are Physical Symptoms, Social Anxiety, Harm Avoidance, Separation/Panic, Anxiety Disorders, Total Anxiety, and Inconsistency index. The MASC yields T-scores. Available in many languages.

Format: Self-administered; untimed: 5 to 15 minutes

Scoring: QuikScore™ forms

Cost: Complete Kit (manual, 25 forms) $60.00

Panic and Agoraphobia Scale (PAS)
Borwin Bandelow

| 1999 | Hogrefe & Huber Publishers |

Population: Adults

Purpose: Assesses the severity of panic disorder with or without agoraphobia

Description: Compatible with both DSM-IV and ICD-10 classifications, and available in both self-rated and observer-rated versions, the PAS was specially developed for monitoring the efficacy of both drug and psychotherapy treatments. In addition to the English scale, translations are available in 16 languages. The PAS has excellent psychometric properties and is quick to use. It has been successfully applied in both double-blind placebo-controlled studies and open treatment trials.

Format: Rating scale; untimed

Scoring: Examiner evaluated

Cost: Complete Test (manual, folder, 50 each of patient questionnaires and observer-rated scales) $79.50

Revised Children's Manifest Anxiety Scale (RCMAS)
Cecil R. Reynolds, Bert O. Richmond

| 1985 | Western Psychological Services |

Population: Ages 6 to 19 years

Purpose: Measures the level and nature of anxiety in children

Description: The RCMAS helps pinpoint the problems in a child's life. A brief self-report inventory provides scores for Total Anxiety and four subscales: Worry/Oversensitivity, Social Concerns/Concentration, Physiological Anxiety, and Lie Scale. It is composed of 37 yes-no items. The scale is useful to clinicians who are treating children for academic stress, test anxiety, peer and family conflicts, or drug problems. It provides objective data on anxiety that can inform and guide treatment.

Format: Self-administered; untimed: 15 minutes

Scoring: Hand key

Cost: Kit (manual, 50 AutoScore™ forms, scoring key) $95.00

Social Phobia and Anxiety Inventory (SPAI)
Samuel M. Turner, Deborah C. Beidel, Constance V. Dancu

| 1996 | Multi-Health Systems, Inc. |

Population: Ages 14 years and older

Purpose: Assesses social anxiety and fear

Description: The 45-item scale measures specific somatic symptoms, cognitions, and behaviors across a wide range of potentially fear-producing situations. The SPAI consists of two subscales: Social Phobia and Agoraphobia.

Format: Self-administered; untimed: 20 to 30 minutes

Scoring: QuikScore™ forms

Cost: Complete Kit (manual, 25 forms) $60.00

Social Phobia and Anxiety Inventory for Children (SPAI-C)
Samuel M. Turner, Deborah C. Beidel, Tracy L. Morris

| 2000 | Multi-Health Systems, Inc. |

Population: Ages 8 to 14 years

Purpose: Assesses social anxiety and phobia

Description: The 26-item questionnaire evaluates the somatic, cognitive, and behavioral aspects of social phobia unique to childhood situations.

Format: Self-administered; untimed: 10 to 15 minutes

Scoring: QuikScore™ forms

Cost: Complete Kit (manual, 25 forms) $60.00

State-Trait Anxiety Inventory for Adults (STAI)
Charles D. Spielberger

| 1983 | Mind Garden, Inc. |

Population: Adolescents, adults

Purpose: Differentiates between long-standing (trait) and temporary (state) anxiety; used for research and clinical practice

Description: Paper-pencil 40-item Likert scale yields State anxiety and Trait anxiety scores. An eighth-grade reading level is required.

Format: Self-administered; suitable for group use; untimed: 5 to 20 minutes

Scoring: Hand key; test scoring service available from publisher

Cost: Sample Set $25.00; Permission for 200 Uses $125.00; 25 Test Booklets $25.00

State-Trait Anxiety Inventory (STAI) for Windows

| 1999 | Multi-Health Systems, Inc. |

Population: Ages 16 years and older

Purpose: Measures two distinct anxiety concepts

Description: The STAI for Windows contains two 20-item scales measuring long-standing (trait) and temporary (state) anxiety. Results are graphically displayed in the Profile Report.

Format: Self-administered on computer; untimed: 20 minutes

Scoring: Computer scored

Cost: $1.50 per administration

State-Trait Anxiety Inventory for Children
Charles D. Spielberger, C. D. Edwards, J. Montuori, R. Lushene

| 1973 | Mind Garden, Inc. |

Population: Grades 4 to 6

Purpose: Assesses anxiety in children; used for research screening and treatment evaluation

Description: Two 20-item scales measure two types of anxiety: state anxiety (current level of anxiety, or S-Anxiety) and trait anxiety (anxiety proneness, or T-Anxiety). The S-Anxiety scales ask how the child feels at a particular moment in time, and the T-Anxiety scales ask how he or she generally feels. The inventory is based on the same concept as the State-Trait Anxiety Inven-

tory for Adults and is used in conjunction with the adult form manual.

Format: Self-administered; suitable for group use; untimed: 10 to 20 minutes

Scoring: Examiner evaluated

Cost: Sample Set $25.00; Permission Set $125.00; Scoring Key $10.00

State-Trait Anxiety Inventory for Children (STAIC) for Windows

| 1999 | Multi-Health Systems, Inc. |

Population: Ages 6 to 14 years

Purpose: Measures two distinct anxiety concepts

Description: The STAIC for Windows contains two 20-item scales measuring long-standing (trait) and temporary (state) anxiety. Results are graphically displayed in the Profile Report.

Format: Self-administered on computer; untimed: 20 minutes

Scoring: Computer scored

Cost: $1.50 per administration

Test Anxiety Inventory (TAI)
Charles D. Spielberger

| 1980 | Mind Garden, Inc. |

Population: Grades 10 and above

Purpose: Measures individual differences in test-taking anxiety; used for research

Description: Paper-pencil 20-item test of two major components of test anxiety: worry and emotionality. Respondents report how frequently they experience specific anxiety symptoms in examination situations. Similar in structure and concept to the T-Anxiety scale of the State-Trait Anxiety Inventory for Adults.

Format: Self-administered; untimed: 5 to 10 minutes

Scoring: Hand key

Cost: Sample Set $25.00; Permission for 200 Uses $125.00

Depression

BDI®-FastScreen for Medical Patients
Aaron T. Beck, Robert A. Steer, Gregory K. Brown

| 2000 | The Psychological Corporation |

Population: Ages 13 through 80 years
Purpose: Screens for depression
Description: This new version of the Beck Depression Inventory is designed specifically for medical patients. The seven-item self-report instrument measures the severity of depressive symptoms corresponding to the psychological, nonsomatic criteria for diagnosing major depressive disorders in the DSM-IV.
Format: Self-report; untimed: less than 5 minutes
Scoring: Examiner evaluated
Cost: Complete Kit (manual, 50 record forms) $61.00

Beck Depression Inventory®-II (BDI®-II)
Aaron T. Beck, Robert A. Steer, Gregory K. Brown

1996	The Psychological Corporation

Population: Ages 13 through 80 years
Purpose: Assesses depression
Description: This revision consists of 21 items to assess the intensity of depression. Each item is a list of four statements arranged in increasing severity about a particular symptom of depression. These new items bring the BDI-II into alignment with DSM-IV criteria.
Format: Self-administered; untimed: 5 minutes
Scoring: Examiner evaluated; computer scoring available
Cost: Complete Kit (manual, 25 record forms) $64.00

Beck Hopelessness Scale® (BHS®)
Aaron T. Beck

1993	The Psychological Corporation

Population: Ages 17 through 80 years
Purpose: Measures negative attitudes about the future
Description: Allows prediction of eventual suicide by measuring three aspects of hopelessness: feelings about the future, loss of motivation, and expectations. Responding to 20 true–false statements, patients either endorse a pessimistic statement or deny an optimistic statement.
Format: Self-administered; untimed: 5 to 10 minutes
Scoring: Examiner evaluated; can be computer scored

Cost: Complete Kit (manual, 25 record forms) $64.00

Beck Scale for Suicide Ideation® (BSS®)
Aaron T. Beck

1991	The Psychological Corporation

Population: Ages 17 years and older
Purpose: Evaluates suicidal thinking
Description: The scale is made up of 21 items. Five screening items reduce the length and the intrusiveness of the questionnaire for patients who are nonsuicidal.
Format: Self-administered; untimed: 5 to 10 minutes
Scoring: Examiner evaluated; can be computer scored
Cost: Complete Kit (manual, 25 record forms) $64.00

Carroll Depression Scales– Revised (CDS-R)
Bernard Carroll

1999	Multi-Health Systems, Inc.

Population: Ages 18 and older
Purpose: Assesses depressive symptom severity
Description: Total of 61 items measure Major Depression, Dysthymic Disorder, Melancholic Features, and Atypical Features. A brief CDS, based on the original CDS, contains 12 items to be used as a screener.
Format: Self-administered; untimed: 20 minutes (full), 5 minutes (brief)
Scoring: QuikScore™ forms, computer scored
Cost: Contact publisher

Children's Depression Inventory (CDI)
Maria Kovacs

1992	Multi-Health Systems, Inc.

Population: Ages 7 to 17 years
Purpose: Measures depressive symptoms
Description: The CDI has 27 items. A 10-item screener (CDI-S) is also available. The CDI yields the following scales: Total CDI score, Negative Mood, Interpersonal Problems, Ineffectiveness, and Negative Self-Esteem. Yields *T*-scores. Also available in Spanish, French-Canadian, Dutch, Hebrew, Hungarian, and more.
Format: Self-administered; untimed: 15 minutes

Scoring: QuikScore™ forms, computer scored

Cost: Contact publisher

Children's Depression Rating Scale, Revised (CDRS-R)

Elva O. Poznanski, Hartmut B. Mokros

1996   Western Psychological Services

Population: Ages 6 to 12 years

Purpose: Used to diagnose depression and determine its severity

Description: In clinical contexts, the CDRS-R can be used to diagnose depression and to monitor treatment response. In nonclinical contexts, such as schools and pediatric clinics, it serves as a screening tool, identifying children who need professional intervention. This is a brief rating scale based on a semistructured interview with the child. The scale requires the interviewer to rate 17 symptom areas (including those that serve as DSM-IV criteria for a diagnosis of depression), including schoolwork, capacity to have fun, social withdrawal, eating patterns, sleep patterns, excessive fatigue, physical complaints, irritability, guilt, self-esteem, depressed feelings, morbid ideation, suicidal ideation, weeping, facial expressions of affect, tempo of speech, and hyperactivity. The majority of these symptom areas are rated on an expanded 7-point scale. The CDRS-R gives a single Summary Score, along with a clear interpretation of and recommendations for six different score ranges.

Format: Examiner required; individual administration; untimed: 15 to 20 minutes

Scoring: Examiner evaluated

Cost: Kit (manual, 25 answer booklets) $55.00

Children's Depression Scale– Second Research Edition

Moshe Lange, Miriam Tisher

1983   Australian Council for Educational Research Limited

Population: Ages 9 to 16 years

Purpose: Measures depression in children; identifies depressed children in need of further evaluation

Description: Scale with 66 items measuring six aspects of childhood depression: affective response, social problems, self-esteem, preoccupation with own sickness or death, guilt, and pleasure. Items are presented on cards that the child sorts into five boxes ranging from *very right* to *very wrong* according to how he or she

feels the item applies to himself or herself. A paper-pencil questionnaire, identical in content to the cards but appropriately reworded, is available for use with parents, teachers, or other adults familiar with the child.

Format: Examiner required; individual administration; untimed

Scoring: Examiner evaluated

Cost: Contact publisher

Draw a Story: Screening for Depression (DAS)

Rawley A. Silver

1993   Ablin Press Distributors

Population: Ages 5 through 21 years

Purpose: Screens for depression; assesses concepts of self and others

Description: The examinee views two sets of stimulus drawings of 14 people, animals, places, or things and is asked to choose two subjects to imagine something happening between them. A picture is then drawn of what is imagined, followed by a written story. The information is rated on a 1- to 5-point scale.

Format: Examiner required; individual administration; suitable for group use; untimed: 10 minutes

Scoring: Examiner administration and interpretation

Cost: $25.00

Hamilton Depression Inventory (HDI)

William H. Reynolds, Kenneth A. Kobak

1995   Psychological Assessment Resources, Inc.

Population: Adults

Purpose: Used as a comprehensive screening for symptoms of depression; used in private practice, hospitals, and correctional institutions

Description: Paper-pencil 3- to 5-point scale with 23 items in the following categories: Depressed Mood, Loss of Interest/Pleasure, Weight Loss, Insomnia/Hypersomnia, Psychomotor Retardation/Agitation, Fatigue, Worthlessness, Indecisiveness, and Suicide Ideation. A fifth-grade reading level is required. Available in PC-administered format. Short form with nine items available.

Format: Self-administered; untimed

Scoring: Examiner evaluated; software scoring available

Cost: Comprehensive Kit (manual, 5 reusable

booklets, 25 each of summary and answer sheets, 5 short form booklets, PC scoring) $179.00

Multiscore Depression Inventory for Adolescents and Adults (MDI)
David J. Berndt

1983	Western Psychological Services

Population: Ages 13 years and older

Purpose: Measures the severity and specific aspects of depression and detects subtle variations in mild forms of depression

Description: Paper–pencil or computer-administered true-false questionnaire containing 118 items and 10 subscales: Low Energy Level, Cognitive Difficulty, Guilt, Low Self-Esteem, Social Introversion, Pessimism, Irritability, Sad Mood, Instrumental Helplessness, and Learned Helplessness. An interpretive report that provides a general score as well as scores for each subscale is available. In addition, one section of the report indicates the probability that the examinee is depressed, conduct disordered, psychotic, suicidal, bulimic, anorexic, or nondepressed; has a mixed diagnosis; has endogenous depression; or is a chronic pain sufferer. A short form consists of the first 47 items of the full-length inventory.

Format: Self-administered; untimed: 20 minutes

Scoring: Examiner evaluated; computer scored

Cost: Kit $110.00

Multiscore Depression Inventory for Children (MDI-C)
David J. Berndt, Charles F. Kaiser

1996	Western Psychological Services

Population: Ages 8 to 17 years

Purpose: Measures the severity and specific aspects of depression and detects subtle variations in mild forms of depression

Description: Paper–pencil or computer-administered inventory containing 79 items on eight scales: anxiety, self-esteem, social introversion, instrumental helplessness, sad mood, pessimism, low energy, and defiance. The inventory yields scores for each of these scales, plus a total score and several validity indicators. This inventory is a downward extension of the Multiscore Depression Inventory for Adolescents and Adults.

Format: Self-administered; untimed: 10 to 20 minutes

Scoring: Examiner evaluated; computer scored

Cost: Kit $305.00

North American Depression Inventories (NADI)
James Battle

1988	James Battle and Associates, Ltd.

Population: Ages 5 years to adult

Purpose: Assesses depression, is applicable for psychotherapy and depression counseling, and is suitable for most populations

Description: Form A for adults has 40 items; Form C for children has 25 items. The following scores are yielded: classifications, percentile ranks, and T-scores. The inventories are available in large print, on audiocassette, and in French and Spanish. The NADI may be used for persons with visual, physical, hearing, or mental impairments.

Format: Examiner required; individual or group administration; untimed: less than 15 minutes

Scoring: Hand key; computer scored; test scoring service available from publisher

Cost: $120.00

Revised Hamilton Rating Scale for Depression (RHRSD)
W. L. Warren

1997	Western Psychological Services

Population: Adults

Purpose: Used to evaluate depression in adult clinical populations, in medical or mental health settings

Description: The RHRSD was developed in a medical setting and used concurrently with antidepressant medication to evaluate treatment response. The instrument covers both psychoaffective and somatic symptoms. It gives three levels of interpretation: Overall Symptom Severity, Groups of Symptoms, and Specific Symptom Areas. It can be used to quickly evaluate symptom severity, to confirm a diagnosis of depression, to explore depressive symptoms, and to measure treatment outcome. The revision includes several new features: a self-report version (can be completed in the waiting room by the client), an AutoScore™ Form, and eight new critical items that help confirm diagnoses of depression.

Format: Self-administered; untimed: 5 to 10 minutes

Scoring: Hand key; computer scored

Cost: Kit (manual, 10 AutoScore™ Clinician Forms, 10 AutoScore™ Self-Report Problem Inventories) $92.50; 20-use PC Disk $180.00

Reynolds Adolescent Depression Scale (RADS)
William M. Reynolds

| 1987 | Psychological Assessment Resources, Inc. |

Population: Ages 13 to 18 years

Purpose: Screens to identify depression in school and clinical groups; used for research on depression, clinical assessment, evaluation of treatment programs, screening of behavior and conduct disorder referrals, and academic problems

Description: Paper–pencil test with 30 items to which students respond on a 4-point Likert-type scale. A clinically relevant cutoff score is provided. Depressive symptomatology includes cognitive, motoric-vegetative, somatic, and interpersonal.

Format: Self-administered; untimed: 5 to 10 minutes

Scoring: Hand key

Cost: Intro Kit $105.00

Reynolds Child Depression Scale (RCDS)
William M. Reynolds

| 1989 | Psychological Assessment Resources, Inc. |

Population: Grades 3 to 6

Purpose: Assesses and screens for depressive symptomatology

Description: Paper–pencil 30-item multiple-choice test. Percentiles by grade and sex are provided for the total score. A second-grade reading level is required. This is one test in the Reynolds Depression Scale series.

Format: Self-administered; untimed: 10 minutes

Scoring: Hand key

Cost: Intro Kit $105.00

Suicidal Ideation Questionnaire (SIQ)
William M. Reynolds

| 1988 | Psychological Assessment Resources, Inc. |

Population: Ages 13 to 18 years

Purpose: Assesses suicidal ideation in adolescents

Description: This 30-item paper–pencil test utilizes a 7-point Likert-type response format. It was designed as a companion instrument to the Reynolds Adolescent Depression Scale. The 15-item SIQ-JR version is appropriate for students in Grades 7 through 9.

Format: Self-administered; untimed: 10 minutes

Scoring: Examiner evaluated

Cost: Kit $119.00

Suicide Behavior History Form (SBHF)
William M. Reynolds, James J. Mazza

| 1992 | Psychological Assessment Resources, Inc. |

Population: Adolescents, adults

Purpose: Documents a history of suicidal behavior

Description: Semi-structured interview with 29 items in the following categories: Client Information, History of Suicide Attempts, Description of Most Recent Attempt, Prior Attempt History, Current Status, Additional Test and Clinical Information, and Recommendations.

Format: Examiner required; individual administration; untimed: 10 to 30 minutes

Scoring: Examiner evaluated

Cost: Intro Kit (clinician's guide, interview book) $72.00

Suicide Probability Scale (SPS)
John G. Cull, Wayne S. Gill

| 1982 | Western Psychological Services |

Population: Ages 14 to 65 years

Purpose: Predicts the probability of suicidal behavior; used by clinicians to assess the probability that an individual may harm himself or herself; may be used for screening, monitoring changes in suicide potential over time, clinical exploration, and research

Description: Paper–pencil or computer-administered 36-item test in which the subject uses a 4-point scale ranging from *none or little of the time* to *most or all of the time* to indicate how often the behavior described in the statements would be descriptive of his or her behavior or feelings. The test itself does not mention suicide. Items are broken down into four subscales: Hopelessness, Suicide Ideation, Negative Self-Evaluation, and Hostility. Scoring yields a total weighted score, a normalized *T*-score, and a Suicide Probability Score. The manual presents cutoff scores indicating the level of probable suicide behavior, interpretive guidelines, and clinical strategies for each level. The computer version is available for PC systems.

Format: Examiner required; individual or group administration; untimed: 5 to 10 minutes

Scoring: Hand key; computer scored

Cost: Kit (manual, 25 tests, 25 profile sheets) $87.50

Trait Anxiety and Depression Scales
Albert Mehrabian

1994	Albert Mehrabian, PhD

Population: Age 14 years to adult

Purpose: Assesses trait anxiety and depression; used for research and in counseling

Description: Paper–pencil test with two subtests: Trait anxiety (16 items) and Depression (20 items). A 10th-grade reading level is required.

Format: Self-administered; suitable for group use; untimed: 10 minutes

Scoring: Hand key; test scoring service available from publisher

Cost: Test Kit $33.00

Weinberg Depression Scale for Children and Adolescents (WDSCA)
Warren A. Winberg

1998	PRO-ED, Inc.

Population: Ages 7 through 18 years

Purpose: Assesses depression in children and adolescents

Description: Comprising 56 yes-no items, this test allows for rapid evaluation. The WDSCA is the only self-report instrument for depression designed for children and adolescents that is based on established criteria for depression. Use it as a screening instrument, an initial assessment tool, or a follow-up test to monitor the effects of depression treatment. The WDSCA can be used as a criterion-referenced or norm-referenced instrument. Two sets of criteria are provided, one based on the Weinberg criteria for depression and the second based on DSM-IV criteria for depression. Nonreferred and identified samples provide two sets of norms.

Format: Rating scale; untimed: 3 to 5 minutes

Scoring: Examiner evaluated

Cost: Complete Kit (manual, 50 summary forms, 50 student response forms, storage box) $98.00

ioral traits common in eating disorders; distinguishes individuals with serious psychopathology from normal dieters; used in the treatment of individuals with eating disorders

Description: Paper–pencil or computer-administered self-report inventory consisting of 91 items and eight subscales (Drive for Thinness, Bulimia, Body Dissatisfaction, Ineffectiveness, Perfectionism, Interpersonal Distrust, Interoceptive Awareness, and Maturity Fear) measuring specific cognitive and behavioral dimensions related to eating disorders. The inventory identifies individuals with serious eating disorders and differentiates between subgroups of eating disorders. The computer version operates on PC systems. Also available in Swedish and Italian.

Format: Self-administered; untimed: 20 minutes

Scoring: Examiner evaluated

Cost: Kit $142.00; Computer Version $379.00

Eating Inventory
Albert J. Stunkard, Samuel Messick

1988	The Psychological Corporation

Population: Ages 17 years and older

Purpose: Measures behavior important to the understanding and treatment of eating-related disorders such as anorexia and bulimia; used to predict response to weight-loss programs, weight gain after quitting smoking, and weight change during depression

Description: Paper–pencil 51-item questionnaire measuring three dimensions of eating behavior: cognitive restraint of eating, disinhibition, and hunger. This test is for use only by persons with at least a master's degree in psychology or a related discipline. Registration is required.

Format: Self-administered; suitable for group use; untimed: 15 minutes

Scoring: Hand key

Cost: Examination Kit (manual, 25 questionnaires, 25 answer sheets) $145.00

Eating Disorders

Eating Disorder Inventory–2 (EDI–2)
David M. Garner

1991	Psychological Assessment Resources, Inc.

Population: Ages 12 years and older

Purpose: Assesses the psychological and behav-

Substance Abuse

Adolescent Chemical Dependency Inventory (ACDI)

1989	Behavior Data Systems, Ltd.

Population: Ages 12 to 18 years

Purpose: Screens for and evaluates adolescent

substance abuse; used in intake/referral settings, adolescent chemical dependency treatment programs, and juvenile court/probation systems

Description: Paper-pencil or computer-administered multiple-choice and true-false inventory containing 104 items and five scales: the Truthfulness scale measures how truthfully the examinee responded to ACDI items; the Alcohol scale measures alcohol-related problems; the Drugs scale measures drug use or abuse-related problems; the Adjustment scale measures overall level of adjustment (personal, home, school, authority, relationship); and the Distress scale measures anxiety and depression levels. Results are reported as percentiles, corrected raw scores, and risk-level classifications (low, low-medium, high-medium, high). Narrative explanations and recommendations are presented in automated reports. The computer version operates on PC-compatible systems. Diskettes containing 50, 100, or 150 ACDS test applications are provided; computer scoring is done on-site. A sixth-grade reading level is required. Also available in Spanish.

Format: Self-administered; untimed: 20 minutes

Scoring: Computer scored

Cost: Contact publisher

Adolescent Diagnostic Interview (ADI)
Ken C. Winters, George H. Henly
1993   Western Psychological Services

Population: Ages 12 to 18 years

Purpose: Systematically assesses psychoactive substance use disorders and evaluates psychosocial stressors, school and interpersonal functioning, and cognitive impairment

Description: Used by chemical dependency therapists, clinical psychologists, and social workers, the ADI consists of a series of questions about behaviors, events, and attitudes related to DSM-III-R and DSM-IV diagnostic criteria for psychoactive substance use disorders. The interviewer reads the questions from the Administration Booklet and enters the client's responses. When the ADI is scored, it yields the following information: presence or absence of a DSM-III-R or DSM-IV diagnosis, level of functioning, severity of psychosocial stressors, and a rating of memory and orientation.

Format: Examiner required; individual administration; untimed: 45 minutes

Scoring: Examiner evaluated

Cost: Kit (manual, 5 administration booklets) $78.00

Adolescent Drinking Index (ADI)
Adele V. Harrell, Philip W. Wirtz
1989   Psychological Assessment Resources, Inc.

Population: Ages 12 to 17 years

Purpose: Assesses alcohol abuse in adolescents with emotional or behavioral problems; used for screening and treatment planning

Description: Rating scale with 24 items. Requires a fifth-grade reading level.

Format: Self-administered; untimed: 5 minutes

Scoring: Hand key

Cost: Kit $48.00

Alcadd Test-Revised
Morse P. Manson, Lisa A. Melchior
1988   Western Psychological Services

Population: Ages 18 years and older

Purpose: Assesses the extent of alcohol addiction; used for diagnosis, treatment, and alcoholism research

Description: Multiple-choice paper-pencil test consisting of 65 items on five subscales measuring regularity of drinking, preference for drinking over other activities, lack of controlled drinking, rationalization of drinking, and excessive emotionality. Materials include Autoscore Form or computer disk. Computer versions available for IBM PC, XT, or AT (or compatible). Fourth-grade reading level is required. This test is suitable for individuals with visual, hearing, and physical impairments. It can be read to individuals with visual impairments. This is a revision of the 1978 test.

Format: Self-administered; untimed: 5 to 15 minutes

Scoring: Hand key; computer scored

Cost: Kit $55.00; Disk (25 uses) $125.00

Alcohol and Drug Use Scales
Albert Mehrabian
1994   Albert Mehrabian, PhD

Population: Ages 14 years and older

Purpose: Measures alcohol and drug abuse; used for research and counseling

Description: Paper-pencil test with 18 items and two subscales: extent of alcohol use/abuse (11 items) and extent of drug use/abuse (7 items). A 10th-grade reading level is required.

Format: Self-administered; suitable for group use; untimed: 10 minutes

Scoring: Hand key
Cost: Test Kit $33.00

Alcohol Use Inventory (AUI)
J. L. Horn, K. W. Wanberg, F. M. Foster

1987	NCS Pearson

Population: Adults

Purpose: Identifies patterns of behavior, attitudes, and symptoms associated with the use and abuse of alcohol; used for planning treatments

Description: Self-report 228-item inventory measuring the alcohol-related problems of addicted, dependent, binge, and violent drinkers along four domains: benefits, styles, consequences, and concerns associated with alcohol use. The test contains 24 scales (17 primary, 6 second order, and 1 general) covering drinking for social or mental improvement, drinking to manage moods, gregarious versus solo drinking, compulsive obsession about drinking, sustained versus periodic drinking, social role maladaptation, loss of control over behavior when drinking, perceptual and somatic withdrawal symptoms, relationship of marital problems and drinking, quantity of alcohol consumed when drinking, guilt and worry associated with drinking, prior attempts to deal with drinking, and awareness of drinking problems and readiness for help. A profile report is included. Items are written at a sixth-grade reading level.

Format: Self-administered; untimed: 35 to 60 minutes

Scoring: Computer scored; hand scoring materials available

Cost: Starter Kit (manual, 10 test booklets, 50 answer sheets, 50 profile forms, answer keys) $137.00

American Drug and Alcohol Survey™ (ADAS)
E. R. Oetting, F. Beauvais, R. Edwards

1999	Rocky Mountain Behavioral Science Institute, Inc.

Population: Grades 4 to 12

Purpose: Assesses substance abuse experience and attitudes; used for prevention program planning and evaluation

Description: Multiple-choice paper–pencil survey. Adolescent Form has 58 questions; Children Form has 51 questions. The ADAS is not an instrument for clinical use with individuals. It is an anonymous survey to be administered to a group. Reports present percentages of respondents who answer in certain ways. The publisher scans the surveys, runs analysis, and produces comprehensive reports on the student population surveyed. Forms are optical scan forms processed by the publisher. Adolescent Form is also available in Spanish.

Format: Self-administered; suitable for group use; untimed: 30 minutes

Scoring: Test scoring available from publisher

Cost: Contact publisher

American Tobacco Survey (ATS)
E. R. Oetting, F. Beauvais, R. Edwards

1999	Rocky Mountain Behavioral Science Institute, Inc.

Population: Grades 4 through 12

Purpose: Measures the rate of use and attitudes regarding tobacco

Description: A 32-item, school-based survey used in assessment needs and program planning and evaluation.

Format: Self-administered; suitable for group use; untimed: 15 minutes

Scoring: Test scoring service available from publisher

Cost: Contact publisher

Children of Alcoholics Screening Test (CAST)
John W. Jones

1983	Camelot Unlimited

Population: Children, adults

Purpose: Identifies children of alcoholics, adult children of alcoholics, and their chemically dependent parents; applicable for school or marital counseling

Description: Paper–pencil true–false test with 30 items yielding an overall score that assists in diagnosis of parental alcoholism. Standard form (alcohol abuse) and Researchers form (drug and alcohol abuse) are used. Available also in Spanish and French. Suitable for individuals with visual, physical, and hearing impairments.

Format: Self-administered; untimed

Scoring: Hand key

Cost: Manual, 50 Forms $30.00

Driver Risk Inventory (DRI)

1987	Behavior Data Systems, Ltd.

Population: Ages 16 years and older

Purpose: Measures the driving risk of DWI (driving while intoxicated) or DUI (driving under the influence) offenders; used to identify problem drinkers, substance abusers, and high-risk drivers

Description: Paper-pencil or computer-administered multiple-choice and true-false screening inventory contains 130 items on five scales. The Validity Scale measures how truthfully the examinee responded to DRI items. The Alcohol Scale measures the examinee's alcohol proneness and related problems. The Drugs Scale measures the examinee's drug use or abuse proneness and related problems and distinguishes between alcohol and drug abuse. The Driver Risk Scale measures driver risk potential, identifying the problem-prone driver independent of the respondent's substance abuse history. The Stress Coping Abilities Scale is a measure of the examinee's ability to cope with stress. Results are presented in the DRI Profile and as percentiles. Risk ranges (low, low-medium, high-medium, high) and scores are provided for all five scales. Also available in Spanish. PC-compatible computer version is available.

Format: Self-administered; untimed: 25 minutes

Scoring: Computer scored

Cost: Contact publisher

Manson Evaluation–Revised
Morse P. Manson, George J. Huba

| 1987 | Western Psychological Services |

Population: Adults

Purpose: Assesses alcohol abuse proneness and eight related personality characteristics

Description: Paper-pencil true-false computer-administered test with 72 items on seven subscales measuring anxiety, depressive fluctuations, emotional sensitivity, resentfulness, incompleteness, aloneness, and interpersonal relations. Raw scores, T-scores, and percentiles are yielded. This revised version provides 1985 norms as well as an easy-to-use test form featuring the AutoScore™ system. This makes it possible for the administrator to score, profile, and interpret the test in just a minute or two. It can be used for personnel screening, diagnosis, therapy, research, and alcohol abuse programs.

Format: Examiner required; group administration; untimed: 5 to 10 minutes

Scoring: Hand key; computer scored; test scoring service available from the publisher

Cost: Kit (manual, 25 AutoScore™ Test/Profile forms) $55.00

Maryland Addictions Questionnaire (MAQ)
William E. O'Donnell, Clinton B. DeSoto, Janet L. DeSoto

| 2000 | Western Psychological Services |

Population: Ages 16 years and older

Purpose: Used for patients entering an addiction treatment program to tell how severe the addiction is, how motivated the patient is, and which treatment approach is most likely to work

Description: A self-report inventory composed of 111 items on the following scales: Substance Abuse Scales, Summary Scores, Treatment Scales, and Validity Scales. The test provides standard scores and percentiles for each scale. Based on the relative elevation of the Summary Scores, the patient is also assigned one of six Summary Codes, indicating his or her ability to benefit from treatment. The MAQ is brief yet multidimensional, the items are easy to complete, the scales are easy to interpret, and the results facilitate treatment planning. Norms are based on a large sample of people receiving substance abuse treatment at clinics. A 30-item Short Form with six scales can be completed in only 5 minutes. A fifth-grade reading level is required.

Format: Self-administered; untimed: 15 to 20 minutes

Scoring: Examiner evaluated; computer scored

Cost: Complete Kit $99.50

Personal Experience Inventory (PEI)
Ken C. Winters, George H. Henly

| 1989 | Western Psychological Services |

Population: Ages 12 to 18 years

Purpose: Assesses chemical dependency of adolescents

Description: Paper-pencil or computer-administered multiple-choice two-part test. Part I contains 129 items relating to personal involvement with chemicals, effects of drug use, social benefits of drug use, consequences of drug use, polydrug use, social-recreational use, psychological benefits of drug use, transitional use, preoccupation with drugs, and loss of control. In addition to documenting the degree, duration, and onset of drug use, this section also provides several clinical scales, validity indexes, and a problem severity section. Part II consists of 147 items that measure aspects of psychosocial functioning related to patterns of drug use and treatment responsiveness. Eight personal risk factor scales and four environmental risk factor scales are included in this section. Scores are used to generate a computer report and chromagraph. A sixth-grade reading level is required.

Format: Self-administered; untimed: 40 to 50 minutes

Scoring: Computer scored; test scoring service available from publisher

Cost: Kit (manual, 5 test reports, 5 answer booklets) $150.00; PC disk (25 uses) $299.00

Personal Experience Inventory for Adults (PEI-A)
Ken C. Winters

| 1996 | Western Psychological Services |

Population: Ages 19 years and older

Purpose: Used to identify alcohol and drug problems, make referrals, and plan treatment

Description: Self-report inventory provides comprehensive information about substance abuse patterns in adults. It was designed to address the broad scope of problems associated with substance abuse. The PEI-A has two parts: the Problem Severity Section (120 items) and the Psychosocial Section (150 items). The interpretive report presents results for each validity indicator; a graphic profile of all scale scores; the raw score, drug clinic *T*-score, and nonclinical *T*-score for each scale; results of the drug use frequency and duration items; and a narrative interpretation, including analysis of the Treatment Receptiveness scale score.

Format: Examiner required; suitable for group use; untimed: 45 to 60 minutes

Scoring: Computer scored; scoring service available from publisher

Cost: Kit (manual, 5 test report prepaid mail-in answer booklets) $138.00; PC disk (25 uses) $290.00

Personal Experience Screening Questionnaire (PESQ)
Ken C. Winters

| 1991 | Western Psychological Services |

Population: Ages 12 to 18 years

Purpose: Used to identify and refer teenagers who may be chemically dependent

Description: This self-report questionnaire identifies teenagers who should be referred for a complete chemical dependency evaluation. The questionnaire includes 40 items divided into three sections: problem severity, psychosocial items, and drug use history. Two validity scales measure response distortion.

Format: Examiner required; suitable for group use; untimed: 10 minutes

Scoring: Hand key

Cost: Kit (manual, 25 AutoScore™ test forms) $70.00

Prevention Planning Survey (PPS)
E. R. Oetting, R. Edwards, F. Beauvais

| 1999 | Rocky Mountain Behavioral Science Institute, Inc. |

Population: Grades 8 through 12

Purpose: Screens for risk and protective factors for substance use and violence

Description: A school-based survey with a total of 57 questions with applications for needs assessment and program planning and evaluation. Available only in booklets combined with the American Drug and Alcohol Survey.

Format: Self-administered; suitable for group use; untimed: 45 minutes

Scoring: Test scoring available from publisher

Cost: Contact publisher

Reinstatement Review Inventory (RRI)

| Date not provided | Behavior Data Systems, Ltd. |

Population: Adults

Purpose: Screens applicants before driver's license reinstatement

Description: The RRI has 124 items with six scales: Truthfulness, Road Rage, Alcohol, Drugs, Comparative Change, and Intervention Checklist. It was designed to answer the question, "Has the applicant changed since his or her driver's license was suspended or revoked?"

Format: Self-administered; untimed: 25 minutes

Scoring: Computer scored

Cost: Contact publisher

Reinstatement Review Inventory-II (RRI-II)

| Date not provided | Behavior Data Systems, Ltd. |

Population: Adults

Purpose: For screening applicants before driver's license reinstatement

Description: The RRI-II has 128 items with six scales: Truthfulness, Stress Coping Abilities, Alcohol, Drugs, Comparative Change, and Intervention Checklist. It was designed to answer the question, "Has the applicant changed since his or her driver's license was suspended or revoked?" The RRI-II differs from the RRI in that the Stress Coping Abilities Scale has replaced the Road Rage Scale.

Format: Self-administered; untimed: 25 minutes

Scoring: Computer scored

Cost: Contact publisher

Smoker Complaint Scale (SCS)
Nina G. Schneider

| 1984 | Nina G. Schneider, PhD |

Population: Adults

Purpose: Assesses withdrawal symptoms of individuals during smoking cessation

Description: A 7-point Likert-type scale with 20 items designed to measure changes in physiological, emotional, and craving states as a function of smoking cessation.

Format: Self-administered; suitable for group use; untimed: 5 to 7 minutes

Scoring: Examiner evaluated

Cost: Free

Substance Abuse Questionnaire (SAQ)

| 1985 | Behavior Data Systems, Ltd. |

Population: Ages 18 years and older

Purpose: Screens and evaluates adult chemical dependency; used as an intake and referral device in chemical dependency treatment settings and in the criminal justice system

Description: Paper–pencil or computer-administered 151-item multiple-choice and true–false test designed to screen for and evaluate chemical dependency. The Truthfulness Scale measures how truthfully the examinee responded to the SAQ items. The Alcohol Scale measures the examinee's alchohol-related problems and proneness. The Drugs Scale measures drug use-or abuse-related problems and proneness. The Aggressivity Scale measures the examinee's risk-taking behavior and aggressiveness. The Resistance Scale measures uncooperativeness and resistance to

assistance. The Stress Coping Abilities Scale measures the examinee's ability to cope with stress, tension, and anxiety. The SAQ Profile reports scores, percentiles, and risk levels (low, low–medium, high–medium, high) for all six scales. The computer version operates on PC-compatible systems. Diskettes containing 50, 100, or 150 test applications are provided. A sixth-grade reading level is required. Also available in Spanish.

Format: Self-administered; untimed: 25 minutes

Scoring: Computer scored

Cost: Contact publisher

Substance Abuse Relapse Assessment (SARA)
Lawrence Schonfeld, Roger Peters, Addis Dolente

| 1993 | Psychological Assessment Resources, Inc. |

Population: Adolescent, adults

Purpose: Used in substance abuse counseling and treatment to assess and monitor relapse causes and coping skills

Description: Oral-response interview with 39 items in the following categories: Substance Abuse Behavior, Antecedents of Substance Abuse, Consequences of Substance Abuse, and Responses to Slips.

Format: Examiner required; individual administration; untimed: 1 hour

Scoring: Examiner evaluated

Cost: Intro Kit (manual, stimulus card, interview record form, relapse prevention planning forms 1, 2, and 3) $105.00

Substance Abuse Screening Test (SAST)
Terry L. Hibpshman, Sue Larson

| 1993 | Slosson Educational Publications, Inc. |

Population: Ages 13 years to adult

Purpose: Facilitates early identification and reliable referral of individuals who are abusing substances or are at risk

Description: The SAST elicits simple yes–no responses to questions that target critical areas of an individual's daily functioning. Responses may be written or verbal. The SAST may be administered by teachers, nurses, counselors, social workers, psychologists, and well-informed adults who are under the supervision of a professional. The respondent's score can be interpreted by the use of a simple pass–fail table or by the use of a traditional standard score table. A comprehensive and user-friendly manual addresses critical sections such as administration, scoring and interpretation, and statistics.

Format: Examiner required; individual or group administration; untimed: 5 minutes

Scoring: Hand key

Cost: Complete $50.50

Substance Abuse Subtle Screening Inventory (SASSI)
Glenn A. Miller

1988	SASSI Institute

Population: Adolescent form: ages 14 to 17 years; Adult form: ages 18 years and older

Purpose: Identifies likelihood of substance use disorders to assist individuals in getting treatment

Description: Computer-administered or paper–pencil test. The substance abuse classification is based on subscale scores. A third-grade reading level is required. Examiner must meet APA guideline qualifications, be alcohol/drug certified, and be SASSI trained. Suitable for individuals with visual and hearing impairments. Clinical support is provided by a toll-free consultation.

Format: Examiner required; individual or group administration; untimed: 10 to 15 minutes

Scoring: Examiner evaluated; computer scoring available

Cost: Contact publisher

Western Personality Inventory (WPI)
Morse P. Manson

1963	Western Psychological Services

Population: Adults

Purpose: Diagnoses the presence and degree of alcoholism; useful in alcohol rehabilitation programs

Description: Paper–pencil or computer-administered test that combines into one booklet the Manson Evaluation, which identifies the potential alcoholic personality, and the Alcadd Test, which measures the extent of alcohol addiction. The computer version is available on IBM PC or compatible systems. Computer scoring is available via mail-in services or on-site.

Format: Examiner required; suitable for group use; untimed:15 to 20 minutes

Scoring: Hand key; computer scored

Cost: Kit (5 AutoScore™ Test Forms, Manson Evaluation Manual, Alcadd Manual, two-use PC disk) $92.50

Personality

Multiage

Adjustment Scales for Children and Adolescents (ASCA)
Paul A. McDermott, Neville C. Marston, Denis H. Stott

1994	Ed & Psych Associates

Population: Ages 5 to 17 years

Purpose: Assesses social and behavioral adjustment for use in educational and psychological diagnosis and intervention

Description: Paper–pencil behavioral rating scales for special education teachers to complete. An adult reading level is required. Examiners must be qualified educational and psychological specialists.

Format: Rating scale; untimed: 10 to 20 minutes

Scoring: Examiner evaluated

Cost: Kit (user's manual, male/female self-scoring forms) $79.95

Anxiety Scales for Children and Adults (ASCA)
James Battle

1993	James Battle and Associates, Ltd.

Population: Ages 5 to adult

Purpose: Measures anxiety, is applicable for psychotherapy and anxiety therapy, and is suitable for most populations

Description: Paper–Pencil instrument with two forms: For children, Form Q has 25 items; for adults, Form M has 40 items. Scores yielded: classifications, percentile ranks, and *T*-Scores. Available in large print, on audiocassette, and in French and Spanish. May be used for individuals with visual, physical, hearing, or mental impairments.

Format: Examiner/self-administration; untimed: less than 15 minutes

Scoring: Hand key/computer scored; test scoring service available from publisher

Cost: $120.00

Automated Child/Adolescent Social History (ACASH)
Mark Rhode

Date not provided	NCS Pearson

Population: Ages 5 to 19 years

Purpose: Assists in obtaining child or adolescent psychosocial history information

Description: Series of computer-administered questions yielding a narrative summary of a child or adolescent seeking counseling treatment. Questions address the following areas: reason for referral and identifying information; developmental history, childhood to present; educational history; current family members and background; and problem identification. Ninth-grade reading level is required of examiner.

Format: Examiner, parent or guardian administered; individual administration; untimed: 45 to 90 minutes

Scoring: Computer administered and scored via Microtest Assessment Software only

Cost: Contact publisher

Bar-Ilan Picture Test for Children
Rivkah Itskowitz, Helen Strauss

1985	Dansk psykologisk Forlag

Population: Ages 4 to 16 years

Purpose: Assesses the child's perception of daily life situations

Description: Nine-item projective verbal test used in child guidance. Measures the child's perception of his or her place at home, in the learning situation, and in the peer group. The materials contain specific gender-related items. Examiner must be a qualified psychologist. Available also in Danish.

Format: Examiner required; individual administration; suitable for group use; untimed

Scoring: Examiner evaluated

Cost: $60.00

BarOn Emotional Quotient-Inventory® (BarOn EQ-i®)
Reuven Bar-On

1997	Multi-Health Systems, Inc.

Population: Ages 16 years and older

Purpose: Measures self-reported emotional intelligence

Description: Consists of 52-item Quikscore™ and 133-item mail-in, fax-in, computer-scored versions. Results include EQ score, five composite scale scores (Intrapersonal EQ, Interpersonal EQ, Adaptability EQ, Stress Management EQ, General Mood EQ), and 15 subscale scores. The subscales are Self-Regard, Emotional Self-Awareness, Assertiveness, Independence, Self-Actualization, Empathy, Social Responsibility, Interpersonal Relationship, Reality Testing, Flexibility, Problem Solving, Stress Management, Impulse Control, Optimism, and Happiness. Several manuals are available. The inventory is available in many languages including French, Spanish, Chinese, Czech, and Danish. It has application for clinical, educational, forensic, medical, corporate, human resources, and research uses.

Format: Self-administered; untimed: 30 to 40 minutes

Scoring: Scoring service available; computer scored

Cost: Preview Kit (manual, booklet, response sheet, development report) $77.50

BarOn Emotional Quotient-Inventory: Youth Version (EQ-i: YV)
Reuven Bar-On, James D. A. Parker

2000	Multi-Health Systems, Inc.

Population: Age 7 to 18 years

Purpose: Measures emotional intelligence

Description: Applications of this 60-item inventory include counseling and development. Scales are intrapersonal abilities, interpersonal abilities, stress management, adaptability, and general mood. A 30-item screener version and a French-Canadian edition are also available.

Format: Self-administered; untimed

Scoring: Hand scored

Cost: Contact publisher

Blue Pearl
Lotte Boeggild, Sonja Overby

| 1992 | Dansk psykologisk Forlag |

Population: Ages 7 to 14 years

Purpose: Evaluates the well-being of immigrant children

Description: Seven-picture projective verbal test measuring seven life situations common in the classroom, schoolyard, shower room, and home. It is used in guidance for children with a background in the Muslim farming culture. Only one form is used, but the material contains specific gender-related items. Assessment must be supervised by a psychologist. Also available in Danish.

Format: Examiner required; individual administration; untimed

Scoring: Examiner evaluated

Cost: $57.00

Bristol Social Adjustment Guides, American Edition (BSAG)
D. H. Stott

| 1970 | EdITS/Educational and Industrial Testing Service |

Population: Ages 5 to 16 years

Purpose: Diagnoses the nature and extent of behavioral disturbances and social adjustment in children; used by teachers and school psychologists

Description: Multiple-item paper–pencil observational instrument consisting of short phrases describing a child's behavior. The phrases that apply to the child being evaluated are underlined by an adult familiar with the child. The guides are concerned with observable behavior, not with inferences based on projective techniques or the child's self-assessment. An overall assessment of maladjustment, subscores for five core syndromes (unforthcomingness, withdrawal, depression, inconsequence, hostility) and four associated groupings (peer-maladaptiveness, nonsyndromic overreaction, nonsyndromic underreaction, and neurological symptoms) are provided. The test is available in separate forms for boys and girls. Separate norms based on students from city, county, and church schools are provided for boys and girls.

Format: Examiner required; suitable for group use; untimed: 10 to 15 minutes

Scoring: Hand key

Cost: Specimen Set (manual, all forms) $7.25

Carey Temperament Scales
William B. Carey, Sean C. McDevitt, Barbara Medoff-Cooper, William Fullard, Robin L. Hegvik

| 1998 | Behavior-Development Initiatives |

Population: Birth to 12 years

Purpose: Designed to assess temperamental characteristics

Description: A series of questionnaires designed to measure nine temperament characteristics: Activity Level, Regularity, Approach–Withdrawal, Adaptability, Intensity, Mood, Persistence, Distractibility, and Sensory Threshold. The five questionnaires (Early Infancy, Revised Infant, Toddler, Behavioral Style, Middle Childhood) in the series use from 75 to 100 descriptions of behavior.

Format: Examiner required; parent ratings; untimed: 15 minutes

Scoring: Examiner evaluated; computer scoring available

Cost: Specimen Set (manual, one of each questionnaire and scoring/profile sheets) $59.95; Report Writer Software with 25 uses $149.95; Unlimited-use Report Writer Software $295.00

Developmental History Report
Giles D. Rainwater, Bonnie B. Slade

| 1988 | Psychometric Software, Inc. |

Population: Children, adolescents

Purpose: Gathers and assesses basic developmental information and generates a written narrative

Description: Computer-administered or paper–pencil 98-item multiple-choice developmental interview that covers all the major developmental areas, including Introduction (10 items), Pregnancy (17 items), Birth (11 items), Development (18 items), Health (9 items), Family (11 items), Education (11 items), and Behavior (9 items). The computer tracks answers that are clinically significant and prints a list of these answers so that follow-up questions can be decided upon. The interview is completed by the person who knows most about the child being evaluated. Computer versions available for IBM PCs and compatibles.

Examiners must be professionals trained in personality assessment.

Format: Examiner required; individual administration; untimed: 30 to 45 minutes

Scoring: Computer scored

Cost: Program $195.95; 20 Paper–Pencil Questionnaires $15.95

d2 Test of Attention
R. Brickenkamp, E. Zillmer

1998	Hogrefe & Huber Publishers

Population: Ages 9 to 59 years

Purpose: Psychodiagnostic instrument used for measuring concentration, particularly visual attention; used for personnel selection and clinical, educational, and developmental psychology assessment

Description: Detail-discrimination paper–pencil test used to assess individuals' visual attention and concentration. Giving the test is virtually language independent because the test taker is intensively engaged in crossing out certain items on a sheet of many possibilities. Also available in German.

Format: Self-administered; suitable for group use; timed: 8 minutes

Scoring: Examiner evaluated

Cost: Complete Test $64.00

Early Memories Procedure (EMP)
Arnold R. Bruhn

1989	Arnold R. Bruhn, Publisher

Population: Adults

Purpose: Exploring personality reorganization

Description: Paper–pencil instrument with short-answer, projective, essay, and verbal-response questions about 21 specific, one-time memories. Fourth-grade reading level is required. Suitable for individuals with visual, physical, or hearing impairments. The EMP is useful for identifying the major unresolved issues in an individual's life.

Format: Examiner required; individual or group administration; untimed: 1.5 to 2.25 hours

Scoring: Examiner evaluated

Cost: 25 Tests $140.00

Emotional Perception Test (EPT)

1992	CogniSyst, Inc.

Population: Sense form: Ages 7 to 15 years; Combined form: Ages 21 to 90 years

Purpose: Measures the ability to judge the emotion expressed in another person's voice tone

Description: The test is a convenient and reliable measure. Impaired emotional perception is believed to be associated with right temporal and parietal lobe lesions. The EPT contains sentences read by an actress on audiocassettes and provided in sense, nonsense, and combined forms. The EPT employs three different sense or nonsense sentences to assess perception of the following emotional tones: Happy, Angry, Frightened, Sad, and Neutral. Single forms contain 45 items (multiple-choice). The combined form contains 90 items and takes 12 minutes. Runs on Windows 95, 98, and NT or MS-DOS.

Format: Self-administered; untimed: 6 minutes

Scoring: Computer scored

Cost: $69.95

Eysenck Personality Questionnaire–Revised (EPQ-R)
H. J. Eysenck, Sybil B. G. Eysenck

1975	EdITS/Educational and Industrial Testing Service

Population: Ages 7 to adult

Purpose: Measures the personality dimensions of extroversion, emotionality, and tough-mindedness (psychoticism in extreme cases); used for clinical diagnosis, educational guidance, occupational counseling, and personnel selection

Description: Paper–pencil 90-item yes–no inventory measuring three important dimensions of personality: extroversion–introversion (21 items), neuroticism–stability (23 items), and psychoticism (25 items). The falsification scale consists of 21 items. The questionnaire deals with normal behaviors that become pathological only in extreme cases; hence, use of the term tough-mindedness is suggested for nonpathological cases. Scores are provided for Extroversion, Neuroticism or emotionality, Psychoticism or toughmindedness, and Lie. College norms are presented in percentile form for Forms A and B, both separately and combined. Adult norms are provided for an industrially employed sample. An 81-item junior form is available for testing young children.

Format: Self-administered; suitable for group use; untimed: 10 to 15 minutes

Scoring: Hand key

Cost: Specimen Set (manual, one copy of each form) $7.75

Group Embedded Figures Test (GEFT)

Philip K. Oltman, Evelyn Raskin,
Herman A. Witkin

Date not provided	Consulting Psychologists Press, Inc.

Population: Ages 10 years to adult

Purpose: Assesses cognitive style in perceptual tasks; used in counseling

Description: Paper–pencil 25-item test of perceptual processes, including field dependence–independence. Performance is related to analytic ability, social behavior, body concept, and preferred defense mechanisms. Subjects find one of eight simple figures in the 18 complex designs.

Format: Examiner required; suitable for group use; untimed: 20 minutes

Scoring: Hand key

Cost: Preview Kit (manual,booklet, scoring keys) $44.55

Hand Test

Edwin E. Wagner

1983	Western Psychological Services

Population: Ages 5 years to adult

Purpose: Used to measure action tendencies such as acting-out and aggressive behavior

Description: Using pictures of hands as the projective medium, the Hand Test elicits responses that reflect behavioral tendencies. The client is shown 10 picture cards containing simple line drawings of a hand in various positions. The client's task is to explain what each hand is doing. It is scored by classifying responses according to clear-cut quantitative and qualitative scoring categories. The quantitative scores reflect the individual's overt behavior. The qualitative scores generally reflect feelings and motivations underlying the impaired action tendencies. The test also provides six summary scores, including an index of overall pathology and an acting-out ratio, which is used to predict aggressive behavior. Manual Supplement: Interpreting Child and Adolescent Responses.

Format: Examiner required; individual administration; untimed: 10 minutes

Scoring: Examiner evaluated

Cost: Kit (25 scoring booklets, picture cards, manual, manual supplement) $130.00

Holtzman Inkblot Technique (HIT)

W. H. Holtzman

1972	The Psychological Corporation

Population: Ages 5 years to adult

Purpose: Assesses an individual's personality characteristics; used for diagnosis and therapy planning

Description: Projective measure of personality in which the examinee responds to 45 inkblots. Some inkblots are asymmetric, and some are in a color other than black. An objective scoring system has been developed. Materials include two alternate and equivalent forms, A and B, for a total of 90 stimulus cards.

Format: Examiner required; individual administration; untimed

Scoring: Examiner evaluated

Cost: Complete Kit—Forms A and B combined (inkblots, 25 record forms, manual) $642.00

House–Tree–Person (H-T-P) Projective Technique

John N. Buck

1970	Western Psychological Services

Population: Ages 3 years and older

Purpose: Assesses personality disturbances in psychotherapy, school, and research settings; may be used with individuals who are culturally disadvantaged, educationally deprived, mentally retarded, or elderly

Description: Multiple-item paper–pencil and oral-response test providing a projective study of personality. The test consists on two steps. The first, which is nonverbal, creative, and almost completely unstructured, requires the subject to make a freehand drawing of a house, a tree, and a person. The second step, which is verbal, apperceptive; and more formally structured, gives subjects an opportunity to describe, define, and interpret the drawings and their respective environments.

Format: Examiner required; individual administration; untimed: 15 minutes

Scoring: Examiner evaluated

Cost: Complete Set (manual and interpretive guide; H-T-P Drawings: An Illustrated Handbook; Catalog of the Qualitative Interpretation of the H-T-P; 25 interpretation booklets; 25 drawing forms) $165.00

Junior Eysenck Personality Questionnaire (JEPQ)

H. J. Eysenck, S. B. G. Eysenck

Date not provided	EdITS/Educational and Industrial Testing Service

Population: Ages 7 to 17 years
Purpose: Measures dimensions of personality
Description: The JEPQ is the revised junior version of the Junior Eysenck Personality Inventory. It is similar to the Eysenck Personality Questionnaire-Revised in that there are four scales: Psychoticism or Tough-Mindedness, Extroversion, Neuroticism or Emotionality, and Lie.
Format: Examiner required; suitable for group use; untimed: 10 to 15 minutes
Scoring: Hand scored
Cost: Specimen Set $7.25; 25 Inventories $10.45; Hand Scoring Keys $12.25

Kinetic Drawing System for Family and School
Howard M. Knoff, H. Thompson Prout

1985	Western Psychological Services

Population: Ages 5 to 20 years
Purpose: Provides personalized themes within school and family contexts; used for school psychology referrals
Description: Paper-pencil oral-response projective system integrating Kinetic Family Drawing and Kinetic School Drawing and therefore covering a broad range of the most frequent areas of child and adolescent distress. It consists of two drawings with a series of suggested projective questions in relation to the action between figures; figure characteristics; position, distance, and barriers style; and symbols. Each has a projective interpretation for family and school forms and a variable number of items subject to examiner discretion.
Format: Examiner required; individual administration; untimed
Scoring: Examiner evaluated
Cost: Kit (manual, 25 scoring booklets) $57.50

M-Scale: Inventory of Attitudes Toward Black/White Relations
James H. Morrison

1969	James H. Morrison

Population: Adolescents, adults
Purpose: Initiates discussions of black-white relations in training sessions; used as a self-examination to sensitize a person to his or her attitudes toward race relations and for research
Description: Paper-pencil 28-item inventory measuring attitudes toward black-white relations in the United States on an integrationist-separa-

tionist continuum. Instructions are read to the subjects, who are allowed as much time as necessary to complete the test. Requires a 10th-grade reading level.
Format: Self-administered; untimed: 25 minutes
Scoring: Examiner interpreted
Cost: $4.00 for 20 Inventories with Manual

Mayer-Salovey-Caruso Emotional Intelligence Test (MSCEIT)
John D. Mayer, Peter Salovey, David R. Caruso

2002	Multi-Health Systems, Inc.

Population: Ages 16 years and older
Purpose: Ability-based measure of emotional intelligence
Description: Because respondents have difficulty faking a good performance, the instrument is ideal for testing respondents who are expected to try to create a positive impression. The MSCEIT yields an overall EI score, two area-level scores (Emotional Experiencing, Emotional Reason), four branch scores (Managing Emotions, Understanding Emotions, Using Emotions, and Perceiving Emotions), and eight task-level scores. The 141-item booklet contains items for each of the tasks.
Format: Self-administered; untimed: 25 to 30 minutes
Scoring: Scoring service
Cost: Kit (manual, item booklet, personal summary report) $50.00

Personality Assessment Questionnaire (PAQ)
Ronald P. Rohner

2000	Rohner Research

Population: Children to adults
Purpose: Predicts personality and mental health outcome of variations in perceived parental acceptance-rejection
Description: Multiple-item paper-pencil instrument measuring seven personality dimensions: Hostility/Aggression, Dependence/Independence, Self-Esteem, Self-Adequacy, Emotional (Un)Responsiveness, Emotional (In)Stability, and World View. Theoretically, these dispositions are linked to the acceptance-rejection process. The test is available in a child version, an adult version, and a mother version. The questionnaire yields seven scale scores in addition to the Total Test score, which is often used as a measure of overall men-

tal health. A computer scoring program is available for PC systems. The examiner may read the items to individuals with visual impairments and explain the meanings of words to individuals who are very young or who have mental impairments. The Handbook for the Study of Parental Acceptance and Rejection contains all versions of the PAQ and provides scoring instructions, descriptions of validity and reliability, and other information needed for administration, scoring, and interpretation.

Format: Examiner/self-administered; suitable for group use; untimed: 10 minutes

Scoring: Self-scored; may be computer scored

Cost: Handbook $15.00

Q-Tags Test of Personality
Arthur G. Storey, Louis I. Masson

Date not provided	Institute of Psychological Research, Inc.

Population: Ages 6 years and older

Purpose: Measures individual personality traits; used for counseling, self-examination, and research

Description: Test measuring five factors of personality: assertive, effective, hostile, reverie, and social. By sorting 54 cards, subjects are able to describe themselves both as they are and as they wish to be. The test was developed with norms for age, grade, occupation, and gender based on a wide range of subjects.

Format: Self-administered; suitable for group use; untimed: 30 minutes

Scoring: Examiner evaluated

Cost: Contact publisher

Rorschach Inkblot Test
Hermann Rorschach

1994	Western Psychological Services

Population: All ages

Purpose: Evaluates personality tendencies

Description: The classic projective technique contains 10 Rorschach color inkblot plates used for psychodiagnostic purposes. The examiner shows one at a time to the client and records responses.

Format: Examiner required; individual administration; untimed

Scoring: Examiner evaluated

Cost: Set (set of plates, 100 miniature inkblots in color/summary forms, 25 each record booklets and summary forms) $155.00

Rorschach Psychodiagnostic Test– Rorschach Inkblot Test
Hermann Rorschach

Date not provided	Hogrefe & Huber Publishers

Population: Ages 3 years and older

Purpose: Evaluates personality through projective technique; used in clinical evaluation

Description: Oral-response projective personality test in which the subject is asked to interpret what he or she sees in 10 inkblots, based on the assumption that the individual's perceptions and associations are selected and organized in terms of his or her motivations, impulses, and other underlying aspects of personality. Extensive scoring systems have been developed. Although many variations are in use, this entry refers only to the Psychodiagnostic Plates first published in 1921. Materials include inquiry charts, tabulation sheets, and a set of 10 inkblots. A set of 10 Kodaslides of the inkblots may be imported on request. Trained examiner required.

Format: Examiner required; individual administration; untimed

Scoring: Examiner evaluated

Cost: $75.00

Rosenzweig Picture-Frustration Study (P-FS)
Saul Rosenzweig

1978	Psychological Assessment Resources, Inc.

Population: Ages 4 years through adult

Purpose: Measures aggression in personality; used in clinical counseling

Description: Paper–pencil semiprojective technique assessing an individual's patterns of response to everyday frustration or stress. It consists of 24 cartoon pictures, each depicting two persons in a frustrating situation. One person is acting as the frustrator. The subject provides a reply for the anonymous frustrated person. The instrument measures three types of aggression (obstacles-dominance, ego-defense, and need-persistence) and three directions of aggression. Nine factors, derived by combining the types and directions of aggression, constitute the score. The scoring guide is provided in the manual. Three versions are available: adult, adolescent, and child.

Format: Examiner required; individual administration; untimed: 15 to 20 minutes

Scoring: Examiner evaluated

Cost: Kit $84.00 (specify version)

Scenotest

G. von Staabs

| 1991 | Hogrefe & Huber Publishers |

Population: Children, adolescents

Purpose: Quickly assesses emotional problems

Description: Specifically developed to evaluate children's and adolescents' unconscious problems, the test is suited for working with adults and families. It permits accessing consciously denied or personally unknown relationships in the attitudes of the subjects to themselves and their social environment. Flexible dolls and a supply of additional materials (selected according to psychological and dynamic considerations), such as animals, trees, symbolic figures, and important objects from everyday life, are used as standard stimuli to prompt the subject to form and play out scenes that reveal real-life experiences, relations, fears, wishes, and coping strategies. Initial sessions reveal considerable matter that could not be tapped by direct questioning. In particular, neurotic disturbances can be revealed, and differential diagnosis is strongly supported. Used as part of an explicit therapy, it helps the patient see his or her problems at a distance and cope with them.

Format: Individual administration; untimed

Scoring: Examiner evaluated

Cost: Complete Test Kit $775.00

TEMAS (Tell-Me-a-Story)

Giuseppe Costantino, Robert G. Malgady, Lloyd Rogler

| 1986 | Western Psychological Services |

Population: Ages 5 to 18 years

Purpose: Measures strengths and deficits in cognitive, affective, interpersonal, and intrapersonal functioning in children and adolescents

Description: Multicultural thematic apperception test designed for use with minority and nonminority children and adolescents. The test, which features 35 scales, uses 23 full-color stimulus cards to elicit stories from the examinee. Two parallel forms, minority and nonminority, are available. Separate norms are available for blacks, Hispanics, and whites.

Format: Examiner required; individual administration; untimed: short form 1 hour, long form 3 hours

Scoring: Examiner evaluated

Cost: Kit (set of stimulus cards, set of minority stimulus cards, 25 record booklets, administration instruction card, manual) $262.50

Test of Basic Assumptions

James H. Morrison, Martin Levit

| 1959 | James H. Morrison |

Population: Adolescents, adults

Purpose: Diagnoses philosophical preferences; used to examine assumptions about reality or philosophy and for research and group discussion

Description: Paper–pencil 20-item measure of realism, idealism, and pragmaticism. Instructions are read to the subjects, who are allowed as much time as they need to complete the test. A minimum 12th-grade reading level is necessary. The test should not be used for prediction purposes.

Format: Self-administered; untimed: 40 minutes

Scoring: Examiner interpreted

Cost: $4.00 for 20 Inventories with Manual

Test of Social Insight: Youth and Adult Editions

Russell N. Cassel

| 1959 | Martin M. Bruce, PhD |

Population: Ages 10 years to adult

Purpose: Measures the subject's understanding of and adaptation to acceptable patterns of culture in the United States

Description: Paper–pencil 60-item multiple-choice test involving five ways of responding to interpersonal problems: withdrawal, passivity, cooperation, competition, and aggression. The potential conflict areas covered include home and family, authority figures, avocational contacts, and work situations. The Youth Edition is appropriate for individuals ages 10 to 18; the Adult Edition is designed for individuals ages 18 and older. A fifth-grade reading level is required. Suitable for individuals with physical, hearing, or visual impairments.

Format: Self-administered; untimed: 30 to 40 minutes

Scoring: Hand key

Cost: Specimen Set $71.40

Welsh Figure Preference Test (WFPT)

George S. Welsh

| 1987 | Mind Garden, Inc. |

Population: Ages 6 years to adult

Purpose: Evaluates individual personality traits through figure identification; used for counseling and research

Description: Paper–pencil 400-item nonverbal test measuring an individual's personality traits by evaluating his or her preference for types of black-and-white figures. The subject responds by indicating "likes" or "dislikes" for each figure. Scales include Conformity, Male–Female, Neuro-Psychiatric, Consensus, Origence, Intellectence, Barron–Welsh Original Art Scale, Revised Art Scale, Repression, Anxiety, Children, Movement, Figure-Ground Reversal, Sex Symbol, and several measuring preferences for specific kinds of geometric figures. All scales need not be scored. The Barron–Welsh Art Scale (86 items) is available separately.

Format: Examiner required; suitable for group use; untimed: 50 minutes

Scoring: Hand key

Cost: Sample Set $25.00; Permission for 200 Uses $125.00

Child

California Q-Sort (Child)
Jeanne Block, Jack Block

1980	Mind Garden, Inc.

Population: Children

Purpose: Describes individual behavior and personality in psychodynamic terms; used for research in child development

Description: A total of 100 descriptive personality statements are sorted from most to least applicable to the subject. Materials include individual cards.

Format: Examiner required; not suitable for group use; untimed

Scoring: Examiner evaluated

Cost: Sampler Set $25.00; Permission Set $125.00 for 200 uses

Children's Apperception Test–Animal Figures (CAT-A)
Leopold Bellak, Sonya Sorel Bellak

1991	C.P.S., Inc.

Population: Ages 3 to 10 years

Purpose: Assesses children's personality; used in clinical evaluation and diagnosis

Description: Oral-response projective personality test measuring the traits, attitudes, and psychodynamics involved in the personalities of children. Each of 10 test items consists of a picture of animals in a human social context through which the child becomes involved in conflicts, identities, roles, and family structures. Examinees are required to tell a story about each picture. The test also includes informational material on the history, nature, and purpose of CAT; Ego Function Graph; test interpretation; use of the Short Form; research possibilities; and bibliography. Available also in Spanish, Indian, French, German, Japanese, Russian, Portuguese, and Italian.

Format: Examiner required; individual administration; untimed: 20 to 30 minutes

Scoring: Examiner evaluated

Cost: Complete Kit (pictures, manual) $28.00

Children's Apperception Test–Human Figures (CAT-H)
Leopold Bellak, Sonya Sorel Bellak

1965	C.P.S., Inc.

Population: Ages 3 to 10 years

Purpose: Assesses children's personality; used for clinical evaluation and diagnosis

Description: Oral-response projective personality test measuring the traits, attitudes, and psychodynamics involved in the personalities of children. The test consists of 10 pictures of human figures in situations of concern to children: conflicts, identities, roles, and family structure. The test also includes a review of the literature concerning the use of animal versus human figures in projective techniques, a discussion of the process of transposing animal figures to human forms, a copy of Haworth's Schedule of Adaptive Mechanisms in CAT Responses, and a bibliography. Available also in Spanish, Portuguese, Flemish, and Japanese.

Format: Examiner required; individual administration; untimed: 20 to 30 minutes

Scoring: Examiner evaluated

Cost: Complete Kit (manual, pictures) $28.00

Children's Apperception Test–Supplement (CAT-S)
Leopold Bellak, Sonya Sorel Bellak

1991	C.P.S., Inc.

Population: Ages 3 to 10 years

Purpose: Assesses children's personality; used for clinical evaluation and diagnosis

Description: Oral-response projective personality test measuring the traits, attitudes, and psychodynamics at work in the personalities of children. The test items consist of 10 pictures of animal figures in family situations that are common, but not as universal as those on the Children's Apperception Test-Animal Figures. Among the situations depicted are prolonged illness, physical disability, mother's pregnancy, and separation of parents. The picture plates are constructed like pieces of a large jigsaw puzzle, with irregularly shaped outlines. Children who do not relate stories readily can manipulate these forms in play techniques. The test also includes informational material on test techniques and a bibliography. Available also in Spanish, French, Flemish, and Italian.

Format: Examiner required; individual administration; untimed: 20 to 30 minutes

Scoring: Examiner evaluated

Cost: Complete Kit (manual, 10 pictures) $32.00

Children's Personality Questionnaire (CPQ)
Rutherford B. Porter, Raymond B. Cattell

1973	Institute for Personality and Ability Testing, Inc.

Population: Ages 8 to 12 years

Purpose: Assesses personality development in children; used for clinical evaluations and educational and personal counseling

Description: Paper–pencil 140-item test measuring 14 primary personality traits useful in understanding and evaluating the course of personal, social, and academic development. The traits measured include emotional stability, self-concept level, excitability, and apprehension. Scores for extroversion, anxiety, and other broad trait patterns are obtained as combinations of the primary scales. Norms are available for both genders together and separately. The test is available in four forms: A, B, C, and D. Each form is divided into two parts for scheduling convenience in school settings. A third-grade reading level is required.

Format: Self-administered; untimed 30 to 60 minutes

Scoring: Computer scored; scoring service available

Cost: CPQ Introductory Kit $23.00; Handbook

$20.00; 25 Reusable Test Booklets $18.00; 25 Answer Sheets $22.00

Children's Problems Checklist
John A. Schinka

1985	Psychological Assessment Resources, Inc.

Population: Parents of children ages 5 to 12 years

Purpose: Assesses children's problems as reported by parent or guardian; used as a survey instrument in clinical and counseling settings to initiate the consultation process and introduce the client to formal diagnostic testing

Description: Paper–pencil 190-item test completed by a parent or guardian and identifying problems in 11 areas: emotions, self-concept, peers/play, school, language/thinking, concentration/organization, activity level/motor control, behavior, values, habits, and health.

Format: Self-administered; suitable for group use; untimed: 10 to 20 minutes

Scoring: Examiner evaluated

Cost: 50 Checklists $42.00

Early School Personality Questionnaire (ESPQ)
Raymond B. Cattell, Richard W. Coan

1966	Institute for Personality and Ability Testing, Inc.

Population: Ages 6 to 8 years

Purpose: Provides insights into the needs and predispositions of young children; used for clinical evaluation and educational and personal counseling

Description: Paper–pencil 160-item test measuring personality in children. Questions are read aloud by the administrator (an optional tape recording may be used instead), and the students mark their answers on the answer sheet. To use the answer sheet, children need only be able to discriminate the letters A and B and common objects. Percentiles and standard scores are provided for both genders separately. The test is divided into two equal parts of 80 items each for scheduling convenience.

Format: Examiner required; suitable for group use; untimed: 1 hour

Scoring: Hand key

Cost: Introductory Kit $37.00

Hirsch Opinions About Psychological & Emotional Disorders in Children (HOPE)
Joseph A. Hirsch

| 1995 | Joseph A. Hirsch, PhD, Psy.D. |

Population: Children

Purpose: Designed for teachers, psychologists, social workers, and day care workers to provide opinions about children's psychological and emotional disorders

Description: Paper-pencil 42-item survey rated using a Likert scale that measures two factors: Biases and Dynamic/Clinical. The Dynamic/Clinical factor assesses treatment efficacy and psychodynamic etiology. Scaled scores are provided for each factor, with separate norms for special populations. Requires a sixth-grade reading level.

Format: Examiner required; individual or group administration; untimed

Scoring: Examiner scoring and interpretation

Cost: 50 Surveys $25.00

Joseph Preschool and Primary Self-Concept Screening Test (JPPSST)
Jack Joseph

| 1979 | Stoelting Company |

Population: Ages 3 years 5 months to 9 years

Purpose: Measures social-emotional development of children; used to identify children who may have learning difficulties due to negative self-appraisals and to monitor progress in early childhood programs and special education classes

Description: Paper-pencil 16-item oral-response test in two parts. First, the child draws his or her own face on a blank figure of the corresponding gender. Next, the child answers two simple oral-response questions and 13 questions asking child to select from pairs of pictures the one with which he or she identifies more closely. The face drawing is evaluated qualitatively, and the 15 questions are scored objectively. The test generates a Global Self-Concept Score based on five dimensions and provides objective high-risk cutoff points. The effects of socially desirable responses are corrected for at upper ranges (ages 5 to 9). Both quantitative and qualitative indexes regarding possible cognitive deficits and experiential or receptive language lags are developed. The manual provides normative data, measures of validity and reliability, item analysis, specific case illustrations, and research considerations.

Format: Examiner required; individual administration; untimed: 5 to 7 minutes

Scoring: Examiner evaluated

Cost: Complete Kit (manual, cards, identity drawings, 50 record forms) $150.00

Junior Eysenck Personality Inventory (JEPI)
Sybil B. G. Eysenck

| 1965 | EdITS/Educational and Industrial Testing Service |

Population: Ages 7 to 16 years

Purpose: Measures the major personality dimensions of children; used as a research instrument

Description: Paper-pencil yes-no inventory measuring extroversion–introversion (24 items) and neuroticism–stability (24 items). A falsification scale (12 items) detects response distortion. Scores are provided for Extroversion, Neuroticism, and Lie. American norms are available for selected samples of majority and minority children. Also available in Spanish.

Format: Examiner required; suitable for group use; untimed: 10 minutes

Scoring: Hand key

Cost: Specimen Set (manual, one copy of all forms) $6.50

Measure of Child Stimulus Screening (Converse of Arousability)
Albert Mehrabian, Carol Falender

| 1978 | Albert Mehrabian, PhD |

Population: Ages 3 months to 7 years

Purpose: Measures major components of a child's arousability and stimulus screening; used for research, counseling, and education program selection purposes

Description: Multiple-item paper-pencil observational inventory measuring parents' descriptions of their children's arousability (responses of one parent are sufficient). Test results indicate the child's characteristic arousal response to complex, unexpected, or unfamiliar situations. Stimulus screening/arousability has been shown to be a major component of many important personality dimensions, such as anxiety, neuroticism, extroversion, or hostility. This test is based on the same conceptual framework used to develop the corresponding adult measure, the Measure of Stimulus Screening (Converse of Arousability).

Format: Examiner required; suitable for group use; untimed: 10 minutes

Scoring: Hand key

Cost: Test Kit (scale, scoring directions, norms, descriptive material) $33.00

Murphy-Meisgeier Type Indicator for Children (MMTIC)
Charles Meisgeier, Elizabeth Murphy

Date not provided	Consulting Psychologists Press, Inc.

Population: Grades 2 to 8

Purpose: Determines the Jungian types of children to identify individual learning styles

Description: Test measuring four preference scales: Extroversion-Introversion (16 items), Sensing-Intuition (18 items), Thinking-Feeling (18 items), and Judgement-Perception (18 items). The inventory is designed to affirm the child's strengths to increase self-esteem; contribute to the rearing, teaching, counseling, and overall understanding of children; and provide a means through which children can understand individual differences. The manual contains statistical information as well as descriptions of learning styles associated with each type. Three booklets introducing the types to children, parents, and teachers are available. The computer report identifies the individual preferences and reports information on learning styles. The reading level of the items is most appropriate for students in Grades 3 through 6; however, teachers may read the items aloud to second graders or any examinee with reading difficulties.

Format: Examiner required; suitable for group use; untimed

Scoring: Hand key; scoring service

Cost: Preview Kit (manual, booklet, answer sheet, teacher's guide) $42.50

Personality Inventory for Children– Second Edition (PIC-2)
David Lachar, Christian P. Gruber

2001	Western Psychological Services

Population: Ages 5 to 19 years

Purpose: Evaluates the personality attributes of children and adolescents; used by professionals for counseling and identification of psychopathology, developmental problems, and social disabilities

Description: Paper-pencil 275-item true-false inventory completed by one of the child's par-

ents, producing a profile of 16 scales: Intellectual Screening, Family Relations, Hyperactivity, Somatic Concern, Social Skills, Achievement, Development, Depression, Delinquency, Withdrawal, Psychosis, Anxiety, Lie Frequency, Defensiveness, and Adjustment. A 420-item version is available for higher scale reliabilities, and a 131-item version is available for screening.

Format: Examiner required; individual administration; untimed: 25 to 30 minutes

Scoring: Hand key; may be computer scored

Cost: Complete Kit $145.00

Adolescent and Adult

16PF Adolescent Personality Questionnaire
James M. Schuerger

2001	Institute for Personality and Ability Testing, Inc.

Population: Ages 11 to 22 years

Purpose: Provides a concise portrait of how an adolescent sees himself or herself

Description: The first three sections elicit valuable information regarding the youth's personal style (normal personality; 135 items), problem-solving abilities (12 items), and preferred work activities (15 items). The optional Life's Difficulties section (43 items) provides an opportunity for the individual to indicate particular problems in areas known to be problematic to adolescents, making the instrument appropriate for screening and for introducing sensitive topics in a counseling situation. Scores are provided for 16 primary personality factor scales, five global factor scales, and six work activity categories (manual, scientific, artistic, helping, sales/management, and procedural), plus additional scores for Impression Management, Missing Responses, Central Responses, and Predicted Grade Point Average. Norms are based on over 1,000 normal adolescents from various parts of the United States.

Format: Self-administered; untimed: 65 minutes

Scoring: Computer scoring; online scoring

Cost: Contact publisher

16PF Fifth Edition Questionnaire
Raymond B. Cattell, A. Karen Cattell, Heather E. P. Cattell

1994	Institute for Personality and Ability Testing, Inc.

Population: Ages 16 years and older

Purpose: Measures 16 personality factors and five global factors; used for personnel selection, individual and couples counseling, career counseling, and management development

Description: Multiple-choice computer-administered or paper–pencil test with 185 items yielding 16 Personality Factors: Warmth, Reasoning, Emotional Stability, Dominance, Liveliness, Rule-Consciousness, Social Boldness, Sensitivity, Vigilance, Abstractedness, Privateness, Apprehension, Openness to Change, Self-Reliance, Perfectionism, and Tension. Global Factors yielded: Extroversion, Anxiety, Tough-Mindedness, Independence, and Self-Control. Response Style Indices yielded: Impression Management, Infrequency, and Acquiescence. Eight unique interpretive reports can be generated from this questionnaire.

Format: Self-administered; untimed: 35 to 50 minutes (paper–pencil), 25 minutes (computer)

Scoring: Hand key, machine scored, computer scored, test scoring service available, online scoring available

Cost: 10 Reusable Questionnaires $18.00; 25 Answer Sheets $15.00

16PF Select Questionnaire
Raymond B. Cattell, A. Karen Cattell, Heather E. P. Cattell, Mary L. Kelly

1999	Institute for Personality and Ability Testing, Inc.

Population: Ages 16 years and older

Purpose: Assesses the degree to which the test taker matches the personality dimensions prespecified by the professional as necessary for effective performance in a particular job

Description: The 16PF Select Report yields an Overall Model Similarity Score as well as scores for 12 primary personality factors (Warmth, Calmness, Dominance, Liveliness, Rule-Consciousness, Social Boldness, Trust, Imagination, Self-Assuredness, Openness, Self-Reliance, and Organization). Scores for three Response Style Indices (Impression Management, Infrequency, and Acquiescence) are also reported.

Format: Self-administered; untimed

Scoring: Computer scored; scoring service available

Cost: Answer Sheet Booklet $30.00 (per 10 pack); Manual (required) $30.00; Report price varies depending on quantity: $30.00 each for 1 to 9; $17.00 each for 10 to 29; $16.00 each for 30 to 99; $15.00 each for 100 or more

Actualizing Assessment Battery (AAB)
Everett L. Shostrom

1976	EdITS/Educational and Industrial Testing Service

Population: Adults

Purpose: Measures an individual's sense of actualization with himself or herself and within his or her relationships with others; used by therapists, marriage and family counselors, personnel administrators, and school psychologists for a wide variety of counseling situations

Description: Four paper–pencil tests measuring 13 dimensions of a person's sense of actualization: being, weakness, synergistic integration, time orientation, core centeredness, love, trust in humanity, creative living, mission, strength, manipulation awareness, anger, and potentiation. The Personal Orientations Dimensions (POD) and the Personal Orientation Inventory (POI) primarily measure intrapersonal actualizing, and the Caring Relationship Inventory (CRI) and the Pair Attraction Inventory (PAI) primarily measure interpersonal actualizing. The AAB may be scored locally by using the POI, CRI, and PAI or may be sent to EdITS for scoring. Results are reported through the AAB Interpretation Brochure, a six-page booklet containing descriptions and profiles for each of the four tests.

Format: Examiner required; suitable for group use; untimed: approximately 3 hours

Scoring: Computer scored

Cost: Contact publisher

Adolescent Dissociative Experiences Scale (A–DES)
Judith Armstrong, Frank W. Putnam, Eve Bernstein Carlson

Date not provided	Sidran Foundation

Population: Ages 10 to 21 years

Purpose: Measures frequency of dissociative experiences

Description: The scale was developed to provide a reliable, valid, and convenient way to quantify dissociative experiences. A response scale that allows subjects to quantify their experiences for each item was used so that scores could reflect a wider range of dissociative symptomatology than possible using a dichotomous format.

Format: Self-report; untimed

Scoring: Examiner evaluated

Cost: Packet (manual, 5 protocols, reference list) $12.00

Assertive Skills Inventory
Millard J. Bienvenu

| 1999 | Northwest Publications |

Population: Ages 14 years and older

Purpose: Assesses the individual's degree of assertiveness

Description: Forty-item yes-no-sometimes test. Seventh-grade reading level is required.

Format: Self-administered; untimed: 12 minutes

Scoring: Hand key

Cost: Guide $1.00; $.25 per inventory copy

Association Adjustment Inventory (AAI)
Martin M. Bruce

| 1959 | Martin M. Bruce, PhD |

Population: Adults

Purpose: Evaluates the extent to which the subject is maladjusted, immature, and deviant in ideation; used as an aid to predicting potential deviant behavior and job tenure

Description: Inventory with 100 items in which the subject matches one of four words with a stimulus word, allowing the examiner to score for ideational deviation, general psychosis, depression, hysteria, withdrawal, paranoia, rigidity, schizophrenia, impulsiveness, psychosomapathia, and anxiety. The scores are compared to norms to measure deviation. Available also in Spanish and German. Suitable for individuals with physical, hearing, or visual impairments.

Format: Examiner/self-administered; suitable for group use; untimed: 10 minutes

Scoring: Hand key

Cost: Specimen Set $76.45

Balanced Emotional Empathy Scale (BEES)
Albert Mehrabian

| 1996 | Albert Mehrabian, PhD |

Population: Ages 14 years and older

Purpose: Assesses emotional empathy (sensitivity) to others; used for research, job placement, and counseling

Description: Paper-pencil 30-item test yielding a single total score. A 10th-grade reading level is required.

Format: Self-administered; untimed: 10 minutes

Scoring: Hand key; test scoring service available from publisher

Cost: Test Kit $33.00

Basic Personality Inventory (BPI)
Douglas N. Jackson

| 1997 | Sigma Assessment Systems, Inc. |

Population: Adolescents, adults

Purpose: Identifies personality dimensions indicating personal strengths as well as psychopathological dimensions; used in psychiatric hospitals, community mental health centers, and psychological, psychiatric, and counseling practices

Description: Paper-pencil or computer-administered true-false multiphasic personality inventory used with both normal and clinical populations to identify personal strengths or sources of maladjustment. The test contains 24 items in 11 substantive clinical scales and one critical item scale. The scales are as follows: Hypochondriasis, Anxiety, Depression, Thinking Disorder, Denial, Impulse Expression, Interpersonal Problems, Social Introversion, Alienation, Self-Deprecation, Persecutory Ideas, and Deviation (critical item scale). The computer version, which operates on IBM PC, AT, XT, and compatible systems, yields scores, profiles, and reports.

Format: Examiner required; suitable for group use; untimed: 20 to 45 minutes

Scoring: Hand key; machine scored; scoring service available from publisher; computer scored

Cost: Examination Kit (test manual, 5 test booklets, 10 answer sheets, 10 profile sheets, scoring template, 1 machine answer sheet, coupon for basic report) $66.00

BASIS-A Inventory (Basic Adlerian Scales for Interpersonal Success–Adult Form)
Mary S. Wheeler, Roy M. Kern, William L. Curlette

| 1993 | TRT Associates, Inc. |

Population: Adults

Purpose: Helps in understanding how an individual's beliefs that developed in early childhood relate to present functioning; used for individual or marital counseling, vocational counseling, organizational settings, and educational settings

Description: Paper-pencil 65-item Likert scale

test with five BASIS-A scales and five HELPS scales. The BASIS-A scales are Belonging-Social Interest, Going Along, Taking Charge, Wanting Recognition, and Being Cautious. The HELPS scales are Harshness (H), Entitlement (E), Liked by All (L), Striving for Perfection (P), and Softness (S). Individuals receive *T*-scores on the five BASIS-A scales and cutoff scores on the five HELPS scales. Profiles are part of the self-scoring test booklet. Materials used include test items, responses, scoring directions, and brief interpretations of scales, all contained in a self-scoring test booklet.

Format: Self- or examiner administered; suitable for group use; untimed: 20 to 30 minutes

Scoring: Self-scored; examiner evaluated

Cost: Instrument $3.40; 25 Interpretive Guides $35.00; Interpretive Manual $17.00; Technical Manual $17.00

Bass Orientation Inventory
Bernard M. Bass

1977	Mind Garden, Inc.

Population: Adults

Purpose: Measures three types of orientation; used for personnel assessment, college vocational counseling, and group research

Description: Paper–pencil 27-item forced-choice test of three types of orientation toward satisfaction and rewards: self-orientation, interaction-orientation, and task-orientation. Results help to predict an individual's success and performance in various types of work. The inventory is based on Bass's theory of interpersonal behavior in organizations.

Format: Self-administered; suitable for group use; untimed: 10 to 15 minutes

Scoring: Hand key

Cost: Sampler Set $25.00; Permission Set $125.00

Bell Object Relations and Reality Testing Inventory (BORRTI)
Morris D. Bell

1995	Western Psychological Services

Population: Adults

Purpose: Used by clinicians to evaluate adults with character disorders and psychoses

Description: Composed of 90 items, the inventory measures object relations and reality testing on seven scales: Object Relations (Alienation, Egocentricity, Insecure Attachment, Social Incompetence) and Reality Testing (Reality Distortion, Uncertainty of Perception, Hallucinations and Delusions). The test report profiles scores, describes client characteristics, makes diagnostic suggestions, provides individualized treatment recommendations, and lists specific clinical themes that apply to client in question.

Format: Examiner required; individual administration; untimed: 15 to 20 minutes

Scoring: Examiner evaluated; scoring service available

Cost: Kit (2 test reports, prepaid mail-in answer sheets, manual) $99.50

Bem Sex-Role Inventory (BSRI)
Sandra L. Bem

1978, 1981	Mind Garden, Inc.

Population: Adults

Purpose: Measures masculinity and femininity; used for research on psychological androgyny

Description: Paper–pencil 60-item measure of integration of masculinity and femininity. Items are three sets of 20 personality characteristics: masculine, feminine, and neutral. The subject indicates on a 7-point scale how well each characteristic describes himself or herself. Materials include a 30-item short form.

Format: Self-administered; untimed: 10 minutes

Scoring: Hand key

Cost: Sampler Set $25.00; Permission Set $125.00; Test Booklets $25.00

Bloom Sentence Completion Attitude Survey
Wallace Bloom

Date not provided	Stoelting Company

Population: Adolescents, adults

Purpose: Assesses adult and student attitudes toward self and important factors in everyday living; used to identify change in an individual over time and to compare individuals and groups

Description: Paper–pencil free-response test consisting of 40 sentence stems that the subject completes in his or her own words. The responses measure attitudes toward agemates or people, physical self, family, psychological self, self-directedness, education or work (depending on which version is used), accomplishment, and irritants. Two versions are available: one for adults and one for unmarried students. The scoring system facilitates use of the test as both an objective and a projective instrument.

Format: Examiner required; suitable for group use; untimed: 25 minutes

Scoring: Examiner evaluated

Cost: Complete Kit, specify version (manual, 30 test forms, 30 analysis record forms) $44.00

California Psychological Inventory™, Third Edition (CPI™)
Harrison G. Gough

1987	Consulting Psychologists Press, Inc.

Population: Ages 14 years to adult

Purpose: Assesses personality characteristics important for daily living; used in business, in schools and colleges, in clinics and counseling agencies, and for crosscultural and other research

Description: Paper–pencil 434-item true–false test measuring behavioral tendencies along 20 scales: Dominance, Capacity for Status, Sociability, Social Presence, Self-Acceptance, Independence, Empathy, Responsibility, Socialization, Self-Control, Good Impression, Communality, Well-Being, Tolerance, Achievement via Independence, Achievement via Conformance, Intellectual Efficiency, Psychological-Mindedness, Flexibility, and Femininity/Masculinity. There are three vector scales that define a theoretical model of personality structure and 13 special-purpose scales, such as Managerial Potential, Work Orientation, Creative Temperament, and Anxiety. Four personality types (Alphas, Betas, Gammas, and Deltas) are described across seven levels. Windows-based scoring and mail-in computer scoring are available. Reports available are the CPI Profile, CPI Narrative Report, CPI Configural Analysis Supplement, and Police and Public Safety Selection Report.

Format: Self-administered; suitable for group use; untimed: 45 to 60 minutes

Scoring: Hand key; may be computer scored

Cost: Profile Starter Kit (manual, 5 reusable item booklets, 10 prepaid mail-in profile answer sheets, guide to interpretation) $238.30

California Q-Sort Revised (Adult)
Jack Block

1990	Mind Garden, Inc.

Population: Adults

Purpose: Describes individual personality in

contemporary psychodynamic terms; used for research

Description: Test used to formulate personality descriptions. Items are 100 descriptive personality statements on cards sorted from most to least applicable to the subject's experience. Materials include individual cards and a sorting guide. Cards may be sorted by professionals or laymen.

Format: Examiner required; individual administration; untimed

Scoring: Examiner evaluated

Cost: Sampler Set $25.00; Permission Set for 200 Uses $125.00

Carlson Psychological Survey (CPS)
Kenneth A. Carlson

1997	Sigma Assessment Systems, Inc.

Population: Adolescents, adults

Purpose: Assesses and classifies criminal offenders; used to evaluate persons presenting behavioral or substance-abuse problems and to analyze the effects of intervention programs

Description: Paper–pencil 50-item questionnaire in a five-category response format with space for the respondent's comments. The scales measured are Chemical Abuse, Thought Disturbance, Antisocial Tendencies, Self-Depreciation, and Validity. The test is designed for offenders, those charged with crimes, and others who have come to the attention of the criminal justice or social welfare systems. The results are classified into 18 offender types. A companion edition, the Psicologico Texto (PT), is designed for use with Spanish-literate offenders. A fourth-grade reading level is required. Also available in French.

Format: Examiner required; suitable for group use; untimed: 15 minutes

Scoring: Hand key; computer scored; scoring service available from publisher

Cost: Examination Kit (manual, 10 question/answer documents, 10 scoring sheets, 10 profile sheets, 1 extended report) $41.00

Chapin Social Insight Test
F. Stuart Chapin

1993	Mind Garden, Inc.

Population: Adults

Purpose: Measures the ability to diagnose situations involving human interaction

Description: Test with 25 items that measure the ability to recognize the dynamics underlying behavior, or to choose the wisest course of action to resolve a difficulty. It helps to measure social insight, appraisal of others, and respondents' evaluations of interpersonal situations.

Format: Examiner required; individual administration; untimed: 20 to 30 minutes

Scoring: Examiner evaluated

Cost: Sampler Set $25.00; Permission Set $125.00

College Adjustment Scales (CAS)
William D. Anton, James R. Reed

| 1991 | Psychological Assessment Resources, Inc. |

Population: Ages 17 to 30 years

Purpose: Used by college counselors to identify psychological adjustment problems experienced by college students

Description: Paper-pencil 108-item 4-point Likert scale measuring anxiety, depression, suicidal ideation, substance abuse, self-esteem problems, interpersonal problems, family problems, academic problems, and career problems. A fifth-grade reading level is required.

Format: Examiner required; individual administration; suitable for group use; untimed

Scoring: Hand scored

Cost: Kit (manual, reusable item booklet, answer sheet) $99.00

Comprehensive Emotional-State Scales
Albert Mehrabian

| 1995 | Albert Mehrabian, PhD |

Population: Ages 14 years and older

Purpose: Measures three basic dimensions of affect: pleasure, arousal, and dominance; used for research and counseling

Description: Paper-pencil 34-item test with three subscales: pleasure-displeasure, arousal-nonarousal, and dominance-submissiveness. A 10th-grade reading level is required.

Format: Self-administered; suitable for group use; untimed: 10 minutes

Scoring: Hand key; test scoring service available from publisher

Cost: Test Kit $59.00

Comrey Personality Scales (CPS)
Andrew L. Comrey

| 1970 | EdITS/Educational and Industrial Testing Service |

Population: Adolescents, adults

Purpose: Measures major personality characteristics of adults and high school and college students; used in educational, clinical, and business settings where personality structure and stability are important

Description: Paper-pencil 180-item test consisting of eight personality dimension scales (20 items each), a validity scale (8 items), and a response bias scale (12 items). The eight personality scales are Trust vs. Defensiveness, Orderliness vs. Lack of Orderliness, Social Conformity vs. Rebelliousness, Activity vs. Lack of Energy, Emotional Stability vs. Neuroticism, Extroversion vs. Introversion, Masculinity vs. Femininity, and Empathy vs. Egocentrism. Subjects respond to items according to 7-point scales ranging from *never* to *always* or from *definitely not,* to *definitely.* The profile presents a description of the personality structure of "normal" socially functioning individuals. Extreme scores on any of the scales may provide a clue to the source of current difficulties, predict future problems, aid in selection of therapy programs, and screen job applicants. Norms are presented as *T*-scores for male and female college students.

Format: Examiner required; suitable for group use; untimed: 30 to 50 minutes

Scoring: Hand key; may be computer scored

Cost: Specimen Set (manual, all forms) $29.25

Coping Operations Preference Enquiry (COPE)
Will Schutz

| 1962 | Mind Garden, Inc. |

Population: Adults

Purpose: Measures individual preference for certain types of coping or defense mechanisms; used for counseling and therapy

Description: Paper-pencil 6-item test measuring the characteristic use of five defense mechanisms: denial, isolation, projection, regression-dependency, and turning-against-the-self. Each item describes a person and his or her behavior in a particular situation. The respondent rank-orders five alternative ways he or she might feel; the alternatives represent the inventory's five coping mechanisms. Materials include separate forms for men and women.

Format: Examiner recommended; may be self-administered; suitable for group use; untimed

Scoring: Examiner evaluated

Cost: Sampler Set $25.00; Permission for 200 Uses $125.00

Coping Resources Inventory (CRI)
Allen L. Hammer, M. Susan Marting

Date not provided	Consulting Psychologists Press, Inc.

Population: Adults

Purpose: Measures an individual's resources for coping with stress; used in individual counseling, workshops, and health settings

Description: Paper–pencil 60-item inventory consisting of five scales measuring an individual's cognitive, social, physical, emotional, and values resources. The results identify the resources a person has developed for coping with stress and those that still must be developed. The manual includes scale descriptions, reliability and validity information, separate norms for males and females, and case illustrations for interpreting the profiles.

Format: Examiner required; suitable for group use; untimed: 10 minutes

Scoring: Hand key; may be computer scored

Cost: Preview Kit (manual, booklet, answer sheet, profile, scoring keys) $95.00

Cornell Index
Arthur Weider

1958	Arthur Weider, PhD

Population: Ages 13 years and older

Purpose: Evaluates an individual's psychiatric history; identifies individuals with serious personal and psychosomatic disturbances; used for clinical evaluations and research purposes

Description: Paper–pencil 101-item questionnaire measuring neuropsychiatric and psychosomatic symptoms. It is administered in the form of a structured interview. Analysis of responses provides a standardized evaluation of an individual's psychiatric history and statistically differentiates individuals with serious personal and psychiatric disturbances.

Format: Self-administered; untimed: 5 to 10 minutes

Scoring: Hand key; self-scored

Cost: Package of 25 $30.00; package of 100 $60.00

Cornell Word Form
Arthur Weider

1958	Arthur Weider, PhD

Population: Ages 13 years and older

Purpose: Assesses an individual's adaptive

mechanisms; used in a variety of clinical and research settings

Description: Multiple-item paper–pencil test employing a modification of the word association technique. For each test item, the subject selects one word of a pair of printed responses that he or she associates with a given stimulus word. Analysis of the responses contributes to a descriptive sketch of the subject's adaptive mechanisms in a manner not easily apparent.

Format: Self-administered; untimed: 5 to 10 minutes

Scoring: Hand key; self-scored

Cost: Package of 25 $30.00; package of 100 $60.00

Defense Mechanisms Inventory
David Ihilevich, Goldine C. Gleser

1993	Psychological Assessment Resources, Inc.

Population: College students and adults

Purpose: Measures style of response to conflict and threat

Description: Ten vignettes (male and female forms) with five defensive responses to a variety of situations are presented to the subject. Each vignette is followed by four questions: "What would you do?" "What would you like to do?" "What do you think?" and "How do you feel?" There are five possible responses to each question corresponding to the following five defense mechanisms: turning against object, projection, principalization, turning against self, and reversal.

Format: Self-administered; untimed: 30 to 45 minutes

Scoring: Examiner evaluated

Cost: Introductory Kit (manual, male and female answer sheets, male and female profile forms) $169.00

Defining Issues Test of Moral Judgment (DIT-1 and DIT-2)
James R. Rest, Darcia Narvaez, Muriel Bebeou

1979 (DIT-1); 1998 (DIT-2)	Center for the Study of Ethical Development

Population: Ages 14+ years

Purpose: Measures development of moral judgment

Description: The DIT has dilemmas and standard items; the subject's task is to rate and rank the items in terms of their moral importance. The DIT-1 has six dilemmas; the DIT-2 has five dilemmas followed by 12 issue-statements. Scores include N-scores, P-scores, and ANOVA. Forms include DIT-1 standard and shortened and DIT-2 standard. May be used for persons with visual, hearing, physical, or mental impairments. An eighth-grade reading level is required.

Format: Examiner required; individual administration; untimed: 1 hour

Scoring: Machine scored; computer scored; scoring service available

Cost: Kit (instructions, 15 answer sheets, guides) $31.00

Dissociative Experiences Scale (DES)
Eve Bernstein Carlson, Frank W. Putnam

Date not provided	Sidran Foundation

Population: Adults

Purpose: Measures frequency of dissociative experiences

Description: The scale was developed to provide a reliable, valid, and convenient way to quantify dissociative experiences. A response scale that allows subjects to quantify their experiences for each item was used so that scores could reflect a wider range of dissociative symptomatology than possible using a dichotomous format. The DES has been translated into over 20 languages.

Format: Self-report; untimed

Scoring: Examiner evaluated

Cost: Packet (manual, 5 protocols, reference list) $12.00

Dissociative Features Profile (DFP)
Joyanna Silberg

Date not provided	Sidran Foundation

Population: Children, adolescents

Purpose: Identifies dissociative pathology

Description: The DFP was developed to be used with a typical psychological testing battery. The DFP may be used if at least two measures were administered.

Format: Examiner required to analyze testing information; untimed

Scoring: Examiner evaluated

Cost: Packet (manual, 5 protocols, reference list) $12.00

Dynamic Factors Survey
J. P. Guilford, Paul R. Christensen, Nicholas A. Bond, Jr.

1993	Mind Garden, Inc.

Population: Adolescents, adults

Purpose: Measures general motivational factors

Description: Used in personality and interest research, personnel selection, and vocational assessment, this 300-item inventory measures general motivational factors, such as Need for Freedom; Cultural Conformity; Need for Precision; Need for Attention; Realistic Thinking; Need for Diversion, Adventure, and Security; Liking for Thinking; Self Reliance vs. Dependence; and Aesthetic Appreciation.

Format: Self-administered; untimed

Scoring: Hand key

Cost: Sampler Set $25.00; Review Set $20.00; Permission Set $125.00

Educational Values (VAL-ED)
Will Schutz

1977	Mind Garden, Inc.

Population: Adults

Purpose: Assesses an individual's attitudes toward education; used to evaluate the working relationships of students, teachers, administrators, and community members

Description: Multiple-item paper–pencil survey of values regarding interpersonal relationships in school settings. The factors included relate to inclusion, control, and affection at both the feeling and the behavioral levels and to the purpose and importance of education.

Format: Examiner/self-administered; suitable for group use; untimed

Scoring: Hand key

Cost: Sampler Set $25.00; Permission Set $125.00

Edwards Personal Preference Schedule (EPPS)
A. L. Edwards

1959	The Psychological Corporation

Population: Ages 18 years and older

Purpose: Assesses an individual's personality

Description: Paper–pencil forced-choice test designed to show the relative importance of 15 needs and motives: achievement, deference, order, exhibition, autonomy, affiliation, intraception, succorance, dominance, abasement, nurturance, change, endurance, heterosexuality, and aggression.

Format: Self-administered; untimed: 45 minutes

Scoring: Hand key; machine scoring

Cost: Examination Kit (manual, schedule booklet, hand-scorable answer sheet, and machine-scored answer sheets) $48.00

Ego Function Assessment (EFA)
Leopold Bellak

1989	C.P.S., Inc.

Population: Ages 13 years and older

Purpose: Assesses ego functions; used for a variety of purposes including personnel assessment, drug effects, and evaluation

Description: Oral-response criterion-referenced test measuring 12 ego functions.

Format: Examiner required; individual administration; untimed: 20 to 30 minutes

Scoring: Examiner evaluated

Cost: Manual and Final Report $19.00

Embedded Figures Test (EFT)
Herman A. Witkin

Date not provided	Consulting Psychologists Press, Inc.

Population: Ages 10 years to adult

Purpose: Assesses cognitive style in perceptual tasks; used in counseling

Description: Twelve-item verbal-manual test of perceptual processes, including field dependence-independence. The task requires the subject to locate and trace a previously seen simple figure within a larger complex figure. Performance is related to analytic ability, social behavior, body concept, and preferred defense mechanisms. Materials include cards with complex figures, cards with simple figures, and a stylus for tracing. A stopwatch with a second hand also is needed. Two alternate forms are available.

Format: Examiner required; individual administration; untimed: 10 to 45 minutes

Scoring: Examiner evaluated

Cost: Test Kit (card sets, stylus, 25 recording sheets) $142.36; Manual $33.80

Emotions Profile Index
Robert Plutcik, Henry Kellerman

1974	Western Psychological Services

Population: Adolescents, adults

Purpose: Measures personality traits and conflicts; used for counseling and guidance, therapy, and diagnostic evaluations

Description: Paper-pencil 62-item forced-choice test in which the subject chooses which of the

two words presented in each item best describes himself or herself. Four bipolar scales measure eight dimensions of emotions: Timed vs. Aggressive, Trustful vs. Distrustful, Controlled vs. Dyscontrolled, and Gregarious vs. Depressed. A unique circular profile displays percentile scores and compares the basic personality dimensions. Norms are provided on 1,000 normal adult men and women. Data also are given for certain special groups.

Format: Examiner required; individual and group administration; untimed: 10 to 15 minutes

Scoring: Examiner evaluated

Cost: Kit (manual, 25 tests and profile sheets) $45.00

Employee Assistance Program Inventory (EAPI)
William D. Anton, James R. Reed

1994	Psychological Assessment Resources, Inc.

Population: Adults

Purpose: Used in employee assistance programs and counseling to screen for identification of common psychological problems in 10 areas

Description: Four-point scale inventory with 120 items on the following 10 scales: Anxiety, Depression, Self-Esteem Problems, Marital Problems, Family Problems, External Stressors, Interpersonal Conflict, Work Adjustment, Problem Minimization, and Effects of Substance Abuse. A third-grade reading level is required.

Format: Self-administered; untimed

Scoring: Hand-scorable answer sheet

Cost: Intro Kit (manual, reusable item booklets, answer profile sheet) $55.00

Eysenck Personality Inventory (EPI)
H. J. Eysenck, Sybil B. G. Eysenck

1963	EdITS/Educational and Industrial Testing Service

Population: Adolescents, adults

Purpose: Measures extroversion and neuroticism, the two dimensions of personality that account for most personality variance; used for counseling, clinical evaluation, and research

Description: Paper-pencil 57-item yes-no inventory measuring two independent dimensions of personality: extroversion-introversion and neuroticism-stability. A falsification scale detects response distortion. Scores are provided for three scales: Extroversion, Neuroticism, and Lie. The inventory is available in two equivalent forms, A and B, for pre- and posttesting. The instrument also is available in Industrial Form A-I for industrial workers. College norms are presented as percentiles for Forms A and B, both separately and combined. Adult norms are presented for Form A-I. Also available in Spanish.

Format: Self-administered; suitable for group use; untimed: 10 to 15 minutes

Scoring: Hand key; may be computer scored

Cost: Specimen Set (manual, one copy of all forms) $7.75

Friedman Well-Being Scale
Philip Friedman

1994	Mind Garden, Inc.

Population: Adults

Purpose: Can easily be used to track changes over time during psychotherapy or during other intervention modalities

Description: The Friedman Well-Being Scale consists of 20 bi-popular adjectives. It is easy to administer, score, and interpret. It can be scored for an overall measure of well-being and for five subscales: emotional stability, self-esteem/self-confidence, joviality, sociability, and happiness. Norms exist for clinical, college, and community populations The scale correlates significantly in the expected directions with over 100 clinical, personality, attitudinal, stress, relational, marital, and interpersonal scales and subscales. It can easily be used to track changes and serves as an excellent outcome measure of change in the current health care environment.

Format: Examiner or self-administered; untimed: 5 to 10 minutes

Scoring: Hand key

Cost: Sampler Set $25.00; Review Set $20.00; Permission Set $125.00

Fundamental Interpersonal Relations Orientation–Behavior (FIRO-B™)
Will Schutz, Marilyn Wood

Date not provided	Consulting Psychologists Press, Inc.

Population: Ages 13 years and older

Purpose: Measures characteristic behavior of children toward other people; used for counseling and therapy

Description: Paper–pencil 54-item test containing six Guttman-type scales measuring the char-

acteristic behavior of children in the areas of inclusion, control, and affection—the three dimensions of interpersonal behavior described by Schutz in his book, *The Interpersonal Underworld.* The test measures the relative strength of the needs within the individual. Because it does not compare a person with a population, norms are not provided.

Format: Self-administered; untimed: 15 minutes

Scoring: Self-scored

Cost: Preview Kit (booklet, introduction, understanding) $26.30

Fundamental Interpersonal Relations Orientation–Feelings (FIRO-F)
Will Schutz

Date not provided	Consulting Psychologists Press, Inc.

Population: Adults

Purpose: Evaluates an individual's characteristic feelings toward others; used to assess both individual and interactional traits as an aid to counseling and therapy

Description: Paper–pencil 54-item test measuring six dimensions of an individual's feelings toward others: expressed significance, expressed competence, expressed lovability, wanted significance, wanted competence, and wanted lovability. Dimensions parallel the three dimensions of the Fundamental Interpersonal Relations Orientation–Behavior (FIRO-B). The FIRO-F is identical to the FIRO-B except the questions are phrased to assess feelings rather than behaviors.

Format: Self-administered; untimed: 15 minutes

Scoring: Hand key

Cost: 25 Test Booklets $43.40; Scoring Key $61.60

Giannetti On-Line Psychosocial History (GOLPH)
Ronald A. Giannetti

1988	NCS Pearson

Population: Adults

Purpose: Gathers information on an individual's background and current life circumstances; used to obtain psychosocial history for general or psychiatric patients, evaluate job applicants' work history, and obtain criminal offenders' history of legal difficulties

Description: Multiple-choice and completion-item questionnaire presented on microcomputer.

Questions and their order of appearance are determined by answers to the preceding items. The examiner selects from the following areas to gather appropriate information: current living situation, family of origin, client development, educational history, marital history/present family, occupational history/current finances, legal history, symptom screening (physical), symptom screening (psychological), and military history. Questions are presented at a sixth-grade reading level. The length of the examination depends on the areas chosen for exploration and the extent of the individual's problems. A 3- to 12-page report presents the individual's responses in narrative fashion.

Format: Computer/self-administered; untimed: 30 minutes to 2 hours

Scoring: PC-based MICROTEST™ system required

Cost: MICROTEST System (10 administrations) $80.00; 50 administrations $337.50; 100 administrations $600.00

Guilford-Zimmerman Temperament Survey (GZTS)
J. P. Guilford, Wayne S. Zimmerman

Date not provided	Consulting Psychologists Press, Inc.

Population: Adults

Purpose: Identifies nonclinical personality and temperament; can be used for crisis intervention, assertiveness training, and desensitization

Description: Records orientation on 10 scales (general activity, restraint, ascendancy, socialibility, emotional stability, objectivity, friendliness, thoughtfulness, personal relations, and masculinity/femininity) to identify positive and negative temperament.

Format: Individual administration; 45 minutes

Scoring: Hand key; scoring service

Cost: Preview Kit (manual, booklet, answer sheet) $52.00

Hassles and Uplifts Scale (HSUP)
Richard S. Lazarus, Susan Folkman

1989	Mind Garden, Inc.

Population: Adults

Purpose: Measures respondents' attitudes about daily situations; used in counseling and in clinical settings

Description: Likert scale measuring the frequency

and severity of hassles and the frequency and intensity of uplifts. An eighth-grade reading level is required.

Format: Self-administered; untimed: 30 minutes

Scoring: Examiner evaluated

Cost: Sampler Set $25.00; Permission for 200 Uses $125.00

Health and Daily Living Form (HDL)
Rudolf H. Moos, Ruth C. Cronkite, John W. Finney

1990	Mind Garden, Inc.

Population: Adolescents, adults

Purpose: Assesses health-related factors, life stressors, social functioning, and resources; used by health psychologists and clinicians

Description: A structured yes–no test for patient and community groups. An eighth-grade reading level is required.

Format: Examiner required; individual administration; untimed

Scoring: Examiner evaluated

Cost: Sampler Set $25.00; Permission for 200 Uses $125.00

Hilson Adolescent Profile (HAP)
Robin E. Inwald

1984	Hilson Research, Inc.

Population: Ages 10 to 18 years

Purpose: Identifies and predicts troubled or delinquent behavior in adolescents

Description: Behaviorally oriented 310-item paper–pencil true-false test consisting of a validity measure and 15 scales assessing specific external behaviors, attitudes and temperament, interpersonal adjustment measures, and internalized conflict measures: Guardedness, Alcohol, Drugs, Educational Adjustment Difficulties, Law/Society Violations, Frustration Tolerance, Antisocial/ Risk-Taking Attitudes, Rigidity/Obsessiveness, Interpersonal/Assertiveness Difficulties, Homelife Conflicts, Social/Sexual Adjustment, Health Concerns, Anxiety/Phobic Avoidance, Depression/ Suicide Potential, Suspicious Temperament, and Unusual Responses. Raw scores and three sets of *t*-scores are provided for each scale. The *t*-scores are based on juvenile offender norms, clinical inpatient norms, and student norms. A fifth- to sixth-grade reading level is required. A computer scoring service available. The publisher provides mail-in and teleprocessing services.

Format: Self-administered; untimed: 30 to 45 minutes

Scoring: Computer scored

Cost: Contact publisher

Human Relations Inventory
Raymond S. Bemberg

1981	Psychometric Affiliates

Population: Adolescents in Grades 10 and above, adults

Purpose: Measures a person's tendency toward social or lawful conformity; differentiates between conformist and nonconformist individuals

Description: Multiple-item paper-pencil test measuring an individual's sense of social conformity. Social conformity is defined and tested in terms of moral values, positive goals, reality testing, ability to give affection, tension level, and impulsivity. The test is constructed using the "direction of perception" technique, and the purpose of the test is disguised from subjects to produce more valid results. The test discriminates between samples of law violators and ordinary conformists. Norms are provided for high school boys, college students, regular churchgoers, Los Angeles police officers, male inmates of a California youth prison, adult male inmates of the Los Angeles County Jail, and adult female inmates of the Los Angeles County Jail.

Format: Examiner required; suitable for group use; untimed

Scoring: Examiner evaluated

Cost: Specimen Set $5.00; 25 Inventories $5.00

Impact Message Inventory
*Donald J. Kiesler, Jack C. Anchin,
Michael J. Perkins, Bernie M. Chirico,
Edgar M. Kyle, Edward J. Federman*

1991	Mind Garden, Inc.

Population: Adolescents, adults

Purpose: Measures the affective, behavioral, and cognitive reactions of one individual to another; is helpful in clarifying interpersonal transactions in any dyad, including teacher-student, friends, employer-employee, and therapist-client

Description: Paper-pencil 90-item inventory assessing one individual's reactions to the interpersonal or personality style of another person. Items describe ways in which people are emotionally engaged or affected when interacting with another person. Individuals respond on a 4-point scale ranging from *not at all* to *very much so* to indicate the extent to which each item describes the feeling aroused by the other person, behaviors they want to direct toward the other person, or descriptions of the other person that come to mind when in the other person's presence. Each test item describes a reaction elicited by a person high on one of 15 interpersonal dimensions. Scores are derived for each of the 15 subscales as well as for four cluster scores. The manual includes descriptions of the subscales and tables for converting raw scores to *T*-scores.

Format: Examiner required; suitable for group use; untimed: 15 minutes

Scoring: Examiner evaluated

Cost: Sampler Set $25.00; Permission for 200 Uses $125.00; Test Booklets $25.00

Interpersonal Adjective Scales (IAS)
Jerry S. Wiggins

1995	Psychological Assessment Resources, Inc.

Population: Adults

Purpose: Used in personality assessment to measure the two most important dimensions of interpersonal behavior: dominance and nurturance

Description: Paper-pencil 64-item 8-point scale with the following categories: Cold Hearted, Aloof-Introverted, Unassured-Submissive, Unassuming-Ingenious, Warm-Agreeable, and Gregarious-Extroverted. A 10th-grade reading level is required. Examiner must be B-level qualified. A computer version using IBM-compatible computers is available. Also available in Spanish.

Format: Self-administered; untimed: 15 minutes

Scoring: Hand-scored answer sheet

Cost: Intro Kit (manual, test booklet, scoring booklet) $96.00

Interpersonal Communication Inventory
Millard J. Bienvenu

1969	Northwest Publications

Population: Ages 13 years and older

Purpose: Assesses the level and characteristics of an individual's communication with others; used in counseling, management training, teaching, research, and communication skills training

Description: Yes-no-sometimes test with 40 items. A seventh-grade reading level is required.

Examiner must have communication skills experience.

Format: Self-administered; suitable for group use; untimed: 15 minutes

Scoring: Hand key

Cost: $.75 per copy; Guide $3.00 (minimum order of $10.00)

Interpersonal Style Inventory (ISI)
Maurice Lorr, Richard P. Youniss

1985	Western Psychological Services

Population: Ages 14 years and older

Purpose: Assesses an individual's manner of interacting with other people and style of impulse control; used for self-understanding, counseling and therapy, personnel guidance; and research

Description: Paper-pencil 300-item true-false inventory assessing an individual's style of interpersonal interactions along 15 primary scales: Directive, Sociable, Help-Seeking, Nurturant, Conscientious, Trusting, Tolerant, Sensitive, Deliberate, Independent, Rule Free, Orderly, Persistent, Stable, and Approval Seeking. Each item is a statement describing ways in which people relate and respond to each other. The individual reads each statement and decides whether it is mostly true or not true for himself or herself. High school and college norms are provided by gender. The computer report includes a full-color ChromaGraph profile of major scores.

Format: Self-administered; untimed: 30 minutes

Scoring: Computer scored

Cost: Test Kit (manual, 2 reusable administration booklets, 20 AutoScore forms, 2-use disk, 2 PC answer sheets) $125.00

Inventory of Altered Self-Capacities (IASC)
John Briere

2000	Psychological Assessment Resources, Inc.

Population: Ages 18 years and older

Purpose: Assesses difficulties in relatedness, identity, and affect control

Description: The IASC is a 63-item self-report with seven scales with nine items each. Two scales have subscales.

Format: Self-administered; untimed: 10 to 15 minutes

Scoring: Examiner evaluated

Cost: Kit (manual, 25 reusable item booklets, 25 handscorable answer sheets, 50 profile forms) $135.00

Inventory of Interpersonal Problems (IIP-64 and IIP-32)
Leonard M. Horowitz, Lynn E. Alden, Jerry S. Wiggins, Aaron L. Pincus

2000	The Psychological Corporation

Population: Ages 18 years and older

Purpose: Assesses interpersonal problems

Description: Identify stressful interpersonal problems people experience with this easily administered self-report inventory. Two versions (64 items and 32 items) measure controlling or manipulative behavior, self-centeredness, and six other personality characteristics.

Format: Self-report; untimed: 10 to 15 minutes

Scoring: Examiner evaluated

Cost: Complete Kit (manual, 25 each of 64- and 32-item scoring and question sheets) $105.00

Inventory of Positive Thinking Traits
Millard J. Bienvenu

1992	Northwest Publications

Population: Ages 13 years and older

Purpose: Assesses negativity and positivity in individuals; used in counseling, human relations, training, and teaching

Description: Yes-no-sometimes test with 34 items. A seventh-grade reading level is required. Examiner must be trained in human relations.

Format: Self-administered; untimed: 10 minutes

Scoring: Hand key

Cost: $.50 each; Guide $1.00 (minimum order of $10.00)

Jackson Personality Inventory Revised (JPI-R)
Douglas N. Jackson

1997	Sigma Assessment Systems, Inc.

Population: Adolescents, adults

Purpose: Assesses personality characteristics of normal people who have average and above-average intelligence; used to evaluate behavior in a wide range of settings, including those involving work, education, organizations, interpersonal, and performance

Description: Paper-pencil 300-item true-false test covering 15 substantive scales and one validity scale. The scales measured are Complexity, Breadth of Interest, Innovation, Tolerance, Empathy, Anxiety, Cooperativeness, Sociability, Social Confidence, Energy Level, Social Astuteness, Risk Taking, Organization, Traditional Values, and Responsibility. Norms include updated college norms, and new norms for blue- and white-collar workers. This test differs from the Personality Research Form in terms of the nature of the variables measured and is a further refinement of substantive psychometric and computer-based strategies for scale development. Machine-readable answer sheets may be mailed to the publisher for a computer-generated report. Test booklets are also available in French.

Format: Examiner required; suitable for group use; untimed: 45 minutes

Scoring: Hand key; computer scored; scoring service available from publisher

Cost: Examination Kit (manual, 10 quick-score answer sheets, 10 profile sheets, 1 report) $62.00

Make a Picture Story (MAPS)
Edwin S. Shneidman

1947	Western Psychological Services

Population: Adolescents, adults

Purpose: Measures fantasies, defenses, and impulses

Description: Projective oral-response test consists of 22 stimulus cards and a set of 67 cutout figures. Stimulus cards range from structured situations (bedroom, bathroom, schoolroom, baby's room) to more ambiguous presentations (a blank doorway, a cave, and a totally blank card). Figures include men, women, boys, girls, policemen, mythical characters, animals, people with disabilities, nudes, and a variety of frequently encountered individuals. The examiner asks the individual to select a stimulus card, place figures on the background stimulus card, and tell a story explaining those choices. The individual may also be asked to act out a story about the figures and their environment. The Location Sheet is used to record the placement of the figures on the stimulus card.

Format: Examiner required; individual administration; untimed

Scoring: Examiner evaluated

Cost: Kit (set of test materials, manual, 25 Location Sheets) $90.00

Mathematics Self-Efficacy Scale
Nancy Betz, Gail Hacket

1993	Mind Garden, Inc.

Population: Adults

Purpose: Measures degree of confidence in person's ability to perform certain math tasks

Description: This scale is intended to measure a person's beliefs regarding his or her ability to perform various math-related tasks and behaviors. Subjects are asked to indicate their degree of confidence in their ability to perform each math task on a 10-point scale ranging from *not at all difficult* to *extremely difficult* .

Format: Individual or group administration; untimed: 15 minutes

Scoring: Examiner evaluated

Cost: Sampler Set $25.00; Review Set $20.00; Permission Set $125.00

Measure of Achieving Tendency
Albert Mehrabian

1994	Albert Mehrabian, PhD

Population: Adults

Purpose: Assesses an individual's motivation to achieve; used for research, counseling, and employee selection and placement purposes

Description: Multiple-item verbal questionnaire assessing all major components of achievement. Test items are based on extensive factor-analytic investigation of most experimentally identified components of achievement.

Format: Self-administered; untimed: 10 minutes

Scoring: Hand key

Cost: Test Kit (test manual, scales, scoring directions, norms) $33.00

Measure of Arousal Seeking Tendency
Albert Mehrabian

1994	Albert Mehrabian, PhD

Population: Adults

Purpose: Assesses an individual's desire for change, stimulation, and arousal; used for research, job placement, and counseling purposes

Description: Multiple-item verbal questionnaire measures individual's arousal-seeking tendencies.

Test items are based on extensive factor-analytic and experimental studies of all aspects of change-seeking, sensation-seeking, variety-seeking, and, generally, desire to master high-uncertainty situations.

Format: Self-administered; untimed: 10 minutes

Scoring: Hand key

Cost: Test Kit (scale, scoring directions, norms, descriptive material) $33.00

Measure of Stimulus Screening (Converse of Arousability)
Albert Mehrabian

1994	Albert Mehrabian, PhD

Population: Adults

Purpose: Measures major components of arousability and stimulus screening; used for research, counseling, and job placement purposes

Description: Multiple-item verbal questionnaire assessing the extent of an individual's arousal response to complex, unexpected, or unfamiliar situations. The test items are based on extensive factor-analytic and experimental investigations of all major components of arousability and stimulus screening. Stimulus screening/arousability has been shown to be a major component of many important emotional characteristics, such as anxiety, neuroticism, extroversion, or hostility.

Format: Self-administered; suitable for group use; untimed: 10 minutes

Scoring: Examiner evaluated

Cost: Test Kit (scales, scoring directions, norms, descriptive material) $33.00

Measures of Affiliative Tendency and Sensitivity to Rejection
Albert Mehrabian

1994	Albert Mehrabian, PhD

Population: Adults

Purpose: Assesses an individual's friendliness, sociability, and general interpersonal and social approach–avoidance characteristics; used for research and counseling purposes

Description: Multiple-item verbal questionnaire consisting of two subscales: affiliative tendency and sensitivity to rejection. The standardized sum of the scores on both subscales also provides a reliable and valid measure of dependency.

Format: Self-administered; untimed: 10 minutes per scale

Scoring: Hand key

Cost: Test Kit (scales, scoring directions, norms, descriptive material) $33.00

Measures of Psychosocial Development (MPD)
Gwen A. Hawley

1988	Psychological Assessment Resources, Inc.

Population: Ages 13 years and older

Purpose: Provides an index of overall psychosocial health and personality development through the eight stages of the life span based on Erik Erikson's criteria

Description: Paper–pencil 112-item multiple-choice test that provides a measure of the positive and negative attitudes or attributes of personality associated with each developmental stage, the status of conflict resolution at each stage, and overall psychosocial health. The items are rated on a 5-point scale ranging from *very much like me* to *not at all like me*. Results are reported as *T*-scores or percentiles and can be plotted on profile forms, which are available separately for males and females by age groups from 13 to 50+. Interpretation of the MPD is consistent with Erikson's focus on healthy personality development and growth, rather than a pathology-oriented focus. A sixth-grade reading level is required.

Format: Examiner required; suitable for group use; untimed: 15 to 20 minutes

Scoring: Hand key

Cost: Kit (manual, reusable item booklets, answer sheets, male and female profile forms) $115.00

Memories of Father (MOF)
Arnold R. Bruhn

1993	Arnold R. Bruhn, Publisher

Population: Adults

Purpose: Designed for individuals who have experienced a conflicted relationship

Description: A structured method of exploring the relationship and lifetime with father (or a paternal surrogate), based on the individual's memories of this relationship. It is recommended for individuals who have experienced a conflicted relationship with their father for some period in their lives and suspect that patterns arising from that relationship may be affecting their lives now.

Format: Examiner required; individual or group administration; untimed

Scoring: Examiner evaluated

Cost: 25 Tests $140.00

Memories of Mother (MOM)
Arnold R. Bruhn

1993	Arnold R. Bruhn, Publisher

Population: Adults

Purpose: Designed for individuals who have experienced a conflicted relationship with their mothers

Description: A structured method of exploring the relationship and lifetime with mother (or a maternal surrogate), based on the individual's memories of this relationship. It is recommended for individuals who have experienced a conflicted relationship with their mother for some period in their lives and suspect that patterns arising from that relationship may be affecting their lives now.

Format: Examiner required; individual or group administration; untimed

Scoring: Examiner evaluated

Cost: 25 Tests $140.00

Millon Adolescent Personality Inventory (MAPI)
Theodore Millon, Catherine J. Green, Robert B. Meagher, Jr.

1982	NCS Pearson

Population: Ages 13 to 18 years

Purpose: Evaluates adolescent personality; used as an aid to clinical assessment and academic and vocational guidance; identifies student behavioral and emotional problems

Description: True–false test with 150 items covering eight personality style scales, eight expressed concern scales (such as peer security), and four behavioral correlate scales (such as impulse control). The clinical version is coordinated with the DSM-III-R and is available to those with experience in the use of self-administered clinical tests.

Format: Examiner required; suitable for group use; untimed: 20 to 30 minutes

Scoring: Computer scored

Cost: Manual $17.50; Clinical Interpretive Report $14.55 to $19.90 depending on quantity and scoring method; Guidance Interpretive Report $6.10 to $9.95 depending on quantity and scoring method

Millon Behavioral Health Inventory (MBHI™)
Theodore Millon, Catherine J. Green, Robert B. Meagher, Jr.

1982	NCS Pearson

Population: Adults

Purpose: Assesses attitudes of physically ill adults toward daily stress factors and health care personnel; used for clinical evaluation of possible psychosomatic complications

Description: True–false inventory with 150 items covering eight basic coping styles (e.g., cooperation), six psychogenic attitudes (e.g., chronic tension), three psychosomatic correlatives (e.g., allergic inclinations), and three prognostic indexes (e.g., pain treatment responsivity). The test is designed for use with medical patients by examiners experienced in the use of clinical instruments.

Format: Self-administered; untimed: 20 minutes

Scoring: Computer scored

Cost: Manual $16.50; Interpretive Report $12.95 to $18.15 depending on quantity and scoring method

Millon Clinical Multiaxial Inventory (MCMI™)
Theodore Millon

1976	NCS Pearson

Population: Adults with psychological or psychiatric disturbances

Purpose: Diagnoses emotionally disturbed adults; used to screen individuals who may require more intensive clinical evaluation and treatment

Description: True–false test with 175 items for evaluating adults who have psychological or psychiatric difficulties. The test covers three categories that include eight basic personality patterns (DSM-III Axis II) reflecting a patient's lifelong traits existing prior to the behavioral dysfunctions; three pathological personality disorders (DSM-III Axis II) reflecting chronic or severe abnormalities, and nine clinical symptom syndromes (DSM-IIII Axis I) describing episodes or states in which active pathological processes are clearly evidenced. The examiner must be experienced in the use of clinical tests. Interpretation is available exclusively from NCS, and test results are available immediately via Arion II teleprocessing or PC-based MICROTEST™ Assessment system. Mail-in computer scoring services also are provided.

Format: Self-administered; untimed: 25 minutes

Scoring: Computer scored; may be hand scored

Cost: Manual $21.00; Interpretive Report $21.25 to $28.35 depending on quantity and scoring method; Profile Report $5.75 to $8.00 depending on quantity and scoring method

Millon Index of Personality Styles (MIPS®)
Theodore Millon

1994	The Psychological Corporation

Population: Ages 18 through 65+ years

Purpose: Assesses normal-range personality

Description: Identify, understand, and assist normally functioning adults who are experiencing difficulties that may show up in work settings, marital or family situations, or other everyday social relationships. The MIPS explores three personality domains and produces the common 16 Jungian types. The unobtrusive item content is readily accepted by clients without serious psychiatric disturbances. Expert interpretive reports are available. An Overall Adjustment Index summarizes client status.

Format: Self-administered; can be administered on computer or on-line; untimed: 30 minutes

Scoring: Hand key; computer scoring; scoring service; on-line

Cost: Contact publisher (depends on scoring method)

Minnesota Multiphasic Personality Inventory–Adolescent™ (MMPI-A™)

Date not provided	NCS Pearson

Population: Ages 14 to 18 years

Purpose: Assists with the diagnosis of mental disorders and the selection of appropriate treatment methods

Description: The MMPI-A provides descriptive and diagnostic information pertinent to today's patients and clients. In addition, tailored reports present interpretive information for specific settings and applications to help meet a wide range of needs. The normative sample is nationally representative, consisting of 805 males and 815 females. Uniform T scores are provided for eight of the clinical scales and the content scales, ensuring percentile equivalency across scales. New validity scales were developed to help refine the clinician's assessment of test-taking attitudes. The test is written at a sixth-grade level.

Format: Self-administration; on-line administration; untimed: 45 to 60 minutes

Scoring: Hand key; software scoring available; scoring service available

Cost: Hand-Scoring Introductory Kit (manual, 10 test booklets, 50 each of answer and profile forms, answer key sets) $415.00

Minnesota Multiphasic Personality Inventory–Second Edition™ (MMPI-2™)

2001	NCS Pearson

Population: Adults

Purpose: Assists with the diagnosis of mental disorders and the selection of appropriate treatment methods

Description: The MMPI-2 provides descriptive and diagnostic information pertinent to today's patients and clients. In addition, tailored reports present interpretive information for specific settings and applications to help meet a wide range of needs. The normative sample is nationally representative, consisting of 1,138 males and 1,462 females between the ages of 18 and 80. Uniform T scores were developed because percentiles for the traditional linear T scores are not strictly comparable from scale to scale. Written at a sixth-grade reading level.

Format: Self-administration; on-line administration; untimed: 60 to 90 minutes

Scoring: Hand key; software scoring available; scoring service available

Cost: Hand-Scoring Introductory Kit (manual, 10 test booklets, 50 each of answer and profile forms, answer key sets) $500.00

MMPI-2 Report
Giles D. Rainwater

2000	Psychometric Software, Inc.

Population: Adults

Purpose: Generates interpretations of the MMPI profiles

Description: This scoring service generates a 27-item report that is derived from the administration of the Minnesota Multiphasic Personality Inventory–Second Edition.

Format: Examiner required; individual administration; untimed

Scoring: Scoring service

Cost: $195.95

Mooney Problem Check Lists
R. L. Mooney, L. V. Gordon

1950	The Psychological Corporation

Population: Grades 7 and above

Purpose: Identifies individuals who want or need help with personal problems; used for individual counseling, increasing teacher understanding of students, and preparing students for counseling interviews

Description: Multiple-item paper–pencil self-assessment of personal problems. The subjects read examples of problems, underline those of "some concern," circle those of "most concern," and write a summary in their own words. The areas covered vary from form to form but include health and physical development, home and family, boy and girl relations, morals and religion, courtship and marriage, economic security, school or occupation, and social and recreational. Materials include separate checklists for junior high students, high school students, college students, and adults.

Format: Self-administered; untimed: 30 minutes

Scoring: Hand key; may be machine scored

Cost: Examination Kit (checklists and manual for all levels combined) $34.00

Multiple Affect Adjective Checklist–Revised (MAACL–R)
Marvin Zuckerman, Bernard Lubin

1965	EdITS/Educational and Industrial Testing Service

Population: High school and college students, adults

Purpose: Measures positive and negative affects as both traits and states; used in studies of stress and stress reduction, diagnosis and treatment of psychological disorders, and in basic research on personality and emotions

Description: Multiple-item paper–pencil inventory measuring the affects of Anxiety (A), Depression (D), Hostility (H), Positive Affect (PA), and Sensation Seeking (SS). This revised edition contains trait and state forms that have been shown to differentiate patients with affective disorders from other types of patients and normal individuals. The test yields two summary scores: Dysphoria (A + D + H) and Positive Affect and Sensation Seeking (PA + SS).

Format: Examiner/self-administered; suitable for group use; untimed: 5 minutes per form

Scoring: Hand key; may be computer scored

Cost: Specimen Set $27.75

Myers–Briggs Type Indicator (MBTI)
Isabel Briggs Myers, Katharine C. Briggs

Date not provided	Consulting Psychologists Press, Inc.

Population: Ages 14 years through adult

Purpose: Measures personality dispositions and interests based on Jung's theory of types; used in executive development programs, educational settings, and personality research, and personal, vocational, and marital counseling

Description: Several forms with different purposes: 166-item Form F for research, 126-item Form G, 94-item Form G self-scorable, 126-item Form G in Spanish, 131-item Form K for understanding differences, or 290-item Form J for clinical settings test of four bipolar aspects of personality: Introversion-Extroversion, Sensing-Intuition, Thinking-Feeling, and Judging-Perceiving. The various combinations of these preferences result in 16 personality types. The inventory is written at the eighth-grade reading level. The available reports are Profile, Narrative Report, Team Report, Organizational Report, Career Report, Expanded Analysis Report, Type Differentiation Indicator Report, and Relationship Report. Many interpretive guides are available to aid the examiner. A software package is available for use with IBM-compatible PCs.

Format: Self-administered; untimed: 20 to 30 minutes

Scoring: Hand key; scoring service

Cost: Contact publisher

NEO Five-Factor Inventory (NEO-FFI)
Paul T. Costa, Jr., Robert R. McCrae

1989	Psychological Assessment Resources, Inc.

Population: Ages 17 years and older

Purpose: Assesses the five major personality domains; used in clinical psychology, psychiatry, behavioral medicine, vocational counseling, and industrial psychology

Description: Paper-pencil 60-item multiple-choice test providing a general description of an adult's personality. The NEO-FFI is a shortened version of the NEO Personality Inventory-Revised. Domains assessed are Neuroticism, Extroversion, Openness to Experience, Agreeableness, and Conscientiousness. The NEO-FFI is based on NEO-PI-R normative data and is interpreted in the same manner. Correlations with NEO-PI-R validimax factors range from .75 to .89. Examiner must meet B-level guidelines.

Format: Examiner required; suitable for group use; untimed

Scoring: Hand key

Cost: Kit (manual, summary sheets, test booklets) $109.00

NEO Personality Inventory–Revised (NEO-PI-R™)
Paul T. Costa, Jr., Robert R. McCrae

| 1992 | Psychological Assessment Resources, Inc. |

Population: Adults

Purpose: Measures five major personality domains of adults; used in clinical psychology, psychiatry, behavioral medicine, vocational counseling, and industrial psychology

Description: Paper–pencil 240-item test providing a general description of an adult's personality. Domains assessed are Neuroticism (N), Extroversion (E), Openness to Experience (O), Agreeableness (A), and Conscientiousness (C). Facet scales for all domains yield a more detailed analysis of personality structure. Domain N scales are anxiety, angry hostility, depression, self-consciousness, impulsiveness, and vulnerability. Domain E scales are warmth, gregariousness, assertiveness, activity, excitement-seeking, and positive emotions. Domain O scales are fantasy, aesthetics, feelings, actions, ideas, and values. Domain A facets are trust, straightforwardness, altruism, compliance, modesty, and tender-mindedness. Domain C facets are competence, order, dutifulness, achievement striving, self-discipline, and deliberation. Two versions (self and other rating) of the inventory are available. Form S and Form R are appropriate for men and women. Answers are provided on a 5-point scale.

Format: Self-administered; untimed: 30 minutes

Scoring: Hand key; may be computer scored; scoring service available

Cost: Comprehensive Kit $182.00

New York Longitudinal Scales: Adult Temperament Inventory

| Date not provided | Behavioral-Developmental Initiatives |

Population: Ages 18 to 40 years

Purpose: Assesses temperament characteristics in adults

Description: Rating scale with 54 items measuring Activity Level, Regularity, Approach, Intensity, Mood, Persistence, and Distractibility Threshold.

Format: Rating scale; untimed: 15 minutes

Scoring: Examiner evaluated; computer scoring available

Cost: Specimen Set (one of each questionnaire, scoring/profile sheets, manual) $69.95; Report Writer Software with unlimited use $495.00

Offer Self-Image Questionnaire for Adolescents–Revised (OSIQ-R)
D. Offer, E. Ostrov, K. I. Howard, S. Dolan

| 1992 | Western Psychological Services |

Population: Ages 13 to 19 years

Purpose: Used to measure adjustment and self-image in adolescents

Description: Composed of 129 simple statements, the questionnaire measures adjustment in 12 areas: impulse control, emotional tone, body image, social functioning, self-reliance, sexuality, family functioning, self-confidence, vocational attitudes, ethical values, mental health, and idealism using a 6-point response scale. The OSIQ-R yields conventional *T*-scores and validity checks.

Format: Examiner required; individual administration; untimed: 30 minutes

Scoring: Examiner evaluated; computer scored; scoring service available

Cost: Kit (manual, 2 reusable administration booklets, 5 prepaid mail-in answer sheets for computer scoring and interpretation) $99.50; PC disk $229.00

Personal Orientation Dimensions (POD)
Everett L. Shostrom

| 1975 | EdITS/Educational and Industrial Testing Service |

Population: Adults

Purpose: Measures attitudes and values in terms of concepts of the actualizing person; used to introduce humanistic value concepts, indicate a person's level of positive mental health, and measure the effects of various treatment and training techniques

Description: Paper–pencil 260-item two-choice test consisting of bipolar pairs of statements of comparative values and behavior judgments. The subject must choose from each pair the statement that is closest to his or her beliefs. Items are stated both negatively and positively;

opposites are dictated not by word choice but by context. Test items are nonthreatening in order to facilitate communication of the results and provide a positive approach for measuring the following personality dimensions: orientation (time orientation and core centeredness), polarities (strength/weakness and love/anger), integration (synergistic integration and potentiation), and awareness (being, trust in humanity, creative living, mission and manipulation awareness). Test results indicate whether (and to what degree) an individual is actualizing or nonactualizing. The inventory may be used as a component of the Actualizing Assessment Battery (AAB).

Format: Examiner required; suitable for group use; untimed: 30 to 40 minutes

Scoring: Computer scored

Cost: Specimen Set (manual, all forms) $7.25

Personal Orientation Inventory (POI)
Everett L. Shostrom

1994-1997	EdITS/Educational and Industrial Testing Service

Population: Adolescents, adults

Purpose: Measures values and behaviors important in the development of the actualizing person; used in counseling and group training sessions and as a pre- and posttherapy measure to indicate a person's level of positive mental health

Description: Paper–pencil 150-item two-choice test containing bipolar pairs of statements of comparative values and behavioral judgments. The subject must choose from each pair the statement that is closest to his or her beliefs. The inventory is scored for two major scales and 10 subscales: Time Ratio, Support Ratio, Self-Actualizing Value, Existentiality, Feeling Reactivity, Spontaneity, Self-Regard, Self-Acceptance, Nature of Man, Synergy, Acceptance of Aggression, and Capacity for Intimate Contact. College norms are presented in percentile scores. Adult mean scores and profiles are provided. Means, standard deviations, and plotted profiles are provided for clinically nominated self-actualized and non–self-actualized groups, as well as for many other clinical and industrial samples. The inventory may be used as a component for group use. Also available in Spanish and French.

Format: Examiner required; suitable for group use; untimed: 30 minutes

Scoring: Hand key; computer scoring service available from EdITS if machine-scoring answer sheets are used

Cost: Specimen Set (manual, all forms) $8.75; Manual $5.00; 25 Test Booklets $21.50; 50 Answer Sheets $14.75

Personality Assessment Inventory (PAI)
Leslie C. Morey

1991	Psychological Assessment Resources, Inc.

Population: Ages 18 years and older

Purpose: Used in forensic psychology and personality assessment to assess adult psychopathology

Description: Paper–pencil 4-point Likert scale with 344 items; four Validity Scales: inconsistency, infrequency, negative impression, and positive impression; 11 Clinical Scales and Subscales: somatic complaints, anxiety, anxiety-related disorders, depression, mania, paranoia, schizophrenia, borderline features, antisocial features, alcohol problems, and drug problems; five Treatment Scales: aggression, suicidal ideation, stress, nonsupport, and treatment rejection; and two Interpersonal Scales: dominance and warmth. A fourth-grade reading level is required. A computer version using PC is available. Spanish version also available.

Format: Examiner required; individual administration; untimed: 50 to 60 minutes

Scoring: Hand key; computer scoring available

Cost: Comprehensive Kit (manual, reusable item book, hand-scorable answer sheets, profile forms, critical items forms) $194.00

Personality Research Form (PRF)
Douglas N. Jackson

1997	Sigma Assessment Systems, Inc

Population: Grades 6 and above

Purpose: Assesses personality traits relevant to the functioning of an individual in a variety of situations; used in self-improvement courses and guidance centers and for personnel selection

Description: True–false paper–pencil or computer-administered test in five forms. Forms AA and BB contain 440 items covering 22 areas of normal functioning. Form E has 352 items in 22 scales. Forms A and B have 300 items in 15 scales. The 22 scales measured are Abasement, Achievement, Affiliation, Aggression, Autonomy, Change, Cognitive Structure, Defendance, Dominance, Endurance, Exhibition, Harm-Avoidance, Impulsivity, Nurturance, Order, Play, Sentience, Social Recognition, Succorance, Understanding,

Infrequency, and Desirability. A 90-minute audio-cassette with simplified wording is available for use with those who have limited verbal skills, sight, or reading abilities. The computer version operates on PC-compatible systems. Form E also available in French and Spanish.

Format: Suitable for group use; Form E 1 hour; Forms A and B 45 minutes; Forms AA and BB 1 hour, 15 minutes; audiocassette 90 minutes

Scoring: Hand key; computer scored; scoring service available from publisher

Cost: Examination Kit (manual, 5 test booklets, 10 scoring answer sheets, 10 profile sheets, scoring template, report) $64.00

Pictorial Study of Values
Charles Shooster

1986	Psychometric Affiliates

Population: Adult

Purpose: Examines personal values; used for self-awareness programs, discussion groups, and research on values and mores

Description: Multiple-item paper–pencil test measuring reactions to six basic value areas: social, political, economic, religious, aesthetic, and theoretical. Test items are composed of photographs. College norms are provided. Suitable for people who are illiterate and non-English-speakers.

Format: Examiner required; suitable for group use; untimed: 20 minutes

Scoring: Examiner evaluated

Cost: Specimen Set $5.00; 25 Tests $5.00

Polyfactorial Study of Personality
Ronald Stark

1959	Martin M. Bruce, PhD

Population: Adults

Purpose: Aids in the clinical evaluation of an individual's personality

Description: Pencil-paper 300-item true–false test measuring 11 aspects of psychopathology: hypochondriasis, sexual identification, anxiety, social distance, sociopathy, depression, compulsivity, repression, paranoia, schizophrenia, and hyperaffectivity. Suitable for individuals with physical, hearing, or visual impairments.

Format: Self-administered; untimed: 45 minutes

Scoring: Hand key

Cost: Specimen Set $53.50

Problem Behavior Inventory– Adolescent Symptom Screening Form
Leigh Silverton

Date not provided	Western Psychological Services

Population: Adolescents

Purpose: Used to help clinicians structure and focus diagnostic interview

Description: This inventory lists more than 100 DSM-IV symptoms in clear, simple language. The adolescent checks those symptoms that he or she has experienced. This inventory identifies areas where personality testing might be helpful.

Format: Self-administered; untimed: 10 to 15 minutes

Scoring: Hand key

Cost: 25 AutoScore™ forms $32.00

Problem Behavior Inventory– Adult Symptom Screening Form
Leigh Silverton

Date not provided	Western Psychological Services

Population: Adults

Purpose: Used to help clinicians structure and focus diagnostic interview

Description: This inventory lists more than 100 DSM-IV symptoms in clear, simple language. The client checks those symptoms that he or she has experienced. This inventory guides the initial interview, provides material for the intake report, and identifies areas where personality testing might be helpful.

Format: Self-administered; untimed: 10 to 15 minutes

Scoring: Hand key

Cost: 25 AutoScore™ forms $34.50

Problem Experiences Checklist– Adolescent Version
Leigh Silverton

Date not provided	Western Psychological Services

Population: Adolescents

Purpose: Used to pinpoint problems and identify areas for discussion prior to the initial clinician interview

Description: This checklist gives the clinician a quick picture of the adolescent's life situation, indicating what kind of difficulties he or she is experiencing. More than 250 problems and troubling life events are listed under the following headings: school, opposite sex concerns, peers, family, goals, crises, emotions, recreation, habits, neighborhood, life phase transition, beliefs and attitudes, and occupational and financial circumstances. The adolescent checks the problems that he or she is experiencing.

Format: Self-administered; untimed: 10 to 15 minutes

Scoring: Hand key

Cost: 25 AutoScore™ forms $32.00

Problem Experiences Checklist–Adult Version
Leigh Silverton

Date not provided	Western Psychological Services

Population: Adults

Purpose: Used to help clinician structure and focus diagnostic interview

Description: This checklist gives the clinician a quick picture of the client's life situation, indicating what kind of difficulties he or she is experiencing. More than 200 problems and troubling life events are listed under the following headings: marital relationship, children-parents, financial-legal, bereavement, personal habits, work adjustment, life transition, beliefs and goals, painful memories, and emotions. The client checks the problems that he or she is experiencing.

Format: Self-administered; untimed: 10 to 15 minutes

Scoring: Hand key

Cost: 25 AutoScore™ forms $32.00

Profile of Mood States (POMS)
Douglas M. McNair, Maurice Lorr, Leo Droppleman

1971	EdITS/Educational and Industrial Testing Service

Population: Ages 18 and older

Purpose: Assesses dimensions of affect or mood in individuals; used to measure outpatient's response to various therapeutic approaches, including drug evaluation studies

Description: Paper-pencil 65-item assessment of six dimensions of affect or mood: tension-anxiety, depression-dejection, anger-hostility, vigor-activity, fatigue-inertia, and confusion-bewilderment. An alternative POMS-Bipolar Form measures the following mood dimensions in terms

of six bipolar affective states identified in recent research: composed-anxious, elated-depressed, agreeable-hostile, energetic-tired, clearheaded-confused, and confident-unsure. Norms are provided for POMS-Bipolar for high school, college, and outpatient populations. POMS is available in a shortened form and large print. Also available in French and Japanese.

Format: Examiner required; suitable for group use; untimed: 3 to 5 minutes

Scoring: Hand key; may be computer scored

Cost: Specimen Set (manual, all forms) $8.25

Psychological Screening Inventory (PSI)
Richard I. Lanyon

1978	Sigma Assessment Systems, Inc.

Population: Adolescents, adults

Purpose: Identifies adults and adolescents who may need a more extensive mental health examination or professional attention; used in clinics, hospitals, schools, courts, and reformatories

Description: True-false 130-item inventory covering five scales: Alienation, Social Nonconformity, Discomfort, Expression, and Defensiveness. Also available in Spanish.

Format: Examiner required; suitable for group use; untimed: 15 minutes

Scoring: Hand key

Cost: Examination Kit (manual, 25 test booklets, scoring templates, 25 profile sheets) $54.00

Psychological/Social History Report

1988	Psychometric Software, Inc.

Population: Adults

Purpose: Gathers basic information relevant to a psychological intake interview; used for initiating discussion between the clinician and patient

Description: Multiple-item paper-pencil or computer-administered psychological intake interview covering presenting problem, family/developmental history, education, financial history/status, employment history, military service, alchohol/drug history, medical history, marital/family life, diet/exercise, and psychological/social stressors. The program generates an Important Responses section of patient responses that may be clinically significant. This section allows the clinician to see areas requiring further evaluation. The program operates on Windows.

Format: Examiner required; individual administration; untimed: 30 to 45 minutes

Scoring: Examiner evaluated; may be computer scored

Cost: Computer Version $295.95; Package of Paper-Pencil Questionnaires $10.95

Purpose in Life (PIL)
James C. Crumbaugh, Leonard T. Maholick

1981	Psychometric Affiliates

Population: Adults

Purpose: Measures degree to which an individual has found meaning in life; used with individuals who are addicted, retired, handicapped, or philosophically confused for purposes of clinical assessment, student counseling, vocational guidance, and rehabilitation

Description: Paper-pencil 34-item test assessing an individual's major motivations in life. Subjects must rate 20 statements according to their own beliefs, complete 13 sentence stems, and write an original paragraph describing their aims, ambitions, and goals in life. Based on Victor Frankl's "Will to Meaning," the test embraces his logotherapeutic orientation in recognition of threat of the existential vacuum. Norms are provided for individuals with and without mental disorders. A fourth-grade reading level is required. Also available in Spanish and Portuguese.

Format: Self-administered; suitable for group use; untimed: 10 to 15 minutes

Scoring: Scoring service available

Cost: Specimen Set (manual, test, bibliography) $4.00; 25 Tests $5.00

Quality of Life Inventory (QOLI)
Michael B. Frisch

1994	NCS Pearson

Population: Adults

Purpose: Measures satisfaction and dissatisfaction with life; used for personal counseling, marriage counseling, and outcomes assessment

Description: Computer-administered or paper-pencil 32-item multiple-choice test with a 3-point rating scale for importance and a 6-point scale for satisfaction. A sixth-grade reading level is required. Examiner must have B-level qualification. A computer version is available using an IBM-compatible 486 PC or higher.

Format: Self-administered; untimed: 5 minutes

Scoring: Hand key; computer scored

Cost: Contact publisher

Quickview® Social History
Ronald A. Giannetti

Date not provided	NCS Pearson

Population: Ages 16 years to adults

Purpose: Provides the clinician with a complete psychosocial history in nine major areas

Description: This instrument enables the clinician or other staff to collect a standardized set of social and clinical data on every client with a minimal amount of administration time. The report format enables all individuals who require a client's information to receive a standardized history. The areas of inquiry are demographics and identifying data, developmental history, family of origin, educational history, marital history, occupational history/financial status, legal history, military history, and symptom screen (physical and psychological). A computer-generated report provides a narrative description of client demographic and clinical information. Each area of inquiry includes a narrative explanation of results.

Format: Self-administered; on-line; untimed: 30 to 45 minutes

Scoring: Hand key, scoring service available; software scoring available

Cost: Administration Booklets (10 softcover and manual) $43; Answer Sheets (25) $18.50

Risk of Eruptive Violence Scale
Albert Mehrabian

1996	Albert Mehrabian, PhD

Population: Adults

Purpose: Identifies adolescents and adults who, although generally quiet and nonaggressive, have a tendency to become extremely violent and destructive

Description: Paper-pencil 35-item measure that deals with a wide range of fantasy, cognitive, emotional, and frustrated violent impulses. It has been shown to be a moderately strong negative correlate of emotional empathy, to be a positive correlate of other measures of aggressiveness and violence, and to clearly differentiate between violent incarcerated adolescents and adults versus controls.

Format: Self-administered; untimed: 10 minutes

Scoring: Hand key

Cost: Test Kit (scale, scoring directions, norms, descriptive material) $33.00

Rotter Incomplete Sentences Blank, Second Edition (RISB™)
Julian B. Rotter, Michael I. Lah, Janet E. Rafferty

| 1992 | The Psychological Corporation |

Population: High school students through adults

Purpose: Assesses overall adjustment

Description: Paper–pencil 40-item test of personality. Items are stems of sentences to be completed by the subject. Responses may be classified into three categories: conflict or unhealthy responses, neutral responses, and positive or healthy responses. The test is available in high school, college, and adult forms.

Format: Self-administered; untimed: 20 to 40 minutes

Scoring: Examiner evaluated

Cost: Incomplete Sentences Blanks (high school, college, or adult) 25 count $32.00, 100-count $119.00; Manual $77.00

Seeking of Noetic Goals Test (SONG)
James C. Crumbaugh

| 1977 | Psychometric Affiliates |

Population: Adolescents, adults

Purpose: Measures the strength of a person's motivation to find meaning in life; used for pre- and posttesting of logotherapy programs with individuals who are addicted, retired, handicapped, or philosophically confused

Description: Paper–pencil 20-item test consisting of statements that the subject rates on a 7-point scale according to his or her beliefs. The test is used in conjunction with the Purpose in Life test to predict therapeutic success. The manual includes a discussion of the test's rationale, validity, reliability, administration, scoring, norms, and other technical data. A fourth-grade reading level is required. Also available in Portuguese.

Format: Self-administered; untimed: 10 minutes

Scoring: Scoring service available

Cost: Specimen Set (test, manual) $4.00; 25 Tests $5.00

Self-Interview Inventory
H. Birnet Hovey

| 1983 | Psychometric Affiliates |

Population: Adults

Purpose: Measures an individual's level of emotional adjustment and identifies individuals with neurotic tendencies; used for self-awareness and counseling programs with both psychiatric and normal patients

Description: Paper–pencil 185-item inventory containing a high loading level of unique content. A Composite Neurotic score is derived from subscores on current complaints, emotional insecurity, and guilt feelings. A Composite Maladjustment score is derived from subscores on prepsychotic and psychotic behavior and childhood illness. Two validating scores are also provided: one on carefulness and one on truthfulness of response. Norms are provided for control groups.

Format: Examiner/self-administered; suitable for group use; untimed: 30 minutes

Scoring: Hand key

Cost: Specimen Set $4.00; 25 Inventories $5.00; 25 Answer Sheets $5.00; 25 Profiles $5.00

Senior Apperception Technique (SAT)
Leopold Bellak, Sonya Sorel Bellak

| 1998 | C.P.S., Inc. |

Population: Adults

Purpose: Assesses personality in individuals ages 60 and older; used by psychiatrists, psychologists, physicians, nurses, and social workers for clinical evaluation and diagnosis

Description: Oral-response 16-item projective personality test measuring the traits, attitudes, and psychodynamics involved in the personalities of individuals ages 60 and older. Each test item consists of a picture of human figures in situations of concern to the elderly. The examinee is asked to tell a story about each picture. The test also includes informational material on technique, administration, research possibilities, and a bibliography. Available also in Spanish, French, and Japanese.

Format: Examiner required; individual administration; untimed: 20 to 30 minutes

Scoring: Examiner evaluated

Cost: Complete Kit (manual, pictures) $22.00

Sentence Completion Series (SCS)
Larry H. Brown, Michael A. Unger

| 1992 | Psychological Assessment Resources, Inc. |

Population: Adolescents, adults

Purpose: Used in counseling to identify themes,

underlying concerns, and specifications of distress

Description: Paper-pencil projective, sentence-completion series with 50 items per form. The categories are as follows: Adult, Adolescence, Family, Marriage, Parenting, Work, Illness, and Aging.

Format: Self-administered; untimed: 10 to 45 minutes

Scoring: Examiner evaluated

Cost: Kit (professional user's guide, forms for each of the categories) $89.00

Singer-Loomis Type Deployment Inventory (SL-TDI)
June Singer, Mary Loomis,
Elizabeth Kirkhart, Larry Kirkhart

1996	Moving Boundaries, Inc.

Population: Ages 17 years and older

Purpose: Assesses personality functioning based on Jungian concepts

Description: Total of 160 items, with 20 on each of eight scales: Introverted Sensing, Extraverted Sensing, Introverted Intuiting, Extraverted Intuiting, Introverted Thinking, Extraverted Thinking, Introverted Feeling, and Extraverted Feeling. There are four aggregate scores (Sensing, Intuiting, Thinking, and Feeling) that bond on 40 items and four aggregate scores (Perceiving, Judging, Introverting, and Extraverting) that bond on 80 items.

Format: Self-administered; computer administration available; untimed: 25 to 40 minutes

Scoring: Self-scored; computer scored; test scoring service available

Cost: Reusable Booklet $6.00; Answer/Scoring Form $4.00; Computer Report $45.00

Six Factor Personality Questionnaire (SFPQ)
Douglas N. Jackson, Sampo V. Paunonen,
Paul F. Tremblay

2000	Sigma Assessment Systems, Inc.

Population: Adults

Purpose: Measures factors underlying basic traits of personality

Description: Assesses normal adult personality in business and industrial settings, in counseling and clinical settings, or for research requiring a broad coverage of personality dimensions. The SFPQ has 108 items, 6 scales, and 18 facet scales.

The six scales are Extroversion, Agreeableness, Independence, Openness to Experience, Methodicalness, and Industriousness. SFPQ provides set scale scores that can be interpreted individually or in series of standardized scale scores. Profiles provided are Typical (percentile comparisons against norms) and Modal (pattern of personality attributes that is characteristic of a subset or cluster of persons in a particular population who share certain personality characteristics). Computer version is available.

Format: Examiner required; individual or group administration; computer administered; untimed

Scoring: Hand key; machine scored; test scoring service available from publisher

Cost: Examination Kit (manual, 5 booklets, 10 quick score answer sheets, 10 profile forms, 1 report) $53.00

Sixteen Personality Factor Questionnaire (16PF)
Raymond B. Cattell

Date not provided	EdITS/Educational and Industrial Testing Service

Population: High school and college students, adults

Purpose: Provides comprehensive profile of the primary dimensions of personality

Description: There are 16 primary scales, five global factors and composite scores for creativity and adjustment, and numerous other criterion-related scales. Stens (10-point scale) given separately for men and women college students, and for a representative sample of the general population. Conversion to stanines and deciles also presented. Norms and profiles are presented for over 100 occupational and clinical syndrome groups.

Format: Examiner required; suitable for group use; untimed: 35 to 50 minutes

Scoring: Hand key

Cost: Complete Kit $107.00; Trial Packet $46.00

Social Reticence Scale (SRS)
Warren H. Jones

1986	Mind Garden, Inc.

Population: Adolescents, adults

Purpose: Assesses shyness and interpersonal problems in high school and college students and adults

Description: Paper-pencil 20-item measure of shyness. Items are answered using a 5-point Likert-type scale. Used to provide client feedback and to assess the effectiveness of therapeutic interventions. Also used in research of interpersonal relationships.

Format: Examiner required; suitable for group use; untimed: 5 to 10 minutes

Scoring: Hand key

Cost: Sampler Set $25.00; Permission Set for 200 Uses $125.00

Structured Interview for the Five-Factor Model of Personality (SIFFM)
Timothy J. Trull, Thomas A. Widiger

| 1997 | Psychological Assessment Resources, Inc. |

Population: Ages 18 years and older

Purpose: Semistructured interview to assess both normal and abnormal personality functioning in specific settings

Description: A total of 120 interview items are rated on a 3-point scale. The interview assesses personality using the Five-Factor Model: Neuroticism (vs. Emotional Stability), Extroversion (vs. Introversion), Openness to Experience (vs. Closedness to Experience), Agreeableness (vs. Antagonism), and Conscientiousness (vs. Negligence).

Format: Examiner required; individual administration; untimed: 60 minutes

Scoring: Examiner evaluated

Cost: Kit (manual, 25 interview booklets) $112.00

Tasks of Emotional Development Test (TED)
Geraldine Weil, Haskel Cohen

| Date not provided | Massachusetts School of Professional Psychology |

Population: Ages 6 to 18 years

Purpose: Used to identify specific areas of emotional difficulty, potential maladaptive behavior, and reasons why a student is having difficulty with academic learning

Description: Projective test uses photographs of children in situations structured to represent the specific emotional developmental tasks that children must meet in the process of growing up. The instrument is grounded in the theoretical framework of psychoanalytic ego psychology, but the photos are less ambiguous than in similar tests. It helps identify core problems of the child and his or her severity, and suggests intervention strategies.

Format: Examiner required; individual administration; untimed: 30 minutes

Scoring: Examiner evaluated

Cost: Complete Set $60.00; Textbook $50.00

Taylor–Johnson Temperament Analysis
Robert M. Taylor, Lucille P. Morrison

| 1996 | Psychological Publications, Inc. |

Population: Ages 13 years to adult

Purpose: Provides a clinical assessment of personality; used for educational and vocational guidance, substance abuse counseling, and individual, premarital, marital, and family counseling

Description: Paper–pencil 180-item test measuring common personality traits to assist in assessing individual adjustment and formulation of an overall counseling plan. The regular edition, for ages 17 to adult, has a special feature allowing "criss-cross" testing in which questions are answered as applied to self and again as applied to significant other, thereby adding the dimension of interpersonal perception to counseling perspective. An eighth-grade reading level is required. The secondary edition, for ages 13 to 17 and adults who are poor readers, is presented in direct-question format with simplified vocabulary for lower level readers. A fifth-grade reading level is required. Evaluation is presented as bipolar graphs of trait pairs: nervous/composed, depressive/lighthearted, active-social/quiet, expressive-responsive/inhibited, sympathetic/indifferent, subjective/objective, dominant/submissive, hostile/tolerant, and self-disciplined/impulsive.

Format: Examiner required; suitable for group use; untimed: 20 to 30 minutes

Scoring: Hand key; may be computer scored

Cost: Basic Package (manual, hand-scoring stencils, pen set, locator ruler, 10 report booklets, 5 question booklets, 50 answer sheets, 50 profiles) $195.00

Temperament Inventory Tests
Peter Blitchington, Robert J. Cruise

| 1979 | Andrews University Press |

Population: Adolescents, adults

Purpose: Assesses an individual's basic temperament traits according to the four-temperament theory; used by professionals and laymen in marital, vocational, social, moral, and spiritual counseling

Description: Paper–pencil 80-item test determining an individual's basic temperamental traits.

The test is available in a self-report form and a group form. The self-report form consists of a 42-page booklet, Understanding Your Temperament, containing the test and instructions for self-administration, self-scoring, and interpreting the scores from a Christian viewpoint. The group form, called the Temperament Inventory, is administered and scored with temperament templates by the examiner or group leader. Interpretive material is not included with the group form. Also available in French, German, and Spanish.

Format: Self-administered; untimed

Scoring: Examiner evaluated

Cost: Test (per copy) $1.25; Scoring Templates $3.95

Trait Arousability Scale (Converse of Stimulus Screening)
Albert Mehrabian

1994	Albert Mehrabian, PhD

Population: Ages 14 years and older

Purpose: Assesses general emotionality or emotional reactivity; used for clinical research and counseling

Description: Paper–pencil 34-item test yielding a single total score. A 10th-grade reading level is required.

Format: Self-administered; untimed: 10 minutes

Scoring: Hand key; test scoring service available from publisher

Cost: Test Kit $33.00

Trait Dominance–Submissiveness Scale
Albert Mehrabian

1994	Albert Mehrabian, PhD

Population: Adults

Purpose: Measures aspects of dominance and submissiveness in an individual's personality; used for research, counseling, job placement purposes, and matching of coworkers

Description: Multiple-item verbal questionnaire assessing personality characteristics related to dominance and submissiveness. Test items are based on extensive factor-analytic and experimental studies on aspects of dominance (con-trolling, taking charge) versus submissiveness characteristics. This measure has been shown to be a basic component of many important personality attributes, such as extroversion, dependency, anxiety, or depression.

Format: Self-administered; untimed: 10 minutes

Scoring: Hand key

Cost: Test Kit (scale, scoring directions, norms, descriptive material) $33.00

Trait Pleasure–Displeasure Scale
Albert Mehrabian

1994	Albert Mehrabian, PhD

Population: Ages 14 years and older

Purpose: Measures general psychological adjustment–maladjustment; used with clinical work, counseling, and research

Description: Paper–pencil 22-item test with a single total score.

Format: Self-administered; untimed: 10 minutes

Scoring: Hand key; test scoring service available from publisher

Cost: Test Kit $33.00

Triadal Equated Personality Inventory

1961	Psychometric Affiliates

Population: Adults

Purpose: Assesses personality; used to predict job success and to measure personal adjustment

Description: Paper–pencil 633-item test of personality. Items are simple adjectives equated for response popularity. The test yields 21 self-image scores: dominance, self-confidence, decisiveness, independence, toughness, suspicion, introversion, activity, depression, foresight, industriousness, warmth, enthusiasm, conformity, inventiveness, persistence, sex drive, recognition, drive, cooperativeness, humility–tolerance, and self-control.

Format: Examiner required; suitable for group use; untimed: 50 to 120 minutes

Scoring: Examiner evaluated

Cost: Professional Examination Kit for 24 Uses $50.00

Relationships

16PF Couple's Counseling Questionnaire
Mary T. Russell

1995	Institute for Personality and Ability Testing, Inc.

Population: Ages 16 years and older

Purpose: Identifies key relationship issues

Description: Enables the counselor to provide possible implications of similarities and differences between two people. The counselor can use the report to help the couple see how their personal qualities may affect their relationship, identify areas that are causing dissatisfaction, and then establish a counseling framework that will result in increased relationship satisfaction for the couple. A valuable tool in relationship counseling that is appropriate for use with cohabiting, premarital, married, separated, divorcing, and same-sex couples. There is one form with 211 items. Items may be administered by computer or on-line.

Format: Self-administered; untimed

Scoring: Computer scored; scoring service available; on-line scoring

Cost: Introductory Kit $33.00

Abortion Scale
Panos D. Bardis

1988	Donna Bardis

Population: Adolescents, adults

Purpose: Measures attitudes toward many aspects of abortion; used in clinical assessment, marriage and family counseling, research on attitudes toward abortion, and discussion in family education

Description: Paper–pencil 25-item instrument in which the subject reads statements about issues concerning abortion and rates them according to his or her personal beliefs on a scale from 0 (*strongly disagree*) to 4 (*strongly agree*). The score equals the sum of the 25 numerical responses. Theoretical range of scores extends from 0 (*lowest approval of abortion*) to 100 (*highest approval*). Suitable for use with individuals who have physical or hearing impairments.

Format: Examiner/self-administered; suitable for group use; untimed: 10 minutes

Scoring: Examiner evaluated

Cost: $1.00

Abuse Risk Inventory (ARI)
Bonnie L. Yegidis

1989	Mind Garden, Inc.

Population: Adult women

Purpose: Identifies women who are abused or at risk for abuse; used for marital or relationship counseling and by social service agencies, physicians, and health care providers

Description: Inventory has 25 items rated using a 4-point Likert scale. Scores provide sociodemographic information. Examiner must be trained in proper use and interpretation.

Format: Self-administered; untimed: 10 to 15 minutes

Scoring: Hand key; examiner evaluated

Cost: Sampler Set $25.00; Permission Set for 200 Uses $125.00

Caring Relationship Inventory (CRI)
Everett L. Shostrom

1966	EdITS/Educational and Industrial Testing Service

Population: Adults

Purpose: Measures the essential elements of caring (or love) in the relationship between a man and a woman; used for evaluation and discussion in marriage and family counseling

Description: Paper–pencil 83-item true-false inventory consisting of a series of statements that the subject applies first to the other member of the couple (spouse, fiance, etc.) and second to his or her "ideal" mate. Responses are scored on seven scales: affection, friendship, eros, empathy, self-love, being love, and deficiency love. Separate forms are available for adult males and females. Items were developed based on the responses of criterion groups of successfully married couples, troubled couples in counseling, and divorced individuals. Percentile norms for successfully married couples are presented separately for men and women. Means and standard deviations are presented for troubled couples and divorced individuals. The CRI is a component of the Actualizing Assessment Battery (AAB).

Format: Examiner required; suitable for group use; untimed: 40 minutes

Scoring: Hand key

Cost: Specimen Set (manual, all forms) $7.00

Coitometer
Panos D. Bardis

1988   Donna Bardis

Population: Adolescents, adults

Purpose: Measures knowledge of the anatomical and physiological aspects of coitus; used for clinical assessment, marriage and family counseling, research on human sexuality, and discussion in family and human sexuality classes

Description: Paper–pencil 50-item true–false four-page instrument consisting of the question-naire and a measure key. Suitable for use with individuals with physical and hearing impairments.

Format: Examiner/self-administered; suitable for group use; untimed: 12 minutes

Scoring: Hand key

Cost: $1.00

Dating Scale
Panos D. Bardis

1988   Donna Bardis

Population: Adolescents, adults

Purpose: Measures attitudes toward various as-pects of dating; used for clinical assessment, marriage and family counseling, research on attitudes toward dating, and discussion in family education

Description: Paper–pencil test in which the subject rates 25 statements about dating from 0 (*strongly disagree*) to 4 (*strongly agree*). The score equals the sum of the 25 numerical responses. Theoretical range of scores extends from 0 (least liberal) to 100 (most liberal). Suitable for use with individuals with physical and hearing impairments.

Format: Examiner/self-administered; suitable for group use; untimed: 10 minutes

Scoring: Examiner evaluated

Cost: $1.00

Dyadic Adjustment Scale (DAS)
Graham Spanier

1989   Multi-Health Systems, Inc.

Population: Adults

Purpose: Measures relationship adjustment for use in marital counseling

Description: Paper–pencil or computer-adminis-tered 32-item self-report measure consisting of four factored subcomponents: Dyadic Satisfac-tion, Dyadic Cohesion, Dyadic Consensus, and Affectional Expression. Windows-based computer version generates interpretive statements.

Format: Self-administered; untimed: 5 to 10 minutes

Scoring: QuikScore™ forms; may be computer scored

Cost: Kit (manual, 20 QuikScore™ Forms) $40.00

Erotic Cyclic Forecast
Thomas J. Rundquist

1998   Nova Media, Inc.

Population: Adults

Purpose: Likelihood of sexual activity

Description: This test can be helpful in coun-seling for couples having marital problems. Total score indicates probability of sexual activity.

Format: Self-administered/on-line administra-tion; untimed

Scoring: Self-scored; computer scored; scoring service available; on-line scoring

Cost: $29.95

Erotometer: A Technique for the Measurement of Heterosexual Love
Panos D. Bardis

1988   Donna Bardis

Population: Adolescents, adults

Purpose: Measures the intensity of an individ-ual's love for a member of the opposite sex; used for clinical assessment, marriage and family coun-seling, research on love, and discussions in fam-ily and sex education

Description: Paper–pencil 50-item test in which the subject reads statements concerning actual feelings, attitudes, desires, and wishes regard-ing one specific member of the opposite sex and rates them on the following scale: 0 (*absent*), 1 (*weak*), or 2 (*strong*). The score equals the sum of the 50 numerical responses. The theoretical range of scores extends from 0 (no love) to 100 (strongest love). Suitable for use with individuals who have physical and hearing impairments.

Format: Self-administered; untimed: 12 minutes

Scoring: Examiner evaluated
Cost: $1.00

Family History Analysis (FHA)
H. Norman Wright

| 1989 | Psychological Publications, Inc. |

Population: Adults

Purpose: A tool for premarital counseling

Description: Eight pages of significant questions designed to help engaged couples thoroughly evaluate their own marriage mode: their marital dreams, marital expectations, attitudes, and behaviors. The tool provides information about family history, parents' history, and personal history.

Format: Self-administered; untimed

Scoring: Examiner evaluated

Cost: Counselor's Guide and 10 Booklets $16.00

Gravidometer
Panos D. Bardis

| 1988 | Donna Bardis |

Population: Adolescents, adults

Purpose: Measures knowledge of the anatomical and physiological aspects of pregnancy; used in clinical assessments, marriage and family counseling, and research on human sexuality and family classes

Description: Paper–pencil 50-item true–false test measuring knowledge of human pregnancy. Suitable for use with individuals who have physical and hearing impairments.

Format: Self-administered; untimed: 12 minutes

Scoring: Hand key

Cost: $1.00

Intimate Adult Relationship Questionnaire (IARQ)
Ronald P. Rohner

| 2000 | Rohner Research |

Population: Adults

Purpose: Assesses current and recent-past intimate adult relationships

Description: Contains a total of 85 items measured on a 4-point Likert scale. This is an adaptation of the adult Parental Acceptance-Rejection Questionnaire instrument.

Format: Examiner/self-administered; suitable for group use; untimed: 10 to 15 minutes

Scoring: Hand key; computer scoring available
Cost: Contact publisher

Intimate Partner Acceptance-Rejection/Control Questionnaire (IPAR/CQ)
Ronald P. Rohner

| 2001 | Rohner Research |

Population: Adults

Purpose: Assesses the quality of the relationship with one's intimate partner in terms of perceived partner acceptance-rejection and partner behavioral control

Description: Paper–pencil questionnaire with 60 items on four scales that comprise the acceptance-rejection component: warmth/affection, hostility/aggression, indifference/neglect, and undifferentiated rejection. The test, designed to cut across social classes, ethnicity, and cultural boundaries, is available in 26 languages. Responses are given using a 4-point scale, with some items reversed when scoring to reduce response bias. The control scale comprises 13 additional items measuring the dimension of partner permissiveness-strictness.

Format: Rating scale; untimed

Scoring: Hand key; computer scoring available

Cost: Contact publisher

Intimate Partner Attachment Questionnaire (IPAQ)
Ronald P. Rohner

| 2001 | Rohner Research |

Population: Adolescents, adults

Purpose: Assesses the nature and quality of attachment with one's intimate partner

Description: Paper–pencil 15-item questionnaire. Results provide information about whether the intimate partner is a true attachment figure, a significant other, or neither. Also measures the quality of the intimate relationship in terms of nine attachment variables.

Format: Examiner/self-administered; suitable for group use; untimed: 10 to 15 minutes

Scoring: Hand key; computer scoring available

Cost: Contact publisher

Marital Attitudes Evaluation (MATE)
Will Schutz

| 1989 | Mind Garden, Inc. |

Population: Adults

Purpose: Explores the relationship between spouses or other closely related persons; measures the amount of satisfaction respondents feel toward someone close to them; used in marital, relationship, and family counseling

Description: The evaluation uses a 6-point Likert scale. An eighth-grade reading level is required.

Format: Examiner required; suitable for group use; untimed: 10 to 15 minutes

Scoring: Hand key; examiner evaluated

Cost: Sampler Set $25.00; Permission for 200 Uses $125.00

Marital Evaluation Checklist
Leslie Navran

1984	Psychological Assessment Resources, Inc.

Population: Adults

Purpose: Assesses common characteristics and problem areas in a marital relationship; used as a survey instrument in clinical and counseling settings to initiate the consultation process and introduce the client to formal diagnostic testing

Description: Paper–pencil test with 140 items organized in three sections: reasons for marrying, current problems, and motivation for counseling. Areas surveyed include interpersonal/emotional, material/economic, social, personal, money and work, sex, personal characteristics, and marital relationships.

Format: Self-administered; untimed: 10 to 20 minutes

Scoring: Examiner evaluated

Cost: 50 Checklists $42.00

Marriage Assessment Inventory (MAI)
H. Norman Wright

1988	Psychological Publications, Inc.

Population: Adults

Purpose: Used prior to seeing a couple or during the process of marriage counseling

Description: The inventory provides the counselor with much of the data needed for planning prior to the first marriage counseling session. It helps the couple to anticipate the kinds of concerns that will be discussed, and in that way helps to introduce them to the process of counseling. Answers to inventory questions also initiate changes in the ways spouses think about their objectives and can bring about some change be-

fore the first interview. Among others, the following topics are included: family structure and background, marital preparation, current levels of satisfaction, and change and commitment level.

Format: Self-administered; untimed

Scoring: Examiner evaluated

Cost: Counselor's Guide and 10 Booklets $16.00

Memories of Spouse
Arnold R. Bruhn

1993	Arnold R. Bruhn, Publisher

Population: Adults

Purpose: Explores the spousal relationship

Description: Recommended for individuals who are considering marital therapy and want to review the relationship and reconnect with what attracted them to their spouse in the first place. Helps to identify the nature of the experiences that have compromised the quality of the relationship.

Format: Examiner required; individual or group administration; untimed

Scoring: Examiner evaluated

Cost: 25 Tests $140.00

Menometer
Panos D. Bardis

1988	Donna Bardis

Population: Adolescents, adults

Purpose: Measures knowledge of the anatomical and physiological aspects of menstruation; used for clinical assessment, marriage and family counseling, research on human sexuality, and discussion in family and human sexuality classes

Description: Paper–pencil 50-item true–false test in which the subject marks the appropriate answers. Suitable for use with individuals who have physical and hearing impairments.

Format: Examiner/self-administered; suitable for group use; untimed: 12 minutes

Scoring: Hand key

Cost: $1.00

Pair Attraction Inventory (PAI)
Everett L. Shostrom

1970	EdITS/Educational and Industrial Testing Service

Population: Adults

Purpose: Measures aspects contributing to adult's selection of a mate or friend; used for premarital, marital, and family counseling

Description: Paper–pencil 224-item test assessing the feelings and attitudes of one member of a male–female pair about the nature of the relationship. Percentile norms are provided based on adult samples. The inventory may be used as a component of the Actualizing Assessment Battery (AAB).

Format: Examiner required; suitable for group use; untimed: 30 minutes

Scoring: Hand key

Cost: Kit (manual, 3 male and 3 female booklets, 50 answer sheets, 50 profiles) $18.75

Pill Scale
Panos D. Bardis
1988　　　　　　　　　　　　　Donna Bardis

Population: Adolescents, adults

Purpose: Measures attitudes toward oral contraceptives; used for clinical assessment, marriage and family counseling, family attitude research, and discussions in family and sex education

Description: Paper–pencil 25-item test in which the subject reads statements concerning moral, sexual, psychological, and physical aspects of "the pill" and rates them on a scale from 0 (*strongly disagree*) to 4 (*strongly agree*). The score equals the sum of the 25 numerical responses. The theoretical range of scores extends from 0 (least liberal) to 100 (most liberal). Suitable for use with individuals who have physical and hearing impairments.

Format: Examiner/self-administered; suitable for group use; untimed: 10 minutes

Scoring: Examiner evaluated

Cost: $1.00

Premarital Communication Inventory
Millard J. Bienvenu
1968　　　　　　　　　　　Northwest Publications

Population: Ages 17 years and older

Purpose: Assesses marriageability of a couple; used in premarital counseling, marriage preparation, and teaching

Description: Yes-no-sometimes inventory with 40 items. A seventh-grade reading level is required. Examiner must have counseling experience.

Format: Self-administered; untimed: 15 minutes

Scoring: Hand key

Cost: $.75 per copy; Guide $2.00 (minimum order $10.00)

PREPARE–Premarital Personal and Relationship Evaluation (Version 2000)
David H. Olson, David G. Fournier, Joan M. Druckman
1996　　　　　　　　　　Life Innovations, Inc.

Population: Adults

Purpose: Premarital counseling in areas of strength and growth

Description: Total of 195 items in 20 categories: Idealistic Distortion, Marriage Expectations, Personality Issues, Communication, Conflict Resolution, Financial Management, Leisure Activities, Sexual Expectations, Children and Parenting, Family and Friends, Role Relationship, Spiritual Beliefs, Couple Flexibility, Family Closeness, Family Flexibility, Self-Confidence, Assertiveness, Avoidance, and Partner Dominance. Results include Revised Individual Scores, Couple Type, Personality Assessment Idealistic Distortion Scores, and Positive Couple Agreement Scores. Also available in Spanish. Also PREPARE-MC for premarital couples with children.

Format: Self-administered; untimed

Scoring: Computer scored; test scoring service available from publisher

Cost: $30.00 for scoring; $125.00 for training

Romantic Relationships Procedure (RRP)
Arnold R. Bruhn
1989　　　　　　　　Arnold R. Bruhn, Publisher

Population: Adults

Purpose: Explores the most significant romantic relationships

Description: A structured method of exploring romantic relationships as a class, or type, of relationship. Measures autobiographical memory.

Format: Examiner required; individual or group administration; untimed

Scoring: Examiner evaluated

Cost: 25 Tests $140.00

Sex-Role Egalitarianism Scale (SRES)
Lynda A. King, Daniel W. King
1993　　　　　　Sigma Assessment Systems, Inc.

Population: Ages 12 years and older

Purpose: Measures attitudes toward equality; used in marital counseling and prevention of sexual harassment

Description: Instrument with 95 items rated on a 5-point Likert scale with five subscales: Educational roles, Marital roles, Employment roles, Social-Interpersonal-Heterosexual roles, and Parental roles. Alternate forms include 25 items. Requires a sixth- to seventh-grade reading level.

Format: Examiner required; individual and group administration; untimed: 25 minutes

Scoring: Examiner evaluated

Cost: Examination Kit (manual, 10 question/answer documents, 10 profile sheets) $33.50

Sexometer
Panos D. Bardis

1988	Donna Bardis

Population: Adolescents, adults

Purpose: Assesses knowledge of human reproductive anatomy and physiology; used for clinical assessment, marriage and family counseling, research on sex knowledge, and discussion in family and sex education

Description: Paper–pencil 50-item test consisting of short-answer and identification questions concerning human reproduction, anatomy, function, physiology, disease, birth control, and sexual behavior. Materials include the test form and answer key. Suitable for use with individuals with physical and hearing impairments.

Format: Examiner/self-administered; suitable for group use; untimed: 15 minutes

Scoring: Hand key

Cost: $1.00

Sexual Communication Inventory
Millard J. Bienvenu

1980	Northwest Publications

Population: Ages 17 years and older

Purpose: Assesses sexual communication in couples; used in marital counseling and in communication skills training for couples

Description: Yes–no–sometimes 30-item test. A seventh-grade reading level is required. Examiner must have couples counseling experience.

Format: Self-administered; untimed: 12 minutes

Scoring: Hand key

Cost: $.50 per copy; Guide $2.00 (minimum order $10.00)

Socio-Sexual Knowledge and Attitudes Test (SSKAT)
Dorothy Griffiths, Yona Lunsky

2002	Stoelting Company

Population: Ages 15 years to adult

Purpose: Measures sexual knowledge and attitudes of individuals with developmental disabilities

Description: The predecessor test was developed in 1979 to obtain an idea of how individuals with special needs understood their own bodies, relationships, and sex. The new version of the test addresses most of the original topics except substance abuse issues, and it adds the topics of HIV/AIDS, sexual health, menopause, age discrimination, appropriate/inappropriate touch, and diversity in sexual activities. There are six subscales: anatomy; male and female bodies (individuals respond only to their own gender); intimacy; pregnancy, childbirth, and childrearing; birth control and STDs; and healthy sexual boundaries. An easy-to-use stimulus picture easel and picture cards present illustrations requiring simple responses to questions. This full revision represents updated and changed materials based on extensive feedback from the field. Subjects must have some visual and verbal comprehension, but expressive language requirements are minimal.

Format: Examiner required; individual administration; untimed: 45 minutes

Scoring: Examiner evaluated

Cost: $175.00

Spousal Assault Risk Assessment Guide (SARA)
P. Randall Kropp, Stephen D. Hart, Christopher D. Webster, Derek Eaves

1999	Multi-Health Systems, Inc.

Population: Adults

Purpose: Helps predict the likelihood of domestic violence

Description: Has forensic applications with a total of 20 items: alleged most recent offense (3 items), criminal history (3 items), psychosocial adjustment (7 items), and spousal assault history (7 items).

Format: Examiner required; individual administration; untimed: 15 to 20 minutes

Scoring: QuikScore™ forms

Cost: Kit (manual, 25 checklists, 25 scoring forms) $55.00

Vasectomy Scale: Attitudes
Panos D. Bardis

| 1988 | Donna Bardis |

Population: Adolescents, adults

Purpose: Measures attitudes toward the social and psychological aspects of vasectomy; used for clinical assessment, marriage and family counseling, research on human sexuality, and discussions in family and sex education

Description: Paper-pencil test in which the subject rates 25 statements concerning vasectomy on a scale from 0 (*strongly disagree*) to 4 (*strongly agree*). The score equals the sum of the 25 numerical responses. The theoretical range of scores extends from 0 (lowest approval of vasectomy) to 100 (highest approval). Suitable for use with individuals who have physical and hearing impairments.

Format: Examiner/self-administered; suitable for group use; untimed: 10 minutes

Scoring: Examiner evaluated

Cost: $1.00

Self-Esteem

Adolescent Coping Scale
Erica Frydenberg, Ramon Lewis

| 1993 | Australian Council for Educational Research Limited |

Population: Adolescents

Purpose: Assesses a broad range of coping strategies, focusing on what an individual does

Description: Paper-pencil instrument in a general and specific Long Form (80 items, 18 scales) and a Short Form (1 item from each scale). The main focus is on psychological well-being and adaptive strategies for coping. It can be used for initiating self-directed and behavioral change and stimulating group discussion. The Long Form can be computer or hand scored. Data can then be transferred to a Profile Chart. A Practitioner's Kit has been specially produced.

Format: Examiner required; individual or group administration; Long form: 10 minutes; Short Form: 2 minutes

Scoring: Hand key; computer scoring; scoring service available

Cost: Contact publisher

Behavioral Academic Self-Esteem (BASE)
Stanley Coopersmith, Ragnar Gilberts

| Date not provided | Consulting Psychologists Press, Inc. |

Population: Grades PreK through 8

Purpose: Measures academic self-esteem; used for counseling and research

Description: Paper-pencil 16-item behavioral rating scale assessing five factors related to self-esteem: student initiative, social attention, success/failure, social attraction, and self-confidence. The BASE may be used with children as young as 4 years old and by teachers, parents, and other professionals who can observe the child directly. It may be used in conjunction with the Coopersmith Self-Esteem Inventories to improve the accuracy and stability of self-esteem measurements.

Format: Self-administered; untimed: 5 minutes

Scoring: Hand key; examiner evaluated

Cost: Manual $35.50; 25 Rating Scales $16.00

Children's Inventory of Self-Esteem– Second Edition (CISE-2)
Richard A. Campbell

| 2001 | Brougham Press |

Population: Ages 5 to 12 years

Purpose: Provides a quick assessment of a child's inferred self-worth and furnishes strategies for improving self-esteem

Description: This 64-item inventory compares the relative strengths and weaknesses of four self-esteem components: Belonging (16 items), Control (16 items), Purpose (16 items), and Self (16 items). Items are divided into defensive and aggressive items to identify favored coping strategies. Male and female forms are provided. The lifetime license entitles the holder to make unlimited copies of all inventory forms and pages.

Examiner must have an advanced degree in mental health or testing field.

Format: Individual/self-administered; suitable for group use; untimed: 10 minutes

Scoring: Hand key; examiner evaluated

Cost: Lifetime Licenses: Individual $99.00; School and Agency $125.00; School District $115.00 per elementary building

Coopersmith Self-Esteem Inventories (SEI)
Stanley Coopersmith

Date not provided	Consulting Psychologists Press, Inc.

Population: Ages 8 years to adult

Purpose: Measures attitudes toward the self in social, academic, and personal contexts; used for individual diagnosis, classroom screening, pre- and posttreatment evaluations, and clinical and research studies

Description: Paper–pencil test of self-attitudes in four areas: social-self-peers, home–parents, school–academic, and general–self. Materials include the 58-item School Form for individuals ages 8 to15 and the 25-item Adult Form for individuals ages 16 and older. The School Form may be used with Behavioral Academic Self-Esteem (BASE).

Format: Self-administered; untimed: 15 minutes

Scoring: Hand key

Cost: School Preview Kit (manual, form, key) $31.50; Adult Preview Kit (manual, form, key) $31.50

Coping Scale for Adults (CSA)
Erica Frydenberg, Ramon Lewis

1997	Australian Council for Educational Research Limited

Population: Adults

Purpose: Measures how frequently 18 coping strategies are used

Description: The CSA can assist individuals and organizations that work with adults in clinical, counseling, and human resource contexts to consider issues surrounding coping and facilitate coping strategies. A self-report inventory with 74 items including 70 structured items that reliably assess 18 conceptually and empirically distinct coping strategies. The Specific Form enables the measurement of responses to a particular concern. There is a 20-item Short Form comprising 19 structured items and a final open-ended response question.

Format: Self-report; untimed

Scoring: Examiner evaluated

Cost: Contact publisher

Culture-Free Self-Esteem Inventories– Third Edition (CFSEI–3)
James Battle

2002	PRO-ED, Inc.

Population: Ages 6 through 18 years

Purpose: Assesses the self-esteem of children and adolescents

Description: There are three age-appropriate self-report versions: Primary, Intermediate, and Adolescent. All three versions provide a Global Self-Esteem Quotient. The Intermediate and Adolescent Forms provide self-esteem scores in four areas: Academic, General, Parental/Home, and Social. The Adolescent Form provides an additional self-esteem score: Personal Self-Esteem. A defensiveness measure is also provided to assess the extent to which an examinee's responses are guarded. The CFSEI–3 was standardized on a sample of 1,727 persons from 17 states. Information is provided on an extensive Canadian sample in reliability and validity chapters of the manual.

Format: Examiner required; suitable for group use; untimed: 10 to 15 minutes

Scoring: Examiner evaluated

Cost: Complete Kit (manual; 50 each of Primary, Intermediate, and Adolescent response and scoring forms, storage box) $179.00

Indiana Student Scale: Self-Esteem
Meryl E. Englander

1997	Meryl E. Englander

Population: Ages 12 years and older

Purpose: Prepares a profile of individual self-esteem

Description: Used in counseling and serves as the basis for designing a learning environment to enhance individual self-esteem. This 63-item scale gives a profile for eight dimensions of self-esteem.

Format: Examiner required; individual or group administration; untimed: 40 minutes

Scoring: Computer scored; test scoring service available from publisher

Cost: $2.00 per student

Multidimensional Self-Esteem Inventory (MSEI)
Edward J. O'Brien, Seymour Epstein

| 1988 | Psychological Assessment Resources, Inc. |

Population: Adults

Purpose: Assesses global self-esteem and its components; used to evaluate job dissatisfaction, eating disorders, anxiety/depression, and treatment intake/outcome

Description: Paper–pencil 116-item multiple-choice inventory that measures global self-esteem and eight components of self-esteem: Competence, Lovability, Likability, Personal Power, Self-Control, Moral Self-Approval, Body Appearance, and Body Functioning. The MSEI uses a a 5-point response format, reporting results as *T*-scores and percentiles. A 10th-grade reading level is required.

Format: Examiner required; suitable for group use; untimed: 15 to 30 minutes

Scoring: Hand key

Cost: Kit (manual, reusable test booklets, rating forms, profile forms) $125.00

Self-Esteem Index (SEI)
Linda Brown, Jacquelyn Alexander

| 1991 | PRO-ED, Inc. |

Population: Ages 8 through 18 years

Purpose: Measures the way individuals perceive and value themselves

Description: Paper–pencil 120-item survey assessing self-esteem. Items are divided into four scales: Perception of Familial Acceptance, Perception of Academic Competence, Perception of Peer Popularity, and Perception of Personal Security. Results are reported as standard scores and percentiles.

Format: Rating scale; untimed: 30 minutes

Scoring: Examiner evaluated

Cost: Complete Kit (manual, 50 student response booklets, 50 profile/record forms, storage box) $124.00

Self-Esteem Inventory
Millard J. Bienvenu

| 1995 | Northwest Publications |

Population: Ages 13 years and older

Purpose: Assesses how an individual perceives himself or herself in positives, negatives, strengths, and weaknesses

Description: Yes–no–sometimes 40-item test. A seventh-grade reading level is required. Examiner must be trained in counseling or human relations.

Format: Self-administered; untimed: 15 minutes

Scoring: Hand key

Cost: $1.00 each; Guide $1.50 (minimum order of $10.00)

Self-Esteem Questionnaire (SEQ–3)
James K. Hoffmeister

| 1971 | Test Analysis and Development Corporation |

Population: Grade 4 to adult

Purpose: Evaluates how individuals feel about various aspects of themselves, including their capabilities, worth, and acceptance by others

Description: Paper–pencil 21-item self-report rating scale consisting of two subscales: Self-Esteem (12 items) and Self–Other Satisfaction (9 items). Items on the Self-Esteem subscale consist of statements, such as "Most of my friends accept me as much as they accept other people," that the individual rates on a 5-point scale from 1 (*not at all*) to 5 (*yes, very much*). Items on the Self–Other Satisfaction subscale immediately follow items on the Self-Esteem subscale and take the form "Does the situation described in [the previous question] upset you?" These items are rated on a 5-point scale also. Scores are provided for both subscales according to the computerized convergence analysis process (a score is computed only if the individual has responded in a reasonably consistent fashion to the items used to measure that factor). The manual includes a description of the test's variables and content and directions for administering and scoring the questionnaire.

Format: Examiner required; suitable for group use; untimed

Scoring: Computer scored

Cost: 50 Questionnaires (includes computer scoring service) $50.00

Smell

Brief Smell Identification Test (B-SIT)
Richard L. Doty

2001	Sensonics, Inc.

Population: Ages 5 years and older

Purpose: Detects smell ability differential and early signs of neurodegenerative disorders (e.g., Alzheimer's disease)

Description: Total of 12 items measure ability to smell. Profiles Anosmia and Normosmia. Provides percentile-ranked scores with age and gender adjustment. Materials used are microencapsulated odorants.

Format: Examiner required; individual administration; untimed: 5 minutes

Scoring: Hand key

Cost: $12.95

Pocket Smell Test (PST)
Richard L. Doty

2001	Sensonics, Inc.

Population: Ages 5 years and older

Purpose: Measures smell ability for differential and early diagnosis of neurodegenerative disorders

Description: Screening test with three items that measure ability to smell. This screening determines if a more detailed test, the Smell Identification Test, should be administered. Materials used are microencapsulated odorants.

Format: Examiner required; individual administration; untimed

Scoring: Hand key

Cost: $1.80 each

Smell Identification Test (SIT)
Richard L. Doty

2001	Sensonics, Inc.

Population: Ages 5 years and older

Purpose: Measures smell ability for detecting Alzheimer's disease and numerous degenerative disorders

Description: Total of 40 items measure ability to smell. Profiles Anosmia (mild to moderate), Severe Hyposmia, and Normosmia, with percentile rankings with age and gender adjustments. Materials used are microencapsulated odorants. Also available in French, Spanish, and German.

Format: Self-administered; untimed: 10 to 15 minutes

Scoring: Hand key

Cost: $26.95 each

Stress

Coping Inventory for Stressful Situations (CISS)
Norman Endler, James Parker

1989	Multi-Health Systems, Inc.

Population: Ages 13 years to adult

Purpose: Measures coping styles in individuals

Description: Paper-pencil 48-item instrument measuring three major types of coping styles: Task-Oriented, Emotion-Oriented, and Avoidance-Coping. The CISS also identifies two types of Avoidance Coping patterns: Distraction and Social Diversion. Scores provide a profile of an individual's coping strategy. Adult and adolescent forms are available. The CISS: Situation Specific Coping (CISS:SSC) is a 21-item measure for adults modified such that responses are given with a particular designated stressful situation in mind.

Format: Self-administered; untimed: 10 minutes

Scoring: QuikScore™ forms

Cost: Kit (test manual, 25 QuikScore™ forms) $45.00

Coping Responses Inventory (CRI)
Rudolf H. Moos

1993	Psychological Assessment Resources, Inc.

Population: Ages 12 years and older

Purpose: Used in counseling and stress management education to identify and monitor coping strategies

Description: Paper-pencil short-answer 4-point scale with the following categories: Logical Analysis, Positive Reappraisal, Seeking Guidance and Support, Problem Solving, Cognitive Avoidance, Acceptance or Resignation, Seeking Alternative Rewards, and Emotional Discharge. Two forms are available: youth and adult. A sixth-grade reading level is required.

Format: Self-administered; untimed

Scoring: Hand-scored answer sheet; scoring software available

Cost: Youth or Adult Kit (adult or youth manual, adult or youth actual and ideal test booklets, and answer sheets) $109.00; Software $375.00

Davidson Trauma Scale (DTS)
Jonathan Davidson

1996	Multi-Health Systems, Inc.

Population: Ages 18 years and older

Purpose: A quick, accurate measure of posttraumatic stress disorder (PTSD) symptoms that corresponds to the DSM-IV

Description: Total of 17 items are rated in terms of both frequency and severity. Yields *T*-scores and percentage of PTSD and non-PTSD individuals who obtained each DTS score. Also available in French and Spanish.

Format: Self-administered; untimed: 10 minutes

Scoring: QuikScore™ forms

Cost: Kit (test manual, 25 QuikScore™ forms) $50.00

Fear Survey Schedule (FSS)
Joseph Wolpe, Peter J. Land

1969	EdITS/Educational and Industrial Testing Service

Population: Adults

Purpose: Evaluates the manner in which an individual deals with fear-related situations; is particularly useful in behavior therapy

Description: Multiple-item paper-pencil survey of a patient's reactions to a variety of possible sources of maladaptive emotional reactions. The reactions are unpleasant and often fearful, fear tinged, or fear related. The schedule reveals reactions to many stimulus classes in a short time.

Format: Examiner required; suitable for group use; untimed: 3 minutes

Scoring: Examiner evaluated

Cost: Manual and Response Forms $11.50

Life Stressors and Social Resources Inventory (LISRES-Adult and LISRES-Youth)
Rudolf H. Moos

1994	Psychological Assessment Resources, Inc.

Population: Ages 12 years to adult

Purpose: Measures ongoing life stressors and social resources and their changes over time

Description: Can be used as a structured interview with individuals whose reading and comprehension skills are below a sixth-grade level. It can be administered and scored by those with no formal training in clinical or counseling psychology. Each version (adult and youth) has its own manual. The adult domains are physical health status, housing and neighborhood, finances, work, and relationships. The youth domains are physical health, home and money, and relationships.

Format: Examiner required; individual administration; untimed: 30 minutes

Scoring: Examiner evaluated

Cost: Adult or Youth Introductory Kit $128.00

Maslach Burnout Inventory (MBI)
Christina Maslach, Susan E. Jackson

Date not provided	Consulting Psychologists Press, Inc.

Population: Adults

Purpose: Measures burnout among social and human service personnel; used in job counseling to reduce burnout symptoms and by school districts to detect potential problems among school staffs

Description: Paper-pencil 22-item inventory consisting of three subscales measuring various aspects of burnout: Emotional Exhaustion, Personal Accomplishment, and Depersonalization. Examinees answer each item on the basis of how frequently they experience the feeling described in the item. The Demographic Data Sheet may be used to obtain biographical information. The revised manual contains more research data and more extensive norms than the previous manual, future research suggestions, and a supplement on burnout in education. In addition, an MBI Educators Survey and an Educators Demographic Data Sheet are available.

Format: Self-administered; untimed: 20 to 30 minutes

Scoring: Hand key

Cost: Preview Kit (manual, Human Services booklet, Educators Survey booklet, General Survey booklet, scoring keys) $52.75

Posttraumatic Stress Diagnostic Scale (PDS)
Edna B. Foa

Date not provided	NCS Pearson

Population: Ages 17 to 65 years

Purpose: Aids in the detection and diagnosis of posttraumatic stress disorder (PTSD)

Description: This brief screening and diagnostic tool parallels DSM–IV criteria. It may be administered repeatedly over time to help monitor changes in symptoms. It enables the examiner to screen for the presence of PTSD in large groups or with patients who have identified themselves as victims of a traumatic event and gauge symptom severity and functioning in patients already identified as suffering from PTSD. The test helps identify the source of a client's pain early on, helping to make treatment planning more effective. The PDS was normed on a group of 248 men and women who had experienced a traumatic event at least 1 month before they took the test. Written at an eighth-grade reading level.

Format: Self-administered; untimed: 10 to 15 minutes

Scoring: Hand key; software scoring available

Cost: Hand-Scoring Starter Kit (manual, 10 test booklets, 10 each of answer and scoring worksheets, scoring sheet) $53.00

School Situation Survey
Barbara J. Helms, Robert K. Gable

1989	Mind Garden, Inc.

Population: Ages 5 to 18 years

Purpose: Identifies the causes of stress that students feel at school

Description: This survey helps identify the causes of stress that students feel at school, as well as the ways in which stress is demonstrated. It is a valuable instrument for those investigating stress-related problems experienced by children in grade school through high school. The 5-point Likert scales are under two categories: Sources of Stress (Teacher Interactions, Academic Stress, Peer Interactions, Academic Self-Concept) and Manifestations of Stress (Emotional, Behavioral, Physiological).

Format: Examiner required; individual or group administration; untimed: 10 to 15 minutes

Scoring: Hand key

Cost: Sampler Set $25.00; Permission Set $125.00; 25 Test Booklets $25.00

Stress Profile
Kenneth M. Nowack

2000	Western Psychological Services

Population: Adults

Purpose: Identifies individual characteristics and behaviors that protect against or contribute to stress-related illness

Description: The Stress Profile measures all personal traits and lifestyle habits that have been shown to moderate the stress–illness relationship. This convenient self–report inventory provides scores in 15 areas related to stress and health risk. Norms are based on an ethnically diverse sample of 1,111 men and women, ages 20 to 68, from various working environments. Computer scoring provides a complete interpretive report, which lists Health Risk Alerts and Health Resources for the individual assessed, showing at a glance the areas in which an individual is vulnerable to stress-related illness.

Format: Self-administered; untimed: 20 to 30 minutes

Scoring: Hand key; computer scored

Cost: Complete Kit $99.50

Wellness

Health Problems Checklist
John A. Schinka

1984	Psychological Assessment Resources, Inc.

Population: Adults

Purpose: Assesses the health problems of adults; used as a survey instrument in clinical and counseling settings to initiate the consultation process and introduce the client to formal diagnostic testing

Description: Paper–pencil 200-item test identify-ing health problems that may affect overall psy-chological well-being. The test, which can be used as a screening tool for medical referrals, covers 13 areas: general health, cardiovascular/pulmon-ary, endocrine/hematology, gastrointestinal, der-matological, visual, auditory/olfactory, mouth/throat/nose, orthopedic, neurological, genitouri-nary, habits, and history. The test is a compo-nent of the Clinical Checklist Series.

Format: Self-administered; untimed: 10 to 20 minutes

Scoring: Examiner evaluated

Cost: 50 Checklists $42.00

Menstrual Distress Questionnaire (MDQ)
Rudolf H. Moos

1991	Western Psychological Services

Population: Ages 13 years and older

Purpose: Assesses the characteristics of a woman's menstrual cycle in order to diagnose and treat premenstrual symptoms

Description: Multiple-item paper–pencil or com-puter-administered questionnaire assessing the examinee on eight characteristics (pain, concen-tration, behavior change, autonomic reactions, water retention, negative affect, arousal, and con-trol) during each of three phases of the men-strual cycle: premenstrual, menstrual, and inter-menstrual. A diskette for administration, scoring, and interpretation on PC-compatible systems is available. The paper–pencil version provides mail-in answer sheets.

Format: Self-administered; untimed

Scoring: Examiner evaluated; computer scored

Cost: Kit $75.00

Quality of Life Questionnaire (QLQ)
David Evans, Wendy Cope

1989	Multi-Health Systems, Inc.

Population: Adults

Purpose: Measures an individual's quality of life

Description: Paper–pencil 192-item self-report measure consisting of 15 content scales and a social desirability scale. The five major domains are General Well-Being, Interpersonal Relations, Organizational Activity, Occupational Activity, and Leisure and Recreational Activity. An overall Quality of Life score is obtained from the ques-tionnaire.

Format: Self-administered; untimed: 30 minutes

Scoring: QuikScore™ forms

Cost: Kit (manual, 10 question booklets, 25 forms) $51.00

SF-36 Health Survey-Research Assistance (RAS)

Date not provided	CogniSyst, Inc.

Population: All ages

Purpose: Monitors general health

Description: The SF-36 Health Survey is a state-of-the-art instrument that can be used to moni-tor general health, estimate the burden of differ-ent health conditions, measure treatment effects from clinical trials, screen medical patients for referral, and monitor outcomes in medical, reha-bilitative, and psychiatric populations. Accepted by countless insurers and managed care organi-zations as a valid and reliable method of assess-ing outcome, the SF-36 often serves as the foun-dation for program evaluation processes. The SF-36 has strong psychometric properties and is supported by a wealth of published research. The survey's extensive normative data are avail-able for a wide array of carefully studied patient groups.

Format: Self-administered; untimed

Scoring: Computer scored

Cost: DOS Version $400.00; Windows Version $700.00

Social Adjustment Scale–Self Report (SAS–SR)
Myrna Weissman

1999	Multi-Health Systems, Inc.

Population: Ages 17 years and older

Purpose: Measures ability to adapt to and be sat-isfied with social roles

Description: Contains 54 items dealing with work, social and leisure, family unit, extended family, parental, and primary relations. Also avail-able in French, Spanish, and 17 other languages.

Format: Self-administered; untimed: 15 to 20 minutes

Scoring: QuikScore™ forms; computer scored

Cost: Complete Kit (manual, 10 question book-lets, 25 forms) $102.00

Spiritual Well-Being Scale
Craig W. Eilison, Raymond F. Paloutzian

1982	Life Advance, Inc.

Population: Ages 16 years and older

Purpose: Measures spiritual wellness; used in medical fields, social science, pastoral counseling, church congregational analysis, and individual counseling

Description: Paper–pencil 20-item multiple-choice test measuring overall spiritual well-being, with religious and existential well-being sub-scales. A high school reading level is required. Also available in French and Spanish.

Format: Self-administered; untimed: 10 to 15 minutes

Scoring: Hand key; examiner evaluated; self-scored

Cost: Contact publisher

Education Instruments

Tests classified in the Education section generally are used in an educational or school setting to assess the cognitive and emotional growth and development of persons of all ages. Typically, professionals who use the tests listed in this section are school psychologists, diagnosticians, school counselors, and classroom teachers. Because the classification of tests by function or usage is somewhat arbitrary, the reader is encouraged to check the Psychology and Business sections for additional tests that may be helpful in meeting assessment needs.

Academic Achievement

Academic Competence Evaluation Scales (ACES)
James C. DiPerna, Stephen N. Elliott

2000	The Psychological Corporation

Population: Grades K through college

Purpose: Standardized instrument to screen students who are having academic difficulty

Description: Facilitates prereferral assessment and identifies at-risk students. Both general and special educators can identify and prioritize skills that may need intervention. Based on these results, child study teams can identify students who would benefit from a comprehensive assessment or early intervention. The Teacher Record Form summarizes all areas necessary for academic competence: Academic Skills, Interpersonal Skills, Academic Motivation, Study Skills, and Classroom Engagement. Multiple teachers may evaluate the same student for a comprehensive view of student functioning. For Grades 6 through 12, a student self-report evaluates academic skills and strategic academic behaviors. College students can also complete a self-report.

Format: Rating scale; untimed: 10 to 15 minutes

Scoring: Examiner evaluated; computer scoring available

Cost: K-12 Complete Kit (manual, 25 each of student and teacher forms, scoring software, box) $193.00; College Complete Kit (manual, 25 forms, scoring software) $160.00

Academic Intervention Monitoring System (AIMS)
Stephen N. Elliott, James C. DiPerna, Edward Shapiro

2000	The Psychological Corporation

Population: Grades K through 12

Purpose: Assists in designing interventions and pinpointing intervention goals

Description: AIMS includes student, parent, and teacher forms for identification, implementation, and monitoring of strategies most likely to enhance student performance, including strategies for use at home. Also available in Spanish.

Format: Rating scale; untimed: 10 to 15 minutes

Scoring: Examiner evaluated

Cost: Complete Kit (manual, 25 each of teacher, parent, student forms) $121.00

ACER Advanced Test B40 (Revised)

1989	Australian Council for Educational Research Limited

Population: Ages 15 years and older

Purpose: Measures intelligence

Description: Paper-pencil 77-item test measuring general mental abilities, including both verbal and numerical reasoning. The revised manual includes norms for adults and supplementary data for 15-year-olds and first-year college students. Materials include an expendable booklet, score key, manual, and specimen set.

Format: Examiner required; suitable for group use; untimed: 1 hour

Scoring: Examiner evaluated

Cost: Contact publisher

ACER Advanced Test BL/BQ– New Zealand Revision
Neil Reid, Cedric Croft, Alison Gilmore, David Philips

1985	New Zealand Council for Educational Research

Population: Ages 17 years and older

Purpose: Measures general scholastic ability

Description: This test has the following applications: vocational, counseling, and occupational selection. Two subtests have a total of 59 items: Quantitative (29 items) and Language (30 items). Results are reported as subtest scores and a total score. Materials used are question/answer booklets and scoring keys.

Format: Examiner required; group administration; timed: 35 minutes

Scoring: Hand key

Cost: Norms Supplements $6.30; 20 Booklets $19.80

ACER Higher Test PL-PQ– New Zealand Revision
Neil Reid, Cedric Croft, Alison Gilmore, David Philips

1986	New Zealand Council for Educational Research

Population: Ages 15 years and older

Purpose: Measures general scholastic ability

Description: This test has the following applications: vocational, counseling, and occupational selection. Two subtests have a total of 68 items: Quantitative (34 items) and Language (34 items). Results are reported as subtest scores and a total score.

Format: Examiner required; group administration; timed: 35 minutes

Scoring: Hand key

Cost: Norms Supplements $6.30; 20 Item/Answer Booklets $19.80

ACER Higher Tests: WL-WQ, ML-MQ (Second Edition), and PL-PQ

1989	Australian Council for Educational Research Limited

Population: Ages 13 years and older

Purpose: Measures the intelligence of students

Description: Paper–pencil 72-item tests of general mental abilities available in three forms: WL-WQ for students ages 13 and older and parallel forms ML-MQ and PL-PQ for students ages 15 and older. The L section (36 items) of each form has a linguistic basis; the Q section (36 items) is quantitative. Australian norms are provided for both sections separately and for a combined score.

Format: Examiner required; suitable for group use; timed: L section 15 minutes; Q section 20 minutes

Scoring: Examiner evaluated

Cost: Contact publisher

ACER Tests of Basic Skills–Orchid Series

1997	Australian Council for Educational Research Limited

Population: Years 3, 5, and 6

Purpose: Measures literacy and numeracy

Description: Tests contain Levels A, B, and C for Literacy and Numeracy. Literacy covers reading, proofreading, listening, and writing. Numeracy covers numbers, measurement, and space. The instrument includes paper–pencil, multiple-choice, short-answer, essay, and show-tell formats.

Format: Examiner required; suitable for group use; timed: from 7 minutes to 55 minutes per section

Scoring: Scored with key; scoring service available from publisher

Cost: Contact publisher

ACT Assessment (ACT)

Yearly	ACT, Inc.

Population: Grades 11 and above

Purpose: Used for college admissions, course placement, and academic advising

Description: Multiple-choice paper–pencil test with the following categories: English Test (75 items, 45 minutes), Math Test (60 items, 60 minutes), Reading Test (40 items, 35 minutes), and Science Reasoning Test (40 items, 35 minutes). The following scores are reported: English Test total score and two subscores: Usage/Mechanics and Rhetorical Skills; Math Test total score and three subscores: Pre-Algebra/Elementary Algebra, Intermediate Algebra/Coordinate Geometry, Plane Geometry/Trigonometry; Reading Test total score and two subscores: Arts/Literature and Social Studies/Sciences; and Science Reasoning Test total score. Raw scores are converted to scale scores; scale scores for the four tests and the composite range from a low of 1 to a high of 36. Subscores are reported on a scale score ranging from a low of 1 to a high of 18. Multiple forms are in use. Test booklets, answer folders, registration forms, and supplemental publications are used. The ACT Assessment Program also collects information about students' career interests, high school courses and grades, educational and career aspirations, extracurricular activities, and special education needs. May be used with individuals with visual, physical, hearing, and mental impairments.

Format: Examiner required; suitable for group use; timed: 175 minutes

Scoring: Machine scored; test scoring service available from publisher

Cost: $24.00 to $27.00

Adult Basic Learning Examination–Second Edition (ABLE)
Bjorn Karlsen, Eric F. Gardner

| 1986 | Harcourt® Brace Educational Measurement |

Population: Ages 17 years and older

Purpose: Measures adult achievement in basic learning

Description: Multiple-item paper–pencil measure of vocabulary knowledge, reading comprehension, spelling and arithmetic computation, and problem-solving skills. The test is divided into three levels. Level 1 is for adults with from 1 to 4 years of formal education. Level 2 is for adults with from 5 to 8 years of schooling. Level 3 is for people who have at least 8 years of schooling and who may or may not have graduated from high school. Because the vocabulary test is dictated, no reading is required. The Arithmetic Problem-Solving test is dictated at Level 1. A short test, SelectABLE, is available for use in determining the appropriate level of ABLE for each applicant. The test is available in two alternate forms, E and F, at each level. SelectABLE is available in only one form. Also available in Spanish. Screening Battery can be used when testing time is limited for Level 2.

Format: Examiner required; suitable for group use; untimed: SelectABLE 15 minutes; Level 1, 2 hours 10 minutes; Levels 2 and 3, 2 hours 55 minutes

Scoring: Hand key; may be computer scored; Levels 2 and 3 self-scored

Cost: ABLE Examination Kit $63.50; SelectABLE Machine Score $68.50; Screening Battery Examination Kit $21.00

AP Examination: Advanced Placement Program®

| Yearly | College Board |

Population: Grades 9 through 12

Purpose: Measures academic achievement in a wide range of fields; used by participating colleges to grant credit and placement in these fields to gifted and advanced students and to measure the effectiveness of a school's Advanced Placement Program

Description: The AP exams are part of the AP Program, which provides course descriptions, exams, and curricular materials to high schools to allow those students who wish to pursue college-level studies while still in secondary school to receive advanced placement or credit when they enter college. The AP Program provides descriptions and exams on 35 introductory college courses in the following 19 fields: art, biology, chemistry, computer science, economics, English, French, German, government and politics, history, Latin, calculus, music, physics, environmental science, psychology, statistics, geography, and Spanish. No test is longer than 3 hours. All exams are paper–pencil tests (except for the art portfolios) with an essay or problem-solving section and a multiple-choice section. Using the operational services provided by the Educational Testing Service, the AP exams are administered in May by schools throughout the world. Any school may participate. Fee reductions are available for students with financial need. Available in Braille and large print. Grades are sent to students, their schools, and colleges in July.

Format: Examiner required; suitable for group use; timed: 3 hours maximum

Scoring: Computer scored; examiner evaluated

Cost: Contact publisher

ASSET

| 1997, 2000, and 2001 | ACT, Inc |

Population: Ages 18 years and older

Purpose: Assesses writing, reading, numerical, and advanced math skills for course placement

Description: Paper–pencil 192-item multiple-choice test with the following categories: Writing

(36 items), Reading (24 items), Numerical (32 items), Elementary Algebra (25 items), Intermediate Algebra (25 items), College Algebra (25 items), and Geometry (25 items). Scores yielded are Entering Student Descriptive Report, Returning Student Retention Report, Course Placement Service, Underprepared Student Follow-up. Forms B, B2, C1, and C2 are used. May be modified for students with disabilities.

Format: Examiner required; individual administration; suitable for group use; timed: 25 minutes per each subtest

Scoring: Hand key; machine scored; computer scored; scoring service available from publisher

Cost: 25 Test Booklets $30.00

Basic Achievement Skills Individual Screener (BASIS)

1983   Harcourt® Brace Educational Measurement

Population: Grades 1 and above

Purpose: Measures achievement in reading, mathematics, and spelling; assesses individual student's academic strengths and weaknesses with both norm-referenced and criterion-referenced information

Description: Subtests assess academic achievement in reading, mathematics, and spelling. Test items are grouped in grade-referenced clusters, which constitute the basic unit of administration. Testing begins at a grade cluster with which the student is expected to have little difficulty and continues until the student fails to reach the criterion for a particular cluster. The clusters range from Readiness through Grade 8 for reading and mathematics and from Grade 1 through Grade 8 for spelling. The reading test assesses comprehension of graded passages. The student is required to read the passages aloud and supply the missing words. Comprehension at the lower levels is assessed by word reading and sentence reading, and readiness is measured by letter identification and visual discrimination. The mathematics test consists of a readiness subtest and assesses computation and problem solving above that level. The student works on the computation items directly in the record form. Word problems are dictated by the teacher and require no reading on the part of the student. The spelling test for Grades 1 through 8 consists of clusters of words that are dictated in sentence contexts. The student writes the words on the record form.

Format: Examiner required; individual administration; untimed: 1 hour

Scoring: Hand key

Cost: Examiner's Kit (manual, content booklet, 2 record forms) $171.00

BRIGANCE® Diagnostic Comprehensive Inventory of Basic Skills–Revised (CIBS-R)

Albert H. Brigance

1999   Curriculum Associates®, Inc.

Population: Grades PreK through 9

Purpose: Measures attainment of basic academic skills; used to meet minimal competency requirements, develop IEPs, and determine academic placement

Description: A total of 154 skill sequences in the following 22 sections: readiness, speech, word recognition grade placement, oral reading, reading comprehension, listening, functional word recognition, word analysis, reference skills, graphs and maps, spelling, writing, math grade placement, numbers, number facts, computation of whole numbers, fractions and mixed numbers, decimals, percents, word problems, metrics, and math vocabulary. Assessment is initiated at the skill level at which the student will be successful and continues until the student's level of achievement for that skill is attained. The following assessment methods may be used to accommodate different situations: parent interview, teacher observation, group or individual assessment, and informal appraisal of student performance in daily work. Two alternate forms, A and B, are available for pre- and posttesting for 51 skill sequences. All skill sequences are referenced to specific instructional objectives and grade-level expectations. The comprehensive book graphically indicates at each testing the level of competency the student has achieved. A videotape for in-service training of examiners is available. The revision includes normed assessments.

Format: Examiner required; many sections are suitable for group use; untimed

Scoring: Examiner evaluated; computer scoring available

Cost: Inventory with Standardization and Validation Manual $185.00

BRIGANCE® Diagnostic Inventory of Essential Skills

Albert H. Brigance

1981   Curriculum Associates®, Inc.

Population: Grades 6 to adult education

Purpose: Measures a student's mastery of academic skills and skills essential to success as a citizen, consumer, worker, and family member; used in secondary programs serving students with special needs; used to develop IEPs

Description: A total of 186 paper–pencil or oral-response skill assessments measuring minimal academic and vocational competencies in reading, language arts, and math. The inventory includes rating scales to measure applied skills that cannot be assessed objectively, such as health and attitude, job interview preparation, and communication. Test results identify basic skills that have and have not been mastered, areas of strengths and weaknesses in academic and practical skills, and instructional objectives for a specified skill level. Individual record books graphically indicate at each testing the level of competency the student has achieved and the student's current instructional goals. An optional class record book monitors the progress of 15 students and forms a matrix of specific student competencies. IEP objective forms are available for reading, writing and spelling, math, and individual use (blank form). Tests may be administered by teachers, aides, or parent volunteers. A videotape program for inservice training of examiners is available.

Format: Examiner required; some sections are suitable for group use; untimed

Scoring: Examiner evaluated

Cost: Assessment Book $168.00; Class Record Book $12.95; 10 Record Books $36.95

BRIGANCE® Diagnostic Life Skills Inventory
Albert H. Brigance

| 1994 | Curriculum Associates®, Inc. |

Population: High school students and adults

Purpose: Assesses basic skills and basic life skills in the context of real-world situations

Description: The inventory serves as a curriculum guide by providing teaching sequences for functional life skills. It provides an in-depth skill assessment with difficulty from grade levels 2 through 8 with 168 skill sequences covered in nine sections: Speaking and Listening, Functional Writing, Words on Common Signs and Warning Labels, Telephone, Money and Finance, Food, Clothing, Health, and Travel and Transportation. Rating scales evaluate subjective items such as aptitude and attitude. The inventory correlates with CASAS and SCANS Foundation Skills, meets

the requirements of the Perkins Act, and supports the Workforce Investment Act.

Format: Examiner required; suitable for group use; untimed: 12 minutes

Scoring: Examiner evaluated

Cost: Inventory $89.95; 10 Record Books $24.95

California Achievement Tests, Fifth Edition (CAT/5)

| 1992 | CTB/McGraw-Hill |

Population: Grades K to 12

Purpose: Assesses academic achievement

Description: A paper–pencil assessment system that evaluates students' academic achievement from Kindergarten through Grade 12. The number of criterion-referenced/multiple-choice items varies from 126 to 408, depending on the format/form. Performance is assessed in reading, language, spelling, mathematics, study skills, science, and social studies. Normative, objectives-based, and other reports are available. Test is available in large print or Braille. May be used for persons with visual, hearing, physical, or mental impairments.

Format: Examiner required; group administration; timed: 1 hour 30 minutes to 5 hours 15 minutes

Scoring: Scoring service or hand key

Cost: Contact publisher

California Diagnostic Tests (CDMT/CDRT)

| 1990 | CTB/McGraw-Hill |

Population: Grades 1 to 12

Purpose: Assesses basic reading and math skills

Description: The California Diagnostic Mathematics Test (CDMT) and the California Diagnostic Reading Test (CDRT) are two assessments that help educators identify strengths and areas of need for students in Grades 1 through 12. The norm-referenced scores produced can be used to evaluate progress.

Format: Examiner required; suitable for group use; approximate total time, including sample items and breaks, 1 hour 40 minutes to 2 hours 30 minutes

Scoring: Hand key or computer scored

Cost: 35 CDRT and CDMT Test Books: Machine Scorable $99.40; Hand-Scorable $61.20; Reusable (answer sheets ordered separately) $45.50

Canadian Achievement Survey Test for Adults (CAST)

| 1994 | Canadian Test Centre |

Population: Adults

Purpose: Measures achievement in reading, language, and mathematics

Description: Items were carefully screened and reviewed by Canadian adult educators and reflect language and content that are appropriate for adults. CAST scores can provide pre- and postinstruction information about an examinee's level of proficiency in the basic skills. Three levels are offered to accommodate the proficiency difference among adults: Level 1 for up to and including Grade 6, Level 2 for Grades 7 through 9, and Level 3 for Grades 10 and above. Each of the six CAST tests (two each in reading, language, and mathematics) were normed with a stratified random sample of over 16,000 senior high school students. Great care was taken to reduce bias from possible sources of greatest concern.

Format: Examiner required; individual or group administration; timed: 10 to 15 minutes for each test

Scoring: Hand key; machine scoring; scoring service available

Cost: Contact publisher

Canadian Achievement Tests–Third Edition (CAT–3)

| 2000 | Canadian Test Centre |

Population: Grades 1 to college

Purpose: Measures reading, language, writing, and mathematics

Description: CAT-3 materials are easy to read and have a contemporary and attractive appearance. The format was finalized after much consultation with teachers, graphic artists, and publishing experts. The content was designed to reflect Canadian society and values. The tests are matched to four major Canadian curricula, those for Western Canada and the Territories, Ontario, Quebec, and Atlantic Canada. The assessments are in a modular and flexible format. The Basic Battery consists of a Reading/Language test that integrates comprehension, vocabulary, and language questions and a Mathematics test that includes questions from all strands as defined by each province. The Basic Battery can be comfortably administered within one morning of class time. Even more in-depth assessments of students' strengths and needs are provided through

the Supplemental Tests: Word Analysis, Vocabulary, Spelling, Language/Writing Conventions, Computation, and Numerical Estimation. Norms are based on 44,000 students across Canada and are representative of the nation.

Format: Examiner required; individual or group administration; timed

Scoring: Hand key; machine scoring; scoring service available

Cost: Contact publisher

Canadian Tests of Basic Skills: High School Battery (CTBS), Levels 15–18, Form K

H. D. Hoover, A. Hieronymus, D. Frisbie

| 1998 | Nelson Thomson Learning |

Population: Grades 9 through 12

Purpose: Assesses students' abilities in academic areas

Description: Four test levels (15 through 18) consisting of a series of paper–pencil multiple-choice subtests: Vocabulary, Reading Comprehension, Quantitative Thinking, Written Expression, Using Sources of Information, and Science. This is a Canadian adaptation of the Iowa Tests of Educational Development published by the Riverside Publishing Company.

Format: Examiner required; suitable for group use; timed: 195 minutes

Scoring: Hand key; machine scored; test scoring service available from publisher

Cost: Contact publisher

Canadian Tests of Basic Skills: Multilevel (CTBS), Levels 9–14, Forms K and L

E. King-Shaw, A. Hieronymus, H. D. Hoover

| 1998 | Nelson Thomson Learning |

Population: Grades K.2 to 12

Purpose: Assesses students' abilities in vocabulary, reading comprehension, spelling, capitalization, punctuation, usage, visual materials, reference materials, mathematics concepts, mathematics problem solving, and mathematics computation

Description: A series of multiple-choice paper-pencil subtests: Vocabulary, Reading Comprehension, Spelling, Capitalization, Punctuation, Usage, Reference Materials, Maps and Diagrams, Mathematics Concepts, Mathematics Problem Solving,

Mathematics Computation, and Science. Materials include test booklets, answer sheets, scoring masks, teacher's guide, and supplementary materials as required. Form L is a shorter battery. This is a Canadian adaptation of the Iowa Tests of Basic Skills published by the Riverside Publishing Company. Examiner must have a teaching certificate.

Format: Examiner required; suitable for group use; timed: Form K 4 hours 40 minutes, Form L 1 hour 40 minutes

Scoring: Hand key; machine scored; test scoring service available from publisher

Cost: Contact publisher

Canadian Tests of Basic Skills: Primary Battery (CTBS), Levels 5–8, Form K
E. King-Shaw, A. Hieronymus, H. D. Hoover

1998	Nelson Thomson Learning

Population: Grades K.2 to 3.5

Purpose: Assesses students' abilities in listening, vocabulary, word analysis, language, reading, mathematics, and work study

Description: Four test levels (5 through 8) consisting of a series of paper–pencil multiple-choice subtests: Listening, Vocabulary, Word Analysis, Language, Reading, Mathematics, and Work Study. Materials include test booklets, scoring masks, a teacher's guide, and supplementary materials as required. Examiner must have a teaching certificate. This test is a Canadian adaptation of the Iowa Tests of Basic Skills published by the Riverside Publishing Company.

Format: Examiner required; suitable for group use; untimed: 2 to 4 hours (varies according to level)

Scoring: Hand key; machine scored; test scoring service available from publisher

Cost: Contact publisher

Career Programs Assessment Test (CPAt)

1997	ACT, Inc.

Population: Ages 18 years and older

Purpose: Used for career college admission and course placement to assess basic language, reading, and numerical skills

Description: Paper–pencil 115-item multiple-choice test with the following categories: Language Usage (60 items), Reading Skills (30 items), and Numerical Skills (25 items). These results are

reported: scores for each content area and composite; standard CPAt Summary Report; Customized CPAt Summary Report; and CPAt Retention Report. Forms B and C are available.

Format: Examiner required; individual and group administration; timed: 60 minutes

Scoring: Hand key; immediate results available

Cost: $165.00 per campus; $1.20 per test booklet; 50 Answer Sheets $125.00 (approximately $3.00 per student)

CASAS Secondary Diploma Program Assessment

1991	Comprehensive Adult Student Assessment System (CASAS)

Population: Adults, adolescents; native and nonnative speakers of English

Purpose: Measures a learner's reading comprehension, critical thinking, and problem-solving capabilities in eight core academic subjects; used to award high school credit and for placement, monitoring progress, and targeting instruction

Description: Multiple-choice tests include Mathematics, Economics, American Government, United States History, English/Language Arts, World History, Biological Science, and Physical Science. CASAS scaled scores identify general skill level and enable comparison of performance across CASAS tests. Training required.

Format: Examiner required; group administration; timed and untimed

Scoring: Self/computer scored

Cost: Each subject area: Set of 5 Pretests, 5 Posttests $48.00; Program Implementation Guide $50.00

College-Level Examination Program (CLEP)

Yearly	College Board

Population: Grades 12 and above

Purpose: Enables any student to earn college credit by recognizing college-level achievement acquired outside the conventional college classroom; used by businesses to allow employees to earn required continuing education credits

Description: Thirty-four subject exams assessing college-level proficiency in a wide range of fields. The material tested is referred to as the general/liberal education requirement. The subject exams measure achievement in specific college courses and are used to grant exemption from and credit in specific college courses. The exams stress concepts, principles, relationships, and applications of course material. They contain questions of varying difficulty. Exams are administered each month via computer at more that 1,000 test centers located on college campuses throughout the country. Test scores are available immediately. Institutions honoring CLEP test scores for credit are listed in "CLEP Colleges," available free from the publisher.

Format: Examiner required; suitable for group use; timed: 90 minutes per test

Scoring: Computer scored

Cost: Contact publisher

Comprehensive Scales of Student Abilities (CSSA)
Donald D. Hammill, Wayne P. Hresko

1994	PRO-ED, Inc.

Population: Ages 6 through 16 years

Purpose: Assesses developmental abilities seen in school settings for identification of need for referral

Description: Multiple-item rating scale to quantify a teacher's knowledge of students' abilities to include in the referral. Nine areas are measured: Verbal Thinking, Speech, Reading, Writing, Handwriting, Mathematics, General Facts in Science and Social Studies, Basic Motor Generalizations, and Social Behavior. The instrument contains a 9-point rating scale for 68 items. Descriptions contain clarifying information to aid the educator in the completion of the checklist. Scores obtained include standard scores and percentiles for the nine areas. Computer administration available in Macintosh and Windows formats.

Format: Rating scale; untimed: 10 minutes

Scoring: Examiner evaluated

Cost: Complete Kit (manual, 100 protocols, storage box) $79.00

Comprehensive Tests of Basic Skills, Fourth Edition (CTBS®/4)

1989	CTB/McGraw-Hill

Population: Grades K to 12

Purpose: Assesses basic skills in reading, language, mathematics, science, and social studies

Description: Paper–pencil multiple-item multiple-choice test measuring basic academic skills. Eleven levels assess the following: visual and sound recognition, word analysis, vocabulary, comprehension, spelling, language mechanics and expression, mathematics computation, mathematics concepts and applications, study skills, science, and social studies. The test is available in 11 Levels (K through 21/22); Level K is a "readiness" rather than "achievement" measure and is not scaled.

Format: Examiner required; suitable for group use; timed: complete battery 2 to 4 hours

Scoring: Hand key; scoring service available from publisher

Cost: Complete Battery (35 booklets) $94.75

Core Knowledge Curriculum-Referenced Tests

2000	Touchstone Applied Science Associates, Inc.

Population: Ages 6 to 10 years

Purpose: Assesses knowledge of core academic skills

Description: Paper–pencil multiple-choice criterion-referenced test with four subtests: Mathematics, Language Arts, History/Geography, and Science (35 to 50 items each, with a total of 140 to 200 items depending on grade). Individual scores for each subtest are obtained. Forms available: A1, A2, A3, A4, and A5.

Format: Examiner required; suitable for group use; untimed: 45 to 55 minutes

Scoring: Machine scored; scoring service available

Cost: 25 Tests $125.00 (A1, A2), $94.00 (A3, A4, A5); Scoring $3.95 per booklet, $2.50 per answer sheet

Criterion Test of Basic Skills (CBS)
Kerth Lundell, William Brown, James Evans

2002	Academic Therapy Publications

Population: Ages 6 through 11 years

Purpose: Assesses reading and arithmetic skills

Description: Paper–pencil multiple-item criterion-referenced test. The Reading subtest measures letter recognition, letter sounding, blending, sequencing, special sounds, and sight words. The Arithmetic subtest measures number and numerical recognition, addition, subtraction, multiplication, and division. Each part of the test offers optional objectives for evaluation. The manual contains over 200 teacher-directed, independent, and peer-tutoring activities correlated to the skill areas assessed, and arranged according to increasing difficulty.

Format: Examiner required; individual or group administration; untimed: 10 to 15 minutes

Scoring: Examiner evaluated

Cost: Test Kit (manual, protocols, and stimulus cards in vinyl folder) $65.00

CTB Performance Assessment
1994   CTB/McGraw-Hill

Population: Grades K to 11

Purpose: Assesses students' complex thinking and learning skills

Description: Short-answer/essay paper–pencil test consisting of 12 to 25 open-ended tasks in four subtest areas: Reading/Language Arts, Mathematics, Science, and Social Studies. Twelve levels. Integrated outcomes report available when used with California Achievement Tests, Fifth Edition, and the California Test of Basic Skills, Fourth Edition.

Format: Examiner required; group or individual administration; timed: 30 minutes to 1 hour each subtest

Scoring: Examiner evaluated; scoring service available from publisher

Cost: Examiner's Manual and 30 Test Books $45.90

CTB Portfolio Assessment
1992   CTB/McGraw-Hill

Population: Grades 1 to 8

Purpose: Assesses classroom performance

Description: Eight to 20 real-life performance tasks that allow students and teachers to work together to monitor development of skills and concepts, emphasizing development and encouraging students to rethink and improve their work. Subcategories include language arts and mathematics. Five levels are available.

Format: Examiner required; suitable for group use; untimed

Scoring: Examiner evaluated

Cost: Classroom Module (Language Arts or Mathematics) with all materials required for instruction and assessment of 35 students $89.60 per level

CTB Task Bank
1994   CTB/McGraw-Hill

Population: Grades 3 to 12

Purpose: Assesses performance on tasks and task-related activities to gain important information on student progress in particular areas of math or language arts

Description: Each task in the bank comprises one or more theme-based activities. Item banks are shipped in electronic form, as a Curriculum Builder bank, or in printed form, as a notebook.

Format: Examiner required; group administration; untimed

Scoring: Examiner evaluated

Cost: Electronic or printed $645.00; electronic and printed $845.00

Diagnostic Achievement Battery–Third Edition (DAB-3)
Phyllis L. Newcomer
2001   PRO-ED, Inc.

Population: Ages 6 through 14 years

Purpose: Assesses a child's ability to listen, speak, read, write, and perform simple mathematics operations; diagnoses learning disabilities

Description: Multiple-item paper–pencil and oral-response subtests assessing the following five components of a child's verbal and mathematical skills: Listening (Story Comprehension and Characteristics), Speaking (Synonyms and Grammatic Completion), Reading (Alphabet/Word Knowledge and Reading Comprehension), Written Language (Capitalization, Punctuation, Spelling, Contextual Language, and Story Construction), and Math (Math Reasoning and Math Calculation). Results, converted to standard scores, provide a profile of the child's strengths and weaknesses. The components of the test may be administered independently, depending on the needs of the child being tested.

Format: Examiner required; individual administration; untimed: 50 minutes

Scoring: Examiner evaluated; computer scoring available

Cost: Complete Kit (manual, student book, 25 record forms, 25 response forms, audiocassette, assessment probes, storage box) $244.00

Diagnostic Achievement Test for Adolescents–Second Edition (DATA-2)
Phyllis L. Newcomer, Brian R. Bryant
1993   PRO-ED, Inc.

Population: Ages 12 through 18 years

Purpose: Assesses a child's ability to listen, speak,

read, write, and perform simple mathematics operations; diagnoses learning disabilities

Description: Multiple-item paper–pencil and oral-response test consisting of 10 core subtests and three supplemental subtests. The core subtests are Receptive Vocabulary, Receptive Grammar, Expressive Grammar, Expressive Vocabulary, Word Identification, Reading Comprehension, Math Calculations, Math Problem Solving, Spelling, and Writing Composition. The supplemental subtests are Science, Social Studies, and Reference Skills. Nine composite standard scores are generated.

Format: Examiner required; individual administration; untimed: 50 minutes

Scoring: Examiner evaluated

Cost: Complete Kit (manual, student book, 25 protocols, 25 student response booklets, storage box) $149.00

Diagnostic Screening Test: Achievement (DSTA)
Thomas D. Gnagey, Patricia A. Gnagey

1977   Slosson Educational Publications, Inc.

Population: Grades K to 14

Purpose: Measures basic knowledge of science, social studies, literature, and the arts to help determine a course of study for special education students

Description: Paper–pencil 108-item multiple-choice test. Scores are obtained for practical knowledge and provide an estimated mental age. The manual discusses subtest pattern analysis of student motivation, cultural versus organic retardation, cultural deprivation, reading and study skill problems, and possession of practical versus formal knowledge. The examiner explains the procedure to individuals or groups and reads the test if the students have poor reading skills.

Format: Examiner required; suitable for group use; untimed: 5 to 10 minutes

Scoring: Hand key

Cost: Manual and 50 Test Forms $52.50

Essential Skills Screener (ESS)
Bradley T. Erford, Gary J. Vitali,
RoseMary Haas, Rita R. Boykin

1995   Slosson Educational Publications, Inc.

Population: Ages 3 to 11 years

Purpose: Identifies children at risk for school readiness or learning problems

Description: Reading, writing, and math skills are assessed for children in three age ranges: 3 to 5, 6 to 8, and 9 to 11. The ESS provides both grade and age norms. Interpretation is simplified through the use of percentile ranks, performance ranges, and standard scores. Age scores and grade scores are provided.

Format: Examiner required; individual or group administration; untimed: 10 minutes

Scoring: Hand key

Cost: Complete Multilevel Kit $178.00

Evaluation of Basic Skills (EBS)
Lee Havis

1996   Trust Tutoring

Population: Ages 3 to 18 years

Purpose: Measures basic skills in reading, writing, and math

Description: Provides a reliable measure of basic skill ability of students enrolled in a program of individualized in-home learning. The EBS is easy to administer and provides raw scores compared to age-level performance on easy-to-read charts. Areas of weakness and lack of concept understanding are revealed. Concepts in math are isolated for clear basic information. Specific rules of phonics are also isolated and sequenced in difficulty.

Format: Examiner required; individual or group administration; timed and untimed

Scoring: Hand key

Cost: $49.95

Evaluation of School-Related Skills (E=MC^2)
Ruth L. Gottesman, Jo Ann Doino-Ingersoll,
Frances M. Cerullo

1996   Slosson Educational Publications, Inc.

Population: Grades K through 5

Purpose: Used to identify children who are at risk for or are experiencing school learning difficulties

Description: The test has six levels, one for each grade. Major skill areas underlying school achievement are measured: Language/Cognition, Letter Recognition, Word Recognition, Oral Reading, Reading Comprehension, Auditory Memory, Arithmetic, and Visual-Motor Integration. The total score reflects the child's overall performance on a variety of tasks that assess school-related skills.

Format: Examiner required; individual administration; untimed: 7 to 10 minutes

Scoring: Hand key

Cost: Complete Multilevel Kit (manual, student booklets, 5 examiner forms for 5 levels) $69.00

EXPLORE

1997 — ACT, Inc.

Population: Grades 8 and 9

Purpose: Measures educational achievement for counseling and evaluation

Description: Paper-pencil 128-item multiple-choice test with the following categories: English (40 items, 30 minutes); Math (30 items, 30 minutes), Reading Test (30 items, 30 minutes), and Science Reasoning (28 items, 30 minutes). The results reported are as follows: an English Test total score and two subscores: Usage/Mechanics and Rhetorical Skills; a Mathematics Test total score; a Reading Test total score; a Science Reasoning Test total score; and a Composite score. Raw scores are converted to scale scores; scale scores for the four tests and the composite range from a low of 1 to a high of 12. The EXPLORE program also collects information about student's career interests, educational plans, and special educational needs. Suitable for individuals with visual, physical, hearing, and mental impairments.

Format: Examiner required; suitable for group use; timed: 120 minutes

Scoring: Test scoring and reporting included in the cost of the student assessment sets

Cost: 30 Reusable Test Booklets $52.50; 30 Consumable Student Assessment Sets $141.00

Graduate Record Examinations (GRE)

Yearly — Educational Testing Service

Population: Adults, college graduates

Purpose: Measures academic abilities and knowledge of graduate school applicants; used by graduate schools for screening the qualifications of applicants and by organizations for selecting fellowship recipients

Description: Multiple-item paper-pencil multiple-choice battery of advanced achievement and aptitude tests. The General Test Measures verbal, quantitative, and analytical abilities. The Subject Tests are available for the following 17 subjects: biology, chemistry, computer science, economics, education, engineering, French, geology, history, literature in English, mathematics, music, physics, political science, psychology, sociology, and Spanish. The tests are administered on specified dates at centers established by the publisher. The General Test is also offered on computer, taken at the examinee's convenience at Sylvan Learning Centers.

Format: Examiner required; suitable for group use; timed: General test 3 hours 30 minutes; subject tests 2 hours, 50 minutes each

Scoring: Computer scored

Cost: Contact publisher

Hammill Multiability Achievement Test (HAMAT)

Donald D. Hammill, Wayne P. Hresko, Jerome J. Ammer, Mary E. Cronin, Sally S. Quinby

1998 — PRO-ED, Inc.

Population: Ages 7 through 17 years

Purpose: Measures achievement in basic academic areas

Description: A content-driven achievement test that measures reading, writing, mathematics, and facts. The Reading Subtest consists of a series of paragraphs, based on the cloze procedure. The Writing Subtest requires the student to write sentences from dictation, stressing correctness. The Mathematics Subtest measures the student's mastery of number facts and ability to complete mathematical calculations. The Facts Subtest requires the student to answer questions based on the content of social studies, science, history, and literature curricula. Scores provided are standard scores (mean of 100, standard deviation of 15), percentiles, and age and grade equivalents. The test was normed on 2,901 students. Alternate equivalent forms are available.

Format: Examiner required; individual or group administration; untimed: 30 to 60 minutes

Scoring: Examiner evaluated

Cost: Complete Kit (manual, 25 each of Form A and B student response and record booklets, storage box) $189.00

Hunter-Grundin Literacy Profiles

Elizabeth Hunter-Grundin, Hans U. Grundin

Date not provided — Test Agency, Ltd.

Population: Ages 6 years 6 months to 12+ years

Purpose: Assesses child's progress in reading and language development

Description: Battery of brief paper-pencil and oral tests measuring five components of literacy skills, including reading for meaning, attitude toward reading, spelling, free writing, and spoken language. The test is available on five levels: Level 1 (ages 6.5 to 8), Level 2 (ages 8 to 9), Level 3 (ages 9 to 10), Level 4 (ages 10 to 11+), and Level 5 (ages 11 to 12+). The Reading for Meaning passage is different at each level. The score correlates with the Schonell Reading Test, Holborn Reading Scale, and Neale Analysis of Reading Ability. Only the Spoken Language subtest must be individually administered.

Format: Examiner required; individual or group administration; timed: 10 minutes

Scoring: Hand key

Cost: Contact publisher

Iowa Tests of Basic Skills® (ITBS®), Form A
H. D. Hoover, S. B. Dunbar, D. A. Frisbie

| 2001 | Riverside Publishing Company |

Population: Grades K through 9

Purpose: Provides a comprehensive assessment of student progress in the basic skills

Description: All new test content is aligned with the most current content standards, curriculum frameworks, and instructional materials. The ITBS measures critical thinking skills across test levels, in every content area. Developed at the the University of Iowa and backed by a tradition of more than 70 years of educational research and test development experience, the ITBS provides an in-depth assessment of students' achievement of important educational objectives. Tests in reading, language arts, mathematics, social studies, science, and information sources yield reliable and comprehensive information both about the development of students' skills and about their ability to think critically. The battery is available as a Complete Battery, a Core Battery (Reading, Language, and Mathematics tests only), and a Survey Battery (a shortened version of the Core Battery).

Format: Examiner required; suitable for group use; time varies according to battery

Scoring: Hand key; may be machine scored; scoring service available

Cost: Contact publisher

Iowa Tests of Basic Skills® (ITBS®), Form M
H. D. Hoover, A. N. Hieronymus, D. A. Frisbie, S. B. Dunbar

| 1996 | Riverside Publishing Company |

Population: Grades K through 9

Purpose: Assesses the development of basic academic skills; identifies individual students' strengths and weaknesses

Description: Paper-pencil multiple-choice tests assess proficiency in the basic skills required for academic success. The Iowa Tests consist of 10 levels: Levels 5 and 6 for Grades K and 1; Levels 7 and 8 for Grades 1 through 3; and for Levels 9 through 14 for Grades 3 through 9. The tests are Vocabulary, Reading, Language, Mathematics, Social Studies, Science, Sources of Information, Student Questionnaire (optional), Performance Assessments (optional), Iowa Writing Assessment (optional), and Listening Assessment (optional). Scores are reported for each of the tests in the Complete and Survey Batteries at each level. Total scores are reported for Reading, Language, Mathematics, and either the Core Battery tests or the Survey Battery. For the Complete Battery, a Source of Information Total and Composite score are also reported. For Title I reporting, Advanced Skills scores are available for Reading, Language, and Mathematics. If the optional Student Questionnaire is used, results are tabulated for teachers and guidance counselors as part of central scoring services.

Format: Examiner required; suitable for group use; time varies according to battery

Scoring: Hand key; may be machine scored; scoring service available

Cost: Contact publisher

Iowa Tests of Basic Skills® (ITBS®), Forms K and L
A. N. Hieronymus, H. D. Hoover, S. B. Dunbar, D. A. Frisbie

| 1993 | Riverside Publishing Company |

Population: Grades K through 9

Purpose: Assesses the development of basic academic skills; identifies individual students' strengths and weaknesses

Description: Available in three different editions: Complete Battery, Core Battery, and Survey Battery. The Complete Battery is a comprehensive battery covering important objectives of the instructional program of a given grade. An optional Questionnaire for Grades 3 through 9 is designed to collect information about students that is useful to counselors and teachers as they work with individual students. The Core Battery contains wholly intact tests from the Complete Battery that provides reading, language, and mathematics scores for Levels 7 through 9. The Survey

Battery is limited to 30 minutes per test in reading, language, and mathematics, plus the Questionnaire.

Format: Examiner required; suitable for group use; time varies according to battery

Scoring: Hand key; may be machine scored; scoring service available

Cost: Contact publisher

Iowa Tests of Educational Development® (ITED®), Form A
Robert A. Forsyth, Timothy N. Ansley, Leonard S. Feldt, Stephanie D. Alnot

2001	Riverside Publishing Company

Population: Grades 9 through 12

Purpose: Assesses academic skills that represent the long-term goals of secondary education, particularly the critical thinking skills of analysis and evaluation

Description: The battery represents an upward extension of the Iowa Tests of Basic Skills. It is available in either a Complete Battery booklet or a Core Battery booklet. The Complete Battery contains nine tests: vocabulary, reading comprehension, language: revision written materials, spelling, mathematics: concepts and problem solving, computation, analysis of social studies materials, analysis of science materials, and sources of information. The Core Battery contains the first six tests of the Complete Battery.

Format: Examiner required; suitable for group use; time varies according to battery

Scoring: Hand key; may be machine scored; scoring service available

Cost: Contact publisher

Kaufman Functional Academic Skill Test (K-FAST)
Alan S. Kaufman, Nadeen L. Kaufman

1994	American Guidance Service

Population: Ages 15 to 85+ years

Purpose: Measures reading and math functional skills

Description: Unlike adaptive behavior inventories that ask an informant to rate how a person functions, the K-FAST requires subjects to show they can perform the requested skills. K-FAST reading and arithmetic tasks relate to everyday activities, such as understanding labels on drug containers, following directions in a recipe, budgeting

monthly expenses, and making price comparisons between products.

Format: Examiner required; individual administration; untimed:15 to 25 minutes

Scoring: Examiner interpreted

Cost: Complete Kit (manual, easel, 25 forms) $111.95

Kaufman Test of Educational Achievement–Normative Update (K-TEA/NU)
Alan S. Kaufman, Nadeen L. Kaufman

1998	American Guidance Service

Population: Ages 6 through 22 years

Purpose: Measures reading, mathematics, and spelling skills

Description: The K-TEA/NU provides a comprehensive and brief form to measure academic achievement. The Brief Form subtests are Mathematics, Reading, and Spelling. The Comprehensive Form subtests are Mathematics Applications, Reading Comprehension, Reading Decoding, Mathematics Computation, and Spelling. Spring and fall grade norms are provided.

Format: Examiner required; individual administration; untimed: Comprehensive Form 60 to 75 minutes, Brief Form 30 minutes

Scoring: Examiner interpreted; computer scoring available

Cost: Complete Kit for Comprehensive and Brief Forms (test easels, manuals, 25 of each protocol, reports to parents, carry bag) $274.95

Metropolitan Achievement Test®, Eighth Edition (METROPOLITAN8)

2000	Harcourt® Brace Educational Measurement

Population: Grades K through 12

Purpose: Assesses school achievement; used for measuring performance of large groups of students

Description: This test combines real-world content and design with cutting-edge reporting information that provides educators and parents with action strategies. Test questions range from measuring foundation skills to critical thinking processes and strategies. This edition reflects what is taught in today's classrooms. Subjects measured are Reading, Mathematics, Language, Writing, Science, and Social Studies. An interactive, online assessment is available for Grades 3 to 8 in Reading Comprehension, Mathematics

Concepts and Problem Solving, and Mathematics Computation. The battery can be easily customized to match local curriculum and testing requirements. Available in 13 levels based on grade.

Format: Examiner required; suitable for group use; timed: varies from 90 minutes to more than 4 hours

Scoring: Hand key; may be machine or computer scored; scoring service available; on-line scoring available

Cost: Examination Kit for Preview only $31.50 per level

Mini-Battery of Achievement (MBA)
Richard W. Woodcock,
Kevin S. McGrew, Judy Werder

1994 Riverside Publishing Company

Population: Ages 4 years through adult

Purpose: Provides a brief screening of achievement

Description: Designed to give broader coverage of the skills included in each achievement area, the MBA has four subtests: reading, mathematics, writing, and factual knowledge. The reading subtest measures a variety of aspects of reading, including sight recognition, comprehension, and vocabulary. The mathematics subtest includes calculation, reasoning, and concepts. The writing skills subtest includes spelling dictation, punctuation, usage, and proofing. The Factual Knowledge subtest helps assess general information in science, social studies, and the humanities. Each of the four subtests can be administered and scored independently of the others. Reading, writing, and mathematics scores can be combined to obtain a Basic Skills Cluster score. The MBA includes a computer program that will print a one-page narrative report summarizing all test results in a matter of seconds.

Format: Examiner required; individual administration; untimed: 20 minutes

Scoring: Computer scored; examiner evaluated

Cost: Complete Test (test book with manual, 25 test records with worksheets, software) $187.00

Monitoring Basic Skills Progress (MBSP)
Lynn S. Fuchs, Carol Hamlett, Douglas Fuchs

Reading 1997; Math Computation 1998; Math Concepts and Applications 1999 PRO-ED, Inc.

Population: Elementary and middle school grades

Purpose: Monitors progress in three academic areas: basic reading, basic math computation, and basic math concepts and applications

Description: Computers automatically conduct curriculum-based measurement, provide students with immediate feedback on their progress, and provide teachers with individual and classwide reports that help them plan more effective instruction. These programs automatically save students' scores and prepare graphs displaying the students' progress over time. The two math programs come with printed copies of tests for Grades 1 through 6. The child works the problems on the reproducible worksheet and inputs the answers for scoring.

Format: Self-administered; untimed

Scoring: Computer scored; Macintosh format only

Cost: Complete Program (one each of basic reading, basic math computation, and basic math concepts and applications; blackline masters for both math programs) $329.00

Multilevel Academic Survey Tests (MAST)
Kenneth W. Howell, Stanley H. Zucker,
Mada K. Morehead

1985 The Psychological Corporation

Population: Grades K through 12

Purpose: Assesses academic performance to ensure meaningful placement and curriculum decisions

Description: Multiple-item paper–pencil test using both Grade Levels and Curriculum Levels. In the Grade Level tests, three levels are available: Primary, Short (reading and mathematics), and Extended (includes reading comprehension and problem solving). The Curriculum Level tests include comprehensive reading and mathematics.

Format: Examiner required; suitable for group use; untimed: 10 to 30 minutes per test

Scoring: Examiner evaluated

Cost: Examination Kit $79.00

National Educational Development Test (NEDT)

1984 CTB/McGraw-Hill

Population: Grades 9 and 10

Purpose: Assesses students' strengths and weaknesses in English, math, social studies, reading, natural sciences, and educational ability

Description: Paper–pencil 209-item test measuring the ability to apply rules and principles of grammar and general English usage, understand mathematical concepts, apply principles in solving quantitative problems, comprehend reading selections, and apply critical reading skills. The test is semisecure (forms and keys are not released). The test is used only in schools that choose to serve as designated test centers.

Format: Examiner required; suitable for group use; timed: 2 hours, 30 minutes

Scoring: Computer scored

Cost: Contact publisher

Norris Educational Achievement Test (NEAT)
Janet Switzer, Christian P. Gruber

| 1992 | Western Psychological Services |

Population: Ages 4 to 17 years

Purpose: Used as a standard assessment of basic educational abilities

Description: A diagnostic achievement battery featuring alternate forms, optional measures of written language and oral reading and comprehension, separate grade and age norms, tables identifying discrepancies between IQ and achievement, and a standardization sample. Readiness Tests are used to assess children between 4 and 6 years of age, and Achievement Tests are used to evaluate examinees ages 6 and older.

Format: Examiner required; individual administration; untimed: 30 minutes

Scoring: Hand key

Cost: Kit (10 test booklets, administration and scoring manual, technical manual) $128.00

Objectives-Referenced Bank of Items and Tests (ORBIT)

| 1982 | CTB/McGraw-Hill |

Population: Grades K to 12

Purpose: Allows the development of customized criterion-referenced tests; offers objectives designed to meet educational needs

Description: Criterion-referenced bank of multiple-choice questions covering objectives in reading, language arts, mathematics, and social studies. Four test items are provided for each objective.

Format: Examiner required; suitable for group use; untimed

Scoring: Machine scored; hand key; computer scored

Cost: Contact publisher

Peabody Individual Achievement Test–Revised/Normative Update (PIAT–R/NU)
Frederick C. Markwardt, Jr.

| 1998 | American Guidance Service |

Population: Ages 5 through 22 years

Purpose: Measure of academic achievement

Description: The PIAT–R/NU is an efficient individual measure of academic achievement. Reading, mathematics, and spelling are assessed in a simple, nonthreatening format that requires only a pointing response for most items. This multiple-choice format makes the instrument idea for assessing low functioning individuals. There are six subtests: General Information, Reading Recognition, Reading Comprehension, Written Expression, Mathematics, and Spelling.

Format: Examiner required; individual administration; untimed: 60 minutes

Scoring: Examiner interpretation; computer scoring is available for Macintosh and Windows formats

Cost: Complete Kit (4 easels, 50 record forms, manual, carry bag) $325.95

Performance Assessments for ITBS® and TAP®/ITED®

| 1993/1994 | Riverside Publishing Company |

Population: Grades 1 through 12

Purpose: Assesses students' strategic thinking and problem-solving capabilities

Description: Norm-referenced, free-response assessments in Integrated Language Arts, Mathematics, Social Studies, and Science. These assessments give students an opportunity to apply content-area concepts and higher-order thinking processes in real-life situations. The assessments are designed to evaluate the application of problem-solving processes; they provide a complement to multiple-choice achievement test batteries. They were developed to minimize the need to apply prior knowledge of specific content information. Performance assessments provide in-depth evaluation of the processes students use to mobilize prior knowledge or solve problems. Tasks in each assessment are weighted toward the higher levels of cognitive complexity. Each assessment uses a scenario to engage students in a real-world situation that requires them to use their strategic-thinking and problem-solving capabilities.

Format: Examiner required; group administration; untimed: 60 minutes

Scoring: Examiner evaluated; scoring service available

Cost: Contact publisher

PLAN

Yearly	ACT, Inc.

Population: Grade 10

Purpose: Used in student guidance and program evaluation to assess educational achievement

Description: Paper–pencil 145-item multiple-choice test with the following categories: English (50 items, 30 minutes), Math (40 items, 40 minutes), Reading (25 items, 20 minutes), and Science Reasoning (30 items, 25 minutes). The following results are reported: English Test total score and two subscores: Usage/Mechanics and Rhetorical Skills; Math Test total score and two subscores: Pre-Algebra/Algebra and Geometry, Reading Test total score; and Science Reasoning Test total score. Raw scores are converted to scale scores; scale scores for the four tests and the composite range from a low of 1 to a high of 32. Subscores are reported on a scale score ranging from a low of 1 to a high of 16. A pencil, test booklet, answer sheet, and supplemental publications are used.

Format: Examiner required; suitable for group use; timed: 115 minutes

Scoring: Machine scored; test scoring service available from publisher

Cost: $8.25 per individual

Pre-Professional Skills Test (PPST)

Date not provided	Educational Testing Service

Population: College students

Purpose: Measures the basic academic skills and achievement of individuals preparing for careers as elementary or high school teachers

Description: Multiple-item paper–pencil multiple-choice and essay test assessing proficiency in reading, writing, and mathematics. The 50-minute Reading test (40 questions) assesses the ability to understand, analyze, and evaluate short passages (100 words), long passages (200 words),

and short statements. The 50-minute Mathematics test (40 questions) evaluates the ability to judge mathematical relations. The two-part Writing test consists of a 45-item multiple-choice test of functional written English (30 minutes) and an essay (30 minutes). Each part is graded separately and combined for a single Writing score.

Format: Examiner required; suitable for group use; timed: 3 hours

Scoring: Computer scored; examiner evaluated

Cost: Contact publisher

Quic Tests
Oliver Anderhalter

1989	Scholastic Testing Service, Inc.

Population: Grades 2 through 12

Purpose: Used as an estimation of grade placement to assess achievement in communications and math

Description: Multiple-choice test with 5 to 8 items per grade. Grade equivalent scores and competency-based grade equivalent scores are yielded. Forms A and B for both Communicative Arts and Mathematics are available. A booklet, answer sheet, and pencil are used. Examiner must be certified for assessment.

Format: Examiner required; group administration; timed: 30 minutes

Scoring: Hand key; examiner evaluated

Cost: Starter Set $59.80

SAT II: Subject Tests

Yearly	College Board

Population: Grades 9 to 12

Purpose: Used to predict college performance and by some schools for admissions selection and course placement in specific subject areas

Description: Paper–pencil multiple-choice tests in Writing, Literature, U.S. History and Social Studies, World History, Math (Levels IC and IIC), Biology, Chemistry, Physics, French, German, Modern Hebrew, Italian, Latin, Korean, English Language Proficiency, and Spanish. An individual may take up to three SAT II: Subject Tests on a single test date. The use of a calculator is allowed on Math Level IC and Math Level IIC; they require a scientific calculator. Fee reductions are available for students with financial need.

Format: Examiner required; suitable for group use; timed: 1 hour

Scoring: Computer scored

Cost: Contact publisher

Scholastic Abilities Test for Adults (SATA)

Brian R. Bryant, James R. Patton, Caroline Dunn

| 1991 | PRO-ED, Inc. |

Population: Ages 16 years and older

Purpose: Measures an individual's scholastic aptitude and achievement; used to identify an individual's strengths and weaknesses and identify persons who may need special assistance in secondary and postsecondary training and educational settings

Description: Multiple-item paper–pencil assessment battery consisting of nine subtests: Verbal Reasoning—understanding verbal analogies; Nonverbal Reasoning—using geometric forms to assess nonverbal problem solving; Quantitative Reasoning—determining problem-solving abilities using numbers; Reading Vocabulary—recognizing synonyms and antonyms in print; Reading Comprehension—reading passages silently and responding to multiple-choice items; Math Calculation—computing arithmetic, geometry, and algebra problems; Math Application—reading and computing story problems; Writing Mechanics—writing sentences that require spelling, capitalization, and punctuation skills; and Writing Composition—writing a story that is checked for content maturity and vocabulary. Individual subtest raw scores are converted to estimated grade equivalents, standard scores ($M = 10$, $SD = 3$), and percentiles. Several composite scores are also generated: General Aptitude, Total Achievement, Reading, Mathematics, and Writing. Composite scores are reported as estimated grade equivalents, standard scores ($M = 100$, $SD = 15$), and percentiles.

Format: Examiner required; suitable for group use; timed: 10 to 15 minutes per subtest

Scoring: Examiner evaluated

Cost: Complete Kit (manual, 10 test books, 25 response booklets, 25 profile/examiner record forms, storage box) $159.00

School Archival Records Search (SARS)

Hill M. Walker, Alice Block-Pedego, Bonnie Todis, Herbert H. Severson

| 1991 | Sopris West Educational Services |

Population: Grades K through 6

Purpose: Provides the school professional with a profile of a student's status on 11 archival variables usually contained in school records

Description: The SARS profile can be used for determining at-risk status for dropout; meeting the requirement that a referred student's school history be systematically examined in eligibility decision-making processes; validating school assessments; and screening in conjunction with the Systematic Screening for Behavior Disorders. Included is a User's Guide, Technical Manual, and Instrument Packet with quantities sufficient to conduct a record search on 50 students.

Format: Records search

Scoring: Examiner evaluated

Cost: $35.00

Secondary School Admission Test (SSAT)

| Date not provided | Educational Testing Service |

Population: Grades 5 to 10

Purpose: Measures the abilities of students applying for admission to Grades 6 through 11 of selective schools; used by independent schools for student selection

Description: Multiple-item paper–pencil multiple-choice test measuring verbal and quantitative abilities and reading comprehension. The test consists of four sections: one measuring verbal ability, two measuring mathematical ability, and one measuring reading comprehension. An upper level form is administered to students in Grades 8 through 10; a lower level form is administered to students in Grades 5 through 7. Scores are normed on the student's grade level at the time of testing. Norms for each grade level are developed annually on the basis of the most recent 3-year sample of candidates tested. The test is administered on specific dates (six Saturdays during the school year and biweekly during the summer) at designated test centers. Students may designate six score recipients. Students with physical or visual disabilities are allowed up to double the amount of testing time per section.

Format: Examiner required; suitable for group use; timed

Scoring: Computer scored; hand key

Cost: Domestic Test Fee (administration, parents' score report, 6 designated school reports) $25.00; Foreign Test Fee (including Canada, Puerto Rico, U.S. territories) $45.00

Stanford Achievement Test™ Series, 9th Edition (Stanford 9)

1996   Harcourt® Brace Educational Measurement

Population: Grades K through 13

Purpose: Assesses school achievement status of children in reading, mathematics, language, spelling, study skills, science, social studies, and listening

Description: Contains multiple-choice and open-ended assessment with a variety of battery configurations to meet individual schools' needs. A separate writing test is available either in paper-pencil format or on-line. Year 2000 norms are available from a norm group sample of more than 10 million students. The sample statistically represents the current U.S. student population. In addition, Stanford 9 offers separate sets of empirical normative information for the following subgroups: Catholic, private, high socioeconomic status, and urban.

Format: Examiner required; suitable for group use; timed

Scoring: Hand key; computer scoring service available

Cost: Examination Kit (for preview only) $34.00 per level

Terranova (CTBS-5)

1996   CTB/McGraw-Hill

Population: Grades K to 12

Purpose: Assesses academic achievement in multiple measures format

Description: Multiple-item paper–pencil norm- and criterion-referenced multiple-choice, short answer and essay assessment system with multiple components. Consists of reading/language arts, mathematics, science, and social studies subtests. Available in Forms A and B. Spanish version available.

Format: Examiner required; suitable for group use; timed

Scoring: Hand key; image scored; hand scored for constructed response

Cost: Contact publisher

Terranova, The Second Edition

2000   CTB/McGraw-Hill

Population: Grades K through 12

Purpose: Measures achievement in reading/language arts, math, science, and social studies

Description: The new edition offers a full range of testing options, from selected-response to open-ended tasks. Together, these assessments give students the best opportunity to show what they know and can do. The examiner can choose the combination that best meets the students' needs, and customize the solution to reflect local and state standards. The publisher offers custom options to complement any of the TerraNova assessments, or to serve as the basis for a local testing program. Two forms are available (C and D). The math requires manipulatives that are included with booklets. Higher-order thinking skills, as well as basic and applied skills, are measured. The test generates norm-referenced achievement scores, criterion-referenced objective mastery scores, and performance-level information.

Format: Examiner required; suitable for group use; timed and untimed

Scoring: Hand key; machine scored; scoring service available

Cost: Contact publisher

Test of Academic Achievement Skills–Revised (TAAS-R)
Morrison F. Gardner

Date not provided   Psychological and Educational Publications, Inc.

Population: Ages 5 to 15 years

Purpose: Measures academic abilities

Description: The revised edition contains the following subtests: Spelling, Letter and Word Reading, Listening Comprehension, Arithmetic, and the new Oral Reading Stories and Comprehension. The revision measures how well a child has mastered various academic subjects. Results are provided in standard scores.

Format: Examiner required; individual administration; untimed: 30 to 40 minutes

Scoring: Examiner evaluated

Cost: Complete Kit (manual, 25 test booklets, oral reading stories booklet, card) $89.95

Test of Academic Performance
Wayne Adams, Lynn Erb, David Sheslow

1989   The Psychological Corporation

Population: Grades K through 12

Purpose: Assesses math, reading, writing, and spelling

Description: The test uses classroom-familiar formats: Spelling is assessed through dictation, mathematics through computation, and reading through decoding and comprehension of material read silently. There are two optional writing subtests.

Format: Examiner required; individual administration; untimed: 20 to 45 minutes

Scoring: Examiner evaluated

Cost: Complete Kit (manual, 25 each of response forms and record forms, cards) $111.00

Tests of Achievement and Proficiency™ (TAP®), Form M
Dale P. Scannell, Oscar M. Haugh, Brenda H. Loyd, C. Frederick Risinger

1996   Riverside Publishing Company

Population: Grades 9 through 12

Purpose: Provides a comprehensive and objective measure of students' progress in a high school curriculum

Description: Paper–pencil multiple-choice battery assessing student achievement in the basic skills of reading, writing, mathematics, social studies, science, and information processing. The tests are organized into four levels that correspond to the four high school grades. Each level is available in a Survey Battery and a Complete Battery. The Survey Battery covers Reading with Vocabulary and Comprehension, Written Expression, Math Concepts and Problem Solving, and optional Math Computation. The Complete Battery consists of Vocabulary, Reading Comprehension, Written Expression, Math Concepts and Problem Solving, optional Math Computation, Social Studies, Science, and Information Processing. For the Complete Battery, scores are reported for each of the seven individual tests, a Reading Total, a Core Total, and a Battery Composite. For the Survey Battery, scores are reported for Reading, Math, and Battery Total. Predicted ACT and SAT scores are available to help with educational guidance.

Format: Examiner required; suitable for group use; complete battery: 255 minutes; survey battery: 90 minutes

Scoring: Hand key; may be machine scored; scoring service available

Cost: Contact publisher

Tests of Achievement and Proficiency™ (TAP®), Forms K and L
Dale P. Scannell, Oscar M. Haugh, Brenda H. Loyd, C. Frederick Risinger

1993   Riverside Publishing Company

Population: Grades 9 through 12

Purpose: Provides a comprehensive and objective measure of students' progress in a high school curriculum

Description: Paper–pencil multiple-choice battery assessing student achievement in the basic skills of reading, writing, mathematics, social studies, science, and information processing. The tests are organized into four levels that correspond to the four high school grades. Each level is available in a Survey, Core, or Complete Battery. The Survey Battery covers Reading with Vocabulary and Comprehension, Written Expression, Math Concepts and Problem Solving, and optional Math Computation. The Complete Battery consists of Vocabulary, Reading Comprehension, Written Expression, Math Concepts and Problem Solving, optional Math Computation, Social Studies, Science, and Information Processing.

Format: Examiner required; suitable for group use; time varies based on battery

Scoring: Hand key; may be machine scored; scoring service available

Cost: Contact publisher

Tests of Adult Basic Education (TABE), Forms 7 and 8

1994   CTB/McGraw-Hill

Population: Adults

Purpose: Measures adult proficiency in reading, mathematics, and language; used to identify individual strengths and needs, establish appropriate level of instruction, and measure growth after instruction

Description: Multiple-item paper–pencil multiple-choice test measuring an adult's grasp of the reading, mathematics, language skills, and spelling required to function in society. The test is available in four levels ranging from easy to advanced. A large-print edition is available. Scores may be used to estimate performance on the GED tests. Spanish version available. Computerized version available.

Format: Examiner required; suitable for group use; complete battery: 2 hours 45 minutes; survey form: 1 hour 30 minutes

Scoring: Hand key; may be computer scored

Cost: Multi-level Review Kit $19.10

Tests of Adult Basic Education (TABE-PC 5.0™)

1994   CTB/McGraw-Hill

Population: Adults

Purpose: Provides automatic scoring of the TABE basic skills assessments

Description: Computerized version of the TABE basic skills assessments. Available for TABE Forms 5 and 6, TABE Forms 7 and 8, TABE Work-Related Foundation Skills (TABE-WF), and TABE Español.

Format: Examiner required; administered on computer; complete battery: 2 hours 45 minutes; survey form: 1 hour, 30 minutes

Scoring: Computer scored

Cost: Contact publisher

Valpar Test of Essential Skills in English and Math (VTES)
Bryan B. Christopherson, Alex Swartz

1998   Valpar International Corporation

Population: Math Grades 4 to 10; English: Grades 6 to 12

Purpose: Measures basic English and math skills for adult basic education

Description: Math skills tested are computation (Grades 4 through 8, 20 items) and usage (Grades 6 through 10, 21 items). English skills assessed are vocabulary (25 items), spelling (5 items), usage (10 items), and reading (10 items). Items are presented in a multiple-choice format. Scores provided are grade equivalents, percent correct by subarea, and GED Math and Language levels.

Format: Examiner required; group or individual administration; untimed: 45 minutes

Scoring: Computer scored; machine scored; test scoring service available from publisher

Cost: Evaluation Kit $50.00 (approximately $1.00 per complete test)

Wechsler Individual Achievement Test®-Second Edition (WIAT®-II)

2001   The Psychological Corporation

Population: Ages 4 years through adult

Purpose: Measures academic abilities to evaluate discrepancies between aptitude and achievement

Description: An expanded age range, more comprehensive items, and streamlined test materials are a few of the benefits of the second edition. The subtests are Oral Language, Listening Comprehension, Written Expression, Spelling, Word Reading, Pseudoword Decoding, Reading Comprehension, Numerical Operations, and Mathematics Reasoning. The examiner can elect to ad-

minister the entire battery or select subtests for a more focused assessment.

Format: Examiner required; individual administration; untimed: 30 to 75 minutes

Scoring: Hand key; computer scoring available

Cost: Complete Kit (manual, stimulus booklets, 25 protocols, bag) $300.00

Wide Range Achievement Test–Expanded Edition (WRAT-Expanded)
Gary J. Robertson

2001   Wide Range, Inc.

Population: Ages 4 to 24 years

Purpose: Measures academic achievement and nonverbal reasoning

Description: Measures achievement in the areas of reading comprehension, mathematics, listening comprehension, oral expression, and written language. The test includes both group administered and individually administered formats. Results on the group and individually administered test forms can be compared, resulting in a number of technical benefits to the user. The Group Form is available in five levels designed for Grades 2 through 12. Each level contains four subtests: Reading Comprehension, Mathematics, Written Language, and Nonverbal Reasoning. The Individual Form contains Pre-reading Skills, Beginning Reading, Reading Comprehension, Beginning Mathematics, Mathematics, Listening Comprehension, and Oral Expression. The same Written Language test is given in groups and individually.

Format: Examiner required; suitable for group administration; untimed: 2 hours 30 minutes

Scoring: Hand key

Cost: Group Package (manual, 25 booklets) $95.00 per level; Individual Package (manual, flipbooks, 25 forms) $195.00

Wide Range Achievement Test–Third Edition (WRAT-3)
Gary S. Wilkinson

1993   Wide Range, Inc.

Population: Ages 5 to 75 years

Purpose: Used in the measurement of basic academic codes and in diagnosing learning disabilities to assess reading, spelling, and arithmetic; intended for school populations, special education, and clinical use

Description: Paper-pencil test with three sub-tests: reading, spelling, and arithmetic. Standard scores, percentiles, absolute scores, and grade ratings are yielded. Reading measures recognizing and naming letters and pronouncing printed words. Spelling tests measure name writing and writing letters and words from dictation. Arithmetic measures counting, reading number symbols, and oral and written computation. Available in large print. Two equivalent forms are provided.

Format: Examiner required; portions suitable for group administration; untimed: 30 minutes

Scoring: Hand key; examiner evaluated

Cost: Starter Set (manual, 25 each of blue and tan test forms, profile/analysis form, cards, case) $135.00

Woodcock-Johnson® III (WJ III®) Tests of Achievement
Richard W. Woodcock, Kevin S. McGrew, Nancy Mather

| 2001 | Riverside Publishing Company |

Population: Ages 2 through 90+ years

Purpose: Provides a comprehensive assessment of oral language and achievement

Description: Comes in two forms that have parallel content. Each form is divided into Standard and Extended batteries. The Standard Battery includes 12 tests that provide a broad set of scores. The Extended Battery contains 10 tests that provide more in-depth diagnostic information on specific academic strengths and weaknesses. With many new features, the WJ III provides broader coverage of key academic areas and more interpretive options than any other achievement battery. The new version includes 7 new tests; 8 new clusters; 4 oral language tests; expanded broad achievement clusters with 3 tests to measure basic skills, fluency, and application; revised procedure for evaluating intra-achievement discrepancies; an ability-achievement discrepancy using oral language; and expanded reading tests containing more items to measure early reading performance. Co-normed with the WJ III Tests of Cognitive Abilities to provide additional ability-achievement discrepancies and intraindividual discrepancy.

Format: Examiner required; individual administration; untimed: 5 minutes per subtest

Scoring: Computer scored; examiner evaluated

Cost: Form A or Form B (standard and extended

test books, 2 manuals, audiocassette, 25 each of test records and response booklets, scoring software, scoring guides, leather case) $500.00

Woodcock-Johnson®-Revised Tests of Achievement (WJ-R®)
Richard W. Woodcock, M. Bonner Johnson

| 1989 | Riverside Publishing Company |

Population: Ages 2 through 90+ years

Purpose: Provides a comprehensive assessment of achievement

Description: The tests are divided into two batteries: standard and supplemental. The Standard Battery contains nine tests covering the areas of reading, mathematics, written language, and knowledge. These tests yield six cluster scores: Broad Reading, Broad Mathematics, Mathematic Reasoning, Broad Written Language, Broad Knowledge, and Skills. The Supplemental Battery contains tests that can be used in conjunction with the tests in the Standard Battery to obtain the following cluster scores: Basic Reading, Reading Comprehension, Basic Mathematics Skills, Basic Writing Skills, and Written Expression. Alternate forms are available for pretest and posttest administration.

Format: Examiner required; individual administration; untimed: 5 minutes per subtest

Scoring: Examiner evaluated; computer scoring available

Cost: Form A or B (standard and supplemental test books, examiner's manual, norm tables, 25 test records, 25 subject response booklets, case) $386.00

Work Sampling System®
Samuel J. Meisels, Judy R. Jablon, Margo L. Dichtelmiller, Dorothea B. Marsden, Aviva B. Dorfman

| 2001 | Rebus, Inc. |

Population: Grades PreK through 5

Purpose: Used to document children's skills, knowledge, behavior, and accomplishments

Description: Measures across a wide variety of curriculum areas on multiple occasions to enhance teaching and learning. The Work Sampling System consists of three complementary elements. Developmental Guidelines and Checklists provide a framework for observation that gives teachers a set of observational criteria that are based on national standards and knowledge of child development. Teachers' observations are recorded three times each year. Portfolios are purposeful collections of children's work that illustrate students' efforts, progress, and achievements. Summary Reports are completed three times a year and are intended to replace conventional reporting systems. Teachers combine information for the Developmental Checklists and Portfolios with their own knowledge of child development to assess students' performance and progress. Seven curriculum domains and eight age/grade levels are covered. The curriculum areas are Personal and Social Development, Language and Literacy, Mathematical Thinking, Scientific Thinking, Social Studies, The Arts, Physical Development, and Health. Spanish forms are also available.

Format: Examiner required; multiple methods of measurement; classroom embedded; untimed

Scoring: Examiner evaluated; computer scoring available

Cost: Single-Grade Classroom Pack for 20 students (manual, developmental guidelines, wall chart, reproducible masters, developmental checklists, portfolio notes and labels, summary report forms, and overview for families) $130.00

Young Children's Achievement Test (YCAT)
Wayne P. Hresko, Pamela K. Peak, Shelley R. Herron, Deanna L. Bridges

| 2000 | PRO-ED, Inc. |

Population: Ages 4 through 7 years

Purpose: Measures early academic achievement

Description: The YCAT represents a major improvement in the early identification of children at risk for school failure. It yields an overall Early Achievement standard score and individual subtest standard scores for General Information, Reading, Writing, Mathematics, and Spoken Language. The YCAT was designed with both the child and the examiner in mind. The individual subtests can be given independent of each other, leading to flexible testing sessions. The YCAT was normed on 1,224 children representing 32 states and Washington, D.C.

Format: Examiner required; individual administration; untimed: 25 to 45 minutes

Scoring: Examiner evaluated

Cost: Complete Kit (manual, picture book, 25 record booklets, 25 response forms, storage box) $179.00

Academic Aptitude

ACER Intermediate Test F

| 1982 | Australian Council for Educational Research Limited |

Population: Ages 10 to 14 years

Purpose: Measures the intelligence of students

Description: Pencil–paper 80-item test measuring general mental abilities in the following areas: classification, jumbled sentences, number series, synonyms and antonyms, arithmetical and verbal problems, and proverbs. Materials include a four-page booklet, scoring key, manual, and specimen set. Australian norms are provided.

Format: Examiner required; suitable for group use; timed: 30 minutes

Scoring: Hand key

Cost: Contact publisher

ACER Intermediate Test G

| 1982 | Australian Council for Educational Research Limited |

Population: Ages 10 to 15 years

Purpose: Measures intelligence of students

Description: Paper–pencil 75-item test measuring general mental abilities: verbal comprehension, verbal reasoning, and quantitative reasoning. Australian age and grade norms are provided. Not available to Australian government schools.

Format: Examiner required; suitable for group use; timed: 30 minutes

Scoring: Hand key

Cost: Contact publisher

ACER Word Knowledge Test: Form F
Marion de Lemos

| 1990 | Australian Council for Educational Research Limited |

Population: Years 9, 10, and 11

Purpose: Measures verbal skills and general reasoning ability

Description: Tests of word knowledge have been found to correlate highly with other measures of verbal skills and general reasoning ability. Because they are relatively quick and easy to administer, they have been widely used as screening tests. This test enables the user to assess quickly student knowledge of word meanings. Students are required to select, from a list of five alternatives, the word or phrase that most closely approximates the meaning of each of the 72 items.

Format: Examiner required; group administration; untimed: 10 minutes

Scoring: Hand key; scoring service available

Cost: Contact publisher

Ann Arbor Learning Inventory
Barbara Meister Vitale, Waneta Bullock

1996 (Levels A and B); 1989 (Level C)	Academic Therapy Publications

Population: Grades K through 8

Purpose: Evaluates the central processing and perceptual skills necessary for reading, writing, and spelling to identify learning difficulties and deficits and suggest appropriate remedial strategies

Description: Multiple-item task-performance oral-response and paper-pencil test measuring the following central processing skills: Visual Discrimination, Visual Memory, Auditory Discrimination, and Auditory Memory. Test items are presented in order of natural cognitive development, beginning with pictures, proceeding to objects and geometric forms, and finally to letters, words, and phrases. Tasks involve listening, manipulating, showing, matching, visualizing, telling, and writing. Results also provide objective data on developmental levels for prereading readiness, precomputational skills, kinesthetic and motor skills, and comprehension and critical thinking. Instrument is criterion referenced.

Format: Examiner required; individual or group administration; untimed

Scoring: Examiner evaluated

Cost: Manuals (Levels A, B, or C) $15.00; Test Booklets (Levels A, B, or C) $12.00; Stimulus Cards (Level C) $8.00

Aptitude Profile Test Series (APTS)
George Morgan, Andrew Stephanou, Brian Simpson

2001	Australian Council for Educational Research Limited

Population: Years 9, 10, and 11

Purpose: Measures verbal, quantitative, abstract, and spatial-visual reasoning

Description: The Verbal Reasoning module tests two kinds of verbal analogy, semantic comprehension, and vocabulary. The Quantitative Reasoning module tests three areas: abstract numeric, short word problems, and problems that require more extensive reading, comprehension and processing of information to find the correct solution. The Abstract Reasoning module assesses a person's ability to reason in an abstract context in which one or more rules must be identified. The module challenges test takers to identify hidden rules that underlie patterns and sequences of patterns, presented in one or more dimensions. The Spatial-Visual module of the APTS involves three kinds of questions: two-dimensional objects/pattern flipping, three-dimensional objects involving maps and side views, and nest of cubes.

Format: Examiner required; suitable for group use; timed: from 30 minutes per section

Scoring: Scored with key, machine scored, computer scored; scoring service available from publisher

Cost: Contact publisher

Ball Aptitude Battery™ (BAB)-Form M

1998	Ball Foundation

Population: Ages 14 through 18 years, and adults

Purpose: Assesses occupation-related aptitudes for career planning and guidance

Description: Consisting of 18 subtests, including several individually administered apparatus tests, these 12 aptitude tests were selected for inclusion in the school battery to provide maximum usefulness. Total of 12 subtests measure seven areas: Speed and Accuracy (clerical, writing speed); Academic (numerical computation, numerical reasoning, vocabulary); Spatial (paper folding); Reasoning (inductive reasoning, analytical reasoning); Personality Orientation (Word Association); Creativity (Idea Generation); and Memory (Associative Memory, Auditory Memory Span). Written on an eighth-grade reading level.

Format: Examiner required; group administration; timed: 2 hours 10 minutes

Scoring: Hand and computer scored; test scoring service available from publisher

Cost: Contact publisher

California Critical Thinking Skills Test (CCTST)
Peter A. Facione

1990 (Form A); 1992 (Form B); 2000 (Form 2000)	California Academic Press

Population: Adults; college and graduate levels

Purpose: Assesses core cognitive skills in critical thinking

Description: Paper-pencil multiple-choice test with five subtests. Categories include analysis, and inference, evaluation, inductive reasoning, and deductive reasoning. Three forms are available. CCTST test booklet (10 pages) used; answer form is optional. Available also in Spanish. Suitable for individuals with hearing impairment.

Format: Examiner required; group administration; timed and untimed

Scoring: Machine scored; scoring service available; Form 2000 scored only by scoring service

Cost: Specimen Kit $60.00

Canadian Test of Cognitive Skills (CTCS)

1992	Canadian Test Centre

Population: Grades 2 to college

Purpose: Measures cognitive abilities important for scholastic success

Description: The CTCS provides the information needed to plan an educational program best suited to the learning and developmental needs of students. It measures selected abilities, such as understanding verbal and nonverbal concepts and comprehending relationships between ideas, so the teacher can screen students for placement in special programs and identify students in need of further diagnosis of learning problems. The CTCS is a thorough Canadian adaptation of the Test of Cognitive Skills–Second Edition published by CTB/McGraw-Hill. The subtests are Sequences, Analogies, Memory, and Verbal Reasoning. Norms were developed from a Canada-wide study involving 78 school jurisdictions. The stratified random sample of over 36,000 students ensured representativeness by region, district size, and degree of urbanization.

Format: Examiner required; individual or group administration; timed: 52 to 55 minutes

Scoring: Hand key; machine scoring; scoring service available

Cost: Contact publisher

Cognitive Abilities Test™ (CogAT®), Form 5
Robert L. Thorndike, Elizabeth P. Hagen

1993	Riverside Publishing Company

Population: Grades K through 12

Purpose: Assesses students' abilities in reasoning and problem solving using verbal, quantitative, and spatial (nonverbal) symbols

Description: Multiple-item paper-pencil multiple-choice test measuring the development of students' cognitive skills. The Primary Battery, organized into two levels (Level 1 for Grades K and 1, Level 2 for Grades 2 and 3), measures the factors of oral vocabulary, verbal classification, figure matricies, and quantitative concepts. The Multilevel/Separate Level Editions are available for Levels A through H for Grades 3 to 12. Each level contains a verbal battery assessing sentence completion, verbal classification, and verbal analogies; a quantitative battery assessing quantitative relations, number series, and equation building; and a nonverbal battery measuring figure classification, figure analogies, and figure analysis. All levels of the test contain three batteries that provide separate scores for verbal, quantitative, and nonverbal reasoning abilities. A composite score is also available. Each item on the verbal tests has been reviewed for appropriateness of vocabulary level and sentence structure. All items have been reviewed to eliminate content that could be biased toward any group of individuals.

Format: Examiner required; suitable for group use; approximately 90 minutes

Scoring: Hand key; may be machine scored; scoring service available

Cost: Contact publisher

Cognitive Abilities Test™ (CogAT®), Form 6
David F. Lohman, Elizabeth P. Hagen

2001	Riverside Publishing Company

Population: Grades K through 12

Purpose: Assesses students' abilities in reasoning and problem solving using verbal, quantitative, and spatial (nonverbal) symbols

Description: An integrated series of tests that provides information on the level of development in general and specific cognitive skills. These abilities have substantial correlations with learning and problem solving both in and out of school. The new edition was developed under the same rigorous standards as The Iowa Tests. Students who would benefit from enrichment or intervention can be easily identified. Individual reports describe the level and pattern of each student's abilities. Profile classifications are made dependable by a careful examination of the consistency of each student's responses to items within a subtest and across subtests within a battery. The following levels are available: K, 1, and 2 (Grades K through 2) and A-H (Grades 3 through 12). National norms are available for fall, midyear, and spring.

Format: Examiner required; suitable for group use; time varies depending on level

Scoring: Hand key; may be machine scored; scoring service available

Cost: Contact publisher

Collegiate Assessment of Academic Progress (CAAP) Critical Thinking Test

| 2001 | ACT, Inc. |

Population: Ages 17 years and older

Purpose: Assesses critical thinking

Description: Paper-pencil 32-item multiple-choice test. Examiner must have experience with test administration at the college level. May be used for persons with visual, physical, hearing, and mental impairments

Format: Examiner required; suitable for group use; timed: 40 minutes

Scoring: Machine scored; test scoring service available

Cost: Kit (test booklet, answer sheet) $10.75

Detroit Tests of Learning Aptitude-Adult (DTLA-A)
Donald D. Hammill, Brian R. Bryant

| 1991 | PRO-ED, Inc. |

Population: Ages 16 to 79 years

Purpose: Measures general and specific aptitudes to identify deficiencies and provide an index of optimal-level performance; permits interpretation in terms of current theories of intellect and behavior domains

Description: The battery's 12 subtests and 16 composites measure both general intelligence and discrete ability areas. The instrument was normed on more than 1,000 adults from more than 20 states. The overall composite is formed by combining the scores of all 12 subtests in the battery. Therefore, the overall composite is prob-

ably the best estimate of Spearman's *g* in that it reflects status on the widest array of different developed abilities. The DTLA-A includes Verbal and Nonverbal Composites, Attention-Enhanced and Attention-Reduced Composites, and Motor-Enhanced and Motor-Reduced Composites.

Format: Examiner required; individual administration; timed and untimed: 90 minutes

Scoring: Examiner evaluated

Cost: Complete Kit (manual, picture books, 25 each of 3 types of protocol, manipulatives, storage box) $279.00

Detroit Tests of Learning Aptitude-Fourth Edition (DTLA-4)
Donald D. Hammill

| 1998 | PRO-ED, Inc. |

Population: Ages 6 through 17 years

Purpose: Measures general and specific aptitudes of children and identifies deficiencies

Description: Includes 10 subtests, the result of which can be combined to form 16 composites that measure both general intelligence and discrete ability areas. This test not only measures basic abilities, but also shows the effects of language, attention, and motor abilities on test performance. The subtests are Word Opposites, Design Sequences, Sentence Imitation, Reversed Letters, Story Construction, Design Reproduction, Basic Information, Symbolic Relations, Word Sequences, and Story Sequences. Subtests are assigned to composites that represent major popular theories. Thus, the subtests can be related to Horn and Cattell's fluid and crystallized intelligence, Jensen's associative and cognitive levels, Das's simultaneous and successive processes, and Wechsler's verbal and performance scales.

Format: Examiner required; individual administration; timed and untimed: 1 to 2 hours

Scoring: Examiner evaluated; computer scoring available

Cost: Complete Kit (manual, 2 picture books, 25 profile/summary forms, 25 record booklets, 25 response forms, story chips, design cubes, storage box) $329.00

Detroit Tests of Learning Aptitude-Primary: Second Edition (DTLA-P:2)
Donald D. Hammill, Brian R. Bryant

| 1991 | PRO-ED, Inc. |

Population: Ages 3 to 9 years

Purpose: Measures general and specific aptitudes of children and identifies deficiencies

Description: Oral-response and paper-pencil battery with 100 items yielding six subtest scores (Verbal and Nonverbal, Attention-Enhanced and Attention-Reduced, Motor-Enhanced and Motor-Reduced) and a General Mental Ability score. These scores provide a detailed profile of a student's abilities and deficiencies. The test is useful with low-functioning school-age children.

Format: Examiner required; individual administration; timed and untimed: 15 to 45 minutes

Scoring: Examiner evaluated

Cost: Complete Kit (examiner's manual, picture book, 25 record forms, 25 response forms, storage box) $159.00

General Processing Inventory (GPI)
Ruth M. Martin-Geiman

1996	ADECCA Educational Alternatives

Population: Ages 5 years through adult

Purpose: Measures processing irregularities in vision, speech, hearing, writing, and memory to develop appropriate educational accommodations

Description: There are two subtests: General Elementary Inventory of Language Skills (GEILS) and General Elementary Inventory of Mathematics and Numeration (GEIMAN). The GEILS measures letter and word processing, and punctuation. There are four levels of 126 to 1,105 items. Each letter of a word counts as an item. The GEIMAN measures number and symbol processing. There are four levels with 109 to 325 items. The results of the GPI are given in a format that can be used directly on IEPs. Adaptation directives are given in four sections: for the student, peers, family members, and teachers or supervisors.

Format: Examiner required; individual administration; untimed: 1 to 2 hours

Scoring: Examiner evaluated; test scoring service available

Cost: $750.00

Gessell School Age Assessment

Date not provided	Modern Learning Press, Inc.

Population: Ages 5 to 9 years

Purpose: Measures developmental skills

Description: Provides a consistent evaluation of eye-hand coordination, motor skills, attention span, visual perception, neuromuscular maturity, perceptual functioning, and thinking.

Format: Examiner required; individual administration; untimed: 40 minutes

Scoring: Examiner evaluated

Cost: 50 Recording Sheets $49.95, Assessment Kit (reusable materials) $30.95

Graduate Management Admissions Test (GMAT)

Yearly	Educational Testing Service

Population: College graduates

Purpose: Measures verbal and quantitative abilities related to success in graduate management schools; used for admission to graduate management school

Description: Paper-pencil multiple-choice test used by many graduate schools of business and management as one criterion for admission. In 1994, an analytical writing assessment was added to the GMAT. The test is administered four times annually at centers established by the publisher, and registration materials are available at no charge. The test is not available for institutional use.

Format: Examiner required; suitable for group use; timed: 4 hours

Scoring: Scored by publisher

Cost: Contact publisher

Henmon-Nelson Test of Mental Ability (Canadian Edition)
M. J. Nelson, Tom Lamke, Joseph French

1989	Nelson Thomson Learning

Population: Grades 3 to 12

Purpose: Assesses students' academic aptitude

Description: Series of multiple-choice paper-pencil subtests that test students' academic aptitude. This is a revision of the Henmon-Nelson Form 1 by Riverside (1973). Materials include test booklets, answer sheets, and record sheets. Examiner must have a teacher certificate.

Format: Examiner required; suitable for group use; timed: 30 minutes

Scoring: Self-scored; hand key; scoring service available from publisher

Cost: Contact publisher

InView and InView Online

2000 and 2001	CTB/McGraw-Hill

Population: Grades 2 through 12

Purpose: Measures aptitude and cognitive ability for learning disabilities and gifted-talented identification

Description: Five subtests have 20 items each: Verbal Reasoning-Context, Verbal Reasoning-Words, Sequences, Analogies, and Quantitative Reasoning. Scores provided are Anticipated Achievement, Cognitive Skills Index, percentiles, scale scores, stanines, and NCEs. Computer version is available for PC format. Web enabled online for any platform.

Format: Examiner required; suitable for group use; timed: 15 to 20 minutes per subtest

Scoring: Hand key; machine scored; computer scored; scoring service available; on-line scoring

Cost: $2.50 for materials, $2.75 for scoring per examinee

Iowa Tests of Educational Development® (ITED®), Form M
Leonard S. Feldt, Robert A. Forsyth, Timothy N. Ansley, Stephanie D. Alnot

1996   Riverside Publishing Company

Population: Grades 9 through 12

Purpose: Assesses intellectual skills that represent the long-term goals of secondary education, particularly the critical thinking skills of analysis and evaluation

Description: Available in a Complete Battery and a Survey Battery. The Complete Battery contains seven tests that require students to apply knowledge and skills in new settings and give students an opportunity to demonstrate different competencies in a variety of contexts: Vocabulary, Ability to Interpret Literary Materials, Correctness and Appropriateness of Expression, Ability To Do Quantitative Thinking, Analysis of Social Studies Materials, Analysis of Science Materials, and Use of Sources of Information. The Survey Battery consists of three tests: Reading, Correctness and Appropriateness of Expression, and Ability To Do Quantitative Thinking. For the Complete Battery, scores are reported for each of the seven tests and a composite. For the Survey Battery, scores are reported for each test and an Advanced Skills Score. Predicted ACT and SAT scores are available to help with educational guidance. If the optional Questionnaire is used, results may be tabulated for teachers and guidance counselors as part of central scoring services.

Format: Examiner required; suitable for group use; time varies according to battery

Scoring: Hand key; may be machine scored; scoring service available

Cost: Contact publisher

Iowa Tests of Educational Development® (ITED®), Forms K and L
Leonard S. Feldt, Robert A. Forsyth, Timothy N. Ansley, Stephanie D. Alnot

1993   Riverside Publishing Company

Population: Grades 9 through 12

Purpose: Assesses intellectual skills that represent the long-term goals of secondary education, particularly the critical thinking skills of analysis and evaluation

Description: Available in a Complete Battery and a Survey Battery. The Complete Battery contains seven tests that require students to apply knowledge and skills in new settings and give students an opportunity to demonstrate different competencies in a variety of contexts: Vocabulary, Ability to Interpret Literary Materials, Correctness and Appropriateness of Expression, Ability To Do Quantitative Thinking, Analysis of Social Studies Materials, Analysis of Science Materials, and Use of Sources of Information. The Survey Battery consists of three tests: Reading, Correctness and Appropriateness of Expression, and Ability To Do Quantitative Thinking. For the Complete Battery, scores are reported for each of the seven tests and an Advanced Skills score. For the Survey Battery, scores are reported for each test and a composite. Predicted ACT and SAT scores are available to help with educational guidance. If the optional Questionnaire is used, results may be tabulated for teachers and guidance counselors as part of central scoring services.

Format: Examiner required; suitable for group use; time varies according to battery

Scoring: Hand key; may be machine scored; scoring service available

Cost: Contact publisher

Kuhlmann-Anderson Tests (KA), 8th Edition
Frederick Kuhlmann, Rose G. Anderson

1981   Scholastic Testing Service, Inc.

Population: Grades K through 12

Purpose: Evaluates students' academic ability and potential; used for placement and diagnosing individual learning abilities

Description: Multiple-item multiple-choice test with eight subtests, four of which are nonverbal in nature. The test is available in seven levels: Kindergarten, Grade 1, Grades 2 to 3, Grades 3 to 4, Grades 5 to 6, Grades 7 to 9, and Grades 9 to 12. The test yields standard scores for verbal, nonverbal, and full battery; national and local percentiles; and stanines. Available in large print.

Format: Examiner required; group administration; timed: 50 to 75 minutes

Scoring: Hand key; machine scored; scoring service available

Cost: Specimen Set (booklet, answer sheet; specify level) $18.40

Measure of Questioning Skills
Ralph Himsl, Garnet W. Miller

1993	Scholastic Testing Service, Inc.

Population: Grades 3 through 10

Purpose: Assesses critical thinking skills development

Description: Short-answer test shows four pictures. Four-minute time limit is given on each item. Forms A and B are available. Examiner must be certified for assessment.

Format: Examiner required; group administration; timed: 20 minutes

Scoring: Examiner evaluated

Cost: Starter Set (booklet) $42.85

Naglieri Nonverbal Ability Test®– Multilevel Form (NNAT®–Multilevel)
Jack A. Naglieri

Date not provided	Harcourt® Brace Educational Measurement

Population: Grades K through 12

Purpose: Measures nonverbal reasoning and problem-solving abilities

Description: The test is independent of educational curricula as well as students' cultural or language background. The test uses progressive matrices in seven grade-based levels with a wide range of items for each age group. The tests at each level contain 38 items, and the brief spoken instructions are available in several different languages. All information needed to solve each task is presented with each diagram, so students do not have to depend on word or mathematical knowledge, or reading skills to answer the questions.

Format: Examiner required; suitable for group use; untimed: 30 minutes

Scoring: Hand key; scoring service available

Cost: Examination Kit $23.50 per level

National Academic Aptitude Tests: Non-Verbal Intelligence
Andrew Kobal, J. Wayne Wrightstone, Karl R. Kuntze

1964	Psychometric Affiliates

Population: Grades 10 and above

Purpose: Assesses mental abilities; used to indicate aptitude for academic training in such areas as engineering, chemistry, and other sciences

Description: Three nonverbal paper–pencil tests measuring mental aptitudes. The tests are Non-verbal Test of Spatial Relations, Comprehension of Physical Relations, and Graphic Relations. The test detects the ability to handle nonverbal materials at a high mental level. Items include pictorial and graphic work.

Format: Examiner required; suitable for group use; timed: 26 minutes

Scoring: Hand key

Cost: Specimen Set $4.00; 25 Tests $13.75

National Academic Aptitude Tests: Verbal Intelligence
Andrew Kobal, J. Wayne Wrightstone, Karl R. Kuntze

1984	Psychometric Affiliates

Population: Adolescents, adults

Purpose: Assesses mental aptitudes important in academic and professional work; used for evaluation of applicants for employment and school programs

Description: Three orally presented paper–pencil tests measuring mental aptitudes. The tests cover general information, academic and general science, mental alertness, comprehension, judgment, arithmetic reasoning, comprehension of relations, logical selection, analogies, and classification. Norms are provided for Grades 7 through 12, college students, administrative and executive employees, physicians, lawyers, and other professionals.

Format: Examiner required; suitable for group use; timed: 40 minutes

Scoring: Hand key

Cost: Specimen Set $4.00; 25 Tests $13.75

Otis-Lennon School Ability Test®, Seventh Edition (OLSAT®7)

Arthur S. Otis, Roger T. Lennon

1995   Harcourt® Brace Educational Measurement

Population: Grades K through 12

Purpose: Assesses general mental ability or scholastic aptitude

Description: Assesses students' reasoning skills and provides an understanding of a student's relative strengths and weaknesses in performing a variety of reasoning tasks. The information allows educators to design programs that will enhance students' strengths while supporting their learning needs. Concepts measured are Verbal Comprehension, Verbal Reasoning, Pictorial Reasoning, Figural Reasoning, and Quantitative Reasoning.

Format: Examiner required; suitable for group use; timed: varies by level, 75 minutes maximum

Scoring: Hand key; may be machine scored; scoring service available

Cost: Examination Kit (test booklet and directions for administering, practice test and directions for administering, machine-scorable answer document, practice test answer document) $25.50

Preliminary SAT/National Merit Scholarship Qualifying Test (PSAT/NMSQT™)

Yearly   College Board

Population: Grades 10 to 12 (Grade 11 score is the only score considered by the National Merit Corporation)

Purpose: Assesses high school students' verbal and math reasoning abilities and writing to evaluate readiness for college-level study

Description: Paper-pencil 131-item multiple-choice test measuring verbal, mathematical, and writing achievement. The verbal section consists of 52 questions of three types: sentence completions, analogies, and critical reading. The mathematical section consists of 40 questions applying graphic, spatial, numerical, symbolic, and logical techniques at a knowledge level no higher than elementary algebra and geometry. The writing section consists of 39 multiple-choice questions. Special testing arrangements can be made for away-from school testing, for students abroad, and for students with visual and other disabilities. Fee reductions are available for students with financial need.

Format: Examiner required; suitable for group use; timed: 2 hours 10 minutes

Scoring: Computer scored

Cost: Contact publisher

Quick Screening Scale of Mental Development

Katherine M. Banham

1963   Psychometric Affiliates

Population: Ages 6 months to 10 years

Purpose: Assesses a child's mental development; identifies children in need of clinical evaluation; used in clinics, hospitals, and special schools

Description: Task-assessment and observational instrument arranged in five behavioral categories to measure a child's mental development. The test booklet consists of brief descriptions of behavior occurring in certain situations. The situations are to be checked and scored directly on the booklet. Instructions for administering are provided in the manual. Professional persons skilled in clinical psychology should interpret the results. The test provides a profile of scores in the five behavior categories for diagnostic purposes and educational guidance. Tentative norms for 50 children, along with the children's scores on the Cattell Infant Scale and the Stanford-Binet Scale, are provided.

Format: Examiner required; individual administration; untimed: 30 minutes

Scoring: Hand key

Cost: Specimen Set $5.00; 25 Tests $5.00

SAT® I: Scholastic Assessment Test-Reasoning Test

Yearly   College Board

Population: Grades 11 and 12

Purpose: Measures developed verbal and mathematical reasoning abilities that are related to successful performance in college

Description: Paper-pencil 138-item multiple-choice test measuring reading comprehension, vocabulary, and mathematical problem-solving ability involving arithmetic reasoning, algebra, and geometry. The test consists of two verbal sections of 78 questions, including 19 analogies, 19 sentence completions, and 40 critical reading questions, and two mathematical sections of 60 questions, including approximately half multiple-choice and the balance quantitative comparison and student-produced questions. Fee reductions are available for students with financial need.

Format: Examiner required; suitable for group use; timed: 3 hours

Scoring: Computer scored

Cost: Contact publisher

Structure of Intellect Learning Abilities Test (SOI-LA)
Mary Meeker, Robert Meeker

1975   Western Psychological Services

Population: Grades K to adult

Purpose: Measures an individual's learning abilities; used for cognitive clinical assessment, diagnosis, screening for giftedness, and identification of specific learning deficiencies

Description: Paper–pencil 430-item multiple-choice free-response test. The test measures 26 factors identified by Guilford's Structure-of-Intellect model. The operations of cognition, memory, evaluation, convergent production, and divergent production are applied to figural, symbolic, and semantic content. The test is available in two equivalent forms, A and B, and five shorter forms (gifted screening, math, reading, primary screening, and reading readiness). The shorter forms use 10 to 12 subtest factors, printed test forms, and a manual with visual aids for group presentations. Training in administration and usage is required.

Format: Examiner required; suitable for group use in some situations; untimed: 2 hours 30 minutes

Scoring: Hand key

Cost: Kit (10 test booklets, 5 each of Form A and Form B, manual, set of scoring keys, set of stimulus cards, 10 worksheets and profile forms) $215.00

STS: High School Placement Test (HSPT)–Closed Form

2002   Scholastic Testing Service, Inc.

Population: Grades 8.3 to 9.3

Purpose: Assesses academic achievement and aptitude

Description: Multiple-choice test with 298 items on five subtests: verbal cognitive skills, quantitative skills, reading, mathematics, and language. Alphabetical lists, rank order lists, group summary reports, performance profiles, and item analysis reports are provided. Optional tests for Catholic religion, mechanical aptitude, and sci-

ence are available. Examiner must be certified for assessment. Available in large print.

Format: Examiner required; individual administration; untimed and timed portions: 2 hours 30 minutes

Scoring: Machine scored; test scoring service available from publisher

Cost: Sample Set (booklet, answer sheet) $19.50

STS: High School Placement Test (HSPT)–Open Form

1982   Scholastic Testing Service, Inc.

Population: Grades 8.3 to 9.3

Purpose: Assesses academic achievement and aptitude

Description: Multiple-choice test with 298 items on seven subtests: verbal cognitive skills, quantitative skills, language, reading comprehension and vocabulary, and math concepts and problem solving. Cognitive Skills Quotients, basic skills scores, and a composite score are yielded. Optional tests available are Catholic Religion, mechanical aptitude, and science. Examiner must be certified for assessment. Available in large print.

Format: Examiner required; individual administration; untimed and timed portions: 2 hours 30 minutes

Scoring: Machine scored; test scoring service available from publisher

Cost: Sample Set (booklet, answer sheet) $19.50

Test of Auditory Reasoning and Processing Skills (TARPS)
Morrison F. Gardner

Date not provided   Psychological and Educational Publications, Inc.

Population: Ages 5 to 14 years

Purpose: Measures the quality and quantity of auditory thinking and reasoning

Description: Although many of the questions and statements reflect what a child has learned from home and formal education, the purpose of this test is to determine what the child does with what he or she has learned. This test measures a child's ability to think logically, conceptually, and abstractly. Another purpose of the TARPS is to assess how well a child can pick out key words in a question or a statement and know that that key word holds the clue to the answer or is the answer. Spanish version also available.

Format: Examiner required; individual administration; untimed: 10 to 15 minutes

Scoring: Examiner evaluated

Cost: Complete Kit (manual, 25 test booklets) $55.95

Test of Cognitive Skills, Second Edition (TCS®/2)

1992	CTB/McGraw-Hill

Population: Grades 2 to 12

Purpose: Assesses skills important for success in school settings; used for predicting school achievement and screening students for further evaluation

Description: Multiple-item paper–pencil multiple-choice test consisting of four subtests (Sequences, Analogies, Memory, and Verbal Reasoning) assessing cognitive skills. The test is divided into six levels spanning Grades 2 through 12. The test yields the following scores: number of correct responses, age or grade percentile rank, scale score, and cognitive skills index.

Format: Examiner required; suitable for group use; timed: 1 hour

Scoring: Hand key; may be computer scored

Cost: Multi-level Examination Kit $52.00

Test of Everyday Reasoning (TER)
Peter A. Facione

2000	California Academic Press

Population: Ages 14 years and older

Purpose: Measures reasoning ability and critical thinking

Description: The TER is based on the Delphi consensus conceptualization of critical thinking and targets those core critical thinking skills regarded to be essential elements for an individual's education. The items range from those requiring an analysis of the meaning of a given sentence to those requiring much more complex integration of critical thinking skills. A total of 35 items are scored in five categories: analysis, evaluation, inference, deductive ability, and inductive.

Format: Examiner required; group administration; timed and untimed

Scoring: Machine scored; scoring service available

Cost: Specimen Kit $25.00

Auditory Skills

Auditory Memory Span Test
Joseph M. Wepman, Anne Morency

1975	Western Psychological Services

Population: Ages 5 to 8 years

Purpose: Measures the ability to retain and recall words as auditory units, an essential capacity for learning how to speak and read accurately

Description: Oral-response test assessing the development of a child's ability to retain and recall familiar, isolated words received aurally. The test items are based on the most frequently used words in the spoken vocabulary of 5-year-old children. Norm-referenced scores are provided. Available in two equivalent forms.

Format: Examiner required; individual administration; untimed: 5 to 10 minutes

Scoring: Hand key

Cost: Complete Kit (100 each of two forms, manual) $55.00

Auditory Sequential Memory Test
Joseph M. Wepman, Anne Morency

1975	Western Psychological Services

Population: Ages 5 to 8 years

Purpose: Measures the child's ability to remember and repeat what he or she has just heard

Description: Oral-response test assessing a child's ability to repeat from immediate memory an increasing series of digits in order of verbal presentation. The test is useful for determining a child's readiness for learning to read and speak with accuracy and is also a determinant of spelling and arithmetic achievement. Norms are provided. Available in two equivalent forms.

Format: Examiner required; individual administration; untimed: 5 minutes

Scoring: Hand key

Cost: Complete Kit (100 each of two forms, manual) $55.00

Denver Audiometric Screening Test (DAST)
William K. Frankenburg, Marion Dreris, Elinor Kuzuk

1973   Denver Developmental Materials, Inc.

Population: Ages 3 years and older

Purpose: Detects hearing deficiencies in children; used to screen for 25-dB loss

Description: Function test in which a trained examiner creates a tone with an audiometer and checks the child's response. The child indicates whether the tone can be heard at different decibel levels. Those who fail the test are referred for additional examination.

Format: Examiner and audiometer required; individual administration; untimed: 5 to 10 minutes

Scoring: Examiner evaluated

Cost: 25 Tests $5.00; Manual/Workbook $28.00

Goldman–Fristoe–Woodcock Test of Auditory Discrimination
Ronald Goldman, Macalyne Fristoe, Richard W. Woodcock

1974   American Guidance Service

Population: Ages 3 years 8 months to 70 years

Purpose: Measures the ability to discriminate speech sounds against two different backgrounds, quiet and noise

Description: Specifically designed to assess young children. Geared to children's vocabulary levels and limited attention spans. The individual responds by pointing to pictures of familiar objects. Writing and speaking are not required. In addition, the test can be used successfully with adults, particularly those with disabilities. Three parts—Training Procedure, Quiet Subtest, and Noise Subtest—provide practice in word-picture associations and provide two measures of speech-sound discrimination for maximum precision. Provides standard scores and error analysis.

Format: Examiner required; individual administration; untimed: 20 to 30 minutes

Scoring: Examiner administered and interpreted

Cost: Complete Kit (easel test plates, manual, 50 response forms, audiocassette) $105.95

Lindamood Auditory Conceptualization Test (LAC)
Charles H. Lindamood, Patricia C. Lindamood

1971   PRO-ED, Inc.

Population: All ages

Purpose: Measures an individual's ability to discriminate one speech sound from another and to perceive the number, order, and sameness or difference of speech sounds in sentences

Description: Forty-item criterion-referenced test in which the person arranges colored blocks (each symbolizing one speech sound) in a row to represent a sound pattern spoken by the examiner. The colors of the blocks indicate sameness or difference, with a repeated sound symbolized by the same color and a different sound by a different color.

Format: Examiner required; individual administration; untimed: 10 minutes

Scoring: Examiner evaluated

Cost: Complete Kit (manual, audiocassette, 24 blocks in 6 colors, cue sheets, 50 each forms A and B, storage box) $98.00

Listening Assessment for ITBS®
H. D. Hoover, A. N. Hieronymus, Kathleen Oberley, Nancy Cantor

1994   Riverside Publishing Company

Population: Grades 3 through 9 (Levels 9 through 14)

Purpose: Monitors the effectiveness of listening instruction

Description: Provided as a supplement to the Iowa Tests of Basic Skills, Forms K, L, and M. Emphasizes learning through reading, listening, and the use of visual materials. Consists of questions that measure Literal Meaning, Inferential Meaning, Following Directions, Visual Relationships, Numerical/Spatial/Temporal Relationships, and Speaker's Purpose, Point of View, or Style. There are a total of 95 questions on the test. Each test level is different, although questions that are included at the end of one test level also appear at the middle of the next level, and toward the beginning of the next higher level. The questions appear at different parts of each level because tasks that would be relatively difficult for a third-grade student would be somewhat easier for a fourth-grade student, and much easier for a fifth-grader.

Format: Examiner required; group administration; untimed: 35 minutes

Scoring: Scoring service

Cost: Mark Reflex® Listening Answer Folder (package of 50, directions for administration and score interpretation, materials needed for machine scoring) $60.50

Listening Assessment for TAP®/ITED®

Oscar M. Haugh, Dale P. Scannell

| 1994 | Riverside Publishing Company |

Population: Grades 9 through 12 (Levels 15 through 18)

Purpose: Assesses the developed listening skills of high school students

Description: Provided as a supplement to the Complete and Survey Batteries of Tests of Achievement and Proficiency (TAP) and the Iowa Tests of Educational Development (ITED). Provides teachers and students with valuable insights into students' strengths and weaknesses in the important art of listening. The assessment consists of questions that measure the following content objectives: Literal Meaning, Inferential Meaning, and Speaker's Purpose or Point of View. In addition, questions are cross-classified according to four levels of cognition: knowledge/information, comprehension, application/analysis, and synthesis/evaluation. The test consists of 100 questions in four overlapping levels.

Format: Examiner required; group administration; untimed: 40 minutes

Scoring: Scoring service

Cost: Mark Reflex® Listening Answer Folder (package of 50, directions for administration and score interpretation, materials needed for machine scoring) $52.00

Listening Test

Mark Barrett, Rosemary Huisingh, Linda Bowers, Carolyn LoGiudice, Jane Orman

| 1992 | LinguiSystems, Inc. |

Population: Ages 6 to 11 years

Purpose: Evaluates the effect of listening on a child's ability to learn in the classroom; helps the child transfer what he or she learns to daily life

Description: Oral-response, verbal, point-to test with 75 items on five subtests (Main Idea, Details, Concepts, Reasoning, and Story Comprehension) and a classroom listening scale. Suitable for individuals with physical, hearing, or mental impairments.

Format: Examiner required; individual administration; untimed: 35 minutes

Scoring: Examiner evaluated

Cost: Manual and 20 Test Forms $89.95

SCAN-A: Test for Auditory Processing Disorders in Adolescents and Adults

Robert W. Keith

| 1994 | The Psychological Corporation |

Population: Ages 12 to 50 years

Purpose: Screens clients for auditory processing disorders

Description: This upward extension of the SCAN-C has four subtests: Filtered Words, Auditory Figure–Ground, Competing Words, and Competing Sentences. Requires a cassette player, two sets of stereo headphones, and a Y adapter. Used with individuals who have normal hearing acuity but poor understanding of speech when listening conditions are less than optimal.

Format: Examiner required; individual administration; untimed: 20 minutes

Scoring: Examiner evaluated

Cost: Complete Kit (manual, audiocassette, 12 record forms) $122.00

SCAN-C: Test for Auditory Processing Disorders in Children–Revised

Robert W. Keith

| 1999 | The Psychological Corporation |

Population: Ages 5 to 11 years

Purpose: Detects auditory processing disorders

Description: Test is for children who have normal peripheral hearing but who appear to have poor listening skills, short auditory attention span, or difficulty understanding speech in the presence of background noise. Administered using a portable CD player. The child repeats the words and sentences heard.

Format: Examiner required; individual administration; untimed: 15 minutes

Scoring: Examiner evaluated

Cost: Complete Program (manual, CD, 25 record forms) $135.00

Screening for Central Auditory Processing Difficulties

Dorothy A. Kelly

| 2001 | Academic Communication Associates |

Population: Grades K through 2 for group; Grades K to 6 for individual

Purpose: Pinpoints a variety of auditory processing difficulties that may be affecting a child's functioning in the classroom

Description: Criterion-referenced instrument that

allows recording observations or is used as a schoolwide screening. Cutoff criteria are included for use in identifying children who should be tested further. The Quick-Checklist, completed by a speech-language pathologist, consists of 20 items assessing the student's ability to perform tasks, such as repeating syllables, following oral directions, associating sounds with their source, and repeating digits. Reproducible checklists for the parent and teacher to complete are included in the manual.

Format: Examiner required; individual and group administration; untimed

Scoring: Hand key

Cost: Complete Kit $69.00

Test of Auditory-Perceptual Skills–Revised (TAPS-R)
Morrison F. Gardner

1997   Psychological and Educational Publications, Inc.

Population: Ages 4 to 13 years

Purpose: Measures ability to perceive auditory matter

Description: The revision, while maintaining the overall concept of the original TAPS, replaces some of the original items with new items. The norms for the revised version of the TAPS are more refined and include standard scores, scaled scores, stanines, and percentiles for each subtest. On some of the subtest items, such as those in Auditory Sentence Memory and Auditory Interpretation of Directions, the numerical value of a correct response has been increased to refine the norms. The seven subtests are Auditory Number Memory Forward, Auditory Number Memory Reversed, Auditory Sentence Memory, Auditory Word Memory, Auditory Interpretation of Directions, Auditory Word Discrimination, and Auditory Processing.

Format: Examiner required; individual administration; untimed: 5 to 10 minutes

Scoring: Examiner evaluated

Cost: Complete Kit (manual, 25 test booklets) $86.50

Test of Auditory-Perceptual Skills–Upper Level (TAPS-UL)
Morrison F. Gardner

1996   Psychological and Educational Publications, Inc.

Population: Ages 12 to 18 years

Purpose: Measures ability to perceive auditory matter

Description: The seven subtests are Auditory Number Memory Forward, Auditory Number Memory Reversed, Auditory Sentence Memory, Auditory Word Memory, Auditory Interpretation of Directions, Auditory Word Discrimination, and Auditory Processing. To challenge individuals, the content of the Upper Level subtests is more difficult than in TAPS-R. A Spanish version is available.

Format: Examiner required; individual administration; untimed: 5 to 10 minutes

Scoring: Examiner evaluated

Cost: Complete Kit (manual, 25 test booklets) $86.50

Wepman's Auditory Discrimination Test, Second Edition (ADT)
Joseph M. Wepman, William M. Reynolds

1987   Western Psychological Services

Population: Ages 4 to 8 years

Purpose: Measures auditory discrimination ability; used to identify specific auditory learning disabilities for possible remediation

Description: Oral-response test in which children are verbally presented pairs of words and asked to discriminate between them. The test predicts articulatory speech defects and certain remedial reading problems. The second edition is identical to the original edition except the scoring. In the second edition, scoring is based on a correct score rather than on the "error" basis of the original edition. The 1987 manual contains standardization tables for children ages 4 to 8, a 5-point qualitative rating scale, an interpretation section discussing how the test results may be used, reports on research using the test, and selected references.

Format: Examiner required; individual administration; untimed: 10 to 15 minutes

Scoring: Hand key

Cost: Complete Kit (100 each of Forms 1A and 2A, manual) $80.00

Wepman's Auditory Memory Battery
Joseph M. Wepman, Anne Morency

Date not provided   Western Psychological Services

Population: Ages 5 to 8 years

Purpose: Assesses auditory memory in young children

Description: Two tests help determine whether children have the basic memory skills required for reading, spelling, and arithmetic. The Auditory Memory Span Test assesses the ability to retain and recall familiar, isolated words received aurally, one of the basic abilities needed to learn to read phonically and to speak accurately. The Auditory Sequential Memory Test assesses the ability to repeat from immediate memory an increasing series of digits.

Format: Examiner required; individual administration; untimed: 5 minutes each

Scoring: Examiner evaluated

Cost: Set (kit for each test: 100 each of Forms 1 and 2, manual) $104.00

Behavior and Counseling

Attitudes

Achievement Identification Measure (AIM)
Sylvia B. Rimm

1985	Educational Assessment Service, Inc.

Population: Grades K through 12

Purpose: Identifies characteristics contributing to underachievement in students; used by teachers and parents for communication and intervention

Description: Paper-pencil 77-item inventory in which parents assess their child's characteristics in five areas (Competition, Responsibility, Independence/Dependence Achievement, Achievement Communication, and Respect/Dominance) by responding "no," "to a small extent," "average," "more than average," or "definitely" to each item. The test distinguishes between achievers and underachievers. Parents receive a computer-scored report with a manual that explains the meaning of the scores.

Format: Self-administered; suitable for group use; untimed: 20 minutes

Scoring: Computer scored

Cost: Class Set (30 tests, computer scoring) $100.00; Specimen Set $15.00

Achievement Identification Measure–Teacher Observation (AIM-TO)
Sylvia B. Rimm

1988	Educational Assessment Service, Inc.

Population: Grades K through 12

Purpose: Identifies characteristics contributing to achievement in students

Description: Paper-pencil 70-item inventory in which teachers assess students' achievement characteristics in five areas (Competition, Responsibility, Achievement Communication, Independence–Dependence, and Respect–Dominance). A computer scoring service is available.

Format: Examiner required; individual administration; timed: 20 minutes

Scoring: Computer scored

Cost: Class Set (30 tests) $100.00; Specimen Set $15.00

Achievement Motivation Profile (AMP)
Jotham Friedland, Harvey Mandel, Sander Marcus

1996	Western Psychological Services

Population: Ages 14 years and older

Purpose: Used to evaluate underachieving or unmotivated students

Description: This self-report inventory is composed of 140 brief, self-descriptive statements that produce scale scores in four areas: motivation for achievement, interpersonal strengths, inner resources, and work habits. Students respond to items using a 5-point scale. The AMP is designed to measure motivation and is validated against objective measures of achievement.

Format: Self-administered; untimed: 20 to 30 minutes

Scoring: Hand key; computer scored

Cost: Kit (20 AutoScore™ forms, manual, 2-use PC disk, 2 PC answer sheets) $99.50; 25-Use PC Disk $199.00

Achieving Behavioral Competencies
Lawrence T. McCarron, Kathleen M. Fad, Melody B. McCarron

1992	McCarron-Dial Systems

Population: Ages 13 years and older

Purpose: Assesses coping skills, work habits, and peer relationships; used for the development of social and emotional skills

Description: Based on the results of the 80-item Teacher Rating Scale, a computer program generates individual and class profiles for 20 competencies within four skill areas. A comprehensive curriculum presents strategies for developing positive social-emotional skills through self-awareness, teacher instruction, teacher demonstration, student interaction, and self-management and generalization. Supplemental, ready-to-use instructor materials to facilitate class participation, generalization, and maintenance of skills are provided.

Format: Teacher rating scale; untimed

Scoring: Computer scored; test scoring software included

Cost: $137.50

Adolescent Anger Rating Scale (AARS)
DeAnna McKinnie Burney

2001	Psychological Assessment Resources, Inc.

Population: Ages 11 to 19 years

Purpose: Assesses anger intensity and frequency as well as typical mode of anger expression and anger control

Description: Used as a screening measure for social maladjustment behavior. Instrumental Anger (IA) has 20 items and measures delayed or covert anger. Reactive Anger (RA) has 8 items and measures angry responses immediately expressed. Anger Control (AC) has 13 items and measures proactive cognitive-behavioral responses. Profile chart is provided in test booklet for plotting IA, RA, AC, and Total Anger *T*-scores.

Format: Self-administered; untimed: 5 to 10 minutes

Scoring: Examiner evaluated

Cost: Test Booklets and Manual $99.00

Children's Academic Intrinsic Motivation Inventory (CAIMI)
Adele E. Gottfried

1986	Psychological Assessment Resources, Inc.

Population: Grades 4 through 8

Purpose: Assesses academic motivation in children

Description: Paper-pencil measure of motivation for learning in both general and specific areas.

The 44 questions comprise five scales: Reading, Math, Social Studies, Science, and General. Results are reported in *T*-scores or percentiles. Used to identify students with academic difficulties and to differentiate motivation from achievement and ability factors. Also used in course selection and individual and district-level program planning.

Format: Self-administered; untimed: 20 to 30 minutes

Scoring: Hand key

Cost: Intro Kit (manual, test booklets, profile forms) $130.00

Group Achievement Identification Measure (GAIM)
Sylvia B. Rimm

1986	Educational Assessment Service, Inc.

Population: Ages 10 to 18 years

Purpose: Identifies students with characteristics that may contribute to underachievement; used by classroom teachers to help underachieving students

Description: Paper–pencil 90-item inventory assessing achievement characteristics. The inventory directs both teachers and parents to the areas in which the child must change in order to achieve in school. The test yields a Total Score and five dimension scores: Competition, Responsibility, Achievement Communication, Independence–Dependence, and Respect–Dominance. A computer scoring service is available from the publisher.

Format: Examiner required; suitable for group use; untimed

Scoring: Computer scored

Cost: Class Set (30 tests) $100.00; Specimen Set $15.00

Interest-a-Lyzer
Joseph S. Renzulli

1997	Creative Learning Press, Inc.

Population: Grades 4 to 8

Purpose: Examines the students' present and potential interests; used as a basis for group discussions and in-depth counseling

Description: Multiple-item paper–pencil instrument consisting of a series of open-ended questions structured to highlight general patterns of interest. Items cover language arts, athletic, leadership, mathematical, historical, political, scientific, artistic, and technical interest areas.

Format: Examiner required; suitable for group use; untimed

Scoring: Examiner evaluated

Cost: 30 Questionnaires $29.95

Inventory of Classroom Style and Skills (INCLASS)
Curtis Miles, Phyllis Grummon

Date not provided — H & H Publishing Company, Inc.

Population: High school and college students

Purpose: Assesses student attitudes and behaviors related to academic learning

Description: Self-assessment instrument designed to assess proficiency in seven competencies (Interest in Life-Long Learning, Having a Sense of Quality, Taking Responsibility, Persisting, Working in Teams, Solving Problems, and Adapting to Change) that affect student performance in the classroom. INCLASS is a diagnostic and prescriptive instrument that provides information to the student and gives teachers and others a framework to develop instructional and other interventions.

Format: Self-assessment; untimed

Scoring: Hand key; also available on the Web

Cost: $3.00 each (for 1 to 99 copies)

Learning Behavior Scale (LBS)
Paul A. McDermott, Leonard F. Green, Jean M. Francis, Denis H. Stott

1999 — Ed & Psych Associates

Population: Ages 5 to 17 years

Purpose: Measures classroom learning behavior in a standardized teacher observation

Description: Test contains 29 items measuring four factors: Competence Motivation, Attitude Toward Learning, Attention/Persistence, and Strategy/Flexibility.

Format: Rating scale; untimed: 10 to 15 minutes

Scoring: Hand score

Cost: $24.95

Learning Process Questionnaire (LPQ)
J. Biggs

1989 — Australian Council for Educational Research Limited

Population: Grades 8 to 12

Purpose: Assesses a student's general orientation toward learning by identifying the motives and strategies that comprise an approach to learning; used by teachers and counselors

Description: Paper–pencil 36-item test identifying the motives and strategies that comprise a student's approach to learning. Items are rated in a Likert-scale format. Stanine and percentile rank scores are yielded for total raw score conversion. Separate profiles are provided for motive and strategy subscales. One of two tests in a series (see entry for Study Process Questionnaire).

Format: Examiner required; suitable for group use; timed: 20 minutes

Scoring: Hand key; may be machine scored

Cost: Contact publisher

My Book of Things and Stuff: An Interest Questionnaire for Young Children
Ann McGeevy

1982 — Creative Learning Press, Inc.

Population: Ages 6 to 11 years

Purpose: Assesses the interests of young children

Description: Multiple-item paper–pencil questionnaire including over 40 illustrated items focusing on the special interests and learning styles of students. The book also includes a teacher's section, an interest profile sheet, sample pages from a journal, and bibliographies of interest-centered books and magazines for children. All questionnaire pages are perforated and prepared on blackline masters so that copies can be made for an entire class.

Format: Examiner required; suitable for group use; untimed

Scoring: Examiner evaluated

Cost: Questionnaire Booklet $14.95

Occupational Self Assessment (OSA)
Kathi Baron, Gary Kielhofner, Victoria Goldhammer, Julie Wolenski

Date not provided — Model of Human Occupation Clearinghouse

Population: Adults

Purpose: Evaluates occupational competence and assesses environmental impact on occupational adaptations

Description: A self-report form that is easily and quickly administered. It explores a client's performance, habits, roles, volition, interests, and environment. The OSA guides clinical practice by identifying clients' perceptions of their strengths and weaknesses as well as their priority goal areas.

Format: Self-administered; untimed

Scoring: Examiner evaluated

Cost: $40.00

Occupational Therapy Psychosocial Assessment of Learning (OT PAL)

Sally C. Townsend, Paula D. Carey,
Nancy L. Hollins, Christine Helfrich,
Melinda Blondis, Amanda Hoffman,
Lara Collins, Julie Knudson

Date not provided	Model of Human Occupation Clearinghouse

Population: Ages 6 to 12 years

Purpose: Examines psychosocial issues and addresses the match between student and environment

Description: Observational and descriptive assessment tool evaluates a student's ability to make choices, habituation, and environmental fit within the classroom setting. The observational component has 21 items.

Format: Examiner required; individual administration; untimed

Scoring: Examiner evaluated

Cost: $40.00

Pediatric Volitional Questionnaire (PVQ)

Rebecca Geist, Gary Kielhofner

Date not provided	Model of Human Occupation Clearinghouse

Population: Children

Purpose: Provides information about volition

Description: Using a variety of settings, various contexts are suggested that enhance motivation and choice. Environments are recommended to enhance motivation and support the child.

Format: Examiner required; individual administration; untimed

Scoring: Examiner evaluated

Cost: $32.00

Primary Interest-A-Lyzer

Joseph S. Renzulli

1997	Creative Learning Press, Inc.

Population: Grades K through 3

Purpose: Examines the child's present and

potential interests; used as a basis for group discussions and in-depth counseling

Description: Multiple-item paper–pencil instrument consisting of a series of open-ended questions structured to highlight general patterns of interest. Items cover language arts, athletics, leadership, mathematical, historical, political, scientific, artistic, and technical interest areas.

Format: Examiner required; suitable for group use; untimed

Scoring: Examiner evaluated

Cost: 30 Questionnaires $29.95

School Setting Interview (SSI)

Oshrat Regev Hoffman, Helena
Hemmingsson, Gary Kielhofner

Date not provided	Model of Human Occupation Clearinghouse

Population: Children

Purpose: Assesses student–environment fit and identifies the need for accommodations in the school setting

Description: The SSI includes 14 content areas that explore the student's functioning in the school setting. Provides suggested interview questions, which facilitate the investigation of the impact of the physical and social environment on the student's occupational performance, habits, meaning, and values.

Format: Examiner required; individual administration; untimed

Scoring: Examiner evaluated

Cost: $32.00

Secondary Interest-A-Lyzer

Joseph S. Renzulli

1997	Creative Learning Press, Inc.

Population: Grades 7 through 12

Purpose: Examines the individual's present and potential interests; used as a basis for group discussions and in-depth counseling

Description: Multiple-item paper–pencil instrument consisting of a series of open-ended questions structured to highlight general patterns of interest. Items cover language arts, athletics, leadership, mathematical, historical, political, scientific, artistic, and technical interest areas.

Format: Examiner required; suitable for group use; untimed

Scoring: Examiner evaluated

Cost: 30 Questionnaires $29.95

Student Adjustment Inventory
James R. Barclay

| 1989 | MetriTech, Inc. |

Population: Grades 5 to 14

Purpose: Assesses common affective-social problem areas; helps students understand their own attitudes and feelings that may interfere with learning and school adjustment

Description: Computer-administered or paper-pencil 78-item inventory yielding scores in self-esteem, group interaction and social processes, self-discipline, communication, energy/effort, learning/studying, and attitude toward the learning environment. PC-compatible computer software administers and scores the test and generates reports.

Format: Self-administered; untimed: 30 minutes

Scoring: Computer scored; scoring service

Cost: 50-Administration Software $225.00; Mail-in Report Kit (test materials, manual, processing fee for 5 reports) $34.00

Student Motivation Diagnostic Questionnaire (Short Form Second Revision)
Kenneth M. Matthews

| 1994 | Kenneth M. Matthews, EdD |

Population: Grades 4 to 12

Purpose: Identifies aspects of student motivation in need of improvement

Description: Paper–pencil 16-item questionnaire assessing teachers' expectations, students' beliefs about relevance, attitudes toward teachers, and calculative self-concepts in language arts, mathematics, science, and social studies.

Format: Self-administered; untimed: 10 to 20 minutes

Scoring: Hand scored

Cost: 25 Forms $55.00

Study Attitudes and Methods Survey (SAMS)
William B. Michael, Joan J. Michael, Wayne S. Zimmerman

| 1985 | EdITS/Educational and Industrial Testing Service |

Population: Grades 7 and above

Purpose: Diagnoses habits and attitudes that may be preventing achievement of full academic potential; used in the classroom and for school-

wide screening to identify students likely to benefit from counseling

Description: Multiple-item paper-pencil inventory assessing dimensions of a motivational, noncognitive nature that relate to school achievement and contribute to a student's performance beyond those measured by traditional ability tests. The student's profile can provide the requisite insights and guidelines for study habit improvement. Scales measured by the SAMS are Academic Interest/Love of Learning, Academic Drive, Study Methods, Lack of Anxiety, Lack of Manipulation, and Lack of Alienation Toward Authority. Norms are provided for high school and college levels.

Format: Examiner required; suitable for group use; untimed: 20 to 30 minutes

Scoring: Hand key; may be computer scored

Cost: Specimen Set (manual, all forms) $8.25; 25 Booklets and Answer Sheets $14.25; Keys $15.50; Manual $4.25

Study Process Questionnaire (SPQ)
J. Biggs

| 1989 | Australian Council for Educational Research Limited |

Population: Tertiary students

Purpose: Assesses a student's general orientation toward learning by identifying the motives and strategies that comprise an approach to learning; used by teachers or counselors

Description: Paper–pencil 42-item test identifying the motives and strategies that comprise the student's approach to learning. Items are rated on a Likert-scale format. Stanine and percentile rank scores are presented for total raw score conversion. Separate profiles are presented for motive and strategy subscales. The test is one of two in a series (see entry for Learning Process Questionnaire).

Format: Examiner required; suitable for group use; timed: 20 minutes

Scoring: Hand key; may be machine scored

Cost: Contact publisher

Subsumed Abilities Test–A Measure of Learning Efficiency (SAT)
Martin M. Bruce

| 1963 | Martin M. Bruce, PhD |

Population: Grades 6 and above

Purpose: Measures, nonverbally, the subject's ability and willingness to learn; used for student placement, vocational counseling, and job selection

Description: Paper–pencil test consisting of 30 pairs of items, each of which is composed of four line drawings. The student analyzes one with three others, resulting in a Potential Abilities Score and a Demonstrated Abilities Score based on the student's ability to conceptualize, form abstractions, and recognize identicals. Designed for individuals with at least a sixth-grade education. Suitable for individuals with physical, hearing, or visual impairments.

Format: Examiner required; suitable for group use; timed: 30 minutes

Scoring: Hand key

Cost: Specimen Set $46.50

Test of Attitude Toward School (TAS)
Guy Thibaudeau

| 1984 | Institute of Psychological Research, Inc. |

Population: Grades 1 through 12

Purpose: Assesses an individual's attitude toward school

Description: Oral-response test assessing two principal components of scholastic attitude: emotional disposition toward school and tendencies to action. The administrator presents to the child drawings showing situations that arise at school and notes how the examinee interprets the situations depicted. The number of situations liked and hated are calculated. Available in English or in French.

Format: Examiner required; individual administration; untimed

Scoring: Examiner evaluated

Cost: Manual $15.00; Set of Drawings $12.00; 25 Questionnaires $18.00

Volitional Questionnaire (VQ)
Carmen Gloria de las Heras,
Rebecca Geist, Gary Kielhofner

| Date not provided | Model of Human Occupation Clearinghouse |

Population: Adults

Purpose: Provides information about volition

Description: Using a variety of settings, the VQ suggests various contexts that enhance motivation and choice. Environmental supports are recommended to facilitate exploration.

Format: Examiner required; individual administration; untimed

Scoring: Examiner evaluated

Cost: $32.00

Learning Styles

Learning and Study Strategies Inventory (LASSI)
Claire E. Weinstein, David Palmer, Ann Schulte

| 1987 | H & H Publishing Company, Inc. |

Population: College freshmen

Purpose: Assesses learning, study practices, and attitudes; used as a counseling tool and a diagnostic measure

Description: Computer-administered or paper–pencil 77-item multiple-choice test measuring attitude, motivation, time management, information processing, test strategies, anxiety, concentration, selecting main ideas, study aid, and self-testing. A chart yielding statistically valid and reliable percentile rankings is available. Computer version (IBM and Macintosh) is available.

Format: Self-administered; untimed: 30 minutes

Scoring: Self- or computer scored; now available on the Web

Cost: $3.00 each (for 1 to 99 copies)

Learning and Study Strategies Inventory–High School (LASSI–HS)
Claire E. Weinstein, David R. Palmer,
Ann Schulte

| 1990 | H & H Publishing Company, Inc. |

Population: Grades 9 to 12

Purpose: Measures learning, study practices, and attitudes; used as a counseling tool and a diagnostic measure

Description: Paper–pencil multiple-choice test measuring attitude, motivation, time management, information processing, test strategies, anxiety, concentration, selecting main ideas, study aid, and self-testing. A chart yielding statistically valid and reliable percentile rankings is used, as is a self-scored form or a scannable NCS form. A seven-page booklet and a pen or pencil are needed.

Format: Self-administered; untimed: 30 minutes

Scoring: Self- or computer scored; now available on the Web

Cost: $2.75 each (for 1 to 99 copies)

Learning and Working Styles Inventory
Helena Hendrix-Frye

1999 — Piney Mountain Press, Inc.

Population: Ages 12 years and older

Purpose: Assesses individual learning styles

Description: Multiple-choice paper–pencil, video, or computer-administered test measuring cognitive learning style, social learning style, expressive learning style, and working (environmental) learning style. Computer printouts for individual and group profiles are provided, graphically indicating major and minor learning styles. Specific teaching and learning strategies are also outlined based on each individual's scores. All results are saved to disk and may be edited or printed at any time. Based on the Hendrix-Frye Working Learning Styles and the CITE Academic Learning Styles. Suitable for individuals with visual, hearing, physical, or mental impairments. Computer versions available for Windows.

Format: Examiner required; suitable for group use; timed: 14 minutes; untimed: 10 to 30 minutes

Scoring: Examiner interpretation; computer scored, hand key, or optical machine

Cost: Stand-Alone Version $195.00; Multi Station Version $395.00; Multimedia Version $595.00; Network Version $995.00

Learning Style Inventory (LSI)
Rita Dunn, Kenneth Dunn, Gary E. Price

1995 — Price Systems, Inc.

Population: Grades 3 to 12

Purpose: Identifies students' preferred learning environments; used for designing instructional environments and counseling

Description: Paper–pencil or computer-administered 104-item Likert-scale inventory assessing the conditions under which students prefer to learn. Individual preferences are measured in the following areas: immediate environment (sound, heat, light, and design), emotionality (motivation, responsibility, persistence, and structure), sociological needs (self-oriented, peer-oriented, adult-oriented, or combined ways), and physical needs (perceptual preferences, time of day, food intake, and mobility). Test items consist of statements about how people like to learn. Students indicate whether they agree or disagree with each item. Results identify student preferences and indicate the degree to which a student's responses are consistent. Suggested strategies for instructional and environmental alternatives are provided to complement the student's revealed learning style. Computerized results are available in three forms: individual profile (raw scores for each of the 22 areas, standard scores, and a plot for each score in each area), group summary (identifies students with significantly high or low scores and groups individuals with similar preferences), and a subscale summary. Available on two levels: Grades 3 to 4 and 5 to 12.

Format: Self-administered; untimed: 30 minutes

Scoring: Computer scored

Cost: Specimen Set (manual, research report, inventory booklet, answer sheet) $12.00; Diskette (100 administrations per licensing agreement) $295.00; each additional 100 administrations $60.00; NCS Scanner Program $395.00; 100 Answer Sheets for NCS $60.00

Learning Style Inventory–Version 3 (LSI-3)
David A. Kolb

1999 — Hay Group

Population: Ages 14 years and older

Purpose: Identifies preferred learning styles and explores the opportunities that different styles present for problem solving, teamwork, conflict resolution, career choice, and communication

Description: On-line and paper–pencil 12-item test. Results are plotted on two graphs: Cycle of Learning and Learning Type Grid. The LSI is also available in French and Spanish.

Format: Self-administered; untimed: 20 to 30 minutes

Scoring: Self-scored

Cost: $10.00 per on-line assessment; 10 Booklets $72.00; Facilitator's Guide $50.00

Learning Styles Inventory
Richard M. Cooper, Jerry F. Brown

1999 — Educational Activities, Inc.

Population: Adolescents

Purpose: Assesses learning styles

Description: Computer-administered 45-item multiple-choice and Likert-scale test assessing learning styles through the following subtests: Visual Language, Visual Numeric, Auditory Language, Auditory Numeric, Tactile Concrete, Social Individual, Social Group, Oral Expressiveness, and Written Expressiveness. The test yields several scores, including Class Composite, Individual vs. Class, Teacher vs. Class, Class Prescriptive Information, and Individual Prescriptive Information. The computer program operates on Windows and Macintosh platforms.

Format: Computer-administered; untimed

Scoring: Computer scored

Cost: CD $98.00

Learning Styles Inventory (LSI)
Joseph S. Renzulli, Linda H. Smith

1997	Creative Learning Press, Inc.

Population: Grades 3 to 8

Purpose: Assesses the methods through which students prefer to learn; used to assist teachers in individualizing the instructional process

Description: Paper–pencil 65-item inventory assessing student attitudes toward nine modes of instruction: projects, drill and recitation, peer teaching, discussion, teaching games, independent study, programmed instruction, lecture, and stimulation. Various classroom learning experiences associated with these nine teaching–learning style approaches are described, and students use a 5-point scale ranging from *very unpleasant* to *very pleasant* to indicate their reaction to each activity. A teacher form is included so that teachers respond to items that parallel those on the student form. The resulting profile of instructional styles can be compared to individual student preferences and serve to facilitate a closer match between how teachers instruct and the styles to which students respond most favorably.

Format: Examiner required; suitable for group use; time varies

Scoring: Examiner evaluated; self-scored

Cost: Class Set (30 student forms, class form, manual) $24.95

Learning Styles Inventory (LSI)
Albert A. Canfield

1988	Western Psychological Services

Population: Adolescents, adults

Purpose: Identifies an individual's preferred learning methods; identifies individuals with little or no interest in independent or unstructured learning situations; used to maximize teaching and learning efficiency

Description: Paper–pencil 30-item forced-rank inventory measuring individual learning needs (interacting with others, goal setting, competition, friendly relations with instructor, independ-

ence in study, classroom authority); preferred mediums (listening; reading; viewing pictures, graphs, slides; or direct experience); and areas of interest (numeric concepts, qualitative concepts, working with inanimate things and people). The inventory also indicates students' perceptions as to how they will perform in the learning situation and identifies learning problems associated with either traditional or innovative teaching methods. The test is available in two forms: Form S-A for use with most adults and Form E for use with persons whose reading level is as low as the fifth grade. The test booklets are reusable. Separate norms are available for males and females.

Format: Self-administered; untimed: 15 to 20 minutes

Scoring: Self-scored

Cost: Kit (8 inventory booklets; 2 each of forms A, B, C, and E; manual; 2-use disk) $99.50

Reading Styles Inventory (RSI)
Marie L. Carbo

2000	National Reading Styles Institute, Inc.

Population: Ages 6 years to adult

Purpose: Assesses learning style for reading; used to implement reading instruction

Description: The RSI reports help the teacher to target and tailor reading instruction so that students enjoy learning to read and learn to read well in the shortest possible time. At a glance, the reports list the child's strengths and weaknesses and the best reading strategies to use for fast progress. There are seven different reports for individuals and groups. Provides descriptions of 14 reading methods and dozens of teaching strategies. Produces personalized letters to parents; plus, a special RSI profile lists extensive recommendations for working with the child at home.

Format: Individual or group administration on computer; untimed

Scoring: Examiner evaluated; computer scored

Cost: $49.95 (35 administrations)

Student Styles Questionnaire
Thomas Oakland, Joseph Glutting, Connie Horton

1996	The Psychological Corporation

Population: Ages 8 through 17 years

Purpose: Measures students' styles of learning, relating, and working

Description: Patterned after the original Jungian constructs in four scales: Extroverted/Introverted, Thinking/Feeling, Practical/Imaginative, and Organized/Flexible. Students respond to 69 forced-choice questions related to real-life situations to express their individual styles; each item is a brief description of an everyday event. Includes classroom applications booklet for activity ideas in specific subject areas appropriate for each student type (personal, educational, and occupational). Optional scoring software generates a report for the child or adolescent and the professional.

Format: Examiner required; suitable for group use; untimed: 30 minutes

Scoring: Examiner evaluated; may be computer scored

Cost: Complete Kit (manual, classroom applications booklet, answer documents, question booklet) $91.00

Surveys of Problem-Solving and Educational Skills (SPRS and SEDS)
Lynn J. Meltzer

| 1987 | Educators Publishing Service, Inc. |

Population: Ages 9 to 15 years

Purpose: Assesses the problem-solving and learning strategies of students in middle childhood

Description: Paper-pencil short-answer test composed of nonlinguistic subtests, linguistic-verbal subtests, reading inventory, writing inventory, spelling inventory, and mathematics inventory. The score provides accurate information to determine the appropriate educational plan. A fourth-grade reading level is required.

Format: Examiner required; individual administration; untimed

Scoring: Examiner evaluated

Cost: Examiner's Manual $10.00; Video $37.90; SPRS Record Forms $18.75; SPRS Stimulus Book $9.45; SEDS Workbook $20.55; SEDS Stimulus Book $7.10; SEDS Record Form $21.75

Your Style of Learning and Thinking (SOLAT)
E. Paul Torrance, Bernice McCarthy, Mary Kolesinski, Jamie Smith

| 1988 | Scholastic Testing Service, Inc. |

Population: Grades K to 12

Purpose: Assesses learning styles

Description: Paper–pencil test with 25 to 28 items per questionnaire. Categories are left-brained, right-brained, or whole-brained. Raw scores, standard scores, and percentiles are yielded. A Youth Form and an Elementary Form are available. Examiner must be certified for assessment.

Format: Individual/self-administered; suitable for group use; untimed

Scoring: Self-scored

Cost: Specimen Set $18.90

Behavior Problems

Behavior Assessment System for Children (BASC)
Cecil R. Reynolds, Randy W. Kamphaus

| 1998 | American Guidance Service |

Population: Ages 2 years 6 months through 18 years

Purpose: Facilitates differential diagnosis and educational classification of a variety of children's emotional and behavioral disorders and aids in the design of treatment plans

Description: The BASC is a multimethod, multidimensional approach to evaluating the behavior and self-perceptions of children. It has five components that can be used individually or in any combination. The three core components are Teacher Rating Scales (TRS), Parent Rating Scales (PRS), and Self-Report of Personality (SRP). Additional components include Structured Developmental History (SDH) and Student Observation System (SOS). The BASC measures positive (adaptive) as well as negative (clinical) dimensions of behavior and personality.

Format: Examiner required; individual administration; TRS/PRS: 10 to 20 minutes, SRP: 30 minutes, SDH varies from family to family, SOS: 15 minutes

Scoring: Computerized scoring available in the BASC Enhanced ASSIST and the BASC Plus software for IBM and compatibles with 640K memory

Cost: Hand-Scored Forms Starter Set $314.95; Windows or Macintosh Starter Set $377.95

Behavior Dimensions Scale (BDS)
Stephen B. McCarney

| 1995 | Hawthorne Educational Services, Inc. |

Population: Ages 5 to 15 years (School Version); Ages 3 to 18 years (Home Version)

Purpose: Assesses dimensions of behavior of attention-deficit/hyperactivity disorder, oppositional defiant disorder, conduct disorder, avoidant personality, anxiety, and depression

Description: Each dimension of behavior is clarified by behavioral items that are observable overt descriptors of the behavior problems documented by primary observers of the child's or adolescent's behavior. Frequency-based quantifiers provide precise measures of the rate of problematic behavior. Available in both a School Version, completed by educators, and a Home Version, completed by the parent or guardian. Windows Quick Score is available. Also available in Spanish.

Format: Rating scale; untimed

Scoring: Examiner evaluated; computer scoring available

Cost: Complete Kit $157.00

Behavior Disorders Identification Scale-Second Edition (BDIS-2)
Stephen B. McCarney, Tamara J. Arthaud

2000   Hawthorne Educational Services, Inc.

Population: Grades K to 12

Purpose: Identifies students with behavior disorders and emotional disturbance

Description: Includes both School and Home Versions to provide a comprehensive profile of student behavior problems. The scale relies on direct behavioral observations by educators and parents or guardians. The BDIS-2 focuses on both the overt indicators of behavior disorders and the more subtle indicators of withdrawal, depression, and suicidal tendencies. The standardized sample represents all geographic regions of the United States, with particular attention given to the inclusion of racial and ethnic minorities in the creation of the national norms. Internal consistency reliability, test-retest reliability, interrater reliability, item analysis, factor analysis, content validity, criterion-related validity, diagnostic validity, and construct validity are all reported. Windows Quick Score is available. Available also in Spanish.

Format: Rating scale; untimed

Scoring: Examiner evaluated; computer scoring available

Cost: Complete Kit $176.00

Behavior Evaluation Scale-Second Edition (BES-2)
Stephen B. McCarney

1990   Hawthorne Educational Services, Inc.

Population: Ages 5 to 19 years

Purpose: Provides results that assist school personnel in making decisions about eligibility, placement, and programming for students with behavior problems who have been referred for evaluation

Description: The scale yields relevant behavioral information about students regardless of disabling conditions, and may be used with students who have learning disabilities, mental retardation, physical impairments, and other disabilities. The scale is based on the Individuals with Disabilities Education Act's definition of behavior disorders and emotional disturbance. Standard scores and percentile ranks are provided for total scale performance across 76 items as well as for each of the five subscales. DOS Quick Score is available. Also available in Spanish.

Format: Rating scale; untimed

Scoring: Examiner evaluated; computer scoring available

Cost: Complete Kit $204.50

Behavior Rating Profile-Second Edition (BRP-2)
Linda L. Brown, Donald D. Hammill

1990   PRO-ED, Inc.

Population: Ages 6 years 6 months to 18 years 6 months

Purpose: Identifies elementary and secondary students with behavior problems and the settings in which those problems seem prominent; also identifies individuals who have differing perceptions about the behavior of a student; may be used for identification of emotional disturbance

Description: Multiple-item paper–pencil battery consisting of six independent, individually normed measures: Student Rating Scales (Home, School, and Peer), Parent Rating Scale, Teacher Rating Scale, and the Sociogram.

Format: Rating scale; untimed

Scoring: Examiner evaluated

Cost: Complete Kit (manual; 50 each of student, parent, and teacher rating forms; 50 profile sheets; storage box) $198.00

Behavioral and Emotional Rating Scale (BERS)
Michael H. Epstein, Jennifer M. Sharma

| 1998 | PRO-ED, Inc. |

Population: Ages 5 through 18 years

Purpose: Measures five aspects of a child's behavioral and emotional strength; used in schools, mental health clinics, and child welfare agencies

Description: The BERS measures interpersonal strength, involvement with family, intrapersonal strength, school functioning, and affective strength. The scale is completed by teachers, parents, or others knowledgeable about the child. An overall strength score and five subtest scores are provided in standard scores and percentiles. The BERS was normed on a representative sample of more than 2,000 children with disabilities and 800 children with emotional and behavioral disorders.

Format: Rating scale; untimed: 10 to 15 minutes

Scoring: Examiner evaluated

Cost: Complete Kit (manual, 50 record forms, storage box) $86.00

Burks' Behavior Rating Scales
Harold F. Burks

| 1977 | Western Psychological Services |

Population: Grades 1 through 9

Purpose: Identifies patterns of behavior problems in children; used as an aid to differential diagnosis

Description: Paper–pencil 110-item inventory used by parents and teachers to rate a child on the basis of descriptive statements of observed behavior. Nineteen subscales measure excessive self-blame, anxiety, withdrawal, dependency, suffering, sense of persecution, aggressiveness, resistance, poor ego strength, physical strength, coordination, intellectuality, academics, attention, impulse control, reality contact, sense of identity, anger control, and social conformity. The Parents' Guide and the Teacher's Guide define each of the scales, present possible causes for the problem behavior, and offer suggestions on how to deal with the undesirable behavior from the point of view of the parent or teacher. The manual discusses causes and manifestations and possible intervention approaches for each of the subscales, as well as use with special groups, such as individuals with educable mental retardation, educational and orthopedic disabilities, and speech and hearing impairments.

Format: Examiner required; individual administration; untimed: 15 to 20 minutes

Scoring: Examiner evaluated

Cost: Kit (25 booklets and profile sheets, manual, 2 parents' guides, 2 teacher's guides) $120.00

Burks' Behavior Rating Scales, Preschool and Kindergarten Edition
Harold F. Burks

| 1977 | Western Psychological Services |

Population: Ages 3 to 6 years

Purpose: Identifies patterns of behavior problems; used to aid differential diagnosis

Description: Paper–pencil 105-item inventory used by parents and teachers to rate a child on the basis of descriptive statements of observed behavior. The inventory contains 18 subscales: excessive self-blame, anxiety, withdrawal, dependency, suffering, sense of persecution, aggressiveness, resistance, poor ego strength, physical strength, coordination, intellectuality, attention, impulse control, reality contact, sense of identity, anger control, and social conformity. This inventory is a downward extension of Burks' Behavior Rating Scales.

Format: Examiner required; individual administration; untimed: 15 to 20 minutes

Scoring: Examiner evaluated

Cost: Kit (25 booklets and profile sheets, manual) $60.00

Child Behavior Checklist for Ages 1½ to 5 (CBCL 1½ to 5)
Thomas M. Achenbach

| 2000 | Research Center for Children, Youth, and Families |

Population: Ages 1 year 6 months to 5 years

Purpose: Used in mental health and special education applications to assess behavioral and emotional problems

Description: Paper–pencil 100-item short-answer rating scales with the following profiles: emotionally reactive, anxious/depressed, somatic complaints, withdrawn, attention problems, and aggressive behavior. A fifth-grade reading level is required. A Windows-based scoring module is available.

Format: Rating scale; untimed: 10 minutes

Scoring: Hand key; computer scored

Cost: 25 Forms $25.00

Child Behavior Checklist for Ages 6 to 18 (CBCL 6 to 18)
Thomas M. Achenbach

2001	Research Center for Children, Youth, and Families

Population: Ages 6 to 18 years

Purpose: Used in mental health and special education applications to assess behavioral and emotional problems

Description: Paper-pencil short-answer rating scales with 120 problem items and 20 competence items. The following profiles are yielded: anxious/depressed, withdrawn/depressed, somatic complaints, rule breaking behavior, aggressive behavior, social problems, thought problems, and attention problems. Separate scoring profiles for males and females ages 6 to 11 and 12 to 18 are available. A form completed by the parent is used. A fifth-grade reading level is required. A computer-administered program and scoring program are available.

Format: Rating scale; untimed: 10 minutes

Scoring: Hand key; machine scored; computer scored

Cost: 50 Forms $50.00

Comprehensive Behavior Rating Scale for Children (CBRSC)
Ronald Neeper, Benjamin B. Lahey, Paul J. Frick

1990	The Psychological Corporation

Population: Ages 6 through 14 years

Purpose: Rates children's behavior

Description: Offers comprehensive coverage of the dimensions that are important in school and clinical settings. Focuses on cognitive, as well as social, emotional, and behavioral, dimensions. Provided with 70 descriptive statements, the teacher indicates, using a 5-point Likert scale, how descriptive each statement is of the child. Nine scales are included.

Format: Rating scale; untimed: 10 to 15 minutes

Scoring: Examiner evaluated

Cost: Complete Kit (manual, 25 forms, scoring key) $113.00

Conduct Disorder Scale (CDS)
James E. Gilliam

2002	PRO-ED, Inc.

Population: Ages 5 through 22 years

Purpose: Designed to help diagnose conduct disorder

Description: An efficient and effective instrument for evaluating students who are exhibiting severe behavior problems and may have conduct disorder. The 40 items describe the specific diagnostic behaviors characteristic of the disorder. These items comprise four subscales necessary for the diagnosis: Aggressive Conduct, Non-Aggressive Conduct, Deceitfulness and Theft, and Rule Violations. The test is useful for screening and clinical assessment in schools, clinics, and correctional facilities. The CDS was normed on a representative sample of over 600 persons who were diagnosed with conduct disorder. A detailed interview form (derived from DSM-IV-TR) is provided to document infrequent but serious behavior problems.

Format: Examiner required; individual administration; untimed: 10 to 15 minutes

Scoring: Examiner evaluated

Cost: Complete Kit (manual, 50 forms, storage box) $86.00

Coping Inventory: A Measure of Adaptive Behavior (Observation Form)
Shirley Zeitlin

1985	Scholastic Testing Service, Inc.

Population: Ages 3 to 16 years

Purpose: Assesses personality

Description: Paper-pencil criterion-referenced test assesses two categories: coping with self (productive, active, flexible) and coping with environment (productive, active, flexible). Scores yielded are not effective (1), minimally effective (2), effective in some but not others (3), effective more often than not (4), and effective most of the time (5). Examiner must be certified for assessment. Available in large print.

Format: Examiner required; individual and group administration; untimed: varies

Scoring: Hand key; examiner evaluated

Cost: Starter Set (manual and 20 forms) $51.20

Coping Inventory: A Measure of Adaptive Behavior (Self-Rated Form)
Shirley Zeitlin

1985	Scholastic Testing Service, Inc.

Population: Ages 15 years and older

Purpose: Assesses personality

Description: Paper-pencil criterion-referenced

test assesses two categories: coping with self (productive, active, flexible) and coping with environment (productive, active, flexible). Scores yielded are not effective (1), minimally effective (2), effective in some but not others (3), effective more often than not (4), and effective most of the time (5). Examiner must be certified for assessment. Available in large print.

Format: Examiner required; individual and group administration; untimed: 45 minutes

Scoring: Examiner evaluated; hand key; self-scored

Cost: Starter Set (manual and 10 forms) $33.35

Developmental Teaching Objectives and Rating Form–Revised (DTORF-R)

| 1996 | Developmental Therapy Institute, Inc. |

Population: Birth to 16 years

Purpose: Assesses social, emotional, and behavioral developments

Description: Four subscales for a total of 171 items: Behavior (33 items), Socialization (41 items), Communication (35 items), and Cognition/Academics (62 items). Yields individual and group developmental profiles, and ratings of items mastered; shows mastered progression sequentially through each category. Three forms are available: Early Childhood, Elementary School, and Middle/High School. Also available in German, Spanish, and Norwegian.

Format: Examiner required; individual administration; untimed

Scoring: Examiner evaluated; test scoring available

Cost: Contact publisher

Devereux Behavior Rating Scale–School Form

Jack A. Naglieri, Paul A. LeBuffe, Steven I. Pfeiffer

| 1993 | The Psychological Corporation |

Population: Ages 5 through 18 years

Purpose: Detects severe emotional disturbances in students

Description: Evaluates the existence of behaviors indicating severe emotional disturbance. The results can be compared across informants and in a variety of settings. The 40-item scale is especially effective when used in conjunction with other findings to monitor and evaluate progress during educational interventions, or to determine whether a child or adolescent with severe emotional disturbance should be placed in a special education program. The four subscales address the individual areas identified in the Individuals with Disabilities Education Act. Two forms are available: a child form for ages 5 to 12 and an adolescent form for ages 13 to 18. Problem Item Scores help identify specific problem behaviors for treatment.

Format: Rating scale; untimed: 5 minutes

Scoring: Examiner evaluated

Cost: Complete Kit (manual, 25 each of child and adolescent answer documents) $142.00

Differential Test of Conduct and Emotional Problems (DT/CEP)

Edward J. Kelly

| 1990 | Slosson Educational Publications, Inc. |

Population: Grades K through 12

Purpose: Differentiates among three critical populations: conduct disorder, emotional disturbance, and noninvolved

Description: The DT/CEP facilitates educational decisions for special education and regular education. Emphasizes simple but effective screening identification, verification, and diagnostic steps to facilitate more accountable placement and programming. Includes nine case studies that illustrate test use and related procedural uses.

Format: Examiner required; group administration; untimed: 15 to 20 minutes

Scoring: Hand key

Cost: Complete Kit $70.50

Direct Observation Form (DOF)

Thomas M. Achenbach

| 1986 | Research Center for Children, Youth, and Families |

Population: Ages 5 to 14 years

Purpose: Used in mental health and special education to assess behavioral and emotional problems for individuals with behavior and emotional disorders and learning disabilities

Description: Paper-pencil short-answer rating scales with 97 problem items; on-task behavior is assessed at 1-minute intervals. The following profiles are yielded: withdrawn–inattentive; nervous-obsessive; depressed; hyperactive; attention demanding; and aggressive. An observation form is used and scored by an observer. Examiner must be an experienced observer. Windows-based scoring is available.

Format: Completed by observer; timed: 10 minutes

Scoring: Hand key; computer scored

Cost: 50 Forms $50.00

Disruptive Behavior Rating Scale (DBRS)
Bradley T. Erford

| 1993 | Slosson Educational Publications, Inc. |

Population: Ages 5 to 10 years

Purpose: Identifies attention-deficit disorder, attention-deficit/hyperactivity disorder, oppositional disorders, and antisocial conduct problems

Description: Administration of the 50-item inventory can be performed by both professionals and paraprofessionals. The DBRS is ideal for individual and mass screenings. The wording of the teacher and parent versions is nearly identical, allowing legitimate comparisons between responses. Scale items were specifically written to allow direct teacher transfer to behavior-modification plans, IEPs, or 504 plans. The DBRS provides separate norms for teacher, mother, and father responses. Normative data were obtained from 1,766 children, mothers of 1,399 children, and fathers of 1,252 children. Normative data are also provided to convert raw scores into T-scores and percentile ranks, as well as standard error of measurement and critical item determination. The computer-generated report calculates a summary statistics table, T-scores, percentile ranks, and interpretation ranges, and also identifies critical items of importance.

Format: Examiner required; individual or group administration; untimed: 7 minutes

Scoring: Hand key; computer scored

Cost: Complete Kit $120.00

Draw A Person: Screening Procedure for Emotional Disturbance (DAP:SPED)
Jack A. Naglieri, Timothy J. McNeish, Achilles N. Bardos

| 1991 | PRO-ED, Inc. |

Population: Ages 6 to 17 years

Purpose: Helps identify children and adolescents who have emotional problems and require further evaluation

Description: The DAP:SPED has items that are used to rate a child's drawings of a man, a woman, and self. The items were based on an exhaustive review of the literature on human figure drawings, and the test was written to be objective and fast to score. The test blends the clinical skills and knowledge reported in the literature over the past 75 years with a modern psychometric approach to test construction. The DAP:SPED was normed on a nationwide sample of 2,260 students representative of the nation as a whole with regard to gender, race, ethnicity, geographic region, and socioeconomic status. Evidence of various types of reliability and validity is well documented in the test manual. The DAP:SPED yields a standard score (T-score) that is used to determine if further assessment is (a) not indicated, (b) indicated, or (c) strongly indicated.

Format: Examiner required; individual or group administration; untimed

Scoring: Examiner evaluated

Cost: Complete Kit (manual, 10 scoring templates, 25 record forms, storage box) $104.00

Emotional and Behavior Problem Scale–Second Edition (EBPS-2)
Stephen B. McCarney, Tamara J. Arthaud

| 2001 | Hawthorne Educational Services, Inc. |

Population: Ages 4 years 5 months to 21 years

Purpose: Provides results for both theoretical and empirical constructs of emotional disturbance/behavioral disorders, providing both an educational and a more clinical perspective of emotional disturbance/behavior disorders

Description: The empirical interpretation provides five "conditions" of behavior, whereas the theoretical interpretation is composed of five subscales representing the five characteristics of emotional disturbance/behavior disorders contained in the Individuals with Disabilities Education Act. Students in the standardization sample represented all geographic regions of the United States, with particular attention given to the inclusion of racial and ethnic minorities in the creation of the national norms. Internal consistency, test-retest, and interrater reliability; item and factor analysis; and content, criterion-related, diagnostic, and construct validity are all well documented and reported for the scale. The School Form is completed by an educator; the Home Form is completed by the parent or guardian. A Windows Quick Score is available.

Format: Rating scale; untimed

Scoring: Examiner evaluated; computer scoring available

Cost: Complete Kit $119.00

Emotional or Behavior Disorder Scale (EBDS)
Stephen B. McCarney

| 1992 | Hawthorne Educational Services, Inc. |

Population: Ages 4 years 5 months through 20 years

Purpose: Contributes to the early identification and service delivery for students with emotional or behavioral disorders

Description: The EBDS is based on the National Mental Health and Special Coalition definition of emotional or behavioral disorder and the theoretical construct of the federal definition the Individuals with Disabilities Education Act. The multiple-item rating scale covers the areas of academic performance, social relationships, and personal adjustment. Both a School Version (completed by an educator) and Home Version (completed by the parent or guardian) are available.

Format: Rating scale; untimed

Scoring: Examiner evaluated

Cost: Complete Kit $118.00

Emotional/Behavioral Screening Program (ESP)
Jack G. Dial, Garry Amann

| 1988 | McCarron-Dial Systems |

Population: Ages 9 years and older

Purpose: Analyzes emotional and behavioral functioning; used with special needs students

Description: Paper-pencil 35-item checklist for rating an individual on the basis of observed behavior, reliable case history reports, or information provided by a reliable informant. The checklist, called the Behavioral Checklist for Students (BCS), contains seven categories of items: Impulsivity-Frustration, Anxiety, Depression-Withdrawal, Socialization, Self-Concept, Aggression, and Reality Discrimination. Raw subtest scores are entered into the computer. Users may choose from three types of reports: The Analysis Report is an analysis of emotional/behavioral functions with possible diagnostic categories; the Classroom Report describes emotional/behavioral characteristics the teacher may anticipate and lists specific recommendations for educational management; and the Comprehensive Report integrates features of both the Analysis Report and the Classroom Report. The software operates on Macintosh and PC systems.

Format: Self-administered; untimed

Scoring: Computer scored; test scoring software included

Cost: Complete Kit (comprehensive manual, 25 copies of BCS, computer program with operating manual) $250.00

Eyberg Child Behavior Inventory (ECBI)/Sutter-Eyberg Student Behavior Inventory-Revised (SESBI-R)
Sheila Eyberg

| 1999 | Psychological Assessment Resources, Inc. |

Population: Ages 2 through 16 years

Purpose: Measures conduct problems reported by parent or teacher

Description: The ECBI consists of 36 items and assesses problem behavior reported by parents. The SESBI-R consists of 38 items and assesses problem behavior reported by teachers.

Format: Self-administered; untimed: 5 to 10 minutes

Scoring: Examiner evaluated

Cost: $109.00

Functional Assessment and Intervention System: Improving School Behavior
Karen Callan Stoiber, Thomas R. Kratochwill

| 2000 | The Psychological Corporation |

Population: Children, adolescents

Purpose: Helps to design interventions based on both socially competent and challenging behaviors

Description: Teachers, parents, and the student complete checklists informed by direct observation or knowledge of the student. The data are used to create an assessment record and design interventions. A detailed list of resources and materials related to promoting social competence in applied settings is included.

Format: Rating scale; untimed

Scoring: Examiner evaluated

Cost: Complete Kit (manual, 25 record forms) $85.00

Life Adjustment Inventory
Ronald C. Doll, J. Wayne Wrightstone

| 1962 | Psychometric Affiliates |

Population: Grades 9 through 12

Purpose: Measures general adjustment to high

school curriculum; used for curriculum surveys and diagnosis of maladjusted pupils for individual guidance

Description: Multiple-item paper-pencil assessment of general adjustment to the high school curriculum. The inventory measures the feeling of needing additional experiences in 13 specific areas, such as consumer education; religion, morals, and ethics; family living; vocational orientation and preparation; reading and study skills; and citizenship education. The test conforms with the U.S. Office of Education's Life Adjustment Program.

Format: Examiner required; suitable for group use; untimed: 25 minutes

Scoring: Hand key

Cost: Specimen Set $5.00; 25 Inventories $8.75

Manifestation of Symptomatology Scale (MOSS)
Neil L. Mogge

2000	Western Psychological Services

Population: Ages 11 to 18 years

Purpose: Assesses individuals who are in trouble at school or with the law to identify personality dynamics, environmental concerns, treatment issues, and placement needs

Description: The MOSS has 124 brief sentences that describe a range of behaviors and emotional states with a true-false format. The MOSS yields 13 content scores, 3 summary indexes, and 4 validity scores. Normed on an ethnically diverse sample of more than 700, the MOSS is designed to evaluate young people who may not have the reading skills and concentration needed for valid administration of other broadband personality instruments. It can be used as a screener, an assessment instrument, or a program evaluation tool.

Format: Examiner required; individual administration or group administration; untimed: 15 to 20 minutes

Scoring: Computer scored; test scoring service available from publisher

Cost: Complete Kit $99.50

Motivation Assessment Scale (MAS)
V. Marvin Durrand, Daniel B. Crimmus

1992	Program Development Associates

Population: Adolescents

Purpose: Assesses the motivation underlying

problem behaviors in order to curb those behaviors

Description: Can be quickly and easily administered to help determine the basis for problem behavior. Tested and validated in home, school, and work settings, the MAS is used to develop individualized, practical solutions that are functionally related to the causes of behavior. The MAS consists of diagnostic questions.

Format: Examiner required; individual administration; untimed

Scoring: Examiner evaluated

Cost: $65.00

Preschool and Kindergarten Behavior Scales-Second Edition (PKBS-2)
Kenneth W. Merrell

2002	PRO-ED, Inc.

Population: Ages 3 through 6 years

Purpose: Assesses social skills and problem behaviors

Description: A rating scale with 76 items on two separate scales, the PKBS-2 provides an integrated and functional appraisal. The scales can be completed by a variety of behavioral informants, such as parents, teachers, and other caregivers. The PKBS-2 was standardized with a nationwide sample of ratings of 3,317 children. A wide variety of reliability and validity evidence in support of the test is included in the manual.

Format: Examiner required; individual administration; untimed: 8 to 12 minutes

Scoring: Examiner evaluated

Cost: Complete Kit (manual, 50 forms, storage box) $107.00

Revised Behavior Problem Checklist (RBPC)-PAR Edition
Herbert C. Quay, Donald R. Peterson

1996	Psychological Assessment Resources, Inc.

Population: Grades K to 12

Purpose: Measures behavior problems in children and adolescents

Description: Paper-pencil 89-item 3-point rating scale with the following categories: Conduct Disorder, Socialized Aggression, Attention Problems/Immaturity, Anxiety/Withdrawal, Psychotic Behavior, and Motor Excess.

Format: Examiner required; individual administration; untimed: 10 minutes

Scoring: Hand key

Cost: Intro Kit (manual, checklist, scoring profile) $140.00

School Social Behavior Scales (SSBS)
Kenneth W. Merrell

1993	Assessment-Intervention Resources

Population: Grades K through 12

Purpose: Provides an integrated rating of both social skills and antisocial problem behaviors

Description: Paper-pencil 65-item multiple-choice two-scale test measuring social competence and antisocial behavior. The Social Competence Scale includes 32 items that measure adaptive, prosocial skills, and includes three subscales (Interpersonal Skills, Self Management Skills, and Academic Skills). The Antisocial Behavior Scale includes 33 items that measure socially linked problem behaviors and also includes three subscales (Hostile-Irritable, Antisocial-Aggressive, and Disruptive-Demanding). This instrument is designed to be used as a screening instrument for early detection of developing social-behavioral problems and as part of a multimethod assessment battery for conducting comprehensive assessments, determining program eligibility, and developing intervention plans.

Format: Examiner required; not suitable for groups; untimed: 5 to 10 minutes

Scoring: Examiner evaluated

Cost: Manual $34.00; 20 Rating Forms $19.00

School Social Skills (S3)
Laura Brown, Donald Black, John Downs

1984	Slosson Educational Publications, Inc.

Population: Grades 1 through 8

Purpose: Assists school personnel in identifying student deficits in school-related social behaviors

Description: The 40-item scale of observable prosocial skills has been socially validated and determined to be important for student school success in the following areas: Adult Relations, Peer Relations, School Rules, and Classroom Behaviors. The S3 Rating Scale is quick and easy to administer, taking approximately 10 minutes per student. Ratings are done on a 6-point Likert scale and are based on observation of student behavior over the previous month. The S3 Manual accompanies the S3 Rating scale and provides complete behavioral descriptions of each of the 40 skills and the conditions under which they should be used. The S3 Rating Scale is a criterion-referenced

instrument that yields knowledge of a student's strengths and deficiencies. Both the test-retest and the interrater reliability data indicate the S3 Rating Scale has comparable reliability with residential, special education, and regular education students.

Format: Rating scale: untimed: 10 minutes

Scoring: Hand key

Cost: Complete Kit $58.00

Semistructured Clinical Interview for Children and Adolescents (SCICA)
Stephanie H. McConaughy, Thomas M. Achenbach

2001	Research Center for Children, Youth, and Families

Population: Ages 6 to 18 years

Purpose: Used in mental health and special education applications to assess behavioral and emotional problems

Description: Paper-pencil short-answer rating scales with 247 problem items. The following profiles are yielded: anxious; anxious/depressed; withdrawn depressed; language/motor problems; aggressive/rule breaking behavior; attention problems; self-control problems; and somatic complaints (ages 12 to 18 only). Protocol and rating forms are used by an interviewer. Examiner must be an experienced interviewer. A Windows-based scoring program is available.

Format: Completed by interviewer; untimed: 60 to 90 minutes

Scoring: Hand key; computer scored

Cost: Package of 50 Forms $50.00

Social Behavior Assessment Inventory (SBAI)
Thomas H. Stephens, Kevin D. Arnold

1992	Psychological Assessment Resources, Inc.

Population: Grades K to 9

Purpose: Used by teachers, counselors, and parents to measure social behaviors

Description: Paper-pencil 136-item rating scale with the following four content areas and 30 subscales: Environmental Behaviors (care for the environment, dealing with emergency, lunchroom behavior, movement around environment), Interpersonal Behaviors (accepting authority, coping with conflict, gaining attention, greeting others, helping others, making conversation, organized play, positive attitude toward others, playing informally, property: own and others), Self-Related Behaviors (accepting consequences, ethical behavior, expressing feelings, positive attitude toward self, responsible behavior, self-care), and Task-Related Behaviors (asking and answering questions, attending behavior, classroom discussion, completing tasks, following directions, group activities, independent work, on-task behavior, performing before others, quality of work). Results can be used to develop instructional strategies.

Format: Rating scale completed by teacher or parent; untimed: 30 to 45 minutes

Scoring: Examiner evaluated

Cost: Intro Kit (Social Skills in the Classroom, manual, and rating booklet) $117.00

Social Skills Rating System (SSRS)
Frank M. Gresham, Stephen N. Elliott

1990	American Guidance Service

Population: Ages 3 to 18 years

Purpose: Assists in obtaining information on social behaviors

Description: The SSRS enables the examiner to obtain a picture of social behaviors from teachers, parents, and students. A broad range of socially validated behaviors are evaluated. The instrument is used to assess and select problem behaviors for treatment. There are three scales: Social Skills Scale, Problem Behavior Scale, and Academic Competence Scale. The Assessment-Intervention Record can be used to combine the perspective of each rater on a single form.

Format: Rating scale; untimed: 15 to 25 minutes for each questionnaire

Scoring: Examiner interpretation; computer scoring is available for Windows

Cost: Starter Set: Preschool/Elementary (10 copies each of teacher, parent, and student questionnaires; 10 assessment-intervention records; manual) $159.95; Secondary Level $144.95

Systematic Screening for Behavior Disorders (SSBD)
Hill M. Walker, Herbert H. Severson

1990	Sopris West Educational Services

Population: Grades K through 6

Purpose: Used in public schools to screen for behavior disorders

Description: The SSBD screening process is proactive and incorporates a three-stage, multi-

gated process. The SSBD relies on teacher judgments and direct observation. The SSBD was extensively field tested. In Stage I, the teacher identifies two groups of 10 students each that most closely resemble behavioral profiles of externalizing and internalizing behavior problems. The teacher then ranks the students, and the three highest ranked students on each list move to Stage II. In Stage II, the teacher completes three brief rating instruments for each of the six students. Only those students who exceed the SSBD Stage II screening criteria move to Stage III. Stage III involves assessing each student in two separate 15-minute classroom and 15-minute playground observations.

Format: Examiner required; judgment and observation; untimed

Scoring: Examiner evaluated

Cost: Kit (user's guide and administration manual, technical manual, observer training manual, videotape, reproducible forms) $95.00

Teacher's Report Form (TRF)
Thomas M. Achenbach

2001	Research Center for Children, Youth, and Families

Population: Ages 6 to 18 years

Purpose: Used in mental health and special education applications to assess behavioral and emotional problems for individuals with behavioral and emotional disorders and learning disabilities

Description: Paper–pencil short-answer rating scales with 120 problem items and five adaptive items. The following profiles are yielded: anxious/depressed, withdrawn/depressed, somatic complaints, rule-breaking behavior, aggressive behavior, social problems, thought problems, and attention problems. Separate scoring profiles for males and females ages 6 to 11 and 12 to 18 available. A computer-administered program and scoring program are available.

Format: Rating scale; untimed: 15 to 20 minutes

Scoring: Hand key; machine scored; computer scored

Cost: 50 Forms $50.00

Walker Problem Behavior Identification Checklist
Hill M. Walker

1983	Western Psychological Services

Population: Grades PreK through 6

Purpose: Identifies children with behavior problems

Description: Paper–pencil 50-item true–false inventory consisting of behavior statements that are applied to the child being rated. The checklist can be completed by anyone familiar with the child, although it is used primarily by teachers. The test provides a Total Score, a cutoff score for classifying children as disturbed, and scores for the following five scales: Acting-Out, Withdrawal, Distractibility, Disturbed Peer Relations, and Immaturity.

Format: Examiner required; suitable for group use; untimed: 5 minutes

Scoring: Hand key

Cost: Kit (200 checklists and profiles, 100 each of male and female forms, manual) $78.00

Young Adult Behavior Checklist, Ages 18–30
Thomas M. Achenbach

1997	Research Center for Children, Youth, and Families

Population: Ages 18 to 30 years

Purpose: Used in mental health and special education applications to assess behavioral and emotional problems

Description: Paper–pencil short-answer rating scales with 115 problem items. The following profiles are yielded: anxious/depressed, withdrawn, somatic complaints, thought problems, attention problems, intrusive, aggression, and delinquent behavior. Choices are presented in a 3-point Likert scale. A Windows-based scoring program is available.

Format: Rating scale; untimed

Scoring: Hand key; computer scored; machine scored

Cost: 50 Forms $50.00

Youth Self-Report (YSR)
Thomas M. Achenbach

1995	Research Center for Children, Youth, and Families

Population: Ages 11 to 18 years

Purpose: Used in mental health and special education applications to assess behavioral and emotional problems

Description: Paper–pencil short-answer rating scales with 102 problem items and 17 competence items. The following profiles are yielded: anx-

ious/depressed, withdrawn/depressed, somatic complaints, rule-breaking behavior, aggressive behavior, social problems, thought problems, and attention problems. A fifth-grade reading level is required. A computer-administered program and scoring program are available

Format: Rating scale; untimed

Scoring: Hand key; machine scored; computer scored

Cost: 50 Forms $50.00

Self-Concept

Dimensions of Self-Concept (DOSC)
William B. Michael, Robert A. Smith

1977	EdITS/Educational and Industrial Testing Service

Population: Grades 4 and above

Purpose: Identifies students who might have difficulty with schoolwork due to low self-esteem and diagnoses factors contributing to low self-esteem

Description: Multiple-item paper–pencil questionnaire assessing level of aspiration, anxiety, academic interest and satisfaction, leadership and initiative, and identification versus alienation. Form E is available for Grades 4 to 6, Form S for Grades 7 to 12, and Form H for college. Percentile ranks are presented for Grades 4 to 6, 7 to 9, and 10 to 12.

Format: Examiner required; suitable for group use; untimed: Form E 20–40 minutes, Forms S and H 15–35 minutes

Scoring: Machine scored by publisher

Cost: 25 Test Forms $11.25; Manual $4.50; Specimen Set $8.25

Multidimensional Self-Concept Scale (MSCS)
Bruce A. Bracken

1992	PRO-ED, Inc.

Population: Grades 5 through 12

Purpose: Assesses global self-concept and six context-dependent self-concept domains that are functionally and theoretically important in the social-emotional adjustment of youth and adolescents

Description: The six self-content domains assessed are Social, Competence, Affect, Academic, Family, and Physical, with 25 items per domain.

The questions are asked in a self-report with a 4-point Likert scale.

Format: Examiner required; individual or group administration; untimed: 20 minutes

Scoring: Examiner evaluated

Cost: Complete Kit (manual, 50 record booklets, storage box) $94.00

Perception of Ability Scale for Students (PASS)
Frederic J. Boersma, James W. Chapman

1992   Western Psychological Services

Population: Grades 3 through 6

Purpose: Used to measure school-related self-concept

Description: The scale includes 70 items with a yes–no response format. Scores are provided for the full scale and for six subscales: general ability, math, reading/spelling, penmanship and neatness, school satisfaction, and confidence in academic ability. Raw scores are convertible to stanines, percentiles, and *t*-scores for comparison to the norm group.

Format: Examiner required; suitable for group use; untimed: 15 minutes

Scoring: Hand key; scoring service available

Cost: Kit (10 AutoScore™ answer forms, manual, 2 test report prepaid mail-in answer sheets) $68.00

Piers–Harris Children's Self-Concept Scale (PHCSCS)
Ellen V. Piers, Dale B. Harris

1984   Western Psychological Services

Population: Grades 4 through 12

Purpose: Measures a child's self-concept and identifies problem areas in a child's self-concept

Description: Paper–pencil 80-item test assessing six aspects of a child's self-esteem: behavior, intellectual and school status, physical appearance and attributes, anxiety, popularity, and happiness and satisfaction. Items are written at a third-grade reading level and require a simple yes–no answer. Percentiles and standard scores are provided for the total score and for each of the six subscales. Scores can be used for research purposes or to identify extreme problem areas. The manual provides the information necessary for administering and interpreting the scale, as well as the information included in Research Monograph #1 concern-

ing use of the scale with minority and special education groups.

Format: Examiner or self-administered; suitable for group use; untimed: 15 to 20 minutes

Scoring: Hand key; may be computer scored

Cost: Kit $99.50

Self Concept Scale
Robert R. Percival

1982   Dallas Educational Services

Population: Grades 7 to 12

Purpose: Measures self concepts in basic living skills

Description: The scale is divided into Decision Making Skills, Interpersonal Relations, Responsibility, Citizenship, and Career Planning. Pupil task books are available to assist in Skill Development.

Format: Examiner required; group administration; untimed

Scoring: Examiner evaluated

Cost: Kit (manual, cards, 35 record forms) $35.80

Self Description Questionnaire I (SDQI)

Date not provided   SELF Research Centre

Population: Ages 8 to 12 years

Purpose: Measures areas of self-concept

Description: The SDQI is a 76-item self-report inventory that measures self-concept in the following areas: Mathematics, Reading, General School, Physical Abilities, Physical Appearance, Peer Relations, and Parent Relations. Global scores are available for Academic, Non-academic, Self, and General. Scores are provided in percentile ranks and *t*-scores by grade level and gender.

Format: Self-administered; untimed: 15 to 20 minutes

Scoring: Examiner evaluated; computer scoring possible

Cost: Package (manual, questionnaire and scoring profile that can be reproduced for 1 year, scoring program) $75.00

Self Description Questionnaire II (SDQII)

Date not provided   SELF Research Centre

Population: Ages 13 to 17 years

Purpose: Measures areas of self-concept

Description: The SDQII is a 102-item self-report

inventory that measures self-concept in the following areas: Mathematics, Verbal, General School, Physical Abilities, Physical Appearance, Peer Relations, Parent Relations, Emotional Stability, and Honesty/Trustworthiness. Global scores are available for Academic and General Self reported in percentile ranks and *t*-scores by grade and gender.

Format: Self-administered; untimed: 20 to 25 minutes

Scoring: Examiner evaluated; computer scoring possible

Cost: Package (manual, questionnaire and scoring profile that can be reproduced for 1 year, scoring program) $75.00

Self Description Questionnaire III (SDQIII)

Date not provided	SELF Research Centre

Population: Ages 16 years through adult

Purpose: Measures areas of self-concept

Description: The SDQIII is a 102-item self-report inventory that measures self-concept in the following areas: Mathematics, Verbal, General School, Physical Abilities, Physical Appearance, Peer Relations, Parent Relations, Spiritual Values/Religion, Emotional Stability, and Honesty/Trustworthiness. Global scores are available for Academic and General Self reported in percentile ranks and *t*-scores by age and gender.

Format: Self-administered; untimed: 20 to 25 minutes

Scoring: Examiner evaluated; computer scoring possible

Cost: Package (manual, questionnaire and scoring profile that can be reproduced for 1 year, scoring program) $75.00

Student Self-Concept Scale (SSCS)
Frank M. Gresham, Stephen N. Elliott, Sally E. Evans-Fernandez

1993	American Guidance Service

Population: Grades 3 through 12

Purpose: Measures self-concept

Description: This flexible 72-item self-report measure of self-concept gives the examiner detailed information from three content areas in each of three dimensions. Based on Bandura's theory of self-efficacy, the SSCS documents the child's confidence level and importance rating of specific behaviors influencing the development of

students' self-concepts. The three dimensions are Self-Confidence, Importance, and Outcome Confidence. The areas in each dimension are Academic, Social, and Self-Image.

Format: Self-administration; untimed: 15 to 25 minutes

Scoring: Examiner evaluated

Cost: Manual $49.95; 25 Level 1 or 25 Level 2 Student Questionnaires $35.95

Tennessee Self Concept Scale– Second Edition (TSCS-2)
William H. Fitts, W. L. Warren

1996	Western Psychological Services

Population: Ages 12 years to adult

Purpose: Measures an individual's self-concept in terms of identity, feelings, and behavior; used for a wide range of clinical applications

Description: Paper–pencil 100-item test consisting of self-descriptive statements that subjects rate on a scale ranging from 1 (*completely false*) to 5 (*completely true*). The test is available in two forms: Counseling (Form C) and Clinical and Research (Form C & R). Form C is appropriate if the results are to be used directly with the subject. It provides a number of measures, including response defensiveness, a total score, and self-concept scales that reflect "What I Am," "How I Feel," and "What I Do." The scales include Identity, Self Satisfaction, Behavior, Physical Self, Moral–Ethical Self, Personal Self, Family Self, and Social Self. It does not require scoring keys. Form C & R yields the same scores as Form C, as well as the following six empirical scales, which require special scoring keys: Defensive Positive, General Maladjustment, Psychosis, Personality Disorder, Neurosis, and Personality Integration. Both forms use the same test booklet, but require different answer-profile sheets.

Format: Self-administered; untimed: 10 to 20 minutes

Scoring: Computer scored; hand key

Cost: Kit (24 AutoScore™ answer forms, manual, 2-use disk, 2 PC answer sheets) $110.00

Study Skills

Test Alert®

1993	Riverside Publishing Company

Population: Grades 1 through 8

Purpose: Develops fundamental test-taking skills to prepare students for standardized achievement tests

Description: This program produces test scores that accurately reflect student achievement. Level A, Grades 1 and 2, attempts to familiarize students with the standardized test format before they are tested. The only prerequisite skill for this program is knowledge of letters and numbers, not reading. It can also be used with kindergarten children toward the end of the school year. It is organized into five lessons, one for each day of the school week, each progressing from simple to more complex skills: Good Listening, Good Guessing, A Closer Look at Numbers, A Closer Look at Words, and Using Clues. At Levels B and C, for Grades 3 through 6, the listening skills that are so important at Level A are re- placed with an emphasis on reading and language. The 10 lessons of Levels B and C are organized into four units: Mechanics of Test Taking, Reading Strategies, Mathematics Strategies, and Language Strategies. At Level D, for Grades 7 and 8, there is more emphasis on interpretive reasoning and less call for practice with separate answer sheets. Level D reflects this change of emphasis in its four units: Mechanics of Test Taking, Reading Strategies, Mathematics Strategies, and Language Strategies.

Format: Examiner required; group administration; Level A, 30–45 minutes per lesson, Levels B and C, 45 minutes per lesson

Scoring: Examiner evaluated

Cost: Classroom Package (25 student books, teacher's guide) $115.50

Development and Readiness

Ages and Stages Questionnaires (ASQ)–Second Edition
Diane Bricker, Jane Squires, Linda Mounts, LaWanda Potter, Robert Nickel, Elizabeth Trimbly, Jane Farrell

1999   Paul H. Brookes Publishing Co., Inc.

Population: Ages 4 months to 5 years

Purpose: Screening and developmental monitoring of at-risk and general preschool populations

Description: The ASQ has 19 age-specific intervals with 30 questions at each interval. The domains covered are Fine Motor, Gross Motor, Communication, Problem Solving, and Personal-Social. Cutoff scores indicate whether further evaluation is warranted. Common materials such as toys and blocks are used. Also available in Spanish, French, and Korean.

Format: Parent rating; untimed: 5 to 10 minutes

Scoring: Examiner evaluated

Cost: Questionnaire and Guide $165.00

Ages and Stages Questionnaires: Social Emotional (ASQ:SE)
Jane Squires, Diane Bricker, Elizabeth Trimbly, Suzanne Yockelson, Maura Schoen, Davis Yoon, Ghee Kim

2001   Paul H. Brookes Publishing Co., Inc.

Population: Ages 3 months to 5 years

Purpose: Used for child-find screening and developmental monitoring for children who are at risk

Description: The ASQ:SE has 19 to 34 items with eight age-specific intervals (6, 12, 18, 24, 30, 36, 48, and 60 months). Deals with social and emotional competence and problem areas. Cutoff scores indicate whether further evaluation is warranted.

Format: Rating completed by parent or caregiver; untimed: 5 to 10 minutes

Scoring: Examiner evaluated

Cost: Questionnaire and Guide $125.00

AGS Early Screening Profiles (ESP)
Patti Harrison, Alan Kaufman, Nadeen Kaufman, Robert Bruininks, John Rynders, Steven Ilmer, Sara Sparrow, Domenic Cicchetti

1990   American Guidance Service

Population: Ages 2 through 6 years

Purpose: Screens the five major developmental areas

Description: The ESP is an ecological assessment battery that uses multiple domains, settings, and sources to measure the cognitive, motor, self-help/social, articulation, health development, and home environment of young children. The ESP screens the five major developmental areas specified by P.L. 99-457: cognitive, language, motor, self-help, and social development. Can be administered by paraprofessionals.

Format: Examiner required; individual administration; untimed: 15 to 30 minutes

Scoring: Two-level scoring system: Level I scores available for two subscales of Cognitive/Language Profile; subscales and subtests of the Cognitive/Language Profile can be scored using Level II scores

Cost: Test Kit (manuals, easel, 25 test records, 25 self-help/social profile questionnaires, 25 score summaries, sample home/health history survey, tape measure, beads) $299.95

Assessment of Behavioral Problems and Intervention Strategies in Early Childhood, Volume II
Louise Ferre

| 1995 | Hawthorne Educational Services, Inc. |

Population: Birth through 6 years

Purpose: Identifies behavioral problems and provides intervention strategies to modify behavior

Description: Pediatric Behavior checklist is included in the book and is reproducible. The checklist has 107 items.

Format: Examiner required; individual administration; untimed

Scoring: Examiner evaluated

Cost: $12.00

Assessment of Developmental Delays and Intervention Strategies in Early Childhood, Volume I
Louise Ferre

| 1993 | Hawthorne Educational Services, Inc. |

Population: Birth through 6 years

Purpose: Identifies children who are at risk in the areas of cognitive, socialization, receptive language, expressive language, self-help, fine motor, and gross motor skills

Description: Ten items in each of seven areas: Cognitive, Socialization, Receptive Language, Expressive Language, Self-Help, Fine Motor, and Gross Motor. Checklists are included and are reproducible.

Format: Examiner required; individual administration; untimed

Scoring: Examiner evaluated

Cost: $12.00

Basic School Skills Inventory–Third Edition (BSSI-3)
Donald D. Hammill, James E. Leigh, Nils A. Pearson, Taddy Maddox

| 1998 | PRO-ED, Inc. |

Population: Ages 4 through 6 years

Purpose: Determines the special learning needs of children by pinpointing both the general areas and the specific readiness skills that need remedial attention

Description: The inventory of 137 items is based on teachers' judgments of desirable school performance in the areas of Daily Living Skills, Spoken Language, Reading, Writing, Mathematics, and Classroom Behavior.

Format: Examiner required; individual administration; checklist format; untimed: 5 to 8 minutes

Scoring: Examiner evaluated

Cost: Complete Kit (manual, 25 summary/response booklets, storage box) $86.00

Battelle Developmental Inventory (BDI)
Jean Newborg, John R. Stock, Linda Wnek, John Guidubaldi, John Svinicki

| 1984 | Riverside Publishing Company |

Population: Birth through 8 years

Purpose: Evaluates the development of children from infant to primary levels; screens and diagnoses developmental strengths and weaknesses

Description: Multiple-item test assesses key developmental skills in five domains: personal-social, adaptive, motor, communication, and cognitive. Information is obtained through structured interactions with the child in a controlled setting, observation of the child, and interviews with the child's parents, caregivers, and teachers. Test items contain content and sequence directly compatible with infant and preschool curricula. The test may be administered by a team of professionals or by an individual service provider. Directions for modifications are included for children with various disabilities. A screening test containing 96 items is included in the complete BDI kit.

Format: Examiner required; individual administration; untimed: 1 to 2 hours for complete; 10 to 30 minutes for screening

Scoring: Examiner evaluated; computer software available

Cost: Complete Kit (test books, examiner's manual, scoring booklets, visuals, case) $325.00; Materials Kit $381.50

Bayley Scales of Infant Development®-Second Edition (BSID-II)
Nancy Bayley

| 1993 | The Psychological Corporation |

Population: Ages 1 through 42 months

Purpose: Assesses mental, motor, and behavioral development; used for assessing developmental progress, comparison with peers, and providing an objective basis for determining eligibility for special services

Description: Two-scale test of infant mental and motor development. The Mental Development portion assesses sensory-perceptual behavior, learning ability, and early communication attempts. The Index-Psychomotor portion measures general body control, coordination of large muscles, and skills in fine-muscle control of hands. The materials include a kit containing stimulus items and the Behavior Rating Scale for noting qualitative aspects of behavior.

Format: Examiner required; individual administration; untimed: 25 to 60 minutes

Scoring: Examiner evaluated; hand scored

Cost: Complete Kit (manual; stimulus booklet; 25 each of mental scale record forms, motor scale record forms, and behavior rating scale record forms; visual stimulus cards; map) $941.00

BCP-Behavioral Characteristics Progression

| 2001 | VORT Corporation |

Population: Ages 1 through 14 years

Purpose: Comprehensive curriculum-based assessment used by special education professionals to assess, set objectives, track progress, and prepare instruction for those with special needs

Description: The BCP Assessment Record booklet helps to quickly screen needs, record skill mastery and dates, and identify target objectives. This continuum of skills and behaviors, without labels or age ranges, focuses on the developmental needs of each individual. It groups the 2,300 skills/behaviors into 56 strands. The BCP Instructional Activities book provides thousands of teacher-developed instructional activities for 1,900 of the BCP skills. For most skills, prerequi-

site abilities and interest levels are listed to help adapt instruction for older individuals.

Format: Examiner required; individual administration; untimed

Scoring: Hand scored

Cost: Assessment Record $4.00 each (quantity 1 to 9), $3.50 each (quantity 10 to 99), $3.00 each (quantity 100 or more); Instructional Activities Book $49.95 each

Birth to Three Assessment and Intervention System-Second Edition (BTAIS-2)
Jerome J. Ammer, Tina E. Bangs

| 2000 | PRO-ED, Inc. |

Population: Birth to 3 years

Purpose: Allows examiners to identify, measure, and address developmental delays

Description: Instrument provides examiners with an integrated, three-component system for screening and assessing. The Screening Test helps examiners know within 15 minutes whether a child has developmental delays, and the Comprehensive Test identifies each child's strengths and weaknesses. Also included is a manual for teaching.

Format: Examiner required; individual administration; untimed

Scoring: Examiner evaluated

Cost: Complete Kit (teaching manual, screening kit, comprehensive kit) $239.00; Screening Kit (manual, 25 record forms, storage box) $79.00; Comprehensive Kit (manual, 25 record forms, storage box) $98.00; Teaching Manual $69.00

Boehm Test of Basic Concepts-Preschool Version
Ann E. Boehm

| 2001 | The Psychological Corporation |

Population: Ages 3 through 5 years

Purpose: Identifies children who lack understanding of basic relational concepts

Description: Measures concepts relevant to today's early childhood curriculum with efficient tests that are quick and easy to administer and score. In addition, children respond favorably to the colorful stimulus materials. Each concept is tested twice to determine the child's understanding of it across contexts.

Format: Examiner required; individual administration; untimed: 20 to 30 minutes

Scoring: Hand key

Cost: Complete Kit (picture book, manual, 20 individual record forms) $125.00

Boehm Test of Basic Concepts–Third Edition (Boehm-3)
Ann E. Boehm

| 2000 | The Psychological Corporation |

Population: Grades K to 2

Purpose: Measures children's mastery of basic concepts used in classroom instruction; identifies individual children with low levels of concept development; targets specific areas for basic concept remediation

Description: Measures 50 basic concepts relevant to today's early childhood curriculum. Has two parallel forms to allow for pre- and posttesting. Directions also available in Spanish.

Format: Examiner required; suitable for group use; untimed: 30 minutes

Scoring: Hand key

Cost: Examination Kit (manual, 1 of each form, directions) $55.00

Bracken Basic Concept Scale–Revised (BBCS-R)
Bruce A. Bracken

| 1998 | The Psychological Corporation |

Population: Ages 2 years 6 months to 8 years

Purpose: Measures a child's acquisition of basic concepts and receptive language skills

Description: This latest version contains colorful artwork, new norms, and new items. Leading directly to IEP development and remediation, the test assesses a child's receptive knowledge of 301 basic concepts in 11 distinct conceptual categories. The BBCS-R can be used for norm-referenced, criterion-referenced, or curriculum-based assessments. A Spanish edition of the Record Form is available for criterion-referenced use.

Format: Examiner required; individual administration; untimed: 20 to 40 minutes

Scoring: Hand key

Cost: Complete Kit (manual, stimulus manual, 15 forms, canvas portfolio) $239.00

BRIGANCE® Inventory of Early Development–Revised
Albert H. Brigance

| 1991 | Curriculum Associates®, Inc. |

Population: Birth to 7 years

Purpose: Measures the development of children functioning below the developmental age of 7 years; diagnoses developmental delays and monitors progress over a period of time; used to develop IEPs

Description: Paper-pencil 200-item oral-response and direct-observation skill assessment measuring psychomotor, self-help, communication, general knowledge and comprehension, and academic skill levels. Test items are arranged in developmental sequential order in the following major skill areas: preambulatory, gross motor, fine motor, prespeech, speech and language, general knowledge and comprehension, readiness, basic reading, manuscript writing, and basic math skills. An introductory section outlines how to administer the tests, assess skill levels, record the results, identify specific instructional objectives, and develop IEPs. Results, expressed in terms of developmental ages, are entered into the individual record book, which indicates graphically at each testing the level of competency the individual has achieved. An optional group record book monitors the progress of 15 individuals.

Format: Examiner required; individual administration; untimed

Scoring: Examiner evaluated

Cost: Assessment Book $124.00; Group Record Book $12.95; Free Test Excerpts available; 10 Developmental Record Books $26.90

BRIGANCE® K & 1 Screen–Revised
Albert H. Brigance

| 1992 | Curriculum Associates®, Inc |

Population: Grades K and 1

Purpose: Screens the basic skills necessary for success in Grades K and 1; identifies students needing special service referral, determines appropriate pupil placement, and assists in planning instructional programs and developing IEPs

Description: Multiple-item paper-pencil oral-response and direct-observation assessments measuring the following basic skills: personal data response, color recognition, picture vocabulary, visual discrimination, visual-motor skills, standing gross-motor skills, draw-a-person, rote counting, identification of body parts, reciting the alphabet, following verbal directions, numeral comprehension, recognizing lowercase letters, auditory discrimination, printing personal data, syntax and fluency, and numerals in sequence. Five optional advanced assessments are included for students scoring 95% or above on the basic first-grade assessment. Optional forms for teacher/parent rating and examiner observations are reproducible. Separate pupil data sheets are required, and class summary record folders are available. Criterion-referenced results are translated directly into curriculum or program objectives to meet the needs of individual pupils. Test items are cross-referenced to the BRIGANCE Inventory of Early Development–Revised to facilitate further evaluation of skill deficiencies. Validation study completed in 1995.

Format: Examiner required; individual administration; untimed: 12 minutes

Scoring: Examiner evaluated

Cost: Assessment Manual $89.00; 30 Pupil Data Sheets $31.00

BRIGANCE® Preschool Screen
Albert H. Brigance

1985	Curriculum Associates®, Inc.

Population: Ages 3 to 4 years

Purpose: Evaluates basic developmental and readiness skills of children; used for program planning, placement, and special service referrals

Description: Multiple-item oral-response and task-performance test evaluating basic developmental and readiness skills. Children identify body parts, objects, and colors; demonstrate gross and visual motor skills; match colors; explain the use of objects; repeat sentences; build with blocks; and provide personal data. Number concepts; picture vocabulary; and use of plural *s*, *-ing*, prepositions, and irregular plural nouns are tested also. Rating forms and supplementary skill assessments allow for additional observations and extended screening options. Validation study completed in 1995.

Format: Examiner required; suitable for group use; untimed: 12 minutes

Scoring: Examiner evaluated

Cost: Manual and Blocks $69.90; 30 Data Sheets $21.00

Cattell Infant Intelligence Scale
Psyche Cattell

1946	The Psychological Corporation

Population: Ages 3 to 30 months

Purpose: Assesses the mental development of infants

Description: Test of early development rates infant verbalizations and motor control, such as the manipulation of cubes, pencils, pegboards, and other stimulus items. The test has been modified with items from the Gesell, Minnesota Preschool, and Merrill–Palmer scales and is applicable to a younger age range than the Stanford-Binet Intelligence Scale. Materials include a kit containing stimulus items.

Format: Examiner required; individual administration; untimed: 20 to 30 minutes

Scoring: Examiner evaluated

Cost: Basic Kit (manipulatives, 25 record forms, case) $764.00; Manual $106.00

Child Development Inventory (CDI)
Harold R. Ireton

1992	Behavior Science Systems, Inc.

Population: Ages 15 months to 6 years

Purpose: Assesses children whose development is a concern

Description: The inventory provides detailed information about the child's development including strengths, delays, and needs. There are 300 items in the developmental scales: social, self-help, motor, language, and preacademic development. Also included is a 30-item Problems List that records the parent's concerns about health, vision and hearing, development, and behavior.

Format: Parents complete by responding to yes-no statements; untimed

Scoring: Examiner evaluated

Cost: Kit (manual, 25 booklets, answer sheets, and profiles) $65.00

Child Development Review (CDR)
Harold R. Ireton

1990	Behavior Science Systems, Inc.

Population: Ages 18 months to 5 years

Purpose: Integrates information from parents with examiner observations and assessment

Description: CDR has six questions, a 28-question Problems checklist, and a child development chart. Parents report on child's present health, development, and behavior. The responses are classified as indicating a problem or not.

Format: Examiner required; individual administration; untimed

Scoring: Examiner evaluated

Cost: Manual $10.00; 25 Questionnaires $10.00

Child Observation Record (COR)

Date not provided	High/Scope Educational Research Foundation

Population: Ages 2 years 6 months to 6 years

Purpose: Measures child's behavior and activities

Description: The trained teacher or observer assesses six categories of development: initiative, social relations, creative representation, music and movement, language and literacy, and logic and mathematics. Over several months, the teacher writes brief notes describing examples of children's behavior. The teacher then uses these notes to rate the child's behavior on 30 five-level COR items. The COR is an observational assessment tool that charts children's development and progress over time.

Format: Examiner required; observation; untimed: several months

Scoring: Examiner evaluated; computer program available

Cost: Kit (manual, 25 assessment booklets, 4 sets of notecards, 50 parent report forms, poster, box) $90.95

Cognitive Abilities Scale–Second Edition (CAS-2)
Sharon Bradley-Johnson, Carl Johnson

2001	PRO-ED, Inc.

Population: Ages 3 months to 3 years 11 months

Purpose: Identifies children who have delays in cognitive development

Description: A General Cognitive Quotient describes overall performance across all test items. A Nonvocal Cognitive Quotient describes children's ability excluding performance on vocal items. Results from the CAS-2 provide detailed information for planning instructional programs. The CAS-2 is playful in nature, and the toys enhance children's interest as well as the validity of the results. Two forms are available in this revision: the Infant Form and the Preschool Form. The Infant Form allows testing of children as young as 3 months. It consists of 79 items divided into three sections: Exploration of Objects, Communication with Others, and Initiation and Imitation. The Preschool Form contains 88 items divided into five sections: Oral Language, Reading, Math, Writing, and Enabling Behaviors. The CAS-2 was normed on 1,106 children from 27 states. Reliability and validity are addressed in the manual.

Format: Examiner required; individual administration; untimed: 20 to 30 minutes

Scoring: Examiner evaluated

Cost: Complete Kit (manual, 25 each profile/examiner record booklets for Infant and Preschool Forms, 25 symbol reproduction forms, 25 copies

of "Mikey's Favorite Things," picture cards, ramp, manipulatives, attache case) $424.00

Cognitive, Linguistic, and Social-Communicative Scales (CLASS)
Dennis C. Tanner, Wendy M. Lamb, Wayne Secord

1997	Academic Communication Associates

Population: Ages Preschool through 6 years

Purpose: Assesses development

Description: Using a parent interview, the examiner assesses a child's basic concepts, comprehension and production of grammar, and communicative effectiveness. Examples of developmental milestones are presented to the parent, and the parent indicates whether the child displays each behavior. The developmental norms in the manual can be used to identify areas in which delays are demonstrated. An interview questionnaire for the classroom teacher is available.

Format: Examiner required; individual administration; untimed

Scoring: Hand key

Cost: Complete Kit $59.00

Communication and Symbolic Behavior Scales (CSBS)
Amy M. Wetherby, Barry M. Prizant

1993	Paul H. Brookes Publishing Co., Inc.

Population: Ages 8 to 24 months

Purpose: Assesses communicative, social-affective, and symbolic abilities; used for intervention planning

Description: Seven clusters and one composite score measure Communication Functions, Communicative Means-Gestures, Communicative Means-Vocal, Communicative Means-Verbal, Reciprocity, Social-Affective Signaling, and Symbolic Behavior Clusters. May be used for persons with visual, physical, hearing, and mental impairments.

Format: Examiner required; individual administration; untimed: 45 to 60 minutes

Scoring: Examiner evaluated

Cost: Complete Kit $599.00

Comprehensive Identification Process (CIP), Second Edition
R. Reid Zehrbach

1997	Scholastic Testing Service, Inc.

Population: Ages 2 years to 6 years 6 months

Purpose: Evaluates the mental and physical development of young children; used to identify children in need of special medical, psychological, or educational help before entering kindergarten or first grade

Description: Criterion-referenced and perceptual multiple-item verbal response and task-assessment test of eight areas of child development: cognitive-verbal, fine motor, gross motor, speech and expressive language, hearing, vision, social/affective behavior, and medical history. The test can be administered by trained paraprofessionals supervised by professionals in the preschool area. The test helps meet the child-find requirements of P.L. 99-457. Also available in Spanish.

Format: Examiner required; individual administration; untimed

Scoring: Examiner evaluated

Cost: Screening Kit (administrator's and interviewer's manuals; screening booklet; 35 each of parent interview forms, observation of behavior forms, speech and expressive language forms; symbol booklet; 35 record folders; materials required for the tasks—blocks, balls, beads, buttons, crayons, etc.) $269.20

Concept Assessment Kit–Conservation (CAK)

Marcel L. Goldschmid, Peter M. Bentler

1968	EdITS/Educational and Industrial Testing Service

Population: Ages 4 to 7 years

Purpose: Assesses the cognitive development of preschool and early school-age children; used to assess the effect of training based on Piaget's theories

Description: Multiple-item task-assessment and oral-response test measuring the development of the concept of conservation. Two parallel forms, A and B, measure conservation in terms of two-dimensional space, number, substance, continuous quantity, discontinuous quantity, and weight. Form C measures conservation in terms of area and length. Test items are constructed to assess the child's conservation behavior and comprehension of the principle involved. The items require the child to indicate the presence or absence of conservation and specify the reason for his or her judgment. The CAK is relatively independent of IQ but correlates significantly with school performance. The two parallel forms assess the effect of training, and Form C tests the transfer effects of

the training. Norms are provided separately for boys and girls.

Format: Examiner required; individual administration; untimed: 15 minutes per form

Scoring: Hand key

Cost: Complete Kit (Forms A, B, C; manual) $52.25

DABERON Screening for School Readiness–Second Edition (DABERON-2)

Virginia A. Danzer, Mary Frances Gerber, Theresa M. Lyons, Judith K. Voress

1991	PRO-ED, Inc.

Population: Age 4 to 6 years

Purpose: Provides a standardized assessment of school readiness in children, including those with learning or behavior problems who are functioning at the early elementary level

Description: Measurement of development, categorization, and other developmental abilities that relate to early academic success. The Learning Readiness Equivalency Age score may be used to identify children at risk for school failure. The test can help identify instructional objectives and develop IEPs. It includes the Classroom Summary Form and the Report on Readiness, a summary of performance and practical suggestions for parents. The test samples knowledge of body parts, color and number concepts, gross motor, and fine motor skills.

Format: Examiner required; individual administration; untimed: 20 to 40 minutes

Scoring: Examiner interpreted

Cost: Complete Kit (manual, 25 screen forms, 25 reports on readiness, 5 classroom summary forms, cards, object kit of manipulatives, storage box) $129.00

Dallas Pre-School Screening Test

Robert R. Percival

1972	Dallas Educational Services

Population: Ages 3 to 6 years

Purpose: Designed to screen the primary learning areas

Description: Test has five subtests that measure psychological, auditory, visual, language, and motor abilities. Also available in Spanish.

Format: Examiner required; individual administration; untimed

Scoring: Examiner evaluated

Cost: Kit (manual, cards, 25 record forms) $36.60

Denver II

William K. Frankenburg, Josiah Dodds, Philip Archer, Howard Shapiro, Beverly Bresnick

1989	Denver Developmental Materials, Inc.

Population: Birth to 6 years

Purpose: Assesses developmental skills

Description: A series of developmental tasks are used to determine if a child's development is within the normal range. The Denver II identifies children likely to have significant motor, social, or language delays.

Format: Examiner required; individual administration; untimed: 10 to 20 minutes

Scoring: Examiner evaluated

Cost: 100 Test Forms $23.00; Kit $48.00; Manual $25.00; Technical Manual $28.00

Denver Prescreening Questionnaire II (DPQ-II)

1998	Denver Developmental Materials, Inc.

Population: Birth to 6 years

Purpose: Determines whether a child possesses developmental skills acquired by most other same-age children; used to indicate need for further testing

Description: Paper-pencil 105-item prescreening test administered by the child's parents. This updated version is designed to include more age-appropriate items, simplified parent scoring, and easier norm comparisons. Forms are available for the following age ranges: 0 to 9 months, 9 to 24 months, 2 to 4 years, and 4 to 6 years. Examiners must have at least a high school education.

Format: Examiner required; suitable for group use; untimed: office assistant 2 minutes; parents 10 minutes

Scoring: Hand key

Cost: 100 forms $19.00 to $22.00

Developing Skills Checklist (DSC)

1990	CTB/McGraw-Hill

Population: Grades PreK through K

Purpose: Evaluates the full range of skills children develop from prekindergarten through the end of kindergarten

Description: Multiple-item point-to and oral-response checklist that measures the following skills and concepts: language, visual, auditory, mathematical concepts and operations, memory, social and emotional, fine and gross motor, and print and writing. The Spanish version is Lista de Destreza en Desarollo.

Format: Examiner required; individual administration; untimed: 30 to 45 minutes

Scoring: Examiner evaluated; machine scored

Cost: Test Kit (materials for 25 students) $259.30

Developmental Activities Screening Inventory-Second Edition (DASI-II)

Rebecca R. Fewell, Mary Beth Langley

1984	PRO-ED, Inc.

Population: Birth to 5 years

Purpose: Detects early developmental disabilities in children

Description: Total-response and task-performance test assessing 67 items in 15 developmental skill categories ranging from sensory intactness, means-end relationships, and causality to memory, seriation, and reasoning. Test items may be administered in different sequences in one or two sittings. Instructions are given either verbally or visually. Each test item includes adaptations for use with children with visual impairment.

Format: Examiner required; individual administration; timed and untimed: 20 to 40 minutes

Scoring: Examiner evaluated

Cost: Complete Kit (manual, 50 protocols, picture cards, configuration cards, numeral cards, word cards, shape cards, storage box) $89.00

Developmental Assessment of Young Children (DAYC)

Judith K. Voress, Taddy Maddox

1998	PRO-ED, Inc.

Population: Birth through 5 years

Purpose: Assesses development in five areas: cognition, communication, adaptive behavior, social-emotional, and physical

Description: The instrument has five subtests for each of the five areas mandated by federal law to identify infants and young children who may benefit from early intervention. Assessment is tailored to each client's needs using any combination of these domains. Parents and caregivers are interviewed as part of the assessment process. Standard scores (mean of 100 and standard deviation of 15), percentiles, and age equivalents are provided. The DAYC may also be used in arena assessment so that each discipline may use the evaluation tool independently.

Format: Examiner required; parental interview; observation; untimed: 10 to 15 minutes per domain

Scoring: Examiner evaluated

Cost: Complete Kit (manual; 25 each of Adaptive, Cognitive, Communication, Physical, Social-Emotional Forms; 25 profile/summary forms; storage box) $174.00

Developmental Indicators for the Assessment of Learning– Third Edition (DIAL-3)
Carol Mardell-Czudnowski, Dorothea S. Goldenberg

1998   American Guidance Service

Population: Ages 3 through 6 years

Purpose: A global screener for assessing large groups of children quickly and efficiently

Description: The DIAL-3 is an individually administered screening test designed to identify young children in need of further diagnostic assessment or curricular modification. Subtests assess behaviors in the motor, concepts, and language areas. The test includes a checklist of social development and self-help development. English and Spanish materials are included. A new feature of the revision is the Speed DIAL, a brief screener that can be given in 5 minutes per area.

Format: Examiner required; individual administration; untimed: 20 to 30 minutes

Scoring: Examiner evaluated

Cost: Complete Kit (manual, 50 English record forms, 1 Spanish record form, 50 cutting cards, 50 parent questionnaires, manipulatives, dials, Spanish and English operator's handbooks for subtests, speed DIAL, training packet) $349.95

Developmental Observation Checklist System (DOCS)
Wayne P. Hresko, Shirley A. Miguel, Rita J. Sherbenou, Steve D. Burton

1994   PRO-ED, Inc.

Population: Ages birth through 6 years

Purpose: Measures the areas of language, motor, social, and cognitive development to identify possible developmental delays

Description: This multiple-item screening questionnaire meets the mandates of P.L. 99-457 and is based on current theory. The checklist can be completed by parents or caregivers. It has a sufficient number of items, interactive play items at the earlier developmental levels, and environmental input on family stress and support, as well as input on problematic child behaviors. Responses are based on careful observation of the child's daily behaviors. The three-part system provides standard scores, percentiles, and NCE equivalents in Overall Development, Developmental Cognition, Developmental Language, Developmental Social Skills, and Developmental Motor Skills.

Format: Examiner required; parental interview; observation; untimed: 10 to 15 minutes per domain

Scoring: Examiner evaluated

Cost: Complete Kit (manual, protocols, storage box) $129.00

Developmental Profile II (DP–II)
Gerald D. Alpern, Thomas Boll, Marsha Shearer

1986   Western Psychological Services

Population: Birth to 9 years 6 months

Purpose: Evaluates the age-equivalent physical, social, and mental development of children with or without disabilities

Description: Paper–pencil 186-item or computer-administered interview test covering five areas: physical, self-help, social, academic, and communication. Developmental age scores are derived by interviewing a parent or through teacher observation. From birth to age 4, the scales are graded by half-year increments. For ages 5 to 9, they are graded in yearly increments. The test also provides an IQ equivalency score. Materials include test books, profile and scoring forms, a manual, and step-by-step procedures for test administration and interpretation. The computer version is suitable for use with PC-compatible systems. The manual must be purchased separately for the computer version. A computer report is available through mail-in service or on-site (if the computer version is used).

Format: Examiner required; individual administration; untimed: 20 to 40 minutes

Scoring: Examiner evaluated; may be computer scored

Cost: Complete Kit (25 scoring/profile forms, manual, 2-use PC disk, 2 PC answer sheets) $120.00

Developmental Tasks for Kindergarten Readiness-II (DTKR-II)
Walter J. Lesiak, Judi Lucas Lesiak

1994   PRO-ED, Inc.

Population: Ages 4 years 6 months to 6 years 2 months

Purpose: Assesses successful performance in kindergarten; intended for preschool and kindergarten students

Description: The DTKR-II has 15 subtests: Social Interaction, Name Printing, Body Concepts-Awareness, Body Concepts-Use, Auditory Sequencing, Auditory Association, Visual Discrimination, Visual Memory, Visual Motor, Color Naming, Relational Concepts, Number Counting, Number Use, Number Naming, and Alphabet Knowledge.

Format: Examiner required; individual administration; untimed: 20 to 30 minutes

Scoring: Examiner evaluated

Cost: Complete Kit (manual, materials book, 25 protocols) $114.00

Devereux Early Childhood Assessment

1999   Kaplan Press

Population: Ages 2 to 5 years

Purpose: Screens for emotional and behavioral concerns

Description: The scale is completed by parents, family caregivers, or early childhood professionals to evaluate the frequency of 27 positive behaviors exhibited by preschoolers. The assessment also contains a 10-item behavioral concerns screener. The three scales measure attachment, self-control, and initiative. It was normed on a representative, nationwide sample of 2,000 children.

Format: Examiner required; individual administration; untimed: 10 minutes

Scoring: Examiner evaluated

Cost: Complete Kit (2 manuals, user's guide, 40 record forms, observation journal, 20 parent strategies) $199.95

Early Childhood Behavior Scale (ECBS)
Stephen B. McCarney

1992   Hawthorne Educational Services, Inc.

Population: Ages 36 to 72 months

Purpose: Provides the standardized profile information and specific indicators necessary to determine which students are in need of intervention, behavioral support, and the opportunity to learn more appropriate behavior

Description: The subscales of Social Relationships, Personal Adjustment, and Academic Progress were carefully developed with the use of behaviors appropriate for children ages 36 to 72 months, in preschool and kindergarten situations. Results provided by primary observers such as teachers, mental health workers, or parents are used to document the behaviors that indicate areas of most concern. Children in the standardization sample represented all geographic regions of the United States, with attention given to racial and ethnic minorities in the creation of the national norms. Internal consistency, test-retest, and interrater reliability; item and factor analysis; and content, criterion-related, diagnostic, and construct validity are well documented and reported for the scale. A computer version using DOS is available.

Format: Rating scale; untimed

Scoring: Examiner evaluated; computer scoring available

Cost: Complete Kit $96.00

Early Coping Inventory: A Measure of Adaptive Behavior
Shirley Zeitlin, G. Gordon Williamson, Margery Szczepanski

1988   Scholastic Testing Service, Inc.

Population: Ages 4 to 36 months

Purpose: Assesses the coping-related behaviors of infants and toddlers

Description: Behavioral observation inventory designed to assess the coping-related behaviors of infants and toddlers. The 48 items are divided into three subtests: sensorimotor organization, reactive behavior, and self-initiated behaviors. The manual contains instructions for rating, scoring, and implementing results. Available in large print.

Format: Examiner required; suitable for group use; untimed

Scoring: Hand key

Cost: Starter Set $51.20

Early School Assessment (ESA)

1990   CTB/McGraw-Hill

Population: Grades PreK to 1

Purpose: Assesses skills that are characteristic

of kindergarten children and prerequisite to formal instruction in reading and mathematics

Description: Multiple-item two-level paper–pencil multiple-choice test used to assess skills in the following areas: language, visual, auditory, math concepts and operations (number concepts), math concepts and operations (logical operations), and memory. Six testing sessions are recommended.

Format: Examiner required; suitable for group use; untimed: 15 to 30 minutes per scale

Scoring: Hand key; scoring service available from publisher

Cost: Review Kit $18.20

Early Screening Inventory–Revised (ESI-R)
Samuel J. Meisels, Dorothea B. Marsden, Martha Stone Wiske, Laura W. Henderson

| 1998 | Rebus, Inc. |

Population: Ages 3 to 6 years

Purpose: Identifies children who may need special education services to perform successfully in school

Description: The revised version is available for two age groups. The ESI-P is for children ages 3 to $4\frac{1}{2}$ years and the ESI-K is for children ages $4\frac{1}{2}$ to 6 years. They are brief developmental screening instruments that measure the following areas: visual motor/adaptive, language and cognition, and gross motor. The instrument was standardized and validated with 6,000 children, many in Head Start. A Spanish language version is available.

Format: Examiner required; individual administration; untimed: 15 to 20 minutes

Scoring: Examiner evaluated

Cost: Kit (manual, 30 score sheets, 30 parent questionnaires, screening materials, tote) $105.00 per level

Early Screening Project (ESP)
Hill H. Walker, Herbert H. Severson, Edward G. Feil

| 1995 | Sopris West Educational Services |

Population: Ages 3 to 5 years

Purpose: Screens for social behaviors that may indicate barriers to learning

Description: Enables educators to proactively screen and identify children who are experiencing preschool adjustment problems, whether internalizing or externalizing. Using standardized criteria to evaluate both the frequency and intensity of adjustment problems, the ESP screens for children whose social behavior may indicate at-risk status for emotional problems, speech and language difficulties, impaired cognitive ability, attention deficits, hyperactivity, and other barriers to learning.

Format: Examiner required; individual or group administration; untimed

Scoring: Examiner evaluated

Cost: Kit (user's manual, reproducibles, social observation training video, stopwatch) $95.00

Egan Bus Puzzle Test
Dorothy F. Egan

| Date not provided | Test Agency, Ltd. |

Population: Ages 2 to 4 years

Purpose: Assesses developmental delay and disability

Description: Multiple-item response screening test consisting of display board with a printed street scene and nine lift-out pieces for assessing verbal labels, comprehension of illustrated situations related to experience, expressive language response, and the beginnings of intuitive verbal thinking.

Format: Examiner required; individual administration; untimed

Scoring: Examiner evaluated

Cost: Contact publisher

Eliot–Price Test
John Eliot, Lewis Price

| 1976 | University of Maryland |

Population: Ages 5 years and older

Purpose: Measures perspective taking for Piagetian research

Description: The test consists of 30 items in a multiple-choice paper–pencil format. Results are to be forwarded to John Eliot.

Format: Examiner required; group or individual administration; untimed: 15 minutes

Scoring: Examiner evaluated

Cost: Free

FirstSTEP Screening Test for Evaluating Preschoolers™
Lucy J. Miller

| 1993 | The Psychological Corporation |

Population: Ages 2 years 9 months to 6 years 2 months

Purpose: Identifies developmental delays

Description: A screening instrument that is sensitive enough to detect even mild developmental delays and identify children who need in-depth diagnostic testing. Addresses the Individuals with Disabilities Education Act domains of Cognition, Communication, Motor, Social-Emotional, and Adaptive. Results are classified as Within Acceptable Limits, Caution, or At-Risk. Available for three levels depending on age of child.

Format: Examiner required; individual administration; untimed: 15 minutes

Scoring: Examiner evaluated

Cost: Complete Kit (manual, stimulus booklet, 5 record forms for each level, 25 social-emotional/adaptive behavior booklets, 25 parent booklets, manipulatives, case) $201.00

Fisher-Landau Early Childhood Screening (FLECS)
Francee R. Sugar, Amy Stone Belkin

| 1995 | Educators Publishing Service, Inc. |

Population: Grades K and 1

Purpose: Assesses a young student's abilities on a range of language, perceptual–motor, and readiness skills

Description: Identifies strengths and weaknesses so that teachers may tailor curriculum to an individual student or whole class.

Format: Examiner required; individual administration; untimed

Scoring: Examiner evaluated

Cost: Examiner's Manual $9.15; Stimulus Book $14.00; Test Booklets $24.00; Specimen Set $25.15

Five P's: Parent/Professional Preschool Performance Profile
Judith Simon Bloch

| 1987 | Variety Child Learning Center |

Population: Ages 2 to 6 years functioning between 6 and 60 months

Purpose: Assesses the development of young children with disabilities in the home and at school; used for the Individualized Family Service Plan

Description: Observational assessment instrument consisting of 458 items on 13 scales grouped in six developmental areas: Classroom Adjustment, Self-Help Skills, Language Development, Social Development, Motor Development, and Cognitive Development. Scale items describe developmental skills and interfering behaviors. Items are observed by teacher and parent on a 3-point Likert scale. The assessment is completed periodically to monitor change and to provide a means of ongoing assessment linked to remediation. Also available in Spanish.

Format: Examiner required; individual administration; time varies

Scoring: Examiner evaluated

Cost: Sample Packet $75.00; Educational Assessment for class of 10 children $125.00; Computerized Preschool Short-Term Instructional Objectives (IBM) $350.00; Video $45.00; Manual $25.00

Gessell Kindergarten Assessment
| Date not provided | Modern Learning Press, Inc. |

Population: Ages 4 to 6 years

Purpose: Measures developmental skills

Description: Provides a consistent evaluation of eye–hand coordination, motor skills, attention span, visual perception, neuromuscular maturity, perceptual functioning, and thinking.

Format: Examiner required; individual administration; untimed: 20 minutes

Scoring: Examiner evaluated

Cost: 50 Recording Sheets $49.95; Assessment Kit (reusable materials) $30.95

Gessell Preschool Assessment
| Date not provided | Modern Learning Press, Inc. |

Population: Ages 2 years 6 months to 6 years

Purpose: Measures developmental skills

Description: This observational and early intervention tool measures four key areas: behavior-motor, adaptive, language, and personal–social. It may be used for diagnostic and prescriptive purposes.

Format: Examiner required; individual administration; untimed: 40 minutes

Scoring: Examiner evaluated

Cost: 50 Recording Sheets $49.95; Assessment Kit (reusable materials) $76.05

Griffiths Mental Development Scales
Ruth Griffiths

| 1996 | Test Agency, Ltd. |

Population: Ages birth to 8 years

Purpose: Measures developmental skills

Description: Multiple-item test of development measuring social development, fine and gross motor skills, hearing, eye-hand coordination, and speech. The test is available on two levels. Scale 1 (35 items) is for children from birth to age 2. Scale 2 (22 items) is for children ages 2 to 8. Some items appear on both scales. Materials include toys, formboards, pictures, and models packed in a carrying case. There are different materials for each age group.

Format: Examiner required; individual administration; untimed

Scoring: Examiner evaluated

Cost: Contact publisher

HELP for Preschoolers (3-6)

2001	VORT Corporation

Population: Ages 3 to 6 years

Purpose: Designed as a curriculum-based assessment

Description: Provides comprehensive coverage of 622 skills in six developmental domains: Cognitive, Language, Gross Motor, Fine Motor, Social, and Self-Help. The Assessment and Curriculum Guide is necessary for proper use of all HELP 3-6 materials. The guide includes sections on Structure and Link to HELP 0-3, Preparing for the Assessment—Overview, Conducting the Assessment, Characteristics of Children: 3-6, General Information on Language Skills, Planning Instructional Techniques for Children with Special Needs, and Tips for Effective Early Childhood Instruction.

Format: Examiner required; individual administration; untimed

Scoring: Examiner evaluated

Cost: $55.95

HELP-Hawaii Early Learning Profile (Inside HELP)

2001	VORT Corporation

Population: Birth to 3 years

Purpose: Developmental assessment, intervention, planning, and instruction with infants and toddlers and their families

Description: Provides comprehensive coverage of 685 skills in six developmental domains: Cognitive, Language, Gross Motor, Fine Motor, Social, and Self-Help. Easy-to-follow developmental sequence, starting at birth to 3 years in month-by-month increments. Used by professionals, the profile provides guidelines for individuals involved in assessment and planning. Designed for use with all young children, including those who have disabilities or are at risk. Focuses on the whole child.

Format: Examiner required; individual administration; untimed

Scoring: Examiner evaluated

Cost: $49.95

Infant Development Inventory
Harold R. Ireton

1994	Behavior Science Systems, Inc.

Population: Birth to 21 months

Purpose: Screens development

Description: There are five developmental scales: social, self-help, gross motor, fine motor, and language. Results are classified as around age level, borderline, or delayed. The parent questionnaire is one page; a child development chart is on the opposite side.

Format: Parent completed; untimed

Scoring: Examiner evaluated

Cost: Manual $10.00; 25 Questionnaires $10.00

Infant/Toddler Symptom Checklist
Georgia DeGangi, Susan Poisson,
Ruth Sickel, Andrea Santman Wiener

1995	The Psychological Corporation

Population: Ages 7 to 30 months

Purpose: Screens for sensory and regulatory diseases

Description: A symptom checklist to determine whether the child may have a predisposition toward developing sensory integrative difficulties. Scores are criterion referenced.

Format: Examiner required; untimed: 10 minutes

Scoring: Hand key

Cost: Test Kit (manual, score sheet sets) $59.00

K1 Assessment Activities

Date not provided	CTB/McGraw-Hill

Population: Grades K and 1

Purpose: Assesses young children's performance in areas of reading/language arts and mathematics

Description: Various group, partner, and individual activities are used to assess outcomes and encourage independent and cooperative work.

Scores are entered on Summary Profiles in back of the book and are based on classroom observation and specific guidelines for evaluating student work.

Format: Examiner required; suitable for group use; untimed

Scoring: Examiner evaluated

Cost: Assessment Activities (includes product overview and all activities, activity sheets, scoring sections) $40.25

Kaufman Developmental Scale (KDS)
Harvey Kaufman

| 1974 | Stoelting Company |

Population: Infants through 9 years

Purpose: Evaluates school readiness, developmental deficits, and all levels of retardation for normal children through age 9 and persons with mental retardation of all ages; used in programming accountability

Description: Task-assessment test consisting of 270 behavioral evaluation items that are actually expandable teaching objectives. The KDS yields a Developmental Age and Developmental Quotient, as well as individual age scores and quotients for the following areas of behavioral development: gross motor, fine motor, receptive, expressive, personal behavior, and interpersonal behavior.

Format: Examiner required; individual administration; untimed: 30 minutes

Scoring: Examiner evaluated

Cost: Complete Kit (testing materials, manual, 25 record forms, carrying case) $425.00; 25 Evaluation Booklets $55.00

Kaufman Infant and Preschool Scale (KIPS)
Harvey Kaufman

| 1981 | Stoelting Company |

Population: Ages 1 month to 4 years

Purpose: Measures early high-level cognitive processes and indicates possible need for intervention in normal children ages 1 month to 4 years and in children and adults with mental ages of 4 years or less

Description: Multiple-item task-assessment and observation measure of high-level cognitive thinking. The child is observed and asked to perform a number of tasks indicative of his or her level. All test items are "maturational prototypes" that can

be taught to enhance maturation. The test covers general reasoning, storage, and verbal communication. The test yields the following scores: Overall Functioning Age (Mental Age) and Overall Functioning Quotient. Based on a child's performance on the scale, the manual suggests types of activities and general experience the child needs for effective general adaptive behavior.

Format: Examiner required; individual administration; untimed: 30 minutes

Scoring: Examiner evaluated

Cost: Complete Kit (manual, manipulatives, stimulus cards, 10 evaluation booklets) $300.00

Kaufman Survey of Early Academic and Language Skills (K–SEALS)
Alan S. Kaufman, Nadeen L. Kaufman

| 1993 | American Guidance Service |

Population: Ages 3 through 6 years

Purpose: Measures language skills, preacademic skills, and articulation

Description: Three subtests (Vocabulary; Numbers, Letters, and Words; and Articulation) provide an expanded and enhanced version of the Cognitive/Language Profile in the AGS Early Screening Profiles. The scores reflect many aspects of the child's language and early academic development.

Format: Examiner required; individual administration; untimed: 15 to 25 minutes

Scoring: Examiner interpreted

Cost: Complete Kit (manual, easel, test protocols, carry bag) $199.95

Kent Inventory of Developmental Skills
Jeanette M. Reuter, Lewis Katoff

| 1978 to 1995 | Western Psychological Services |

Population: Developmental ages birth to 14 months

Purpose: Uses caregiver reports to screen and assess the developmental strengths and needs of infants and young children with disabilities

Description: Paper–pencil or computer-administered 252-item inventory that has caregivers describe behaviors characteristic of infants in the first year of life. Test items cover five behavioral domains: cognitive, motor, language, self-help, and social. Developmental ages for each domain and for the full scale are based on a normative sample of healthy infants. Specifically, the test can be used to assess the developmental status of healthy infants (0 to 14 months), infants at risk (0 to 20 months), and young children with severe handicaps (2 to 8 years). The scale has been used for evaluating early intervention projects; monitoring the developmental progress of neonatal intensive care unit graduates; teaching teenage mothers about their children's development, and evaluating at-risk infants. Also available in Spanish, Dutch, German, Russian, and Hungarian.

Format: Examiner required; individual administration; untimed: 30 to 40 minutes

Scoring: Hand key; computer scored

Cost: Kit (administration booklet, 25 answer sheets, 25 profile forms, manual, scoring templates, developmental time tables, 2-use disk) $99.50

Kindergarten Diagnostic Instrument– Second Edition (KDI–II)
Daniel C. Miller

2000	Kindergarten Interventions and Diagnostic Services, Inc.

Population: Ages 4 through 6 years

Purpose: Designed to assess developmental readiness skills

Description: A comprehensive and time-efficient screening instrument measuring 13 areas: body awareness, concept mastery, form/letter identification, general information, gross motor, memory for sentences, number skills, phonemic awareness, verbal associations, visual discrimination, visual memory, visual-motor integration, and vocabulary. My Kindergarten Fun Book contains over 90 learning activities related to the KDI-II areas.

Format: Examiner required; individual administration; untimed: 35 minutes

Scoring: Examiner evaluated; computer scoring available

Cost: Complete Kit (manual, 3 stimulus booklets, blocks, 25 forms, carrying case) $165.00

Kindergarten Inventory of Social-Emotional Tendencies (KIST)
Daniel C. Miller

1997	Kindergarten Interventions and Diagnostic Services, Inc.

Population: Ages 4 through 6 years

Purpose: Designed to provide information about social-emotional status

Description: The KIST has seven domains that

measure the following areas: communication, daily living, hyperactivity/inattentive behaviors, maladaptive behaviors, separation anxiety symptoms, sleeping and eating behaviors, and socialization.

Format: Examiner required; individual administration; untimed: 35 minutes

Scoring: Examiner evaluated; computer scoring available

Cost: Starter Set (manual, 25 rating forms, 25 interpretation forms) $59.00

Kindergarten Readiness Test (KRT)
Sue Larson, Gary J. Vitali

1988	Slosson Educational Publications, Inc.

Population: Ages 4 to 6 years

Purpose: Identifies school readiness

Description: Consolidates critical areas of various developmental tests into one single form, making identification of school readiness more efficient and valid. The KRT targets and screens key developmental traits across a broad range of skills necessary to begin school: Reasoning, Language, Auditory and Visual Attention, Numbers, Fine Motor Skills, and several other cognitive and sensory-perception areas. Test booklet and additional forms are designed for use in parent conferences or interprofessional presentations. The KRT may be used to identify possible disabilities at an early age and facilitate writing developmental objective programs for teachers or parents. Tasks are presented in a sequential developmental-maturational format.

Format: Examiner required; individual administration; 15 minutes

Scoring: Hand key

Cost: Complete Kit $97.00

McCarthy Screening Test (MST)
Dorothea McCarthy

1978	The Psychological Corporation

Population: Age 4 years through 6 years 6 months

Purpose: Screens for potential learning problems

Description: Includes six component scales, all drawn from the McCarthy Scales of Children's Abilities, that are predictive of a child's ability to cope with schoolwork in the early grades. The MST helps educators identify children who may be at risk for learning problems. The subtests measure cognitive and sensorimotor functions central to the successful performance of school tasks, including Verbal Memory, Right-Left Orientation, Leg Coordination, Draw-A-Design, Numeric Memory, and Conceptual Grouping. Although interpretation of the MST requires training in psychology, it can be easily administered and scored by the classroom teacher or trained paraprofessional.

Format: Examiner required; individual administration; untimed: 20 minutes

Scoring: Examiner evaluated

Cost: Complete Set (manual, 25 record forms, 25 drawing booklets, case) $1,216.00

Merrill-Palmer Scale-Revised
Gale H. Roid, Jacqueline Sampers

2003	Stoelting Company

Population: Birth through 6 years

Purpose: Measures early development in cognition, communication, physical, social-emotional, and adaptive areas

Description: Developed to examine prematurity and children with talents or disabilities. The scales for younger children are based on play with enticing toys. With removal of the language scale and a few others, the test can be used with limited verbal interaction. Cognitive items fall into small, highly unified subtests showing progression and high relationship to total scale scores. Rasch scaling allows the cognitive scale to be used as a criterion measure with precise intervals between items.

Format: Examiner required; individual administration; timed and untimed

Scoring: Examiner evaluated

Cost: Complete Kit (manual, picture stimuli, manipulatives, record forms, easel) $850.00

Metropolitan Performance Assessment (MPA)
Joanne R. Nurss

1995	Harcourt® Brace Educational Measurement

Population: Ages 4 to 7 years

Purpose: Measures skills in playlike activities

Description: Tasks in Level 1 for prekindergarten and beginning kindergarten children involve playlike interactions to hold the child's interest and maximize performance. Level 2 has more complex language/literacy and quantitative/mathematics tasks for children in kindergarten

and beginning Grade 1. Included are a Developmental Inventory, Classroom Literacy Environment Inventory, Home Literacy Environment Inventory, Portfolio Assessment Guideline, and Preliteracy Inventory.

Format: Examiner required; group administration; untimed

Scoring: Hand key

Cost: Exam Kit $38.50 per activity

Metropolitan Readiness Tests: Sixth Edition (MRT6)
Joanne R. Nurss

1995	Harcourt® Brace Educational Measurement

Population: Ages 4 to 7 years

Purpose: Assesses underlying skills important for early school learning; used in identifying each child's needs

Description: Multiple-item paper-pencil test of skills important for learning reading and mathematics and for developing language. The test is divided into two levels. Level 1 assesses literacy development in prekindergarten and beginning kindergarten children. Level 2 assesses beginning reading and mathematics development in the middle and end of kindergarten and at the beginning of Grade 1.

Format: Examiner required; Level 1—individual administration, Level 2—suitable for group use; timed: Level 1—85 minutes, Level 2—100 minutes

Scoring: Hand scored; scoring service available

Cost: Level 1 Exam Kit $28.00; Level 2 Exam Kit $16.00

Miller Assessment for Preschoolers™ (MAP™)
Lucy J. Miller

1982	The Psychological Corporation

Population: Ages 2 years 9 months though 5 years 8 months

Purpose: Identifies preschoolers with moderate to severe developmental delays

Description: The MAP can be used for screening or for the in-depth assessment needed for formulating IEPs. There are five indexes (neural foundations, coordination, verbal, nonverbal, and complex tasks) that help identify developmental delays in sensorimotor and cognitive abilities. The scoring is divided by age into six levels.

Format: Examiner required; individual administration; untimed: 30 to 40 minutes

Scoring: Examiner evaluated

Cost: Complete Kit (manual, 6 levels of 25 score sheets, manipulatives, briefcase) $686.00

Missouri Kindergarten Inventory of Developmental Skills (KIDS)

| 1982 | Assessment Resource Center |

Population: Ages 4 to 6 years

Purpose: Assesses the development of academic skills

Description: The KIDS is a screening battery developed by a State Task Force on Early Childhood Screening. A parent questionnaire is included to obtain additional relevant information about each child's development. The following areas of development are surveyed: Number Concepts, Language Concepts, Auditory Skills, Visual Skills, Paper and Pencil Skills, and Gross Motor Skills. Revised and Alternate editions are available.

Format: Examiner required; individual administration; untimed: 35 minutes

Scoring: Examiner evaluated

Cost: Contact publisher

Mullen Scales of Early Learning: AGS Edition
Eileen M. Mullen

| 1995 | American Guidance Service |

Population: Birth to 68 months

Purpose: A comprehensive scale of cognitive functioning in multiple developmental domains; used to assess learning styles, strengths, and weaknesses

Description: Consists of a Gross Motor Scale (birth to 33 months) together with four cognitive scales: Visual Reception, Fine Motor, Receptive Language, and Expressive Language (birth to 68 months each). An Early Learning Composite score is derived from the scores on the cognitive scales. Results provide a profile of cognitive strengths and weaknesses that can be used to develop individualized program plans. Items are performance based, involving the child in a variety of activities.

Format: Examiner required; individual administration; 15 to 30 minutes (birth to 2 years), 40 to 60 minutes (3 to 5 years)

Scoring: Examiner interpreted; computer

scoring is available for Macintosh and Windows formats

Cost: Complete Kit (manuals, picture books, 25 record forms, all manipulatives, briefcase) $599.95

Parents' Evaluations of Developmental Status (PEDS)
Frances Page Glascoe

| 1998 | Ellsworth & Vandemeer Press, Ltd. |

Population: Birth through 8 years

Purpose: Detects developmental and behavioral problems

Description: A screening test and tool for managing a wide range of developmental, behavioral, and family issues. With 10 short questions to parents, PEDS helps professionals identify children at risk for school problems and those with undetected developmental and behavioral disabilities. The questions are written at the fifth-grade level, which ensures that most parents can read and respond independently to the items. There is also a Spanish version.

Format: May be completed independently; untimed: 2 minutes

Scoring: Examiner evaluated

Cost: Complete Set (guide, 50 response forms, 50 scoring forms) $30.00

Pediatric Evaluation of Disability Inventory (PEDI)
Stephen M. Haley, Wendy J. Coster, Larry H. Ludlow, Jane Haltiwanger, Peter J. Andrellos

| 1992 | Center for Rehabilitation Effectiveness |

Population: Ages 6 months to 7 years 6 months

Purpose: Comprehensive clinical assessment of children with disabilities

Description: Clinical assessment of functional capabilities and functional performance. Functional skills measured are self-care (73 items), mobility (59), and social function (65); caregiver-assisted skills are self-care (8), mobility (7), and social function (5). Yields normative standard score and scaled score for each domain. May be used for persons with physical or mental impairments. Can be used for the evaluation of older children if their functional abilities fall within the age range of the test. Functional performance is measured by the level of caregiver assistance needed to accomplish major functional activities.

Format: Examiner required; individual administration; untimed

Scoring: Examiner evaluated; computer scored; test scoring service available from publisher

Cost: Complete Kit (manual, 25 score forms, scoring software) $185.95

Phelps Kindergarten Readiness Scale
Leadelle Phelps

1991	Psychology Press, Inc.

Population: PreK and early K

Purpose: Assesses kindergarten readiness

Description: Paper–pencil oral-response short-answer point-to test with eight subtests: Vocabulary, Verbal Reasoning, Analogies, Visual Discrimination, Perceptual Motor, Auditory Discrimination, Auditory Digit Memory, and Memory of Sentences and Stories. Also available in Spanish.

Format: Examiner required; individual administration; untimed: 15 to 20 minutes

Scoring: Examiner evaluated

Cost: Evaluation Set $25.00 (cost of materials is determined on a sliding scale)

Pre-Kindergarten Screen (PKS)
Raymond E. Webster, Angela Matthews

2000	Academic Therapy Publications

Population: Ages 4 through 5 years

Purpose: Measures kindergarten readiness and detects at-risk difficulties due to experiential or neurological immaturity

Description: The PKS identifies deficiencies in skills shown by research to be indicators of a child's later academic success: fine- and gross-motor skills, following directions, visual-spatial ability, elementary number and color concepts, letter identification, and impulse control. Administered prior to kindergarten entry, it allows teachers to provide extra help in areas that are problematic for the child. The PKS reliably identified children who later had academic problems in first grade. Thirty-nine items are clustered within five subtests. Cutoff scores are provided; standard scores and percentiles define the child's risk category.

Format: Examiner required; individual administration; timed and untimed: 10 to 15 minutes

Scoring: Examiner evaluated

Cost: Complete Kit $65.00

Preschool Evaluation Scale (PES)
Stephen B. McCarney

1992	Hawthorne Educational Services, Inc.

Population: Birth to 72 months

Purpose: Used in child development to screen for developmental delays and behavior problems

Description: Subscales are large muscle skills, small muscle skills, cognitive thinking, expressive language, social/emotional behavior, and self-help skills. Irregularities in normal development are determined in order to provide an appropriate intervention plan. Two forms are available: birth through 35 months (94 items) and 36 through 72 months (85 items). A DOS Quick Score is available.

Format: Rating scale; untimed

Scoring: Examiner evaluated; computer scoring available

Cost: Complete Kit $80.00

Preschool Screening Instrument (PSI)
Stephen Paul Cohen

1994	Stoelting Company

Population: Ages 4 years to 5 years 3 months

Purpose: Identifies prekindergarten children with learning disabilities

Description: Multiple-item task-assessment test in which the child is told he or she will be "playing some games" with the examiner, who administers the following subtests: Figure Drawing, Circle Drawing, Tower Building, Cross Drawing, Block Design, Square Drawing, Broad Jumping, Balancing, Ball Throwing, Hopping, Whole Name, Picture Responses, Comprehension, and Oral Vocabulary. The child's responses are evaluated in seven developmental areas: visual-motor perception, fine-motor development, gross-motor skills, language development, verbal fluency, conceptual skills, and speech and behavioral problems.

Format: Examiner required; individual administration; untimed: 5 to 8 minutes

Scoring: Examiner evaluated

Cost: Complete Kit (25 each of student record books and parent questionnaires, manual, manipulatives, story card) $75.00

Primary Test of Cognitive Skills (PTCS)

1990	CTB/McGraw-Hill

Population: Grades K and 1

Purpose: Assesses intellectual functioning of young children, including verbal, spatial, memory, and concepts; used by teachers to identify students who may be gifted, have learning disabilities, or have developmental delays

Description: Multiple-item paper–pencil multiple-choice test divided into four subtests: verbal, spatial, memory, and concepts. It yields four subscales that combine with the child's age to produce a single Cognitive Skills Index (CSI). May be used with the California Achievement Test, Fifth Edition, or California Test of Basic Skills, Fourth Edition, to produce an Anticipated Achievement score to screen children for potential learning disabilities.

Format: Examiner required; suitable for group use; untimed: 30 minutes per subtest

Scoring: Machine scored; examiner evaluated

Cost: Review Kit $18.20

Reading Readiness Test: Reversal Tests (Bilingual)
Ake W. Edfeldt

Date not provided	Institute of Psychological Research, Inc.

Population: Grade 1

Purpose: Measures degree of speech reversal tendencies in young children before they learn to read; used by educators and speech therapists to predict reading problems in first grade

Description: Oral-response test based on research into the cause and effect of word transposition tendencies of children. The test was developed to diagnose and prevent these difficulties. A child who is scored either as "control case" or as "not yet ready to read" is not considered ready to master reading and therefore should postpone instruction.

Format: Examiner required; individual administration; untimed

Scoring: Hand key; examiner evaluated

Cost: Contact publisher

Revised Pre-Reading Screening Procedures To Identify First Grade Academic Needs
Beth H. Slingerland

1977	Educators Publishing Service, Inc.

Population: Grades K and 1

Purpose: Evaluates auditory, visual, and kines-

thetic strengths to identify children who may have some form of dyslexia or specific language disability; should be used with students who have had no introduction to reading

Description: Series of 12 verbal–visual subtests measuring visual perception; visual discrimination; visual recall; visual-motor skills; auditory recall; auditory discrimination; auditory perception; letter knowledge; and language skills, such as vocabulary, enunciation, comprehension of oral directions, oral expression, and recall of new words. The test also evaluates motor coordination, hobbies and interests, attention span, and mental growth. The test identifies children who are ready for formal instruction in reading, writing, and spelling and are able to learn through conventional methods; children who, while appearing to be ready, reveal indications of a language disability and need immediate multisensory instruction; children who show language confusion but whose maturity indicates a need to begin strengthening their language background; and children of any age who are unready to begin reading instruction and who would benefit from more readiness and social development training. The examiner first explains the directions to the students and then they proceed with the task.

Format: Examiner required; suitable for group use; untimed: 2 to 3 hours

Scoring: Examiner evaluated

Cost: 12 Test Booklets $15.95; Teacher's Manual $5.75; Teachers Cards and Chart $7.45; Specimen Set (teacher's manual, test booklet) $6.00

Ring and Peg Tests of Behavior Development for Infants and Preschool Children
Katherine M. Banham

1963	Psychometric Affiliates

Population: Birth to 6 years

Purpose: Measures the development of infants and preschool children and helps identify the social and motivational factors influential in a child's development; used for clinical assessment of infant and child development

Description: Task-assessment test measures five categories of behavioral performance and ability: ambulative, manipulative, communicative, social-adaptive, and emotive. The test covers a wider range of items than standard intelligence tests to provide the clinical psychologist with diagnosis information. The scale yields a point score and a behavior age for the whole test, as well as for each of the five categories. A developmental quotient may be derived from the full-scale behavior age. The test kit includes minimally culture-bound manipulation objects, manual, test booklet, and scoring sheet.

Format: Examiner required; individual administration; untimed: 45 minutes

Scoring: Hand key

Cost: Professional Examination Kit (25 tests, handbook) $20.00; 25 Score Sheets $5.00

Rockford Infant Developmental Evaluation Scales (RIDES)

Date not provided	Scholastic Testing Service, Inc.

Population: Birth to 4 years

Purpose: Evaluates the level of a child's skill and behavioral development

Description: Multiple-item criterion-referenced evaluation of 308 developmental behaviors in five skill areas: personal–social/self-help, fine motor/adaptive, receptive language, expressive language, and gross motor. Children respond verbally or by pointing. Each behavioral item is determined to be present, emerging, or absent in the child. Test results relate these single items to major developmental patterns and competencies and provide an informal indication of a child's development. The format calls for one eight-page booklet per child. An Individual Child Progress Graph on the back page shows progress and allows comparison of levels across developmental areas. The manual contains a section detailing development, use, and interpretation of the test. The entries for all 308 behaviors provide scoring criteria, developmental significance, equipment specifications, and references to further information. Examiner must be certified for assessment.

Format: Examiner required; individual administration; untimed

Scoring: Examiner evaluated

Cost: Starter Set $80.65

Rossetti Infant–Toddler Language Scale
Louis Rossetti

1990	LinguiSystems, Inc.

Population: Birth to 3 years

Purpose: Assesses language skills

Description: Oral-response 291-item criterion-referenced projective, verbal, point-to, gesture, vocalization test composed of six domains: interaction attachment, pragmatics, gesture, play, language comprehension, and language expression. An examiner's manual with scoring standards and interpretation is available.

Format: Examiner required; individual administration; untimed

Scoring: Examiner evaluated

Cost: Kit (manual, 10 test forms, 10 parent questionnaires) $69.95

School Readiness Test (SRT)
O. F. Anderhalter, Jan Perney

1990	Scholastic Testing Service, Inc.

Population: Grades K to 1

Purpose: Determines individual and group readiness for first grade

Description: Multiple-choice criterion-referenced test designed for children entering first grade. The test reveals readiness for formal instruction by assessing eight skill areas: number knowledge, handwriting ability, vocabulary, identifying letters, visual discrimination, auditory discrimination, comprehension and interpretation, and spelling ability. Raw scores, national percentiles, stanines, and norm curve equivalents are yielded. The test results, which can be used as the basis for placement, show a child at one of six readiness levels. A booklet and pencil are used. Examiner must be certified for assessment.

Format: Examiner required; individual administration; untimed and timed portions: 90 minutes

Scoring: Hand key

Cost: Starter Set $59.45

Screening Test for Educational Prerequisite Skills (STEPS)
Frances Smith

1990	Western Psychological Services

Population: Ages 4 to 5 years

Purpose: Provides a clear picture of needs and skills of beginning kindergartners

Description: STEPS screens five areas: intellectual skills, verbal information skills, cognitive strategies, motor skills, and attitudes in learning styles. The child performs several tasks: copying shapes and words, identifying colors, classifying objects, following directions, and remembering digits. The test is scored as it is given.

Format: Examiner required; individual administration; untimed: 8 to 10 minutes

Scoring: Hand key; computer scored

Cost: Kit (set of test materials, 25 AutoScore™ forms, 25 AutoScore™ home questionnaires, manual) $145.00; 50-use PC disk $99.95

Slosson Test of Reading Readiness (STRR)
Leslie Anne Perry, Gary J. Vitali

| 1991 | Slosson Educational Publications, Inc. |

Population: Late K to Grade 1

Purpose: Assesses reading readiness in young children

Description: The test was designed to identify children who are at risk of failure in programs of formal reading instruction. STRR subtests include recognition of capital letters, recognition of lowercase letters, matching capital and lowercase letters, visual discrimination, auditory discrimination, sequencing, and opposites. Test items focus on cognitive, auditory, and visual abilities.

Format: Examiner required; individual administration; untimed: 15 minutes

Scoring: Examiner evaluated

Cost: Complete Kit $65.00

Sugar Scoring System for the Bender Gestalt Visual Motor Test
Francee R. Sugar

| 1995 | Educators Publishing Service, Inc. |

Population: Grades K and 1

Purpose: Assesses visual-motor functions and developmental problems in young children

Description: The system is designed for teachers and psychologists to assess a young child's production of six of the Bender designs from both qualitative and quantitative points of view.

Format: Examiner required; individual administration; untimed

Scoring: Examiner evaluated

Cost: $3.15

Survey of Early Childhood Abilities (SECA)
Karen Gardner Codding

| Date not provided | Psychological and Educational Publications, Inc. |

Population: Ages 3 years 6 months to 7 years

Purpose: Determines a child's readiness for kindergarten or first grade

Description: The SECA consists of four individual tests that evaluate the following skills: Visual Motor; Reading, Spelling, Arithmetic Readiness; Auditory Perceptual; and Visual Perceptual: Non Motor.

Format: Examiner required; individual administration; untimed: 40 minutes

Scoring: Examiner evaluated

Cost: Complete Kit (manual, 25 profile sheets, 25 record booklets, 25 test booklets, test plates) $89.95

Teacher's Observation Guide (TOG)
Harold R. Ireton

| 1995 | Behavior Science Systems, Inc. |

Population: Birth to 6 years

Purpose: Assesses development in eight areas

Description: There are 400 items in these categories: Social Development, Self Help, Gross Motor, Fine Motor, Expressive Language, Language Comprehension, Letters, and Numbers. Development is classified in each area as around age level, borderline, or delayed. Twenty-three items record the teacher's concerns about the child's social adjustment/behavior problems, maturity, motor, and language development.

Format: Teacher observation; untimed

Scoring: Examiner evaluated

Cost: Manual $10.00; 10 Booklets $15.00

Test of Kindergarten/First Grade Readiness Skills (TKFGRS)
Karen Gardner Codding

| Date not provided | Psychological and Educational Publications, Inc. |

Population: Ages 3 years 6 months to 7 years

Purpose: Evaluates the basic skills in reading, spelling, and arithmetic

Description: The areas measured in the TKFGRS are Reading (letter, phonetic, and word identification, story comprehension), Spelling (letter and word identification), and Arithmetic (number identification, written computation, time identification, verbal word problems). Results are given in standard scores.

Format: Examiner required; individual administration; untimed: 10 minutes

Scoring: Examiner evaluated

Cost: Complete Kit (manual, 25 record booklets, 8 cards) $50.95

Test of Sensory Functions in Infants (TSFI)

Georgia A. DeGangi, Stanley I. Greenspan

| 1989 | Western Psychological Services |

Population: Ages 4 to 18 months

Purpose: Used to identify infants with sensory integrative dysfunction

Description: Composed of 24 items, the test provides objective criteria for determining the presence and extent of deficits in sensory functioning in infants. The TSFI provides an overall measure of sensory processing and reactivity and also assesses these subdomains: reactivity to tactile deep pressure, visual tactile integration, adaptive motor function, ocular motor control, and reactivity to vestibular stimulation.

Format: Examiner required; individual administration; untimed: 20 minutes

Scoring: Examiner evaluated

Cost: Kit (set of test materials, 100 administration and scoring forms, manual, plastic carrying case) $165.00

Tests of Basic Experiences, Second Edition (TOBE 2)

Margaret H. Moss

| 1978 | CTB/McGraw-Hill |

Population: Grades K and 1

Purpose: Measures the degree to which young children have acquired concepts and experiences related to effective school participation; used for evaluation of school readiness

Description: Multiple-item battery of paper-pencil tests measuring quantity and quality of children's early learning experiences. The test is divided into two overlapping levels, covering programs from preschool through first grade. Each level contains a language, mathematics, science, and social studies test. Each test item consists of a verbal stimulus and four pictured responses. An instructional activities kit contains materials for teaching concepts and skills.

Format: Examiner required; suitable for group use; untimed: 45 minutes per test

Scoring: Hand key

Cost: 30 Test Books $58.90

Vineland Social-Emotional Early Childhood Scales (Vineland SEEC)

Sara Sparrow, David Balla, Domenic Cicchetti

| 1998 | American Guidance Service |

Population: Birth through 5 years 11 months

Purpose: Measures social-emotional skills

Description: Information is collected by interview with the parent or caregivers. The SEEC Scales identify strengths and weaknesses in specific areas of social-emotional behavior. The results can be used to plan a program and select activities best suited to a child's needs.

Format: Examiner required; untimed: 15 to 25 minutes

Scoring: Examiner evaluated

Cost: Complete Kit (manual, 25 record forms) $54.95

Vulpe Assessment Battery– Revised (VAB-R)

Shirley German Vulpe

| 1994 | Slosson Educational Publications, Inc. |

Population: Birth to 6 years

Purpose: Evaluates the developmental status of atypically developing children

Description: Performance analysis/developmental assessment of functioning with 1,127 items in multiple developmental skill areas (basic senses and functions, gross-motor behaviors, fine-motor behaviors, language behaviors, cognitive processes and specific concepts, the organization of behavior, activities of daily living) and an environmental domain. Information about an individual child is obtained through direct observation or from a knowledgeable informant.

Format: Examiner required; individual or group administration; untimed

Scoring: Examiner evaluated

Cost: Complete Battery $99.00

English as a Second Language and Bilingual Education

Adult Language Assessment Scales (Adult LAS®)
Sharon E. Duncan, Edward A. DeAvila

1991	CTB/McGraw-Hill

Population: Adults

Purpose: Assesses English language proficiency in adults whose primary language is not English

Description: Multiple-item paper–pencil multiple-choice, oral-response and short-answer test available in two levels. The test consists of oral language, writing, reading, and mathematics components. There are four subtests, divided into subsections that allow for identification of problem areas. Results of all test components are combined to give one measure of language proficiency.

Format: Examiner required; suitable for group use; untimed: 5 to 30 minutes per subsection

Scoring: Examiner evaluated; hand key

Cost: Oral Examiner's Kit (Form A) $201.95; 50 Oral Answer Books $51.85; 25 Reading/Math Test Books $110.15; 50 Reading/Math Answer Sheets $43.20; 50 Writing Combination Test Books and Answer Sheets $76.50

Adult Rating of Oral English (AROE)

1995	Development Associates, Inc.

Population: Adults

Purpose: Informally assesses oral proficiency

Description: Eleven categories are rated to guide instruction, track progress, and guide placement. The instructor rates the individual based on interaction over time. Subtotals for each of two matrices are available: Building Blocks and Discourse Matrices.

Format: Rating scale; untimed

Scoring: Examiner evaluated

Cost: Introductory Kit (5 user handbooks, 25 matrices) $75.00

Basic English Skills Test (BEST)

Date not provided	Center for Applied Linguistics

Population: Adults

Purpose: Measures basic oral and literacy skills

Description: The BEST is a competency-based survival-level ESL performance test that is widely used in adult ESL literacy programs. It includes a structured oral interview component. The Oral Interview Section measures communication, fluency, pronunciation, and listening comprehension. The Literacy Skills Section provides scores for reading and writing. The BEST is available in two parallel forms.

Format: Examiner required; individual/group administration; timed: 45 minutes

Scoring: Examiner evaluated; test scoring service available from publisher

Cost: Complete Kit $150.00

Batería Woodcock-Muñoz–Revisada
Richard W. Woodcock, Ana F. Muñoz-Sandoval

1996	Riverside Publishing Company

Population: Ages 2 through 90+ years

Purpose: Assesses cognitive abilities and achievement levels in Spanish-speaking individuals

Description: A comprehensive, technically excellent set of conormed tests, thereby allowing meaningful comparison between cognitive abilities and achievement levels. This is a parallel version of the Woodcock-Johnson–Revised, so information can be directly compared. A comparative language index is available when oral language, reading, or written language clusters have been administered in both languages. An ancillary examiner procedure is designed to help a qualified, English-speaking examiner prepare a Spanish-speaking individual to help administer the instrument.

Format: Examiner required; individual administration; timed: 5 minutes per subtest

Scoring: Examiner evaluated

Cost: Complete Battery (cognitive test books, achievement test books, audiocassettes, manuals, 25 each of test records and response booklets, norm tables, 2 cases) $926.00

Ber-Sil Spanish Tests: Elementary Test 1987 Revision
Marjorie L. Beringer

1987	Ber-Sil Company

Population: Ages 5 to 12 years

Purpose: Assesses the functioning level of children in Spanish; used to assist in placing Spanish speakers and students with speech impairments for efficient instruction

Description: Multiple-item paper–pencil criterion-referenced test consisting of five sections: Vocabulary (Spanish; 100 words), Action Responses to directions (13 items), Visual-Motor Activity (3 parts), Mathematics (70 items), and Vocabulary (English; 100 words). Writing samples, geometric figures, and figure drawing are included in the test. Spanish Vocabulary, Comprehension of Spanish, Visual-Motor Abilities, Math Skills, and English Vocabulary scores are yielded. The revision includes the math and English vocabulary tests. Directions are on an audiocassette tape. Translations are available in Spanish, Mandarin, Cantonese, Tagalog, Ilocano, Korean, and Persian.

Format: Examiner required; individual administration; untimed: 30 to 60 minutes

Scoring: Hand key; examiner evaluated

Cost: Complete Kit $60.00; Combination Kit (elementary/secondary) $100.00; Translation Tapes $15.00

Ber-Sil Spanish Tests: Secondary Test
Marjorie L. Beringer

| 1984 | Ber-Sil Company |

Population: Ages 13 to 17 years

Purpose: Assesses Spanish language and mathematics abilities of junior and senior high school students; used to assist in placing secondary Spanish-speaking students or students with speech impairments for efficient instruction

Description: Multiple-item multiple-choice paper–pencil and point-to criterion-referenced test in four sections: Spanish Vocabulary (100 words), Dictation in Spanish (4 sentences), Draw a Boy or Girl (maturity level), and Mathematics (70 items). Scores indicating the level of the examinee's ability in Spanish vocabulary, Spanish grammar and spelling, maturity level, and mathematical processes are generated. The test is administered with audiocassette tape instructions by psychologists, pschometricians, counselors, and speech specialists. It is useful for curriculum planning and academic counseling. Translations are available in Ilocano and Tagalog.

Format: Examiner required; individual administration; untimed: 20 to 30 minutes

Scoring: Hand key; examiner evaluated

Cost: Complete Kit $60.00; Combination Kit (elementary/secondary) $100.00; Translation Tapes $15.00

Bilingual Verbal Ability Tests (BVAT)
Ana F. Muñoz-Sandoval, Jim Cummins, Criselda G. Alvarado, Mary L. Ruef

| 1998 | Riverside Publishing Company |

Population: Ages 5 years through adult

Purpose: Provides a measure of overall verbal ability for bilingual individuals

Description: A test of the unique combination of cognitive–academic language abilities possessed by bilingual individuals in English and another language. The need for this test is based on the reality that bilingual persons know some things in one language, some things in the other language, and some things in both languages. Traditional procedures measure a person's ability in only one language, usually the one considered dominant. The BVAT may be administered either by one examiner who is fluent in the individual's two languages, or by a primary and ancillary examiner team. The test can be used to determine entry and exit criteria for bilingual programs or to assess the academic potential of a bilingual student. The BVAT comprises three subtests from the Woodcock-Johnson-Revised Tests of Cognitive Ability: Picture Vocabulary, Oral Vocabulary, and Verbal Analogies. The subtests have been translated from English into 17 languages. The subtests are administered in English first. Items that were missed are then administered in the individual's native language and added to the score.

Format: Examiner required; individual administration; untimed: 30 minutes

Scoring: Computer scored; examiner evaluated

Cost: English Test Kit (English test book, manual, scoring software) $159.50; Languages $64.00 each

Bilingual Vocabulary Assessment Measure
Larry J. Mattes

| 1995 | Academic Communication Associates |

Population: Ages 3 through 11 years

Purpose: Determines if basic picture-naming vocabulary for common nouns has been acquired

Description: Measures basic expressive vocabulary in a variety of languages. The instrument is criterion referenced and designed for use as an initial screening. It is helpful in determining whether the child is able to label articles of clothing, tools, motor vehicles, and other nouns commonly encountered in school, in the supermarket, and at home. The standard record forms are designed so that responses can be recorded in any language spoken by the child.

Format: Examiner required; individual administration; untimed

Scoring: Hand key

Cost: Complete Kit $52.00

BRIGANCE® Diagnostic Assessment of Basic Skills–Spanish Edition

Albert H. Brigance

1984	Curriculum Associates®, Inc.

Population: Grades PreK through 9

Purpose: Measures the academic skills of Spanish-speaking students; distinguishes language barriers from learning disabilities; used by bilingual, ESL, migrant, and bilingual special educators to identify, develop, and implement academic programs

Description: A total of 102 skill sequences assess Spanish-speaking students' abilities in readiness, speech, functional word recognition, oral reading, reading comprehension, word analysis, listening, writing and alphabetizing, numbers and computation, and measurement. Directions to the examiner are written in English; directions to the student are written in Spanish. Assessments used for dominant language screening present directions to the student in English and Spanish. The diagnostic tests identify skills the student has and has not mastered and students who might have learning disabilities. The diagnostic tests help to determine individual instructional objectives. The dominant language screening form provides a means of comparing a student's performance in English and Spanish on all of the oral language and literacy diagnostic assessments. Results of the screening are used to place students in appropriate ESL and bilingual programs. The seven grade-level screens assess skills that indicate grade-level competency in Grades K through 6. The results are used to place students at their appropriate instructional levels and to identify students who need further evaluation. Individual student record books record the level of competency the student has achieved.

Format: Examiner required; many sections are suitable for group use; untimed

Scoring: Examiner evaluated

Cost: Assessment Book $149.00; Class Record Book $12.95; 10 Student Record Books $27.90

Computerized Adaptive Placement Assessment and Support System and English as a Second Language (COMPASS/ESL)

2000	ACT, Inc.

Population: Ages 18 years and older

Purpose: Used for placement and diagnosis to assess writing, reading, and math skills

Description: Multiple-choice computer-administered test with placement tests (7 separate scores) and diagnostic tests (28 separate scores). The categories are Writing Skills Placement (465 items), Reading Placement (205 items), Math Placement: Prealgebra (234 items), Algebra (235 items), College Algebra (165 items), Geometry (187 items), Trigonometry (200 items), Math Diagnostic Tests (20 items per category): Operations with Integers, Operations with Fractions, Operations with Decimals, Exponents, Ratios and Proportions, Percentages, Averages; Reading Diagnostic Tests: Main Idea (30 items), Implicit Information (90 items), Explicit Information (60 items), Vocabulary (100 items); Writing Skills Diagnostic Tests: Punctuation (40 items), Verbs (40 items), Usage (40 items), Relationships of Clause (40 items), Shifts in Construction (40 items), Organization (40 items), Spelling (40 items), and Capitalization (40 items). Contact publisher about computer requirements.

Format: Examiner required; computer administered; untimed

Scoring: Computer scored

Cost: Site License $450.00; Administration Unit $1.30 each

English Placement Test (EPT)

Mary Spann, Laura Strowe, A. Corrigan, B. Dobson, E. Kellman, S. Tyma

1993	English Language Institute Test Publications

Population: Adults

Purpose: Assesses facility with the English language; used to group adult nonnative speakers of English into homogeneous ability levels (low to advanced intermediate proficiency) as they enter an intensive English course

Description: Paper–pencil 100-item multiple-choice test of listening comprehension, grammar in conversational contexts, vocabulary recognition, and reading comprehension of sentences. An audiocassette is available for use with the listening comprehension items. Three forms (A, B, C) are available.

Format: Examiner required; suitable for group use; timed: 1 hour 15 minutes

Scoring: Hand key

Cost: Testing Package (examiner's manual, scoring stencil, 20 test booklets, 100 answer sheets, audiocassette) $65.00

Expressive One-Word Picture Vocabulary Test–Spanish Bilingual Edition
Rick Brownell

| 2001 | Academic Therapy Publications |

Population: Ages 4 through 12 years

Purpose: Measures speaking vocabulary in Spanish and English

Description: Provides a measure of total acquired expressive vocabulary. Examinees may respond in both languages. The test was conormed with the Receptive One Word Picture Vocabulary Test–Spanish Bilingual Edition on a national sample of Spanish-bilingual individuals. Administration procedures permit examiners to cue examinees so that they will attend to the relevant aspects of each illustration. Record forms provide cues and acceptable responses in both languages and common Spanish dialects. Raw scores are converted to standard scores, percentiles, and age equivalents. The test uses the same plates as the English version, so users of the English version should order only the Spanish-Bilingual Manual and Record Forms.

Format: Examiner required; individual administration; untimed: 20 minutes

Scoring: Examiner evaluated

Cost: Test Kit (manual, test plates, 25 forms, portfolio) $140.00; Manual $38.00; Forms $27.00

Institutional Testing Program (ITP)

| Date not provided | Educational Testing Service |

Population: Adolescents, adults

Purpose: Measures English proficiency of nonnative speakers of English

Description: Multiple-choice test composed of Listening Comprehension (50 items), Structure and Written Expression (40 items), and Vocabulary and Reading Comprehension (60 items). This test uses retired forms of the Test of English as a

Foreign Language (TOEFL). The test yields three section scores and one total score. Suitable for individuals with visual, physical, and hearing impairment.

Format: Examiner required; suitable for group use; timed: 150 minutes

Scoring: Hand key; test scoring service available from publisher

Cost: 200 or fewer tests $14.00 each; more than 200 tests $12.00 each (minimum order of 10 tests)

IRCA Pre-Enrollment Appraisal

| 1988 | Comprehensive Adult Student Assessment System (CASAS) |

Population: Adult ESL students

Purpose: Measures learners' English ability in the context of basic life skills as well as the history and government of the United States

Description: Includes a multiple-choice reading test, a short oral interview, and a two-sentence listening dictation to assess basic writing ability. The appraisal is a screening and placement test battery for beginning and intermediate limited-English speaking adults. May be used in private postsecondary ESL programs that receive Pell Grants and are required to administer a test to show students' "ability to benefit" from instruction. The test is approved by the U.S. Department of Education only for students enrolling in ESL programs.

Format: Examiner required; group administration; untimed

Scoring: Self-scored

Cost: Set of 25 Reusable Tests $65.00; Set of 25 Answer Sheets $25.00; Administration Manual $45.00

Language Assessment Scales–Oral (LAS-O)
Sharon E. Duncan, Edward A. DeAvila

| 1990 | CTB/McGraw-Hill |

Population: Grades 1 to 12

Purpose: Assesses oral language abilities of students whose primary language is not English

Description: Multiple-item paper-pencil multiple-choice and oral-response test available in two levels and two forms in English, and in two levels and one form in Spanish. The test is based on an analysis of four primary language subsystems: phonemic, lexical, syntactical, and pragmatic. Its five sections are divided into two components:

the Oral Language Component and the Pronunciation Component. Can be used with LAS® Reading/Writing.

Format: Examiner required; individually administered; untimed 10 to 20 minutes

Scoring: Examiner evaluated

Cost: Examiner's Kit $108.50

Language Proficiency Test (LPT)
Joan E. Gerald, Gloria Weinstock

1981	Academic Therapy Publications

Population: Ages 15 years to adult

Purpose: Evaluates ability to use English language; identifies competency levels and detects specific deficiencies of ESL students

Description: Multiple-item paper–pencil criterion-referenced test in three major sections: aural/oral, reading, and writing. An optional translation section is included for ESL students. Materials were designed to be appropriate for older students. The majority of the nine subtests can be group administered. Raw scores are converted to a percentage and plotted on a profile chart that indicates level of English language competency.

Format: Examiner required; individual and group administration; untimed: 90 minutes

Scoring: Examiner administered and interpreted

Cost: Test Kit (manual and protocols in vinyl folder) $50.00

Language Proficiency Test Series (LPTS)

1999	MetriTech, Inc.

Population: Grades K through 12

Purpose: Measures English proficiency; identifies students requiring services, monitors student progress over time, and provides information for mainstreaming

Description: Categories are Reading, Writing, and Listening/Speaking, each available for Grades K to 2, 3 to 5, 6 to 8, and 9 to 12. There are four proficiency levels for Reading and Writing. Proficiency cut scores are provided for Listening/Speaking. Forms A and B are available for each genre at each of four grade clusters, for a total of 24 test booklets.

Format: Examiner required; group administration; untimed: 15 to 60 minutes

Scoring: Hand key; examiner evaluated; scoring

service available from publisher (additional consultation/customization available)

Cost: Contact publisher

LAS® Reading/Writing (LAS R/W)
Sharon E. Duncan, Edward A. DeAvila

1994	CTB/McGraw-Hill

Population: Grades 2 through 12

Purpose: Assesses reading and writing proficiency of nonnative English-speaking students

Description: Multiple-item paper–pencil multiple-choice and essay test available in two forms and three levels in English, and one form and three levels in Spanish. Vocabulary, fluency, reading comprehension, and mechanics are assessed objectively with multiple-choice items, and writing is evaluated directly using performance assessment.

Format: Examiner required; suitable for group use; timed 90 minutes

Scoring: Examiner evaluated; hand key

Cost: Review Kit $20.85 (English or Spanish version)

Listening Comprehension Test (LCT)
John Upshur, H. Koba, Mary Spaan, Laura Strowe

1986	English Language Institute Test Publications

Population: Adults

Purpose: Measures a nonnative speaker's understanding of spoken English; used to predict readiness to pursue studies in an English-speaking institution

Description: Paper–pencil 45-item multiple-choice test of aural comprehension of English. The student is read a short question or statement and responds by marking the appropriate written answer. A tape recording of the verbal questions and statements is available. The test is available in three forms: 4, 5, and 6. This test is a retired, nonsecure component of the Michigan Test Battery. It is sold only to educational institutions for internal use (e.g., to measure the learning progress of ESL or EFL students who have already been admitted to a program or to confirm the level of proficiency of matriculated students). The tests are not to be used for initial university admission purposes or to report scores to other institutions.

Format: Examiner required; suitable for group use; timed: 15 minutes

Scoring: Hand key

Cost: Testing Package (manual, 20 test booklets, 100 answer sheets, 3 scoring stencils) $70.00

MAC II Test of English Language Proficiency

2001	Touchstone Applied Science Associates, Inc.

Population: Ages 5 years and older

Purpose: Measures English language proficiency

Description: Applications include placement, measuring progress, determining readiness for ESL program exit, evaluating ESL programs. Four subtests measure English proficiency: Speaking, Listening, Reading, and Writing. Results are reported as standard scores, Degrees of Reading Power scores (Grades 4 and up), and percentiles. Forms available: A1, A2, A3, A4, A5, B1, B2, B3, B4, and B5. Materials used: manuals, picture booklets, test booklets, record forms, writing forms, and answer sheets.

Format: Examiner required; suitable for group use; both timed and untimed

Scoring: Hand key; machine scored; scoring service available

Cost: $95.00 to $120.00 per pack of 25; Basic Scoring $2.05 to $2.90

Michigan Test of English Language Proficiency (MTELP)
John Upshur

1977	English Language Institute Test Publications

Population: Adults

Purpose: Assesses the English language proficiency of nonnative speakers of English; used to predict the readiness to study at the college level or in a professional training program in an English-speaking institution

Description: Paper–pencil 100-item multiple-choice test of grammar, reading comprehension, and vocabulary. Available in eight alternate forms (G, H, J, K, L, P, Q, R). These materials are retired, nonsecure components of the Michigan Test Battery and should not be used as an admission test; however, the test is suitable for placement of students who already have been admitted.

Format: Examiner required; suitable for group use; timed: 1 hour 15 minutes

Scoring: Hand key

Cost: Testing Package (manual, scoring stencil, 20 test booklets, 100 answer sheets) $50.00

Oral Communication Applied Performance Appraisal (OCAPA)

1991	Comprehensive Adult Student Assessment System (CASAS)

Population: Adults, adolescents; native and nonnative speakers of English

Purpose: Assesses speaking, listening, reading, writing, and thinking skills in functional contexts; used as an appraisal of a client's communication skills upon entry into a job training program or to determine readiness for program exit

Description: Eight competency tasks set in an employment (primarily office) context, are presented in a modified role-play format. Examiner training is recommended. Checklist for scoring of performance on competency tasks is provided.

Format: Individual administration; responses are oral and written

Scoring: Test administrator uses standardized scoring rubric

Cost: Reusable Test and 50 Sets of Scoring Materials $57.00

Oral English or Spanish Proficiency Placement Test

1995	Moreno Educational Company

Population: Grades 1 through 6 and Grades 7 through 12

Purpose: Designed to measure oral English-speaking ability of limited English-speaking students

Description: Oral test is administered in English to measure language-speaking ability. Initial directions are given in the student's native language. Spanish placement test measures the oral Spanish speaking ability of the student. May also be used with adults.

Format: Examiner required; individual administration

Scoring: Examiner evaluated

Cost: $20.00

Pre-LAS
Sharon E. Duncan, Edward A. DeAvila

1985	CTB/McGraw-Hill

Population: Ages 4 to 6 years

Purpose: Assesses oral language abilities of nonnative English-speaking children

Description: Multiple-item paper–pencil verbal-oral response test available in two forms in English and one form in Spanish. The test assesses expressive and receptive abilities in three linguistic components of oral language: morphology, syntax, and semantics.

Format: Examiner required; individual administration; untimed 15 to 20 minutes

Scoring: Examiner evaluated

Cost: Examiner's Kit $110.75

Receptive One-Word Picture Vocabulary Test–Spanish Bilingual Edition
Rick Brownell

2001	Academic Therapy Publications

Population: Ages 4 through 12 years

Purpose: Measures receptive vocabulary in Spanish and English

Description: Provides a measure of total acquired receptive vocabulary. Examinees may respond to stimulus words in both languages. The test was conormed with the Expressive One Word Picture Vocabulary Test–Spanish Bilingual Edition on a national sample of Spanish-bilingual individuals. Administration procedures permit examiners to cue examinees so that they will attend to the relevant aspects of each illustration. Record forms include acceptable responses and stimulus words in both languages and common Spanish dialects. Raw scores are converted to standard scores, percentiles, and age equivalents. The test uses the same plates as the English version, so users of the English version should order only the Spanish-Bilingual Manual and Record Forms.

Format: Examiner required; individual administration; untimed: 20 minutes

Scoring: Examiner evaluated

Cost: Test Kit (manual, test plates, 25 forms, in portfolio) $140.00; Manual $38.00; Forms $27.00

Secondary Level English Proficiency Test (SLEP)

Date not provided	Educational Testing Service

Population: Ages 12 to 17 years

Purpose: Assesses English language proficiency of nonnative speakers; used as an admissions test by private secondary schools and as a placement test by both public and private secondary schools

Description: Paper–pencil 150-item multiple-choice test measuring two components (75 items each) of English proficiency: listening comprehension and reading comprehension (structure and vocabulary). The test does not measure productive language skills. A tape recorder is required to administer the listening comprehension sections. An audiocassette tape is included. Raw and converted scores are provided for both listening comprehension and reading comprehension sections. The test is available in three equivalent forms.

Format: Examiner required; suitable for group use; timed: 1 hour 20 minutes

Scoring: Hand key

Cost: Complete Kit (reusable materials, 25 test booklets, 100 answer sheets, audiocassette, 2 keys, manual) $100.00

Spanish and English Reading Comprehension Test

1993	Moreno Educational Company

Population: Grades 1 through 6 and Grades 7 through 12

Purpose: Measures Spanish reading achievement based on Mexican norms to determine learning ability and learning potential; used as a tool to evaluate bilingual education programs, and for research

Description: Compares Spanish reading ability with that of Mexican neighbors. Based on Mexican curriculum materials, standardized and normed in Mexico. Measures both Spanish and English reading comprehension. Developed and designed for use in the United States. Can be used by psychologists and evaluators for the identification of students who are mentally gifted or who have learning disorders.

Format: Individual administration; suitable for group use; 25 minutes

Scoring: Examiner administration and interpretation

Cost: Elementary $20.00; Secondary $20.00 (Answer sheets may be duplicated as needed)

Spanish Articulation Measures (SAM)
Larry J. Mattes

1995	Academic Communication Associates

Population: Ages 3 years through adult

Purpose: Measures articulation and phonological processes in Spanish

Description: Vocabulary words that are familiar to young children are emphasized in the tasks. The Spontaneous Word Production Task is used to assess production of individual phonemes and use of phonological processes such as cluster reduction, stridency deletion, velar fronting, stopping, and syllable reduction. The instrument is criterion referenced.

Format: Examiner required; individual administration; untimed

Scoring: Hand key

Cost: Complete Kit $70.00

Spanish Language Assessment Procedures (SLAP)

Larry J. Mattes

| 1995 | Academic Communication Associates |

Population: Ages 3 to 9 years

Purpose: Assesses pragmatic and structural aspects of the Spanish language

Description: A criterion-referenced measure of the ability to understand basic concepts, communicate basic needs, follow oral directions, retell short stories, request information, describe events in sequence, make inferences, express opinions, ask questions, and so on. An articulation screening instrument is included. The manual includes guidelines for using the assessment results in the identification of children with communication disorders.

Format: Examiner required; individual administration; untimed

Scoring: Hand key

Cost: Complete Kit $75.00

Spanish Reading Comprehension Test (Evaluación de Comprensión de la Lectura)

| 1994 | Comprehensive Adult Student Assessment System (CASAS) |

Population: Spanish-speaking adults and adolescents

Purpose: Assesses basic reading comprehension in Spanish

Description: Multiple-choice competency-based test of reading comprehension in Spanish. Contains reading selections drawn from authentic Spanish-language material in functional life skill contexts. Difficulty levels range from 3 to 9 years of schooling. May be used as entrance appraisal, progress test, or exit measure in Spanish-language instructional programs. Two forms are available.

Format: Group administration

Scoring: Self-scoring answer sheets

Cost: Set of 25 Reusable Answer Sheets $65.00; Set of 25 Answer Sheets $25.00; Administration Manual $40.00

Spanish Test for Assessing Morphologic Production (STAMP)

Therese M. Nugent, Kenneth G. Shipley, Dora O. Provencio

| 1991 | Academic Communication Associates |

Population: Ages 5 through 11 years

Purpose: Assesses production of Spanish morphemes

Description: An incomplete sentence is presented to the child and the child is asked to complete that sentence using a pictorial prompt. Plurals, verb endings, and various other structures are examined. The instrument was developed based on an analysis of structure of the Spanish language. Means and standard deviations are reported for Spanish-speaking students. The test can be adapted for use with speakers of different Spanish dialects. When used in conjunction with conversational speech samples, the results are helpful in identifying children with communication disorders.

Format: Examiner required; individual administration; untimed

Scoring: Hand key

Cost: Complete Kit $70.00

Speaking Proficiency English Assessment Kit (SPEAK)

| Yearly | Educational Testing Service |

Population: Adults; international teaching assistants

Purpose: Assesses spoken English for international teaching assistants

Description: Oral-response 12-item test available for purchase by institutions. Under this program, test forms are administered and scored by institutions, at their convenience, using their own facilities and staff. Scores are reported on a scale from 20 to 60 in 5-point increments. Materials used include a test book, test audiocassette, and an answer audiocassette/response tape.

Format: Examiner required; suitable for group use; timed: 30 minutes total

Scoring: Examiner evaluated

Cost: Contact publisher

Student Oral Proficiency Rating (SOPR)

1986   Development Associates, Inc.

Population: Grades K to 12

Purpose: Informally assesses oral proficiency

Description: Five categories are rated to guide instruction, track progress, and guide placement. The instructor rates the individual based on interaction over time.

Format: Rating scale; untimed

Scoring: Examiner evaluated

Cost: Introductory Information and Matrix $5.00; Teacher's Training Packet $10.00

Test de Vocabulario en Imágenes Peabody (TVIP)

Lloyd M. Dunn, Delia E. Lugo, Eligio R. Padilla, Leota M. Dunn

1986   American Guidance Service

Population: Ages 2 years 6 months through 17 years

Purpose: Measures receptive vocabulary for Spanish-speaking individuals

Description: Based on the Peabody Picture Vocabulary Test-Revised, the TVIP contains 125 translated items to assess the vocabulary of Spanish-speaking and bilingual students. Items were carefully selected through rigorous item analysis for their universality and appropriateness to Spanish-speaking communities.

Format: Examiner required; individual administration; untimed: 10 to 15 minutes

Scoring: Examiner evaluated

Cost: Test Kit (test easel, Spanish manual, 25 record forms, shelf box) $112.95

Test of English as a Foreign Language (TOEFL)

Date not provided   Educational Testing Service

Population: Adults

Purpose: Assesses proficiency in English for nonnative speakers; used as a college admission and placement test

Description: Paper–pencil 150-item multiple-choice test measuring three aspects of English ability: listening comprehension, structure and written expression, and reading comprehension. Items involve comprehension of spoken and written language. The test is administered monthly on either Friday or Saturday.

Format: Examiner required; suitable for group use; timed: 3 hours

Scoring: Computer scored

Cost: Contact publisher

Test of Spoken English (TSE)

Date not provided   Educational Testing Service

Population: Adults

Purpose: Assesses nonnative speakers' proficiency in spoken English; used to evaluate applicants whose native language is not English for graduate-level teaching assistantships and for certification in health-related professions

Description: Oral-response 12-item test assessing nonnative speakers' proficiency in spoken English. A test audiocassette leads the examinee through questions requiring controlled responses or less structured answers that demand more active use of English. The subject's answers are taped and evaluated by two raters at the Educational Testing Service (ETS). The test yields scores in three areas: grammar, fluency, and pronunciation. The TSE is part of the Test of English as a Foreign Language (TOEFL) program and is designed to complement the TOEFL, which does not measure oral English proficiency. The institutional version, the Speaking Proficiency English Assessment Kit (SPEAK), is available for local testing.

Format: Examiner required; individual administration; untimed: 20 minutes

Scoring: Computer scored; examiner evaluated

Cost: Contact publisher

Test of Written English (TWE)

Velma R. Andersen, Sheryl K. Thompson

1986   Educational Testing Service

Population: Students entering college

Purpose: Measures written English ability of nonnative speakers of English who wish to study at the college level; used for admissions and placement

Description: Paper–pencil criterion-referenced essay test on a specific topic using answer sheets, paper, pencil, and a test booklet. The TWE uses a 6-point holistic score scale. This is a secure test; the publisher arranges all administrations, scoring, and so on. The TWE is suitable for individuals with visual, physical, or hearing impairments.

Format: Examiner evaluated; group administration; timed: 30 minutes

Scoring: Examiner evaluated; test scoring service required from publisher

Cost: TWE is given with the TOEFL test; no additional fee

Woodcock Language Proficiency Battery-Revised (WLPB-R) Spanish Form
Richard W. Woodcock, Ana F. Muñoz-Sandoval

| 1995 | Riverside Publishing Company |

Population: Ages 2 through 90+ years

Purpose: Assess language skills in Spanish; used for purposes of eligibility and determination of level of language proficiency

Description: Provides an overall measure of language proficiency in measures of oral language, reading, and written language. The subtests are Memory for Sentences, Picture Vocabulary, Oral Vocabulary, Listening Comprehension, Verbal Analogies, Letter-Word Identification, Passage Comprehension, Word Attack, Reading Vocabulary, Dictation, Writing Samples, Proofing, Writing Fluency, Punctuation and Capitalization, Spelling and Usage, and Handwriting. There are cluster scores for Oral Language, Reading, and Written Language. The tests are primarily measures of language skills predictive of success in situations characterized by cognitive-academic language proficiency (CALP) requirements. CALP levels from advanced to negligible are provided. When the WLPB-R English Form also has been administered, a comparative language index that allows direct comparison between English and Spanish scores can be obtained.

Format: Examiner required; individual administration; untimed: 20 to 60 minutes depending on number of subtests

Scoring: Examiner evaluated; computer software available

Cost: Complete Program (test book, audiocassette, 25 each of test records and response booklets, English manual, English norm tables, supplemental manual) $307.50

Woodcock-Muñoz Language Survey (WMLS) Normative Update
Richard W. Woodcock, Ana F. Muñoz-Sandoval

| 2001 | Riverside Publishing Company |

Population: Ages 4 years through adult

Purpose: Establishes language proficiency level in English or Spanish

Description: Provides a broad overview of language ability in oral language, reading, and writing. Use of the English Form in conjunction with the Spanish Form enables examiners to obtain information about the individual's dominant language and information regarding the subject's proficiency in each language compared to others at the same age or grade level. The Language Survey provides five cognitive-academic language proficiency (CALP) levels. This survey gives examiners a sound procedure for classification of a subject's English or Spanish language proficiency, for determining eligibility for bilingual services, and for assessing a subject's progress or readiness for English-only instruction. Age and grade equivalents can be obtained directly from the test record. Percentile ranks, standard scores, relative proficiency indexes, and CALP levels can be obtained through use of the Scoring and Reporting Program, which comes with the test.

Format: Examiner required; individual administration; untimed: 5 minutes per subtest

Scoring: Computer scored; examiner evaluated

Cost: Complete Kit English or Spanish (comprehensive manual, 25 test records, test book, software) $225.00

Fine Arts

Art Interest-A-Lyzer
Joseph S. Renzulli

| 1997 | Creative Learning Press, Inc. |

Population: Grades 4 through 8

Purpose: Examines present and potential interests; used as a basis for group discussions and in-depth counseling

Description: Multiple-item paper-pencil instrument consisting of a series of open-ended questions structured to highlight general patterns of interest. Items cover visual art interest areas.

Format: Examiner required; suitable for group use; untimed

Scoring: Examiner evaluated

Cost: 30 Questionnaires $29.95

Harmonic Improvisation Readiness Record and Rhythm Improvisation Readiness Record
Edwin E. Gordon

| Date not provided | GIA Publications, Inc. |

Population: Grades 3 through music graduate school

Purpose: Helps determine objectively whether individual students have the necessary harmonic and rhythmic readiness to learn to improvise

Description: The tests indicate what types of general instruction in improvisation are most beneficial for individual students and assist teachers in adapting instruction to each student's individual needs.

Format: Examiner required; individual administration; untimed: 20 minutes

Scoring: Hand key; machine scoring available

Cost: Complete Kit (enough to test 100 students) $95.00

Instrument Timbre Preference Test
Edwin E. Gordon

| 1984 | GIA Publications, Inc. |

Population: Ages 9 years and older

Purpose: Assesses the timbre preference of students; used to help students select appropriate brass or woodwind instruments

Description: Multiple-item paper–pencil test identifying the timbre preferences of students. Students listen to different melodic synthesized sounds on an audiocassette recording and indicate their preferences on an answer sheet. Results help students choose instruments that match their timbre preferences, which improves the performance of beginning band students and reduces dropout rates.

Format: Examiner required; group administration; untimed: 30 minutes

Scoring: Hand key

Cost: Complete Kit (audiocassette, 100 test sheets, scoring masks, manual) $44.00

Intermediate Measures of Music Audiation
Edwin E. Gordon

| 1986 | GIA Publications, Inc. |

Population: Grades 1 through 6

Purpose: Measures the music aptitude of children

Description: Multiple-item paper–pencil test measuring and discriminating among the music aptitudes of children who obtained exceptionally high scores on the Primary Measures of Music Audiation or who are slightly older than the students targeted for the primary test. The test requires no language or music skills. Children lis-

ten to tonal and rhythm tape recordings, decide whether pairs of patterns are the same or different, and circle an appropriate picture on the answer sheet. The manual contains information on converting raw scores to percentile ranks, interpreting results, and formal and informal music instruction suggestions.

Format: Examiner required; suitable for group use; untimed: 24 minutes

Scoring: Hand key

Cost: Complete Kit $85.00

Iowa Tests of Music Literacy (ITML)
Edwin E. Gordon

| 1991 | GIA Publications, Inc. |

Population: Grades 4 through 12

Purpose: Assesses strengths and weaknesses in music achievement

Description: Six-level multiple-choice paper–pencil test with two categories: Tonal Concepts (45 minutes) and Rhythm Concepts (45 minutes). Listening, reading, and writing reports are available. A rhythm sheet, tonal sheet, audiocassette, and scoring mask are used.

Format: Examiner required; suitable for group use; timed: 90 minutes

Scoring: Hand key

Cost: Entire Kit $350.00

Keynotes–Music Evaluation Software Kit
Jenny Bryce, Margaret Wu

| 2001 | Australian Council for Educational Research Limited |

Population: Upper primary, junior secondary

Purpose: Provide information about a student's existing strengths and weaknesses in pitch, rhythm, and music notation

Description: A computer interactive measure in two parts. Part I is multiple choice with three domains: Pitch and Intervals Discrimination, Recognition of Rhythmic and Melodic Patterns, and Music Reading (traditional Western notation). Part II provides video clips of students demonstrating their musical instruments and discussing why they decided to learn particular instruments. The clips cover instruments commonly available in school instrumental programs.

Format: Examiner required; computer administered; individual administration; untimed: varies

Scoring: Computer scored

Cost: Contact publisher

Modern Photography Comprehension
Martin M. Bruce

1969	Martin M. Bruce, PhD

Population: Adolescents, adults

Purpose: Assesses knowledge of photography; used for vocational guidance and as a measure of classroom progress

Description: Paper–pencil 40-item multiple-choice test measuring photographic understanding. Individuals are rated on a scale of superior, high average, average, and low average. Materials include a manual and grading keys. Suitable for individuals with physical, hearing, or visual impairments.

Format: Self-administered; untimed: 20 to 25 minutes

Scoring: Hand key

Cost: Specimen Test $9.50

Music Aptitude Profile (MAP)
Edwin E. Gordon

1995	GIA Publications, Inc.

Population: Grades 5 through 12

Purpose: Measures a student's aptitude for music

Description: MAP is a complete test with seven components: tonal imagery (melody and harmony), rhythm imagery (tempo and meter), and musical sensitivity (phrasing, balance, and style). Features remastered recordings and an updated manual.

Format: Examiner required; individual administration; untimed: 3 hours 30 minutes

Scoring: Hand key

Cost: Complete Kit $99.00

Primary Art Interest-A-Lyzer
Joseph S. Renzulli

1997	Creative Learning Press, Inc.

Population: Grades K through 3

Purpose: Examines present and potential interests; used as a basis for group discussions and in-depth counseling

Description: Multiple-item paper–pencil instrument consisting of a series of open-ended questions structured to highlight general patterns of interest. Items cover visual art interest areas.

Format: Examiner required; suitable for group use; untimed

Scoring: Examiner evaluated

Cost: 30 Questionnaires $29.95

Primary Measures of Music Audiation
Edwin E. Gordon

1986	GIA Publications, Inc.

Population: Grades K through 3

Purpose: Measures the music aptitude of students

Description: Multiple-item paper–pencil test diagnosing the musical potential of students with average to low musical aptitudes. The test requires no language or musical skills. Children listen to tonal and rhythm recordings, decide whether patterns sound the same or different, and circle an appropriate picture on the answer sheet. The manual contains information on converting raw scores to percentile ranks, interpreting results, and formal and informal music instruction.

Format: Examiner required; suitable for group use; untimed: 24 minutes

Scoring: Hand key

Cost: Complete Kit $85.00

Foreign Language

AATG First Level Test

Yearly	American Association of Teachers of German

Population: High school and college students

Purpose: Measures knowledge of basic German; used with secondary and college-level students

Description: Paper–pencil 70-item test assessing understanding of the German language by secondary school students completing one year of study and by college or university students completing one semester of study. Knowledge of German is not necessary for the examiner.

Format: Examiner required; individual or group administration

Scoring: Hand key

Cost: $3.00

AATG National German Examination for High School Students

Yearly — American Association of Teachers of German

Population: Grades 9 to 12

Purpose: Measures German language achievement of students in their second, third, and fourth years of study; assesses the progress of individual students and entire classes

Description: Multiple-item paper–pencil test assessing German language competency. Test sections include listening comprehension, grammar, situational questions, and comprehension of connected passages. Questions are of graded difficulty. Tests are administered annually in school under the supervision of the school's testing personnel. The test company returns scores to test administrators. Scores for the total test and for each section of the test are provided. Practice tests are available. Knowledge of German is not necessary for the examiner.

Format: Examiner required; individual or group administration

Scoring: All tests scored by Software Design, Inc.

Cost: $4.00 per student

Advanced Russian Listening Comprehension/Reading Proficiency Test (ARPT)

Date not provided — Educational Testing Service

Population: Adults, college students

Purpose: Measures the listening comprehension and reading proficiency of native English-speaking students' Russian; appropriate for use with students who have completed the equivalent of 3 to 5 years or more of college-level study

Description: Multiple-item orally administered and paper–pencil test in two major sections: Listening Comprehension and Reading Proficiency. The Listening Comprehension section is administered via an audiocassette recording that presents the student with a variety of material spoken in Russian. Questions about this material are printed in a test booklet, and students respond on machine-scorable answer sheets. In the Reading Proficiency section, the students read passages printed in Russian and select responses that complete or answer the questions.

Format: Examiner required; suitable for group use; timed: 2 hours

Scoring: Computer scored

Cost: Test Booklet $15.00 each

Arabic Proficiency Test (APT)

Raji M. Rammuny

1992 — Center for Applied Linguistics

Population: Adolescents, adults; college and above

Purpose: Measures reading and listening proficiency for placement, selection, and evaluation

Description: Paper–pencil 100-question multiple-choice test comprised of Listening and Reading Comprehension. Forms A and B are available. Materials used include an audiocassette player, test booklet, and test answer sheet. Suitable for individuals with physical impairments.

Format: Examiner required; individual or group administration; timed: 110 minutes

Scoring: Hand key; machine scored; test scoring service available from publisher

Cost: $14.00 to $25.00 per examinee depending on the number of examinees

Arabic Speaking Test (AST)

Raji M. Rammuny

1992 — Center for Applied Linguistics

Population: Adolescents, adults; college and above

Purpose: Measures oral proficiency in Arabic

Description: Oral-response 15-item test measuring oral language proficiency in Arabic. Ratings are based on the speaking proficiency scale of the American Council on the Teaching of Foreign Languages (ACTFL). Available in Forms A and B. Playback and tape-recording equipment used. Test is available on audiocassette. May be used with individuals with physical impairments.

Format: Examiner required; timed: 55 minutes

Scoring: Examiner evaluated; test scoring service available

Cost: $115.00 per examinee for operational costs and certified rating service

Chinese Proficiency Test (CPT)

1983 — Center for Applied Linguistics

Population: Adolescents, adults; high school and above

Purpose: Measures listening and reading proficiency used for placement, evaluation, and selection

Description: Paper–pencil 150-question multiple-choice test comprised of Listening Comprehension, Reading Comprehension, and Structure. Materials used include an audiocassette player, test booklet, and test answer sheet. Suitable for those with physical impairments.

Format: Examiner required; individual or group administration; timed: 120 minutes

Scoring: Machine scored

Cost: $14.00 to $25.00 per examinee depending on the number of examinees

Chinese Speaking Test (CST)

1994	Center for Applied Linguistics

Population: Adolescents, adults; college and above

Purpose: Assesses the ability to speak Chinese in contemporary, real-life language-use contexts

Description: Oral-response test measuring oral language proficiency in Chinese. Test is administered via a question tape and test booklet. The examinees are asked six types of questions: Personal Conversation, Giving Directions, Detailed Descriptions, Picture Sequences, Topical Discourse, and Situations. The examinee's oral responses to the six item types are recorded and then sent to the publisher for scoring. Ratings are based on the speaking proficiency scale of the American Council on the Teaching of Foreign Language (ACTFL). Three forms (A, B, and C) are available. May be used with individuals with physical impairments.

Format: Examiner required; suitable for group use; timed: 45 minutes

Scoring: Publisher scored

Cost: $115.00 per examinee for operational costs and certified rating service

French Computerized Adaptive Placement Exam (F-CAPE)

Jerry W. Larson, Kim L. Smith, Don C. Jensen

1996	Brigham Young University Foreign Language Testing

Population: Adults

Purpose: Measures the student's achievement level in French; used for placement into first-, second-, and third-semester university or college classes

Description: Total number of items varies according to the ability of the examinee. Categories include grammar, vocabulary, and reading. Full performance or simplified compiled reports are available. A PC computer test disk is used. Now available on the Web.

Format: Individually/self-administered; untimed

Scoring: Computer scored

Cost: $995.00 for site license

French Speaking Test (FST)

1995	Center for Applied Linguistics

Population: Adolescents, adults; high school and above

Purpose: Measures oral proficiency in French

Description: Oral-response 16-item test measuring oral language proficiency in French. Via playback and tape-recording equipment, the oral response is recorded. Forms A, B, and C are available. Ratings are based on the speaking proficiency scale of the American Council on the Teaching of Foreign Languages (ACTFL). Available on audiocassette. Suitable for individuals with physical impairments.

Format: Examiner required; individual or group administration; timed: 45 minutes

Scoring: Examiner evaluated; test scoring service available from publisher

Cost: $115.00 per examinee for operational costs and certified rating service

German Computerized Adaptive Placement Exam (G-CAPE)

Jerry W. Larson, Kim L. Smith, Randall L. Jones

1996	Brigham Young University Foreign Language Testing

Population: Adults

Purpose: Measures the achievement level in German; used for placement into first-, second-, and third-semester university or college classes

Description: Total number of items varies according to the ability of the examinee. Categories include grammar, vocabulary, and reading. Full performance or simplified compiled reports are available. A PC computer test disk is used. Now available on the Web.

Format: Self-administered; untimed

Scoring: Computer scored

Cost: $995.00 for site license

German Speaking Test (GST)

1995	Center for Applied Linguistics

Population: Adolescents, adults; high school and above

Purpose: Measures oral proficiency in German

Description: Oral-response 16-item test measuring oral language proficiency in German. Via playback and tape-recording equipment, the examinee's oral response is recorded. The test is available on audiocassette. Forms A, B, and C are available. Suitable for individuals with physical impairments.

Format: Examiner required; individual or group administration; timed: 45 minutes

Scoring: Examiner evaluated; test scoring service available

Cost: $115.00 per examinee for operational costs and certified rating service

Hausa Speaking Test (HAST)
1989	Center for Applied Linguistics

Population: Adolescents, adults; college and above

Purpose: Assesses the ability to speak Hausa in contemporary, real-life language-use contexts

Description: Oral-response 16-item test measuring oral language proficiency in Hausa. Via a question tape and test booklet, the examinee's oral responses to five item types are recorded and then sent to the publisher for scoring. Ratings are based on the speaking proficiency scale of the American Council on the Teaching of Foreign Languages (ACTFL). Forms A and B, and male and female forms are available. May be used with individuals with physical impairments.

Format: Examiner required; suitable for group use; timed: 45 minutes

Scoring: Publisher scored

Cost: $115.00 per examinee for operational costs and certified rating service

Hebrew Speaking Test (HEST)
1989	Center for Applied Linguistics

Population: Adolescents, adults; college and above

Purpose: Assesses the ability to speak Hebrew in contemporary, real-life language-use contexts

Description: Oral-response 16-item test measuring oral language proficiency in Hebrew. Via a question tape and test booklet, the examinees are asked six types of questions: Personal Conversation, Giving Directions, Detailed Descriptions, Picture Sequences, Topical Discourse, and Situations. The examinee's oral responses to the six item types are recorded and then sent to the publisher for scoring. Ratings are based on the speaking proficiency scale of the American Council on the Teaching of Foreign Language

(ACTFL). Israeli and U.S. versions are available for males and females, Forms A and B. May be used with individuals with physical impairments.

Format: Examiner required; suitable for group use; timed: 45 minutes

Scoring: Publisher scored

Cost: $115.00 per examinee for operational costs and certified rating service

Indonesian Speaking Test (IST)
1989	Center for Applied Linguistics

Population: Adolescents, adults; college and above

Purpose: Assesses the ability to speak Indonesian in contemporary, real-life language-use contexts

Description: Oral-response 27-item test measuring oral language proficiency in Indonesian. Via a question tape and test booklet, the examinees are asked five types of questions: Personal Conversation, Giving Directions, Picture Sequences, Topical Discourse, and Situations. The examinee's oral responses to the five item types are recorded and then sent to the publisher for scoring. Ratings are based on the proficiency scale of the American Council on the Teaching of Foreign Language (ACTFL). Two forms (A and B) are available. May be used with individuals with physical impairments.

Format: Examiner required; suitable for group use; timed: 45 minutes

Scoring: Publisher scored

Cost: $60.00

Japanese Speaking Test (JST)
1992	Center for Applied Linguistics

Population: Adolescents, adults; college and above

Purpose: Measures oral proficiency in Japanese for evaluation, placement, and selection

Description: Oral-response 15-item test using playback and tape-recording equipment to record examinee's oral response. Ratings are based on the speaking proficiency scale of the American Council on the Teaching of Foreign Languages (ACTFL). Suitable for individuals with physical impairments.

Format: Examiner required; individual or group administration; timed: 45 minutes

Scoring: Examiner evaluated; test scoring service available

Cost: $115.00 per examinee for operational costs and certified rating service

LOTE Tests

1998	Australian Council for Educational Research Limited

Population: Primary to year 10

Purpose: A competency analysis for listening and reading comprehension after a minimum of 80 hours of instruction

Description: These tests are based on Australian Language Level Guidelines. Languages available are Italian, German, French, Modern Greek, and Japanese. Responses are given using paper–pencil and orally. An audiocassette is used.

Format: Examiner required; individual or group administration; untimed: 60 minutes

Scoring: Examiner evaluated

Cost: Contact publisher

National Spanish Examinations

Yearly	National Spanish Exam

Population: Grades 6 to 12

Purpose: Motivational competition to assess reading and listening comprehension skills in Spanish

Description: Proficiency-based Spanish exams covering six levels developed each year by teachers who are members of the American Association of Teachers of Spanish and Portuguese. Multiple-choice test has both aural and written sections that measure the knowledge of Spanish after each year of study at the secondary school level. There are 30 listening comprehension questions, 30 reading comprehension questions, and an additional 10 reading comprehension questions for bilingual-native students.

Format: Examiner required; suitable for group use; timed: 1 hour

Scoring: Examiner evaluated; computer scored

Cost: Contact publisher

Polish Proficiency Test (PPT)

1992	Center for Applied Linguistics

Population: Adolescents, adults; college and above

Purpose: Measures listening and reading proficiency; used for placement, evaluation, and selection

Description: Paper–pencil 135-question multiple-

choice test composed of listening comprehension, reading comprehension, structure, and total. Test available on audiocassette. Suitable for individuals with physical impairments.

Format: Examiner required; individual or group administration; timed: 150 minutes

Scoring: Machine scored; test scoring service available from publisher

Cost: $14.00 to $25.00 per examinee depending on the number of examinees

Portuguese Speaking Test (PST)

1988	Center for Applied Linguistics

Population: Adolescents, adults; college and above

Purpose: Assesses the ability to speak Portuguese in contemporary, real-life language-use contexts

Description: Oral-response 16-item test measuring oral language proficiency in Portuguese. Via a question tape and test booklet, the examinees are asked six types of questions: Personal Conversation, Giving Directions, Detailed Descriptions, Picture Sequences, Topical Discourse, and Situations. Their oral responses are recorded and then sent to the publisher for scoring. Ratings are based on the speaking proficiency scale of the American Council on the Teaching of Foreign Languages (ACTFL). Forms A, B, and C are available. Available also in Brazilian and Lusitanian.

Format: Examiner required; suitable for group use; timed: 45 minutes

Scoring: Scored by publisher

Cost: $115.00 per examinee for operational costs and certified rating service

Preliminary Chinese Proficiency Test (Pre-CPT)

1991	Center for Applied Linguistics

Population: Adolescents, adults; high school and above

Purpose: Measures reading and listening proficiency for placement, evaluation, and selection

Description: Paper–pencil 125-question multiple-choice test composed of Listening Comprehension, Reading Comprehension, and Structure. Materials used include audiocassette player, test booklet, and test answer sheet. Suitable for individuals with physical impairments.

Format: Examiner required; individual or group administration; timed: 90 minutes

Scoring: Machine scored; test scoring service available

Cost: $14.00 to $25.00 per examinee depending on the number of examinees

Preliminary Japanese Speaking Test (Pre-JST)

1991	Center for Applied Linguistics

Population: Adolescents, adults; high school and above

Purpose: Measures oral proficiency in Japanese for placement, evaluation, and selection

Description: Oral-response 8-item test using playback and tape-recording equipment to record oral response. Forms A and B available. Ratings are based on the speaking proficiency scale of the American Council on the Teaching of Foreign Languages (ACTFL). Suitable for individuals with physical impairments.

Format: Examiner required; individual or group administration; timed: 25 minutes

Scoring: Examiner evaluated; test scoring service available

Cost: $90.00 per examinee for operational costs and certified rating service

Russian Computerized Adaptive Placement Exam (R-CAPE)

Jerry W. Larson, Kim L. Smith, Marshall R. Murray

1996	Brigham Young University Foreign Language Testing

Population: Adults

Purpose: Measures achievement level in Russian; used for placement into first-, second-, and third-semester university or college classes

Description: Total number of items varies according to the ability of the examinee. Categories include grammar, vocabulary, and reading. Full performance or simplified compiled reports are available. A PC computer test disk is used.

Format: Self-administered; untimed

Scoring: Computer scored

Cost: $995.00 for site license

Spanish Assessment of Basic Education, Second Edition (SABE®/2)

1991	CTB/McGraw-Hill

Population: Grades 1 to 8

Purpose: Assesses the basic reading and mathematics skills of Spanish-speaking students with limited English proficiency

Description: Multiple-item paper–pencil multiple-choice test covering word attack, vocabulary, reading comprehension, mathematics computation, mathematics concepts and applications, spelling, language mechanics, language expression, and study skills. The examiner must speak fluent Spanish.

Format: Examiner required; suitable for group use; timed: 180 to 255 minutes

Scoring: Hand key; machine scored; test scoring service available

Cost: Package of 35 Tests $87.00

Spanish Computerized Adaptive Placement Exam (S-CAPE)

Jerry W. Larson, Kim L. Smith

1995	Brigham Young University Foreign Language Testing

Population: Adults

Purpose: Measures achievement level in Spanish; used for placement into first-, second-, and third-semester university or college classes

Description: Total number of items varies according to the ability of the examinee. Categories include grammar, vocabulary, and reading. Full performance or simplified compiled reports are available. A PC computer test disk is used. Now available on the Web.

Format: Self-administered; untimed

Scoring: Computer scored

Cost: $995.00 for site license

Spanish Proficiency Test (SPT)

1994	Educational Testing Service

Population: Adolescents, adults

Purpose: Assesses Spanish language proficiency of nonnative speakers of Spanish; used for assessment, placement, evaluation of programs, and selection of students for immersion programs

Description: Multiple-choice paper–pencil oral-response, essay, and verbal test composed of four categories: Listening (25 multiple-choice questions), Reading (40 multiple-choice questions), Writing (3 essay or constructed response prompts), and Speaking (simulated dialog with 15 inquiries). Raw scores and American Council on the Teaching of Foreign Languages (ACTFL) proficiency ratings for Listening and Reading (scored by the Educational Testing Service); ACTFL proficiency ratings for Writing and Speaking (scored at institutions).

Format: Examiner required; suitable for group use; timed: 90 minutes

Scoring: Scoring service available

Cost: 4 Skills $25.00; Listening and Reading $17.00; Writing and Speaking $15.00

Spanish Speaking Test (SST)
1995   Center for Applied Linguistics

Population: Adolescents, adults; high school and above

Purpose: Measures oral proficiency in Spanish for placement, evaluation, and selection

Description: Oral-response 16-item test. Oral response of examinee is recorded using playback and tape-recording equipment. Forms A, B, and C are available. Ratings are based on the speaking proficiency scale of the American Council on the Teaching of Foreign Languages (ACTFL).

Format: Examiner required; individual or group administration; timed: 45 minutes

Scoring: Examiner evaluated; test scoring service available

Cost: $115.00 per examinee for operational costs and certified rating service

Guidance

General

APTICOM
1985   Vocational Research Institute

Population: High school to adult

Purpose: Assesses aptitudes, interests, and work-related math and language skills; used for vocational guidance and counseling

Description: Multiple-item aptitude battery measuring general learning ability, verbal aptitude, numerical aptitude, spatial aptitude, form perception, clerical perception, motor coordination, finger dexterity, manual dexterity, and eye-hand-foot coordination. The Interest Inventory assesses preference for U.S. Department of Labor interest areas. The Educational Skills Development Battery assesses math and language achievement levels defined by the U.S. Department of Labor as General Educational Development. Tests are presented via panels mounted on APTICOM, a portable computerized desktop console. APTICOM times and scores tests and generates score and recommendation reports when interfaced with a printer. The aptitude battery has separate norm bases for three levels: adult/Grades 11 to 12, Grade 10, and Grade 9. The Interest Inventory has vocational (i.e., adult) and prevocational (roughly 17 years and younger) norm bases. Also available in Spanish.

Format: Examiner required; suitable for use with groups of four using optional master con-

trol; timed: Aptitude 29 minutes; Educational Skills Development Battery 25 minutes; untimed: Interest Inventory 10 minutes

Scoring: Computer scored

Cost: Contact publisher

Armed Services Vocational Battery (ASVAB)
Department of Defense
Yearly   ASVAB Career Exploration

Population: Grades 10 and above

Purpose: Evaluates high school students' vocational interests and aptitudes; used for counseling and by the military services to identify eligible graduates for possible recruitment

Description: Paper-pencil 334-item test of aptitudes in various vocational and technical fields. Factors measured include electronics, mechanical comprehension, general science, automotive and shop information, numerical operations, coding speed, word knowledge, arithmetic, reasoning, paragraph comprehension, and mathematics knowledge. Indicates ability in the following areas: verbal; math; academic; mechanical and crafts; business and clerical; electronics and electrical; and health, social, and technologies. A military service recruiter assists each school in administering the test, and the Defense Manpower Data Center provides the examiner. Individual test results are delivered to school counselors, and copies of the scores are given to the recruiting services.

Format: Examiner required; suitable for group use; timed: 3 hours

Scoring: Computer scored

Cost: No charge to schools for administration, materials, and scoring

Assessment of Career Decision Making (ACDM)
Vincent A. Harren, Jacqueline N. Buck

1985	Western Psychological Services

Population: High school and college students

Purpose: Used to help students select careers

Description: Comprises 96 true-false items covering six scales: decision-making styles (rational, intuitive, and dependent) and decision-making tasks (school adjustment, occupation, and major). Inventory is designed to help students select a career that is compatible with their particular interests and abilities, and can identify students who need career counseling.

Format: Self-administered; untimed

Scoring: Scoring service

Cost: Kit (4 test reports, prepaid mail-in answer sheets, manual) $68.00

Barriers to Employment Success Inventory, Second Edition (BESI)
John J. Liptak

2002	JIST Publishing

Population: Adolescents, adults

Purpose: Identifies key barriers that keep people from conducting successful job searches; used for work with the unemployed

Description: Fifty-statement multiple-choice, short-answer, and true-false test with the following categories: Personal/Financial, Emotional/Physical, Career Decision-Making/Planning, Job Seeking Knowledge, and Education and Training. Reports a person's barrier to a successful job search. An eighth-grade reading level is required.

Format: Self-administered; untimed: 20 minutes

Scoring: Self-scored

Cost: 25 Forms and User's Guide $39.95

Becker Work Adjustment Profile (BWAP)
Ralph L. Becker

1989	Elbern Publications

Population: Ages 15 years to adult

Purpose: Assesses vocational adjustment and competency

Description: Likert-type questionnaire completed by someone familiar with the individual's work behavior. Two editions of the questionnaire are available: Short Scale and Full Scale. Vocational adjustment and competency are evaluated in four domains: Work-Habits/Attitudes (10 items), Interpersonal Relations (12 items), Cognitive Skills (19 items), and Work Performance Skills (22 items). In addition to scores in each domain, a global score is obtained. The raw scores are converted to percentiles, T-scores, and stanines using an appropriate norm for individuals with mental retardation, physical disabilities, emotional disturbance, or learning disability. Two profiles are available: a Peer Profile to interpret an individual's work adjustment compared with other people who have the same disability, and an Employability Status Profile to provide a graphic picture of the person's vocational competency for placement in one of five program tracks (Day Care, Work Activity, Sheltered Workshop, Transitional, and Community-Competitive). A complete report-analysis is given on different individuals with disabilities.

Format: Examiner required; individual administration; untimed: 10 to 20 minutes

Scoring: Examiner required

Cost: Starter Set (2 short scales, 2 full scales, 2 profiles, manual) $35.00

BRIGANCE® Diagnostic Employability Skills Inventory
Albert H. Brigance

1995	Curriculum Associates®, Inc.

Population: High school students and adults

Purpose: Assesses basic skills and employability skills in job-seeking and employment contexts

Description: The inventory provides specific feedback on curriculum needs, allowing instructors to plan, monitor, and assess learning growth. A total of 124 in-depth skill sequences are covered in eight life-skill sections: Reading Grade Placement, Career Awareness and Self-Understanding, Job-Seeking Skills and Knowledge, Rating Scales, Reading Skills, Speaking and Listening, Preemployment Writing, and Math Skills and Concepts. The inventory correlates with the Comprehensive Adult Student Assessment System (CASAS) and SCANS Foundation Skills and meets the requirements of the Perkins Act.

Format: Examiner required; suitable for group use; untimed: 12 minutes
Scoring: Examiner evaluated
Cost: Inventory $89.95; 10 Record Books $24.95

California Critical Thinking Disposition Inventory (CCTDI)

Peter A. Facione, Noreen C. Facione

| 1992 | California Academic Press |

Population: Grades 7 to 12
Purpose: Measures disposition toward critical thinking; used for evaluation of groups and programs, personnel development, and management training
Description: Paper–pencil 75-item test. Five-page test booklet includes specialized answer sheet. Categories include truth-seeking, inquisitiveness, analyticity, systematicity, open-mindedness, cognitive maturity, and reasoning confidence. Available also in Spanish, French, Hebrew, Chinese, Thai, Korean, Finnish, and Japanese. May also be used with adults.
Format: Self-administered; untimed: 20 minutes
Scoring: Hand key; machine scored; scoring service available
Cost: Specimen Kit $75.00

CAM 2001 Computerized One-Stop

| 1989 | PESCO International |

Population: Ages 14 years and older
Purpose: Assesses interests, aptitudes, attitudes, temperament, and learning styles
Description: A comprehensive, flexible career assessment and placement solution. The system supports individual or multiuser group testing in local or wide area networks. Job applicants may be simultaneously assessed from different locations. Testing addresses many skills, including general, verbal, and numerical abilities, clerical aptitude, and language skills. The system incorporates the latest technologies to make it easy to use, highly flexible, responsive, and accurate. It is a menu-driven system that supports multiple-choice testing. Tests can be taken immediately, with all responses automatically scored, tabulated, and matched to the requirements established by the Department of Labor, *Dictionary of Occupational Titles*, and O*Net. A 3-day on-site training program is offered.
Format: Computer administered; untimed

Scoring: Computer scored
Cost: Contact publisher

Campbell™ Interest and Skill Survey (CISS®)

David Campbell

| 1992 | NCS Pearson |

Population: Ages 15 years and older
Purpose: Assesses self-reported interests and skills for individuals who are college bound or college educated
Description: Multiple-choice 320-item computer-administered or paper–pencil test divided into 200 interest categories and 120 skill categories. A sixth-grade reading level is required. Examiner must have a bachelor's degree and have completed a test measurement course, or attended a CISS workshop.
Format: Self-administered; on-line administration available; untimed: 25 minutes
Scoring: Computer scored; test scoring service available
Cost: Preview Package with Profile Reports $45.95

Career Assessment Inventory™– Enhanced Version (CAI-E)

Charles B. Johansson

| 1986 | NCS Pearson |

Population: Grades 9 and above
Purpose: Assesses the career interests of students and individuals reentering the job market or considering a career change; used for making decisions about career interests, screening job applicants, and providing career and vocational assistance
Description: Paper–pencil 370-item test in which items are answered on a 5-point Likert-type scale ranging from *like very much* to *dislike very much*. Items are divided into three major categories: activities, school subjects, and occupations. The test, which focuses on careers requiring up to and including 4 years of college, covers 111 occupations. Six General Occupational Theme scores (Holland's RIASEC model: Realistic, Investigative, Artistic, Social, Enterprising, and Conventional) and 25 Basic Interest scale scores that divide the six general scores into specific areas are provided. A narrative report, profile report, and optional group reports are available. Items are written at an eighth-grade reading level. This

is a revision of the Career Assessment Inventory–The Vocational Version, which focuses on skilled trade occupations and careers requiring little or no postsecondary education. The inventory may be computer scored in one of three ways: via mail-in services, Arion II teleprocessing, or MICROTESTQ Assessment system.

Format: Self-administered; untimed: 40 minutes

Scoring: Scoring service

Cost: Preview Package with Interpretive Reports $42.00

Career Beliefs Inventory (CBI)
John D. Krumboltz

| 1991 | Consulting Psychologists Press, Inc. |

Population: Ages 13 years and older

Purpose: Assesses individuals' beliefs and assumptions about themselves and the world of work

Description: Paper–pencil 96-item multiple-choice test intended for career counseling for use in high school, in college, or during midlife career transitions. The profile yields 25 scales organized into five categories: My Current Career Situation, What Seems Necessary for My Happiness, Factors That Influence My Decisions, Changes I Am Willing To Make, and Effort I Am Willing To Initiate. Response choices range from *strongly agree* to *strongly disagree*. An eighth-grade reading level is required. Also available in French Canadian. Materials used include an item booklet, prepaid answer sheet or nonprepaid answer sheet, a report booklet and a scoring key. A client workbook is also available.

Format: Self-administered; untimed: 45 minutes

Scoring: Self-scored; scoring service

Cost: Profile Preview Kit (item booklet, answer sheet, guide, manual) $64.50

Career Decision Scale
*Samuel H. Osipow, Clarke G. Carney,
Jane Winer, Barbara Yanico,
Maryanne Koschir*

| 1987 | Psychological Assessment Resources, Inc. |

Population: Grades 9 to college

Purpose: Identifies barriers preventing an individual from making career decisions; used as a basis for career counseling, to monitor the effectiveness of career counseling programs, and for research on career indecisiveness

Description: Paper–pencil 10-item inventory as-

sessing a limited number of circumstances that cause problems in reaching and implementing educational and career decisions. Items 1 and 2 measure degree of certainty (Certainty scale). Items 3 to 18 measure career indecision (Indecision scale). Item 19 is open-ended. Individuals rate each item on a 4-point scale from 1 (*not like me*) to 4 (*like me*) to indicate the extent to which each item describes their personal situations. Scores are reported as percentiles. The manual includes data regarding validity and reliability and norms for various age and grade levels. This edition is a revision of the Career Decision Scale.

Format: Self-administered; untimed: 10 to 15 minutes

Scoring: Examiner evaluated

Cost: Kit $52.00

Career IQ and Interest Test (CIQIT)

| 1997 | PRO-ED, Inc. |

Population: Age 13 through adult

Purpose: Assists individuals in identifying jobs they would likely enjoy and do successfully

Description: The self-administering CD-ROM contains a vocational aptitude test and an interest test, along with a searchable database containing the entire Occupational Outlook Handbook published by the U.S. Department of Labor. The Aptitude Survey measures six broad factors: General Ability, Verbal Aptitude, Numerical Aptitude, Spatial Aptitude, Perceptual Aptitude, and Manual Dexterity. The Interest Schedule measures 12 factors: Artistic, Scientific, Nature, Protective, Mechanical, Industrial, Business Detail, Selling, Accommodating, Humanitarian, Leading–Influencing, and Physical Performing. The tests are scored automatically, test profiles are displayed, and interpretive information is provided. Works on PC computers.

Format: Self-administered on computer; untimed: Aptitude 25 minutes, Interest 15 minutes

Scoring: Computer scored

Cost: $59.00

Career Planning Survey

| 1997 | ACT, Inc. |

Population: Grades 8 to 10

Purpose: Measures and profiles students' work-relevant interests and abilities; used in guidance and vocational counseling

Description: A comprehensive guidance-oriented career (educational and vocational) assessment system designed to help students in Grades 8 through 10 identify and explore personally relevant occupations and high school courses. The formal assessment components consist of an interest inventory (90 items), an inventory of ability self-estimates (15 items), and two optional academic ability tests: Reading Skills (32 items) and Numerical Skills (24 items). In addition, the Career Planning Guide workbook provides students the opportunity to complete checklists examining their work-relevant experiences and the job characteristics they want in a work setting. Testing can be scheduled in one, two, or more sessions. The interest and ability scales were built around a two-dimensional model: people–things and data–ideas.

Format: Self-administered; timed: 45 minutes for each

Scoring: Scoring service

Cost: $3.80 per Assessment Set Option A (with Ability Measures); $3.25 per Assessment Set Option B (without Ability Measures) (answer sheet, student guidebook, prepaid scoring, 2 copies of the student report)

Career Scope–Version 5

Yearly   Vocational Research Institute

Population: Adolescents and adults (middle school and above)

Purpose: Measures career interest and aptitudes

Description: Interest section with 141 items measures 12 interest areas used by the U.S. Department of Labor. The Aptitude section has seven subtests with 203 items: Object Identification (30 items), Abstract Shape Matching (30 items), Clerical Matching (30 items), Pattern Visualization (30 items), Computation (30 items), Numerical Reasoning (23 items), and Word Meanings (30 items). Results are reported as standardized scores, a profile, a Counselor's Report, and a Summary Report.

Format: Self-administered; Interest: untimed; Aptitude: timed

Scoring: Computer scored

Cost: Contact publisher

CASAS Employability Competency System

1994   Comprehensive Adult Student Assessment System (CASAS)

Population: Adults, adolescents; native and nonnative speakers of English

Purpose: Helps programs identify the skills needed by adults and youth in today's workforce and place them into appropriate education and employment training programs and jobs; helps agencies place learners into appropriate instructional levels

Description: Multiple-choice survey achievement tests assess reading comprehension and basic math skills at four levels, and listening comprehension tests assess English as a second language (ESL) at three levels. Each test has two forms, for pre-and posttesting. Includes an appraisal for placement purposes, certification tests, preemployment and work maturity checklists, critical thinking assessment, and occupation-specific tests. Tests are competency based. Content covers a range of employment-related contexts. CASAS scaled scores identify general skill level and enable comparison of performance across CASAS tests. Scannable answer sheets are available.

Format: Examiner required; group administration

Scoring: Self- or computer scored

Cost: 25 Reusable Tests $65.00; 25 Listening Tests with Audiocassette $70.00

Computerized Assessment (COMPASS)

1994   Valpar International Corporation

Population: Ages 9 years and older

Purpose: Used in occupational exploration and career counseling to screen for work-related factors from the Department of Labor's *Dictionary of Occupational Titles*

Description: Multiple-choice computer-administered test with 12 computer-based subtests plus three short work samples, and a paper–pencil survey. The three work samples are Alignment and Driving, Machine Tending, and Writing. The 12 subtests are Placing, Color Discrimination, Reading, Size Discrimination, Shape Discrimination, Short-Term Visual Memory, Spelling, Vocabulary, Mathematics, Language Development (Editing), Problem Solving, and Eye–Hand–Foot Coordination. The paper–pencil survey is the Guide to Occupational Exploration (GOE). Subtest level scores and DOT-type factors are yielded. A computer, control panel, foot pedal, and three out-of-computer work samples are used. A fourth-grade reading level is required. Designed to quickly establish that evaluees have various degrees of work-related and academic skills.

Format: Examiner required; individual administration; timed and untimed

Scoring: Computer scored
Cost: Contact publisher

Developmental History Checklist
Edward H. Dougherty, John A. Schinka

1989	Psychological Assessment Resources, Inc.

Population: Ages 5 to 12 years
Purpose: Assesses development of children
Description: Designed to be completed by a parent, guardian, or clinician. The checklist has 136 items that cover family history, developmental history, educational history, family background, medical history, and current behavior. A computer version using PCs is available.
Format: Rating scale; untimed
Scoring: Examiner evaluated; scoring software available
Cost: 25 Checklists $42.00; Computer Version $305.00

Differential Aptitude Tests™, Fifth Edition (DAT™)
G. K. Bennett, H. G. Seashore, A. G. Wesman

1990	Harcourt® Brace Educational Measurement

Population: Grades 7 through 12 and adults
Purpose: Assesses aptitudes and interests; used for educational and vocational guidance in junior and senior high schools
Description: Multiple-item paper–pencil test of eight abilities: verbal reasoning, numerical ability, abstract reasoning, clerical speed and accuracy, mechanical reasoning, space relations, spelling, and language usage. A ninth score is obtained by summing the verbal reasoning and numerical ability scores. The Career Planning Questionnaire is optional. Two levels: Level 1 for Grades 8 and 9, and Level 2 for Grades 10 through 12.
Format: Examiner required; suitable for group use; timed: complete battery 2.5 hours; partial battery 1.5 hours
Scoring: Hand key; may be machine scored; scoring service available
Cost: Examination Kit with Career Interest Inventory $32.50

Educational Development Series
O. F. Anderhalter, Jan Perney,
Sandra Carlson, Peter Fisher,
Sharon Weiner, Stephen Bloom,
Charles Hamburg, Carol F. Larson

1999	Scholastic Testing Service, Inc.

Population: Grades K through 12
Purpose: Assesses academic achievement, aptitude, and career interests
Description: The multiple-choice battery has eight subsets: Reading, Language Arts, Mathematics, Science, Social Studies, Reference Skills, Nonverbal Cognitive Skills, and Verbal Cognitive Skills. Future Plans and School Interests sections are also included in the battery. These 10 areas can be administered in one of four ways: Complete Battery (all subsets), Core Achievement Battery (R, LA, M, S, SS, RS), Cognitive and Basic Skills Battery (R, LA, M, S, SS, NC, VC), and Basic Skills Battery (FP, SI, R, LA, M). Various reports are provided.
Format: Examiner required; suitable for group use; timed: $2\frac{1}{2}$ to $5\frac{1}{2}$ hours
Scoring: Machine scored; hand key; computer scored; test scoring service available
Cost: Specimen Set (specify level and form) $18.40

Explore the World of Work (E-WOW)
Lori Constantino, Bob Kauk

1991	CFKR Career Materials

Population: Children
Purpose: Develops career awareness
Description: Students rate their interests, match job activities with job groups, and select a specific job to research.
Format: Examiner required; individual or group administration; untimed
Scoring: Examiner evaluated; scoring software available
Cost: $1.28 each (1 to 9 copies)

Guilford–Zimmerman Aptitude Survey (GZAS)
J. P. Guilford, Wayne S. Zimmerman

Date not provided	Consulting Psychologists Press, Inc.

Population: Adults
Purpose: Measures areas of aptitude
Description: Instrument tests verbal comprehension, general reasoning, numerical operation, perceptual speed, spatial orientation, and spatial visualization. The measures can be used independently or in combination.
Format: Self-administration; untimed
Scoring: Hand key

Cost: Assessment Kit (manual, scoring keys, materials for 25 examinees) $379.00

Harrington–O'Shea Career Decision-Making System–Revised (CDM-R)
Thomas F. Harrington, Arthur J. O'Shea

1993   American Guidance Service

Population: Grade 7 through adult

Purpose: Involves the client with self-understanding of values and abilities needed for successful career choices and development

Description: The CDM-R is an interest inventory with a sound theoretical basis that provides valid and reliable assessment of career interests. It also surveys values, training plans, and abilities. It incorporates career information and presents a model for career decision making. The CDM-R is based on the Holland theory of vocational development—that is, that most people can be categorized by a single type or a combination of personality types. The CDM-R uses these six types: Crafts, Scientific, The Arts, Social, Business, and Office Operations. These six areas provide raw scores that are used to define a client's preferred work environment. Spanish and English versions are available.

Format: Individual or group administration: Level 1: 20 minutes; Level 2: 30 to 40 minutes

Scoring: Level 1 is hand scored; Level 2 is hand or machine scored

Cost: Classroom Set (25 workbooks, teacher's guide, video) $349.95

Job Readiness Skills Pre/Post Assessment
Shelley M. Mauer

2000   Education Associates, Inc.

Population: Ages 14 years and older

Purpose: Measures job readiness and employability skills for workforce, school-to-work, and career counseling

Description: Ten multiple-choice questions in each of the following sections: career goals, finding job opportunities, job applications, interviewing, positive attitudes, good appearance, written communication, communication, and resumes. Based on the score, a self-prescribed plan of study is provided.

Format: Examiner required; individual administration; untimed

Scoring: Hand key

Cost: 25 Pretests or Posttests $52.00

Job Search Attitude Inventory, Second Edition (JSAI)
John J. Liptak

2002   JIST Publishing

Population: High school students through adults

Purpose: Measure self-motivation for job searching

Description: Test takers agree or disagree with each of 32 statements on a 4-point scale. They then self-score the instrument, turn the page, and place their scores on a graphic profile that shows four measures: Luck vs. Planning, Involved vs. Uninvolved, Self-Directed vs. Other-Directed, Active vs. Passive. Higher scores indicate the belief that persons can find their own jobs. Can be used as a pre- and posttest.

Format: Self-administered; untimed: 20 minutes

Scoring: Self-scored

Cost: Administrator's Guide and 25 Forms $39.95

JOB-O A (Advanced)
Arthur Cutler, Francis Ferry, Bob Kauk, Robert Robinett

1991   CFKR Career Materials

Population: High school and college students

Purpose: Assesses work interests

Description: This career planner provides students with the opportunity to make a self-assessment of their interests and work skills. After they have completed the assessment, the students match their responses with occupational families, as well as with specific occupations contained within each family. In addition, students develop job research skills and make a career decision based on their skill and interest assessments.

Format: Examiner required; individual or group administration; untimed

Scoring: Examiner evaluated; scoring software available

Cost: $4.20 each (1 to 9 copies)

Jobs Observation and Behavior Scales (JOBS)
Howard Rosenberg, Michael P. Brady

2000   Stoelting Company

Population: Ages 15 years to adult

Purpose: Measures job performance for entry-level workers and individuals transitioning from high school to work

Description: This employee performance evaluation is for use by educators, job coaches, rehabilitation professionals, and employers involved in the evaluation, training, and placement of secondary students or adults, with and without disabilities, into the competitive workforce. The 30 items that make up the three subscales are designed to represent critical patterns of performance in work-required daily living skills, work-required behavior, and work-required job duties.

Format: Examiner required; individual administration; untimed: 5 to 8 minutes

Scoring: Examiner evaluated

Cost: Complete Kit (manual, 25 record forms) $75.00

Key Educational Vocational Assessment System (KEVAS)
2000   Key Education, Inc.

Population: Adolescents, adults

Purpose: Measures vocational interests and aptitudes and matches individual interests and functional capabilities with locally available jobs and training programs; used with normal and special needs populations

Description: Computer-administered (Windows 98) norm- and criterion-referenced test measuring Auditory Acuity, Auditory Localization, Auditory Memory, Visual Acuity, Color Vision, Visual Memory, Persistence, Eye–Hand Coordination, Reaction Times, Spatial Reasoning, Problem Solving, Language Series, Reading Level Locator, Arithmetic Series, Vocational Interest, and Independent Living Skills. The KEVAS software also enables scoring and on-site report production. Group data are aggregated, and statistical reports and research services are available.

Format: Some of the tests require an examiner; some parts are self-administered; untimed: 1 to 2 hours

Scoring: Computer scored automatically; immediate results

Cost: Contact publisher

Leisure to Occupations Connection Search (LOCS)
Carl McDaniels, Sue Mullins
1999   JIST Publishing

Population: Grade 7 through adult

Purpose: Designed to measure vocational interest through leisure activities

Description: The LOCS takes a nontraditional approach by presenting 100 leisure activities, such as gardening or learning a new language, and asking test takers to rate their level of activity and skill in each. It then lists related occupations for each leisure activity and helps test takers identify jobs they want to know more about. A large chart presents information on 250 major jobs, including earnings, training or education required, and projected growth.

Format: Self-administered; untimed

Scoring: Self-scoring

Cost: $29.95 (administrator's guide and 25 forms)

Life Style Questionnaire (LSQ)
Jim Barrett
Date not provided   Test Agency, Ltd.

Population: Adolescents

Purpose: Provides insight regarding interests, attitudes, and behaviors of people about to begin work or already working

Description: The LSQ is a 132-item paper–pencil multiple-choice test for self-assessment of vocational interests and attitudes. Items are statements about work activities. Scores are provided on 13 scales: six deal with general motivation, five examine consistency of outlook with interest, and two estimate the degree of certainty about questionnaire responses. The test booklet contains instructions on how to respond to test items.

Format: Examiner required; suitable for group use; untimed

Scoring: Test scoring service available

Cost: Contact publisher

Major–Minor Finder
Arthur Cutler, Francis Ferry, Bob Kauk, Robert Robinett
1996   CFKR Career Materials

Population: High school and college students

Purpose: Designed to assist students in planning college courses

Description: An assessment survey that ties college planning with career planning. The program helps the student to assess aptitudes and interests, learn about jobs in each college major and their projected growth, learn about the skills and interests required for different majors, list college majors that are most compatible with their educational and career interests, and find community college programs related to 4-year programs.

Format: Examiner required; individual or group administration; untimed

Scoring: Examiner evaluated; scoring software available

Cost: $4.20 each (1 to 9 copies)

MATCH
Lisa Knapp-Lee

Date not provided	EdITS/Educational and Industrial Testing Service

Population: High school graduates, college students, and adults

Purpose: Provides a comprehensive narrative report for job market exploration

Description: The MATCH is designed for use in guiding examinees in self-evaluation and exploration of careers with the goal of finding a good match with each individual and the job market. It may be used for career outplacement or with individuals just entering the market or those returning to the workforce. Self-scoring form is designed for immediate feedback, with examinee participation in scoring and interpretation through use of self-scoring booklets.

Format: Self-administered; untimed

Scoring: Self-scored

Cost: Single Self-Scoring Form $12.25; 10 Forms $110.00

Mini-Hilson Personnel Profile (MHPP)
Robin E. Inwald

1991	Hilson Research, Inc.

Population: Ages 9 to 19 years

Purpose: Measures work-related strengths and weaknesses

Description: Total of 50 items to measure Social Ability, Achievement History, and Goal Orientation with these applications: Adolescent, Teen, High School, College, and Career Counseling.

Format: Self-administration; untimed

Scoring: Self-scored

Cost: Contact publisher

Missouri Comprehensive Student Needs Survey

1989	Assessment Resource Center

Population: Grades 4 through 12

Purpose: Identifies need to develop guidance programs

Description: Students are asked to respond to needs grouped into areas of concern. Some of the categories are Exploring and Planning Careers, Understanding and Accepting Self, Making Decisions, Finding Jobs, and Learning To Use Leisure Time. Three levels of the instrument are available: elementary (Grades 4 to 6), middle (Grades 6 to 9), and senior (Grades 9 to 12). Teacher versions are available for the same groups.

Format: Rating scale; group administration; untimed

Scoring: Machine-scored; test scoring service available from publisher

Cost: Survey Instruments $.50; Adult/Teacher Version $.30; Scoring Services: $.75 (student), $.50 (adult)

Missouri Guidance Competency Evaluation Surveys (MGCES)

Date not provided	Assessment Resource Center

Population: Grades 6 through 12

Purpose: Assesses the impact of guidance curriculum units on student attainment of guidance competencies

Description: The areas targeted are career planning and exploration, knowledge of self and others, and educational and vocational development. The surveys have two forms for middle school (Grades 6 to 9) and high school (Grades 9 to 12) students. The MGCES provides school counselors and teachers with measures of students' self-reported confidence in their achievement of guidance curriculum competencies. The items are rated on a 7-point scale.

Format: Rating scale; group administration; untimed

Scoring: Machine-scored; test scoring service available

Cost: Package (50 surveys, identification sheets, manual) $35.00; Scoring Service $.40 each

My Vocational Situation
John L. Holland

Date not provided	Consulting Psychologists Press, Inc.

Population: Adults

Purpose: Assesses the problems that may be troubling an individual seeking help with career decisions; used in career counseling and guidance

Description: Two-page multiple-item paper–pencil questionnaire is used to determine which of three difficulties may be troubling an individual in need of career counseling: lack of vocational identity, lack of information or training, or environmental or personal barriers. The questionnaire is completed by the individual just prior to the counseling interview and may be tabulated by the counselor at a glance. Responses may offer clues for the interview itself and treatments relevant to each individual's need. The manual discusses development of the diagnostic scheme and reports statistical properties of the three variables.

Format: Self-administered; untimed: 5 to 10 minutes

Scoring: Examiner evaluated

Cost: Booklets $13.10; Manual $5.00

O*NET Career Values Inventory

| 2002 | JIST Publishing |

Population: Grade 8 through adult

Purpose: Used in career exploration

Description: Relates work values to jobs described in the Department of Labor's O*NET database.

Format: Self-administered; untimed

Scoring: Self-scored

Cost: Administrator's Guide and 25 Forms $29.95

Occupational Clues
J. Michael Farr

| 1993 | JIST Publishing |

Population: High school students, adults

Purpose: Explores career alternatives; used in career counseling with adults with above average reading skills

Description: Multiple-choice, true–false test with six groups of checklists: occupational interests, work-related values, leisure activities, home activities, school, training, and work experience. Short and long versions exist.

Format: Self-administered; untimed: 60 minutes

Scoring: Self-scored

Cost: 25 Long Version Forms $48.95; 25 Short Version Forms $37.95

Perceptions, Expectations, Emotions, and Knowledge about College (PEEK)
Claire E. Weinstein, David R. Palmer

| 1995 | H & H Publishing Company, Inc. |

Population: High school seniors and college freshmen

Purpose: Assesses thoughts, beliefs, and expectations about personal, social, and academic changes that may occur in a college setting; used for counseling, course development, and college success courses

Description: Three-scale multiple-choice paper–pencil or computer-administered test measuring academic experiences (10 items), personal experiences (10 items), and social experiences (10 items). Assessment yields a Distribution Report showing responses, percents, median, mode, mean, and standard deviation; a Student Profile; and a Summary Report.

Format: Self-administered; untimed: 20 to 30 minutes

Scoring: Machine scored; test scoring service available; computer version available

Cost: Up to 500 Forms $1.25 each; Computer Version up to 99 Administrations $2.25 each

Program for Assessing Youth Employment Skills (PAYES)

| Date not provided | Educational Testing Service |

Population: Adolescents

Purpose: Measures the attitudes, knowledge, and interests of students preparing for entry-level employment; used by program directors, counselors, and teachers working with dropouts and disadvantaged youth in government training programs and skill centers

Description: Three orally administered paper–pencil tests assessing attitudes, knowledge, and interests related to entry-level employment. Test Booklet I measures attitudes toward job-holding skills (supervisor's requests, appropriate dress, punctuality), attitudes toward supervision by authority figures, and self-confidence in social and employment situations. Measurements are made by assessing responses to multiple-choice questions based on statements, real-life situations, and scenes. Test Booklet II provides cognitive measures, including job knowledge, job-seeking skills, and practical job-related reasoning in situations that require following directions. Test Booklet III measures seven vocational interest clusters. Respondents indicate their degree of interest in specific job tasks that are described verbally and pictured. Students mark answers directly in test booklets.

Format: Examiner required; suitable for group use; untimed

Scoring: Examiner evaluated

Cost: Complete Set (20 each of Test Booklets I, II, and III; score sheets) $90.00; User's Guide $4.50; Administrators' Manual $5.50

PSB Health Occupations Aptitude Examination

1995	Psychological Services Bureau, Inc.

Population: Adults; health occupations students

Purpose: Measures abilities, skills, knowledge, and attitudes important to successful performance in various health care occupations; used as an admission test for schools and programs in health occupations

Description: Multiple-item paper–pencil or electronic battery of five tests assessing areas important to performance in health care occupations: academic aptitude, spelling, reading comprehension, the natural sciences, and vocational adjustment. The test predicts an individual's readiness for specialized instruction in numerous health care positions, including medical record technician, dental assistant, psychiatric aide, histologic technician, nursing assistant, respiratory therapy technician, and radiologic technologist.

Format: Examiner required; suitable for group use; timed: 2 hours 15 minutes

Scoring: Machine and electronically scored

Cost: Reusable Test Booklets $10.00; Answer Sheets (scoring and reporting service) $10.00; Electronic Version $15.00

Responsibility and Independence Scale for Adolescents (RISA)
John Salvia, John T. Neisworth, Mary W. Schmidt

1990	Riverside Publishing Company

Population: Ages 12 through 19

Purpose: Measures adolescents' adaptive behavior

Description: Nationally standardized instrument specifically designed to measure adolescents' behavior in terms of responsibility and independence. Whereas most measures of adaptive be-

havior target low-level skills, the RISA assesses higher level behaviors. Subscales include domestic skills, money management, citizenship, personal planning, transportation skills, career development, self-management, social maturity, and social communication.

Format: Examiner required; individual administration; untimed: 30 to 45 minutes

Scoring: Examiner evaluated

Cost: Complete Program (test book, examiner's manual, 25 response forms) $169.50

Rothwell Miller Values Blank (RMVB)
Jack W. Rothwell, Kenneth M. Miller

1968	Miller & Tyler, Ltd.

Population: Ages 14 and older

Purpose: Assesses work-related values; used in career guidance and personal counseling

Description: The RMVB has a total of 50 items within five categories: Rewards, Interest, Security, Pride, and Autonomy. Results include Total Importance and rank scores and percentile scores (by age, grade, and gender). The authors recommend that the RMVB be used in conjunction with the Rothwell Miller Interest Blank or other interest measure, or with a comprehensive personality questionnaire.

Format: Examiner required; suitable for group use; untimed: 5 to 10 minutes

Scoring: Self-scored; computer scored; examiner evaluated

Cost: 25 forms £16.00 + Value Added Tax; Manual £16.00

Self-Directed Search® Career Planner (SDS®) Form CP: Career Planning
John L. Holland

1990	Psychological Assessment Resources, Inc.

Population: Adults

Purpose: Used in career counseling as an assessment for long-term career planning; intended for individuals on the career development path

Description: Paper–pencil yes–no test. Materials used include a professional user's guide, technical manual, Form CP assessment booklets, career option finders, and exploring career options booklet. An eighth-grade reading level is required. A computer version using PC compatibles is available.

Format: Self-administered; untimed: 20 to 30 minutes

Scoring: Self-scored; computer scored; scoring service available

Cost: Intro Kit $158.00

Student Adaptation to College Questionnaire (SACQ)
Robert W. Baker, Bohad Siryk

1999   Western Psychological Services

Population: Adults

Purpose: Measures overall student adjustment to college; used for college counseling

Description: Multiple-choice 67-item questionnaire with four subscales that measure academic adjustment, social adjustment, personal–emotional adjustment, and attachment to the college. Yields *T*-scores. A computer version for PC computers is available.

Format: Self-administered; untimed: 30 minutes

Scoring: Machine scored; computer scored; self-scored; test scoring service available

Cost: Kit (25 hand-scored questionnaires, manual, 2-use PC disk, 2 PC answer sheets) $92.50

Student Developmental Task and Lifestyle Assessment (SDTLA)
Roger B. Winston, Jr., Theodore K. Miller, Diane L. Cooper

1999   Student Development Associates, Inc.

Population: Ages 17 to 25 years

Purpose: Measures the psychosocial development of traditional-aged college students

Description: The SDTLA is a major revision of the Student Developmental Task and Lifestyle Inventory. It represents a sample of behavior and reports about feelings and attitudes that are indicative of students who have satisfactorily achieved certain developmental tasks common to young adult college students. The phenomena with which the SDTLA are concerned are the changes produced in individuals as a result of accomplishing a developmental task or having addressed important life events or issues within the context of higher education. The instrument is composed of both developmental tasks (and subtasks) and scales. There are three developmental tasks—Establishing and Clarifying Purpose, Developing Autonomy, and Developing Mature Interpersonal Relationships—and two scales—Salubrious Lifestyle and Response Bias.

There are four forms of the SDTLA. The overall reading level ranges from Grade 11.2 to Grade 11.5.

Format: Self-administered; untimed: varies depending on form (10 to 35 minutes)

Scoring: Self-scored; computer scoring available

Cost: Licensing Options: Hard Copy or Computer Administered $1,000.00 for 12-month period

Student Profile and Assessment Record (SPAR)
Theodore K. Miller, Roger B. Winston, Jr.

1985   Student Development Associates, Inc.

Population: Ages 17 to 23 years

Purpose: Assesses perceptions of students entering college; used by academic advisers, counselors, residence hall staff, and others

Description: Multiple-item paper–pencil comprehensive self-assessment tool providing information in six categories: general (home address, marital status, disabilities, need for financial assistance, emergency contact person); academic (perceptions of subjects, decisions about major, noncredit academic interests and long-range plans, instructional approach preference, academic strengths and weaknesses); career; health and wellness; activities and organizations; and special concerns and other considerations. The SPAR folder has space for recording the student's test profile, high school academic record, and other pertinent information, including educational goals and objectives. The instrument is useful in the initial phases of orientation. It is recommended for use in conjunction with the Student Developmental Task and Lifestyle Assessment.

Format: Self-administered; untimed

Scoring: Self-scored

Cost: 50 Folders $10.00

System for Assessment and Group Evaluation (SAGE)

1980   PESCO International

Population: Ages 14 years and older

Purpose: Measures educational development, vocational aptitudes, vocational interests, temperaments, and work attitudes

Description: Paper–pencil, multiple-choice, hands-on assessment battery measuring four categories. A fourth-grade reading level is required. Used for vocational planning and guidance with populations who have physical or mental disabilities, are disadvantaged, or are dislocated or injured workers.

Format: Examiner required; suitable for groups; timed and untimed

Scoring: Machine/computer scored

Cost: Contact publisher

Transition Behavior Scale–Second Edition (TBS-2)
Stephen B. McCarney, Paul D. Anderson

| 2000 | Hawthorne Educational Services, Inc. |

Population: Ages 12 through 18 years

Purpose: Provides a measure of behaviors necessary for success in employment and independent living

Description: The subscales measure a student's behavior in the areas of Work Related Behavior, Interpersonal Relations, and Social/Community Expectations. The TBS-2 provides teachers with a convenient mechanism for measuring the student's skills and readiness for transition activities. Students in the standardization sample represented all geographic regions of the United States, with particular attention given to the inclusion of racial and ethnic minorities in the creation of the national norms. Internal consistency, test-retest, and interrater reliability; item and factor analysis; and content, criterion-related, diagnostic, and construct validity are well documented and reported for the scale. The School Form is completed by an educator; the Self-Report Form is completed by the student.

Format: Rating scale; untimed

Scoring: Examiner evaluated

Cost: Complete Kit $116.00

Transition Planning Inventory (TPI)
Gary M. Clark, James R. Patton

| 1997 | PRO-ED, Inc. |

Population: Ages 14 to 22 years

Purpose: Provides school personnel with a systematic way to address critical transition planning areas that are mandated by the Individuals with Disabilities Education Act

Description: Information on transition needs is gathered from the student, parents or guardians, and school personnel through the use of three separate forms designed specifically for each of the target groups. The forms contain the same 46 items. The student form also contains 15 open-ended questions. The Administration and Resource Guide includes three extensive case studies, blackline master of the Planning Notes Form, and an extensive list of more than 600 transition goals that are correlated to each planning statement. Informal Assessments for Transition Planning consists of three major components. This is a criterion-referenced instrument. A set of Home Forms Spanish Version is also available as an optional component.

Format: Rating scales; untimed

Scoring: Examiner evaluated

Cost: Complete Kit (administration and resource guide, 25 profile and further assessment recommendation forms, 25 school forms, 25 home forms, 25 student forms, informal assessments for transition planning, storage box) $154.00

VCWS 201—Physical Capacities/Mobility Screening

| 1993 | Valpar International Corporation |

Population: Ages 13 years and older

Purpose: Screens physical demands required in work and training settings; used for placement and career planning

Description: Criterion-referenced test consisting of demonstrated performance of lifting, continuous lifting, two-handed grip, palm press, horizontal press, vertical press, balancing, walk forward, walk backward, walk heel-toe, and climbing. Examiner qualifications as required by testing site. Materials include weight scale, standing platform, lifting apparatus, hinged climbing board, and tape measure. This test is suitable for individuals with hearing, physical, and mental impairments. Signing for hearing impairment is necessary.

Format: Examiner required; individual administration; untimed: 10 to 15 minutes

Scoring: Examiner evaluated

Cost: $725.00

Vocational Decision-Making Interview
Shirley Chandler, Thomas Czerlinsky

| 1999 | JIST Publishing |

Population: Grade 7 through adult

Purpose: Designed to improve vocational decision making of people with learning and other disabilities

Description: This revised edition has high reliability, validity, and consistency measures that are important in vocational guidance instruments. A professional asks the 54 structured questions. Three scales provide immediate feedback: decision-making readiness, employment readiness, and self-appraisal. Problems that need to be corrected are clarified.

Format: Examiner required; individual administration; untimed: 20 to 40 minutes

Scoring: Examiner evaluated

Cost: Manual $24.95; 10 Forms $29.95

Vocational Interest, Temperament, and Aptitude System (VITAS)

| 1981 | Vocational Research Institute |

Population: High school students and adults

Purpose: Assesses aptitudes, vocational interests, and work-related temperaments of individuals who are disadvantaged and who have educable mental retardation; used for vocational guidance

Description: Performance test of vocational aptitudes consisting of work samples in 21 areas: nuts, bolts, and washers assembly; packing matchbooks; tile sorting and weighing; collating material samples; verifying numbers; pressing linens; budget book assembly; nail and screw sorting; pipe assembly; filing by letters; lock assembly; circuit board inspection; calculating; message taking; bank teller; proofreading; payroll computation; census interviewing; spot welding; laboratory assistant; and drafting. The assessment process includes orientation, assessment, a motivational group session, feedback, and an interest interview. The test hardware is provided for all work samples.

Format: Examiner required; suitable for group use (10 persons per week); untimed: 2$\frac{1}{2}$ days

Scoring: Examiner evaluated

Cost: Contact publisher

Work Adjustment Inventory (WAI)
James E. Gilliam

| 1994 | PRO-ED, Inc. |

Population: Ages 12 to 22 years

Purpose: Assesses work-related temperament

Description: A multidimensional, norm-referenced instrument designed for use in schools and clinics, the WAI provides vital information to counselors, psychologists, personnel directors, and others. It can be used in the development of individual transition plans for students with disabilities (required under the Individuals with Dis-

abilities Education Act) and has application for at-risk students. Six scales measure six work-related temperament traits: Activity, Empathy, Sociability, Assertiveness, Adaptability, and Emotionality. Each scale provides a standard score for age and gender, and a combination of the standard scores generates an overall quotient of work temperament and adjustment. These scores can be displayed graphically. The WAI standardization (on more than 7,000 students, 10% with disabilities) is the largest and most representative of the 1990 U.S. population of any test of temperament. Studies of both internal consistency and test–retest reliability produced appropriately high coefficients. Evidence of reliability of the WAI is provided in the form of coefficients alpha.

Format: Rating scale; timed: 20 minutes

Scoring: Examiner evaluated

Cost: Complete Kit (manual, 50 response record forms, storage box) $86.00

Work Adjustment Scale (WAS)
Stephen B. McCarney

| 1991 | Hawthorne Educational Services, Inc. |

Population: Grades 11 and 12

Purpose: Provides the profile necessary to determine a student's readiness for success in the workplace

Description: Includes 54 items easily observed and documented by educational personnel. Separate norms are provided for male and female students.

Format: Rating scale; untimed

Scoring: Examiner evaluated

Cost: Complete Kit $65.00

Workforce Skills Certification System

| 2000 | Comprehensive Adult Student Assessment System (CASAS) |

Population: Grade 11 to adult

Purpose: Measures job readiness skills in reading, math, critical thinking, problem solving, and oral communication in specific job areas; provides job readiness certification

Description: Includes 13 subtests plus portfolio assessment system. Each subtest is individually scored. Reading and Math test yields scaled score. Tests: Reading and Math; Critical Thinking and Problem Solving tests in Banking, Health, High-Tech, and Telecommunication; Applied Performance Test in Banking, Health, and Telecommunications. Test includes multiple-choice, paper-pencil, oral response, and short answer items.

Format: Examiner required; individual and group administration; timed and untimed

Scoring: Machine scored; hand key; examiner evaluated

Cost: Contact publisher

World of Work and You, Third Edition
J. Michael Farr

2002	JIST Publishing

Population: Grades 8 to 12

Purpose: Used in career exploration; teaches the importance of values and education in career planning

Description: Career exploration booklet (32 pages) identifies such factors as work satisfiers, values, and training in educational options. Job matching chart included. Eighth-grade reading level is required.

Format: Self-administered; untimed

Scoring: Self-scored

Cost: 10 Forms $24.95

Aptitude

Ability Explorer
Thomas F. Harrington, Joan C. Harrington

1996	Riverside Publishing Company

Population: Level 1: Grades 6 to 8; Level 2: Grades 9 to 12 and adults

Purpose: Helps students and adults in transition explore their abilities as they relate to the world of work and career and educational planning

Description: The Ability Explorer is a measure of self-reported abilities that provides information on 14 work-related abilities relevant to the workplace of today and the future. The work-related ability areas include Artistic, Clerical, Interpersonal, Language, Leadership, Manual, Musical/Dramatic, Numerical/Mathematical, Organizational, Persuasive, Scientific, Social, Spatial, and Technical/Mechanical. Level 1 helps middle school and junior high school students explore abilities and careers, begin career planning, and select courses for high school. Level 2 helps high school students and adults learn about their abilities, do advanced career or educational exploration, develop career plans and portfolios, and begin the transition from school to work and

postsecondary education or training. Spanish version is available.

Format: Examiner required; group or individual administration; untimed: less than one class period

Scoring: Examiner/student evaluated; scoring service available

Cost: 25 Hand-Scorable Assessment Documents and Directions for Administration $35.00

Career Ability Placement Survey (CAPS)
Lila F. Knapp, Robert R. Knapp

1994	EdITS/Educational and Industrial Testing Service

Population: Adolescents, adults

Purpose: Measures abilities keyed to entry requirements for the majority of jobs in each of the 14 COPSystem Career Clusters; used with students for career and vocational guidance and academic counseling

Description: Eight paper–pencil subtests measuring career-related abilities: Mechanical Reasoning, Spatial Relations, Verbal Reasoning, Numerical Ability, Language Usage, Word Knowledge, Perceptual Speed and Accuracy, and Manual Speed and Dexterity. The eight tests are keyed to the COPSystem Career Clusters. An audiocassette tape of recorded instructions is available.

Format: Self-administered; timed: 51 minutes

Scoring: Self-scored; may be computer scored

Cost: Specimen Set (one copy of each test, manual) $7.00

McCarron-Dial System (MDS)
Lawrence T. McCarron, Jack G. Dial

1986	McCarron-Dial Systems

Population: Ages 16 years and older

Purpose: Assesses verbal-spatial-cognitive, sensory, motor, emotional, and integration-coping factors; used primarily in educational and vocational programming, development, and placement of special education and rehabilitation populations

Description: Multiple-item paper–pencil oral-response point-to task-performance battery consisting of six separate instruments: Peabody Picture Vocabulary Test–Third Edition (PPVT–III), Bender Visual Motor Gestalt Test (BVMGT), Behavior Rating Scale (BRS), Observational Emotional Inventory (OEI), Haptic Visual Discrimination Test (HVDT), and McCarron Assessment of Neuromuscular Development (MAND). The standard format for comprehensive reporting includes specific scores, vocational and residential place-ment scores, behavioral observations, case his-tory information, lists of strengths and weak-nesses, programming priorities, and program-ming recommendations. The system is designed to predict the level of vocational and residential functioning the individual may achieve after train-ing. This level can be used to establish vocational goals or appropriate vocational program place-ment. The system is targeted toward individuals with learning disabilities, emotional disturbance, mental retardation, cerebral palsy, closed head injuries, social disabilities, and cultural disadvan-tages. It also can be used with persons who are blind or deaf. The examiner must be trained.

Format: Examiner required; individual admin-istration; untimed: varies

Scoring: Hand key; examiner evaluated

Cost: Complete MDS $2,825.00; HVDT $1,040.00; MAND $1,260.00

Non-Verbal Reasoning

1994	Valpar International Corporation

Population: Ages 12 years and above

Purpose: Assesses nonverbal reasoning of the Department of Labor's GED R Levels 4, 5, and 6; used in career counseling and vocational explo-ration

Description: The examinee is presented with a series of 3 × 3 grids. Eight of the cells contain geometric pictures that bear some relationship to one another. From a list, the examinee must choose the item that best completes the grid. A test booklet, answer sheet, and manual are used.

Format: Examiner required; individual or group administration; timed: 20 minutes

Scoring: Machine scored; computer scored

Cost: Contact publisher

Occupational Aptitude Survey and Interest Schedule–Third Edition: Aptitude Survey (OASIS-3:AS)
Randall M. Parker

2002	PRO-ED, Inc.

Population: Grade 8 through adult

Purpose: Evaluates a student's aptitude for vari-ous occupations; used for occupational guidance and counseling

Description: Paper–pencil 245-item survey meas-uring general, verbal, numerical, spatial, percep-tual, and manual abilities through five subtests: Vocabulary (40 items, 9 minutes), Computation (30 items, 12 minutes), Spatial Relations (20 items, 8 minutes), Word Comparison (95 items, 5 min-utes), and Making Marks (60 items, 1 minute). Subtest raw scores, percentiles, stanines, and 5-point scores are yielded. A companion test to the OASIS Interest Schedule, scores for both sur-veys are keyed directly to the *Dictionary of Occu-pational Titles*, *Guide for Occupational Explora-tion*, and *Worker Trait Group Guide*.

Format: Examiner required; suitable for group use; timed: 35 minutes

Scoring: Examiner evaluated; scoring service available

Cost: Complete Kit (manual, 10 student test booklets, 50 hand-scorable answer sheets, 50 profile sheets, interpretation workbook, storage box) $159.00

Skills Assessment Module (SAM)
Michelle Rosinek

1999	Piney Mountain Press, Inc.

Population: Ages 14 years and older

Purpose: Assesses basic skill level in 12 work-performance and basic skills locator test areas; used for career training placement

Description: Paper–pencil show–tell format with 12 hands-on modules: Digital Discrimination, Clerical Verbal Perception, Motor Coordination, Clerical Numerical Perception, Written Instruc-tions, Aiming Finger Dexterity, Form Perception, Spatial Perception, Color Discrimination, Dia-gramed Instructions, and Oral Instructions. Basic skills assessment of person's function in math and reading. A Career Training Performance ma-trix is generated. Computer version for Windows computers is available. Also available in Spanish.

Format: Examiner required; suitable for group or individual use; timed: 1 hour 45 minutes

Scoring: Examiner evaluated; computer scored

Cost: $1,995.00

Spatial Aptitude

1994	Valpar International Corporation

Population: Ages 12 years and older

Purpose: Used in career counseling and voca-tional exploration to assess the top three levels of the APT-S

Description: The examinee is presented with a series of two-dimensional drawings that could fold into three-dimensional objects. The examinee must select the proper object from a group of three-dimensional projections. Department of Labor Spatial Aptitude Levels 1 and 2 scores are yielded. A test booklet, answer sheet, and manual are used.

Format: Examiner required; individual or group administration; timed: 10 minutes

Scoring: Machine scored; computer scored

Cost: Contact publisher

Interest

Career Assessment Battery (CAB)

1999	Piney Mountain Press, Inc.

Population: Ages 13 years to adult

Purpose: Measures career interests for career counseling

Description: A live-action video and multimedia CD provide participants access to 12 occupational situations to make informed choices. Each category takes 3 minutes and provides aptitude, career cluster, and job title matches. Computer scoring on Windows systems is included in the package.

Format: Examiner required; individual or group administration; untimed: 40 minutes

Scoring: Examiner interpretation; computer scored, machine scored, or scoring service

Cost: Stand-alone Version $195.00; Multi-station Version $395.00; Multimedia Version $595.00; Network Version $995.00

Career Assessment Inventory™– Vocational Version (CAI-V)

Charles B. Johansson

1982	NCS Pearson

Population: Adolescents, adults

Purpose: Measures occupational interests of high school students who want immediate, non-college-graduate business or technical training; used for employment decisions, vocational rehabilitation, and self-employment

Description: Compares an individual's vocational interests to those of individuals in 91 specific careers that reflect a range of positions in today's workforce requiring 2 years or less of postsecondary training. Helps to guide students to focus

on the patterns of interest that are important in making educational and occupational choices. Has 305 items with a 5-point rating scale.

Format: Self-administered; on-line administration available; untimed: 25 to 30 minutes

Scoring: Computer scored; scoring service available

Cost: Preview Package with Interpretive Reports $42.00

Career Directions Inventory

Douglas N. Jackson

2001	Sigma Assessment Systems, Inc.

Population: Adolescents, adults

Purpose: Helps evaluate career interests of high school and college students, and adults

Description: Paper–pencil or computer-administered 100-item inventory consisting of a triad of statements for each item, describing job-related activities. Computer scoring yields a gender-fair profile of 15 basic interest scales. The pattern of these interests is compared to the interest patterns shown by individuals in a wide variety of occupations. This new test evolved from the Jackson Vocational Interest Survey; the content and vocabulary are easier, and more emphasis is placed on activities involved in sales, service, and technical occupations. Reports are available through the mail-in batch scoring service. The computer version operates on PC systems.

Format: Examiner required; suitable for group use; untimed: 30 to 45 minutes

Scoring: Computer scored; scoring service available from publisher

Cost: Examination Kit (manual, machine-scorable question–answer document for extended report) $35.00

Career Exploration Inventory, Second Edition (CEI)

John J. Liptak

2001	JIST Publishing

Population: Grades 7 and above

Purpose: Integrates work, leisure, and learning interests; used for career guidance

Description: The CEI asks individuals to consider their past, present, and future activities by reflecting on 120 brief activity statements. They then indicate whether they like or would like to engage in that activity. By assessing leisure interests, the CEI can be used successfully with people who have limited work or education experience. The responses are totaled on a grid, and the Interest Profile provides an immediate graphic picture of interest levels in 15 categories. The guide then provides the areas of strongest interest, and information is given on related occupations, typical leisure activities, and related education and training programs. Results are related to codes in the *Guide for Occupational Exploration*. Formal validity data are provided.

Format: Self-administered; untimed

Scoring: Self-scored

Cost: 25 Forms $34.95; Professional Manual $34.95; Workshop Manual $19.95

Career Gateways

Date not provided	CFKR Career Materials

Population: Junior and high school students

Purpose: Designed to help students focus on work interests

Description: Students will become familiar with the 14 families in the Skill-Based Job Family Matrix. The instrument involves students in their future career planning using a self-directed program. Helps students develop career planning skills to locate, understand, and use career information; identify the education and training required for job entry; identify interests, abilities, values, and their relationship to careers; and develop an individualized career plan.

Format: Examiner required; individual or group administration; untimed

Scoring: Examiner evaluated; scoring software available

Cost: $6.36 each (1 to 9 copies)

Career Journeys

Date not provided	CFKR Career Materials

Population: Junior and high school students

Purpose: Designed to help students develop a career-oriented educational program

Description: Emphasizes the 14 families within the Skill-Based Job Family Matrix and the importance of cross-functional job skills. This knowledge helps students identify abilities that can be used in many occupations, making it easier for them to find several jobs in which they can excel.

Format: Examiner required; individual or group administration; untimed

Scoring: Examiner evaluated; scoring software available

Cost: $6.36 each (1 to 9 copies)

Career Orientation Placement and Evaluation Survey (COPES)

1995	EdITS/Educational and Industrial Testing Service

Population: Grades 8 and above

Purpose: Measures personal values related to the type of work an individual chooses and the satisfactions derived from the occupation; used for career evaluation and guidance and to supplement other types of information used to improve self-awareness

Description: Multiple-item paper–pencil inventory measuring the following 16 value dimensions related to career evaluation and selection: investigative vs. accepting, practical vs. carefree, independent vs. conformity, leadership vs. supportive, orderliness vs. flexibility, recognition vs. privacy, aesthetic vs. realistic, and social vs. reserved. The COPES value dimensions are based on theoretical and factor analytic research and are keyed to the COPSystem Career Clusters. Norms are provided for high school and college levels. Measures both ends of each scale.

Format: Self-administered; untimed: 30 minutes

Scoring: Self-scored; may be computer scored

Cost: Specimen Set (manual, all forms) $6.25

Chronicle Career Quest® (CCQ)

2001	Chronicle Guidance Publications, Inc.

Population: Grades 7 through 12 and adults

Purpose: A comprehensive interest inventory used for career counseling

Description: A series of statements of work-related activities grouped in 12 interest areas. Two forms based on grade and abilities of the user are available. Form S consists of 108 statements with 9 in each interest area for Grades 7 through 10. Form L consists of 144 statements with 12 in each interest area for Grades 9 through 12 and adults. Suitable for individuals with hearing impairments.

Format: Self-administered; untimed: 30 to 35 minutes

Scoring: Hand key

Cost: Form S (package of 25) $63.25; Form L (package of 25) $63.50

COPS Interest Inventory
Lisa Knapp-Lee, Robert R. Knapp,
Lila F. Knapp

Date not provided	EdITS/Educational and Industrial Testing Service

Population: Grades 7 and above

Purpose: Job activity items reflecting the increased use of computers along with similar other current trends in occupations

Description: The COPS (blue form) provides job activity interest scores related to occupational clusters. Each cluster is keyed to curriculum choice and major sources of detailed job information, including the *Dictionary of Occupational Titles, Occupational Outlook Handbook*, COPSystem Career Briefs, and COPSystem Career Cluster Booklets. Low-cost, on-site scoring provides immediate feedback of results, and the use of one instrument for vocationally oriented and college-oriented individuals are major features of this instrument. Also available in Spanish. Percentile norms are presented separately at the high school and college levels.

Format: Examiner required; suitable for group use; untimed: 20 minutes

Scoring: Self-scored; machine scored

Cost: Specimen Set $30.50; 25 Self-Scoring Booklets $13.75; 25 Machine-Scoring Booklets $14.25

COPS Intermediate Inventory (COPS II)
Robert R. Knapp, Lila F. Knapp

1994	EdITS/Educational and Industrial Testing Service

Population: Grades 4 through 7

Purpose: Measures the career-related interests of students in Grades 4 through 7 and older students for whom language or reading might present more difficulty; used for academic counseling and guidance

Description: Multiple-item paper–pencil inventory provides a rating of student's job-related interests based to a large extent on knowledge of school activities. COPS II extends interest measurement to younger students and to older students with reading or language difficulties for whom motivational considerations are of special concern. Items are written at a fourth-grade reading level.

Format: Self-administered; untimed: 20 to 30 minutes

Scoring: Self-scored

Cost: Specimen Set (includes manual) $5.00; 25

Self-Scoring Forms $24.25 (combined self-scoring booklet and self-interpretation guide); Set of 14 COPSystem Occupational Cluster Charts with COPSystem II Cartoons $44.00; 25 Pocket-Size Cluster Charts $6.50

COPS Picture Inventory of Careers (COPS–PIC)
Lisa Knapp-Lee

Date not provided	EdITS/Educational and Industrial Testing Service

Population: Elementary students through adults

Purpose: Provides job activity interest scores using pictures only

Description: The COPS–PIC yields measurement of the 14 COPSystem Clusters for nonreaders. The same interpretive material is provided as for the COPS Interest Inventory.

Format: Examiner required; individual administration; untimed

Scoring: Hand scored with keys; machine scoring available from publisher

Cost: Specimen Set $3.50; 25 Booklets/Answer Sheets $31.25

COPS–P Interest Inventory
Lisa Knapp-Lee, Lila F. Knapp,
Robert. R. Knapp

1995	EdITS/Educational and Industrial Testing Service

Population: Grades 7 and above

Purpose: Measures job activity interests related to occupational clusters appropriate for college-bound and vocationally oriented individuals; used for academic counseling, career planning, and vocational guidance

Description: Multiple-item paper–pencil inventory (brown form) measuring interests related to both professional and skilled positions in science, technology, business, arts, and service and to occupations in communication, consumer economics, clerical, and outdoor fields. Each cluster is keyed to curriculum choice and major sources of detailed job information, including the *Dictionary of Occupational Titles* and the *Occupational Outlook Handbook*. On-site scoring provides immediate feedback of results. The instrument may be used with the Career Ability Placement Survey and the Career Orientation Placement and Evaluation Survey as part of the COPSystem. Percentile norms are presented separately for high school and college levels. Also available in Spanish and French Canadian.

Format: Self-administered; untimed: 20 minutes

Scoring: Self-scored; may be computer scored

Cost: Specimen Set (all forms, technical manual) $8.25; 25 Self-Scoring Test Booklets $11.75; 25 Self-Interpretation Guides and Profile Guides $11.50; 25 Machine-Scoring Booklets and Answer Sheets $12.25; Handscoring Keys $17.75; Examiner's Manual $2.50

COPS-R Interest Inventory

Lisa Knapp-Lee, Lila F. Knapp,
Robert R. Knapp

1994	EdITS/Educational and Industrial Testing Service

Population: Grades 6 to 12

Purpose: Measures job activity interests related to occupational clusters; used for academic counseling, career planning, and vocational guidance

Description: Multiple-item paper–pencil inventory (green form) measuring interests related to both professional and skilled positions in science, technology, business, arts, and service and to occupations in communication, consumer economics, clerical, and outdoor fields. COPS-R is parallel to the COPS Interest Inventory but uses simpler language and a single norms profile. Items are written at a sixth-grade reading level, and the whole unit is presented in a single booklet. The instrument may be used with the Career Ability Placement Survey and the Career Orientation Placement and Evaluation Survey as a part of the COPSystem. A self-scoring form and a machine-scoring form for processing and scoring by EdITS are available. Percentile norms are provided at the high school level.

Format: Self-administered; untimed: 20 minutes

Scoring: Self-scored; may be computer scored

Cost: Specimen Set (manual, all forms) $6.50; 25 Self-Scoring Forms (includes self-scoring booklet and self-interpretation guide) $23.00; 25 Machine-Scoring Booklets and Answer Sheets $12.25; Examiner's Manual $2.50

Educational Opportunities Finder (EOF)

Donald Rosen, Kay Holmberg, John L. Holland

1997	Psychological Assessment Resources, Inc.

Population: Adolescents

Purpose: Used in college counseling to aid in identifying fields of study that match one's interests; intended for college students or college-bound individuals

Description: The EOF is used with the Self-Directed Search Career Planner.

Format: Self-administered; untimed: 20 to 30 minutes

Scoring: Hand key

Cost: Package of 25 $45.00

E-WOW-A (Explore the World of Work, Grades 9–Adult)

Date not provided	CFKR Career Materials

Population: High school students through adults

Purpose: Assesses career interests

Description: This is a partly visual instrument with a very easy reading level. It matches job interests, job requirements, and job working conditions with job families. The E-WOW-A user accomplishes the following: rate responses to work activities, rate responses to work conditions, choose a job to explore and get realistic information, and develop a training plan through practical questions and activities. Also available in Spanish.

Format: Examiner required; individual or group administration; untimed

Scoring: Examiner evaluated; scoring software available

Cost: $1.28 each (1 to 9 copies)

Geist Picture Interest Inventory

Harold Geist

1975	Western Psychological Services

Population: Grades 8 and above

Purpose: Identifies an individual's vocational and avocational interests

Description: Multiple-item paper–pencil multiple-choice test requiring minimal language skills. The subject circles one of three pictures depicting preferred vocational and avocational scenes. Occupational norms are provided A Motivation Questionnaire can be administered separately to explore motivation behind occupational choices.

Format: Self-administered; suitable for group use; untimed: 20 to 30 minutes

Scoring: Hand key

Cost: Kit (10 male and 10 female tests, manual) $79.95

Gordon Occupational Check List II

Leonard V. Gordon

1981	Harcourt® Brace Educational Measurement

Population: Grades 8 and above

Purpose: Identifies areas of job interest; used

for counseling of non–college-bound high school students

Description: Multiple-item paper–pencil test consisting of 240 activities, each related to a different occupation within six broad vocational interest categories: business, arts, outdoors, technical-mechanical, technical-industrial, and service. The categories are further divided into the area and work group classifications used in the Department of Labor's *Guide for Occupational Exploration*.

Format: Examiner required; suitable for group use; untimed: 20 to 25 minutes

Scoring: Hand scored by the examinee

Cost: Examination Kit (checklist, manual, job title supplement) $36.50

Guide for Occupational Exploration Interest Inventory, Second Edition (GOE)
J. Michael Farr

2002	JIST Publishing

Population: Adolescents, adults

Purpose: Explores career, education, and lifestyle options; used in career counseling

Description: Multiple-choice and true–false test yielding a graphic interest profile on seven factors leading to career options: Leisure Activities, Home Activities, Education and School Subjects, Training, Work Settings, Work Experience, and Overall Interest. An eighth-grade reading level is required.

Format: Self-administered; untimed

Scoring: Self-scored

Cost: $29.95 (administrator's guide, 25 forms)

Hall Occupational Orientation Inventory (HALL)–Adult Basic Form
Lacy G. Hall

2000	Scholastic Testing Service, Inc.

Population: Adults with reading deficiencies

Purpose: Used in career counseling and guidance to assess vocational interests for adults in basic education programs

Description: Paper–pencil criterion-referenced test with 175 items focusing on 35 occupational and personality characteristics. A booklet, response sheet, and interpretive folder are used. Examiner must be certified for assessment. Reading level can be modified for the test. Available in large print.

Format: Examiner required; individual and group administration; untimed: 45 minutes

Scoring: Self-scored; examiner evaluated

Cost: Sample Set with Manual $21.75

Hall Occupational Orientation Inventory (HALL)–Form II
Lacy G. Hall

1989	Scholastic Testing Service, Inc.

Population: Adolescents, adults

Purpose: Used in career guidance and counseling to assess vocational interests

Description: Paper–pencil criterion-referenced test with 150 items focusing on career opportunities and development. Items are referenced to six interest scales, eight worker trait scales, and nine value/needs scales. A booklet, response sheet, and interpretive folder are used. Examiner must be certified for assessment. Available in large print.

Format: Examiner required; individual and group administration; untimed: 45 minutes

Scoring: Self-scored; examiner evaluated

Cost: Sample Set with Manual $25.75

Hall Occupational Orientation Inventory (HALL)–Intermediate Form
Lacy G. Hall

1976	Scholastic Testing Service, Inc.

Population: Grades 3 through 7

Purpose: Used in elementary career guidance to assess vocational interests

Description: Paper–pencil criterion-referenced test with 110 school-focused items and 22 work and personality characteristics. A booklet, response sheet, and interpretive folder are used. Examiner must be certified for assessment. Available in large print.

Format: Examiner required; individual and group administration; untimed: 45 minutes

Scoring: Self-scored; examiner evaluated

Cost: Sample Set with Manual $21.75

Hall Occupational Orientation Inventory (HALL)–Young Adult/College Form
Lacy G. Hall

2000	Scholastic Testing Service, Inc.

Population: High school and above

Purpose: Used in career guidance and counseling to assess vocational interests

Description: Paper–pencil criterion-referenced test with 175 items focusing on 35 occupational and personality characteristics. A booklet, response sheet, and interpretive folder are used. Examiner must be certified for assessment. Available in large print.

Format: Examiner required; individual and group administration; untimed: 45 minutes

Scoring: Self-scored; examiner evaluated

Cost: Sample Set with Manual $21.75

High School Career Course Planner

1990	CFKR Career Materials

Population: Grades 8 and 9

Purpose: Designed to develop a high school course plan that is consistent with self-assessed career goals

Description: Allows students to match interests with 16 occupational groups and job requirements. Also provides a choice of an occupational group that matches students' interests, and enables students to research job titles for educational planning and to develop a high school educational plan.

Format: Examiner required; individual or group administration; untimed

Scoring: Examiner evaluated; scoring software available

Cost: $1.28 each (1 to 9 copies)

Interest Determination, Exploration, and Assessment System (IDEAS™)
Charles B. Johansson

1990	NCS Pearson

Population: Grades 6 to 12

Purpose: Measures career-related interests of junior high and high school students; used in career planning and occupational exploration

Description: Paper–pencil 128-item inventory assessing a range of career interests. The areas covered are mechanical/fixing, nature/outdoors, science, writing, child care, protective services, mathematics, medical, creative arts, community service, educating, public speaking, business, sales, office practices, and food service. The test is scored on a 5-point Likert-type scale and is sold in a self-contained package that can be scored and interpreted by the student. A sixth-grade reading level is required.

Format: Self-administered; untimed: 30 to 40 minutes

Scoring: Self-scored

Cost: Preview Package with Self-Scored Reports $18.50

Inventory of Vocational Interests
Andrew Kobal, J. Wayne Wrightstone, Karl R. Kuntze, Andrew J. MacElroy

1966	Psychometric Affiliates

Population: Grade 10 to adult

Purpose: Assesses vocational interests; used for vocational guidance

Description: Paper–pencil 25-subject test of occupational interests. Each of the 25 topics contains 10 responses. The test, which provides insight into both major and minor interests, measures academic, artistic, mechanical, business and economic, and farm–agricultural areas. Materials include an inventory and occupation index arranged by vocational categories in the manual.

Format: Examiner required; suitable for group use; timed: 35 minutes

Scoring: Examiner evaluated

Cost: Specimen Set $4.00; 25 Tests $5.00; 25 Answer Sheets $5.00

Jackson Vocational Interest Survey (JVIS)
Douglas N. Jackson

1999	Sigma Assessment Systems, Inc.

Population: Grades 9 and above

Purpose: Helps evaluate career interests of high school students, college students, and adults in career transition; used for educational and vocational planning and counseling and for personnel placement

Description: Paper–pencil or computer-administered 289-item inventory consisting of paired statements covering 34 basic interest scales and 10 occupational themes: expressive, logical, inquiring, practical, assertive, socialized, helping, conventional, enterprising, and communicative. The subject marks one of two responses. Scoring yields a gender-fair profile of 34 basic interest scales. A seventh-grade reading level is required. The computer version operates on PC systems. Also available in French and Spanish.

Format: Examiner required; suitable for group use; untimed: 45 to 60 minutes

Scoring: Hand key; computer scored; scoring service available

Cost: Examination Kit (manual, handbook, guide, machine-scorable answer sheet for extended report, test booklet, hand-scorable answer sheet, profile sheet) $79.00

JOB-O 2000
Arthur Cutler, Francis Ferry,
Bob Kauk, Robert Robinett

| 2000 | CFKR Career Materials |

Population: Junior high students through adults

Purpose: Assesses work interests

Description: A comprehensive program of self-awareness, job exploration, and career planning. The answer folder contains information on 120 of the most popular, fastest growing occupations, with a listing of approximately 1,000 related jobs. Students match their interests with different education and training levels, examine career preparation options in the school and community, identify a tentative career choice and update individual career plans, and develop an educational plan to meet tentative career choices.

Format: Examiner required; individual or group administration; untimed

Scoring: Examiner evaluated

Cost: $4.20 each (1 to 9 copies)

JOB-O E (Elementary)
Arthur Cutler, Francis Ferry,
Bob Kauk, Robert Robinett

| 1991 | CFKR Career Materials |

Population: Grades 4 to 7

Purpose: Assesses work interests

Description: This is an activity-centered career awareness and career planning program. The program provides students with an opportunity to become aware of various occupational groups and occupations within the group.

Format: Examiner required; individual or group administration; untimed

Scoring: Examiner evaluated

Cost: $4.20 each (1 to 9 copies)

JOB-O Enhanced Second Edition
Arthur Cutler, Francis Ferry,
Bob Kauk, Robert Robinett

| 2000 | CFKR Career Materials |

Population: Junior high students through adults

Purpose: Assesses work interests

Description: Provides the student with the op-

portunity to explore occupations within eight occupational groups. The jobs are sorted by level of education and training. The first edition is available in Spanish.

Format: Examiner required; individual or group administration; untimed

Scoring: Examiner evaluated; scoring software available

Cost: $4.20 each (1 to 9 copies)

Leisure/Work Search Inventory
John J. Liptak

| 1994 | JIST Publishing |

Population: Adolescents, adults

Purpose: Connects leisure interests with employment opportunities; used for employment counseling

Description: Test takers respond to 96 leisure activity statements by circling the degree to which they like or dislike that activity. The Interest Profile provides an immediate graphic picture of interest levels in 12 categories. The Career Exploration chart provides the areas of strongest interest and information on sample occupations, self-employment options, and related education and training programs.

Format: Self-administered; untimed: 30 minutes

Scoring: Self-scored

Cost: Administrator's Guide and 25 Forms $32.95

My eCareers 101 Internet Application

| 2001 | Chronicle Guidance Publications, Inc. |

Population: Grades 7 to 12 and adults

Purpose: A comprehensive interest inventory used for career counseling

Description: A series of statements of work-related activities grouped in 12 interest areas. Two forms based on the grade and abilities of the user are available. Form S consists of 108 statements with 9 in each interest area for Grades 7 through 10. Form L consists of 144 statements with 12 in each interest area for Grades 9 through 12 and adults. The results take the user directly to a list of matching occupations. The user selects from the list of occupations and views a detailed job description, working conditions, salary, education requirements, and job outlook. The user then researches and compares several occupations against his or her own skills, work objectives, interests, and the education sought.

Format: Self-administered; untimed: 30–35 minutes

Scoring: Scored on-line automatically

Cost: $600.00 (1,000 uses)

O*NET Career Interest Inventory

2002	JIST Publishing

Population: Grade 8 through adult

Purpose: Used in career exploration

Description: Relates career interests to jobs described in the Department of Labor's O*NET database.

Format: Self-administered; untimed

Scoring: Self-scored

Cost: Administrator's Guide and 25 Forms $29.95

Occupational Aptitude Survey and Interest Schedule–Third Edition: Interest Survey (OASIS-3:IS)
Randall M. Parker

2002	PRO-ED, Inc.

Population: Grades 8 to 12

Purpose: Evaluates a student's areas of interest, as related to various occupations; used for occupational guidance and counseling

Description: Paper–pencil or computer-administered 240-item self-rating scale measuring the following interest areas: artistic, scientific, nature, protective, mechanical, industrial, business detail, selling, accommodating, humanitarian, leading/influencing, and physical performing. The test yields scale raw scores, percentiles, and stanines. A companion test is the OASIS Aptitude Survey. Scores for both surveys are keyed directly to the *Dictionary of Occupational Titles, Guide for Occupational Exploration,* and *Worker Trait Group Guide.* Questions may be read aloud to students with visual impairments or reading disabilities.

Format: Examiner required; suitable for group use; untimed: 30 minutes

Scoring: Examiner evaluated; scoring service available

Cost: Complete Kit (manual, 25 student test booklets, 50 hand-scorable answer sheets, 50 profile sheets, 50 scoring forms, interpretation workbook, storage box) $169.00

Ohio Vocational Interest Survey–Second Edition (OVIS-II)

1981	Harcourt® Brace Educational Measurement

Population: Grades 7 through adult

Purpose: Assesses occupational and vocational interests; used for educational and vocational counseling

Description: Paper–pencil 253-item test of job-related interests. Items are job activities to which the student responds on a 5-point scale ranging from *like very much* to *dislike very much.* Used in conjunction with the *Dictionary of Occupational Titles,* the OVIS-II classifies occupations according to three elements: data, people, and things. Materials include a Career Planner Workbook, Handbook for Exploring Careers, and filmstrips to aid counselors in administering and interpreting the test. The interest inventory is combined with an optional Career Planning Questionnaire and Local Survey and includes 23 Interest Scales.

Format: Examiner required; suitable for group use; untimed: 45 minutes

Scoring: Hand key; may be machine scored

Cost: 35 Test Booklets and Directions $127.00; 35 Hand-Scorable Answer Sheets $111.50

Reading Free Vocational Interest Inventory:2 (R-FVII:2)
Ralph Leonard Becker

2000	Elbern Publications

Population: Ages 13 and older

Purpose: Measures vocational interests of individuals in job areas that may be within the individuals' capabilities

Description: Consists of a series of 55 sets of three drawings each, depicting different job tasks. The individual is asked to mark the one occupational activity most preferred in each set. Responses are keyed to yield scores in 11 interest areas and five clusters. The interest areas are Animal Care, Automotive, Building Trades, Clerical, Food Service, Horticulture, Housekeeping, Laundry Service, Materials Handling, Patient Care, and Personal Service. The clusters are Mechanical, Outdoor, Mechanical/Outdoor, Clerical/Personal Care, and Food Service/Handling Operations. A Cluster Quotient is obtained for each examinee from a combination of related interest area scores. The manual contains the normative tables and a description of the scales and clusters and suggested jobs within each of the categories. A single booklet is used for both males and females. Each booklet has two detachable pages that provide a complete record of interest and cluster scores that is used as a permanent record.

Format: Examiner required; suitable for group use; untimed: 20 minutes or less

Scoring: Hand key; self-scored

Cost: Sample Set (10 test booklets, 1 manual) $52.00

Rothwell Miller Interest Blank (RMIB)
Jack W. Rothwell, Kenneth M. Miller

| 1994 | Miller & Tyler, Ltd. |

Population: Ages 14 and older

Purpose: Measures occupational interests; used in career guidance and personal counseling

Description: Appropriate for school, college or university, rehabilitation, company (selection, development, mid-career change, etc.), and counseling services. The RMIB has 12 categories: Outdoor, Mechanical, Computational, Scientific, Persuasive, Aesthetic, Literary, Musical, Social Service, Clerical, Practical, and Medical. The test has a total of 108 items. Obtain total Interest and rank scores and percentile scores. For some purposes, a simple interpretation, based purely on the psychometric scores, can be appropriate. However, the format is designed to facilitate a more in-depth exploration of motivational aspects in a counseling interview. The RMIB is available in French, Greek, and Romanian, with other languages pending. May be used for individuals with hearing and physical impairments.

Format: Examiner required; portions are self-administered; suitable for group use; untimed: 20 minutes

Scoring: Self-scored; computer scored; examiner evaluated

Cost: 25 Forms £23.50 + Value Added Tax; Manual £46.50

Safran Students Interest Inventory (Third Edition)
C. Safran

| 1985 | Nelson Thomson Learning |

Population: Grades 5 to 12

Purpose: Assesses occupational interests of students

Description: Multiple-item three-part paper–pencil inventory determining the relationship of students' interests and occupational characteristics. Section 1 requires students to choose one alternative from 168 pairs of occupational alternatives categorized in the areas of economic, technical, outdoor, service, humane, artistic, and scientific preferences. Section II measures school subject interests, and Section III contains a self-rated Levels of Ability Chart (academic, mechanical, social, and clerical). Student interests are referenced to the Canadian Classification and Dictionary of Occupations (CCDO) and the Student Guidance Information System (SGIS). The inventory is available on two levels: Level 1 (Grades 5 to 9) and Level 2 (Grades 8 to 12). Reading levels are matched to the grades indicated for test levels. For remedial and special education students in Grades 8 and 9, the Level 1 instrument should be used. This edition includes occupational selections relevant to a student's world.

Format: Examiner/self-administered; suitable for group use; untimed: 40 minutes

Scoring: Hand key

Cost: Specimen Set (test booklets Levels 1 and 2, student manual, counselor's manual) $33.95; 35 Student Booklets $59.00

Self-Directed Search® Career Explorer (SDS® CE)
John L. Holland, Amy B. Powell

| 1994 | Psychological Assessment Resources, Inc. |

Population: Grades 5 through 8

Purpose: Used to help students assess and explore interests for future education and career planning

Description: Paper–pencil yes–no test. Materials used include a technical information book, teacher's guide, self-assessment booklet, careers booklet, and guidance booklet. A sixth-grade reading level is required. A computer version using PCs is available.

Format: Self-administered; untimed: 30 minutes

Scoring: Self-scored; computer scored

Cost: Intro Kit $133.00

Self-Directed Search® (SDS®) Form E–4th Edition
John L. Holland

| 1990 | Psychological Assessment Resources, Inc. |

Population: Adolescents, adults

Purpose: Used in career counseling to assess career interests among individuals with lower educational levels

Description: Paper-pencil yes-no form. An SDS summary code is yielded. Materials used include a user's guide, technical manual, assessment booklet, jobs finder, and informational booklet. Also available in Spanish and Canadian.

Format: Self-administered; untimed: 20 to 30 minutes

Scoring: Self-scored

Cost: Intro Kit $124.00

Self-Directed Search® Form R– 4th Edition (SDS® Form R)
John L. Holland

1994	Psychological Assessment Resources, Inc.

Population: Adolescents, adults

Purpose: Used to explore career interests

Description: Paper-pencil yes-no test. Materials used include professional user's guide, technical manual, Form R assessment booklet, occupations finder, career booklet, leisure activity finder, and educational opportunity finder. Computer version using Windows is available. An eighth-grade reading level is required.

Format: Self-administered; untimed: 20 to 30 minutes

Scoring: Self-scored; computer scored; scoring service available

Cost: Comprehensive Kit $155.00

Strong Interest Inventory
E. K. Strong, Jr., Jo-Ida C. Hansen, David P. Campbell

1994	Consulting Psychologists Press, Inc.

Population: Grades 8 and above

Purpose: Measures occupational interests in a wide range of career areas; used to make long-range curricular and occupational choices and for employee placement, career guidance, development, and vocational rehabilitation placement

Description: Paper-pencil 317-item multiple-choice test requiring the examinee to respond in various ways to items covering a broad range of familiar occupational tasks and daily activities. Topics include occupations, school subjects, activities, leisure activities, types of people, preference between two activities, "your characteristics," and preference in the world of work. The response is scored on six general occupational themes, 25 basic interest scales, occupational scales, and four personal style scales. The scoring services provide 11 additional nonoccupa-

tional and administrative indexes as a further guide to interpreting the results. Also available in Spanish, French Canadian, and Hebrew.

Format: Self-administered; untimed: 35 to 40 minutes

Scoring: Scoring service; software and on-line scoring

Cost: High School Preview Kit $10.75; Self-Scorable Preview Kit $4.75; College Preview Kit $10.75

Vo-Tech Quick Screener (VTQS)
Bob Kauk, Robert Robinett

1990	CFKR Career Materials

Population: Non-college-bound high school students and adults

Purpose: Designed to identify job interests

Description: A self-assessment inventory that helps the student match interests and goals with jobs, learn about training programs, and make career decisions. The student rates occupational interests to find out what job activities are preferred, matches occupational interests with 14 vocational-technical occupational groups, and selects the three most preferred groups. The student then examines specific jobs, training required, and the job outlook.

Format: Examiner required; individual or group administration; untimed

Scoring: Examiner evaluated; scoring software available

Cost: $1.28 each (1 to 9 copies)

Vocational Interest Exploration (VIE) System
Lawrence T. McCarron, Harriette P. Spires

1991	McCarron-Dial Systems

Population: Ages 14 years and above

Purpose: Assesses preferences for work conditions and orientation to work; used for vocational guidance, work adjustment, and occupational planning

Description: Six to 10 entry-level jobs (computer-generated) are described with matching responses from a multiple-choice work preference questionnaire. Each job can then be reviewed in the VIE Job Manuals that contain color photographs and descriptive information about job duties, abilities required, training needed, suggestions on where to look for the job, occupational outlook, and estimated earnings. A fourth-grade reading level is required.

Format: Examiner required; individual or group administration; untimed

Scoring: Test scoring software included

Cost: $350.00

Vocational Interest Inventory–Revised (VII-R)
Patricia W. Lunneborg

| 1981 | Western Psychological Services |

Population: Grades 11 and above

Purpose: Measures high school students' interests in a number of vocational areas

Description: Paper-pencil or computer-administered 112-item inventory measuring the relative strengths of students' interests in eight occupational areas: service, business contact, organization, technical, outdoor, science, general culture, and arts and entertainment. Each item is a forced-choice statement that pulls interests apart. Two copies of a narrative report are provided for each student. The report includes a profile of scores by percentile; a summary of percentiles and T-scores for each scale; an analysis and discussion of all scores at or above the 75th percentile; a college majors profile, which compares a student's scores with the mean scores of college majors who took the VII when they were in high school; and a discussion of nontraditional areas for exploration for students who scored between the 50th and 75th percentiles in an area that has been considered nontraditional for his or her gender (test items are controlled for gender bias). An eight-page Guide to Interpretation describes the types of people typical of each of the eight interest groups and gives examples of jobs typical of each group for five levels of education and training.

Format: Self-administered; untimed: 20 minutes

Scoring: Scoring service

Cost: Kit (4 Test Report answer sheets, manual) $69.50

Vocational Interest, Experience and Skill Assessment (VIESA), Second Canadian Edition

| 1995 | Nelson Thomson Learning |

Population: Grades 8 and above

Purpose: Measures vocational interests, experiences, and skills of individuals; used by educators and professionals in career counseling with individuals and group programs

Description: Multiple-item two-part paper-pencil assessment providing career counseling information. Individuals link personal characteristics determined using the Career Guidebook to more than 500 occupations on a World of Work Map that shows how occupations relate to each other. The Job Family Charts list occupations according to typical preparation level, including high school courses, post-high school preparation, and college majors. Occupations are referenced to National Occupational Classification (NOC) and the Canadian Classification and Dictionary of Occupation (CCDO). The test is available on two levels: Level 1 (Grades 8 to 10) and Level 2 (Grades 11 to adult). A seventh-grade reading level is required.

Format: Examiner/self-administered; suitable for group use; untimed: 40 to 45 minutes

Scoring: Hand key

Cost: Examination Kit Levels 1 and 2 $28.65; 25 Student Booklets $55.00

Vocational Training Inventory and Exploration Survey (VOC-TIES)
Nancy Scott

| 1999 | Piney Mountain Press, Inc. |

Population: Ages 13 years to adult

Purpose: Identifies technical training interests of junior high and high school students

Description: Video and CD are used to examine technical training interests. A descriptive report of the examinee's technical training interests is generated. Computer scoring in Windows format is included. This instrument does not require reading ability.

Format: Group administration, presented in video or CD format

Scoring: Examiner evaluated

Cost: Stand-Alone Version $195.00; Multi-Station Version $395.00; Multimedia Version $595.00; Network Version $995.00

Wide Range Interest–Opinion Test (WRIOT)
Joseph F. Jastak, Sarah Jastak

| 1979 | Wide Range, Inc. |

Population: Ages 5 years to adult

Purpose: Provides information about vocational interests (without language requirements)

Description: Paper–pencil 150-item test measuring an individual's occupational motivation according to his or her likes and dislikes. The test booklet contains three pictures on each page. Each picture shows an individual or group performing a specific job. The subject selects the picture he or she likes the most and the picture he or she likes the least for each page. The results are presented on a report form that graphically shows the individual's strength of interest in 18 interest and eight attitude clusters (normed on seven age groups, separately for males and females). The occupational range is from unskilled labor to the highest levels of training. The test may be used with individuals with educational and cultural disadvantages, learning dis-

abilities, mental retardation, and deafness. The picture titles can be read to those with visual impairments. Individual administration is necessary for those unable to complete a separate answer sheet.

Format: Examiner required; suitable for group use (except where noted); untimed: 40 minutes

Scoring: Hand key; computer scoring available; scoring service available

Cost: Starter Set (manual, 50 profile/report forms, picture book, 50 answer sheets, scoring stencils, case) $150.00

Health Education

Missouri Safe and Drug-Free Schools and Communities Survey

1993	Assessment Resource Center

Population: Grades 6 to 12

Purpose: Assesses use of alcohol, tobacco, and drugs, as well as AIDS awareness

Description: An anonymous 51-item questionnaire designed to determine high school students' attitudes toward, observations of, and experiences with tobacco, alcohol, driving under the influence, drugs (legal and illegal), weapons, violence, vandalism, and suicide (on and off school property). Administered biannually by districts receiving Drug-Free Schools funds, the survey is an adaptation of the longer Youth Risk Behaviors Survey administered by the federal Centers for Disease Control.

Format: Examiner required; group administration; 50 minutes

Scoring: Machine scored; test scoring service available

Cost: Contact publisher

National Achievement Tests: Health and Science Tests—Health Education

John S. Shaw, Maurice E. Troyer, Clifford L. Brownell

1964	Psychometric Affiliates

Population: Grades 7 and above

Purpose: Assesses health knowledge; used for educational evaluation

Description: Paper–pencil test of health information. The test contains problems with which students in high school and college should be familiar. Two equivalent forms, A and B, are available.

Format: Examiner required; suitable for group use; timed: 40 minutes

Scoring: Hand key

Cost: Specimen Set (test, manual, key) $4.00; 25 Tests $8.75; 25 Answer Sheets $4.00

Industrial Arts

VCWS 202—Mechanical Assembly/ Alignment and Hammering

1993	Valpar International Corporation

Population: Ages 13 years and older

Purpose: Assesses worker qualification to profile factors for job, curricula placement, and career planning

Description: Criterion-referenced test consisting of demonstrated performance of block assembly, alignment driving, block disassembly, and hammering. Spatial aptitude, motor coordination, finger dexterity, and manual dexterity are measured. The test yields Methods-Time Measurement standard and percentile scores. Materials include assembly block, assorted small tools and parts, and hammering cards. This test is suitable for individuals with hearing, physical, and mental impairments. Signing for individuals with hearing impairment is necessary.

Format: Examiner required; individual administration; untimed: 10 to 15 minutes

Scoring: Examiner evaluated

Cost: $1,035.00

VCWS 203—Mechanical Reasoning and Machine Tending

1993	Valpar International Corporation

Population: Ages 13 years and older

Purpose: Assesses worker qualification to profile factors for job, curricula placement, and career planning

Description: Criterion-referenced test consisting of demonstrated performance of platform assembly and disassembly using fingers and small tools. Measures vocational reasoning, motor coordination, manual dexterity, finger dexterity, and general learning ability. The test yields Methods-Time Measurement standard and percentile scores. Materials include four-legged platform, machine tending board, nut driver, and felt marker. This test is suitable for individuals with hearing, physical, and mental impairments. Signing for individuals with hearing impairment is necessary.

Format: Examiner required; individual administration; timed: 10 to 15 minutes

Scoring: Examiner evaluated

Cost: $1,035.00

Library Skills

Essential Skills Assessments: Information Skills (ESA:IS)
Cedric Croft, Karyn Dunn, Gavin Brown

2000	New Zealand Council for Educational Research

Population: Ages 10 to 15 years

Purpose: Measures information-finding skills

Description: Educational assessment applications (curriculum), with 14 tests in six modules:

finding information in a library, in books, in reference sources, in graphs and tables, in phrase text, and in text. Primary, Intermediate, and Secondary forms are available. Yields raw scores and stanines.

Format: Examiner required; group administration; timed: 30 minutes

Scoring: Hand key

Cost: Manual $9.90; 10 Booklets $9.90

Mathematics

Basic

ACER Mathematics Tests

1989	Australian Council for Educational Research Limited

Population: Ages 4 to 7 years

Purpose: Measures achievement in mathematics; used for diagnosing student strengths and weaknesses

Description: Multiple-choice paper–pencil tests of basic mathematics skills: addition, subtraction, multiplication, and division. Tests are for years 4 to 5 and for years 6 to 7.

Format: Examiner required; suitable for group use; timed: varies

Scoring: Hand key

Cost: Contact publisher

College Basic Academic Skills Examination (C-BASE)

S. J. Osterlind

1995	Assessment Resource Center

Population: College students

Purpose: Assesses knowledge of basic academic skills

Description: The instrument has 180 multiple-choice items that evaluate knowledge and skills in English, mathematics, science, and social studies. Each subject is further defined by clusters, skills, and subskills. Optional essay prompt evaluates students' writing abilities. Provides assessment of students' higher order thinking skills. Institutional and individual student reports with composite score are available. Test available in large print and audiocassette.

Format: Examiner required; group administration; untimed: 45 minutes per subject, 40 minutes for essay

Scoring: Examiner evaluated; machine scored; test scoring service available from publisher

Cost: Contact publisher

Collegiate Assessment of Academic Progress (CAAP) Mathematics Test

2001	ACT, Inc.

Population: Ages 17 years and older

Purpose: Assesses mathematics skills

Description: Paper-pencil 35-item multiple-choice test. A test booklet, answer sheet, and pencil are used. May be used for persons with visual, physical, hearing, and mental impairments.

Format: Examiner required; suitable for group use; timed: 40 minutes

Scoring: Machine scored; test scoring service available from publisher

Cost: $10.75

I Can Do Maths . . .

Brian Doig, Marion de Lemos

2000	Australian Council for Educational Research Limited

Population: First 3 years of school

Purpose: Assesses early numeracy skills

Description: This test comes in two levels to enable continuous monitoring focusing on number, space, and measurement. It provides a basis for planning programs to match individual needs. Administration is oral. Suitable to assess children whose knowledge of English may be limited.

Format: Examiner required; individual or group administration; untimed: 20 minutes

Scoring: Examiner evaluated

Cost: Contact publisher

Mathematics Competency Test

John F. Izard, Ken M. Miller

1996	Australian Council for Educational Research Limited

Population: Ages 11 to 18 years

Purpose: Used for general screening and identification of strengths and weaknesses to provide a profile of math competency

Description: Paper-pencil 46-item multiple-choice short-answer and true-false test. Scores yielded are Full Test, Using and Applying Mathematics, Number and Algebra, Shape and Space, and Data.

Format: Examiner required; individual administration; suitable for group use; timed

Scoring: Hand key; examiner evaluated

Cost: Contact publisher

National Achievement Tests for Arithmetic and Mathematics— American Numerical Test

John J. McCarty

1962	Psychometric Affiliates

Population: Adolescents, adults

Purpose: Assesses arithmetic and numerical ability; used for educational evaluation and vocational guidance

Description: Paper-pencil 60-item test arranged in sequences of the four basic arithmetical operations. Items require numerical alertness and adaptation. Validity studies include specific fields of secretarial training, automotive, machine tools, construction technology, accounting, and machine drafting and design.

Format: Examiner required; group administration; 4 minutes

Scoring: Hand key

Cost: Specimen Set (test, key, manual) $4.00; 25 Tests $5.00

National Achievement Tests for Elementary Schools: Arithmetic and Mathematics—Fundamentals and Reasoning (Grades 3-6)

Robert K. Speer, Samuel Smith

1962	Psychometric Affiliates

Population: Grades 3 to 6

Purpose: Assesses students' achievement in arithmetic; used to identify strengths and weaknesses as part of an educational evaluation

Description: Paper-pencil five-part test of arithmetic reasoning and fundamentals, including computation, arithmetical judgments, problem reading, and problem solving. Special norms for students with high and low IQs are provided. Two equivalent forms are available.

Format: Examiner required; suitable for group use; timed: 30 minutes per part

Scoring: Hand key

Cost: Specimen Set (test, key, manual) $4.00; 25 Tests $5.00

National Achievement Tests for Elementary Schools: Arithmetic and Mathematics–Fundamentals and Reasoning (Grades 6–8)
Robert K. Speer, Samuel Smith

1962	Psychometric Affiliates

Population: Grades 6 to 8

Purpose: Assesses students' achievement in arithmetic; used to identify strengths and weaknesses as part of an educational evaluation

Description: Paper-pencil five-part test of arithmetic reasoning and fundamentals, including fundamentals, number comparisons, mathematical judgments, problem reading, and problem solving. Special norms are provided for students with high and low IQs. Two equivalent forms are available.

Format: Examiner required; suitable for group use; timed: 30 minutes per part

Scoring: Hand key

Cost: Specimen Set (test, key, manual) $4.00; 25 Tests $5.00

National Achievement Tests for Elementary Schools: Arithmetic and Mathematics–General Mathematics (Grades 3–8)
Robert K. Speer, Samuel Smith

1962	Psychometric Affiliates

Population: Grades 3 to 8

Purpose: Assesses students' achievement in basic arithmetic skills; used to identify strengths and weaknesses as part of an educational evaluation

Description: Multiple-item paper-pencil test covering three basic areas of arithmetic skills: speed and accuracy in computation; judgment, speed, and accuracy in comparing computations; and skill and understanding, without special reference to speed. Two equivalent forms are available.

Format: Examiner required; suitable for group use; timed: 45 minutes

Scoring: Hand key

Cost: Specimen Set (test, key, manual) $4.00; 25 Tests $5.00

National Achievement Tests for Elementary Schools: Arithmetic and Mathematics–General Mathematics (Grades 4–6)
Stanley J. Lejeune

1969	Psychometric Affiliates

Population: Grades 4 to 6

Purpose: Assesses students' achievement in general mathematics; used to identify strengths and weaknesses as part of an educational evaluation

Description: Multiple-item paper-pencil power test of student comprehension of 11 major topics in general mathematics: the numeration system; addition, subtraction, multiplication, and division; common fractions; decimal fractions and percentages; measurements; geometry; solving written problems; graphs and scale drawings; set terminology; mathematical structure; and money. Two equivalent forms are available.

Format: Examiner required; suitable for group use; untimed: approximately 2 to 3 class periods

Scoring: Hand key

Cost: Specimen Set (test, key, manual) $5.00; 25 Tests $9.00; 25 Answer Sheets $3.50

National Achievement Tests for Elementary Schools: Arithmetic and Mathematics–General Mathematics (Grades 7–9)
Harry Eisner

1962	Psychometric Affiliates

Population: Grades 7 to 9

Purpose: Assesses students' achievement in general mathematics; used to identify strengths and weaknesses as part of an educational evaluation

Description: Multiple-item paper-pencil test of students' knowledge of essential concepts, skills, and insights that should be developed in junior high school mathematics. The abilities measured are arithmetic, algebraic, and geometric concepts; applications; problem analysis; and reasoning. Two equivalent forms are available.

Format: Examiner required; suitable for group use; timed: Section 1, 10 minutes; Section 2, 15 minutes; Section 3, 27 minutes

Scoring: Hand key

Cost: Specimen Set (test, key, manual) $4.00; 25 Tests $9.00

Slosson-Diagnostic Math Screener (S-DMS)
Bradley T. Erford, Rita R. Boykin

1996	Slosson Educational Publications, Inc.

Population: Ages 6 to 13 years

Purpose: Assesses children's mathematical skills

Description: Test assesses conceptual development, problem solving, and computation skills in five grade ranges. Provides an overall view for entire class when group scored. Used for screening at-risk students, checking new school entrants, or making eligibility assessments. Criterion or norm-referenced curriculum evaluation.

Format: Examiner required; suitable for group use; untimed: 30 to 50 minutes

Scoring: Examiner evaluated

Cost: Complete Multilevel Kit $168.00

Comprehensive

Arithmetic Skills Assessment Test
Howard Behrns

1995	Educational Activities, Inc.

Population: Children to adults

Purpose: Provides profile of students' strengths and weaknesses in 119 math skills

Description: Computer-generated test measuring students' math skills, including addition, subtraction, multiplication, and division of whole numbers, fractions, and decimals. Students work out problems on worksheets and enter answers in the computer. Results may be printed or viewed on screen. Macintosh and Windows versions available. Approximate grade level is given.

Format: Computer administered; untimed

Scoring: Computer scored

Cost: CD and Worksheets $89.00

Booker Profiles in Mathematics
George Booker

2000	Australian Council for Educational Research Limited

Population: Children, adolescents

Purpose: Measures capacity to think, reason, and problem solve in mathematics

Description: The assessment reflects contemporary approaches to the development of mathematical problem solving. The instrument contains an easel of items organized in four levels of difficulty, a set of laminated blackline masters containing the protocol, and a manual containing directions for administering, recording, and interpreting the assessment items and ideas for a follow-up program.

Format: Examiner required; suitable for group use; timed: 30 minutes

Scoring: Scored with key

Cost: Contact publisher

Collis-Romberg Mathematical Problem-Solving Profiles
Kevin Collis, Thomas Romberg

1992	Australian Council for Educational Research Limited

Population: Ages 9 to 17+ years

Purpose: Assesses mathematical problem solving

Description: The test profiles assessment items in five aspects of mathematics: Algebra, Chance and Data, Measurement, Number, and Space. Suggestions for further teaching based on the student's current level of functioning are provided.

Format: Examiner required; suitable for group use; timed: 40 to 50 minutes

Scoring: Examiner evaluated

Cost: Contact publisher

Comprehensive Mathematical Abilities Test (CMAT)
Wayne P. Hresko, Paul L. Schlieve, Shelley R. Herron, Colleen Swain, Rita J. Sherbenou

2002	PRO-ED, Inc.

Population: Ages 7 through 18 years

Purpose: Measures all aspects of mathematics

Description: The CMAT has 12 subtests: Addition; Subtraction; Multiplication; Division; Problem Solving; Charts, Tables, and Graphs; Algebra; Geometry; Rational Numbers; Time; Money; and Measurement. They are combined into six composites: General Mathematics, Basic Calculations, Reasoning Core, Advanced Calculations, Practical Applications, and Overall Mathematics. The General Mathematics Composite provides a concise analysis of the two critical areas used in defining mathematical learning disabilities: Basic Calculations and Reasoning Core. These two areas are included in the federal definition of learning disabilities.

Format: Examiner required; individual administration; untimed

Scoring: Examiner evaluated; computer scoring available

Cost: Complete Kit (manual, picture book, 25 record forms, 25 each of two response books, storage box) $267.00

DART (Developmental Assessment Resource for Teachers) Mathematics
E. Recht, M. Forster, G. Masters

1998	Australian Council for Educational Research Limited

Population: Children, adolescents

Purpose: Assesses a student's level of performance in mathematics

Description: Forms A and B each contain five strands: Number, Space, Measurement, Chance and Data, and Data Sense. They are designed to be integrated into day-to-day teaching program and are aligned with outcome statements. The questions are grouped around specific stimuli related to the workings and life of the zoo.

Format: Examiner required; suitable for group use; untimed: 60 minutes each strand

Scoring: Examiner evaluated

Cost: Contact publisher

Diagnostic Screening Test: Math, Third Edition (DSTM)
Thomas D. Gnagey

1980	Slosson Educational Publications, Inc.

Population: Grades 1 to 10

Purpose: Determines a student's conceptual and computational mathematical skills

Description: Multiple-item paper–pencil test with Basic Processes Section and Specialized Section. The Basic Processes Section consists of 36 items arranged developmentally within four major areas: addition skills, subtraction skills, mul-

tiplication, and division. Each area yields a separate Grade Equivalent Score and Consolidation Index Score and scores in nine supplemental categories: process, sequencing, simple computation, complex computation, special manipulations, use of zero, decimals, simple fractions, and manipulation in fractions. The Specialized Section consists of 37 to 45 items evaluating conceptual and computational skills in five areas: money, time, percent, U.S. measurement, and metric measurement. The examiner explains the procedure, and the student completes the problems. The test is available in two alternate forms.

Format: Examiner required; suitable for group use; untimed: 5 to 20 minutes

Scoring: Hand key

Cost: Complete Kit (manual, 25 each of Forms A and B) $52.50

KeyMath-Revised/NU: A Diagnostic Inventory of Essential Mathematics-Revised-Normative Update
Austin J. Connolly

1998	American Guidance Service

Population: Ages 5 to 22 years

Purpose: Measures understanding and application of important mathematics concepts and skills

Description: Provides an accurate measurement of students' math skills with 516 items in 13 subsets. Because the test does not require reading ability, it is easy to administer to a wide range of students. The age range has been extended in the update. National Council of Teachers of Mathematics' standards are reflected. The test includes estimating, interpreting data, problem solving, and knowledge of the metric system.

Format: Examiner required; individual administration; untimed: 35 to 50 minutes depending on grade level

Scoring: Examiner interpreted; computer scoring available

Cost: Complete Form A and Form B Kit (2 easels, 25 of each record form, manual, sample report to parents, carry bag) $445.95

Progressive Achievement Test (PAT): Mathematics (Revised)
Neil Reid

1993	New Zealand Council for Educational Research

Population: Ages 8 to 14 years

Purpose: Measures mathematical achievement

Description: An educational assessment with 50 items, yielding a total score. Forms A and B for alternate years: primary, intermediate, and secondary.

Format: Examiner required; group administration; timed: 55 minutes

Scoring: Hand key

Cost: Manual $6.75; Booklets $1.80; 10 Answer Sheets $1.80; Keys $.99

Progressive Achievement Tests in Mathematics–Revised

1997	Australian Council for Educational Research Limited

Population: Years 4 through 9

Purpose: Assesses levels of achievement in mathematics

Description: Provides information to teachers about the level of achievement attained by their students in skills and understanding of mathematics. All items have been assigned to an appropriate level from the National Profiles. The features of the tests are a battery of six tests covering levels 1 through 5 of the National Profiles; tests arranged in three parallel pairs for test-retest options; reusable test booklets; multiple-choice format; and calculator- and noncalculator-use items provided.

Format: Examiner required; group administration; timed: 45 minutes

Scoring: Examiner evaluated; scoring service available

Cost: Contact publisher

Quant Q
Stephen W. Blohm

2000	California Academic Press

Population: Ages 18 years and older

Purpose: Measures quantitative reasoning

Description: The instrument (17 items) measures reasoning skills in relation to quantitatively oriented problems. They are designed to measure one's ability to think outside of the box when solving quantitative problems.

Format: Examiner required; group administration; timed and untimed

Scoring: Machine scored; scoring service available

Cost: Contact publisher

Stanford Diagnostic Mathematics Test, Fourth Edition (SDMT 4)

1995	Harcourt® Brace Educational Measurement

Population: Grades 1 through 13

Purpose: Measures competence in the basic concepts and skills that are prerequisite to success in mathematics

Description: The SDMT 4 was created to identify specific areas of difficulty for each student so that appropriate intervention may be planned. A complete revision of the previous version, the test reflects current trends in mathematics instruction. Each test provides both multiple-choice and free-response assessment formats. Students select and apply problem-solving strategies and use their reasoning and communication skills. Norm- and criterion-referenced information is provided. Calculators may be used in Grades 3.5 through 13.

Format: Examiner required; suitable for group use; timed

Scoring: Hand key; scoring service available

Cost: Examination Kit $35.50

Test of Early Mathematics Ability–Second Edition (TEMA-2)
Herbert P. Ginsburg, Arthur J. Baroody

1990	PRO-ED, Inc.

Population: Ages 3 to 8 years

Purpose: Measures the mathematics performance of children; identifies individual strengths and weaknesses

Description: Oral-response and paper–pencil 50-item test assessing mathematical abilities in two domains: informal mathematics (concepts of relative magnitude, counting, and calculation) and formal mathematics (knowledge of convention, number facts, calculation, and base-ten concepts). A picture card is used to present test items. Raw scores may be converted to standard scores, percentiles, and age equivalents. Criterion-referenced interpretation leads directly to instructional objectives.

Format: Examiner required; individual administration; untimed: 20 to 45 minutes

Scoring: Examiner evaluated

Cost: Complete Kit (manual, picture book, 50 profile/examiner record forms, assessment probes, storage box) $169.00

Test of Mathematical Abilities–Second Edition (TOMA-2)
Virginia L. Brown, Mary E. Cronin, Elizabeth McEntire

| 1994 | PRO-ED, Inc. |

Population: Grades 3 to 12

Purpose: Assesses the mathematical attitudes and aptitudes of students; used to plan and assess instructional programs in mathematics, identify students who are gifted or have learning disabilities, determine strengths and weaknesses, document progress, and conduct research

Description: Five paper-pencil subtests assess knowledge, mastery, and attitudes in two major skill areas: story problems (17 items) and computation (25 items). In addition to measuring the student's abilities, the TOMA-2 assesses the following broad diagnostic areas: expressed attitudes toward mathematics (15 items) and understanding of vocabulary as applied to mathematics (20 items). Normative information related to age, as well as graded mastery expectations for the "400" basic number facts, is provided. Scores differentiate diagnostically between students who have problems in mathematics and those who do not.

Format: Examiner required; suitable for group use; untimed: 60 to 90 minutes

Scoring: Examiner evaluated

Cost: Complete Kit (manual, 25 profile/record forms, storage box) $89.00

Specific

Diagnostic Test for Pre-Algebra Math (DT-PAM)

| 1992 | Applied Personnel Research |

Population: Grades 7 through 12

Purpose: Identifies specific areas of weakness

Description: Objective multiple-choice paper-pencil test that produces diagnostic scores in 21 areas, including whole numbers, common fractions, signed numbers, word problems, and reading tables and graphs. Provides diagnostic scores for individual students, as well as class and school summaries.

Format: Examiner required; individual or group administration; timed: 45 minutes

Scoring: Scoring service provided; turnaround 1 week

Cost: Specimen Set (test, sample test report, test manual) $55.00

Iowa Algebra Aptitude Test™ (IAAT™)
Harold L. Schoen, Timothy N. Ansley, H. D. Hoover, Beverly S. Rich, Sheila I. Barron, Robert A. Bye

| 1993 | Riverside Publishing Company |

Population: Grades 7 and 8; suitable for high school or junior college testing

Purpose: Assesses student readiness for Algebra 1

Description: Mathematics educators have long recognized that Algebra 1 classes tend to have high student failure rates. That failure creates frustration and lost time for both teacher and students. The IAAT can promote student success in algebra classes by helping educators more accurately determine which students should be placed into Algebra 1 or into prealgebra courses. The content of the IAAT has been aligned with current recommendations of the National Council of Teachers of Mathematics, both for prealgebra and algebra curricula and for testing.

Format: Examiner required; group administration; untimed: 50 minutes

Scoring: Examiner evaluated; machine scoring available

Cost: Test Booklets (25, includes Directions for Administration) $85.25 per level; 25 Self-Scoring Answer Sheets $38.50

National Achievement Tests for Arithmetic and Mathematics—Algebra Test for Engineering and Science
A. B. Lonski

| 1973 | Psychometric Affiliates |

Population: Adolescents, adults

Purpose: Assesses achievement in intermediate algebra; used for screening students planning to register in an engineering college or technical school

Description: Paper-pencil test of algebra knowledge. Items represent mistakes made in algebra by college freshman who failed the subject in engineering and science courses. The test represents minimum essentials for entry into regular freshman mathematics.

Format: Examiner required; suitable for group use; untimed

Scoring: Hand key

Cost: Specimen Set (test, key, manual) $4.00; 25 Tests $17.50; 25 Answer Sheets $3.00

National Achievement Tests for Arithmetic and Mathematics— First Year Algebra Test
Ray Webb, Julius H. Hlavaty

| 1962 | Psychometric Affiliates |

Population: Adolescents

Purpose: Assesses achievement in first-year algebra; used to identify strengths and weaknesses as part of an educational evaluation

Description: Paper-pencil test measuring students' knowledge of first-year algebra. Two equivalent forms are available.

Format: Examiner required; suitable for group use; timed: 40 minutes

Scoring: Hand key

Cost: Specimen Set (test, key, manual) $4.40; 25 Tests $6.00; 25 Answer Sheets $4.50

National Achievement Tests for Arithmetic and Mathematics— Plane Geometry, Solid Geometry, and Plane Trigonometry Tests
Ray Webb, Julius H. Hlavaty

| 1970 | Psychometric Affiliates |

Population: Adolescents

Purpose: Assesses achievement in geometry and trigonometry; used to identify strengths and weaknesses as part of an educational evaluation

Description: Three paper-pencil tests measuring essential concepts, skills, and insight in three content areas: plane geometry, solid geometry, and plane trigonometry. Two equivalent forms are available.

Format: Examiner required; suitable for group use; timed: 40 minutes

Scoring: Hand key

Cost: Specimen Set (test, key, manual) $4.00; 25 Tests $8.75; 25 Answer Sheets $3.50

Orleans-Hanna Algebra Prognosis Test–Third Edition
Gerald S. Hanna

| 1998 | Harcourt® Brace Educational Measurement |

Population: Grades 7 through 11

Purpose: Determines algebra readiness

Description: This edition retains the reliability of the previous edition, but aligns with the National Council of Teachers of Mathematics' Curriculum and Evaluation Standards for School Mathematics. More problem-solving items are included. The items cover algebraic topics such as exponents, integers, and algebraic expressions. A new, open design makes it easy for students to proceed through the test.

Format: Examiner required; suitable for group use; timed: 40 minutes

Scoring: Hand key; may be machine scored

Cost: 25 Test Booklets and Directions $71.50; 25 Hand-Scorable Answer Sheets $29.00

TerraNova Algebra

| 2000 | CTB/McGraw-Hill |

Population: Grades 7 to 12

Purpose: Measures end-of-course achievement in algebra

Description: Students use algebraic processes to manipulate expressions and model mathematical situations. They demonstrate the ability to recognize, interpret, solve, and graph linear and basic quadratic equations and to apply algebraic formulas in geometric contexts.

Format: Examiner required; suitable for group use; timed: 45 minutes

Scoring: Hand key; machine scored; scoring service available

Cost: $3.00 per student for materials; $1.70 for scoring

Motor Skills

Bruininks-Oseretsky Test of Motor Proficiency
Robert H. Bruininks

| 1978 | American Guidance Service |

Population: Ages 4 years 6 months to 14 years 6 months

Purpose: Provides a comprehensive picture of a child's motor development

Description: The test provides a comprehensive index of motor proficiency as well as differentiated measures of gross and fine motor skills. The Complete Battery contains eight subtests comprising 46 separate items. The Short Form consists of 14 items from the Complete Battery and provides a quick, brief survey. One score provides an index of general motor proficiency. The Short Form may be used to test large numbers of children in a limited amount of time.

Format: Examiner required; individual administration; Complete Battery 45 to 60 minutes, Short Form 15 to 20 minutes

Scoring: Examiner evaluated

Cost: Test Kit (manual; 25 each of student booklets, individual record forms for Complete Battery and Short Form; sample of alternate Short Form; testing equipment; canvas carry bag) $524.95

Functional Fitness Assessment for Adults over 60 Years
Wayne H. Osness, Marlene Adrian, Bruce Clark, Werner Hoeger, Diane Raab, Robert Wiswell

| 1996 | American Association for Active Lifestyles and Fitness |

Population: Ages 60 years and older

Purpose: Assesses physical well-being

Description: Assesses six items: flexibility, agility, strength, endurance, balance, and coordination. Results are given as means and standard deviations of raw scores in 5-year intervals from ages 60 to 90, for males and females. A training video is available.

Format: Examiner required; individual administration

Scoring: Examiner evaluated

Cost: $12.00

Functional Writing Assessment

| 1995 | Comprehensive Adult Student Assessment System (CASAS) |

Population: Adolescents, adults; native and nonnative speakers of English

Purpose: Assesses learners' general writing level and provides diagnostic information about which writing skills the learner needs to target; appropriate for low literacy levels

Description: Three writing tasks: Process Task, Picture Task, and Form Task. Students describe the process or picture, or fill out the form. Students choose writing prompt and write in test booklet. Training is required for examiners.

Format: Examiner required; individual or group administration; untimed

Scoring: Writing samples are scored analytically or holistically using standardized detailed rubrics and annotated scoring anchors.

Cost: Contact publisher

Jordan Left-Right Reversal Test-Revised (JLRRT)
Brian T. Jordan

| 1990 | Academic Therapy Publications |

Population: Ages 5 through 12 years

Purpose: Assesses the extent to which a child reverses letters, numbers, and words

Description: Multiple-item paper-pencil examination on two levels. Level I measures reversals of letters, numerals, and words. Level II reveals reversed lowercase letters within words and whole-word reversals within sentences. The manual includes detailed remediation exercises for reversal problems. The Laterality Checklist is an informal survey that determines whether a student prefers use of one side of his or her body, and the Remedial Checklist provides a list of activities that can be used to develop laterality. Norm-referenced instrument provides developmental age and percentile ranks.

Format: Examiner required; individual and group administration; untimed: 20 minutes

Scoring: Examiner administered and interpreted

Cost: Test Kit (manual, protocols, and checklists in vinyl folder) $90.00

Occupational Performance History Interview II (OPHI-II)

Gary Kielhofner, Trudy Mallinson,
Carrie Crawford, Meika Nowak,
Matt Rigby, Alexis Henry, Deborah Walens

Date not provided	Model of Human Occupation Clearinghouse

Population: Adults

Purpose: Explores occupational life history

Description: A semistructured interview in the areas of work, leisure, and daily life activities. Enhances the therapeutic relationship by facilitating rapport with the client. Flexible interview formats are designed for both novice and experienced interviewers.

Format: Examiner required; individual administration; untimed

Scoring: Examiner evaluated

Cost: $40.00

Peabody Developmental Motor Scales–Second Edition (PDMS-2)

M. Rhonda Folio, Rebecca R. Fewell

2000	PRO-ED, Inc.

Population: Birth through 5 years

Purpose: Assesses students' thinking and process skills, and problem-solving strategies

Description: An early childhood motor development program that provides both in-depth assessment and training or remediation of gross and fine motor skills in six subtests: reflexes, stationary, locomotion, object manipulation, grasping, and visual-motor integration. The normative sample consisted of 2,003 persons residing in 46 states. The PDMS-2 can be used by an occupational therapist, physical therapist, diagnostician, early intervention specialist, adapted physical education teacher, and psychologist. There are three composite scores: Gross Motor Quotient, Fine Motor Quotient, and Total Motor Quotient. The Illustrated Guide to Item Administration provides detailed descriptions of every item in the PDMS-2. The Examiner Record Booklets contain all of the items to be given to the child and allow the examiner to use the same form for four administrations to one child. The Peabody Motor Activities Program is the instruction and treatment program. It contains units organized developmentally by skill area. The Peabody Motor Development Chart provides a convenient reference for the motor skills measured and the ages at which 50% of the normative sample performed the skill.

Format: Examiner required; individual administration; untimed: 20 to 30 minutes

Scoring: Examiner evaluated; computer scoring program available for Windows

Cost: Complete Kit (manual, guide to item administration, 25 profile/summary forms, 25 examiner record booklets, Peabody Motor Activities Program Manual, Peabody Motor Development chart, manipulatives, storage box) $389.00

Test of Gross Motor Development–Second Edition (TGMD-2)

Dale A. Ulrich

2000	PRO-ED, Inc.

Population: Ages 3 through 10

Purpose: Assesses common motor skills of children; used for educational planning and research and to evaluate existing special education programs

Description: Multiple-item task-performance test consists of two subtests. The Locomotor Skills subtest measures the run, gallop, hop, horizontal jump, and slide. The Object Control Skills subtest measures striking of a stationary ball, stationary dribble, catch, kick, overhand throw, and underhand roll. Test findings are reported in terms of subtest standard scores, percentiles, and a composite quotient that represents total gross motor development performance.

Format: Examiner required; individual administration; untimed: 15 minutes

Scoring: Examiner evaluated

Cost: Complete Kit (manual, 50 protocols, storage box) $96.00

VCWS 204—Fine Finger Dexterity

1993	Valpar International Corporation

Population: Ages 13 years and older

Purpose: Assesses worker qualification to profile factors for job or curricula placement, and career planning

Description: Criterion-referenced test consisting of demonstrated performance of dominant and nondominant fine finger dexterity. The test yields Methods-Time Measurement standard and percentile scores. Materials include wiring box and tweezers. This test is suitable for individuals with hearing, physical, and mental impairments. Signing for hearing impairment is necessary.

Format: Examiner required; individual administration; timed: 10 to 15 minutes

Scoring: Examiner evaluated

Cost: $725.00

Work Environment Impact Scale (WEIS)
Renee Moore-Corner, Linda Olson, Gary Kielhofner

Date not provided	Model of Human Occupation Clearinghouse

Population: Adults

Purpose: Measures impact on work of injury or illness

Description: Interview conducted with an injured worker who is having difficulty on the job or whose work has been interrupted by injury or illness. Shows environmental barriers and issues with supervisors and coworkers.

Format: Examiner required; individual administration; untimed

Scoring: Examiner evaluated

Cost: Manual $30.00; Manual and Video $44.00

Worker Role Interview (WRI)
Craig Velozo, Gary Kielhofner, Gail Fisher

Date not provided	Model of Human Occupation Clearinghouse

Population: Adults

Purpose: Examines the effects of injury on the client

Description: Used to evaluate injured workers in the areas of personal causation, values, interests, roles, habits, and perception of environmental supports. Looks at life outside work, past and present work experience, and plans for return to work.

Format: Examiner required; individual administration; untimed

Scoring: Examiner evaluated

Cost: Manual $30.00; Manual and Video $44.00

Reading, Language Arts, and English

Elementary

An Observation Survey: Of Early Literacy Achievement
Marie M. Clay

1985	Heinemann

Population: Grades K to 2

Purpose: Assesses reading skills; used for diagnosing individual reading deficiencies

Description: Multiple-item test for observing and screening the emergent reading skills of children in Grades 1 and 2. Materials include a set of two test booklets, a guide, and a textbook, The Patterning of Complex Behavior: Sand and Stones. Another book, The Early Detection of Reading Difficulties, presents the theoretical background, administration details, and scoring interpretation of the tests.

Format: Examiner required; suitable for group use; untimed

Scoring: Hand key

Cost: $19.50

Burt Word Reading Test– New Zealand Revision
Alison Gilmore, Cedric Croft, Neil Reid

1981	New Zealand Council for Education Research

Population: Ages 6 to 13 years

Purpose: Measures word recognition

Description: Assessment of reading skills, with a total of 110 items. Gives total score.

Format: Examiner required; individual administration; timed: 30 minutes

Scoring: Examiner evaluated

Cost: Manual $6.30; Card $.99; 20 Forms $3.60

Diagnostic Reading Scales, Revised Edition (DRS)
George D. Spache

1982	CTB/McGraw-Hill

Population: Children

Purpose: Identifies a student's reading strengths and weaknesses; used by educators to determine placement and to prescribe instruction

Description: Multiple-item reading skills test consisting of a series of graduated scales containing 3 word-recognition lists, 22 reading sections, and 12 phonics and word analysis tests.

Format: Examiner required; individual administration; timed: 1 hour

Scoring: Examiner evaluated

Cost: Specimen Set (test book, record book, manual, test reviewer's guide) $34.65

Durrell Analysis of Reading Difficulty: Third Edition (DARD)
Donald D. Durrell, Jane H. Catterson

1980   Harcourt® Brace Educational Measurement

Population: Grades 1 through 6

Purpose: Assesses reading behavior; used for diagnosis, measurement of prereading skills, and planning remedial programs

Description: Multiple-item series of tests and situations measuring 10 reading abilities: oral reading, silent reading, listening comprehension, listening vocabulary, word recognition/word analysis, spelling, auditory analysis of words and word elements, pronunciation of word elements, visual memory of words, and prereading phonics abilities. Supplementary paragraphs for oral and silent reading are provided for supplementary testing or retesting. Materials include a spiral-bound booklet containing items to be read and a tachistoscope with accompanying test card.

Format: Examiner required; individual administration; untimed: 30 to 45 minutes

Scoring: Examiner evaluated

Cost: Examiner's Kit (5 record booklets, tachistoscope and test card, reading booklet, manual) $129.00

Graded Nonword Reading Test
Margaret Snowling, Susan Stothard, Janet McLean

1996   Thames Valley Test Company, Ltd.

Population: Ages 5 to 11

Purpose: Assesses whether a child's nonword reading score is at the expected level for his or her age; used in the diagnosis of developmental dyslexia

Description: This test has been developed on the basis of some 20 years of research with children who have reading difficulties. A recent review of more than 25 studies of nonword reading in children with dyslexia points to the importance of the assessment of these skills. This test

has high internal and test–retest reliability, and it correlates well with performance on other standardized reading tests. Five practice items and 20 nonwords are graded in difficulty. Children who fail to reach criterion on the practice items are not tested further.

Format: Individual administration; untimed: 15 minutes

Scoring: Examiner evaluated

Cost: $97.00

Language Arts Assessment Portfolio (LAAP)
Bjorn Karlsen

1992   American Guidance Service

Population: Grades 1 through 6

Purpose: Provides an alternative assessment of language arts (reading, writing, listening, speaking)

Description: Alternative classroom assessment system for the language arts that makes use of both portfolio and performance-based assessment techniques. The Evaluation Booklet is used by the teacher to observe and rate students' performance in language arts. The Self-Evaluation Booklet is used by the student to help develop self-awareness of language arts skills. Portfolio folders and blackline masters are used together to assemble and evaluate samples of the student's work. Available in three Levels for Grade 1, Grades 2 and 3, and Grades 4 to 6.

Format: Individual administration; untimed

Scoring: For each language arts area, both the Self-Evaluation Booklet and the Evaluation Booklet list specific skills, which the student and teacher use as the basis of their ratings.

Cost: Complete Kit: Level I $104.95; Level II $104.95; Level III $104.95

Phonemic-Awareness Skills Screening (PASS)
Linda Crumrine, Helen Lonegan

2000   PRO-ED, Inc.

Population: Grades 1 and 2

Purpose: Identifies specific weaknesses in phonological processing ability

Description: The PASS includes eight sections: Rhyme, Sentence Segmentation, Blending, Syllable Segmentation, Deletion, Phoneme Isolation, Phoneme Segmentation, and Phoneme Substitution.

Format: Examiner required; individual administration; untimed: 15 minutes

Scoring: Examiner evaluated

Cost: Complete Kit (manual, 25 record forms) $29.00

Pre-Literacy Skills Screening (PLSS)

Linda Crumrine, Helen Lonegan

| 1999 | PRO-ED, Inc. |

Population: Kindergarten

Purpose: Identifies incoming kindergarten children who may be at risk for literacy failure

Description: The PLSS incudes nine subtests: Rhyme, Sentence Repetition, Naming, Blending, Sentence Segmentation, Letter Naming, Syllable Segmentation, Deletion, and Multisyllabic Word Repetition.

Format: Examiner required; individual administration; untimed: 15 minutes

Scoring: Examiner evaluated

Cost: Complete Kit (manual, picture book, 25 record forms) $49.00

Predictive Reading Profile (PRP)

Jane Flynn

| 2001 | LinguiSystems, Inc. |

Population: Ages 5 and 6 years

Purpose: Identifies children at risk of reading failure and identifies special instructional needs in literacy

Description: The PRP has six subtests—Syllable-Sound Counting (20 items), Sound Recognition (30 items), Visual Matching (20 items), Alphabet-Word (30 items), Vocabulary (26 items), and Syntax (26 items)—and two optional subtests—Story Writing and Phonemic Segmentation. Results include individual subtest scores, Early Achievement Cluster, Language Cluster, and Individual and Group Profiles.

Format: Examiner required; individual or group administration; untimed

Scoring: Examiner evaluated; computer scoring available

Cost: $89.95

Process Assessment of the Learner™ (PAL™): Test Battery for Reading and Writing

Virginia Wise Beringer

| 2000 | The Psychological Corporation |

Population: Grades K through 6

Purpose: Examines processes underlying reading and writing skills

Description: The PAL screens by identifying students at risk, monitors by tracking progress, and diagnoses by evaluating the nature of reading- and writing-related processing problems. The subtests are developmentally appropriate, and the examiner may choose which subtests to administer; the test does not need to be given in its entirety. The PAL was standardized with the Wechsler Individual Achievement Test-Second Edition, providing an empirically based sequence of decision making. The battery includes measures of phonological processing; orthography coding; rapid automatized naming; and integration of listening, note taking, and summary writing skills.

Format: Examiner required; individual administration; untimed

Scoring: Examiner evaluated

Cost: Complete Kit (manual, stimulus booklets, 25 each of record forms and response forms, word card, audiocassette, manipulatives, bag) $275.00

Roswell-Chall Screening Tests

Florence G. Roswell, Jeanne S. Chall

| Date not provided | Educators Publishing Service, Inc. |

Population: Grades K to 4

Purpose: Evaluates skills necessary for success in reading

Description: The Auditory Blending Test assesses phonemic awareness by having the student blend sounds to form words presented orally. The Diagnostic Reading Test measures basic word analysis and word recognition skills at approximately first- through fourth-grade levels. The test yields both qualitative and quantitative results. For test-retest purposes, Forms A and B are equivalent.

Format: Examiner required; individual administration; untimed

Scoring: Examiner evaluated

Cost: Each test $15.25 for 1 to 5 forms; Auditory Manual $5.45; Diagnostic Manual $6.20

Signposts Early Literacy Battery

| 2000 | Touchstone Applied Science Associates, Inc. |

Population: Ages 5 to 8 years

Purpose: Measures language arts competency

(reading and prereading), helps to design instruction, and evaluates progress

Description: A total of 68 to 88 items, depending on level, with four categories (Speaking, Listening, Reading, and Writing) that measure a number of different elements of emerging literacy. Pre-DRP and DRP (Degrees of Reading Power) subscores, battery scale score, and percentile rank scores are provided. Materials used: test booklets and administration manuals. Forms available: SA-1, SA-2, SA-3, SA-4, and SA-5.

Format: Examiner required; suitable for group use; untimed: 110 to 165 minutes

Scoring: Hand key

Cost: 25 Booklets $72.00; Scoring Key $10.00

Signposts Pre-DRP Test

2000	Touchstone Applied Science Associates, Inc.

Population: Ages 5 to 8 years

Purpose: Measures reading ability of emerging and beginning readers, monitors progress, and matches ability with appropriate reading materials

Description: A total of 28 to 32 items depending on level. Yields Pre-DRP (Degrees of Reading Power) scale score and percentile rank. Materials used: test booklets and administration manual. Forms available: J-P2, K-P2, J-P3, K-P3, J-P4, and K-P4.

Format: Examiner required; suitable for group use; untimed: 45 to 50 minutes

Scoring: Hand Key

Cost: 25 Booklets $47.50; Scoring Key $10.00

STAR Supplementary Test of Achievement in Reading
Warwick B. Elley

2000	New Zealand Council for Educational Research

Population: Ages 9 to 11 years

Purpose: Measures reading achievement

Description: Educational application intended for school children. Four subtests: Word Recognition (10 items), Sentence Comprehension (10 items), Paragraph Comprehension (20 items), and Vocabulary Range (10 items). Yields scores on Forms A and B, and a total score. Materials include Forms A and B, manual, test/answer booklet, and answer key.

Format: Examiner required; group or individual administration; timed: 30 minutes

Scoring: Hand key

Cost: Manual $18.00; Keys $9.00; 10 Booklets $9.90

Test of Children's Language (TOCL)
Edna Barenbaum, Phyllis Newcomer

1996	PRO-ED, Inc.

Population: Ages 5 through 8

Purpose: Identifies students' specific strengths and weaknesses in language components and recognizes students who are at risk for failure in reading and writing; helps with documentation of students' progress as a consequence of early intervention

Description: Unit 1 uses a storybook format featuring the antics of animal characters to assess children's ability in spoken language and reading. In Unit 2, students undertake a series of writing tasks that range from basic writing skills to creative writing. Materials in the TOCL are familiar to primary-level classrooms. Test results provide the teacher with authentic information about specific students' performances in all aspects of language, permit comparisons with national norms, and yield useful guidelines for further assessment and instruction. The skills included in Unit 1 of the TOCL include aspects of spoken language known to be correlates of reading and writing, including semantics, syntax, and listening comprehension, as well as three other skills related to reading: knowledge about print, phonological awareness, and letter knowledge. Additional items in this section assess the two major components of reading: word recognition and reading comprehension. Unit 2 is divided into three parts: Part A measures various types of writing ability, Part B requires the children to write the story they have read previously, and Part C requires children to write an original story about the animal characters in the storybook.

Format: Individual administration; untimed: 30 to 40 minutes

Scoring: Examiner evaluated

Cost: Complete Kit (manual, "A Visit with Mr. Turtle" storybook, story picture sheet, 25 student workbooks, 25 profile/examiner record forms, storage box) $144.00

Test of Early Reading Ability–Third Edition (TERA–3)
D. Kim Reid, Wayne P. Hresko, Donald D. Hammill

2001	PRO-ED, Inc.

Population: Ages 3 years 6 months to 8 years 6 months

Purpose: Measures mastery of early developing reading skills

Description: Three subtests: Alphabet (measuring knowledge of the alphabet and its uses), Conventions (measuring knowledge of the conventions of print), and Meaning (measuring knowledge of the construction of meaning from print). Standard scores are provided for each subtest. An overall Reading Quotient is computed using all three subtest scores. New items have been added to make the test more reliable and valid for the upper and lower ages covered by the test. All pictures have been drawn in color to present a more appealing look to children. All logos and labels are included.

Format: Examiner required; individual administration; untimed: 30 minutes

Scoring: Examiner evaluated

Cost: Complete Kit (manual, picture books, 25 each of Form A and Form B profile/examiner record forms, storage box) $229.00

Test of Early Written Language– Second Edition (TEWL-2)
Wayne P. Hresko, Shelley R. Herron, Pamela K. Peak

| 1996 | PRO-ED, Inc. |

Population: Ages 3 through 10

Purpose: Measures the emerging written language skills of young children; used to identify students with mild impairments and to document student growth and program effectiveness

Description: Multiple-item paper–pencil test covering areas with a direct relationship to a young child's school-related activities, including transcription, conventions of print, communication, creative expression, and record keeping. Picture cards are used to prompt writing samples. The test yields standard scores and percentiles, which can be used with other cognitive and academic measures to identify intraindividual abilities. The scores obtained are Global Writing Quotient, Basic Writing Quotient, and Contextual Writing Quotient.

Format: Examiner required; individual administration; untimed: 30 to 45 minutes

Scoring: Examiner evaluated

Cost: Complete Kit (manual, 10 each of Forms A and B, 10 each of student workbooks Forms A and B, storage box) $159.00

Test of Handwriting Skills (THS)
Morrison F. Gardner

| 1998 | Psychological and Educational Publications, Inc. |

Population: Ages 5 to 11 years

Purpose: Assesses handwriting skills in manuscript or cursive

Description: The THS measures neurosensory integration ability. Manuscript or cursive, upper- and lowercase forms are assessed through the following tasks: writing letters of the alphabet in alphabetical sequence from memory; writing letters of the alphabet out of alphabetical order from dictation; writing eight numerals out of numerical order from dictation; copying 12 uppercase and 10 lowercase letters; copying six words and two sentences; and writing six words from dictation.

Format: Examiner required; individual administration; untimed: 30 to 40 minutes

Scoring: Examiner evaluated

Cost: Complete Test (manual, 15 each of cursive and manuscript booklets, 30 record forms) $89.95

Test of Oral Reading and Comprehension Skills (TORCS)
Morrison F. Gardner

| Date not provided | Psychological and Educational Publications, Inc. |

Population: Ages 5 to 15 years

Purpose: Measures reading skills

Description: Measures what the child reads or what is read to the child to determine how well a child will perform other academic subjects. Words, phrases, and sentences are arranged developmentally. Information on reliability and validity is well documented in the manual.

Format: Examiner required; individual administration; untimed: 20 minutes

Scoring: Examiner evaluated

Cost: Complete Kit (manual, 15 test booklets, oral reading stories booklet) $39.95

Test of Silent Reading Skills (TSRS)
Morrison F. Gardner

| Date not provided | Psychological and Educational Publications, Inc. |

Population: Ages 7 to 14 years

Purpose: Measures ability to gain information from silent reading

Description: Measures not only story comprehension and paragraph comprehension, but also word meaning, word identification, and speed of reading. All six stories and all six paragraphs are followed by multiple-choice questions. A Spanish version is available.

Format: Examiner required; individual or group administration; untimed: 25 to 35 minutes

Scoring: Examiner evaluated

Cost: Complete Kit (manual, 25 test booklets, template, reading card) $89.95

High School and College

Collegiate Assessment of Academic Progress (CAAP) Reading Test

2001	ACT, Inc.

Population: Ages 17 years and older

Purpose: Assesses reading skills

Description: Paper-pencil 36-item multiple-choice test with two categories: Referring and Reasoning. A test booklet, answer sheet, and pencil are used. May be used for persons with visual, physical, hearing, and mental impairments.

Format: Examiner required; suitable for group use; timed: 40 minutes

Scoring: Machine scored; test scoring service available

Cost: $10.75

Collegiate Assessment of Academic Progress (CAAP) Writing Essay Test

2001	ACT, Inc.

Population: Ages 17 years and older

Purpose: Assesses writing skills

Description: Paper-pencil essay test. A test booklet, answer sheet, and pencil are used. May be used for persons with visual, physical, hearing, and mental impairments.

Format: Examiner required; suitable for group use; timed: 40 minutes

Scoring: Examiner evaluated; test scoring service available

Cost: $10.75

Collegiate Assessment of Academic Progress (CAAP) Writing Skills Test

2001	ACT, Inc.

Population: Ages 17 years and older

Purpose: Assesses English usage/mechanics and rhetorical skills

Description: Paper-pencil 72-item multiple-choice test with the following categories: Usage/ Mechanical and Rhetorical Skills. Two subscores are yielded. A test booklet, answer sheet, and pencil are used. May be used for persons with visual, physical, hearing, and mental impairments.

Format: Examiner required; suitable for group use; timed: 40 minutes

Scoring: Machine scored; test scoring service available

Cost: $10.75

English Language Understanding Test (ELT)
Geoff Williams

2000	Test Agency, Limited

Population: Ages 16 years and older

Purpose: Measures an individual's level of competence in, understanding of, and ability to work effectively with the English language

Description: The test consists of two short sections. In part one the candidate chooses, from a selection of four words, the one word that best fits the meaning of the text. This part is primarily word knowledge but also requires a basic understanding of grammar in looking at contextual cues. Part two is more concerned with accuracy and understanding. The examinee is required to read a passage of text and find the errors, which can be spelling, punctuation, grammar, or the use of inappropriate words. In addition, the topic of the text is unlikely to be familiar to the candidates, and therefore the ability to grasp new topics can also be assessed.

Format: Examiner required; individual administration; timed: 14 minutes

Scoring: Hand key; test scoring service available

Cost: Contact publisher

National Achievement Tests: English, Reading, Literature, and Vocabulary Tests—American Literacy Test
Andrew Kobal

1962	Psychometric Affiliates

Population: Adults

Purpose: Assesses literacy in adults; used for detecting functional illiteracy

Description: Paper–pencil 50-item test measuring vocabulary or depth of literacy. Items require knowledge of approximate synonyms. The test discriminates degrees of literacy from illiterate to highly sophisticated.

Format: Examiner required; suitable for group use; timed: 4 minutes

Scoring: Hand key

Cost: Specimen Set (test, manual, key) $4.00; 25 Scales $5.00

National Achievement Tests: English, Reading, Literature, and Vocabulary Tests—College English for High School and College

A. C. Jordon

1961	Psychometric Affiliates

Population: Grades 10 and above

Purpose: Assesses English achievement of high school and college students; used for evaluating prospective college students

Description: Multiple-item paper–pencil test measuring a range of English skills, including the ability to use correct capitalization, punctuate correctly, use proper syntax, determine subject–verb agreement, vary sentence structure, use modifiers correctly, and apply language principles. Two equivalent forms are available.

Format: Examiner required; suitable for group use; timed: 45 minutes

Scoring: Hand key

Cost: Specimen Set (test, manual, key) $4.00; 25 Tests $8.75

Nelson-Denny Reading Test: Forms G and H

James I. Brown, Vivian Vick Fishco, Gerald S. Hanna

1993	Riverside Publishing Company

Population: Grades 9 through adult

Purpose: Assesses student achievement and progress in vocabulary, comprehension, and reading rate

Description: Part I (Vocabulary) is a 15-minute timed test; Part II (Comprehension and Rate) is a 20-minute test. The vocabulary section focuses on words students need for success in today's classroom, and the comprehension passages are drawn from widely used current high school and college texts.

Format: Examiner required; suitable for group use; untimed: 35 minutes

Scoring: Hand key; may be machine scored

Cost: Contact publisher

PSB Reading Comprehension Examination

1993	Psychological Services Bureau, Inc.

Population: Health occupations students

Purpose: Measures an individual's ability to understand material read; used to identify students in the health professions who need counseling or remedial assistance

Description: Multiple-item paper–pencil or electronic test sampling essential functional elements of reading comprehension. It is specifically designed for secondary, postsecondary, and professional programs and may be used as an adjunct to PSB tests in practical nursing, health occupations, and nursing.

Format: Examiner required; suitable for group use; timed: 60 minutes

Scoring: Machine and electronically scored

Cost: Reusable Test Booklets $10.00; Answer Sheets (scoring and reporting service) $10.00; Electronic Version $15.00

Multiage

American Literacy Profile Scales

Patrick Griffin, Patricia Smith, Lois Burrill

1995	Heinemann

Population: Primary to middle school students

Purpose: Describes students' accumulation of literacy related to behaviors and attributes; provides a framework for authentic assessment

Description: The scales provide a manageable way of observing, interpreting, and recording children's progress. They merge assessment and teaching to map indicators of progress in nine levels, from primary to middle school. The instruments were developed with educators in Australia and the United States.

Format: Examiner required; individual administration; untimed

Scoring: Examiner interpretation

Cost: $34.00

Bench Mark Measures
Aylett Cox

| 1986 | Educators Publishing Service, Inc. |

Population: Children, adolescents

Purpose: Assesses a student's general phonic knowledge, including reading, alphabet and dictionary skills, handwriting, and spelling, as a means of diagnosing particular deficiencies and to gauge progress during remediation

Description: Three paper–pencil verbal tests are arranged in sequence to cover four areas of remedial language: alphabet and dictionary skills, reading, handwriting, and spelling. The alphabet and reading sections must be administered individually, but the handwriting and spelling schedules may be administered to groups. A Guide to Bench Mark Measures contains testing, scoring, and interpretation information. Designed for use with the Alphabetic Phonics curriculum, but can be used independently.

Format: Examiner required; individual and group (last two sections) administration; 30 minutes to 1 hour for each of the four areas

Scoring: Examiner interpretation

Cost: $64.40

Classroom Reading Inventory, Ninth Edition
Nicholas J. Silvaroli, Warren H. Wheelock

| 2001 | McGraw-Hill Companies |

Population: All school ages

Purpose: Measures reading recognition and comprehension to help identify students' reading problems

Description: Informal reading inventory for in-service and preservice teachers who have little or no experience with informal reading inventories. Form A follows a subskills format, and Form B follows a reader response format designed around the predicting and retelling of stories. Both forms include a pretest and a posttest. Eighty percent of the stories used in the ninth edition are new. Form C, available from McGraw-Hill College Custom Publishing, targets high school and adult readers.

Format: Examiner required; individual administration; untimed: 15 minutes

Scoring: Examiner evaluated

Cost: Contact publisher

CTB Writing Assessment System®

| 1993 | CTB/McGraw-Hill |

Population: Grades 2 to 12

Purpose: Assesses reading-related and independent writing skills

Description: Multiple-item paper–pencil essay test used independently or combined with results from the California Achievement Test, Fifth Edition. The test offers two kinds of writing assignments or prompts: independent and reading related. Independent prompts test writing ability independent of the ability to comprehend a reading passage. Reading-related prompts combine reading comprehension with writing tasks to reflect the whole-language instructional approach. Writing tasks elicit one of the following types of writing: personal expression (narrative or descriptive), informative, or persuasive. The assessment has four levels ranging from Grades 2 through 12.

Format: Examiner required; suitable for group use; timed

Scoring: Examiner evaluated; scoring service available

Cost: 30 Tests and Scoring Service $33.80 per writing type

DART (Developmental Assessment Resource for Teachers) English
W. Bodey, L. Darkin, M. Forster, G. Masters

| 1997 | Australian Council for Educational Research Limited |

Population: Levels 1 to 5

Purpose: Assesses students' level of performance in terms of skills and understanding

Description: The tests contain five strands: viewing, reading, listening, speaking, and writing. DART activities can be used as the basis for a classroom language unit. Descriptive and Diagnostic reports are provided.

Format: Examiner required; suitable for group use; untimed

Scoring: Examiner evaluated

Cost: Contact publisher

Degrees of Reading Power® (DRP)

| 2000 | Touchstone Applied Science Associates, Inc. |

Population: Grades 1 through 12+, college

Purpose: Assesses reading comprehension of students; used to identify and place students in reading programs, assess reading goals and standards, relate reading ability to appropriate reading materials, and make admission decisions

Description: Multiple-item multiple-choice text-referenced paper–pencil test in which students read a series of nonfiction prose passages, each with seven deleted words. Students supply the missing word from among five choices provided for each deletion. The passages progress from easy to difficult. The test yields six scores: raw score, independent level score (indicates the difficulty of books the student can read with a 90% chance of understanding the material), three instructional level scores (70%, 75%, and 80% chance of student comprehending materials), and frustration level score (indicates probability of comprehension of 50% or less). Percentile ranks and NCEs are available for Grades 1 through 12. The test is available in two alternate series, J and K, for Grades 1 through 12. Both Primary Forms (machine scorable) and Standard Forms (reusable) are available for the various grades.

Format: Examiner required; suitable for group use; untimed: about one class period

Scoring: Hand key; scoring service available

Cost: DRP Examination Set $50.00

Diagnostic Assessments of Reading with Trial Teaching Strategies™ (DARTTS®)
Florence G. Roswell, Jeanne S. Chall

| 1992 | Riverside Publishing Company |

Population: Prereading through high school

Purpose: Assesses individual student achievement in word recognition, word analysis, oral reading, silent reading comprehension, spelling, and word meaning to discover appropriate methods and materials to enhance learning

Description: Comprises tests and related diagnostic lessons. There are six tests of Reading and Language in a multilevel, ungraded format. Results reveal strengths and weaknesses. TTS Manual suggests ways to interpret the DAR results with students, provides model case studies, and describes common patterns of strengths and weaknesses in reading. Storybooks are filled with interesting, high-quality stories, poems, riddles, and sayings at reading Levels 1 through 6 that are of proven interest even to reluctant readers. The companion book *Creating Successful Readers: A Practical Guide to Testing and Teaching at All Levels* provides the theoretical and research bases for the program and also includes 20 annotated case studies. The book outlines the

stages of normal reading development and describes remedies for less-than-average progress.

Format: Examiner required; suitable for group use; untimed: 50 to 60 minutes

Scoring: Examiner evaluated

Cost: Program Kit (2 manuals, student book, A–J envelopes, 6 storybooks, package of consumable materials, response record, 2 record booklets) $213.00

Diagnostic Screening Test: Language, Second Edition (DSTL)
Thomas D. Gnagey, Patricia A. Gnagey

| 1980 | Slosson Educational Publications, Inc. |

Population: Grades 1 through 13

Purpose: Determines a student's ability to write English and diagnoses common problems in use of the language

Description: Paper–pencil 110-item multiple-choice test yielding six scores: total, sentence structure, grammar, punctuation, capitalization, and formal spelling rules. All subtests yield applied versus formal knowledge for a total of 12 scores in all. The examiner explains the procedure to individuals or groups and reads the test if the students have poor reading skills.

Format: Examiner required; suitable for group use; untimed: 5 to 10 minutes

Scoring: Hand key

Cost: Manual and 50 Test Forms $52.50

Diagnostic Screening Test: Reading, Third Edition (DSTR)
Thomas D. Gnagey, Patricia A. Gnagey

| 1982 | Slosson Educational Publications, Inc. |

Population: Grades 1 to junior college

Purpose: Determines reading achievement levels and diagnoses common reading problems by testing word recognition, reading, and listening comprehension

Description: Paper–pencil 84-word test yielding two major scores (Word Recognition and Reading Comprehension Grade Equivalents) and eight diagnostic scores that reflect skills in using seven basic word attack skills, as well as sight vocabulary. The student reads a word list and comprehension passages aloud and answers prescribed questions. The examiner then reads a passage aloud and the student answers questions. The test yields a consolidation index that reflects how solid or spotty each skill is. The test is available in two equivalent forms.

Format: Examiner required; individual administration; untimed: 5 to 10 minutes

Scoring: Hand key

Cost: Complete Kit (manual, 25 each of Forms A and B) $52.50

Diagnostic Screening Test: Spelling, Third Edition (DSTS)
Thomas D. Gnagey

1982	Slosson Educational Publications, Inc.

Population: Grades 1 to 12

Purpose: Measures a student's ability to spell words and diagnoses common spelling problems

Description: Pencil-paper 78-item test measuring sight or phonics orientation for spelling instruction; relative efficiency of verbal and written testing procedures; analysis of sequential and gross auditory memory; and spelling potential. A pretest is available to determine the appropriate level of entry. The examiner, using the test form, pronounces 78 developmentally arranged words and the student spells them orally; the examiner then repronounces difficult words and the student writes them. When administered to groups, the test yields a grade equivalent score. The test is available in Forms A and B.

Format: Examiner required; individual administration; untimed: 5 to 10 minutes

Scoring: Hand key

Cost: Complete Kit (manual, 25 each of Forms A and B) $52.50

Diagnostic Word Patterns: Tests 1, 2, and 3
Evelyn Buckley

1978	Educators Publishing Service, Inc.

Population: Grades 3 and above

Purpose: Assesses basic phonic knowledge; used to help classroom teachers determine general word attack concepts to review with an entire class and to identify individual student's strengths and weaknesses to develop suitable reading programs

Description: Three verbal paper–pencil 100-word tests. Each can be used as a spelling or word recognition test. Test 1 deals with short vowels, nonphonetic words, and consonant digraphs. Test 2 covers vowel digraph and dipthong patterns and nonphonetic words. Test 3 contains suffixes, two-syllable words, and more material from Tests 1 and 2.

Format: Examiner required; Spelling: group administration; Word Recognition: individual administration; 20 to 45 minutes

Scoring: Examiner evaluation

Cost: Manual $4.60; Individual Student Charts $4.50; Cards for Word Recognition Tests $5.15

Gates-MacGinitie Reading Tests®, Second Canadian Edition (GMRT®)
Walter MacGinitie

1992	Nelson Thomson Learning

Population: Grades K to 12

Purpose: Measures students' reading and vocabulary achievement levels; used for placement and class planning

Description: Multiple-item paper–pencil test of vocabulary and reading comprehension. The basic Level R contains 54 items. Levels A through F contain 85 to 89 items.

Format: Examiner required; suitable for group use; timed 55 minutes; untimed: Level R 65 minutes

Scoring: Hand key; may be computer scored

Cost: Contact publisher

Gates-MacGinitie Reading Tests®, Fourth Edition (GMRT®-4)
Walter H. MacGinitie, Ruth K. MacGinitie, Katherine Maria, Lois G. Dreyer

2000	Riverside Publishing Company

Population: Grades K through 12, adults

Purpose: Measures the general level of reading achievement

Description: The test places emphasis on comprehension at all levels. Each level is developmentally appropriate and alternate forms provide for pre- and posttesting. Level AR is designed for adult education programs. The tests were standardized nationally in the 1998–1999 school year. The empirical norms dates for most levels are November 9 and April 22, except for Level 1, which are February 24 and April 22. National norms are available for all times of the year. A broad range of out-of-level norms is also available.

Format: Examiner required; suitable for group use; timed

Scoring: Hand key; may be machine scored; scoring service available

Cost: Contact publisher

Gates-MacGinitie Reading Tests®, Third Edition (GMRT®-3)

Walter H. MacGinitie, Ruth K. MacGinitie

| 1989 | Riverside Publishing Company |

Population: Grades K through 12

Purpose: Measures reading achievement; used to identify students who would benefit from remedial or accelerated programs, to evaluate instructional programs, and to counsel students and report progress to parents

Description: Multiple-item paper–pencil test assesses reading comprehension and vocabulary development. The test is available on nine levels: PRE (Grade K), R (Grade 1), 1 (Grade 1.3 to 1.9), 2 (Grade 2), 3 (Grade 3), 4 (Grade 4), 5/6 (Grades 5 to 6), 7/9 (Grades 7 to 9), and 10/12 (Grades 10 to 12). Level PRE is a readiness test that assesses the student's knowledge of important background concepts on which beginning reading skills are built. Level R measures beginning reading achievement in four skill areas: Initial Consonants and Consonant Clusters, Final Consonant and Consonant Clusters, Vowels, and Use of Context. Test levels 1 through 10/12 each includes two tests, a Vocabulary test and a Comprehension test.

Format: Examiner required; suitable for group use; timed

Scoring: Hand key; may be machine scored; scoring service available

Cost: Contact publisher

Gray Oral Reading Tests– Diagnostic (GORT–D)

Brian R. Bryant, J. Lee Wiederholt

| 1991 | PRO-ED, Inc. |

Population: Ages 5 years 6 months through 12 years 11 months

Purpose: Evaluates specific abilities and weaknesses in reading

Description: Multiple-item test uses two alternate equivalent forms to assess students' specific abilities and weaknesses. Seven subtests are organized under the three major cue systems believed to affect reading proficiency: meaning cues, function cues, and graphic/phonemic cues. Paragraph Reading requires the student to orally read passages and respond to comprehension questions. If the student performs poorly on the first subtest, the remaining subtests are administered: Decoding (Consonant/Cluster Recognition, Phonogram Recognition, Blending), Word

Identification Attack, Morphemic Analysis, Contextual Analysis, and Word Ordering. Standardized scores are provided for the three components and a composite.

Format: Examiner required; individual administration; untimed: 15 to 30 minutes

Scoring: Examiner evaluated

Cost: Complete Kit (manual, student book, 25 each of Forms A and B, storage box) $169.00

Gray Oral Reading Tests– Fourth Edition (GORT–4)

J. Lee Wiederholt, Brian R. Bryant

| 2001 | PRO-ED, Inc. |

Population: Ages 7 through 18

Purpose: Measures growth in oral reading and diagnoses reading difficulties in students

Description: Multiple-item oral-response test with two alternate, equivalent forms. The student reads aloud 14 developmentally sequenced passages and responds to five comprehension questions. The Passage Score, derived from reading rate and errors, and Oral Reading Comprehension are reported as standard scores, percentiles, and grade equivalents. A system of miscue analysis provides criterion information in Meaning Similarity, Function Similarity, Graphic/Phonemic Similarity, and Self-Correction. A total standard score for Oral Reading is also provided.

Format: Examiner required; individual administration; portions timed; 15 to 30 minutes total testing time

Scoring: Examiner evaluation

Cost: Complete Kit (manual, student book, 25 each of Forms A and B, storage box) $189.00

Gray Silent Reading Tests (GSRT)

J. Lee Weiderholt, Ginger Blalock

| 2000 | PRO-ED, Inc. |

Population: Ages 7 through 25 years

Purpose: Measures an individual's silent reading comprehension ability

Description: Test consists of two parallel forms, each containing 13 developmentally sequenced reading passages with five multiple-choice questions. Each form of the test yields raw scores, grade equivalents, age equivalents, percentiles, and a Silent Reading Quotient. Unlike many other tests of reading, the GSRT reports internal consistency is reported for each 1-year interval. Sources of cultural, racial and gender bias are eliminated. Validity data also show that the GSRT can be used with the Gray Oral Reading Tests–Fourth Edition.

Format: Examiner required; individual and group administration; untimed: 15 to 30 minutes

Scoring: Examiner evaluated

Cost: Complete Kit (manual, 25 Forms A and B, 10 reading booklets A and B, storage box) $134.00

Informal Reading Comprehension Placement Test
Eunice Insel, Ann Edson

1994	Educational Activities, Inc.

Population: Reading levels Grades 1 to 12

Purpose: Measures reading comprehension; determines students' instructional placement level

Description: Computer-administered test assessing word and passage comprehension. The 60-item word comprehension test uses a word analogy format to measure students' knowledge of word meanings and thinking skills. The passage comprehension test consists of a series of eight graded selections and questions ranging in difficulty from the primary level through Grade 8. Students are placed in an instructional reading range of Grade 1 through Grade 12 in word comprehension and passage comprehension. Correlates to Tests of Adult Basic Education (Mac and Windows versions).

Format: Computer administered; untimed

Scoring: Computer scored

Cost: CD $59.95

Iowa Writing Assessment
H. D. Hoover, A. N. Hieronymus, D. A. Frisbie, S. B. Dunbar, L. S. Feldt, R. A. Forsyth, T. N. Ansley, S. D. Alnot

1994	Riverside Publishing Company

Population: Grades 3 through 12

Purpose: To assess students' ability to generate, organize, and express ideas in a variety of written forms

Description: Measures students' ability to generate, organize, and express ideas in four different modes of discourse: narrative, descriptive, persuasive, and expository. Used in conjunction with the Iowa Tests of Basic Skills, Tests of Achievement and Proficiency, and Iowa Tests of Educational Development, the Iowa Writing Assessment provides a measure of students' productive writing skills in response to specific writing tasks.

Format: Examiner required; suitable for group use; untimed: 50 minutes

Scoring: Examiner evaluated

Cost: Classroom Test Packages (directions and testing materials for 25 students) $37.50 per level/writing mode; Manual for Scoring and Interpretation $23.00 per level/writing mode

National Achievement Tests: English, Reading, Literature, and Vocabulary Tests—Reading
Robert K. Speer, Samuel Smith

1961	Psychometric Affiliates

Population: Grades 7 and above

Purpose: Assesses students' reading achievement; used to identify student strengths and weaknesses as part of an educational evaluation

Description: Multiple-item paper–pencil test of reading skills important for achievement, including vocabulary, word discrimination, sentence meaning, noting details, and interpreting paragraphs. Two equivalent forms are available.

Format: Examiner required; suitable for group use; timed: 40 minutes

Scoring: Hand key

Cost: Specimen Set (test, manual, key) $5.00; 25 Tests $13.75

National Achievement Tests: English, Reading, Literature, and Vocabulary Tests—Vocabulary (Grades 3–8)
Robert K. Speer, Samuel Smith

1961	Psychometric Affiliates

Population: Grades 3 through 8

Purpose: Assesses the vocabulary knowledge of children; used as part of an educational evaluation

Description: Multiple-item paper–pencil test of vocabulary knowledge. For each item, the base word is printed in capital letters in a meaningful sentence. The pupil selects a synonym for the base word from a group of words. The base words are more difficult than synonyms. Two equivalent forms are available.

Format: Examiner required; suitable for group use; timed: 15 minutes

Scoring: Hand key

Cost: Specimen Set (test, manual, key) $4.00; 25 Tests $3.50

National Achievement Tests: English, Reading, Literature, and Vocabulary Tests—Vocabulary (Grades 7–College)
Robert K. Speer, Samuel Smith

| 1971 | Psychometric Affiliates |

Population: Grades 7 and above

Purpose: Assesses students' vocabulary knowledge; used as part of an educational evaluation

Description: Multiple-item paper–pencil test measuring knowledge and judgment related to word meaning and word discrimination. Two equivalent forms are available.

Format: Examiner required; suitable for group use; timed: 15 minutes

Scoring: Hand key

Cost: Specimen Set (test, manual, key) $4.00; 25 Tests $3.50

Neale Analysis of Reading Ability– Third Edition
Marie D. Neale

| 1999 | Australian Council for Educational Research Limited |

Population: Ages 6 through 12+ years

Purpose: Assesses reading progress objectively

Description: Series of reading passages that the student reads aloud. The test is available in two parallel forms, Forms 1 and 2, and a Diagnostic Tutor Form that extends test options. The test yields stanine and percentile rank and range scores, Neale (Rasch) scale scores, and reading ages. This test is a revised version of the Neale Analysis of Reading Ability published by Macmillan Education.

Format: Examiner required; individual administration; timed and untimed

Scoring: Hand key; examiner evaluated

Cost: Contact publisher

Phonological Awareness and Reading Profile–Intermediate
Wanda Salter, Carolyn Robertson

| 2001 | LinguiSystems, Inc. |

Population: Ages 8 through 14 years

Purpose: Assesses phonological awareness, decoding, spelling, and fluency skills of students who continue to have difficulty with reading and spelling skills past second grade

Description: Oral-response criterion-referenced test with five subtests: Phonological Awareness (65 items measuring blending, isolation, segmentation, deletion, and manipulation skills), Decoding (41 items assessing phonetic patterns), Spelling (20 items assessing phonetic patterns), and Fluency (rapid letter naming and paragraph reading tasks).

Format: Examiner required; individual administration; untimed: 25 to 35 minutes

Scoring: Examiner evaluated

Cost: Test Kit (manual, 15 forms, cubes) $41.95

Progressive Achievement Test (PAT) Reading: Comprehension and Vocabulary
Neil Reid, Warwick B. Elley

| 1990 | New Zealand Council for Educational Research |

Population: Ages 8 to 14 years

Purpose: Assesses comprehension and vocabulary skills

Description: Educational application with two subtests: Comprehension (41 items) and Vocabulary (45 to 54 items). Forms available: A, B, Primary, Intermediate, and Secondary.

Format: Examiner required; group administration; timed: 75 minutes

Scoring: Hand key

Cost: Manual $6.75; 10 Answer Sheets $1.98; Booklets $1.80; Keys $.99

Progressive Achievement Tests: Reading, Forms A and B

| 1985 | Australian Council for Educational Research Limited |

Population: Years 3 through 9

Purpose: Assesses reading abilities in vocabulary and comprehension

Description: Vocabulary questions are presented with each test word in context in a short sentence. The task is to select the best synonym from a choice of five. Comprehension questions are designed to measure factual and inferential comprehension. Multiple-choice items follow each reading passage. Available in parallel forms.

Format: Examiner required; individual and group administration; untimed: Vocabulary, 30 minutes; Comprehension, 40 minutes

Scoring: Examiner evaluated; scoring service available

Cost: Contact publisher

Proof Reading Test of Spelling (PRETOS)
Cedric Croft, Alison Gilmore, Neil Reid, Peter Jackson

1981	New Zealand Council for Educational Research

Population: Ages 8 through 13 years

Purpose: Measures discrimination between misspelled and correctly spelled words in meaningful text

Description: Separate test for each grade. Each test has three or four paragraphs consisting of 12 to 14 lines of text, with two lines having no misspelled words. Class percentile ranks are provided for both production and recognition scores.

Format: Examiner required; group administration; timed: 30 minutes

Scoring: Hand key

Cost: Manual $7.20; 10 Booklets $5.40; Keys $.63

Slosson Oral Reading Test-Revised (SORT-R)
Richard L. Slosson, Charles L. Nicholson

1990	Slosson Educational Publications, Inc.

Population: Grades 1 through 12

Purpose: Measures reading ability and identifies reading handicaps

Description: Oral screening test provides an estimate of a person's word recognition level. The SORT-R is based on the ability to pronounce words at different levels of difficulty.

Format: Examiner required; individual administration; untimed: 3 to 5 minutes

Scoring: Examiner evaluated

Cost: Complete Kit $48.00

Slosson Written Expression Test (SWET)
Donald B. Hofler, Bradley T. Erford, William J. Amoreill

2002	Slosson Educational Publications, Inc.

Population: Ages 8 to 17 years

Purpose: Measures spontaneous written expression skills

Description: The test allows for description of the individual child's authentic written expressive skills and a comparison of the child's performance to his or her age peers. Student responses are analyzed in the context of an authentic composition. The SWET's dinosaur, space, and shipwreck themes are highly stimulating picture prompts that help tap creative writing skills and are ideal for portfolio and performanced-based assessment approaches. The standardized scoring system, featuring specially designed, user-friendly scoring and profile forms, yields subscale scores for spelling, capitalization, and punctuation, as well as two writing maturity measures: sentence length and type-token ratio.

Format: Examiner required; individual and group administration; untimed: 15 minutes

Scoring: Examiner evaluated

Cost: Complete Kit (manual, 25 each of student response forms and scoring/profile forms) $95.00

Spadafore Diagnostic Reading Test (SDRT)
Gerald J. Spadafore

1983	Academic Therapy Publications

Population: Ages 6 years to adult

Purpose: Assesses reading skills; used as a screening and diagnostic instrument for academic placement and career guidance counseling

Description: Four subtests assess word recognition, oral reading and comprehension, silent reading comprehension, and listening comprehension. Criterion-referenced test items are graded for difficulty. Independent, Instructional, and Frustration reading and comprehension levels are designated for performance at each grade level. Test results may be used for screening to determine whether reading problems exist at a student's current grade placement. Administration for diagnostic purposes requires 30 minutes for all four subtests and yields a comparison of decoding reading skills. Guidelines are provided for interpreting performance in terms of vocational literacy. Provisions for conducting a detailed error analysis of oral reading are included.

Format: Examiner required; individual administration; screening 30 minutes, diagnosis 1 hour

Scoring: Examiner evaluated

Cost: Test Kit (manual, test plates, 10 test booklets) $65.00

Standardized Reading Inventory-Second Edition (SRI-2)
Phyllis L. Newcomer

1999	PRO-ED, Inc.

Population: Grades 1 to 8

Purpose: Evaluates a student's idiosyncratic reading skills

Description: In addition to being criterion referenced, the instrument is now norm referenced. The subtests include a measure of vocabulary proficiency and a supplemental measure of predictive comprehension. Designed like an informal reading inventory, each of the two forms consists of 10 graded passages, ranging from the lowest reading level (preprimer) to the highest level (eighth grade). Evidence of construct validity is presented showing that the SRI-2 discriminates between good and poor readers. The comprehension questions are open-ended.

Format: Examiner required; individual administration; untimed: 30 to 90 minutes

Scoring: Examiner evaluated

Cost: Complete Kit (manual, storybook, 25 each Forms A and B vocabulary sheets, 25 each Forms A and B examiner record booklets, 50 profile scoring forms, storage box) $224.00

Stanford Diagnostic Reading Test, Fourth Edition (SDRT 4)

Bjorn Karlsen, Eric F. Gardner

1995	Harcourt® Brace Educational Measurement

Population: Grades 1.5 through 13

Purpose: Measures major components of the reading process

Description: Provides formal and informal diagnostic measures for determining students' strengths and needs in reading. The information is used to evaluate students for program placement or to design an appropriate instructional program. High-quality selections provide relevant information. There are six test levels with a single form at each of the first three levels and two alternate and equivalent forms at each of the upper three levels. The SDRT 4 enables teachers to determine how students' comprehension can vary according to the reading selection: recreational, textual, and functional.

Format: Examiner required; suitable for group use; timed

Scoring: Hand key; scoring service available

Cost: Examination Kit $35.50

Test of Reading Comprehension– Third Edition (TORC-3)

Virginia L. Brown, Donald D. Hammill, J. Lee Wiederholt

1995	PRO-ED, Inc.

Population: Grades 2 to 12

Purpose: Assesses students' reading comprehension; used to diagnose reading problems in terms of current psycholinguistic theories of reading comprehension as a constructive process involving both language and cognition

Description: Eight multiple-item paper–pencil subtests measuring aspects of reading comprehension. Three of the subtests (General Vocabulary, Syntactic Similarities, and Paragraph Reading) are combined to determine a basic Comprehension Core, which is expressed as a Reading Comprehension Quotient (RCQ). Three subtests measure students' abilities to read the vocabularies of math, science, and social studies. Subtest 7, Reading the Directions of Schoolwork, is a diagnostic tool for younger or remedial students. The eighth subtest is Sentence Sequences. Scaled scores are provided for each subtest.

Format: Examiner required; individual or group administration; untimed: 30 to 90 minutes

Scoring: Examiner evaluated

Cost: Complete Kit (manual, 50 answer sheets, 50 Subtest 8 forms, 50 profile/examiner record forms, 10 student booklets, storage box) $159.00

Test of Word Reading Efficiency (TOWRE)

Joseph K. Torgesen, Richard Wagner, Carol Rashotte

1999	PRO-ED, Inc.

Population: Ages 6 through 24

Purpose: Measures word-reading accuracy and fluency

Description: Because it can be administered very quickly, the test provides an efficient means of monitoring the growth of two kinds of word reading skills that are critical in the development of overall reading ability: the ability to accurately recognize familiar words as whole units and the ability to "sound out" words quickly. The TOWRE contains two subtests: Sight Word Efficiency and Phonetic Decoding Efficiency. Each subtest has two forms that are of equivalent difficulty. Percentiles, standard scores, and age and grade equivalents are provided.

Format: Examiner required; individual administration; timed: 5 to 10 minutes

Scoring: Examiner evaluated

Cost: Complete Kit (manual, 25 each of Form A and Form B record booklets, word cards, storage box) $119.00

Test of Written Expression (TOWE)
Ron McGhee, Brian R. Bryant,
Stephen C. Larsen, Diane M. Rivera

| 1995 | PRO-ED, Inc. |

Population: Age 6 years 6 months through 14 years 11 months

Purpose: Provides a comprehensive assessment of writing achievement

Description: The TOWE uses two assessment methods to evaluate a student's writing skills. The first method involves administering a series of 76 items that tap different skills associated with writing. The second method requires students to read or hear a prepared story starter and use it as a stimulus for writing an essay (i.e., the beginning of the story is provided, and the writer continues the story to its conclusion). The TOWE provides an excellent source of writing samples that can be used independently in a norm-referenced assessment of writing or as a component of a student's portfolio of written products. The 76 items assess a broad array of writing skills (i.e., ideation, vocabulary, grammar, capitalization, punctuation, and spelling) to determine the student's general writing proficiency. The overall writing score derived can be converted to normative data. Examiners also can conduct an item analysis to examine strengths and weaknesses across the content assessed by the items.

Format: Examiner required; individual administration; untimed: 60 minutes

Scoring: Examiner evaluated

Cost: Complete Kit (manual, 25 profile/examiner record forms, 25 student booklets, storage box) $129.00

Test of Written Language– Third Edition (TOWL-3)
Donald D. Hammill, Stephen C. Larsen

| 1988 | PRO-ED, Inc. |

Population: Ages 7 years 6 months to 17 years 11 months

Purpose: Identifies students who have problems in written expression and pinpoints specific areas of deficit

Description: Paper–pencil test in which students write a story about a given theme. The test yields information in eight areas of writing competence, in contrived and spontaneous formats: Vocabulary, Spelling, Style, Logical Sentences, Sentence Combining, Contextual Conventions, Contextual

Language, and Story Construction. The information is derived from an analysis of a sample of continuous writing, as well as from an analysis of subtest performance. Subtest raw scores, standard scores, percentiles, a Contrived Writing Quotient, Spontaneous Writing Quotient, and Overall Written Language Quotient are generated. The test is available in Forms A and B.

Format: Examiner required; suitable for group use; untimed: 90 minutes

Scoring: Examiner evaluated; computer scoring available

Cost: Complete Kit (manual, 25 each of student response booklets A and B, 50 profile/story scoring forms, storage box) $179.00

Test of Written Spelling– Fourth Edition (TWS-4)
Stephen C. Larsen, Donald D. Hammill,
Louisa Moats

| 1999 | PRO-ED, Inc. |

Population: Grades 1 through 12

Purpose: Identifies individuals whose scores are below those of their peers and who might need interventions designed to improve spelling

Description: The TWS-4 is a norm-referenced test of spelling. The test is administered using a dictated word format. The TWS-4 has two alternate or equivalent forms that make it more useful in test-teach-test situations. This test was developed after a review of 2,000 spelling rules. The words to be spelled are drawn from 10 basal spelling programs and popular graded word lists.

Format: Examiner required; suitable for group or individual use; untimed: 20 minutes

Scoring: Examiner evaluated

Cost: Complete Kit (manual, 50 summary/response forms, storage box) $79.00

Tests of Reading Comprehension (TORCH)
L. Mossenson, P. Hill, G. Masters

| 1989 | Australian Council for Educational Research Limited |

Population: Grades 3 to 10

Purpose: Assesses the extent to which a student is able to obtain meaning from the text

Description: Multiple-item paper–pencil modified-cloze-response reading comprehension test yielding both diagnostic and achievement information. The test consists of 14 passages of graded difficulty. Each passage contains approximately 24 items. The test yields both stanine and percentile rank scores and scale scores.

Format: Examiner required; suitable for group use; untimed: 30 minutes

Scoring: Hand key; examiner evaluated

Cost: Contact publisher

Woodcock Diagnostic Reading Battery (WDRB)
Richard W. Woodcock

1997   Riverside Publishing Company

Population: Ages 4 through 90+ years

Purpose: Provides a diagnostic test that assesses reading achievement and important related abilities

Description: The test can be used to determine reading aptitude, reading achievement levels, phonological awareness, and oral comprehension. There are 10 subtests: letter-word identification, passage comprehension, word attack, reading vocabulary, memory for sentences, visual matching, incomplete words, sound blending, oral vocabulary, and listening comprehension. These are combined into seven clusters: Total Reading, Broad Reading, Basic Reading Skills, Reading Comprehension, Phonological Awareness, Oral Comprehension, and Reading Aptitude.

Format: Examiner required; individual administration; untimed: 5 minutes per subtest

Scoring: Examiner evaluated; computer scoring available

Cost: Complete Kit (test book, audiocassette, manual, norms tables, 25 test records) $301.00

Woodcock Reading Mastery Tests-Revised-Normative Update (WRMT-R/NU)
Richard W. Woodcock

1998   American Guidance Service

Population: Ages 5 through 75+ years

Purpose: Assesses reading skills

Description: The WRMT-R/NU is a comprehensive individual assessment of reading ability and is available in two parallel forms: Forms G and H. Six tests: (1) Visual-Auditory Learning (Form G) measures ability to form associations between visual stimuli and oral responses; (2) Letter Identification (Form G) measures ability to identify letters presented in uppercase or lowercase

forms; Supplementary Letter Checklist (Form G) is used to determine which letters the subject can name or identify by sound; (3) Word Identification requires the subject to identify isolated words that appear in large type on the subject pages in the test easel; (4) Word Attack requires the subject to read either nonsense words or words with a very low frequency of occurrence in English, thus measuring ability to apply phonic and structural analysis skills to pronounce unfamiliar words; (5) Word Comprehension measures reading vocabulary at several different levels of cognitive processing and consists of three subtests (Antonyms, Synonyms, and Analogies); and (6) Passage Comprehension measures ability to identify a key word.

Format: Examiner required; individual administration; 10 to 30 minutes for each cluster of tests

Scoring: Examiner evaluated; computer scoring available for Macintosh and Windows

Cost: Combined Kit (Form G and H test books, 25 each Form G and H test records, sample Form G and H summary record form, pronunciation guide audiocassette, sample report to parents, manual) $367.95

Writing Process Test (WPT)
M. Robin Warden, Thomas A. Hutchinson

1992   PRO-ED, Inc.

Population: Ages 8 through 19 years

Purpose: Assesses both written product and writing process

Description: The norm-referenced WPT is a direct measure of writing that requires the student to plan, write, and revise an original composition. The written product is measured by scoring the first draft (or the revision if a student is given time to revise the composition). The same set of scales is used to analyze all students' writing, regardless of age or grade. The scales rate the writer's effort on two scales, Development and Fluency. The six Development Scales assess Purpose and Focus, Audience, Vocabulary, Style and Tone, Support and Development, and Organization and Coherence. The six Fluency Scales assess Sentence Structure and Variety, Grammar and Usage, Capitalization and Punctuation, and Spelling.

Format: Examiner required; suitable for group use; untimed: 45 minutes, then 30 minutes for revision

Scoring: Examiner evaluated

Cost: Complete Kit (2 manuals, 25 analytical record forms, 25 each of Form A and B first draft booklets, 25 training and calibration record forms, 25 revision booklets, scorer folder) $174.00

Written Language Assessment (WLA)
J. Jeffrey Grill, M. M. Kirwin

1989	Academic Therapy Publications

Population: Ages 8 to 18+ years

Purpose: Assesses written language

Description: Essay test offering direct assessment of written language through an evaluation of writing samples that reflect three modes of discourse: expressive, instructive, and creative writing. Analytic scoring techniques are used to yield scores in General Writing Ability, Productivity, Word Complexity, and Readability. A Written Language Quotient that is a composite of the four subscores is also reported. Raw scores for the four subskill areas and the Written Language Quotient can be converted to scaled scores and percentile ranks and plotted on the scoring/profile form.

Format: Examiner required; individual or group administration; untimed: 1 hour

Scoring: Examiner evaluated

Cost: Test Kit (manual, 25 each of three writing record forms, 25 scoring/profile forms, hand counter, in vinyl folder) $80.00

Religion

Bible Major Test–Forms A and B

1996	Accrediting Association of Bible Colleges

Population: College freshmen and seniors

Purpose: Assesses general biblical knowledge

Description: Test with 135 items. Results are given as percentile scores. Old Testament (OT) and New Testament (NT) questions are in separate sections, thus enabling differentiation or comparison of OT and NT scores.

Format: Examiner required; group administration; untimed

Scoring: Hand key; machine scored

Cost: Test $1.00 each or 100 for $75.00; Answer Sheets $.10 each or 100 for $7.50; Scoring Keys $2.00

New Testament Diagnostic
Fred R. Johnson

1985	Accrediting Association of Bible Colleges

Population: Ages 17 years and older

Purpose: Measures and assesses New Testament knowledge

Description: Paper–pencil 150-item multiple-choice test with five subtests: Introduction to New Testament World and Records, Gospels, Acts, Epistles, and Revelation. Raw scores are converted to 100% scale and percentile ranks.

Format: Examiner required; group administration; untimed: 45 minutes

Scoring: Hand key

Cost: Test $1.00 each or 100 for $75.00; Answer Sheets $.10 each or 100 for $7.50; Scoring Keys $2.00

Partial Index of Modernization: Measurement of Attitudes Toward Morality
Panos D. Bardis

1972	Donna Bardis

Population: Adolescents, adults

Purpose: Measures attitudes toward traditional concepts of sin; used for clinical assessment, counseling, research on religion and morals, and discussions in religion and social science classes

Description: Paper–pencil 10-item test in which the subject rates 10 statements about sin and morality from 0 (*least agreement*) to 10 (*highest agreement*). The score equals the sum of the 10 numerical responses. The theoretical range of scores extends from 0 (*least modern*) to 100 (*most modern*).

Format: Group and individual administration; untimed: 5 minutes

Scoring: Examiner evaluated and interpreted

Cost: $1.00

Standardized Bible Content Tests: A, B, C, D

1959	Accrediting Association of Bible Colleges

Population: Adults

Purpose: Evaluates knowledge of the Bible; used for college entrance examinations, class assignment, assessment (pretest and posttest), and comparing national and institutional norms

Description: Paper–pencil 150-item multiple-choice test measuring biblical knowledge: people, history, doctrine, geography, and quotations. The test is recommended for institutions of higher education. Form D is available in Spanish.

Format: Examiner required; group administration; untimed: 45 minutes

Scoring: Examiner evaluated; hand key

Cost: Test $1.00 each or 100 for $75.00; Answer Sheets $.10 or 100 for $7.50; Scoring Keys $2.00

Standardized Bible Content Tests: E, F

1976	Accrediting Association of Bible Colleges

Population: Adults

Purpose: Measures and assesses biblical knowledge; used for college admissions, class assignments, assessment (pretest–posttest), and comparing national and institutional norms

Description: Paper–pencil 150-item multiple-choice test measuring biblical knowledge: people, history, doctrine, geography, and quotations. The test is recommended for institutions of higher education. Form E is available in Spanish.

Format: Examiner required; group administration; untimed: 45 minutes

Scoring: Examiner evaluated; hand key

Cost: Test $1.00 each or 100 for $75.00; Answer Sheets $.10 each or 100 for $7.50; Scoring Keys $2.00

Standardized Bible Content Tests: G, H, GS, HS

1993	Accrediting Association of Bible Colleges

Population: Adults

Purpose: Assesses biblical knowledge for evaluating teaching effectiveness, learning, and curriculum design

Description: GS and HS: 50-item multiple-choice paper–pencil tests. Scores are reported as percentiles relative to Accrediting Association of Bible Colleges member colleges. G and H: 150-item multiple-choice paper–pencil tests. Tests measure areas of history, geography, facts about people, doctrine, identification of Bible quotes, and general book content.

Format: Examiner required; group administration; untimed: 45 minutes

Scoring: Examiner evaluated; hand key

Cost: G or H $1.00 each or $75.00 for 100; GS or HS $.40 each or $30.00 for 100; Answer Sheets $.10 each or 100 for $7.50; Scoring Keys $2.00

Standardized Bible Content Tests: Form SP

1976	Accrediting Association of Bible Colleges

Population: Ages 15 years and older

Purpose: Measures and assesses biblical knowledge for counseling, Bible college readiness, and missionary candidacy

Description: Paper–pencil 150-item multiple-choice test. Scores are reported as percentiles relative to Accrediting Association of Bible Colleges member colleges.

Format: Examiner required; group administration; untimed: 45 minutes

Scoring: Examiner evaluated; hand key

Cost: Test $1.00 each or 100 for $75.00; Answer Sheets $.10 each or 100 for $7.50; Scoring Keys $2.00

Thanatometer
Panos D. Bardis

1986	Donna Bardis

Population: Adolescents, adults

Purpose: Measures awareness and acceptance of death

Description: Paper–pencil 20-item Likert-type scale assessing attitudes toward death and dying. Examinee responds by indicating degree of agreement with each item. Suitable for use with individuals with physical and hearing impairments.

Format: Self-administered; untimed: 12 minutes

Scoring: Hand key

Cost: $1.00

Speech and Language

Aphasia, Apraxia, Dysarthria, and Dysphagia

Aphasia Diagnostic Profiles (ADP)
Nancy Helm-Estabrooks

1992	PRO-ED, Inc.

Population: Adults

Purpose: Measures language and communication impairments associated with aphasia

Description: Designed to meet the demands of today's medical climate, the test contains nine brief subtests. Each subtest yields standard scores and percentile ranks. Subtest results are used to create composite scores and a series of five profiles addressing critical areas of the patient's performance: Aphasia Classification Profile, Aphasia Severity Profile, Alternative Communication Profile, Error Profiles, and Behavioral Profile. The ADP was standardized on 290 adults with neurological impairments and 40 nonaphasic adults (median age 70).

Format: Examiner required; individual administration; untimed: 40 to 45 minutes

Scoring: Examiner evaluated

Cost: Complete Kit (manual, stimulus cards/letter board, 25 record forms) $164.00

Apraxia Battery for Adults– Second Edition (ABA-2)
Barbara L. Dabul

2000	PRO-ED, Inc.

Population: Adults

Purpose: Used in supporting or refuting a prior impression of apraxia to gain an estimate of severity

Description: Measures the presence and severity of apraxia in adolescents and adults. The instrument has six subtests: Diadochokinetic Rate, Increasing Word Length, Limb and Oral Apraxia, Latency Time and Utterance Time for Polysyllabic Words, Repeated Trials Test, and Inventory of Articulation Characteristics of Apraxia.

Format: Examiner required; individual administration; untimed: 20 minutes

Scoring: Examiner evaluated

Cost: Complete Kit (manual, picture book, 25 profile/examiner record forms, storage box) $119.00

Apraxia Profile
Lori A. Hickman

1997	The Psychological Corporation

Population: Ages 3 to 13 years

Purpose: Identifies the presence of developmental verbal apraxia and documents a child's progress over time

Description: Used to assist in the differential diagnosis of developmental verbal apraxia, identify the presence of oral apraxia, and reveal the most problematic oral-motor sequences and movements. Documents a child's oral-motor sequencing deficits and establishes the level of oral movements and sequences produced successfully.

Format: Examiner required; individual administration; untimed: 25 to 35 minutes

Scoring: Examiner evaluated

Cost: Complete Kit (manual, 10 each of record form for ages 2 to 5 and 5 to 12) $55.00

Assessment of Intelligibility of Dysarthric Speech
Kathryn Yorkston, David Beukelman, Charles Traynor

1984	PRO-ED, Inc.

Population: Adolescents, adults

Purpose: Quantifies the single-word intelligibility, sentence intelligibility, and speaking rates of individuals with dysarthria

Description: Multiple-item verbal and listening test containing speaker tasks, recording techniques, and listener response formats to obtain a variety of intelligibility and communication efficiency measures. The clinical software version provides for quick and efficient quantifying without tedious stimuli selection or computation. Both versions can be readministered repeatedly with reliable results.

Format: Speech pathologist required; individual administration

Scoring: Examiner evaluated

Cost: Complete Kit (manual with reproducible forms, picture book, storage box) $98.00

Bedside Evaluation of Dysphagia (BED)
Edward Hardy

| 1995 | PRO-ED, Inc. |

Population: Adults with neurological impairment

Purpose: Assesses adult patients with dysphagia at bedside

Description: Comprises a Screening of behavior, cognition, and communication abilities; Oral Motor assessment of structure and function of the lips, cheeks, tongue, soft palate, mandible, and larynx; and Oral-Pharyngeal Dysphagia Symptoms assessment of oral and, to some degree, pharyngeal abilities. The Summary Report is detachable. A bedside screening form is also available.

Format: Examiner required; individual administration; untimed

Scoring: Examiner evaluated

Cost: Kit (manual, 25 evaluation forms, 25 screening forms) $89.00

Bedside Evaluation Screening Test–Second Edition (BEST–2)
Joyce Fitch-West, Elaine S. Sands, Deborah Ross-Swain

| 1998 | PRO-ED, Inc. |

Population: Adults

Purpose: Assesses language deficits of patients to provide a profile of severity of aphasia

Description: Used to assess and quantify language disorders resulting from aphasia. Highly efficient and effective tool for assessing communicative modalities. Pathologists, psychologists, neuropsychologists, and physicians using this test will obtain sufficient clinical information to set treatment goals and objectives.

Format: Examiner required; individual administration; untimed: 20 minutes

Scoring: Examiner evaluated

Cost: Complete Kit (manual, picture book, 25 record forms, 25 profile/summary sheets, storage box) $139.00

Boston Assessment of Severe Aphasia (BASA)
Nancy Helm-Estabrooks

| 1989 | PRO-ED, Inc. |

Population: Adults

Purpose: Provides diagnostic information needed for immediate treatment of stroke patients

Description: This test is designed to be given to poststroke patients soon after the onset of aphasia symptoms, preferably at bedside. It can be given long before most other assessments are appropriate. The BASA probes the spared language abilities of persons with severe aphasia and provides diagnostic information needed for immediate treatment. The 61 items measure a wide variety of tasks and modalities, including auditory comprehension, buccofacial or limb praxis, gesture recognition, oral and gestural expression, reading comprehension, writing, and visual-spatial tasks. Both gestural and verbal responses to the items are scored, and refusals, affective responses, and perseverative responses are recorded. Gestural and verbal responses may be scored in combination or separately, and both scores may be expressed as fully or partially communicative.

Format: Examiner required; individual administration; untimed

Scoring: Examiner evaluated

Cost: Complete Kit (manual, custom clipboard, manipulatives, stimulus cards, 25 record forms, briefcase) $269.00

Boston Diagnostic Aphasia Examination–Third Edition (BDAE–3)
Harold Goodglass, Edith Kaplan, Barbara Barresi

| 2000 | Lippincott Williams & Wilkins |

Population: Ages 5 years 6 months to 10 years 6 months, adults

Purpose: Measures the presence and type of aphasic syndrome, leading to inferences concerning cerebral localization for both initial determination and detection of change over time, as well as comprehensive assessment of the patient's assets and liabilities

Description: Multiple-item instrument provides severity rating in fluency, auditory comprehension, naming, oral reading, repetition, paraphasia, automatic speech, reading comprehension, writing, visual-spatial, and computational areas. The patient responds to oral, pictorial, and written prompts. Also includes the former Boston Naming Test, a 60-item test of line-drawn objects of graded difficulty from *bed* to *abacus*. The individual is provided with the initial sound if he or she is unable to name it correctly. Norms are provided for children ages 5½ to 10½ and adults.

Format: Examiner required; individual administration; untimed

Scoring: Examiner evaluated

Cost: Complete Kit (manual, standard form stimulus cards, 25 standard record booklets, short form stimulus cards, 25 short form record booklets, 25 Boston Naming Test record booklets, videotape, box) $169.00

Complete Clinical Dysphagia Evaluation
Nancy B. Swigert

| 2001 | LinguiSystems, Inc. |

Population: Adults with dysphagia

Purpose: Assesses swallowing skills, oral-motor skills

Description: Summary sheet and dysphagia evaluation for overview. Six subtests with multiple-choice questions: behavioral, oral-motor, laryngeal, respiratory, cognitive, and swallowing abilities and limitations. The evaluation has no formal scoring system and no severity norms.

Format: Examiner required; individual administration

Scoring: Examiner evaluated

Cost: $41.95

Dysarthria Examination Battery
Sakina S. Drummond

| 1993 | The Psychological Corporation |

Population: Children, adults

Purpose: Assesses motor speech disorders

Description: Helps to identify and characterize speech production and obtain objective data for five processes: respiration, phonation, resonation, articulation, and prosody. Used to determine the appropriateness of augmentative communication.

Format: Examiner required; individual administration; untimed: 40 minutes

Scoring: Examiner evaluated

Cost: Test Kit (manual, test, stimulus cards, 20 scoring forms) $73.00

Dysphagia Evaluation Protocol
Wendy Avery-Smith, Abbey Brod Rosen, Donna Dellarosa

| 1997 | The Psychological Corporation |

Population: Adults

Purpose: Evaluates patients for swallowing problems

Description: Results help determine whether a patient is appropriate for videofluoroscopy and assist in defining variables and factors that need to be evaluated further with videofluoroscopy. A pocket-sized version of the evaluation in a flip-book format is included for easy bedside administration.

Format: Examiner required; individual administration; untimed: 30 minutes

Scoring: Examiner evaluated

Cost: Complete Kit (manual, flipbook, 15 record forms) $63.00

Examining for Aphasia– Third Edition (EFA-3)
Jon Eisenson

| 1994 | PRO-ED, Inc. |

Population: Adolescents, adults

Purpose: Helps determine areas of strength and weakness for receptive and expressive functions

Description: A revised version of a classic assessment of aphasia and aphasic impairments relative to receptive and evaluative (decoding) and expressive and productive (encoding) impairments. The EFA-3 acknowledges cognitive, personality, and linguistic modifications that are associated with acquired aphasia. The test reflects current positions and interpretations of aphasic impairments on subsymbolic and symbolic levels. The 33 subtests help determine areas of strength and weakness for receptive and expressive functions. The EFA-3 tests for agnosia (visual, auditory, and tactile); linguistic reception (oral and written) of words, sentences, and paragraphs; and expressive impairments, including simple skills, automatic language, arithmetic computations, and language items that parallel those for receptive tasks. An optional Tell a Story test in response to a picture assesses self-organized language content. The Examiner's Manual includes the author's position on the nature and purposes of assessment for diagnosis, prognosis, and therapy.

Format: Examiner required; individual administration; time varies

Scoring: Examiner evaluated

Cost: Complete Kit (manual, picture book, 25 profile/response forms, 25 examiner record booklets, object kit, storage box) $149.00

Frenchay Dysarthria Assessment
Pamela M. Enderby

| 1983 | PRO-ED, Inc. |

Population: Ages 12 years to adult

Purpose: Assesses and provides differential description and diagnosis of dysarthria

Description: Task-performance and behavioral-observation test with 29 items measuring speech impairment due to neuromuscular disorders. The test items cover reflex, respiration, lips, jaw, palate, larynx, tongue, intelligibility, influencing factors (sight, teeth, language, mood, posture), rate, and sensation. The results are recorded graphically on multicopy forms using a 9-point rating scale.

Format: Examiner required; individual administration; untimed: 20 minutes

Scoring: Examiner evaluated

Cost: Complete Kit (manual and 25 protocols) $54.00

Psycholinguistic Assessments of Language Processing in Aphasia (PALPA)
Janice Kay Ruth, Lesser Max Coltheart

| 1992 | Psychology Press |

Population: Adults

Purpose: Measures comprehensive psycholinguistic abilities in adults with acquired aphasia

Description: Intended both as a clinical instrument and research tool, this is a set of resource materials enabling the user to select language tasks that can be tailored to the investigation of a patient's impaired and intact abilities. The detailed profile that results can be interpreted within current cognitive models of language. The materials consist of 60 rigorously controlled tests of components of language structure such as orthography and phonology, word and picture semantics, and morphology and syntax. The tests make use of simple procedures, such as lexical decision, repetition, and picture naming, and have been designed to assess spoken and written input and output modalities. Particular attention has been paid to practical use of the tests in the clinic.

Format: Examiner required; individual administration; untimed

Scoring: Hand key

Cost: $397.00

Reading Comprehension Battery for Aphasia–Second Edition (RCBA-2)
Leonard L. LaPointe, Jennifer Horner

| 1998 | PRO-ED, Inc. |

Population: Preadolescent through geriatric clients

Purpose: Evaluates the nature and degree of reading impairment in adults with aphasia and provides a focus for therapy

Description: Multiple-item stimulus-response test using pictures to assess the reading comprehension of adults with aphasia. The 10 subtests are Single Word Comprehension (Visual Confusions, Auditory Confusions, and Semantic Confusions), Functional Reading, Synonyms, Sentence Comprehension (Picture), Short Paragraph Comprehension (Picture), Paragraphs (Factual and Inferential Comprehension—two subtests), and Morpho-Syntactic Reading with Lexical Controls.

Format: Examiner required; individual administration; untimed: 3 to 10 minutes

Scoring: Examiner evaluated

Cost: Complete Kit (manual, picture book, supplementary picture book, 25 profile/summary record forms, storage box) $159.00

Screening Test for Developmental Apraxia of Speech–Second Edition (STDAS-2)
Robert W. Blakeley

| 2000 | PRO-ED, Inc. |

Population: Ages 4 to 12 years

Purpose: Assists in the differential diagnosis of developmental apraxia of speech

Description: Multiple-item test for diagnosing the developmental apraxia of speech through eight subtests: Expressive Language Discrepancy, Vowels and Diphthongs, Oral Motor Movement, Verbal Sequencing, Motorically Complex Words, Articulation, Transpositions, and Prosody. The testing results of 169 children of normal intelligence with multiple articulation errors are reported.

Format: Examiner required; individual administration; untimed: 15 minutes

Scoring: Examiner evaluated

Cost: Complete Kit (examiner's manual, 50 response record forms, storage box) $86.00

Swallowing Ability and Function Evaluation (SAFE)

Deborah Ross-Swain,
Peggy Kipping, Patricia Yee

| 2002 | PRO-ED, Inc. |

Population: Adolescents and adults

Purpose: Comprehensive evaluation of swallowing

Description: Based on the findings of the latest research in swallowing disorders and the practical needs of therapists conducting such assessments, the test is designed to assist in providing a definitive diagnosis or label of dysphagia. Its results help generate treatment plans or suggest the need for referral to other professionals for further assessment. The SAFE's primary focus is on the oral and pharyngeal phases of the swallow. There are three stages of the SAFE: Evaluation of General Information Related to Swallowing Ability, Physical Examination of the Oropharyngeal Mechanism, and Functional Analysis of Swallowing. The results can be used to determine the effectiveness of various interventions on test performance.

Format: Examiner required; individual administration; untimed

Scoring: Examiner evaluated

Cost: Complete Kit (examiner's manual, treatment manual, 50 record forms, storage box) $114.00

Western Aphasia Battery (WAB)

Andrew Kertesz

| 1982 | The Psychological Corporation |

Population: Adolescents, adults

Purpose: Tests for aphasia syndromes and measures their severity

Description: Evaluates information, content, fluency, auditory comprehension, repetition, and naming. An Aphasia Quotient helps categorize clients according to various aphasia taxonomic classifications and determine the degree of severity. Koh's Blocks and Raven's Coloured Progressive Matrices are needed to obtain a Cortical Quotient.

Format: Examiner required; individual administration; timed: 1 hour

Scoring: Examiner evaluated

Cost: Complete Kit (manual, 25 test booklets, stimulus cards) $115.00

Articulation and Phonology

Arizona Articulation Proficiency Scale: Third Edition

Janet Barker Fudala

| 2001 | Western Psychological Services |

Population: Ages 1 year 6 months to 18 years

Purpose: Measures articulation skills

Description: The edition retains the features from previous editions and adds a number of improvements: updated picture cards, gender-specific norms up to age 6 years, expanded age range, optional assessment tasks, and improved test booklet. It covers all major speech sounds in the English language, including initial and final consonants and blends, vowels, and diphthongs. Scores are provided in several formats: intelligibility descriptions, severity designations, percentile rankings, and standardized scores. Three optional tasks are included: Word Reading Administration, Language Screening Task, and Spontaneous Speech Task.

Format: Examiner required; individual administration; untimed: 3 minutes

Scoring: Examiner evaluated

Cost: Kit (picture cards, 25 protocols, manual) $118.00

Assessment of Phonological Processes–Revised (APP-R)

Barbara Williams Hodson

| 1986 | PRO-ED, Inc. |

Population: Ages 3 through 12 years

Purpose: Evaluates the ability of children with severe speech disorders to use phonetics

Description: Fifty-item test measuring spontaneous utterances naming three-dimensional stimuli. The examiner records speech deviations using narrow phonetic transcription. Materials include recording, analysis, summary, and preschool and multisyllabic screening forms, as well as 12 pictures for multisyllabic screening and 12 picture cards for hard-to-find objects. Explicit descriptions for more than 30 phonological processes, along with examples and clear instructions for scoring, are found in the manual.

Format: Speech pathologist required; individual administration; untimed: 15 to 20 minutes

Scoring: Examiner evaluated

Cost: Complete Kit (manual, all protocols, storage box) $109.00; Object Kit $36.00

Bankson-Bernthal Test of Phonology (BBTOP)
Nicholas W. Bankson, John E. Bernthal

| 1990 | PRO-ED, Inc. |

Population: Ages 3 through 9 years

Purpose: Assesses articulation and phonology

Description: Three different points of view are represented: a whole word accuracy analysis, a traditional consonant articulation analysis, and a phonological process analysis. Practice exercises for scoring the phonological process inventory are included.

Format: Examiner required; individual administration; untimed: 15 to 20 minutes

Scoring: Examiner evaluated

Cost: Complete Kit (manual, picture book, 25 record booklets, easel) $159.00

Children's Speech Intelligibility Measure (CSIM)
Kim Wilcox, Sherrill Morris

| 1999 | The Psychological Corporation |

Population: Ages 3 through 10 years

Purpose: Measures the intelligibility of children's speech

Description: Can be used to establish baseline information and to monitor progress during the course of articulation and phonological treatment. The manual provides over 100 versions of the stimulus list, so the examiner can test a child frequently using a different word list each time. To administer, the examiner models 50 words and the child repeats each one for tape recording. Intelligibility is determined by a second individual (listening to the tape) who is not familiar with the child's speech errors or patterns. The CSIM meets new Individuals with Disabilities Education Act regulations for progress reports to parents on the same schedule as report cards for regular education.

Format: Examiner required; individual administration; untimed: 20 minutes

Scoring: Examiner evaluated

Cost: Complete Kit (manual, 15 record forms, microphone switch) $79.00

Comprehensive Test of Phonological Processing (CTOPP)
Richard Wagner, Joseph K. Torgesen, Carol Rashotte

| 1999 | PRO-ED, Inc. |

Population: Ages 5 through 24 years

Purpose: Assesses phonological awareness, phonological memory, and rapid naming

Description: The CTOPP was developed to aid in the identification of individuals from kindergarten through college who may profit from instructional activities to enhance their phonological skills. There are two versions of the instrument: a primary version for ages 5 to 6 that contains seven core subtests and one supplemental subtest. The second version, for individuals ages 7 through 24, contains six core subtests and six supplemental subtests. The test contains the following subtests: Elision, Blending Words, Sound Matching (only for 5- to 6-year-olds), Memory for Digits, Nonword Repetition, Rapid Color Naming, Rapid Digit Naming, Rapid Letter Naming, Rapid Object Naming, Blending Nonwords, Phoneme Reversal, Segmenting Words, and Segmenting Nonwords. There are three composites: Phonological Awareness Quotient, Phonological Memory Quotient, and Rapid Naming Quotient. Percentiles, standard scores, and age and grade equivalents are provided. The CTOPP was normed on more than 1,600 individuals.

Format: Examiner required; individual administration; untimed: 30 minutes

Scoring: Examiner evaluated

Cost: Complete Kit (manual, 25 each of Ages 5 to 6 and 7 to 25 protocols, picture book, audiocassette, storage box) $224.00

Compton Phonological Assessment of Children
Arthur J. Compton

| Date not provided | Carousel House |

Population: Children

Purpose: Evaluates and analyzes patterns of speech errors in children

Description: Evaluation tool that uses a step-by-step approach that provides a visual display of error patterns, provides phonological rule analysis, and does a phonological process analysis. The first 15 items can function as a screening evaluation. Pictures are used as prompts.

Response booklet provides results in a color-coded, easy-to-read format.

Format: Examiner required; individual administration; untimed: 45 to 60 minutes

Scoring: Examiner interpreted

Cost: Set (manual, pictures, protocols) $45.00

Compton Phonological Assessment of Foreign Accent
Arthur J. Compton

Date not provided   Carousel House

Population: All ages

Purpose: Identifies the accent patterns of non-native English speakers

Description: Evaluation kit gives a quick, detailed analysis of client's problem sounds and accent patterns. Assessment is based on research on over 1,500 people and 95 different languages. A tape-recorded speech analysis gives a phonetically balanced sampling of speech sounds in single words, sentences and phrases, oral reading, and conversational speech. The results are organized in a clear, color-coded display of problem sounds and accent patterns.

Format: Examiner required; individual administration; untimed: 90 minutes

Scoring: Examiner interpreted

Cost: Set (manual, stimulus words, reading passage, protocols) $45.00

Compton Screening Assessment of Foreign Accent
Arthur J. Compton

Date not provided   Carousel House

Population: Adults

Purpose: Identifies the accent patterns of non-native English speakers

Description: Based on 15 stimulus words and a three-sentence reading passage that samples 70% of all consonants and 100% of the vowels and diphthongs, the instrument helps potential clients discover their degree of accent. The test is normed on 200 clients from 40 language backgrounds and objectively locates the person's accent into one of three categories: very mild, average, or severe. Speaking rate, volume, intonation, vocal quality, grammar, and perceived degree of accent are assessed from a conversational speech sample.

Format: Examiner required; individual administration; untimed: 6 to 10 minutes

Scoring: Examiner evaluated; Spanish version requires bilingual pathologist or aide

Cost: Set (stimulus items, instructions, and response booklets) $10.50

Compton Speech and Language Screening Evaluation
Arthur J. Compton

Date not provided   Carousel House

Population: Ages 3 to 6 years

Purpose: Estimates articulation and language development of young children

Description: Multiple-item oral-response test utilizing common objects to elicit verbal responses from the child. The test, which measures both production and comprehension, covers the following areas: articulation, vocabulary, colors, shapes, memory span, language (plurals, opposites, progressive and past tenses, prepositions, multiple commands, possessive pronouns), spontaneous language, fluency, voice, and oral mechanism. The materials include revised response forms with age profiles, pass–fail guidelines, and an audiogram. Available in Spanish.

Format: Examiner required; individual administration; untimed: 6 to 10 minutes

Scoring: Examiner evaluated; Spanish version requires bilingual pathologist or aide

Cost: Complete Kit (manual, carrying case, stimulus objects, pictures, 25 response forms) $50.00

Computerized Articulation and Phonology Evaluation System
Julie Masterson, Barbara Bernhardt

2001   The Psychological Corporation

Population: Ages 2 years through adult

Purpose: Analyzes articulation and phonology

Description: This easy-to-use software provides a thorough, individualized evaluation and analysis in a few minutes, and it includes treatment suggestions based on the respondent's error patterns, strengths, and weaknesses. The respondent states answers to on-screen stimuli and the administrator enters the answers into the computer. The system consists of two separate evaluations: The Phonemic Profile—a quick screen of sound production—and the Individualized Phonological Evaluation—a deeper analysis of 10 to 100 words that consists of multiple examples of target phonemes, phonological processes, or features that need remediating. A dialect filter is used to help determine which phonemes are produced in error.

Format: Examiner required; computer administered; untimed: 15 to 40 minutes

Scoring: Computer scored; examiner evaluated

Cost: Contact publisher

Denver Articulation Screening Exam (DASE)
Amelia F. Drumwright

| 1971 | Denver Developmental Materials, Inc. |

Population: Ages 2 years 6 months to 7 years

Purpose: Detects speech articulation problems in children; screens for more sophisticated testing

Description: Test measures a child's intelligibility (does not assess language ability, vocabulary, school readiness, or intelligence). The examiner shows 22 pictures displayed on 11 cards to the child, says a word, and the child repeats it. The test is not recommended for shy or younger children.

Format: Examiner required; individual administration; untimed: 5 minutes

Scoring: Examiner evaluated

Cost: 25 Tests $8.00; Manual/Workbook $19.00; Picture Cards $8.00

Fisher-Logemann Test of Articulation Competence (F-LOTAC)
Hilda B. Fisher, Jerilyn A. Logemann

| 1971 | PRO-ED, Inc. |

Population: Children, adults

Purpose: Implements the examination of the phonological system, provides ease in recording and analyzing phonetic notations of articulation, and facilitates accurate analysis of articulation errors

Description: Two test forms (pictures and sentences) provide a method for eliciting spontaneous responses that are prestructured for required phonemic occurrence and analyzed and summarized according to distinctive features that are violated. The test consists of a Test Portfolio of 35 cards with 109 large, full-color illustrations and a Sentence Test with 15 sentences to be repeated.

Format: Examiner required; individual administration; time varies

Scoring: Examiner evaluated

Cost: Complete Kit (manual, portfolio, 50 record forms) $164.00

Goldman Fristoe Test of Articulation–Second Edition
Ronald Goldman, Macalyne Fristoe

| 2000 | American Guidance Service |

Population: Ages 2 through 21 years

Purpose: Provides descriptive information about an individual's articulation skills

Description: The test provides information about a child's articulation ability by sampling both spontaneous and imitative sound production. Examinees respond to picture plates and verbal cues from the examiner with single-word answers that demonstrate common speech sounds. Additional sections provide further measures of speech production. The revision contains new items, new artwork, and new norms.

Format: Examiner required; individual administration; untimed: 10 to 15 minutes

Scoring: Examiner evaluated

Cost: Complete Kit (test easel, manual, 25 response forms, canvas bag) $179.95

Khan-Lewis Phonological Analysis (KLPA)
Linda Khan, Nancy Lewis

| 1986 | American Guidance Service |

Population: Ages 2 through 5 years

Purpose: Measures phonological processes

Description: Used by transferring the scores of the Sounds-in-Words section of the Goldman Fristoe Test of Articulation to the KLPA Analysis Form. Easy to read and color coded, the form gives diagnostic information at a glance. A Goal Selection Worksheet is provided for developing treatment strategies.

Format: Uses administration of GFTA; untimed: 15 to 40 minutes

Scoring: Examiner evaluated

Cost: Complete Kit (manual, 25 analysis forms) $83.95

Phonological Awareness Profile
Carolyn Robertson, Wanda Salter

| 1995 | LinguiSystems, Inc. |

Population: Ages 5 to 8 years

Purpose: Used to diagnose deficits in phonological processing and phoneme-grapheme correspondence

Description: Oral-response criterion-referenced test. Nine total tasks are assessed, divided into two areas. Suitable for individuals with visual, physical, hearing, or mental impairments.

Format: Examiner required; individual administration; untimed: 10 to 20 minutes

Scoring: Examiner evaluated

Cost: Manual and 20 Test Forms $34.95

Phonological Awareness Test
Carolyn Robertson, Wanda Salter

1997	LinguiSystems, Inc.

Population: Ages 5 through 9 years

Purpose: Measures phonological processing skills and phoneme-grapheme correspondence

Description: A total of 278 on eight subtests: rhyming discrimination and production; segmentation for sentences, syllables, and phonemes; isolation for initial, medial, and final sounds; deletion for compound words, syllables, and phonemes; substitution with and without manipulatives; blending syllables and phonemes; graphemes; and decoding. Standard score, percentile rank, and age equivalency are given for each subtest and the total test.

Format: Examiner required; individual administration; untimed: 40 minutes

Scoring: Examiner evaluated; computer scoring available

Cost: $109.95

Photo Articulation Test–Third Edition (PAT–3)
Barbara A. Lippke, Stanley E. Dickey, John W. Selmar, Anton L. Soder

1997	PRO-ED, Inc.

Population: Ages 3 to 11 years

Purpose: Measures articulation skills; used for screening and analysis in schools and clinics to plan therapy

Description: The PAT–3 meets the nationally recognized need for a standardized way to document the presence of articulation errors. Enables clinicians to rapidly and accurately assess and interpret articulation errors. Some features of the PAT–3 include full-color photos used to elicit words, stimulus pictures that appeal to students, quick test administration, and easily scored and interpreted test results.

Format: Examiner required; individual administration; untimed: 5 minutes

Scoring: Examiner evaluated

Cost: Complete Kit (manual, photo album picture book, picture card deck, 50 summary/response forms, storage box) $154.00

Riley Articulation and Language Test: Revised
Glyndon D. Riley

1971	Western Psychological Services

Population: Grades K through 2

Purpose: Measures the language proficiency of young children; used to identify children most in need of speech therapy

Description: Oral-response screening test consisting of three subtests (Language Proficiency and Intelligibility, Articulation Function, and Language Function) measuring phonemic similarity, stimulability, number of defective sounds, error consistency, frequency of occurrence, and developmental expectancy. The test yields an objective articulation loss score and standardized language loss and language function scores.

Format: Examiner required; individual administration; untimed: 2 to 3 minutes

Scoring: Examiner evaluated

Cost: Kit (25 tests, manual) $42.50

Slosson Articulation, Language Test with Phonology (SALT-P)
Wilma Jean Tade

1986	Slosson Educational Publications, Inc.

Population: Ages 3 to 5 years

Purpose: Assesses articulation, phonology, and language in young children

Description: Indicates the communicative competency of a young child. Screening format uses structured conversation centering around stimulus pictures. The articulation section assesses 22 initial and 18 final consonants, 10 clusters/blends, and 8 vowels and diphthongs. Phonological processes probed are initial and final consonant deletion, fronting, stopping, and cluster reduction. The language subscore reflects errors on 31 language behaviors normally acquired between ages 2¹/₂ and 6. Statistical section is included in the manual.

Format: Individual administration; examiner required; untimed: 7 to 10 minutes

Scoring: Examiner evaluated

Cost: Complete Kit (manual, 50 scoring forms, picture plates) $68.00

Speech-Ease Screening Inventory (K–1)
Teryl Pigott, Jane Barry, Barbara Hughes, Debra Eastin, Patricia Titus, Harriett Stensel, Kathleen Metcalf, Belinda Porter

| 1985 | PRO-ED, Inc. |

Population: Grades K and 1

Purpose: Assesses the articulation and language development of children; used to identify students needing speech–language services

Description: Multiple-item response test evaluating the speech and language development of children. The basic section assesses articulation, language association, auditory recall, expressive vocabulary, and concept development. An optional section includes additional auditory items, a section on similarities and differences, a language sample, and a section on linguistic relationships.

Format: Examiner required; individual administration; untimed: 7 to 10 minutes

Scoring: Examiner evaluated

Cost: Complete Kit (manual, 100 screening forms, 50 summary sheets each for kindergarten and first grade, 3 picture plates, storage box) $109.00

Structured Photographic Articulation and Phonological Test II featuring Dudsberry® (SPAT-D II)
Janet I. Dawson, Patricia Tattersall

| Date not provided | Janelle Publications, Inc. |

Population: Ages 3 to 9 years

Purpose: Assesses phonological repertoire in a natural manner and provides a systematic means of assessing the child's articulation

Description: The second edition includes 40 full-color photographs that are used to assess 59 consonant singletons and 10 consonant blends as well as 7 phonological processes. The full-color photographs portray Dudsberry interacting with objects that contain the target phonemes. For optional assessment, 8 photographs depicting the story of "Dudsberry's 1st Birthday" are included in the album to elicit phoneme production in connected speech. A color-coded response form allows for ease in recording. Errors can be transferred to the Consonant Classification Chart, enabling the examiner to immediately analyze articulation errors according to syllabic function and manner of articulation. Further, the child's consonant inventory, percentage of consonants correct, word shapes, and usage of seven common phonological processes can be evaluated. No whole word transcription is necessary.

Format: Examiner required; individual administration; untimed: 10 to 15 minutes

Scoring: Examiner evaluated

Cost: Complete Kit (manual, picture book, 30 response forms, storage box) $140.00

Test of Minimal Articulation Competence (T-MAC)
Wayne A. Secord

| 1981 | The Psychological Corporation |

Population: Ages 3 years to adult

Purpose: Assesses the severity of articulation disorders; used to identify children needing therapy, monitor speech development in terms of research-based minimal expectations for age level, and target the most trainable phonemes for remediation

Description: Multiple-item verbal-response test using one of the following procedures: picture identification, sentence reading, or sentence repetition. The test provides a flexible format for obtaining a diagnostic measure of articulation performance on 24 consonant phonemes; frequently occurring *s*, *r*, and *l* blends; 12 vowels; 4 diphthongs; and variations of vocalic *r*.

Format: Examiner required; individual administration; untimed: 10 to 20 minutes

Scoring: Examiner evaluated

Cost: Complete Program (manual, 25 protocols) $111.00

Test of Phonological Awareness (TOPA)
Joseph K. Torgesen, Brian R. Bryant

| 1994 | PRO-ED, Inc. |

Population: Grades K to 2

Purpose: Measures young children's awareness of the beginning and ending sounds in words

Description: The TOPA can be used to identify children in kindergarten who may profit from instructional activities to enhance their phonological awareness in preparation for reading instruction. Additionally, because kindergarten scores on the TOPA are strongly related to reading growth in first grade, the TOPA is also useful as part of kindergarten screening activities to identify children who are at risk for learning difficulties in school. The Early Elementary version of the TOPA can be used to determine if first- and second-grade students' difficulties in early reading are associated with delays in development of phonological awareness. The test has been standardized on a large sample of children representative of the population characteristics reported in the U.S. census. The manual provides information to generate percentiles and a variety of standard scores.

Format: Examiner administered; suitable for group use; untimed: 15 to 20 minutes

Scoring: Examiner evaluated

Cost: Complete Kit (manual, 25 student booklets each for kindergarten and early elementary, 25 profile/examiner record forms each for kindergarten and early elementary, storage box) $149.00

Weiss Comprehensive Articulation Test (WCAT)
Curtis E. Weiss

| 1980 | PRO-ED, Inc. |

Population: Ages 2 years 6 months to 7 years

Purpose: Determines articulation disorders or delays and identifies misarticulation patterns and other problems; used in articulation therapy

Description: Multiple-item criterion-referenced test in two forms: an easel-stand flipbook of 85 pictures for subjects who cannot read and a card with 38 sentences for those who can. With the pictures, the child supplies the missing word in a sentence spoken by the examiner; with the sentences, the child does the reading. Materials include the picture cards and forms.

Format: Examiner required; individual administration; untimed: 20 minutes

Scoring: Examiner evaluated

Cost: Complete Kit (manual, picture cards, sentence card, 50 picture response forms, 50 sentence response forms) $98.00

Comprehensive Language

Adapted Sequenced Inventory of Communication Development for Adolescents and Adults with Severe Handicaps
Sandra E. McClennen

| 1989 | Western Psychological Services |

Population: Adolescents, adults

Purpose: Evaluates the communication abilities of individuals with severe disabilities whose language skills are in the range of birth to 4 years; used for remedial programming by speech-language pathologists, audiologists, psychologists, and teachers

Description: Inventory with 76 items assessing and diagnosing language disorders in adolescents and adults. The receptive communication section (27 items) includes a processing profile for auditory perception and pragmatic, semantic, and syntactic language, and a concepts profile for awareness, words, directions, questions, and attributes. The expressive communication section (31 items) includes a processing profile for pragmatic and semantic/syntactic language and imitation, and a behavioral profile for imitating motor behavior, motor and/or vocal/verbal initiating behavior, and motor and/or vocal/verbal responding behavior. An observation/interview section (18 items) is also included. Approach is based on order of difficulty concept, and mode of expression is defined to recognize alternatives to vocal communication. The resulting Communication Profile provides guidelines for developing remedial programs for adolescents and adults who have little or no speech or who are understood only by those closest to them. Handicapping conditions represented in the norm group include severe hearing loss, legal blindness, epilepsy, spastic quadriplegia, and nonambulation. Adaptations are described for clients with cerebral palsy and other motor handicaps.

Format: Examiner required; individual administration; untimed

Scoring: Examiner evaluated

Cost: Complete Kit (manuals, 50 receptive skills checklists and profiles, 50 expressive skills checklists and profiles, 50 assessment booklets, plastic carrying case) $350.00

Adolescent Language Screening Test (ALST)

Denise L. Morgan, Arthur M. Guilford

1984	PRO-ED, Inc.

Population: Ages 11 through 17 years

Purpose: Screens the dimensions of oral language use, content, and form

Description: Multiple-item, thorough method of screening through seven subtests: Pragmatics, Receptive Vocabulary, Concepts, Expressive Vocabulary, Sentence Formulation, Morphology, and Phonology. The results provide the clinician with a solid foundation for recommending a total communication evaluation and outline the language dimensions on which extension testing should focus.

Format: Examiner required; individual administration; untimed: 15 minutes

Scoring: Examiner evaluated

Cost: Complete Kit (manual, picture book, 50 protocols, storage box) $124.00

Assessment of Communication and Interaction Skills (ACIS)

Kristy Forsyth, Marcille Salamy, Sandy Simon, Gary Kielhofner

Date not provided	Model of Human Occupation Clearinghouse

Population: Adults

Purpose: Measures impact of communication deficits on task performance

Description: Assists clinicians in identifying areas of strengths and limitations in communication and interaction through observational assessment.

Format: Examiner required; individual administration; untimed

Scoring: Examiner evaluated

Cost: $32.00

Assessment of Language-Related Functional Activities (ALFA)

Kathleen A. Baines, Ann W. Martin, Heidi McMartin Heeringa

1999	PRO-ED, Inc.

Population: Ages 16 years and older

Purpose: Assesses language-related functional activities

Description: The ALFA consists of 10 subtests: Telling Time, Counting Money, Addressing an Envelope, Solving Daily Math Problems, Writing a Check/Balancing a Checkbook, Understanding Medicine Labels, Using a Calendar, Reading Instructions, Using the Telephone, and Writing a Phone Message. The patient performs each functional activity, and the examiner records an objective, quantitative score. The subtests require use of all language modalities (auditory comprehension, verbal expression, reading, and writing) as well as cognitive and motor skills. The ALFA was standardized on 495 patients between the ages of 20 and 95 who had a history of neurological episodes, as well as 150 normally functioning adults.

Format: Examiner required; individual administration; untimed: 30 to 90 minutes

Scoring: Examiner evaluated

Cost: Complete Kit (manual, picture book, 25 record booklets, materials kit, storage box) $159.00

Bankson Language Test–Second Edition (BLT-2)

Nicholas W. Bankson

1990	PRO-ED, Inc.

Population: Ages 3 years to 6 years 4 months

Purpose: Provides examiners with a measure of children's psycholinguistic skills

Description: The test is organized into three general categories that assess a variety of areas: Semantic Knowledge—body parts, nouns, verbs, categories, functions, prepositions, and opposites; Morphological/Syntactical Rules—pronouns, verb usage/verb tense, verb usage (auxiliary, modal, copula), plurals, comparatives/superlatives, negation, and questions; and Pragmatics—ritualizing, informing, controlling, and imagining. The selection of subtests to be included in the BLT-2 was predicated on a review of those areas that language interventions frequently test and remediate in younger children. Results are reported as standard scores and percentile ranks. The normative sample consisted of more than 1,200 children living in 19 states. The demographic features of the sample are representative of the U.S. population on a variety of variables. Evidence of internal consistency reliability is provided in the test manual, and reliability coefficients exceed .90. Support for content, concurrent, and construct validity also is provided.

Format: Examiner required; individual administration; untimed: 30 minutes

Scoring: Examiner evaluated

Cost: Complete Kit (manual, 25 profile/examiner's record booklets, 25 screen record forms, picture book, storage box) $139.00

CAT/5 Listening and Speaking Checklist

1993	CTB/McGraw-Hill

Population: Grades K to 12

Purpose: Assesses oral language proficiency in children and adolescents

Description: Oral-response checklist is teacher scored and individually administered to evaluate students' listening behavior, listening comprehension, critical listening, speaking behavior, and participation. The teacher uses one checklist per student to rate each student's ability based on classroom observation and experience. Students receive an overall rating that classifies them as basic, proficient, or advanced.

Format: Examiner required; individual administration; untimed

Scoring: Examiner evaluated

Cost: Classroom Package (30 checklists, teacher's guide, class summary folder) $22.80

CELF™-3 Observational Rating Scales
Eleanor Semel, Elisabeth H. Wiig, Wayne A. Secord

1996	The Psychological Corporation

Population: Ages 6 through 21 years

Purpose: Provides descriptive indicators of students' language performance in class and at home

Description: Each of three parallel Rating Scale Forms (Teacher, Parent, and Student) contains 40 statements that describe problems in listening, speaking, reading, and writing. Can be used during the prereferral process or as part of an assessment battery. Information is used to target the most important classroom language needs of the student. Companion to Clinical Evaluation of Language Fundamentals–Third Edition.

Format: Rating scale; untimed: 30 to 60 minutes

Scoring: Examiner evaluated

Cost: Complete Kit (guide; 25 each of teacher, parent, and student forms; summary) $55.00

CELF™-Preschool
Elisabeth H. Wiig, Wayne A. Secord, Eleanor Semel

1992	The Psychological Corporation

Population: Ages 3 through 6 years

Purpose: Measures a broad range of expressive and receptive language skills

Description: Child-sized stimulus manuals feature interesting, full-color pictures. Companion to Clinical Evaluation of Language Fundamentals–Third Edition.

Format: Examiner required; individual administration; untimed: 30 to 45 minutes

Scoring: Examiner evaluated

Cost: Complete Kit (manual, 25 record forms, 3 stimulus manuals) $225.00

Child Language Ability Measures (CLAM)
Albert Mehrabian, Christy Moynihan

1979	Albert Mehrabian, PhD

Population: Ages 2 to 7 years

Purpose: Measures the language production and language comprehension abilities of children; identifies linguistic abilities and difficulties

Description: Six multiple-item oral-response and nonverbal task-performance tests measuring a child's expressive and receptive language abilities, including vocabulary comprehension, grammar comprehension, inflection production, grammar imitation, "grammar formedness" judgment, and grammar equivalence judgment. The tests assess a child's knowledge of syntactic, semantic, and phonological rules and do not confound measurement of language development with intellectual skills such as memory span, knowledge of real world facts, or ability to form abstract relationships. Administration procedures contain built-in safeguards against tester bias (such as encouraging one child more than another). The six tests may be administered separately or together. Norms are provided to calculate standardized scores for each test and for combinations of tests. The manual includes details regarding the construction of the tests, statistics on item selection and test reliabilities, appropriate age ranges for each test, and scoring procedures and norms. Two administration books are available with sample answer sheets at the end of each test booklet that can be copied by the examiner for use in recording children's answers.

Format: Examiner required; individual administration; untimed: 15 minutes per test

Scoring: Examiner evaluated

Cost: Contact publisher

Clinical Evaluation of Language Fundamentals–Third Edition (CELF™-3)
Eleanor Semel, Elisabeth H. Wiig, Wayne A. Secord

1995	The Psychological Corporation

Population: Ages 6 through 21 years

Purpose: Yields detailed diagnostic information on language processing and production skills to identify children with language disabilities

Description: Multiple-item oral-response assessment consisting of two screening tests (Elementary for Grades K to 5 and Advanced for Grades 5 to 12) and a diagnostic battery. The Elementary screening test is administered using a "Simon Says" format. The Advanced screening test uses playing cards to elicit language processing skills. The Diagnostic Battery employs 13 criterion- and norm-referenced subtests to probe language processing, language production, and receptive and expressive phonological factors. These 13 subtests can be administered in their entirety, in part, or in any sequence. A Spanish edition is available.

Format: Examiner required; individual administration; untimed: 1 to 2 hours, screening 10 to 15 minutes

Scoring: Examiner evaluated; computer scoring available

Cost: Complete Kit (2 manuals, 2 stimulus manuals, 12 record forms, briefcase) $360.00; Screening Kit (manual, stimulus manual, 25 record forms, case) $172.00

Communication Activities of Daily Living–Second Edition (CADL-2)
Audrey L. Holland, Carol M. Frattali, Davida Fromm

1999	PRO-ED, Inc.

Population: Adults with aphasia

Purpose: Assesses functional communication skills; used for planning treatment programs

Description: Assessment of the functional communication skills of adults with neurogenic communication disorders. The test contains 50 items

that assess communication activities in seven areas: Reading, Writing, and Using Numbers; Social Interaction; Divergent Communication; Contextual Communication; Nonverbal Communication; Sequential Relationships; and Humor/Metaphor Absurdity.

Format: Examiner required; individual administration; untimed: 30 minutes

Scoring: Examiner evaluated

Cost: Complete Kit (manual, picture book, 25 record booklets, 25 response forms, storage box) $177.00

Communication and Symbolic Behavior Scales: Developmental Profile (CSBS:DP)
Amy M. Wetherby, Barry M. Prizant

1998	Paul H. Brookes Publishing Company, Inc.

Population: Ages 6 to 24 months to 6 years

Purpose: Screens and evaluates communicative and symbolic abilities

Description: The instrument has seven clusters—Emotion and Eye Gaze, Communication, Gestures, Sounds, Use of Words, Understanding of Words, and Use of Objects—and three composites—Social Communication, Expressive Speech, and Symbolic. Standard scores and percentiles are given on each cluster and composite. May be used for persons with visual, physical, hearing, and mental impairments.

Format: Examiner required; individual administration; untimed: 25 to 30 minutes

Scoring: Examiner evaluated

Cost: Complete Kit $399.00

Communication Competency Assessment Instrument (CCAI)
Rebecca R. Rubin

Date not provided	SPECTRA, Inc.

Population: Adults

Purpose: Assesses level of communication competency

Description: Assessment instrument for college- or high school-level speaking and listening skills. Measures four competencies: Communication Codes, Oral Message Evaluation, Basic Speech Communication Skills, and Human Relations.

Format: Examiner required; individual administration; untimed

Scoring: Examiner evaluated

Cost: High School (manual, 50 scoring sheets) $39.95; College (2 manuals, video, 50 two-part scoring sheets) $185.00

Comprehensive Assessment of Spoken Language (CASL)
Elizabeth Carrow-Woolfolk

Date not provided — American Guidance Service

Population: Ages 3 through 21 years

Purpose: Assesses oral language skills

Description: Fifteen tests measure language processing skills—comprehension, expression, and retrieval—in four language structure categories: Lexical, Semantic, Syntactic, Supralinguistic, and Pragmatic. In-depth assessment capabilities provide a precise picture of problems with language processing skills and structural knowledge.

Format: Examiner required; individual administration; untimed: 30 to 45 minutes for core battery

Scoring: Examiner evaluated; computer scoring available

Cost: Complete Kit (3 test books, 12 each of 2 record forms, manual, norms book, carry bag) $299.95

Early Language Milestone Scale– Second Edition (ELM Scale-2)
James Coplan

1993 — PRO-ED, Inc.

Population: Birth to 36 months

Purpose: Assesses speech and language development

Description: The ELM Scale-2 is ideally suited to help clinicians implement the mandate to serve the developmental needs of children. It also can be used with older children with developmental delays whose functional level falls within this range. The ELM Scale-2 consists of 43 items arranged in three areas of language function: Auditory Expressive (which is further subdivided into Content and Intelligibility), Auditory Receptive, and Visual. The ELM Scale-2 may be used by examiners with varying levels of prior knowledge of early language development. It may be administered using either a pass-fail or a point-scoring method. The pass-fail method yields a global "pass" or "fail" rating for the test as a whole, whereas the point-scoring method yields percentile values, standard score equivalents, and age equivalents for each area of language func-

tion, as well as a Global Language score. The pass-fail method is preferred whenever large numbers of low-risk subjects must be evaluated. The point-scoring method is preferred whenever more detailed information is desired.

Format: Examiner required; individual administration; untimed: 1 to 10 minutes

Scoring: Examiner evaluated

Cost: Complete Kit (manual, object kit, 100 record forms, storage box) $139.00

Evaluating Acquired Skills in Communication–Revised (EASIC-R)
Anita Marcott Riley

1991 — PRO-ED, Inc.

Population: Ages 3 months to 8 years

Purpose: Assesses the language abilities of individuals with a language age of 3 months to 8 years and an interest level age of 4 to 20 years; used for planning therapy programs for clients with severe language impairments

Description: Multiple-item oral-response test consisting of five inventories assessing a child's abilities in semantics, syntax, morphology, and pragmatics. The examiner uses picture stimuli to elicit spontaneous, cued, imitated, manipulated, noncompliant, or incorrect responses. The test helps determine emerging communication skills, including before meaningful speech; understanding of simple noun labels, action verbs, and basic concepts; emerging modes of communication; understanding of more complex language functions; and use of more complex communication. The test includes goals for individual education prescriptions. It is used with children and adolescents with autism, mental impairments, developmental delays, and preschool language delays.

Format: Examiner required; individual administration; untimed: 15 to 30 minutes

Scoring: Examiner evaluated

Cost: Complete Kit (manual, picture book, cards, test booklets, skill profiles, storage box) $149.00

Fluharty Preschool Speech and Language Screening Test– Second Edition (Fluharty-2)
Nancy Buono Fluharty

2000 — PRO-ED, Inc.

Population: Ages 3 through 6

Purpose: Measures early speech and language performance

Description: Contains five subtests: Articulation, Repeating Sentences, Responding to Directives and Answering Questions, Describing Actions, and Sequencing Events. The Fluharty-2 is a complete revision, normed on 705 children in 21 states. Standard scores and age equivalents are provided for the subtests and composites.

Format: Examiner required; individual administration; untimed: 45 minutes

Scoring: Examiner evaluated

Cost: Complete Kit (manual, picture book, 12 blocks, 25 record forms, storage box) $149.00

Fullerton Language Test of Adolescents–Second Edition (FLTA-2)
Arden R. Thorum

| 1986 | PRO-ED, Inc. |

Population: Ages 11 years through adult

Purpose: Measures receptive and expressive language skills to identify language impairment

Description: Standardized instrument contains eight subtests: Auditory Synthesis, Morphology Competency, Oral Commands, Convergent Production, Divergent Production, Syllabication, Grammatic Competency, and Idioms. The test diagnoses strengths and weaknesses and makes remediation suggestions.

Format: Examiner required; individual administration; untimed: 1 hour

Scoring: Examiner evaluated

Cost: Complete Kit (manual, stimulus items, protocols) $76.00

Functional Communication Profile
Larry I. Kleiman

| 1994 | LinguiSystems, Inc. |

Population: Ages 3 years through adult

Purpose: Measures communicative effectiveness in clients with developmental delays; used in speech and language therapy and family counseling with individuals with developmental delays, autism, cerebral palsy, Down syndrome, and other chromosomal abnormalities

Description: Oral-response criterion-referenced verbal show-tell, point-to test comprising nine categories: sensory/motor functioning, attentiveness, receptive language, expressive language, pragmatic/social skills, speech, voice, oral functioning, and fluency. Interpretation of results

is in the manual. Examiner must be a qualified speech pathologist or intern, special education teacher, or graduate student in communicative disorders.

Format: Examiner required; individual administration; untimed

Scoring: Examiner evaluated

Cost: Manual and 15 Forms $37.95

HELP Test–Elementary
Andrea M. Lazzari

| 1996 | LinguiSystems, Inc. |

Population: Ages 6 through 11 years

Purpose: Assesses general language functioning for students with language disorders

Description: A total of 84 items in six subtests: semantics, specific vocabulary, word order, general vocabulary, question grammar, and defining. Standard score, percentile rank, and age equivalency are provided for each subtest and the total test.

Format: Examiner required; individual administration; untimed: 20 to 30 minutes

Scoring: Examiner evaluated

Cost: $99.95

Illinois Test of Psycholinguistic Abilities–Third Edition (ITPA-3)
Donald D. Hammill, Nancy Mather, Rhia Roberts

| 2001 | PRO-ED, Inc. |

Population: Ages 5 through 12

Purpose: Measures spoken and written language

Description: All of the subtests measure some aspect of language, including oral language, writing, reading, and spelling. The content in this edition is consistent with Charles Osgood's original Communication Model and also with the adaptations of that model made by Samuel Kirk, James McCarthy, and Winifred Kirk. The test can contribute to an accurate diagnosis of dyslexia and identify children with general linguistic delays in the development of spoken and written language. There are 12 subtests: Spoken Analogies, Spoken Vocabulary, Morphological Closure, Syntactic Sentences, Sound Deletion, Rhyming Sequences, Sentence Sequencing, Written Vocabulary, Sight Decoding, Sound Decoding, Sight Spelling, and Sound Spelling. The subtests can be combined to form 11 composites: General Language, Spoken

Language, Written Language, Semantics, Grammar, Phonology, Comprehension, Word Identification, Spelling, Sight-Symbol Processing, and Sound–Symbol Processing. Scores provided are standard scores, percentiles, and age equivalents.

Format: Examiner required; individual administration; untimed: 45 to 60 minutes

Scoring: Examiner evaluated; computer scoring available

Cost: Complete Kit (manual, 25 record booklets, 25 student response booklets, audiocassette, storage box) $159.00

Interaction Checklist for Augmentative Communication (INCH)
Susan Oakander Bolton, Sallie E. Dashiell

1991	PRO-ED, Inc.

Population: Children, adults

Purpose: Evaluates and remediates the interaction skills of nonspeaking individuals

Description: The INCH checklist evaluates responding to greetings from others, introducing self when appropriate, using AAC system without prompting, seeking help when needed, using pauses or spaces for greater clarity, and restating a message. Can be used as an initial and follow-up measure of communicative effectiveness with either an electronic or manual device. Authors include suggestions for remediating interaction skills and for writing goals and objectives.

Format: Examiner required; individual administration; untimed

Scoring: Examiner evaluated

Cost: Manual and 25 Checklists $49.00

Kindergarten Language Screening Test–Second Edition (KLST–2)
Sharon V. Gauthier, Charles L. Madison

1998	PRO-ED, Inc.

Population: Ages 3 years 6 months to 6 years 11 months

Purpose: Tests receptive and expressive language competency and assesses language deficits that may cause kindergartners to fail academically

Description: Oral-response 8-item test identifying children for further diagnostic testing for language deficits that may accelerate academic fail-

ure. The child identifies name, age, colors, and body parts; demonstrates knowledge of number concepts; follows commands; repeats sentences; and engages in spontaneous speech. The test is based on the verbal language abilities considered average for children of kindergarten age.

Format: Examiner required; individual administration; untimed: 4 to 5 minutes

Scoring: Examiner evaluated

Cost: Complete Kit (manual, 50 profile/examiner record forms, picture book, picture cards, storage box) $109.00

Kohlman Evaluation of Living Skills (KELS)
Linda Kohlman Thomson

1992	American Occupational Therapy Association, Inc.

Population: Adults

Purpose: Measures ability to function in basic living skills

Description: Tests 17 basic living skills under five areas: self-care, safety and health, money management, transportation and telephone, and work and leisure. Used with the elderly and with persons who have cognitive disabilities, in court for the determination of commitment, and in discharge planning at acute-care hospitals.

Format: Examiner required; individual administration; untimed: 30 to 45 minutes

Scoring: Examiner evaluated

Cost: $35.00

Language Processing Test–Revised (LPT–R)
Gail J. Richard, Mary Anne Hanner

1995	LinguiSystems, Inc.

Population: Ages 5 through 11 years

Purpose: Evaluates the ability to attach increasingly more meaning to information received auditorily and to handle the increasing language demands of the classroom

Description: Oral-response verbal test with 84 items. The two pretests are Labeling and Stating Functions. The six subsets are Associations, Categorization, Similarities, Differences, Multiple Meanings, and Attributes. The numbers of subjects, means, medians, and standard deviations are given for each subtest and total test by 6-month age groups; age equivalents of raw scores are provided for each subtest and the total test;

and percentile ranks and standard score values are given for each subtest and total test raw score by age. The manual includes test–retest reliability coefficients and standard errors of measurement for each subtest and total test by age; reliability based on item homogeneity; and point biserial correlations between subjects with and without language disorder by age level. The LPT-R tests for differences between male and female mean scores for each subtest and total test by age. Suitable for individuals with physical, hearing, and mental impairments.

Format: Examiner required; individual administration; untimed: 35 minutes

Scoring: Examiner evaluated

Cost: Manual and 20 Test Forms $89.95

Preschool Language Scale–3 (PLS–3)
Irla Lee Zimmerman, Violette G. Steiner, Robert Evatt Pond

| 1992 | The Psychological Corporation |

Population: Birth through 6 years

Purpose: Measures receptive and expressive language

Description: Multiple-item test assessing both auditory comprehension and verbal ability. Items measure sensory discrimination, logical thinking, grammar and vocabulary, memory and attention span, temporal/spatial relations, and self-image at most age levels in each of the two domains. Also available in Spanish.

Format: Examiner required; individual administration; untimed: 20 to 30 minutes

Scoring: Examiner evaluated

Cost: Complete Kit (picture book, manual, record forms) $145.00

Receptive-Expressive Emergent Language Scale– Second Edition (REEL-2)
Kenneth R. Bzoch, Richard League

| 1991 | PRO-ED, Inc. |

Population: Infants and toddlers to age 3 years

Purpose: Used for the multidimensional analysis of emergent language

Description: Designed for use with a broad range of infants and toddlers who are at risk in the multidisciplinary programs developed under P.L. 99-457. The REEL-2 is a system of measurement and intervention planning based on neurolinguistic development and is designed to help

public health nurses, pediatricians, and educators identify young children who have specific language problems based on specific language behaviors. These behaviors have been systematically selected based on extensive research, and all are age related. Results of the evaluation are given in terms of an Expressive Language Age, Receptive Language Age, and Combined Language Age.

Format: Examiner required; parent interview; untimed: 15 minutes

Scoring: Examiner evaluated

Cost: Complete Kit (examiner's manual, 25 profile/test forms, storage box) $86.00

Revised Token Test (RTT)
Malcolm M. McNeil, Thomas E. Prescott

| 1978 | PRO-ED, Inc. |

Population: Ages 20 through 80 years

Purpose: Used for designing effective auditory rehabilitation programs and in quantifying small amounts of patient change for both clinical and research purposes

Description: A revision of the Token Test by DeRenzi and Vignolo, the RTT is a sensitive quantitative and descriptive test battery for auditory processing inefficiencies and disorders associated with brain damage, aphasia, and certain language and learning disabilities. Percentile ranks are available for normal adults and for adults with right- and left-hemisphere brain damage for each of the 10 subtests and for overall performance. Experimental evidence is reported for concurrent and construct validity, as well as for test–retest, intrascorer, and interscorer reliability.

Format: Examiner required; individual administration; untimed: 30 minutes

Scoring: Examiner evaluated

Cost: Complete Kit (examiner's manual, administration manual, scoring forms, profile forms, tokens, storage box) $149.00

Reynell Developmental Language Scales
Joan K. Reynell, Christian P. Gruber

| 1990 | Western Psychological Services |

Population: Ages 1 through 6 years

Purpose: Assesses two processes essential to language development: verbal comprehension and expressive language

Description: Battery of 134 items includes colorful test materials. Useful in evaluating language processes in young children, the test identifies the nature and extent of each child's language difficulty.

Format: Examiner required; individual administration; untimed: 30 minutes

Scoring: Examiner evaluated

Cost: Kit (set of stimulus materials, 10 test booklets, manual, carrying case) $499.00

Screening Kit of Language Development (SKOLD)

Lynn S. Bliss, Doris V. Allen

1983   Slosson Educational Publications, Inc.

Population: Ages 2 years 6 months to 4 years

Purpose: Assesses language disorders and delays in young children

Description: Oral-response 135-item test measuring language development in children speaking either Black English or Standard English. Picture stimuli are used to assess vocabulary, comprehension, story completion, individual and paired sentence repetition with pictures, individual sentence repetition without pictures, and comprehension of commands. The test consists of six subtests, three for Black English and three for Standard English, in each of the following age ranges: 30 to 36 months, 37 to 42 months, and 43 to 48 months. Norms are provided for speakers of Black and Standard English. The manual includes guidelines for administration and scoring and the linguistic characteristics of Black English.

Format: Examiner required; individual administration; untimed: 15 minutes

Scoring: Examiner evaluated

Cost: Complete Kit (manual, stimulus materials, scoring guidelines, 25 of either Standard or Black English scoring forms) $84.00

Speech and Language Evaluation Scale (SLES)

Diane R. Fressola, Sandra Ciponeri Hoerchler, Jacquelyn S. Hagan, Steven B. McDannold, Jacqueline Meyer

1989   Hawthorne Educational Services, Inc.

Population: Ages 4 years 5 months to 18 years

Purpose: Aids in the diagnosis of speech and language disorders

Description: The SLES is designed for in-school screening and referral of students with speech and language problems. The scale is designed to provide the clinician with input from classroom teachers, without requiring anecdotal reporting. The scale includes the most commonly recognized subscales of speech (articulation, voice, fluency) and language (form, content, and pragmatics). A DOS QuikScore is available.

Format: Rating scale; untimed

Scoring: Examiner evaluated; computer scoring available

Cost: Complete Kit $125.00

Test for Auditory Comprehension of Language–Third Edition (TACL-3)

Elizabeth Carrow-Woolfolk

1999   PRO-ED, Inc.

Population: Ages 3 through 9 years

Purpose: Measures auditory comprehension of children

Description: Test consists of 142 items divided into three subtests (Vocabulary, Grammatical Morphemes, Elaborated Phrases and Sentences) that assess a child's ability to understand English language forms. Ceiling rules for scoring are provided for each section. The Examiner's Manual includes a comprehensive discussion of the test's theoretical and research-based foundation, item development, standardization, administration and scoring procedures, norms tables, and guidelines.

Format: Examiner required; individual administration; untimed: 15 to 25 minutes

Scoring: Examiner evaluated

Cost: Complete Kit (manual, picture book, 25 profile/examiner record booklets, storage box) $254.00

Test for Examining Expressive Morphology (TEEM)

Kenneth G. Shipley, Terry A. Stone, Marlene B. Sue

1983   PRO-ED, Inc.

Population: Ages 3 to 16 years

Purpose: Assesses the expressive morpheme development of children (language age of 3 to 8 years; interest level age of 3 to 16 years), measures general language level, and monitors student progress

Description: Oral-response 54-item sentence-completion test assessing the allomorphic variations of six major morphemes: present progressives, plurals, possessives, past tenses, third-person singulars, and derived adjectives. The examiner presents each stimulus picture while reading the stimulus phrase, and the child completes the phrase while viewing the picture. Results identify specific morphemes and allomorphic variations requiring stimulation or instruction. The manual includes administration instructions and technical data.

Format: Examiner required; individual administration; untimed: 7 minutes

Scoring: Examiner evaluated

Cost: Test Kit (manual, 25 scoring forms, picture book) $69.00

Test of Adolescent and Adult Language–Third Edition (TOAL-3)
Donald D. Hammill, Virginia L. Brown, Stephen C. Larsen, J. Lee Wiederholt

| 1994 | PRO-ED, Inc. |

Population: Ages 12 through 24 years

Purpose: Assesses the linguistic aspects of listening, speaking, reading, and writing

Description: The TOAL-3 distinguishes between groups known to have language problems and those known to have normal language. The 10 composites are Listening—the ability to understand the spoken language of other people; Speaking—the ability to express one's ideas orally; Reading—the ability to comprehend written messages; Writing—the ability to express thoughts in graphic form; Spoken Language—the ability to listen and speak; Written Language—the ability to read and write; Vocabulary—the ability to understand and use words in communication; Grammar—the ability to understand and generate syntactic (and morphological) structures; Receptive Language—the ability to comprehend both written and spoken language; and Expressive Language—the ability to produce written and spoken language.

Format: Examiner required; individual or group administration; untimed: 1 to 3 hours

Scoring: Examiner evaluated

Cost: Complete Kit (manual, 50 answer booklets, 10 test booklets, 50 profile/examiner record forms, storage box) $172.00

Test of Early Language Development–Third Edition (TELD-3)
Wayne P. Hresko, D. Kim Reid, Donald D. Hammill

| 1999 | PRO-ED, Inc. |

Population: Ages 2 through 7 years

Purpose: Measures content and form in the receptive and expressive language abilities of children; used to identify problems, document progress, conduct research, and guide instructional practices

Description: This edition is a major revision. Like the previous edition, the TELD-3 yields an overall Spoken Language score, but now it includes scores for Receptive Language and Expressive Language subtests. The TELD-3 was standardized on 2,127 children representing 35 states. Pictures are presented in color to make them more attractive to children. Standard scores (with a mean of 100 and a standard deviation of 15) and percentiles are provided for subtest and composite scores. Age-equivalent scores are also reported for the subtests. The test is quick and easy to administer and score. The attractive pictures and content, along with the untimed nature of the items, allow for optimal assessment. The kit now includes all the manipulatives the examiner needs.

Format: Examiner required; individual administration; untimed: 15 to 45 minutes

Scoring: Examiner evaluated

Cost: Complete Kit (manual, 25 each of Form A and Form B, picture book, manipulatives, storage box) $264.00

Test of Language Competence–Expanded (TLC-Expanded)
Elisabeth H. Wiig, Wayne A. Secord

| 1989 | The Psychological Corporation |

Population: Ages 5 through 18 years

Purpose: Measures metalinguistic higher-level language functions

Description: Multiple-item response test for diagnosing language disabilities by assessing language strategies rather than language skill. The Recreating Sentences subtest examines the ability to perceive the nature of a communication and recreate a semantically, syntactically, and pragmatically appropriate sentence. The Understanding Metaphoric Expressions subtest has students interpret an expression and select another one with the same meaning. The Understanding Ambiguous Sentences subtest evaluates the ability to recognize and interpret alternative meanings of lexical and structural ambiguities. The Making Inferences subtest has students identify permissible inferences based on causal relationships or chains. The test's features include norm-referenced scores, extension teaching and testing formats for each subtest, and individual education program guidelines. Two levels for different age groups.

Format: Examiner required; individual administration; untimed: less than an hour

Scoring: Examiner evaluated

Cost: Complete Kit (manuals, materials, 25 protocols for both levels, briefcase) $384.50

Test of Language Development–Intermediate: Third Edition (TOLD–I:3)
Donald D. Hammill, Phyllis L. Newcomer

1997   PRO-ED, Inc.

Population: Ages 8 through 12 years

Purpose: Assesses the expressive and receptive language abilities of children

Description: Different components of spoken language are measured by five subtests: Generals, Malapropisms with Picture Vocabulary, Sentence Combining, Word Ordering, and Grammatic Comprehension. The TOLD–I:3 was standardized on more than 700 children from 19 states.

Format: Examiner required; individual administration: untimed: 30 minutes to 1 hour

Scoring: Examiner evaluated; computer scoring available

Cost: Complete Kit (manual, picture book, 25 profile/examiner record forms, storage box) $174.00

Test of Language Development–Primary: Third Edition (TOLD–P:3)
Phyllis L. Newcomer, Donald D. Hammill

1997   PRO-ED, Inc.

Population: Ages 4 through 8 years

Purpose: Assesses the expressive and receptive language abilities of children

Description: Nine subtests measure different components of spoken language. Picture Vocab-

ulary, Relational Vocabulary, and Oral Vocabulary assess the understanding and meaningful use of spoken words. Grammatic Understanding, Sentence Imitation, and Grammatic Completion assess differing aspects of grammar. Word Articulation, Phonemic Analysis, and Word Discrimination are supplemental subtests that measure the abilities to say words correctly and to distinguish between words that sound similar. The test was completely renormed in 1996 on more than 1,000 children from 30 states.

Format: Examiner required; individual administration: untimed: 30 minutes to 1 hour

Scoring: Examiner evaluated; computer scoring available

Cost: Complete Kit (manual, picture book, 25 profile/examiner record forms, storage box) $239.00

Token Test for Children (TTFC)
Frank DiSimoni

1978   PRO-ED, Inc.

Population: Ages 3 to 12 years

Purpose: Measures functional listening ability in children and identifies receptive language dysfunction

Description: Test with 61 items in which the child arranges wooden tokens in response to the examiner's oral directions. The results indicate a need for further testing of lexicon and syntax or to rule out language impairment in a child with reading difficulties. Materials include the tokens, manual, and scoring forms. Age and grade scores are available.

Format: Examiner required; individual administration; untimed: 10 minutes

Scoring: Examiner evaluated

Cost: Complete Kit (manual, 20 tokens, 50 scoring forms, storage box) $98.00

TOPS–R Elementary (Test of Problem Solving)
Linda Bowers, Rosemary Huisingh, Mark Barrett, Jane Orman, Carolyn LoGiudice

1994   LinguiSystems, Inc.

Population: Ages 6 through 11 years

Purpose: Assesses how children use language to think; used for children with communicative disorders, social or psychological difficulties, behavior disorders, and cognitive disorders

Description: Oral-response 72-item verbal test. Profiles and reports yielded are as follows: numbers of subjects, means, medians, and standard deviations by age in 6-month age groupings; age equivalents of raw scores; percentile ranks and standard score values for raw scores by age; test-retest reliability coefficients and standard errors of measurement by age; reliability based on item homogeneity; Kuder Richardson coefficients by age; point biserial correlations between item scores and total test by age; T values for differences between subjects with and without language disorders by age level for raw score means; T-tests for differences between male and female mean scores by age; numbers, means, and standard deviations for raw scores for normal subjects for the Classroom Problem Solving Scale; and T values for differences between subjects with and without language disorders by age level for raw score means for the Classroom Problem Solving Scale. Suitable for individuals with physical, hearing, and mental impairments.

Format: Examiner required; individual administration; untimed: 35 minutes

Scoring: Examiner evaluated

Cost: Manual and 20 Test Forms $89.95

Utah Test of Language Development–Third Edition (UTLD-3)
Merlin J. Mecham

| 1989 | PRO-ED, Inc. |

Population: Ages 3 through 9 years

Purpose: Identifies children with language-learning disabilities who may need further assistance

Description: Task-assessment oral-response 51-item test measuring the following factors: receptive semantic language, expressive semantic language, receptive sequential language, and expressive sequential language. Test items are arranged in developmental order.

Format: Examiner required; individual administration; untimed: 20 to 30 minutes

Scoring: Examiner evaluated

Cost: Complete Kit (manual, administration/picture book, 50 profile/examiner record forms, storage box) $119.00

Wiig Criterion-Referenced Inventory of Language (Wiig CRIL)
Elisabeth H. Wiig

| 1990 | The Psychological Corporation |

Population: Ages 4 through 13 years

Purpose: Obtains information to plan and implement effective language intervention

Description: Language probe sets are organized into four modules: Semantics, Pragmatics, Morphology, and Syntax. The record form provides space for three administrations to determine progress over time. Can be used as follow-up for norm-referenced testing.

Format: Examiner required; individual administration; untimed

Scoring: Examiner evaluated

Cost: Complete Kit (guide, 4 stimulus manuals, 10 of each record form) $267.50

Woodcock Language Proficiency Battery–Revised (WLPB-R) English Form
Richard W. Woodcock

| 1991 | Riverside Publishing Company |

Population: Ages 2 through 90+ years

Purpose: Assesses language skills in English; used for purposes of eligibility and determination of language proficiency level

Description: Provides an overall measure of language proficiency in measures of oral language, reading, and written language. The subtests are Memory for Sentences, Picture Vocabulary, Oral Vocabulary, Listening Comprehension, Verbal Analogies, Letter-Word Identification, Passage Comprehension, Word Attack, Reading Vocabulary, Dictation, Writing Samples, Proofing, Writing Fluency, Punctuation and Capitalization, Spelling and Usage, and Handwriting. There are cluster scores for Oral Language, Reading, and Written Language. The tests are primarily measures of language skills predictive of success in situations characterized by cognitive-academic language proficiency (CALP) requirements. CALP levels from advanced to negligible are provided.

Format: Examiner required; individual administration; untimed: 20 to 60 minutes depending on number of subtests

Scoring: Examiner evaluated; computer software available

Cost: Complete Test (test book, audiocassette, 25 each of test records and response booklets, manual, norm tables) $307.50

Fluency and Voice

Computerized Scoring of Stuttering Severity (CSSS)
Klaas Bakker, Glyndon D. Riley

1997	PRO-ED, Inc.

Population: Children, adults

Purpose: Allows repeated measures of stuttering severity

Description: Designed for PC computers with Windows or DOS. Types of measurement include percentage of stuttered syllables, mean duration of three longest stuttering events, mean duration of all stuttering events, fluent rate, and length of periods of fluent speech. These data are useful for tracking stuttering severity during treatment or in research over time. Results of scoring can be displayed as graphs to illustrate each measure to a client or audience.

Format: Examiner required; individual administration; untimed

Scoring: Computer evaluated; examiner interpretation

Cost: $89.00

Oral Speech Mechanism Screening Examination–Third Edition (OSMSE-3)
Kenneth O. St. Louis, Dennis M. Ruscello

2000	PRO-ED, Inc.

Population: All ages

Purpose: Evaluates speech, language, and other related skills; used for examining oral speech mechanisms in language and speech clients of all ages

Description: Provides an efficient, quick, and reliable method to examine the oral speech mechanism in individuals with all types of speech, language, and related disorders where oral structure and function is of concern. The third edition has a number of new features designed to make the instrument easier to administer and score than the previous revision. Included is a demon-

stration audiotape recorded to assist in giving instructions, and an updated manual has 16 new photographs.

Format: Examiner required; individual administration; untimed: 5 to 10 minutes

Scoring: Examiner evaluated

Cost: Complete Kit (manual, 50 scoring forms, audiocassette, storage box) $98.00

Stuttering Prediction Instrument for Young Children (SPI)
Glyndon D. Riley

1981	PRO-ED, Inc.

Population: Ages 3 to 8 years

Purpose: Determines whether a child should be scheduled for therapy to treat stuttering

Description: Diagnostic test uses pictures, parent interview, observation, and taped recordings of the child's speech to assess the child's history, reactions, part-word repetitions, prolongations, and frequency of stuttered words.

Format: Examiner required; individual administration; timed speech sample

Scoring: Examiner evaluated

Cost: Complete Kit (manual with picture plates and test forms, storage box) $74.00

Stuttering Severity Instrument for Children and Adults–Third Edition (SSI-3)
Glyndon D. Riley

1994	PRO-ED, Inc.

Population: Ages 2 years 10 months through adult

Purpose: Measures the severity of stuttering and evaluates the effects of treatment

Description: The third edition of this widely used test includes the following features: new and updated procedures, new normative data, and expanded picture plates to simplify speaking samples. The SSI-3 can be used in conjunction with the Stuttering Prediction Instrument for Young Children.

Format: Examiner required; individual administration; untimed: 15 to 20 minutes

Scoring: Examiner evaluated

Cost: Complete Kit (manual, picture plates, 50 test record and frequency computation forms, storage box) $94.00

Test of Oral Structures and Functions (TOSF)
Gary J. Vitali

1986   Slosson Educational Publications, Inc.

Population: Ages 7 years to adult

Purpose: Assesses oral structures, nonverbal oral functioning, and verbal oral functioning; used by speech pathologists for screening, differential diagnosis, caseload management decisions, and pre- and posttreatment assessment

Description: Multiple-item paper–pencil and oral-response test assessing oral structures and motor integrity during verbal and nonverbal oral functioning and establishing the nature of structural, neurological, or functional disorders. The test is composed of five subtests: Speech Survey, Verbal Oral Functioning, Nonverbal Motor Functioning, Orofacial Structures, and History/Behavioral Survey. The Speech Survey targets articulation, rate/prosody, fluency, and voice during spontaneous or elicited speech. The Verbal Oral Functioning subtest assesses the integrity of oral-nasal resonance balance during imitated and spontaneous speech and articulatory precision and rate/prosody during tests that control for performance loading effects, syllable position effects, voicing, manner of articulation, and placement of articulation. The Nonverbal Motor Functioning subtest assesses volitional and automatic oral functioning during essentially static and sequenced activities controlled for general anatomic site of functioning. The Orofacial Structures subtest is an observational survey of intra-oral and orofacial structures at rest.

Format: Examiner required; individual administration; untimed: 20 minutes

Scoring: Examiner evaluated

Cost: Complete Kit (manual, 25 test booklets, finger cots, tongue blades, balloons, oroscope penlight) $79.00

Verbal Motor Production Assessment for Children (VMPAC)
Deborah Hayden, Paula Square

1999   The Psychological Corporation

Population: Ages 3 through 12 years

Purpose: Assesses the neuromotor integrity of the motor speech system

Description: Identifies children with motor issues that have negative effects on the development of normal speech control. Items are arranged from basic to complex to pinpoint where the child begins to have difficulty. A training video demonstrates administration and scoring. Three main areas are assessed (Global Motor Control, Focal Oromotor Control, and Sequencing), as well as two supplemental areas (Connected Speech and Language Control and Speech Characteristics).

Format: Examiner required; individual administration; untimed: 30 minutes

Scoring: Examiner evaluated

Cost: Complete Kit (manual, cards, 15 record forms, videotape) $125.00

Voice Assessment Protocol for Children and Adults (VAP)
Rebekah H. Pindzola

1987   PRO-ED, Inc.

Population: Ages 4 years through adult

Purpose: Evaluates voice pitch, loudness, quality, breath features, and rate/rhythm

Description: Clinical tasks are guided step by step, and immediate interpretations of normalcy are facilitated by a grid-marking system. The VAP is equally applicable to functional and neurogenic voice disorders. The VAP includes a pitch level sample audiocassette for clinical use. By using these taped samples, examiners do not need musical instruments and sophisticated pitch determination equipment for a voice assessment. The cassette contains whole notes of the musical scale between E2 and C6. The tape is arranged for clinical practicality. Each whole note and octave is identified, played on a piano, then followed by a vocal demonstration.

Format: Examiner required; individual administration; untimed

Scoring: Examiner evaluated

Cost: Complete Kit (manual, audiocassette, 25 protocols, storage box) $59.00

Pragmatics

Test of Pragmatic Language (TOPL)
Diana Phelps-Terasaki

1992   PRO-ED, Inc.

Population: Kindergarten through junior high; adult remedial

Purpose: Assesses the student's ability to effectively use pragmatic language

Description: Test items provide information within six core subcomponents of pragmatic language: physical setting, audience, topic, purpose (speech acts), visual-gestural cues, and abstraction. The test includes 44 items, each of which establishes a social context. After a verbal stimulus prompt from the examiner, who also displays a picture, the student responds to the dilemma presented. The TOPL is designed for use by speech-language pathologists, teachers, counselors, psychologists, mental health professionals, and administrators. It is also appropriate for use as part of a comprehensive psychological battery of tests to aid in the evaluation of social skills and social language use. Norms are provided for individuals from 5 through 13 years of age; however, test items can be used as a criterion-referenced assessment for older individuals. The TOPL was standardized on a sample of 1,016 children residing in 21 states. Characteristics of the normative sample match those from the 1990 U.S. census data with regard to gender, residence, race, geographic region, and ethnicity. Internal consistency of the TOPL was determined using the coefficient alpha technique at each age level.

Format: Examiner required; individual administration; timed: 15 minutes

Scoring: Examiner evaluated

Cost: Complete Kit (examiner's manual, picture book, 25 profile/examiner record forms, storage box) $134.00

Semantics

Assessing Semantic Skills Through Everyday Themes (ASSET)
Mark Barrett, Linda Bowers, Rosemary Huisingh

| 1988 | LinguiSystems, Inc. |

Population: Ages 3 through 9 years

Purpose: Assesses the receptive and expressive vocabulary and semantic skills of preschool and early elementary children

Description: Test with 150 items examines semantics through theme approach that utilizes 20 pictures depicting the day-to-day life experiences of preschool and early elementary children. The themes include learning and playing, shopping, around the house, working, eating, and health and fitness. The types of tasks that are evaluated receptively and expressively are labeling, categorizing, attributes, functions, and definitions. The test provides standardized analyses of a child's strengths and weaknesses as well as an overall estimate of the individual child's semantic and vocabulary abilities in relation to same-age children. Standard scores, percentile ranks, age equivalents, and standard deviations are available. In addition, the normative data from a sample of children with language disorders who were administered the test are available.

Format: Examiner required; individual administration; untimed: 30 to 40 minutes

Scoring: Examiner evaluated

Cost: Test Kit (manual, picture stimuli book, 20 test forms) $89.95

Category-Specific Names Test
Pat McKenna

| 1998 | Psychology Press |

Population: Children, adults

Purpose: Measures naming ability of objects and their semantic categories

Description: The test is unique in allowing for the detection of a category-specific deficit both in naming and in comprehension of the spoken or written name within four semantic categories. Two of the categories are living things: fruits and vegetables and animals. The other two categories are manmade objects: praxic objects, which need a particular skilled action for their use, and nonpraxic objects, which are not associated with a specific action. Each object is presented in a clear colored photograph. Thirty objects for each category are graded in difficulty to sample the full range of knowledge within that category, making the test appropriate for all levels of ability within the normal population. The test was standardized on 400 adults and 81 children and has been validated on a series of patients with focal lesions restricted to the right or left cerebral hemisphere. The test has separate norms for men, women, and children.

Format: Examiner required; individual administration; untimed

Scoring: Hand key

Cost: Kit (manual, 6 booklets, 3 scoring sheet masters) $415.00

Joliet 3-Minute Preschool Speech and Language Screen

Mary C. Kinzler

1993   The Psychological Corporation

Population: Ages 2 years 6 months and 4 years 6 months

Purpose: Identifies students' potential problems in grammar, semantics, and phonology

Description: Multiple-item individually administered oral-response test assessing receptive vocabulary, expressive syntax, voice, fluency, and phonological competence. Line drawings are used to elicit receptive vocabulary. Sentences are used to identify expressive syntax, morphology, and phonological competence.

Format: Examiner required; individual or group administration; untimed: 3 minutes

Scoring: Examiner evaluated

Cost: Test Kit (manuals, Apple II disk, vocabulary plates, scoring sheets, ring binder) $69.50

Joliet 3-Minute Speech and Language Screen (Revised)

Mary C. Kinzler, Constance Cowing Johnson

1992   The Psychological Corporation

Population: Kindergarten, Grades 2 and 5

Purpose: Identifies students' potential problems in grammar, semantics, and phonology

Description: Multiple-item individually administered oral-response test assessing receptive vocabulary, expressive syntax, voice, fluency, and phonological competence. Line drawings are used to elicit receptive vocabulary. Sentences are used to identify expressive syntax, morphology, and phonological competence.

Format: Examiner required; individual or group administration; untimed: 3 minutes

Scoring: Examiner evaluated

Cost: Test Kit (manuals, Apple II disk, vocabulary plates, scoring sheets, ring binder) $69.50

Pyramids and Palm Trees

David Howard, Karalyn Patterson

1992   Thames Valley Test Company, Ltd.

Population: Adults

Purpose: Determines the degree to which meaning from pictures and words can be accessed

Description: Information from the test enables the examiner to establish whether difficulty in naming or pointing to a named picture is due to a difficulty in retrieving semantic information from pictures or words or in retrieving the appropriate spoken form of the word. Six different versions of the test are possible by using pictures, written words, or spoken words to change the modality of stimulus or response items. The test is short and easily administered.

Format: Examiner required; individual administration; untimed: 25 minutes

Scoring: Examiner evaluated

Cost: $112.00

Test of Adolescent/Adult Word Finding (TAWF)

Diane J. German

1990   PRO-ED, Inc.

Population: Ages 12 to 80 years

Purpose: Assesses word finding abilities to identify disorders

Description: Test with 70 items (or 40 in the brief test) with five naming sections: Picture Naming: Nouns; Picture Naming: Verbs; Sentence Completion Naming; Description Naming; and Category Naming. The TAWF includes a special sixth comprehension section that allows the examiner to determine if errors are a result of word finding problems or are due to poor comprehension. The test provides formal and informal analyses of two dimensions of word finding: speed and accuracy. The formal analysis yields standard scores, percentile ranks, and grade standards for item response time. The informal analysis yields secondary characteristics (gestures and extra verbalization) and substitution types. Speed can be measured in actual or estimated item response time. The estimated response time can be done during testing and eliminates the need for a stopwatch or tape recorder.

Format: Examiner required; individual administration; untimed: 20 to 30 minutes

Scoring: Examiner evaluated

Cost: Complete Kit (examiner's manual, technical manual, test book, 25 response forms) $179.00

Test of Word Finding in Discourse (TWFD)

Diane J. German

1991   PRO-ED, Inc.

Population: Ages 6 years 6 months to 12 years 11 months

Purpose: Helps answer questions related to word finding difficulties

Description: The child views three stimulus pictures contained in the manual and responds to standard auditory prompts. The elicited language sample is audiorecorded and then scored through a process of transcribing and segmenting the child's narrative. Scores obtained include the Productivity Index, a quantitative measure of how much language is produced in a child's discourse, and the Word Finding Behaviors Index, a frequency measure of specific word finding behaviors present in a child's discourse, such as repetitions, reformulations, substitutions, insertions, empty words, time fillers, and delays. Percentile ranks and standard scores can be obtained for both indexes.

Format: Examiner required; individual administration; untimed: 20 minutes

Scoring: Examiner evaluated

Cost: Complete Kit (manual, 25 record forms) $106.00

Test of Word Finding–Second Edition (TWF-2)
Diane J. German

2000	PRO-ED, Inc.

Population: Ages 4 through 12

Purpose: Diagnoses expressive language problems resulting from word retrieval difficulties

Description: Uses four different naming sections to test a student's word finding ability (picture naming nouns, sentence completion naming, picture naming verbs, picture naming categories). In addition, five supplemental analyses are provided as follow-up procedures to the word finding measures. The examiner gains critical information from these analyses that will both enhance the interpretation of a student's test performance and help to formulate a word finding intervention plan. The TWF-2 was normed on 1,836 students residing in 26 states from 1996 to 1999. Correlations between the TWF-2 and other tests of vocabulary showed a considerable relationship.

Format: Examiner required; individual administration; untimed: 20 to 30 minutes

Scoring: Examiner evaluated

Cost: Complete Kit (manual; 2 picture books; 10 each of preprimary, primary, and intermediate

profile/examiner record forms; storage box) $339.00

Test of Word Knowledge (TOWK)
Elisabeth H. Wiig, Wayne A. Secord

1992	The Psychological Corporation

Population: Ages 5 to 18 years

Purpose: Evaluates deficits in semantic knowledge

Description: Designed for use as part of a total diagnostic language battery, the test helps evaluate the student's ability to understand and use words.

Format: Examiner required; individual administration; untimed

Scoring: Examiner evaluated

Cost: Complete Kit (manual, stimulus manual, 12 record forms) $163.00

Uncritical Inference Test
William V. Haney

1982	International Society for General Semantics

Population: Adolescents, adults

Purpose: Measures uncritical inferencing

Description: Multiple-choice paper-pencil test helps students learn to distinguish between observations and inferences.

Format: Examiner required; group or individual administration; untimed

Scoring: Examiner interpretation; self-scored

Cost: $.75 each (minimum of 10)

WORD Test–Adolescent
*Linda Bowers, Rosemary Huisingh,
Mark Barrett, Jane Orman,
Carolyn LoGiudice*

1989	LinguiSystems, Inc.

Population: Ages 12 through 18 years

Purpose: Assesses students' expressive vocabulary and semantic skills using common as well as unique contexts

Description: A 60-item oral-response test assessing a student's facility with language and word meaning. The four subtests assess the following expressive vocabulary and semantic tasks: Brand Names, Synonyms, Sign of the Times, and Definitions. Tasks reflect language usage typical of school assignments and life experiences. Tasks are presented both auditorily and in printed or graphic form. Test results yield age equivalencies, standard scores, standard deviations, and percentile ranks for students ages 12 to 18. Demonstration items are provided. A discussion of performance and suggestions for remediation are included in the test manual.

Format: Examiner required; individual administration; untimed: 25 minutes

Scoring: Examiner evaluated

Cost: Manual and 20 Test Forms $89.95

WORD Test–Revised (Elementary)
Rosemary Huisingh, Mark Barrett, Linda Bowers, Carolyn LoGiudice, Jane Orman

1990	LinguiSystems, Inc.

Population: Ages 7 through 11 years

Purpose: Assesses expressive vocabulary and semantics; evaluates how a child understands and uses critical semantic features to attach meaning to words; used for students with communicative disorders and low academic performance, especially in vocabulary and language arts

Description: Oral-response 90-item verbal test with six subtests: Associations, Synonyms, Semantic Absurdities, Antonyms, Definitions, and Multiple Definitions. Profiles and reports yielded are as follows: number of subjects, means, medians, and standard deviations of each task and total test by age in 6-month intervals; age equivalents of raw scores for each task and total test; percentile ranks and standard score values for each task and total test raw scores by age in 6-month intervals; test-retest reliability coefficients and standard errors of measurement of each task and total test by age; reliability based on item homogeneity: Kuder Richardson coefficients of each task by age; point biserial correlations between item scores and task scores by age; average task intercorrelations and average correlations between tasks and total test across all ages; task intercorrelations and correlations between tasks and total test across all ages; correlations between the original and revised editions for each task and total test by age; *t* values for differences between subjects with and without language disorders by age level for raw score means by task and total test; and subject distribution for item selection study.

Format: Examiner required; individual administration; untimed: 25 to 35 minutes

Scoring: Examiner evaluated

Cost: Manual and 20 Test Forms $89.95

Syntax

Language Sampling, Analysis, and Training–Third Edition (LSAT-3)
Dorothy Tyack, Gail Portuff Venable

1998	PRO-ED, Inc.

Population: Ages 2 years to adult

Purpose: Assesses the use of morphological and syntactical elements in sentences; also used as a resource for training children whose language delays are serious enough to warrant intervention

Description: Based on established linguistic and behavioral principles, this method is appropriate for both group or individual teaching. The child's speech sample demonstrates the rules that each child has acquired to form sentences. Analyzing the sample enables teachers and clinicians to write Individualized Education Programs that are precisely tailored to specific linguistic needs. The book contains four main chapters: Eliciting and Transcribing Language, Analyzing the Sample, Training Programs, and Measuring Change. Included with the handbook are the following worksheets: Transcription, Word-Morpheme Tally and Summary, Sequence of Language Acquisition, Baseline Analysis, Training Worksheet, and Score Sheet. Scored and unscored samples are provided for practice.

Format: Examiner required; individual administration; untimed

Scoring: Examiner evaluated

Cost: Complete Kit (manual, 25 analysis forms, 25 transcription sheets, storage box) $89.00

Patterned Elicitation Syntax Test (PEST) (Revised)
Edna Carter Young, Joseph J. Perachio

1993	The Psychological Corporation

Population: Ages 3 years to 7 years 6 months

Purpose: Determines whether a child's expressive grammatical skills are age appropriate; identifies children needing further evaluation

Description: Multiple-item oral-response test using the delayed imitation technique to assess a child's use of 44 syntactic structures. The child listens to three consecutive modeled sentences with a common syntactic pattern but varying vocabulary while looking simultaneously at corresponding illustrations. The child then repeats the sentences with the aid of the drawings. The first two sentences serve as models. The third sentence, which is most distant from the examiner's model, is scored. In addition to determining the child's language age, criterion-referenced interpretation of the child's responses provides an in-depth analysis of the child's use of grammatical structures. The manual includes stimulus pictures, a demonstration page, normative data, and instructions for administration and scoring. The response form is used to record the child's utterances, the assessment form includes grammatical analysis, and the individual data form is used for record keeping.

Format: Examiner required; individual administration; untimed: 20 minutes

Scoring: Examiner evaluated

Cost: Test Kit (picture book, manual, 10 forms) $65.50

Vocabulary

Comprehensive Receptive and Expressive Vocabulary Test–Computer Administered (CREVT-CA)
Gerald Wallace, Donald D. Hammill

1997	PRO-ED, Inc.

Population: Ages 4 through 89 years

Purpose: Measures both receptive and expressive vocabulary

Description: The receptive portion is completely computer administered and scored. The expressive portion requires examiner input. The computer gives instructions and asks the individual to define a series of words. The examiner then scores using criteria on the screen. Report is provided on-screen or may be exported to word processor.

Format: Examiner required; computer administration; untimed

Scoring: Examiner and computer scoring

Cost: Complete Kit (disks, manual, 25 administrations, installation guide) $249.00

Comprehensive Receptive and Expressive Vocabulary Test–Second Edition (CREVT-2)
Gerald Wallace, Donald D. Hammill

2002	PRO-ED, Inc.

Population: Ages 4 through 89 years

Purpose: Measures receptive and expressive oral vocabulary

Description: Receptive vocabulary is measured with the use of a picture book that has 10 color pictures for 61 items for the "point-to-the-picture-of-the-word-I-say" technique. Five to eight words are associated with each picture plate, spread evenly across ability levels. On the Expressive Vocabulary subtest, the 25 words pertain to the same 10 common themes used in the Receptive Vocabulary subtest. The individual defines the word given. A combined score is provided on two equivalent forms.

Format: Examiner required; individual administration; untimed: 20 to 30 minutes

Scoring: Examiner evaluated

Cost: Complete Kit (manual, photo album, 25 each of Form A and B protocols, storage box) $219.00

Expressive Language Test
Linda Bowers, Rosemary Huisingh, Jane Orman, Carolyn LoGiudice

1998	LinguiSystems, Inc.

Population: Ages 5 through 11 years

Purpose: Assesses overall expressive language functioning

Description: An oral-response standardized test with eight subtests: Sequencing (13 items), Metalinguistics—Defining (15 items), Metalinguistics—Generating Examples (15 items), Grammar and Syntax (15 items), Concepts (15 items), Categorizing and Describing—Identifying Categories (10 items), Categorizing and Describing—Defining Categories (10 items), and Categorizing and Describing—Generating Examples (10 items).

Format: Examiner required; individual administration; untimed: 40 to 45 minutes

Scoring: Examiner evaluated

Cost: Test Kit (manual, sequencing cards, stimuli book, 20 forms) $99.95

Expressive One-Word Picture Vocabulary Test–2000 (EOWPVT-2000)
Morrison F. Gardner

2000	Academic Therapy Publications

Population: Ages 4 through 18 years

Purpose: Provides assessment of English speaking vocabulary

Description: This 170-item test is conormed with the Receptive One-Word Picture Vocabulary Test-2000 on a representative national sample of over 2,000 individuals. New administration procedures permit examiners to cue examinees so that they will attend to the relevant aspects of each illustration. Record forms provide cues, acceptable alternate answers, and age-related start points. Newly rendered test plates provide full-color drawings; a number of test items are new to this edition. Raw scores are converted to standard scores, percentile ranks, and age equivalents.

Format: Examiner required; individual administration; untimed: 20 minutes

Scoring: Examiner evaluated

Cost: Test Kit (manual, test plates, 25 English forms, portfolio) $140.00

Expressive Vocabulary Test (EVT)
Kathleen T. Williams

Date not provided   American Guidance Service

Population: Ages 2 years 6 months through 90+ years

Purpose: Measures expressive vocabulary and word retrieval for standard English

Description: The EVT has 38 labeling items and 152 synonym items. For the labeling items, the examiner points to a picture or a part of the body and asks a question. On the synonym items, the examiner presents a picture and stimulus word(s) within a carrier phrase. The examinee responds to each item with a one-word answer. All stimulus pictures are in full color, carefully balanced for gender and ethnic representation.

Format: Examiner required; individual administration; untimed: 15 minutes

Scoring: Examiner evaluated; computer scoring available

Cost: Complete Kit (easel, manual, 25 record forms) $139.95

OWLS: Oral and Written Language Scales Listening Comprehension and Oral Expression; Written Expression
Elizabeth Carrow-Woolfolk

1995   American Guidance Service

Population: Ages 3 through 21 years

Purpose: Assessment of receptive and expressive language

Description: OWLS consists of three scales: Listening Comprehension (LC), Oral Expression (OE), and Written Expression (WE). The scales were developed and normed as part of the same assessment. The oral language components (LC and OE) are packaged together with one manual. The WE scale is packaged separately with its own manual. The LC scale is designed to measure the understanding of spoken language. The OE scale is designed to measure the understanding and use of spoken language. The WE scale is designed to measure the ability to communicate meaningfully using written linguistic forms. Tasks in LC address the lexical (vocabulary), syntactic (grammar), and supralinguistic (higher-order thinking) skills. Tasks in OE address lexical, syntactic, supralinguistic, and pragmatic or functional language skills. Tasks address conventions (rules of spelling, capitalization, punctuation, etc.), linguistics (modifiers, phrases, verb forms, etc.), and content (ability to communicate meaningfully). Items are administered in age-appropriate item sets.

Format: Examiner required; individual administration; untimed: LC 5 to 15 minutes, OE 10 to 25 minutes, WE 10 to 40 minutes

Scoring: Examiner interpreted; computer scoring available for Macintosh and Windows platforms

Cost: Complete Kit (Listening, Oral, and Written manuals, easels, 25 of each record form) $249.95

Peabody Picture Vocabulary Test–Third Edition (PPVT–III)
Lloyd M. Dunn, Leota M. Dunn

1998   American Guidance Service

Population: Ages 2 to 90+ years

Purpose: Measures hearing vocabulary for standard English

Description: Like the first two editions, the PPVT–III is a measure of listening comprehension for spoken words in standard English and a screening test of verbal ability. Items are arranged in 17 sets of 12 items each for more efficient and accurate application of basal and ceiling rules. There are many new illustrations for better gender and ethnic balance. Alternate equivalent forms are available.

Format: Examiner required; individual administration; untimed: 10 to 15 minutes

Scoring: Examiner interpretation; computer scoring is available for Macintosh and Windows platforms

Cost: Complete Kit (easels, manuals, 25 each of Forms A and B) $239.95

Progressive Achievement Test (PAT): Listening Comprehension-Revised
Neil Reid, Ian C. Johnstone, Warwick B. Elley

1994	New Zealand Council for Educational Research

Population: Ages 7 to 14 years

Purpose: Assesses comprehension of orally presented material

Description: Educational assessment applications with 25 to 30 items with eight overlapping levels for Primary, Intermediate, and Secondary. Forms A and B for alternate years. Materials used: manual, script, audiocassette, answer sheets, scoring keys, and test booklets. Yields total scores.

Format: Examiner required; group administration; timed: 55 minutes

Scoring: Hand key

Cost: Manual $6.75; Booklet $1.80; 10 Answer Sheets $1.44; Key $.99

Receptive One-Word Picture Vocabulary Test-2000 (ROWPVT-2000)
Morrison F. Gardner

2000	Academic Therapy Publications

Population: Ages 2 through 18 years

Purpose: Provides assessment of English hearing vocabulary

Description: This 170-item test provides a measure of receptive vocabulary. The test is conormed with the Expressive One-Word Picture Vocabulary Test-2000 on a representative national sample of over 2000 individuals. Pronunciation guides are provided for the more difficult words. Record forms include detailed instructions for test administration. Newly rendered test plates provide full-color drawings. A number of test items are new to this edition. Raw scores are converted to standard scores, percentile ranks, and age equivalents.

Format: Examiner required; individual administration; untimed: 20 minutes

Scoring: Examiner evaluated

Cost: Test Kit (manual, test plates, 25 English record forms, in portfolio) $140.00

Structured Photographic Expressive Language Test-Preschool (SPELT-P)
Ellen O'Hara Werner, Janet I. Dawson

1983	Janelle Publications, Inc.

Population: Ages 3 to 5 years 11 months

Purpose: Measures abilities in expression of early developing morphological and syntactic features

Description: Twenty-five items, using photographs, are used to assess skills. Target structures include prepositions, plurals, possessive nouns and pronouns, plurals, possessive nouns, regular and irregular past tense, contractible and uncontractible copula, and negation. An Articulation Screening form is available.

Format: Examiner required; individual administration; untimed: 10 to 15 minutes

Scoring: Examiner evaluated

Cost: Complete Kit (manual, picture book, 50 response forms) $99.00

Structured Photographic Expressive Language Test-II (SPELT-II)
Janet I. Dawson

1983, manual updated 1995	Janelle Publications, Inc.

Population: Ages 4 years to 9 years 5 months

Purpose: Measures expressive use of morphology and syntax

Description: Oral-response verbal test with 50 photographs. Standard scores, percentile ranks, and age equivalent scores are yielded. Photographs are used to examine use of morphology and syntax. A modified version is available in Spanish. The standardization sample included over 1,000 children throughout the United States.

Format: Examiner required; individual administration; untimed: 15 to 20 minutes

Scoring: Examiner evaluated

Cost: Complete Kit (manual, picture book, 50 response forms) $109.00

School and Institutional Environments

Classroom Environment Scale (CES)
Rudolf H. Moos, Edison J. Trickett

Date not provided	Consulting Psychologists Press, Inc.

Population: Grades 7 through 12

Purpose: Assesses the teaching atmosphere of junior and senior high school classrooms to evaluate the effects of course content, teaching methods, teacher personality, and class composition

Description: Paper–pencil 90-item test measuring nine dimensions of classroom atmosphere: involvement, affiliation, teacher support, task orientation, competition, order and organization, rule clarity, teacher control, and innovation. These dimensions are grouped into four sets: relationship, personal development, system maintenance, and system change. Materials include four forms: the Real Form (Form R), which measures current perceptions of classroom atmosphere; the Ideal Form (Form I), which measures conceptions of the ideal classroom atmosphere; the Expectations Form (Form E), which measures expectations about a new classroom; and a 36-item Short Form (Form S). Forms I and E are not published, although reworded instructions and items are listed in the manual.

Format: Examiner required; suitable for group use; untimed

Scoring: Examiner evaluated

Cost: Preview Kit (booklet, profile, answer sheet, scoring keys, manual) $74.80

Community College Student Experiences Questionnaire (CCSEQ)
Jack Friedlander, C. Robert Pace, Patricia H. Murrell, Penny Lehman

1999	Center for the Study of Higher Education

Population: Ages 18 years and older

Purpose: Intended for community and technical college students, to measure student progress, involvement, and experiences, as well as institutional effectiveness

Description: Multiple-choice, self-report (Likert scale) instrument with 170 items plus 20 optional locally developed questions on six subtests: Student Background, College Program, Courses, College Activities, Estimate of Gains, and Campus Environment. Results include frequency reports of all data and Quality of Effort scores. The CCSEQ can be used for individuals with visual, hearing, and physical impairments.

Format: Self-administered; untimed: 20 to 30 minutes

Scoring: Computer scored; scoring service available from publisher

Cost: $125.00 for print report and data on diskette; $2.25 per instrument

Community Oriented Programs Environment Scale (COPES)
Rudolf H. Moos

1996	Mind Garden, Inc.

Population: Adults

Purpose: Assesses the social environments of community-based psychiatric treatment programs

Description: Paper–pencil 100-item true–false test of 10 aspects of social environment: involvement, support, spontaneity, autonomy, practical orientation, personal problem orientation, anger and aggression, order and organization, program clarity, and staff control. Materials include the Real Form (Form R), which measures perceptions of a current program; the 40-item Short Form (Form S); and the Ideal Form (Form I), which measures conceptions of a new program. Forms I and E are not published, but items and instructions are printed in the appendix of the COPES manual. Items are modified from the Ward Atmosphere Scale. One in a series of nine Social Climate Scales.

Format: Examiner required; untimed: 20 minutes

Scoring: Hand key

Cost: Sampler Set $25.00; Permission for up to 200 Uses $125.00

Correctional Institutions Environment Scale (CIES)
Rudolf H. Moos

1974, 1987	Mind Garden, Inc.

Population: Adults

Purpose: Assesses the social environment of juvenile and adult correctional programs

Description: Paper-pencil 90-item true-false test of nine aspects of social environment: involvement, support, expressiveness, autonomy, practical orientation, personal problem orientation, order and organization, clarity, and staff control. Materials include four forms: the Real Form (Form R), which measures perceptions of the current correctional program; the 36-item Short Form (Form S); the Ideal Form (Form I), which measures conceptions of an ideal program; and the Expectations Form (Form E), which measures expectations of a new program. Forms I and E are not published, but items and instructions appear in the appendix of the CIES manual. Items and subscales are similar to those used in the Ward Atmosphere Scale. One of a series of nine Social Climate Scales.

Format: Examiner administered; suitable for group use; untimed:

Scoring: Hand key

Cost: Sampler Set $25.00; Permission for up to 200 Uses $125.00

Early Childhood Environment Rating Scale-Revised (ECERS)
Thelma Harms, Richard M. Clifford, Debby Cryer

| 1998 | Teachers College Press |

Population: Adults

Purpose: Measures the quality of educational programs

Description: The revision has been expanded to 43 items and includes many improvements. Examples of new items and improvements are as follows: Interaction items, such as staff-child interactions, interactions among children, and discipline; Curriculum items, such as nature/science and math/numbers; Health and Safety items; more inclusive and culturally sensitive indicators for many items; and more items focusing on staff needs. Training video available.

Format: Rating scale; untimed

Scoring: Examiner evaluated

Cost: $10.95

Elementary Program Implementation Profile (PIP)

| Date not provided | High/Scope Educational Research Foundation |

Population: Adults

Purpose: Rates a program

Description: An evaluation tool for all elemen-

tary grade settings. Rates the site according to physical environment, daily schedule, adult-child interaction, instructional methods, staff development, and home-school collaboration. The PIP can also be used for training and pinpointing specific areas needing improvement.

Format: Self-administered; untimed

Scoring: Self-scored

Cost: Manual $6.95; 25 Forms $14.95

Family Day Care Rating Scale (FDCRS)
Thelma Harms, Richard M. Clifford

| 1989 | Teachers College Press |

Population: Adults

Purpose: Designed to measure the quality of educational programs

Description: Consists of 32 items, organized under six major headings: Space and Furnishings for Care and Learning, Basic Care, Language and Reasoning, Learning Activities, Social Development, and Adult Needs. Eight additional items are included for rating a day care home's provisions for children with special needs. Video training program is available.

Format: Rating scale; untimed

Scoring: Examiner evaluated

Cost: $10.95

Functional Assessment of Academic Behavior (formerly The Instructional Environment System-II [TIES-II])
James Ysseldyke, Sandra Christenson

| 2002 | Sopris West Educational Services |

Population: Grades 1 to 12

Purpose: Assesses the instructional needs of students in relation to the learning environment

Description: Based on the belief that student performance in school is a function of an interaction between the student and the learning (instructional) environment, this assessment provides a set of observational and interview forms, administration procedures, and an organizational structure that allows educators to both identify and address the instructional needs of individual students. It can be used to assess the learning needs of all students, but it is especially useful when applied to the needs of students who are tough to teach. The assessment enables education professionals to identify ways to change instruction—or the learning environment—so that the student will respond to instruction more positively, and thus more successfully. It provides education professionals with essential information for prereferral intervention, instructional consultation, student–staff support teams, intervention assistance, and collaborative intervention planning. This new edition contains a section on interventions associated with the student's specific areas of need.

Format: Examiner required; individual administration; untimed

Scoring: Examiner evaluated

Cost: $59.00

Infant/Toddler Environment Rating Scale (ITERS)
Thelma Harms, Debby Cryer, Richard M. Clifford

| 1990 | Teachers College Press |

Population: Adults

Purpose: Measures the quality of educational programs

Description: The 35 items in the ITERS are divided into seven categories: Furnishings and Display for Children, Personal Care Routines, Listening and Talking, Learning Activities, Interactions, Program Structure, and Adult Needs. A video training program is available.

Format: Rating scale; untimed

Scoring: Examiner evaluated

Cost: $10.95

Institutional Functioning Inventory
Earl J. McGrath

| Date not provided | Educational Testing Service |

Population: Adults

Purpose: Evaluates functioning of educational institutions; used in self-studies for accreditation, planning, and research

Description: Paper-pencil 132-item test assessing 11 dimensions of institutional functioning: intellectual-aesthetic, extracurricular, freedom, human diversity, concern for undergraduate learning, democratic governance, meeting local needs, self-study and planning, concern for advanced knowledge, concern for innovation, and institutional esprit. The inventory is distributed to a random sample of college community members, including the faculty, administration, and students. Available in French for Canadian institutions.

Format: Self-administered; untimed: 45 minutes

Scoring: Computer scored

Cost: Reusable Faculty Booklet $.50; Reusable Student Booklets $.35; Answer Sheet $.10

Instructional Climate Inventory–Students
Larry A. Braskamp, Martin L. Maehr

| 1988 | MetriTech, Inc. |

Population: Grades 3 to 12

Purpose: Assesses school culture from the students' perspective; used by elementary and secondary school administrators to assess student attitudes toward the school and its instructional learning climate

Description: Paper-pencil 20-item multiple-choice test measuring school loyalty and the strength of the school's climate. Additional scales describe the climate on four dimensions: accomplishment, recognition, power, and affiliation.

Format: Self-administered; untimed: 5 to 10 minutes

Scoring: Scoring service

Cost: Booklets/Answer Sheets $.25 each; Computer Report (up to 250 students) $150.00

Instructional Climate Inventory–Teachers
Larry A. Braskamp, Martin L. Maehr

| 1988 | MetriTech, Inc. |

Population: Adults

Purpose: Assesses instructional leadership behavior, satisfaction, and school culture from the teachers' perspective; used by elementary and secondary school administrators to assess teacher attitudes toward the school and the effectiveness of school leadership

Description: Paper-pencil 108-item multiple-choice test measuring instructional leadership and school climate. Climate is described on four dimensions: accomplishment, recognition, power, and affiliation. Additional scales measure strength of culture, degree of commitment or loyalty to the school, job satisfaction, and the following research-based dimensions of instructional leadership: Defines Mission, Manages Curriculum, Supervises Teaching, Monitors Student Progress, and Promotes Instructional Climate. Items were adapted from the Organizational Assessment Survey.

Format: Self-administered; untimed: 25 minutes

Scoring: Scoring service

Cost: Booklets/Answer Sheets $1.75 each; Computer Report (up to 15 teachers) $100.00

Military Environment Inventory (MEI)
Rudolph H. Moos

1986	Mind Garden, Inc.

Population: Adults

Purpose: Assesses the social environment of various military contexts; used to detect individuals and units at risk of morale and performance problems

Description: Multiple-item paper–pencil inventory assessing individuals' and units' perceptions of the military environment. The test yields seven scores: Involvement, Peer Cohesion, Officer Support, Personal Status, Order and Organization, Clarity, and Officer Control. Additional subscales are related to military performance and sick-call rates.

Format: Self-administered; untimed

Scoring: Hand key

Cost: Sampler Set $25.00; Permission Set $125.00; Test Booklets $25.00

My Class Activities

2001	Creative Learning Press, Inc.

Population: Children, adolescents

Purpose: Examines student perceptions of Interest, Challenge, Choice, and Enjoyment in the classroom; used to assist teachers in adapting instruction so that it is more effective and increases student motivation

Description: Paper–pencil 31-item instrument asks students to indicate, using a 5-point scale from *never* to *always*, how often a statement applies to their classroom. A sample item is "My class has helped me explore my interests." Data gleaned from the survey can help teachers modify classroom activities to make school a more relevant and engaging place to be.

Format: Examiner required; suitable for group use; untimed

Scoring: Examiner evaluated

Cost: Manual and 1 Reproducible Questionnaire $15.95

Opinion Inventories for Students, Teachers, Parents, and Community Members

Date not provided	National Study of School Evaluation

Population: All ages

Purpose: Measures the opinions of the school's stakeholders

Description: The Opinion Inventories address a series of issues of particular concern to teachers, students, parents, and community members. In addition, each inventory contains a section for up to 20 additional questions that can be developed by the school to address specific issues of concern or interest to the school. The inventories also include a section on which respondents can write additional comments. Each of the Opinion Inventories has been designed to incorporate the survey questions directly on optical scan answer sheets to provide for ease of administration. Consequently, survey participants do not need to transfer their responses to a separate answer sheet.

Format: Self-administered; untimed

Scoring: Scoring service

Cost: Administrator's Manual $6.50; all inventories are $15.00 for package of 25

Preschool Program Quality Assessment (PQA)

Date not provided	High/Scope Educational Research Foundation

Population: Adults

Purpose: Rates a program

Description: A comprehensive rating instrument for evaluating program quality and identifying staff training needs. It contains sections on the learning environment, daily routine, parent involvement and family services, staff qualifications and development, curriculum planning and assessment, adult–child interaction, and program management. A separate guide is available for using the PQA in Head Start program evaluation.

Format: Self-administered; untimed

Scoring: Self-scored

Cost: Package (manual, Head Start user guide, form) $22.85

School Environment Preference Survey (SEPS)
Leonard V. Gordon

1978	EdITS/Educational and Industrial Testing Service

Population: Grades 1 through 12

Purpose: Measures work role socialization as it occurs in the traditional school setting; used for academic and disciplinary student counseling, vocational counseling, and instructional planning

Description: Paper-pencil 24-item test measuring a student's levels of commitment to the set of attitudes, values, and behaviors that are necessary for employment and are fostered and rewarded in most school settings. The scales measured are structured role orientation, self-subordination, traditionalism, rule conformity, and uncriticalness. High and low scores have differential behavioral implications. Norms are provided for high school level.

Format: Examiner required; suitable for group use; untimed: 10 to 15 minutes

Scoring: Hand key; may be computer scored

Cost: Specimen Set $6.75; 25 Forms $9; Keys $13.50; Manual $3.75

School Improvement Follow-Up Survey

1994	Assessment Resource Center

Population: Adults

Purpose: Measures success of academic programs and the extracurricular climate for learning

Description: Multiple-choice response format with comments section. For students in their first and fifth years following graduation.

Format: Survey mailed

Scoring: Machine-scored; test scoring service available from publisher

Cost: $50.00 (50 surveys, supportive materials); Scoring $.75 per survey

School-Age Care Environment Rating Scale (SACERS)
Thelma Harms, Ellen Vineberg Jacobs, Donna Romano White

1996	Teachers College Press

Population: Adults

Purpose: Designed to measure the quality of educational programs

Description: Provides an easy-to-use resource for defining high-quality care and assessing levels of quality in child care programs offered by schools and other organizations. It consists of 49 items, organized under seven categories: Space and Furnishings, Health and Safety, Activities, Interactions, Program Structure, Staff Development, and Supplementary Items (for children with special needs).

Format: Rating scale; untimed

Scoring: Examiner evaluated

Cost: $10.95

Small College Goals Inventory (SCGI)

Date not provided	Educational Testing Service

Population: College students

Purpose: Assesses the educational goals of small colleges; used to establish priorities and to provide direction for present and future planning

Description: Paper-pencil 90-item test assessing the educational goals of small colleges. The 20 goal areas are divided into two types: outcome goals and process goals. The outcome goals are academic development, intellectual orientation, individual personal development, humanism/altruism, cultural/aesthetic awareness, traditional religiousness, vocational preparation, advanced training, research, meeting local needs, public service, social egalitarianism, and social criticism/activism. The process goals are freedom, democratic governance, community, intellectual/aesthetic environment, innovation, off-campus learning, and accountability/efficiency. The inventory is distributed to a random sample of students, faculty, and administrators. Materials include space for 20 additional locally written goals.

Format: Self-administered; untimed: 45 minutes

Scoring: Computer scored

Cost: Booklets $.65; Processing $1.75

Student Instructional Report (SIR)

Date not provided	Educational Testing Service

Population: College students

Purpose: Measures teacher performance; used for instructional improvement, administrative decisions, and student course selection

Description: Paper-pencil 39-item test assessing six aspects of teacher performance: course organization and planning, faculty-student interaction, communication, course difficulty and workload, textbooks and readings, and tests and exams. The instrument is administered to students during regular class sessions. Available in Spanish and French (for Canadian universities).

Format: Examiner required; suitable for group use; untimed: 50 minutes

Scoring: Computer scored

Cost: First 20,000 Forms $.18 each; Processing First 5,000 Forms $.35 each

Student Reactions to College: Four Year College Edition (SRC/4)

| Date not provided | Educational Testing Service |

Population: College students

Purpose: Assesses the needs and concerns of students enrolled in 4-year colleges; used in institutional self-assessment for developing programs and services for students

Description: Paper–pencil 150-item test assessing four dimensions of student concerns: processes of instruction, program planning, administrative affairs, and out-of-class activities. These four dimensions are divided further into such areas as content of courses, appropriateness of course work to occupational goals, satisfaction with teaching procedures, student–faculty relations, educational and occupational decisions, effectiveness of advisers and counselors, registration, regulations, availability of classes, housing, employment, financial aid, and satisfaction with campus environment. The test is distributed to random samples of students.

Format: Self-administered; untimed: 50 minutes

Scoring: Computer scored

Cost: Booklet $.65; Processing $1.75

Student Reactions to College: Two Year College Edition (SRC/2)

| Date not provided | Educational Testing Service |

Population: College students

Purpose: Assesses the needs and concerns of students enrolled in 2-year colleges; used in institutional self-assessment for developing programs and services for students

Description: Paper–pencil 150-item test assessing four dimensions of student concerns: processes of instruction, program planning, administrative affairs, and out-of-class activities. These four dimensions are divided further into such areas as content of courses, appropriateness of course work to occupational goals, satisfaction with teaching procedures, student–faculty relations, educational and occupational decisions, effectiveness of advisers and counselors, registration, regulations, availability of classes, housing, employment, financial aid, and satisfaction with campus environment. The test is distributed to a random sample of students.

Format: Self-administered; untimed: 50 minutes

Scoring: Computer scored

Cost: Booklet $.65; Processing $1.75

Survey of Goals for Student Learning

| Date not provided | National Study of School Evaluation |

Population: Students

Purpose: Assesses the quality of students' work across the curriculum

Description: The National Study of School Evaluation, working together with the Alliance for Curriculum Reform, conducted a comprehensive review of the subject area expectations for student learning defined by each of the national curriculum associations. Based on the results of this interdisciplinary analysis of the national standards, the following schoolwide goals for student learning were identified: Learning-to-Learn Skills, Expanding and Integrating Knowledge, Communications Skills, Thinking and Reasoning Skills, Interpersonal Skills, and Personal and Social Responsibility. Part 1 of the survey helps schools assess the extent to which students are achieving these goals for their learning. In Part 2 of the survey, the respondents are asked to determine the level of priority for improvement that should be assigned to each goal. Schools can further customize the survey by including additional goals on the survey. Included with the survey is a comprehensive set of rubrics for the six schoolwide goals.

Format: Self-administered; untimed

Scoring: Scoring service

Cost: 10 Surveys and Answer Sheets $30.00

Survey of Instructional and Organizational Effectiveness

| Date not provided | National Study of School Evaluation |

Population: Schools

Purpose: This survey provides a tool to help schools identify strengths and limitations

Description: This survey is not designed for staff evaluation. The focus is on assessing the overall effectiveness of the school for the purpose of school improvement. This survey is based on the NSSE's Indicators of Schools of Quality, which includes a comprehensive set of research-based principles and indicators that consistently distinguish the work of top-performing schools. The principles are defined within seven categories of instructional and organizational effectiveness: Curriculum Development, Instructional Strategies, Assessment of Student Learning, Educational Agenda, Leadership for School Improvement, Community-Building, and Culture of Continuous Improvement and Learning.

Format: Self-administered; untimed

Scoring: Scoring service

Cost: 10 Surveys and Answer Sheets $30.00

University Residence Environment Scale (URES)
Rudolf H. Moos

1988   Mind Garden, Inc.

Population: College students, adults

Purpose: Assesses the social environment of university residence halls and dormitories

Description: Paper-pencil 100-item true–false test of 10 dimensions of the social climate of college dormitories: involvement, emotional support, independence, traditional social orientation, competition, academic achievement, intellectuality, order and organization, student influence, and innovation. Materials include the Real Form (Form R), which measures current perceptions of a residence; the 40-item Short Form (Form S); the Expectations Form (Form E), which measures expectations of a new residence; and the Ideal Form (Form I), which measures conceptions of an ideal residence hall environment. Forms I an E are not in published form, but items and instructions appear in the appendix of the URES manual. One in a series of nine Social Climate scales.

Format: Examiner required; suitable for group use; untimed

Scoring: Hand Key; examiner evaluated

Cost: Sample Set $25.00; Permission for up to 200 Uses $125.00

Ward Atmosphere Scale (WAS)
Rudolf H. Moos

1996   Mind Garden, Inc.

Population: Adolescents, adults

Purpose: Assesses the social environments of hospital-based psychiatric treatment programs; used to evaluate organizational effectiveness

Description: Paper–pencil 100-item true–false test covering 10 aspects of social environment. Yields 10 scores: involvement, support, spontaneity, autonomy, practical orientation, personal problem orientation, anger and aggression, order and organization, program clarity, and staff control. Three treatment outcome scales may be used: Dropout, Release Rate, and Community Tenure. Materials include the Real Form (Form R), which measures perceptions of a current program; the 40-item Short Form (Form S); the Ideal Form (Form I), which measures conceptions of an ideal program; and the Expectations Form (Form E), which measures expectations of a new program. Forms I and E are not published, but items and instructions appear in the appendix of the WAS manual. One in a series of nine Social Climate scales.

Format: Examiner required; suitable for group use; untimed: 20 minutes

Scoring: Hand key; examiner evaluated

Cost: Sample Set $25.00; Permission for up to 200 Uses $125.00

School Leadership

Instructional Leadership Inventory
Martin L. Maehr, Russell Ames

1985   MetriTech, Inc.

Population: Adults

Purpose: Evaluates the leadership goals and behaviors of school administrators

Description: Paper–pencil 100-item multiple-choice inventory evaluating the leadership goals and behaviors of school administrators on five broad categories of instructional leadership: Defines Mission, Manages Curriculum, Supervises Teaching, Monitors Student Progress, and Promotes Instructional Climate. An additional set of items assesses the individual's perception of contextual factors relating to staff, students, and community. A mail-in scoring service is available from the publisher. American Psychological Association purchase guidelines apply.

Format: Self-administered; untimed: 30 to 60 minutes

Scoring: Scoring service

Cost: $35.00 per report; Booklets/Answer Sheets $1.75 each

School Administrator Assessment Survey
Larry A. Braskamp, Martin L. Maehr

1988	MetriTech, Inc.

Population: Adults

Purpose: Assesses organizational culture and employee commitment, assesses worker motivation by determining personal values and incentive, and evaluates the opportunities for fulfillment that individuals perceive in their present jobs

Description: Likert scale with 200 items measuring four aspects of the person, the job, and the culture of the school. Each element is assessed in terms of the same four characteristics: accomplishment, recognition, power, and affiliation. Reports help administrators identify specific objectives for individual improvement and personal development. This instrument is an adaptation of the Organizational Assessment Survey.

Format: Self-administered; untimed: 1 hour

Scoring: Scoring service

Cost: $35.00 per report; Booklets/Answer Sheets $1.75 each

School Principal Job Functions Inventory (SP-JFI)
Melany E. Baehr, Frances M. Burns,
R. Bruce McPherson, Columbus Salley

1976	NCS Pearson Reid London House

Population: Adults

Purpose: Assesses the relative importance of functions performed in a particular type of principalship and the principal's ability to perform the functions; used to clarify a school principal's job responsibilities and to diagnose training needs

Description: Multiple-item paper–pencil inventory assessing the relative importance of 17 basic functions for overall successful performance in a given principalship: personal handling of student adjustment problems, organizations and extracurricular activities, individual student development, utilization of specialized staff, evaluation of teacher performance, collegial contacts, racial and ethnic group problems, troubleshooting and problem solving, community involvement and support, dealing with gangs, curriculum development, instructional materials, staffing, working with unions, working with central office, safety regulations, and fiscal control. Items are rated by the incumbent principal. The inventory also may be used to have incumbents rate their relative ability to perform these functions. Separate forms are available for rating the importance of various functions and for a self-rating of the incumbent's abilities.

Format: Self-administered; untimed: 45 to 60 minutes

Scoring: Hand key

Cost: 25 Test Booklets $30.00; 25 Score Sheets $10.00; Examiner's Manual $15.00

Science

General

Collegiate Assessment of Academic Progress (CAAP) Science Reasoning Test

2001	ACT, Inc.

Population: Ages 17 years and older

Purpose: Assesses science reasoning

Description: Paper–pencil 36-item multiple-choice test with two categories: Referring and Reasoning. A test booklet, answer sheet, and pencil are used. May be used for persons with visual, physical, hearing, and mental impairments.

Format: Examiner required; suitable for group use; timed: 40 minutes

Scoring: Machine scored; test scoring service available from publisher

Cost: $10.75

Specific

Dental Admission Test (DAT)

Updated annually	American Dental Association

Population: Ages 21 to 22; college students applying to dental schools; 63% have completed 60 to 120 semester hours

Purpose: Used for admission to dental school

Description: The testing program is designed to measure general academic ability, comprehension of scientific information, and perceptual ability. Completion of at least one year of collegiate education, which should include courses in biology, general chemistry, and organic chemistry, is required. The examinations have multiple-choice items. Four examinations are included: Survey of the Natural Sciences (Biology, General Chemistry, Organic Chemistry), Perceptual Ability, Reading Comprehension, and Quantitative Reasoning. The test is administered on computer almost any day of the year at Sylvan Technology Test Centers only in the United States.

Format: Computer administered; individual administration; timed: 4 hours 15 minutes

Scoring: Computer scored; candidate receives official DAT scores immediately

Cost: Candidate Fee $160.00

PSB Aptitude for Practical Nursing Examination

1997	Psychological Services Bureau, Inc.

Population: Adults; practical nursing students

Purpose: Measures abilities, skills, knowledge, and attitudes important to successful performance as a practical nurse; used as an admission test for schools and programs of practical nursing

Description: Multiple-item paper–pencil or electronic battery of five tests assessing areas important for performance as a practical nurse: general mental ability, spelling, the natural sciences, judgment in practical nursing, and readiness for specialized instruction in practical nursing.

Format: Examiner required; suitable for group use; timed: 2 hours, 15 minutes

Scoring: Machine and electronically scored

Cost: Reusable Test Booklets $10.00; Answer Sheets (scoring and reporting service) $10.00; Electronic Version $15.00

PSB Nursing School Aptitude Examination (RN)

1996	Psychological Services Bureau, Inc.

Population: Adult nursing school candidates

Purpose: Measures abilities, skills, knowledge, and attitudes important to successful performance as a professional nurse; used as an admission test for schools and departments of nursing

Description: Multiple-item paper–pencil or electronic battery of five tests assessing areas important for performance as a nurse: academic aptitude, spelling, reading comprehension, information in the natural sciences, and vocational adjustment. The battery predicts readiness for instruction in nursing at the diploma or associate degree levels.

Format: Examiner required; suitable for group use; timed: 1 hour, 45 minutes

Scoring: Machine and electronically scored

Cost: Reusable Test Booklets $10.00; Answer Sheets (scoring and reporting service) $10.00; Electronic Version $15.00

Special Education

General

Adaptive Behavior Evaluation Scale–Revised (ABES–R)
Stephen B. McCarney

1995	Hawthorne Educational Services, Inc.

Population: Ages 5 through 18 years

Purpose: Used as a measure of adaptive skills in the identification of individuals with mental retardation; behavior disorders; learning disability; and visual, hearing, or physical impairments

Description: The ABES–R represents the 10 adaptive behavior skill areas of Communication Skills, Self-Care, Home Living, Social Skills, Community Use, Self-Direction, Health and Safety, Functional Academics, Leisure, and Work Skills. The School Form is completed by an educator; the Home Form is completed by a parent or guardian. A DOS Quick Score is available. Also available in Spanish.

Format: Individual administration; untimed

Scoring: Examiner evaluated; computer scoring available

Cost: Complete Kit $155.00

Analytic Learning Disability Assessment (ALDA)
Thomas D. Gnagey, Patricia D. Gnagey

1982   Slosson Educational Publications, Inc.

Population: Ages 8 to 14 years

Purpose: Measures the skills necessary to read, spell, write, and work with numbers; aids in the neuropsychological evaluation of individuals with learning disability, mental retardation, and behavior disorders

Description: Multiple-item test assessing a student's strengths and weaknesses in 77 skills underlying basic school subjects. The strengths and weaknesses are matched with the student's most appropriate learning method for each subject: 11 reading methods, 23 spelling methods, 6 math computation methods, and 8 handwriting methods. The results are transferred to the Recommendation Pamphlet to create an individualized teaching plan providing specific procedures and methods for teachers. The test should not be used unless a learning dysfunction is suspected.

Format: Examiner required; individual administration; untimed: 75 minutes

Scoring: Hand key; computer scoring available

Cost: Complete Kit (test book, manual, scoring straight edge, four colored scoring pencils, tape, chalk, 20 complete testing forms, teaching plan, carrying case) $148.00

Anser System—Aggregate Neurobehavioral Student Health and Educational Review
Melvin D. Levine

1989   Educators Publishing Service, Inc.

Population: Ages 3 to 18 years

Purpose: Gathers information from parents and teachers for the educator or clinician who has questions about a child with learning or behavioral problems

Description: Three separate short-answer paper-pencil questionnaires for parents and school personnel to evaluate three age groups: Form 1 (ages 3 to 5), Form 2 (ages 6 to 11), and Form 3 (ages 12 and over). Form 4 is a self-administered student profile to be completed by students ages 9 and older. The parent questionnaire surveys family history, possible pregnancy problems, health problems, functional problems, early development, early educational experience, skills and interests, activity-attention problems, associated behaviors, and associated strengths. The school questionnaire covers the educational program and setting, special facilities available, the results of previous testing. The self-administered Student Profile asks the student to rate himself or herself on a series of statements in the following categories: fine motor, gross motor, memory, attention, language, general efficiency, visual-spatial processing, sequencing, general academic performance, and social interaction. Follow-up questionnaires document frequency and changes of behaviors and environment, assisting in monitoring and evaluation of progress and deficiency of intervention programs.

Format: Examiner required; individual administration; untimed: 30 to 60 minutes

Scoring: Examiner evaluated

Cost: Interpreter's guide for Forms 1 to 6 $10.25; Specimen Set (guide, sample of each Form 1-6) $10.25; all questionnaires available for purchase in 1- or 2-dozen lots

CASAS Life Skills Assessment System

1994   Comprehensive Adult Student Assessment System (CASAS)

Population: Adult and adolescent native and nonnative speakers of English

Purpose: Used by programs to identify basic skills in reading, math, and listening needed by individuals to function successfully in today's workplace, community, and society; learners can be placed into educational programs to assess learning gains

Description: Multiple-choice survey achievement series includes reading comprehension and math tests at four levels (A-D) and, for assessment in English as a second language (ESL), listening comprehension tests at three levels (A-C). Each test has two forms, for pre- and posttesting. Includes a life skills appraisal and an ESL appraisal for placement purposes, a reading certification test, and a beginning literacy reading assessment. Tests are competency based; content covers general life skills in a variety of content areas. CASAS scaled scores identify general skill level and enable comparison of performance across CASAS tests. Scannable answer sheets are available.

Format: Self-administered

Scoring: Self/computer scored

Cost: 25 Reusable Tests $65.00; 25 Listening Tests with Audiocassette $70.00

Checklist of Adaptive Living Skills (CALS)
Lanny E. Morreau, Robert H. Bruininks

| 1991 | Riverside Publishing Company |

Population: All ages

Purpose: Targets specific behaviors each individual needs to develop

Description: Comprehensive, criterion-referenced checklist organized into four broad domains: Personal Living Skills, Home Living Skills, Community Living Skills, and Employment Skills. The CALS presents 24 specific skill modules spanning a wide range of behaviors. Evaluates 794 important life skills. It can be used to determine instructional needs, develop individual training objectives, and provide continuous record of progress. Linked to two norm-referenced tests: Scales of Independent Behavior and Inventory for Client and Agency Planning.

Format: Examiner required; individual administration; untimed

Scoring: Examiner evaluated

Cost: Complete Program (manual, 25 checklists) $94.50

Dynamic Assessment of Test Accommodations™ (DATA)
Lynn Fuchs, Douglas Fuchs, Susan Eaton, Carol Hamlett

| 2000 | The Psychological Corporation |

Population: Grades 2 through 7

Purpose: Helps to determine appropriate test accommodations based on empirical evidence

Description: Practitioners administer brief tests, with and without testing accommodations. Student scores are compared to those of a nondisabled normative sample. When scores indicate that a student benefits from an accommodation more than would be expected, the accommodation is recommended. DATA includes tests that assess the following areas under various testing conditions: math computation, math concepts and applications, and reading comprehension. There are three grade-appropriate levels.

Format: Examiner required; appropriate for group use; untimed

Scoring: Examiner evaluated

Cost: Complete Kit (manual, 25 each of 3 booklets) $150.00 per level

Scales for Predicting Successful Inclusion (SPSI)
James E. Gilliam, Kathleen S. McConnell

| 1997 | PRO-ED, Inc. |

Population: Ages 5 to 18 years

Purpose: Helps in predicting which students with disabilities are likely to be successful in general education

Description: The SPSI is a norm-referenced instrument that can be an excellent source of data for completion of functional behavior assessments. Designed for use in schools and clinics, the test is easily completed by teachers, parents, and others who are knowledgeable about the student. The SPSI contains 60 items that describe four major factors of school adjustment: work habits, coping skills, peer relationships, and emotional maturity. The items on these scales represent essential behaviors necessary for successful inclusion.

Format: Rating scale; untimed

Scoring: Examiner evaluated

Cost: Complete Kit (manual, 50 record booklets, storage box) $86.00

Scales of Independent Behavior–Revised (SIB-R)
Robert H. Bruininks, Richard W. Woodcock, Richard F. Weatherman, Bradley K. Hill

| 1996 | Riverside Publishing Company |

Population: Infants through adults

Purpose: Measures adaptive and problem behavior; used to determine independence of individuals with varying degrees of mental, emotional, behavioral, or physical disability

Description: Multiple-item structured interview or checklist procedure with 14 subtests assessing motor skills, social interaction and communication skills, personal living skills, community living skills, and problem behaviors. In addition, four maladaptive behavior indexes measure frequency and severity of problem behaviors: General Maladaptive Index, Internalized Maladaptive Index, Externalized Maladaptive Index, and Asocial Maladaptive Index. Age scores, percentile ranks, standard scores, relative mastery indexes, expected range of independence, and training implication range are obtained. The SIB-R offers five administration options: full battery, short form, early development scale, individual clusters, and a problem behavior scale.

This test is related structurally and statistically to the WJ-R. Because common norms are provided for the two tests, an individual's adaptive behavior may be interpreted in relation to cognitive ability.

Format: Examiner required; individual administration; time varies

Scoring: Examiner evaluated; computer software available

Cost: Complete Program (interview book, manual, 15 full scale response booklets, 5 short form response booklets, 5 early development response booklets) $193.00

School Function Assessment (SFA)
Wendy Coster, Theresa Deeney, Stephen Haley

1998   The Psychological Corporation

Population: Grades K through 6

Purpose: Evaluates and monitors a student's performance of functional tasks and activities

Description: The instrument helps elementary school students with disabilities succeed by identifying their strengths and needs in important nonacademic functional tasks. Three scales are included for evaluating students: Participation, Task Supports, and Activity Performance. Criterion cutoff scores help establish eligibility for special services.

Format: Examiner required; individual administration; untimed: 5 to 10 minutes

Scoring: Examiner evaluated

Cost: Complete Kit (manual, 25 record forms, 3 rating scales) $139.00

Teaching Resource and Assessment of Critical Skills (TRACS)
Lauren Meiklejohn, Mark Rice

1989   Program Development Associates

Population: Individuals with special needs

Purpose: Assists in decision making about an individual's skills and potential to live in an unsupervised setting

Description: A criterion-referenced teaching and assessment tool based on an individualized, community-based, functional skills mode. It was designed to help staff transition individuals with developmental, mental, or learning disabilities.

Format: Examiner required; individual administration; untimed

Scoring: Unscored

Cost: $124.00

Vineland Adaptive Behavior Scales
Sara S. Sparrow, David A. Balla, Dominic V. Cicchetti

1984, 1985   American Guidance Service

Population: Birth through 18 years

Purpose: Measures personal and social skills

Description: Semi-structured interviews and a questionnaire that assess personal and social skills. Available in an Expanded Form (577 items), Survey Form (297 items), and Classroom Edition (244 items). Four domains are measured: Communication, Daily Living Skills, Socialization, and Motor Skills. The Survey Form is available in Spanish, as are all of the Reports to Parents.

Format: Interview and questionnaire; untimed: 20 to 90 minutes

Scoring: Examiner evaluated; computer scoring available for Macintosh and Windows

Cost: Complete Starter Set (one each of the manuals and 25 forms for each version) $169.95

Autism

Adolescent and Adult Psychoeducational Profile (AAPEP)
Gary B. Mesibov, Eric Schopler, Bruce Schaffer, Rhoda Landrus

1988   PRO-ED, Inc.

Population: Adolescents and adults with developmental disabilities

Purpose: Measures the learning abilities and characteristics of individuals with severe developmental disabilities; used by service providers, teachers, and parents for preparing and maintaining individuals in community-based programs

Description: Multiple-item task-performance test assessing the learning abilities of individuals with autism and developmental disabilities. The test results are profiled to reflect the individual characteristics of the person. Emphasis is on evaluating functional skills from three areas: direct observation, home, and schoolwork. The profile is translated into an appropriately individualized set of goals and objectives for each individual.

Format: Examiner required; individual administration; untimed: 60 minutes

Scoring: Examiner evaluated

Cost: Manual (includes reproducible protocol) $69.00

Asperger Syndrome Diagnostic Scale (ASDS)

Brenda Myles, Stacy Jones-Bock, Richard Simpson

2000   PRO-ED, Inc.

Population: Ages 5 to 18 years

Purpose: Helps determine presence of Asperger syndrome

Description: Completed by anyone who knows the child, the rating scale has 50 yes-no items. The items were drawn from five specific areas of behavior: cognitive, maladaptive, language, social, and sensorimotor. The ASDS was normed on 227 persons with various disabilities. All items included represent behaviors that are symptomatic of Asperger syndrome.

Format: Rating scale; untimed: 10 to 15 minutes

Scoring: Examiner evaluated

Cost: Complete Kit (manual, 50 record forms, storage box) $89.00

Autism Diagnostic Observation Schedule (ADOS)

Catherine Lord, Michael Rutter, Pamela C. DiLavore, Susan Risi

1999   Western Psychological Services

Population: All ages

Purpose: Evaluates anyone suspected of having autism

Description: The ADOS consists of various activities that allow the examiner to observe social and communication behaviors related to the diagnosis of pervasive developmental disorders (PDDs). These activities provide interesting, standard contexts in which interaction can occur. The ADOS consists of four modules. The individual being evaluated is given only one module, depending on his or her expressive language level and chronological age. Following guidance provided in the manual, the examiner selects the appropriate module for each person. Observations are recorded, then coded later to formulate a diagnosis. Cutoff scores are provided for both the broader diagnosis of PDD, atypical autism, or autism spectrum, as well as the traditional, narrower conceptualization of autism.

Format: Examiner required; individual administration; untimed: 35 to 40 minutes

Scoring: Examiner evaluated

Cost: Complete Kit $1,325.00

Autism Screening Instrument for Educational Planning–Second Edition (ASIEP-2)

David A. Krug, Joel R. Arick, Patricia J. Almond

1993   PRO-ED, Inc.

Population: Ages 18 months to adult

Purpose: Assesses the behavioral, social, and educational development of students with autism, mental retardation, deafness, blindness, and emotional disturbance; used to establish Individualized Education Programs, evaluate program effectiveness, and monitor student progress

Description: Multiple-item paper-pencil observational inventory consisting of five subtests: Autism Behavior Checklist (ABC), Sample of Vocal Behavior, Interaction Assessment, Educational Assessment, and Prognosis of Learning Rate. The observational methods involved in all five subtests allow all students to be "testable."

Format: Examiner required; individual administration; untimed

Scoring: Examiner evaluated

Cost: Complete Kit (manual, 25 each of all record forms, manipulatives, storage box) $198.00

Behavior Rating Instrument for Autistic and Other Atypical Children–Second Edition (BRIAAC)

Bertram Ruttenberg, Charles Wenar, Enid G. Wolf

1991   Stoelting Company

Population: Children

Purpose: Evaluates the status of low-functioning, atypical, and autistic children of all ages; used to evaluate children who will not or cannot cooperate with formal testing procedures

Description: Paper-pencil inventory of observations taken over a 2-day period assessing a child's present level of functioning and measuring behavioral change in eight areas: relationship to an adult, communication, drive for mastery, vocalization and expressive speech, sound and speech reception, social responsiveness, body movement (passive and active), and psychobiological development. Each of the eight scales begins with the most severe autistic behavior and progresses to behavior roughly comparable to that of a normally developing $3\frac{1}{2}$- to $4\frac{1}{2}$-year-old. The complete BRIAAC includes a manual, report forms, individual scale score sheet, total score sheet, intrascale and interscale profile forms, descriptive guides, and suggested individual plans.

Format: Examiner required; individual administration; untimed

Scoring: Examiner evaluated

Cost: Complete Kit (manual, all required forms) $124.50

Childhood Autism Rating Scale (CARS)
Eric Schopler, Robert J. Reichler,
Barbara Rochen Renner

1988	Western Psychological Services

Population: Children, adolescents

Purpose: Diagnoses children with autism syndrome and distinguishes them from children with developmental disabilities who are not autistic

Description: Items on this behavior rating scale include relating to people; imitation; emotional response; body use; object use; adaptation to change; visual response; listening response; taste, smell, and touch response and use; fear or nervousness; verbal communication; nonverbal communication; activity level; level and consistency of intellectual response; and general impression. The child is rated on each of the 15 items using a 7-point scale that indicates the degree to which the child's behavior deviates from that of a normal child of the same age. A total score is then computed by summing the individual ratings. Children who score above a given point are categorized as autistic. Scores within the autistic range can then be divided into two categories: mild-to-moderate autism and severe autism.

Format: Examiner required; individual administration; untimed

Scoring: Examiner evaluated

Cost: Kit (25 rating scales, manual) $60.00

Gilliam Asperger Disorder Scale (GADS)
James E. Gilliam

2001	PRO-ED, Inc.

Population: Ages 3 to 22 years

Purpose: Evaluates unique behavioral problems of individuals who may have Asperger's disorder

Description: Based on the most current and relevant definitions and diagnostic criteria of Asper-

ger's disorder, the rating scale is completed by a parent or professional who knows the child. The 32 items are divided into four subscales that describe specific, observable, and measurable behaviors. Eight additional items are included for parents to contribute data about their child's development during the first 3 years of life. Standard scores and percentiles are provided.

Format: Rating scale; untimed: 5 to 10 minutes

Scoring: Examiner evaluated

Cost: Complete Kit (manual, 25 protocols, storage box) $89.00

Gilliam Autism Rating Scale (GARS)
James E. Gilliam

1995	PRO-ED, Inc.

Population: Ages 3 through 22 years

Purpose: Helps identify and diagnose autism and estimates the severity

Description: Items on the GARS are based on the definitions of autism adopted by the Autism Society of America and the *Diagnostic and Statistical Manual of Mental Disorders: Fourth Edition.* The items are grouped into four subtests: Stereotyped Behaviors, Communication, Social Interaction, and Developmental Disturbances. Three core subtests describe specific and measurable behaviors. An optional subtest (Developmental Disturbances) allows parents to contribute data about their child's development during the first 3 years of life. The test was normed on 1,092 representative subjects with autism from 45 states, Puerto Rico, and Canada. Both validity and reliability of the instrument are high. Behaviors are assessed using objective, frequency-based ratings. The scale is easily completed by those who have knowledge of the subject's behavior.

Format: Rating scale; untimed: 5 to 10 minutes

Scoring: Examiner evaluated

Cost: Complete Kit (manual, 25 summary/ response forms, storage box) $86.00

Psychoeducational Profile–Revised (PEP-R)
Eric Schopler, Robert J. Reichler, Ann Bashford, Margaret D. Lansing, Lee M. Marcus

1990	PRO-ED, Inc.

Population: Children with developmental disabilities functioning between the ages of 6 months and 7 years

Purpose: Measures the learning abilities and characteristics of autism and related developmental disabilities; used to establish individualized special education curricula or home programs

Description: Multiple-item task-performance test assessing the learning abilities of children with autism and developmental disabilities. The test results are profiled to reflect the individual characteristics of the child. This profile is translated into an appropriately individualized special education curriculum or home program according to the teaching strategies described in Volume II of the manual. Volume III contains a collection of more than 250 teaching activities.

Format: Examiner required; individual administration; untimed: 45 to 90 minutes

Scoring: Examiner evaluated

Cost: Volume I Complete Kit (manual, 10 forms) $74.00; Volume II $36.00; Volume III $74.00

Deaf and Hearing Impairment

Carolina Picture Vocabulary Test (CPVT)
Thomas L. Layton, David W. Holmes

1985	PRO-ED, Inc.

Population: Ages 4 to 11 years 6 months

Purpose: Measures receptive sign vocabulary in individuals who use manual signing as their primary mode of communication

Description: Norm-referenced, validated, receptive sign vocabulary test for children who are deaf or hearing impaired. The population ($N = 767$) used in the standardization research was based on a nationwide sample of children who use manual signs as their primary means of communication. Stratification of the sample was based on geographic region, educational facility, parental occupation, gender, race, age, grade, etiology, age of onset of hearing impairment, number of years of signing, IQ, and threshold of hearing loss in the better ear. The CPVT consists of 130 items with suggested basal and ceiling levels. Scale scores, percentile ranks, and age equivalency scores are provided.

Format: Examiner required; individual administration; untimed: 10 to 15 minutes

Scoring: Examiner evaluated

Cost: Complete Kit (manual, picture book, 50 record forms, storage box) $129.00

Central Institute for the Deaf Preschool Performance Scale (CID-PPS)
Ann E. Geers, Helen S. Lane

1984	Stoelting Company

Population: Ages 2 to 6 years

Purpose: Measures intellectual potential using completely nonverbal testing procedures; predicts school achievement in preschoolers with hearing impairment

Description: Multiple-item task-performance test assessing the intellectual abilities of preschoolers without requiring a single spoken word from either the examiner or the child (optional verbal clues are provided for hearing children). Six subtests assess intellectual abilities in the following areas: manual planning (block building, Montessori cylinders, and two-figure formboard); manual dexterity (buttons and Wallin pegs); form perception (Decroly pictures, Seguin formboard); perceptual/motor skills (Knox cube, drawing, and paper folding); preschool skills (color sorting and counting sticks); and part/whole relations (Manikin and Stutsman puzzles). Test materials were selected from existing mental tests for children ages 2 to 5 to obtain a broad, clinical picture of the child's ability and a numerical rating (Deviation IQ) that would correlate with a Stanford-Binet IQ. The test is an adaptation of the early Randall's Island Performance Series.

Format: Examiner required; individual administration; untimed: 40 minutes

Scoring: Examiner evaluated

Cost: Complete Kit (manual, 30 record forms, manipulatives) $850.00

CID Phonetic Inventory
Jean S. Moog

1988	Central Institute for the Deaf Publications

Population: Ages 3 years to adolescents with severe to profound hearing impairment

Purpose: Measures speech production in individuals with hearing impairment

Description: This is a rating form on which the teacher can record the child's ability to produce speech sounds. The Phonetic Skills Profile graphically illustrates the child's skills and progress. There are six subtests: Suprasegmental Aspects, Vowels/Diphthongs, Initial Consonants, Alternating Vowels, Final Consonants, and Alternating Consonants.

Format: Examiner required; individual administration; untimed: 30 minutes

Scoring: Examiner evaluated

Cost: Kit (manual, forms, cards) $24.00

Early Speech Perception Test (ESP)
Jean S. Moog, Ann E. Geers

1990	Central Institute for the Deaf Publications

Population: Ages 3 years to adolescents with severe to profound hearing impairment

Purpose: Measures speech perception skills

Description: The ESP may be used to establish objectives and to measure effects of a hearing aid or cochlear implant on the child's speech perception ability. There are two versions: standard and low verbal.

Format: Examiner required; individual administration; untimed: 20 to 30 minutes

Scoring: Examiner evaluated

Cost: Kit (manual, forms, toys, full-color picture cards, audiocassette) $150.00

Grammatical Analysis of Elicited Language–Pre-Sentence Level (GAEL-P)
Ann E. Geers, Victoria J. Kozak, Jean S. Moog

1983	Central Institute for the Deaf Publications

Population: Ages 3 to 6 years

Purpose: Measures grammatical aspects of spoken or signed English in a standardized test setting

Description: These subtests measure comprehension, prompted production, and imitated production. Items measure readiness skills (6), single words (90), and word combinations (39).

Format: Examiner required; individual administration; untimed: 30 minutes

Scoring: Examiner evaluated

Cost: Kit (manual, manipulatives, forms, video) $320

Rhode Island Test of Language Structure (RITLS)
Elizabeth Engen, Trygg Engen

1983	PRO-ED, Inc.

Population: Ages 3 to 20 years

Purpose: Measures English language development in hearing children ages 3 to 6 years or in children and adults with hearing impairment ages 3 to 20 years

Description: Multiple-choice 100-item verification test assessing understanding of language structure (syntax). The test presents 20 sentence types, both simple and complex. The test is used for educational planning, such as determination of school readiness, bilingual programming, and language introduction procedures. It can also be used where language development is a concern, including for individuals with mental retardation or learning disabilities, and in bilingual programs.

Format: Examiner required; individual administration; timed: 30 minutes

Scoring: Examiner evaluated

Cost: Complete Kit (test booklet, 10 response sheets, 10 analysis sheets, manual) $139.00

Scales of Early Communication Skills (SECS)
Jean S. Moog, Ann E. Geers

1975	Central Institute for the Deaf Publications

Population: Ages 2 to 8 years

Purpose: Evaluates speech and language development of children with hearing impairment

Description: Four scales measure receptive language, expressive language, nonverbal receptive skills, and nonverbal expressive skills. Ratings are based on observation of the child in structured lessons and in natural communication settings.

Format: Examiner required; individual administration; untimed

Scoring: Examiner evaluated

Cost: Manual $12.00; 25 Forms $10.00

Speech Perception Instructional Curriculum and Evaluation (SPICE)
Julia J. Biedenstein, Lisa S. Davidson, Jean S. Moog

1995	Central Institute for the Deaf Publications

Population: Ages 3 years through adult

Purpose: Measures auditory speech perception and is an auditory training curriculum for individuals with hearing impairment

Description: There are four subtests: detection of speech, suprasegmental perception of speech, vowel and consonant perception of speech, and auditory speech perception in connected speech activities. The evaluation and curriculum are used with children with cochlear implants or hearing aids.

Format: Examiner required; individual administration; untimed

Scoring: Examiner evaluated

Cost: Kit (manual, forms, toys, full-color illustrated word and sentence cards, auditory training screen, instructional video) $300.00

Teacher Assessment of Grammatical Structures (TAGS)
Jean S. Moog, Victoria J. Kozak

1983	Central Institute for the Deaf Publications

Population: Children

Purpose: Measures grammatical language use

Description: There are three levels of assessment of syntactic ability: Pre-Sentence, Simple Sentence, and Complex Sentence. The results assist teachers in planning goals and are used to rate progress.

Format: Examiner required; individual administration; untimed

Scoring: Examiner evaluated

Cost: Manual $15.00; 25 Forms $10.00

Test of Early Reading Ability–Deaf or Hard of Hearing (TERA-D/HH)
D. Kim Reid, Wayne P. Hresko, Donald D. Hammill, Susan Wiltshire

1991	PRO-ED, Inc.

Population: Ages 3 through 13 years

Purpose: Measures early literacy of individuals with hearing impairment

Description: This is the only individually administered test of reading designed for children with moderate to profound hearing loss (ranging from 41 to beyond 91 decibels, corrected). The TERA-D/HH is also the only individually administered reading test designed for children younger than age 8 who are deaf or hard of hearing. It has equivalent forms and taps the child's ability to construct meaning, knowledge of the alphabet and its functions, and awareness of print conventions. Results are reported as standard scores, percentile rankings, and normal curve equivalents. The test was standardized on a national sample of more than 1,000 students from 20

states who are deaf or hard of hearing. Normative data are given for every 6-month interval. Internal consistency and test–retest reliability coefficients approach or exceed .90. Validity coefficients for the TERA-D/HH with other reading, language, intelligence, and achievement tests frequently used with students who are deaf or hard of hearing are reported in the manual.

Format: Examiner required; individual administration; untimed: 20 to 30 minutes

Scoring: Examiner evaluated

Cost: Complete Kit (manual, picture book, 25 each of Form A and Form B profile/examiner record forms, storage box) $179.00

Emotional Disturbance

Scale for Assessing Emotional Disturbance (SAED)
Michael H. Epstein, Douglas Cullinan

1998	PRO-ED, Inc.

Population: Ages 5 through 18 years

Purpose: Identifies children and adolescents who qualify for the federal special education category emotional disturbance (ED); the SAED is based on the federal terminology and definition as presented in the Individuals with Disabilities Education Act

Description: The SAED contains 52 items that measure the following seven areas of child functioning: inability to learn, relationship problems, inappropriate behavior, unhappiness or depression, physical symptoms or fears, social maladjustment, and overall competence. The scale is completed by teachers, counselors, parents, or other individuals familiar with the child. Information from the SAED is useful in understanding the emotional and behavioral disorders of children, identifying students who may meet the criteria for the ED educational disability category, selecting appropriate education goals for an IEP, and periodically evaluating student progress toward desired outcomes. The SAED was normed on a nationally representative sample of students without disabilities and students with ED.

Format: Rating scale; untimed

Scoring: Examiner evaluated

Cost: Complete Kit (manual, 50 record booklets, storage box) $86.00

Gifted and Talented

California Measure of Mental Motivation (CM3)
Carol A. Giancarlo

1998	California Academic Press

Population: Ages 12 years and older

Purpose: Measures attitudes and inclinations about thinking

Description: Total of 72 items that measure mental focus, learning orientation, creative problem solving, and cognitive integrity. Three versions of the CM3 are available: Level I targets students in 6th grade and below; Level II targets 6th grade through high school students; and Level III targets college students, adults, and professionals. Level I is still in development.

Format: Examiner required; group administration; timed and untimed

Scoring: Machine scored; scoring service available

Cost: Specimen Kit $25.00

California Reasoning Appraisal (CRA)

1999	California Academic Press

Population: Ages 18 years and older

Purpose: Measures reasoning and critical thinking; used in screening, placement, and outcomes assessments

Description: The CRA has 78 multiple-choice items intended for individuals with advanced reasoning skills (in the top 20% of the general population).

Format: Examiner required; group administration; timed and untimed

Scoring: Machine scored; scoring service available

Cost: Contact publisher

Cornell Critical Thinking Test Software
Robert Ennis, Jason Millman

2001	Critical Thinking Books & Software

Population: Grades 7 through adult

Purpose: Assesses an individual's ability to think critically; used for research, for teaching of critical thinking, or as one of several criteria for admission to positions or areas requiring ability for critical thinking

Description: The examiner can set up a test and have students take it from the same computer or from many computers (either on stand-alone stations or over a network). Students can also take the test as a group or at different times. The administration program can be used to create student records, assign tests (individually or in batches), check testing status in progress, then grade and print.

Format: Group or individual administration; computer administered; timed and untimed: 50 minutes

Scoring: Computer scored

Cost: Administrator CD $39.95; $.95 per student

Cornell Critical Thinking Test, Level X
Robert H. Ennis, Jason Millman

1985	Critical Thinking Books & Software

Population: Grades 5 to 14

Purpose: Assesses an individual's ability to think critically; used for research, for teaching of critical thinking, or as one of several criteria for admission to positions or areas requiring ability to think critically

Description: Paper–pencil 71-item multiple-choice measure of critical thinking divided into four sections. In the first section, the examinee reads a conclusion and decides which of several premises supports the conclusion. The second section measures the examinee's ability to judge the reliability of information. The third section tests the examinee's ability to judge whether a statement follows from premises. The fourth section involves the identification of assumptions. Level X is easier than Level Z.

Format: Examiner required for Grades 4 to 6; suitable for group use; timed: 50 to 62 minutes depending on grade

Scoring: Machine or hand scored

Cost: Specimen Set (1 of each test, manual) $17.95

Cornell Critical Thinking Test, Level Z
Robert H. Ennis, Jason Millman

1985	Critical Thinking Books & Software

Population: Advanced secondary grades to adult

Purpose: Assesses an individual's ability to think critically; used for research, for teaching critical thinking, or as one of several criteria for admission to positions or areas requiring ability for critical thinking

Description: Paper–pencil 52-item multiple-choice measure of critical thinking divided into seven sections directed at assessing the examinee's ability to decide whether a statement follows from a given premise, detect equivocal arguments, judge reliability of observation and authenticity of sources, judge direction of support for a hypothesis, judge possible predictions for their value in guiding experiments, and find assumptions of various types. Level Z is more difficult than Level X.

Format: Self-administered; suitable for group use; timed: 50 minutes

Scoring: Machine or hand scored

Cost: Specimen Set (1 of each test, manual) $17.95

Creativity Assessment Packet (CAP)
Frank E. Williams

| 1980 | PRO-ED, Inc. |

Population: Ages 6 through 18 years

Purpose: Measures cognitive thought factors of fluency, flexibility, elaboration, originality, vocabulary, and comprehension that are related to the creative process; identifies gifted students

Description: Instrument consists of two group-administered instruments for children: the Test of Divergent Thinking (Forms A and B) and the Test of Divergent Feeling. A third instrument, The Williams Scale, is a rating instrument for teachers and parents of the same tested factors among children. All three instruments can be used to evaluate, screen, and identify the most important factors of creativity found in some degree among all children.

Format: Examiner required; group administration; untimed

Scoring: Examiner evaluated

Cost: Complete Kit (manual, forms, storage box) $109.00

Gifted and Talented Evaluation Scales (GATES)
James E. Gilliam, Betsy O. Carpenter, Janis R. Christensen

| 1996 | PRO-ED, Inc. |

Population: Ages 5 to 18 years

Purpose: Identifies students who are gifted and talented

Description: Assesses the characteristics, skills, and talents of gifted students in a quick rating scale approach. Completed by someone who knows the child. Ratings are obtained in Intellectual Ability, Academic Skills, Creativity, Leadership, and Artistic Talent. The norms are based on a sample of gifted students. Scores are identified with the likelihood of giftedness from very unlikely to extremely probable.

Format: Rating scale; untimed: 5 to 10 minutes

Scoring: Examiner evaluated

Cost: Complete Kit (manual, 50 protocols, storage box) $86.00

Gifted Evaluation Scale– Second Edition (GES-2)
Stephen B. McCarney, Paul D. Anderson

| 1998 | Hawthorne Educational Services, Inc. |

Population: Ages 5 through 18 years

Purpose: Contributes to the identification of gifted and talented students based on the current federal definition of giftedness adopted by the U.S. Office of Education in 1978 and P.L. 95-561

Description: The scale has five subscales: Intelligence, Creativity, Specific Academic Aptitude, Leadership Ability, and Performing and Visual Arts Skills. An optional subscale, Motivation, is available. The completed rating form and student profile provide standard scores for the five subscales, a quotient score, and a percentile score based on the national standardization sample. The School Form is completed by an educator; the Home Form is completed by the parent or guardian. A Windows QuikScore is available.

Format: Rating scale; untimed

Scoring: Examiner evaluated; computer scoring available

Cost: Complete Kit $69.00

Group Inventory for Finding Creative Talent (GIFT)
Sylvia B. Rimm

| 1980 | Educational Assessment Service, Inc. |

Population: Grades K through 6

Purpose: Assesses creativity; used to identify gifted students

Description: Multiple-item paper–pencil test of interests and attitudes related to creativity. The test yields the following dimension scores: Imagination, Independence, and Many Interests. Validation groups include minorities, urban and suburban students, students with learning disabilities, and gifted students. Available also in Spanish.

Format: Examiner required; suitable for group use

Scoring: Scoring service

Cost: Specimen Set $15.00; Class Set of 30 $90.00 (indicate grade level) (scoring included in price)

Group Inventory for Finding Interests (GIFFI)
Sylvia B. Rimm, Gary A. Davis

1979   Educational Assessment Service, Inc.

Population: Grades 6 through 12

Purpose: Assesses creativity in children; used to identify gifted children

Description: Multiple-item paper–pencil test of interests and attitudes related to creativity. The test yields the following dimension scores: Creative Art and Writing, Confidence, Imagination, Challenge-Inventiveness, and Many Interests. Validation groups include minorities, urban and suburban students, students with learning disabilities, and gifted children. Also available in Spanish.

Format: Self-administered; suitable for group use; untimed: 20 to 40 minutes

Scoring: Scoring service

Cost: Specimen Set $15.00; Class Set of 30 $100.00 (indicate grade level) (scoring included in price)

Khatena-Morse Multitalent Perception Inventory (KMMPI)
Joe Khatena, David T. Morse

1998   Scholastic Testing Service, Inc.

Population: Grades 5 and above

Purpose: Assesses giftedness in art, music, and leadership

Description: Paper–pencil criterion-referenced test that measures five factors: art, music, creative imagination, initiative, and leadership. Form A has 19 items; Form B has 20 items. Raw scores, national percentile ranks, standard scores, and stanines are yielded. Examiner must be certified for assessment. Available in large print.

Format: Examiner required; individual and group administration; untimed: 20 to 40 minutes

Scoring: Examiner evaluated; self-scored

Cost: Starter Set $56.60

Khatena Torrance Creative Perception Inventory (KTCPI)
Joe Khatena, E. Paul Torrance

1994   Scholastic Testing Service, Inc.

Population: Ages 12 years and older

Purpose: Identifies candidates for gifted programs

Description: Paper–pencil criterion-referenced test with two subtests: Something About Myself (SAM) and What Kind of Person Are You (WKOPAY). Both subtests have 50 items each. Raw scores and standard scores are yielded. Examiner must be certified for assessment. Available in large print.

Format: Examiner required; individual and group administration; untimed: 20 to 40 minutes

Scoring: Examiner evaluated; self-scored

Cost: Starter Set $57.65

Preschool and Kindergarten Interest Descriptor (PRIDE)
Sylvia B. Rimm

1983   Educational Assessment Service, Inc.

Population: Ages 3 to 6 years

Purpose: Identifies creatively gifted preschool and kindergarten children; used for academic placement in gifted programs

Description: Paper–pencil 50-item inventory in which parents assess their child's attitudes and interests by responding "no," "to a small extent," "average," "more than average," or "definitely" to each item. Scores are provided on four dimensions: Many Interests, Independence-Perseverance, Imagination-Playfulness, and Originality.

Format: Self-administered; untimed: 20 to 35 minutes

Scoring: Scoring service

Cost: Specimen Set $15.00; Class Set of 30 $90.00 (indicate grade level) (scoring included in price)

Scales for Rating the Behavioral Characteristics of Superior Students (SRBCSS)
Joseph S. Renzulli, Linda H. Smith, Alan J. White, Carolyn M. Callahan, Robert K. Hartman, Karen Westberg

1997   Creative Learning Press, Inc.

Population: Children, adolescents

Purpose: Assesses the behavioral characteristics related to the objectives of gifted and talented elementary and junior high school programs; used to supplement measures of intelligence, achievement, and creativity in selecting students for gifted programs

Description: Paper-pencil 95-item inventory consisting of 10 subscales, each of which assesses a different dimension of behavioral characteristics related to gifted and talented educational objectives. The following 10 dimensions are evaluated: learning, motivation, creativity, leadership, art, music, dramatics, planning, precise communication, and expressive communication. Each scale consists of 4 to 15 statements describing behaviors attributed to gifted and talented students. The teacher rates each item on a 4-point scale from *seldom* to *almost always*, reflecting the degree to which the presence or absence of each characteristic has been observed. The 10 subscales represent 10 distinct sets of behavioral characteristics; therefore, no total score is derived. Only scales relevant to program objectives should be selected for use in a given program.

Format: Self-administered; untimed

Scoring: Examiner evaluated

Cost: Test Kit $8.95

Screening Assessment for Gifted Elementary and Middle School Students–Second Edition (SAGES-2)
Susan Johnsen, Anne Corn

2001	PRO-ED, Inc.

Population: Grades K through 8

Purpose: Assesses aptitude and achievement; used to identify gifted children

Description: Three subtests sample aspects of two of the most commonly used areas for identifying gifted students: aptitude and achievement. Aptitude is measured via the Reasoning subtest. The student is asked to solve analogical problems by identifying relationships among pictures and figures. The other two subtests assess achievement, one for language arts and social studies, the other for math and science. The SAGES-2 was normed on two large samples: a normal sample of 3,023 students who were in heterogeneous classrooms and a sample of 2,290 students who were identified as gifted by their local school districts. Reliability and validity are reported in the manual. There are separate forms for Grades K to 3 and 4 to 8.

Format: Examiner required; group administration; untimed: 20 minutes each subtest

Scoring: Examiner evaluated

Cost: Complete Kit (manual, 10 each of 3 forms for Grades K–3 and 4–8, storage box) $179.00

Teacher Observation Scales–For Identifying Children with Special Abilities
Don McAlpine, Neil Reid

1996	New Zealand Council for Educational Research

Population: Ages 8 to 13 years

Purpose: Measures educational ability

Description: Educational applications for the possibly gifted and other children. Includes five scales: Learning Characteristics (13 items), Social Leadership (12 items), Creative Thinking (11 items), Self-Determination (9 items), and Motivational (8 items).

Format: Examiner required; individual administration; untimed

Scoring: Hand key

Cost: Manual $12.60; 20 Record Forms $12.60

Test of Mathematical Abilities for Gifted Students (TOMAGS)
Gail R. Ryser, Susan K. Johnsen

1998	PRO-ED, Inc.

Population: Grades K to 6

Purpose: Measures students' ability to use mathematical reasoning and mathematical problem solving

Description: There are two forms of the test: Primary Level (Grades K to 3) and Intermediate Level (Grades 4 to 6). The TOMAGS is a standardized, norm-referenced test to identify children gifted in mathematics. One composite score is provided that can be interpreted using two sets of national norms: for children who are identified as gifted in mathematics and for normal children. The items were written to reflect the following National Council of Teachers of Mathematics curriculum and evaluation standards: Number Sense and Numeration, Concepts of Whole Number Operations, Whole Number Computation, Number and Number Relationships, Number Systems and Number Theory, Estimation, Geometry and Spatial Sense, Measurement, Statistics and Probability, Patterns and Relationships, and Algebra.

Format: Examiner required; group administration; untimed: 30 to 60 minutes

Scoring: Examiner evaluated

Cost: Complete Kit (manual, 25 each of Primary and Intermediate student booklets, 25 each of Primary and Intermediate scoring forms, storage box) $149.00

Thinking Creatively in Action and Movement (TCAM)

E. Paul Torrance

| 1981 | Scholastic Testing Services, Inc. |

Population: Ages 3 to 8 years

Purpose: Assesses the creativity of young children; used as part of a program to develop promising creative talent among young children

Description: Show-tell test assessing the creativity of young children, especially preschoolers. The responses are appropriate to the developmental characteristics of the younger child and are physical in nature, although verbal responses are acceptable. A booklet, manual, and set of equipment are used. Raw scores and standard scores are yielded. Examiner must be certified for assessment.

Format: Examiner required; individual administration; untimed: 10 to 30 minutes

Scoring: Examiner evaluated; machine scored; scoring service available from publisher

Cost: Starter Set $38.55

Thinking Creatively with Sounds and Words (TCSW)

E. Paul Torrance, Joe Khatena, Bert F. Cunnington

| 1973 | Scholastic Testing Service, Inc. |

Population: Grades 3 and above

Purpose: Measures ability to create images for words and sounds; used to identify gifted and creative individuals and to teach imagery

Description: Two-test battery assessing creativity by measuring the originality of ideas stimulated by abstract sounds and spoken onomatopoeic words. The TCSW is a battery of two tests: Sounds and Images and Onomatopeia and Images. It is available in equivalent forms (A and B) on two levels: Level I (Grades 3 to 12) and Level II (Adult). One audiocassette provides the stimuli

for each level. Raw scores are yielded. A booklet and pencil are used. Examiner must be certified for assessment.

Format: Examiner required; suitable for group use; untimed: 30 minutes per test

Scoring: Examiner evaluated; machine scored; scoring service available from publisher

Cost: Specimen Set $18.90

Torrance Tests of Creative Thinking (TTCT)–Figural

E. Paul Torrance

| 1990 | Scholastic Testing Service, Inc. |

Population: Grades K to adult

Purpose: Assesses figural creativity

Description: The TTCT assesses mental characteristics of fluency, originality, elaboration, abstractness of titles, and resistance to closure. The tests have three main activities or categories with 41 items: Picture Construction, Picture Completion, and Lines. The TTCT yields an individual student report. Materials used are a manual, test booklets, scoring worksheets, pencils, and crayons.

Format: Examiner required; administered to groups or individuals; timed: 30 minutes

Scoring: Hand key; examiner evaluated; scoring service available

Cost: Administration Set $40.80; Specimen Set $18.90

Torrance Tests of Creative Thinking (TTCT)–Verbal

E. Paul Torrance

| 1990 | Scholastic Testing Service, Inc. |

Population: Grade 1 to adult

Purpose: Assesses fluency, flexibility, and originality

Description: Paper-pencil and short-answer measure of verbal creativity with six categories: Asking, Guessing Causes, Guessing Consequences, Product Improvement, Unusual Uses, and Just Suppose. Materials used are a manual, test booklets, and scoring sheets.

Format: Examiner required; administered to groups or individuals; timed: 40 minutes

Scoring: Hand key; examiner evaluated; scoring service available

Cost: Administration Set $40.80; Examiner's Kit $29.90

Tracking Talents
Francoys Gagné

| 1999 | Prufrock Press, Inc. |

Population: Grades 4 to 7

Purpose: Helps in identifying multiple talents through peer, teacher, and self-nomination

Description: Offers an innovative component to a comprehensive screening and identification process. The instrument is unique in that it identifies these talent areas using many different sources and identifies multiple abilities, including cognitive abilities, academic talents, social and physical abilities, and technological and artistic talents. There are two forms composed of 12 items each. There are at least two items for each ability domain, with no overlap between the two forms.

Format: Examiner required; suitable for group administration; untimed: 60 minutes

Scoring: Hand key; scoring software included

Cost: Complete Kit (manual, 25 each of Forms A and B, scoring software) $69.00

Learning Disabilities

Boder Test of Reading–Spelling Patterns
Elena Boder, Sylvia Jarrico

| 1982 | The Psychological Corporation |

Population: All ages

Purpose: Differentiates specific reading disability (developmental dyslexia) from nonspecific reading disability through reading and spelling performance; used to classify readers with dyslexia into one of three subtypes

Description: Paper–pencil 300-item tests of reading and spelling ability. The Reading Test uses 13 graded word lists of 20 words each, half of which are phonetic and half of which are nonphonetic. The words, which are presented timed and untimed, require sight vocabulary and phonic word analysis skills. The Spelling Test uses two individualized spelling lists (10 known and 10 unknown words) based on the student's reading performance. Both the reading and spelling tests tap the

central visual and auditory processes required for reading and spelling, making it possible to diagnose developmental dyslexia by the joint analysis of reading and spelling as interdependent functions. The results should be supplemented with testing that uses instructional materials to which the child already has been and will be exposed.

Format: Examiner required; timed: 30 minutes

Scoring: Examiner evaluated

Cost: Complete Kit (manual, stimulus materials, 25 each of 4 forms) $164.00

Dyslexia Screening Instrument
Kathryn B. Coon, Mary Jo Polk,
Melissa McCoy Waguespack

| 1994 | The Psychological Corporation |

Population: Ages 6 to 21 years

Purpose: Screens for characteristics of dyslexia

Description: The test measures a cluster of characteristics associated with dyslexia and discriminates between those who have the cluster and those who do not. The classroom teacher rates 33 statements using a 5-point scale.

Format: Rating scale; untimed: under 20 minutes

Scoring: Computer scored

Cost: Complete Kit (manual, rating scale, scoring software) $79.00

Learning Disabilities Diagnostic Inventory (LDDI)
Donald D. Hammill, Brian R. Bryant

| 1998 | PRO-ED, Inc. |

Population: Ages 8 through 17 years

Purpose: Helps in the diagnosis of learning disability (LD)

Description: Rating scale designed to help identify intrinsic processing disorders and learning disabilities. This is not an ability or achievement measure (i.e., it will not indicate how well or how poorly students read, write, or speak). Instead, the LDDI results indicate the extent to which a student's skill patterns in a particular area are consistent with those of individuals known to have LD in that area. Thus, using the LDDI shifts the diagnostic emphasis away from interpreting norm-referenced ability test scores and toward studying an individual's skill patterns, especially those patterns that are indicative of people who are known to have specific learning disabilities. The test was normed on 2,152 students residing in 43 states and Washington, DC. The scores are reported in terms of stanines and percentiles.

Format: Rating scale; untimed: 10 to 20 minutes

Scoring: Examiner evaluated

Cost: Complete Kit (manual, 50 record booklets, storage box) $109.00

Learning Disabilities Evaluation Scale (LDES)-Renormed
Stephen B. McCarney

1996   Hawthorne Educational Services, Inc.

Population: Ages 4 years 5 months to 18 years

Purpose: Aids in the diagnosis of learning disability

Description: The instrument uses performance observations of the classroom teacher or other instructional personnel. The instrument is designed to provide a profile based on the most commonly accepted definition (P.L. 94-142) of learning disabilities. This profile classifies whether the student's difficulties are in the areas of listening, thinking, speaking, reading, writing, spelling, or mathematical calculations. Appropriate for initial referral and screening procedures. The School Form is completed by an educator; the Home Form is completed by a parent or guardian. A DOS Quick Score is available.

Format: Rating scale; untimed

Scoring: Examiner evaluated; computer scoring available

Cost: Complete Kit $143.00

Slingerland High School Screening
Carol Murray, Patricia Beis

1993   Educators Publishing Service, Inc.

Population: Grades 9 to 12

Purpose: Screens for dyslexia and specific language disabilities; shows how the student learns by identifying strengths and weaknesses

Description: Paper-pencil 10-item multiple-choice and short-answer test with the following items: visual to kinesthetic motor, visual perception and memory, visual discrimination, visual perception memory to kinesthetic motor, auditory to visual-kinesthetic, auditory to visual, comprehension, and auditory to kinesthetic.

Format: Examiner required; individual or group administration; untimed

Scoring: Examiner evaluated

Cost: Manual $11.35; Tests $15.95; Cards and Charts $15.95

Slingerland Screening Tests for Identifying Children with Specific Language Disability
Beth H. Slingerland

1984   Educators Publishing Service, Inc.

Population: Grades 1 to 6

Purpose: Screens elementary school children for indications of specific language disabilities in reading, spelling, handwriting, and speaking

Description: Four forms (A, B, C, and D), each containing eight subtests. Five of the subtests evaluate visual-motor coordination and visual memory linked with motor coordination. Three subtests evaluate auditory–visual discrimination or auditory-memory-to-motor ability. Form D contains a ninth subtest that evaluates personal orientation in time and space and the ability to express ideas in writing. All the forms contain separate echolalia tests and include individual auditory tests. Also available in Spanish.

Format: Examiner required; individual or group administration; untimed: 90 minutes

Scoring: Examiner evaluated

Cost: Forms A, B, C, and D $13.65 per dozen; Manual for A, B, and C $6.85; Manual for Form D $5.15

Specific Language Disability Tests
Neva Malcomesius

1967   Educators Publishing Service, Inc.

Population: Grades 6 to 8

Purpose: Screens entire classroom groups or individual students and identifies those who show specific language disability

Description: Subtests I through V evaluate perception in visual discrimination, visual memory, and visual-motor coordination. Subtests VI through X evaluate perception in auditory discrimination, auditory-visual coordination, auditory-motor coordination, and comprehension.

Format: Examiner required; group administration; untimed: 90 minutes

Scoring: Examiner evaluated

Cost: Test $14.10; Charts and Cards $14.10; Manual $1.90; Specimen Set $2.10

TOPS–Adolescent (Test of Problem Solving)

Linda Bowers, Mark Barrett, Rosemary Huisingh, Jane Orman, Carolyn LoGiudice

| 1991 | LinguiSystems, Inc. |

Population: Ages 12 through 17 years

Purpose: Measures expressive language, thinking, and problem-solving skills for students with language learning disabilities

Description: Test has 50 items in six subtests that measure evaluating, fair-mindedness, analyzing, thinking independently, clarifying, and affect. Standard score, percentile rank, and age equivalent are given for the total test.

Format: Examiner required; individual administration; untimed: 40 minutes

Scoring: Examiner evaluated

Cost: $89.95

Mental Retardation

AAMR Adaptive Behavior Scale–Residential and Community: Second Edition (ABS-RC:2)

Kazuo Nihira, Henry Leland, Nadine Lambert

| 1993 | PRO-ED, Inc. |

Population: Ages 18 to 60+ years

Purpose: Identifies individuals who are significantly below their peers in important areas of adaptive behavior to determine strengths and weaknesses among adaptive domains and factors

Description: Items measure the following domains: Independent Functioning, Physical Development, Economic Activity, Language Development, Numbers and Time, Domestic Activity, Prevocational/Vocational Activity, Self-Direction, Responsibility, Socialization, Social Behavior, Conformity, Trustworthiness, Stereotyped/Hyperactive Behavior, Sexual Behavior, Self-Abuse Behavior, Social Engagement, and Disturbing Interpersonal Behavior. Factor scores of Personal Self-Sufficiency, Community Self-Sufficiency, Personal-Social Responsibility, Social Adjustment, and Personal Adjustment are available from the domain scores.

Format: Individual interview format; untimed: 15 to 30 minutes

Scoring: Examiner evaluated

Cost: Complete Kit (manual, 25 protocols, 25 scoring forms, storage box) $124.00

AAMR Adaptive Behavior Scale–School: Second Edition (ABS-S:2)

Nadine Lambert, Kazuo Nihira, Henry Leland

| 1993 | PRO-ED, Inc. |

Population: Ages 3 through 18 years

Purpose: Identifies individuals who are significantly below their peers in important areas of adaptive behavior to determine strengths and weaknesses among adaptive domains and factors

Description: Items in Part One measure the following domains: Independent Functioning, Physical Development, Economic Activity, Language Development, Numbers and Time, Prevocational/ Vocational Activity, Self-Direction, Responsibility, and Socialization. Items in Part Two measure Social Behavior, Conformity, Trustworthiness, Stereotyped/Hyperactive Behavior, Self-Abusive Behavior, Social Engagement, and Disturbing Interpersonal Behavior. Factor scores of Personal Self-Sufficiency, Community Self-Sufficiency, Personal-Social Responsibility, Social Adjustment, and Personal Adjustment are available from the domain scores.

Format: Individual interview format; untimed: 15 to 30 minutes

Scoring: Examiner evaluated

Cost: Complete Kit (manual, 25 protocols, 25 scoring forms, storage box) $124.00

Aberrant Behavior Checklist (ABC)

Michael G. Aman, Nirbhay N. Singh

| Residential 1986; Community 1999 | Slosson Educational Publications, Inc. |

Population: Children to adults

Purpose: Assesses problem behaviors of children and adults with mental retardation at home and in residential facilities, ICFs/MR, and work training centers

Description: Checklist with 58 items in five subscales: Irritability, Agitation; Lethargy, Social Withdrawal; Stereotypic Behavior; Hyperactivity, Noncompliance; and Inappropriate Speech. The ABC asks for degree of retardation, the person's medical status, and current medication condition; then 58 specific symptoms are rated. An extensive manual gives comprehensive descriptions for each assessed behavior. The checklist can be completed by parents, special educators, psychologists, direct caregivers, nurses, and others with knowledge of the person being assessed. Average subscale scores are available for both U.S. and overseas residential facilities and for children and adults living in the community.

Format: Rating scale; untimed: 25 minutes

Scoring: Examiner evaluated

Cost: Residential Complete $57.00; Community Complete $63.00

Adaptive Behavior Assessment System (ABAS)
Patti Harrison, Thomas Oakland

2000	The Psychological Corporation

Population: Ages 5 to 89 years

Purpose: Provides complete assessment of adaptive skills functioning

Description: Assesses 10 areas of adaptive skills specified by the American Association of Mental Retardation and the DSM-IV: communication, community use, functional academics, home living, health and safety, leisure, self-care, self-direction, social, and work. Separate forms for teacher and parent are available for ages 5 to 21 years. The adult form can be completed by the individual's caretaker or by the individual. The ABAS can also be used to determine if adults can live independently.

Format: Examiner required; appropriate for group use; untimed: 15 minutes

Scoring: Examiner evaluated

Cost: School Kit (manual, 25 each of teacher and student forms) $139.00; Adult Kit (manual, 25 forms) $99.00

Adaptive Behavior Inventory (ABI)
Linda Brown, James E. Leigh

1986	PRO-ED, Inc.

Population: Ages 6 through 18 years

Purpose: Evaluates the functional, daily living skills of school-aged children; used to identify children with mental retardation and emotional disturbance

Description: Paper–pencil 150-item inventory assesses functional skills in five scale areas: Self-Care Skills, Communication Skills, Social Skills, Academic Skills, and Occupational Skills. The test yields an Adaptive Behavior Quotient, standard scores, and percentiles. The ABI–Short Form, which contains 50 items and yields the same scores as the complete form, is also available.

Format: Individual interview format; untimed: 15 to 30 minutes

Scoring: Examiner evaluated

Cost: Complete Kit (manual, short and long form protocols, storage box) $89.00

Assessment for Persons Profoundly or Severely Impaired (APPSI)
Patricia Connrad, Sharon Bradley-Johnson

1998	PRO-ED, Inc.

Population: All ages

Purpose: Assesses communication and motor performance of students and adults whose communication performance is between the developmental range of birth to 9 months; diagnoses communication needs and evaluates prelinguistic behavior of preverbal individuals

Description: Discover clients' preferences for visual, auditory, and tactile stimuli on the receptive side; social interaction; and methods of communicative output. The APPSI is not normed, but it was piloted in three states with 32 individuals (ages 2 through 24) who have severe and profound impairments. Reliability coefficients range from .76 to .92, indicating a very high level of reliability. The APPSI aids in defining individuals' preferred methods of communication.

Format: Examiner required; individual administration; untimed: 30 to 60 minutes

Scoring: Examiner evaluated

Cost: Complete Kit (manual, 25 record booklets, 25 profile/summary forms, set of cards and manipulatives, storage box) $149.00

CASAS STRETCH Competency Tests

1992	Comprehensive Adult Student Assessment System (CASAS)

Population: Adults, adolescents

Purpose: Assesses life skill competencies for use with learners with developmental disabilities

Description: Set of 15 tests, each targeting one of the following transition domains: domestic self-care, domestic home care, vocational, recreation/leisure, and community resources. The tests consist of informal inventories and are used with the STRETCH Curriculum Guide that coincides with each transition domain.

Format: Checklist

Scoring: Standardized observational scoring rubric provided

Cost: 15 Reusable Tests $95.00

CASAS Tests for Special Populations

2000	Comprehensive Adult Student Assessment System (CASAS)

Population: Adults, adolescents

Purpose: Used with learners with developmental disabilities to assess competencies across a range of life skills; may be used to measure learning progress

Description: Multiple-choice tests with four levels. Highest test level provides transition into regular CASAS life skill series. Training required to implement the program. CASAS scaled scores identify general skill level and enable comparison of performance across CASAS tests.

Format: Examiner required; individual administration

Scoring: Hand scored

Cost: $20.00 per Reusable Test

Developmental Assessment for Students with Severe Disabilities– Second Edition (DASH-2)
Mary K. Dykes, Jane N. Erin

1999	PRO-ED, Inc.

Population: Developmental ages birth through 6 years

Purpose: Assesses the development of individuals with severe disabilities; used to establish Individualized Education Programs

Description: Five Pinpoint Scales assess performance in Language, Sensory-Motor Skill, Activities of Daily Living, Basic Academic Skills, and Social-Emotional Skill. The skills assessed are identified as present, emerging, task-resistive, nonrelevant, or unknown. This is a criterion-referenced instrument.

Format: Examiner required; individual administration; untimed

Scoring: Examiner evaluated

Cost: Complete Kit (manual, 5 each of 5 Pinpoint Scales, 25 daily plan sheets, 1 pad comprehensive program records, and 25 individualized education plans) $189.00

Inventory for Client and Agency Planning (ICAP)
Robert H. Bruininks, Bradley K. Hill, Richard F. Weatherman, Richard W. Woodcock

1986	Riverside Publishing Company

Population: Infants through Adults

Purpose: Measures adaptive and problem behav-iors and service needs of individuals with moderate to severe disabilities or mental retardation in residential rehabilitation, education, and human service programs; also used by geriatric service agencies

Description: Multiple-item paper–pencil self-report inventory provides client information in the following areas: diagnostic and health status, adaptive behavior, problem behavior, service history, residential placement, projected service needs, functional limitations, and social/leisure history. The results can be used by administrators and supervisors to determine the client's current status and eligibility for services and to manage programs and facilities by assisting in their accreditation, coordinating and planning project costs and reimbursement, and obtaining funding. Age scores, adaptive behavior indexes, standard scores, and service level index scores are obtained. Response booklets are available in Spanish.

Format: Examiner required; individual administration; untimed: 20 to 30 minutes

Scoring: Examiner evaluated; software scoring available

Cost: Complete Program (manual, 25 response booklets) $134.50

Progress Assessment Chart (PAC)
Herbert C. Gunzburg

Date not provided	SEFA (Publications) Ltd.

Population: All ages

Purpose: Assesses the ability to cope with everyday situations; intended for use with individuals with mental disabilities.

Description: Paper–pencil criterion-referenced assessment of abilities composed of four subcategories: socialization, occupation, self-help, and communication. Also available in German, French, Spanish, Dutch, Norwegian, Polish, Icelandic, and Danish.

Format: Examiner required; individual administration; untimed

Scoring: Examiner evaluated

Cost: Contact publisher

Street Survival Skills Questionnaire (SSSQ)
Dan Linkenhoker, Lawrence T. McCarron

1993	McCarron-Dial Systems

Population: Ages 9 years and older

Purpose: Measures specific aspects of the adaptive

behavior of special education students; used as a baseline behavioral measure of the effects of training and to predict one's potential for adapting to community living conditions and vocational placement

Description: Oral-response and point-to test consisting of 216 items on nine subtests, each containing 24 picture plates. The examiner orally presents the question, and the examinee responds by pointing to one of the four pictures presented. Fundamental reading skills are required. The large print and graphic format are designed for use with individuals with visual acuity of 20/200 or better in either eye. A booklet for administering the SSSQ in sign language is available. The SSSQ Report (sold separately) provides narrative interpretations of the examinee's performance in each area as well as more specific area analyses.

Format: Examiner required; individual administration; untimed: 30 to 45 minutes

Scoring: Hand key; may be computer scored

Cost: Complete $350.00; Computer Scoring Service $225.00

VCWS 17—Pre-Vocational Readiness Battery

1978   Valpar International Corporation

Population: Adults

Purpose: Measures an individual's ability to function independently; may be used with individuals with mental retardation to determine whether the individual requires a sheltered environment or can function independently

Description: Assessment and training tool contains five subtests. The Development Assessment subtest contains functional nonmedical measures of physical and mental abilities. The Workshop Evaluation subtest is a simulated assembly process designed to determine if the examinee is appropriately placed in a work or training setting. The Vocational Interest Screening subtest, presented in an audiovisual format, identifies job interests. The Interpersonal/Social Skills subtest identifies barriers to employment or independent living. The Independent Living Skills subtest measures skill and knowledge in transportation, money handling, grooming, and living environment. The tasks in each subtest vary in difficulty from very simple recognition of rooms to more complex processes relating to work. The test is designed in such a way that a lack of language or reading skills does not present a barrier to evaluation. The test should not be administered to in-

dividuals with severe impairment of the upper extremities.

Format: Examiner required; individual administration; timed

Scoring: Examiner evaluated

Cost: $3,845.00

Vocational Adaptation Rating Scales (VARS)
Robert G. Malgady, Peter R. Barcher, John Davis, George Towner

1980   Western Psychological Services

Population: Adolescents, adults

Purpose: Measures maladaptive behavior in individuals with mental retardation

Description: The rating can be done by any adult who has had sufficient contact with the individual being rated and covers maladaptive behavior in six areas: verbal manners; communication skills; interpersonal skills; respect for property, rules, and regulations; attendance and punctuality; and grooming and personal hygiene. Ratings are totaled to produce frequency and severity scores for each area and are used to make placement decisions. Used to help determine individual vocational activity.

Format: Self-administered; untimed: 30 minutes

Scoring: Examiner evaluated

Cost: Kit (25 rating booklets, 25 profile forms, manual) $59.50

Washer Visual Acuity Screening Technique (WVAST)
Rhonda Wiczer Washer

1984   Scholastic Testing Service, Inc.

Population: Ages 2 years to adult

Purpose: Measures the visual abilities of individuals with severe mental challenges (mental ages 2.6 years to adult), those who are low functioning, and very young children; used for screening groups of children to identify those with possible visual impairments

Description: Point-to vision test for screening both near and far-point acuity. The testing procedure omits as many perceptual, motor, and verbal skills as possible. A conditioning process is outlined for familiarizing individuals with the symbols, matching skills, and eye occlusion used in the screening. Examiner must be certified for assessment.

Format: Examiner required; suitable for group use; untimed

Scoring: Examiner evaluated

Cost: Specimen Set $22.00

Wisconsin Behavior Rating Scale (WBRS)
Agnes Y. Song, Stephen E. Jones

1980	Central Wisconsin Center for the Developmentally Disabled

Population: Ages birth to 3 years

Purpose: Measures adaptive behavior in individuals with severe or profound mental retardation

Description: The standard test has 176 items that measure 11 areas: Gross Motor, Fine Motor, Expressive Language, Receptive Language, Play Skills, Socialization, Domestic Activity, Eating, Toileting, Dressing, and Grooming. A variation for individuals who are deaf and blind has 159 items, with four substitute items used for individuals who are only blind. Items are measured in a third-party interview.

Format: Examiner required; individual administration; untimed: 15 minutes

Scoring: Examiner evaluated

Cost: Specimen Set (manual and protocol) $5.00

Visual Impairment

Hill Performance Test of Selected Positioned Concepts
Everett Hill

1981	Stoelting Company

Population: Ages 6 to 10 years

Purpose: Measures the development of spatial concepts in children with visual impairment

Description: Task assessment of basic spatial concepts such as front, back, left, and right. The development of these positional concepts is tested through performance on 72 items in four types of tasks: identifying body relationships, demonstrating positional concepts of body parts to one another, demonstrating positional concepts of body parts to other objects, and forming object-to-object relationships. The test may be used as a criterion-referenced instrument to identify individual strengths and weaknesses in the area of spatial concepts or as a norm-referenced test.

Format: Examiner required; individual administration; untimed

Scoring: Examiner evaluated

Cost: Complete Kit (20 record forms, manual) $35.00

VCWS 18—Conceptual Understanding Through Blind Evaluation (CUBE)

1980	Valpar International Corporation

Population: Adults who are blind or visually impaired

Purpose: Measures the perceptive abilities that help a person compensate for visual impairment; used with individuals who are congenitally and adventitiously blind

Description: Performance-based battery of five subtests assessing a person's perceptual skills in meeting the basic needs of judgment, mobility, orientation, discrimination, and balance. The subtests are Tactual Perception, Mobility/Discrimination Skills, Spatial Organization and Memory, Assembly and Packaging, and Audile Perception. Administration of the tests varies according to the factors being assessed: mobility or job skills.

Format: Examiner required; individual administration; timed

Scoring: Examiner evaluated

Cost: $4,075.00

Social Studies

Informeter: An International Technique for the Measurement of Political Information
Panos D. Bardis

1972	Donna Bardis

Population: Grades 10 and above

Purpose: Measures political knowledge and awareness of local, national, and international affairs; used for research on political information in the general population and discussion in social sciences classes

Description: Paper-pencil 100-item test in which the subject is asked to list important names, dates, events, and issues in response to specific questions about politics, government, and current events. Suitable for use with individuals with physical or hearing impairments.

Format: Self-administered; 15 minutes
Scoring: Examiner evaluated
Cost: $1.00

Irenometer
Panos D. Bardis

1985	Donna Bardis

Population: Adolescents, adults

Purpose: Measures attitudes and beliefs concerning peace; used for discussion purposes

Description: Paper–pencil 10-item inventory in which an individual rates 10 statements about peace and its effects on individuals and society on a 5-point scale ranging from 0 (*strongly disagree*) to 4 (*strongly agree*). All statements express positive attitudes toward peace. The score equals the sum of the 10 numerical responses. Suitable for use with individuals with physical or hearing impairments.

Format: Self-administered; untimed

Scoring: Self-scored
Cost: $1.00

World Government Scale
Panos D. Bardis

1985	Donna Bardis

Population: Adolescents, adults

Purpose: Measures attitudes and beliefs concerning world government and the possible effects that world government might have on society; used for discussion and educational purposes

Description: Paper–pencil 6-item inventory in which individuals rate six statements about world government and its effects on society on a 5-point scale from 0 (*strongly disagree*) to 4 (*strongly agree*). All statements express positive attitudes toward world government. The score equals the sum of the six numerical responses. The theoretical range extends from 0 (complete rejection of the concept of world government) to 24 (complete acceptance). Suitable for use with individuals with physical and hearing impairments.

Format: Self-administered; untimed
Scoring: Self-scored
Cost: $1.00

Teacher Attitude

Instructional Styles Inventory (ISI)
Albert A. Canfield, Judith S. Canfield

1986	Western Psychological Services

Population: Adults

Purpose: Identifies a teacher's preferred instructional methods; used in conjunction with the Canfield Learning Styles Inventory to maximize teaching and learning efficiency

Description: Paper–pencil 25-item forced-rank inventory assessing a teacher's preferences concerning learning environments, instructional modalities, and topical interests. The inventory also measures how much responsibility the instructor will assume for student learning (instead of measuring performance expectancy), identifies areas where instructional training would be most beneficial, provides information to help instructors interpret classroom problems and student reactions, and measures the same dimensions as the Canfield Learning Styles Inventory to allow for one-to-one comparison between the two inventories. The test booklets are reusable. Separate norms are provided for male and female instructors.

Format: Self-administered; untimed: 20 to 30 minutes
Scoring: Self-scored
Cost: Kit (5 inventories, manual) $65.00

Music Teacher Self-Assessment
James O. Froseth, Molly A. Weaver

Date not provided	GIA Publications, Inc.

Population: Music teachers

Purpose: Evaluates teaching abilities

Description: Comes with an instructional videotape to help the teacher recognize the teaching style used. A simple and convenient manual/ workbook and self-assessment forms, along with regular taping of teaching, help the teacher analyze his or her teaching style and directly affect student motivation and achievement.

Format: Self-administered; untimed
Scoring: Hand key
Cost: $34.95

Teacher Motivation Diagnostic Questionnaire
Kenneth M. Matthews

1985	Kenneth M. Matthews, EdD

Population: Adults

Purpose: Used for improving teacher motivation

Description: Paper–pencil 16-item questionnaire using a Likert scale. Assesses self-concept, principal expectations, future utility, and attitudes toward principal.

Format: Examiner required; self-administered; untimed: 10 to 20 minutes
Scoring: Examiner evaluated
Cost: 25 Forms $55.00

Visual Processing

Basic Visual Motor Association Test
James Battle

1990	James Battle and Associates, Ltd.

Population: Ages 6 to 15 years

Purpose: The test measures visual-motor skills; applicable for tutoring and remediation

Description: Multiple-item paper–pencil test of visual integration, symbol integration, visual association, recall of visual symbols, and visual sequencing. Available in two forms (60 items each). Also available in large print and in French.

Format: Examiner required; individual/group administration; timed: 3 minutes
Scoring: Hand key; test scoring service available from publisher
Cost: $20.00

Benton Visual Retention Test®, Fifth Edition
Abigail Benton Sivan

1991	The Psychological Corporation

Population: Ages 8 years through adult

Purpose: Measures visual memory, visual perception, and visual attention

Description: Ten-item test of visual perception, visual memory, and visuo-constructive abilities. Items are designs that are shown to the subject one by one. The subject studies each design and reproduces it as exactly as possible by drawing it

on plain paper. Materials include Design Cards and three alternate and equivalent forms.

Format: Examiner required; individual administration; untimed: 15 minutes
Scoring: Examiner evaluated
Cost: Complete Set (manual, stimulus booklet, scoring templates, 25 response booklets–record forms) $164.00

Comprehensive Test of Visual Functioning (CTVF)
Sue Larson, Evelyn Buethe, Gary J. Vitali

1990	Slosson Educational Publishing, Inc.

Population: Ages 8 years to adult

Purpose: Provides a profile of a person's ability in total visual processing

Description: The CTVF was designed to be a brief and meaningful assessment device to accurately detect and discriminate visual processing problems. The CTVF is an excellent complement to traditional assessments of IQ, and standardized reading and neuropsychological evaluations. It is appropriate for multiple professions. No specific training is required. The CTVF may be used with populations manifesting visual-perceptual problems secondary to acute or chronic disorder processes.

Format: Examiner required; individual administration; untimed: 25 minutes

Scoring: Examiner evaluated

Cost: Complete Kit (manual, protocol, test booklets, cards) $98.00

DeGangi-Berk Test of Sensory Integration (TSI)
Georgia A. DeGangi, Ronald A. Berk

1983	Western Psychological Services

Population: Ages 3 to 5 years

Purpose: Measures overall sensory integration in preschool children; screens for young children with delays in sensory, motor, and perceptual skills in order to facilitate intervention programs

Description: Performance test with 36 items in three subdomains of sensory integration: postural control, bilateral motor integration, and reflex integration. The examiner rates the child's response to each item on a numerical scale indicating abnormal to normal development.

Format: Examiner required; individual administration; untimed: 30 minutes

Scoring: Examiner required

Cost: Kit (test materials, 25 star design sheets, 25 protocol booklets, manual, carrying case) $168.00

Denver Eye Screening Test (DEST)
William K. Frankenburg,
J. Goldstein, A. Barker

1973	Denver Developmental Materials, Inc.

Population: Ages 6 months to 7 years

Purpose: Helps evaluate eye problems and strabismus in children to determine if a child needs specialized testing

Description: Performance test in which the examiner shows seven picture cards and asks the child to name the pictures at 15 feet. For children ages 6 months to 2 years 5 months old, the examiner uses an "E" card and a spinning toy to attract the child's attention and examines the child's eyes one at a time to see if they track. Materials consist of picture cards, cord, toy, and "E" card. A flashlight is required. The alternate cover test and pupillary light reflex test are used to detect strabismus.

Format: Examiner required; individual administration; untimed: 10 minutes

Scoring: Examiner evaluated

Cost: Complete Kit $20.00; Manual/Workbook $20.00; 25 Test Forms $6.00

Developmental Test of Visual Perception–Adolescent and Adult (DTVP-A)
Cecil R. Reynolds, Nils A. Pearson,
Judith K. Voress

2002	PRO-ED, Inc.

Population: Ages 11 through 74 years

Purpose: Measures visual-perceptual and visual-motor abilities

Description: The DTVP-A is the latest version of Marianne Frostig's milestone test battery. The DTVP-A is an extension and redevelopment of this classic work, designed for use with adolescents and adults. The test is especially useful in the evaluation of the neuropsychological integrity of traumatic brain injury (TBI) and stroke patients in whom right hemisphere function may be at issue. There is sufficient floor to allow accurate assessment even of individuals with severe TBI and other neurological impairments. The reliability of the various subtests and index scores indicates that the DTVP-A will be sensitive to improvement over the course of treatment. The six subtests were built to conform to the visual-perception constructs espoused by Frostig: Copying, Figure-Ground, Visual-Motor Search, Visual Closure, Visual-Motor Speed, and Form Constancy. There are three index scores: General Visual Perceptual, Motor-Reduced Visual Perception, and Visual-Motor Integration. Validity evidence shows that all DTVP-A subtests and indexes are useful for measuring visual-perceptual and visual-motor integration skills.

Format: Examiner required; individual administration; untimed: 25 minutes

Scoring: Examiner evaluated

Cost: Complete Kit (manual, picture book, 25 protocols, 25 response booklets, storage box) $164.00

Developmental Test of Visual Perception–Second Edition (DTVP-2)
Donald D. Hammill, Nils A. Pearson,
Judith K. Voress

1993	PRO-ED, Inc.

Population: Ages 4 through 10 years

Purpose: Distinguishes between visual-perceptual and visual-motor problems

Description: Multiple-item instrument that yields scores for both pure visual perception with no motor response and visual-motor integration ability. The eight subtests are Eye-Hand Coordination, Copying, Spatial Relations, Position in Space, Figure–Ground, Visual Closure, Visual-Motor Speed, and Form Constancy. Standard scores, percentiles, and age equivalents are provided for each subtest as well as the composites of General Visual Perception, Motor-Reduced Perception, and Visual-Motor Integration.

Format: Examiner required; individual administration; untimed: 35 minutes

Scoring: Examiner evaluated

Cost: Complete Kit (manual, picture book, 25 protocols, 25 scoring forms, storage box) $174.00

Developmental Test of Visual-Motor Integration–Third Edition (VMI)
Keith E. Beery, Norman A. Buktencia

1996	Pearson Learning/ Modern Curriculum Press, Inc.

Population: Ages 3 to 18 years

Purpose: Measures students' visual-motor skills by duplicating geometric figures

Description: Multiple-item paper–pencil test measuring the integration of visual perception and motor behavior. Test items, arranged in order of increasing difficulty, consist of geometric figures that the children are asked to copy. The Short Test Form (18 figures) is used with children ages 3 to 8. The Long Test Form (27 figures) is used with children ages 3 to 18 and adults with developmental delays. The manual includes directions for administration, scoring criteria, developmental comments, age norms, suggestions for teaching, percentiles, and standard score equivalents.

Format: Examiner required; individual administration; timed: 10 to 15 minutes

Scoring: Examiner evaluated

Cost: Complete Kit (manual, 25 each of short form, long form, motor, visual) $208.30

Dvorine Color Vision Test
Israel Dvorine

Date not provided	The Psychological Corporation

Population: Adults

Purpose: Screens applicants for jobs that require color-discrimination abilities

Description: This test can ascertain type, as well as severity, of color blindness. Consists of a bound set of color plates that feature a number of designs made of colored dots against a background of contrasting dots. The figures are easily identified by persons with normal vision, but not by those with color blindness. There are two parts: nomenclature and tracing.

Format: Examiner required; individual administration; untimed: 2 minutes

Scoring: Examiner evaluated

Cost: Color Plates $335.00; 35 Record Forms $29.00

Farnsworth Color Deficiency Test

1940	Richmond Products, Inc.

Population: Ages 5 years and older

Purpose: Diagnoses color deficiencies

Description: Measures color deficiencies as to color and depth of problem. This is a modification of the well-known Farnsworth-Munsell 100 Hue Test intended for classification instead of in-depth study of color vision defects. The Farnsworth Color Deficiency Test is called dichotomous because it was designed to separate subjects into one of two groups: (1) strongly color deficient or (2) mildly color deficient or color normal. This is accomplished by the arrangement of vivid (saturated) color discs. This makes the test fairly easy, and a nonperfect score is indicative of a strong color deficiency.

Format: Examiner required; individual administration; untimed: 10 to 15 minutes

Scoring: Hand key

Cost: $165.00

HRR Pseudoisochromatic Plates
LeGrand Hardy, Gertrude Rand, M. Catherine Rittler

1960	Richmond Products, Inc.

Population: All ages, 3 years and older

Purpose: Screens for color perception deficiency

Description: Measures color deficiency separately for red, green, blue, and yellow. The HRR screener has three purposes: a screening test to separate those with defective color vision from those with normal color vision; a qualitative diagnostic test to classify the type of color defect, whether protan or duetan, tritan, or tetartan; and a quantitative test to indicate the degree of the defect, whether mild, medium, or strong. There is growing evidence that adult-acquired color deficiency, especially in the yellow and blue perception, can indicate medicinal toxicity and other problems. Included in the HRR are 4 demonstration plates, 6 screener plates, and the 14 diagnostic series.

Format: Examiner required; individual administration; untimed: 10 to 15 minutes

Scoring: Hand key

Cost: $100.00 to $200.00

Inventory of Perceptual Skills (IPS)
Donald R. O'Dell

1983	Stoelting Company

Population: Ages 5 to 10 years

Purpose: Assesses visual and auditory perceptual skills and provides the structure for individual remedial programs

Description: Oral-response and task-performance test with 79 items assessing perceptual skills in the following areas: visual discrimination, visual memory, object recognition, visual-motor coordination, auditory discrimination, auditory memory, auditory sequencing, and auditory blending. Once scored and recorded on the student profile (included in the student record booklet), a graphic comparison can be made of all the subtests. A score below the mean on any subtest indicates a weakness in that area. The test may be administered by teachers, aides, or specialists without special training. The teacher's manual contains many educational activities in visual and auditory perception. Games, exercises, and activities provide the teacher with a variety of approaches and materials to use with the student. The student workbook includes 18 exercises to improve the areas in need of remediation.

Format: Examiner required; individual administration; untimed: 15 minutes

Scoring: Examiner evaluated

Cost: Complete Set (manual, student workbook, 10 student record booklets, stimulus cards) $45.00

Kent Visual Perceptual Test (KVPT)
Lawrence E. Melamed

2000	Psychological Assessment Resources, Inc.

Population: Ages 5 to 11, 18 to 22, and 55 to 91 years

Purpose: Evaluates ability to discriminate, copy, or recall items

Description: The KVPT is a three-part test. KVPT-D (Discrimination) requires the individual to select from a set of alternatives the item that matches a standard form. The KVPT-C (Copy) consists of three increasingly difficult subtests

that require the individual to reproduce forms of the same type as the discrimination forms. The KVPT-M (Immediate Memory) requires the individual to locate a target form within a set of alternatives immediately following a brief exposure to the form. Stimuli are presented in a binder.

Format: Examiner required; individual administration; untimed: 25 to 30 minutes

Scoring: Examiner evaluated

Cost: $179.00

Learning Efficiency Test–II (LET–II)
Raymond E. Webster

1992	Academic Therapy Publications

Population: Ages 4 through 75+ years

Purpose: Used in education, rehabilitation, and cognitive assessment to measure information processing in auditory and visual modalities

Description: The LET–II provides a quick and reliable measure of visual and auditory information processing characteristics and is useful in determining sequential processing deficits that may be related to learning problems in the classroom. The test yields information about a person's preferred modality for learning, and provides valuable insights about the impact of interference on information storage and retrieval. The revised edition features an updated literature review, new case studies, expanded remediation strategies, and an improved record form and scoring system. The norms have been expanded to include adult values. Processing is assessed in two modalities (visual and auditory) and in three recall conditions (immediate recall, short-term recall, and long-term recall). The six subtest scores can be collapsed into Modality Scores and into a Global Memory Score; each score can be converted into standard scores and percentiles for comparison with other tests.

Format: Examiner required; individual administration; timed presentation, untimed response

Scoring: Examiner evaluated

Cost: Test Kit (manual, stimulus cards, 50 record forms, vinyl folder) $92.00

McDowell Vision Screening Kit
P. Marlene McDowell, Richard L. McDowell

1994	Western Psychological Services

Population: Children

Purpose: Used for testing preschoolers and children with severe disabilities for vision problems

Description: This test assesses the functional vision of children previously considered untestable. It gives a behavioral assessment of visual performance in five areas: distance visual acuity, near point visual acuity, ocular alignment and motility, color perception, and ocular function. The kit contains all the toys, objects, and recording forms necessary for a comprehensive screening. The test requires no matching or verbal skills.

Format: Examiner required; individual administration; 10 to 20 minutes

Scoring: Examiner evaluated

Cost: Kit (includes all test materials, 100 recording forms, 1 manual) $118.00

Motor-Free Visual Perception Test–Third Edition (MVPT-3)
Ronald R. Colarusso, Donald D. Hammill

2002	Academic Therapy Publications

Population: Ages 4 through 85+ years

Purpose: Assesses visual perception without reliance on an individual's motor skills

Description: Measures skills without copying tasks. Contains many new, more difficult, items at the upper end for older children and adults. Tasks include matching, figure–ground, closure, visual memory, and form discrimination. Stimuli are line drawings. Answers are presented in multiple-choice format. Responses may be given verbally or by pointing. Standard scores and percentiles are provided. Item response times may be interpreted in terms of functional behavioral categories. Clinical population comparisons are also provided.

Format: Examiner required; individual administration; untimed: 20 minutes

Scoring: Examiner evaluated

Cost: Contact publisher

Neitz Test of Color Vision
Jay Neitz, Phyllis Summerfelt, Maureen Neitz

2000	Western Psychological Services

Population: All ages

Purpose: Tests for color blindness

Description: The Neitz accurately identifies the type and severity of color vision deficiency in less than 5 minutes. It can be easily administered to people of any age, including very young children. It can be given to large groups in school, military, and work settings at a low cost. The test includes

nine items on a single sheet of paper, which is given to the examinee. Below each pattern are five smaller response options; the examinee simply marks the response that represents what he or she sees.

Format: Examiner required; individual or group administration; untimed: 5 minutes

Scoring: Examiner evaluated

Cost: Complete Kit $75.00

Ontario Society of Occupational Therapists–Perceptual Evaluation Kit (OSOT)
Marian Boys, Pat Fisher, Claire Holzberg

1991	Nelson Thomson Learning

Population: Adults

Purpose: Assesses perceptual impairment; used for identification and monitoring of perceptual dysfunction

Description: Paper–pencil short-answer, oral-response, show–tell, and point-to test with 18 subtests: scanning, spatial neglect, motor planning, copying 2-D designs, copying 3-D designs, body puzzle, draw-a-person, r–l discrimination, clock, pegboard, draw-a-house, shape recognition, color recognition, size recognition, f–g discrimination, proprioception, stereognosis r, and stereognosis l. Examiner must be a qualified occupational therapist. Also available with French manual.

Format: Examiner required; individual administration; timed and untimed

Scoring: Hand key; no scoring service available

Cost: Kit $725.00

Perceptual Memory Task (PMT)
Lawrence T. McCarron

1985	McCarron-Dial Systems

Population: Ages 4 years and older

Purpose: Assesses individual learning style; used with special education and rehabilitation populations at any level of intellectual functioning and with physical, mental, emotional, or functional behavior disabilities

Description: Oral-response and show–tell 62-item test using stimulus materials to assess fundamental information processing skills essential for learning and performance, including perception and memory for spatial relationships, visual and auditory sequential memory, intermediate term memory, and discrimination of detail. To test examinees with hearing and visual impairments (visual acuity of 20/400 or worse in either eye), supplementary procedures involving two alternate subtasks are provided. The instrument also assesses information processing skills dependent on right and left cerebral functioning. Age-corrected norms tables are used to convert each subtest score to a standard score that can be profiled on the PMT Score Form to portray graphically the individual's relative strengths and weaknesses. Factor scores also may be determined and compared to indicate relative strengths and weaknesses in specific memory processes.

Format: Examiner required; individual administration; untimed

Scoring: Hand key

Cost: Complete Set $420.00; Computer Report $350.00

Perceptual-Motor Assessment for Children (P-MAC)
Jack G. Dial, Lawrence T. McCarron, Garry Amann

1988	McCarron-Dial Systems

Population: Ages 4 to 15 years 11 months

Purpose: Screens perceptual-motor skills; used by diagnosticians and classroom teachers to identify needs and provide educational management for the student with special needs

Description: Multiple-item oral-response point-to task-performance battery of perceptual-motor skills. The battery consists of selected subtests from the McCarron Assessment of Neuromuscular Development (MAND), Haptic Visual Discrimination Test (HVDT), and Perceptual Memory Task (PMT). The P-MAC Computer Program provides scores for each area assessed. Four types of printed reports are offered: Educational Analysis Report, Classroom Report, Report of Trait Scores, and Comprehensive Evaluation Report. The computer program operates on Apple, PC, and Macintosh systems.

Format: Examiner required; individual administration; untimed

Scoring: Examiner evaluated; hand key; computer scored

Cost: Complete Set (assessment battery in single case, comprehensive manual, scoring forms, 5-volume set of Guides for Educational Management, computer program, and operating manual) $1,995.00

Sensory Integration and Praxis Tests (SIPT)
A. Jean Ayres

1987	Western Psychological Services

Population: Ages 4 through 8 years

Purpose: Measures sensory integration processes that underlie learning problems and emotional disorders; used for analyzing sensory integrative dysfunction and planning treatment for disorders

Description: Seventeen tests assessing aspects of sensory processing in the vestibular, proprioceptive, kinesthetic, tactile, and visual systems, as well as the behavior and learning disorders (including learning disabilities, emotional disorders, and minimal brain dysfunction) associated with inadequate integration of sensory input from these systems. The subtests are Space Visualization, Figure–Ground Perception, Manual Form Perception, Kinesthesia, Finger Identification, Graphesthesia, Localization of Tactile Stimuli, Praxis on Verbal Command, Design Copying, Constructional Praxis, Postural Praxis, Oral Praxis, Sequencing Praxis, Bilateral Motor Coordination, Standing and Walking Balance, Motor Accuracy, and Postrotary Nystagmus. Computer scoring and interpretation are available. The ChromaGraph for SIPT provides an eight-color single-page visual summary of major testing and statistical results.

Format: Examiner required; individual administration; untimed

Scoring: Computer scored

Cost: Set (all test materials, 25 copies of all consumable test forms, 10 complete sets of all 17 computer-scored answer sheets, 10 transmittal sheets, manual, carrying case) $1,150.00

Spatial Orientation Memory Test
Joseph M. Wepman, D. Turaids

1985	Western Psychological Services

Population: Ages 5 to 9 years

Purpose: Measures a child's ability to retain and recall the orientation of visually presented forms; used to identify children facing potential learning difficulties

Description: Multiple-item response test. The examiner presents a target page with a nonalphabetic design to the child and asks the child to select the same design from the response page, which contains four or five samples of the same design in different rotational positions. Spatial orientation ability prepares the child for individ-

ual letter discrimination recall, sequential ordering of letters in words, and related skills essential for reading. Adequacy scores are indicated.
The test is available in two forms for retesting.

Format: Examiner required; individual administration; untimed: 10 to 15 minutes

Scoring: Hand key

Cost: Complete Kit (set of reusable stimulus
cards, 25 score sheets, manual) $78.00

Standard Pseudoisochromatic Plates, Book 1
H. Ichikawa

1978	Richmond Products, Inc.

Population: Ages 6 years and older

Purpose: Screens for red and green color
deficiencies

Description: A series of color plates designed to
discriminate subjects with color deficiency from
those without. The screening plates are accurate
in the detection of even mild color defects. The
diagnostic plates are effective for accurate classification of mild, moderate, and severe color defects. This series of pseudoisochromatic plates
provides a rapid and easily administered test that
lends itself especially well to mass screening.

Format: Examiner required; individual administration; untimed: 8 to 10 minutes

Scoring: Hand key

Cost: $155.00

Standard Pseudoisochromatic Plates, Book 2
H. Ichikawa

1983	Richmond Products, Inc.

Population: Adults

Purpose: Screens for adult acquired color
deficiency

Description: In this set of plates, emphasis is on
the blue-yellow defect because it is often a presenting sign of various diseases. Plates for the
acquired red-green defect, as well as two plates
for scotopic vision, have been included to complete the series with appropriate plates to test all
acquired color vision problems.

Format: Examiner required; individual administration; untimed: 8 to 10 minutes

Scoring: Hand key

Cost: $155.00

Test of Pictures/Forms/Letters/ Numbers Spatial Orientation and Sequencing Skills (TPFLNSOSS)
Morrison F. Gardner

Date not provided	Psychological and Educational Publications, Inc.

Population: Ages 5 to 9 years

Purpose: Measures the ability to visually form
letters and numbers in the correct direction and
to visually perceive words with the letters in the
correct sequence

Description: There are seven subtests: Spatial
Relationships (Pictures and Forms), Reversed Letter and Numbers, Reversed Letter(s) in Words,
Reversed Letters from non-Reversed Letters and
Numbers, and Letter Sequencing. No verbal responses are required; all responses are made in
the test booklet.

Format: Examiner required; individual or group
administration; untimed: 10 to 15 minutes

Scoring: Examiner evaluated

Cost: Complete Kit (manual, 25 test booklets)
$49.95

Test of Visual Motor Integration (TVMI)
Donald D. Hammill, Nils A. Pearson, Judith K. Voress

1996	PRO-ED, Inc.

Population: Ages 4 through 17

Purpose: Measures visual-motor ability

Description: Multiple-item paper-pencil test consisting of 30 items (12 for ages 4 to 8 and 12 for
ages 8 to 17) that are copied by students. Each
item is rated 0, 1, 2, or 3. This range of points
makes it possible for the examiner to distinguish
readily among students with severe visual-motor
problems and students with exceptional copying
skills. Results are reported in standard scores,
percentiles, and age equivalents.

Format: Examiner required; individual or group
administration; untimed: 20 minutes

Scoring: Examiner evaluated

Cost: Complete Kit (manual, 50 protocols,
storage box) $116.00

Test of Visual-Motor Skills-Revised (TVMS-R)
Morrison F. Gardner

Date not provided	Psychological and Educational Publications, Inc.

Population: Ages 3 to 14 years

Purpose: Measures visual-motor abilities

Description: The test contains 23 geometric forms that are scored based on eight classifications: closure, angles, intersecting lines, size, rotation or reversal, length of lines, overpenetration or underpenetration, and modification of form. Norms for an individual's errors and accuracies are included. The TVMS–R was standardized on approximately 1,500 individuals.

Format: Examiner required; individual or group administration; untimed: 3 to 6 minutes

Scoring: Examiner evaluated; 15 to 20 minutes

Cost: Complete Test (manual, 15 test booklets, 15 scoring-criterion forms, protractor) $79.95

Test of Visual-Motor Skills–Revised Alternate Scoring Method [TVMS–R (ASM)]
Morrison F. Gardner

Date not provided	Psychological and Educational Publications, Inc.

Population: Ages 3 to 14 years

Purpose: Measures visual-motor abilities

Description: The purpose of this method of scoring the geometric forms is to give examiners a more refined diagnosis of an individual's visual-motor strengths and weaknesses in eight categories. With the Alternate Scoring Method, the examiner assigns a score from 0 to 3.

Format: Examiner required; individual administration; untimed: 10 to 20 minutes

Scoring: Examiner evaluated

Cost: Complete Test (manual, 15 test booklets, 15 profile forms) $62.95

Test of Visual-Motor Skills: Upper Level [TVMS(UL)]
Morrison F. Gardner

Date not provided	Psychological and Educational Publications, Inc.

Population: Ages 12 to 40 years

Purpose: Measures visual-motor abilities

Description: The test comprises 16 geometric figures arranged in increasing order of difficulty, each of which is to be copied. Each figure is scored for a variety of discrete errors (from a minimum of 9 to a maximum of 22 errors per figure). Standard scores are provided. A specific feature is having only one form per page. All 16 forms are in a single test booklet.

Format: Examiner required; individual or group administration; untimed: 5 to 10 minutes

Scoring: Examiner evaluated; 15 to 20 minutes

Cost: Complete Kit (manual, 25 test booklets, 25 scoring sheets, protractor) $59.00

Test of Visual-Perceptual Skills (non-motor)–Revised [TVPS(n-m)–R]
Morrison F. Gardner

1996	Psychological and Educational Publications, Inc.

Population: Ages 4 through 13 years

Purpose: Assesses visual-perceptual skills with no motor response other than pointing

Description: The format and arrangement of the forms in this revision remain the same. New norms, up-to-date standardization, and updated items are included. The test assesses a child using subtests in these areas: visual discrimination, visual memory, visual-spatial relationships, visual form constancy, visual sequential memory, visual-figure ground, and visual closure. The standardization sample included approximately 1,000 individuals.

Format: Examiner required; individual administration; untimed: 10 to 20 minutes

Scoring: Examiner evaluated

Cost: Complete Test (manual, test plates, 25 record forms) $155.95

Test of Visual-Perceptual Skills (non-motor) Upper Level–Revised [TVPS(n-m)UL–R]
Morrison F. Gardner

Date not provided	Psychological and Educational Publications, Inc.

Population: Ages 12 to 18 years

Purpose: Assesses visual-perceptual skills with no motor response other than pointing

Description: The format and arrangement of the forms in this revision remain the same. New norms, up-to-date standardization, and updated items are included. The test assesses a child using subtests in these areas: visual discrimination, visual memory, visual-spatial relationships, visual form constancy, visual sequential memory, visual-figure ground, and visual closure. Easier items are included.

Format: Examiner required; individual administration; untimed: 10 to 20 minutes

Scoring: Examiner evaluated

Cost: Complete Test (manual, test plates, 25 record forms) $120.95

Useful Field of View (UFOV)
Karlene Ball, Daniel Roenker

1998   The Psychological Corporation

Population: Adults

Purpose: Predicts a driver's risk of accident involvement

Description: A computer-administered and scored test of visual attention that determines the size of a driver's perceptual window. Three parts measure components of an examinee's useful field of view: central vision and processing speed, divided attention, and selective attention. Rapidly presented target objects are viewed on a computer monitor, with the information displayed progressing from simple to complex. The software administers, scores, interprets responses, and prints a report that may be given to an examinee unedited. A risk level is assigned for each part.

Format: Computer administered; untimed: 15 minutes

Scoring: Computer scored

Cost: Complete Kit (manual, reference card, CD, 5 uses) $126.00

VCWS 205—Independent Perceptual Screening (Special Aptitude)

1993   Valpar International Corporation

Population: Ages 13 years and older

Purpose: Assesses worker qualification and profiles factors for job, curricula placement, and career planning

Description: Criterion-referenced test consisting of demonstrated performance of pin placement, pin assembly, six-part assembly, and three-dimensional assembly. Measures special aptitude, reasoning, general learning ability, form perception, motor coordination, and finger and manual dexterity. The test yields Methods-Time Measurement standard and percentile scores. Materials include assembly board, parts bin, and assorted assembly parts. This test is suitable for individuals with hearing, physical, and mental impairments. Signing for hearing impairment is necessary.

Format: Examiner required; individual administration; timed: 25 to 30 minutes

Scoring: Examiner evaluated

Cost: $625.00

Visual Memory Test
Joseph M. Wepman,
Anne Morency, Maria Seidl

1983   Western Psychological Services

Population: Ages 5 to 8 years

Purpose: Measures a child's ability to remember nonalphabetical, visual forms; used to identify any perceptual inadequacy that might reduce the ability to learn to read

Description: Sixteen-item test measuring a child's ability to recall unfamiliar forms that cannot readily be named. The examiner shows the child a design on a target page, and the child chooses the design from four designs on a response page. Norms are provided. Adequacy threshold scores indicate the need for additional evaluation.

Format: Examiner required; individual administration; untimed: 10 to 15 minutes

Scoring: Hand key

Cost: Kit (set of stimulus cards, 25 score sheets, manual) $87.50

Visual-Aural Digit Span Test (VADS)
Elizabeth M. Koppitz

1977   The Psychological Corporation

Population: Ages 5 years 6 months to 12 years

Purpose: Diagnoses specific problems in reading recognition and spelling for children who can read and write digits; used to develop individual educational programs for children with learning disabilities

Description: Multiple-item test in which digit sequences on 26 test cards must be reproduced from memory, first orally; then in writing after being presented orally; and finally as a separate series, visually. The test measures auditory, visual, visual-auditory, and auditory-visual integration; sequence and recall of digits; and organization of written material. There are 11 scores, which are interpreted individually. Also available in Spanish.

Format: Examiner required; suitable for group use; untimed: 10 minutes

Scoring: Examiner evaluated

Cost: Complete Kit (cards, directions, 100 scoring sheets) $55.00; Manual $75.00

Wepman's Visual Assessment Battery
Joseph M. Wepman, Anne Morency, Maria Seidl, D. Turaids

Date not provided	Western Psychological Services

Population: Ages 5 to 9 years

Purpose: Used to measure visual skills essential to reading

Description: Battery of three tests: The Visual Memory Test measures ability to retain immediate memory of visually presented, nonalphabetic forms; the Visual Discrimination Test measures ability to discriminate between similar visually perceived forms; and the Spatial Orientation Memory Test measures a child's ability to retain and recall the orientation of visually presented forms.

Format: Examiner required; individual administration; untimed: 5 minutes each

Scoring: Hand key

Cost: Set (includes one kit for each of the three tests) $234.00

Wide Range Assessment of Visual Motor Ability (WRAVMA)
Wayne Adams, David Sheslow

1995	Wide Range, Inc.

Population: Ages 3 to 17 years

Purpose: Measures visual-motor intregration

Description: Visual-motor integration is assessed by measuring its component parts, Visual-Motor, Visual-Spatial, and Fine-Motor abilities. These three areas can be measured individually or in combination. Each of the three subtests was standardized nationally on the same stratified sample of over 2,600 children.

Format: Examiner required; suitable for group administration; untimed: 5 to 10 minutes per subtest

Scoring: Hand key; examiner evaluated

Cost: Kit (manual; 25 each of drawing forms, matching forms, and examiner forms; pegboard and pegs; pencils and markers; case) $255.00

Wilson Driver Selection Test
Clark L. Wilson

1986	Martin M. Bruce, PhD

Population: Adults

Purpose: Evaluates visual attention, depth visualization, eye-hand coordination, steadiness, and recognition of details; used by driver selection, evaluation companies, and schools to screen personnel to reduce the risk of operator-caused accidents

Description: Six-part paper-pencil nonverbal test measuring visual attention, depth perception, recognition of simple and complex details, eye-hand coordination, and steadiness. The booklet includes norms for males and females, as well as items on the subject's accident record and personal history. Suitable for individuals with physical, hearing, and visual impairments.

Format: Examiner required; suitable for group use; timed: 26 minutes

Scoring: Hand key

Cost: Specimen Set $58.80

Business Instruments

T he tests described in the Business section generally are used for personnel selection, evaluation, development, and promotion. In addition, the reader is encouraged to consult the Psychology and Education sections for other assessment instruments that may be of value in the area of business.

Attitudes

Abridged Job Descriptive Index (AJDI)
Jeffrey M. Stanton, Evan F. Sinar,
William K. Balzer, Amanda L. Julian,
Paul Thoreson, Shahnaz Aziz,
Patricia C. Smith

2000	Bowling Green State University

Population: Ages 8 years and older

Purpose: Measures job satisfaction

Description: There are 25 items in five categories: work on present job (5 items), present day (5 items), opportunities for promotion (5 items), supervision (5 items), and coworkers (5 items). Scores range from 0 to 15 on each scale.

Format: Self-administered; untimed: 10 minutes

Scoring: Hand key; may be computer scored; may be machine scored

Cost: $1.00 per scale

Advocacy/Inquiry
Skill Inventory (AISI)
Kittie W. Watson, Larry L. Barker

Date not provided	SPECTRA, Inc.

Population: Adults

Purpose: Assesses preference for using advocacy or inquiry communication skills

Description: Initiating communication, being direct, comprehending others, and respecting others' preferences can help or hinder relationships with others. Participants quickly score and receive immediate feedback on their preferences. The guide provides details on how the AISI was developed and validated and how to best administer it. Learn how to incorporate the inventory in communication, management, and leadership workshops.

Format: Self-administered; untimed

Scoring: Self-scored

Cost: Guide and Sample Instrument $24.95

Applicant Potential Inventory (API™)

Date not provided	NCS Pearson Reid London House

Population: Adults

Purpose: Evaluates attitudes that can improve employee productivity

Description: The API assessment evolved from the Personnel Selection Inventory. Each version of the API may contain the following scales: honesty, drug avoidance, employee relations, work values, supervision attitudes, tenure, safety, customer service, validity/candidness, and validity/accuracy. Results in an Employability Index.

Format: Self-administered; untimed: 15 minutes

Scoring: Software scoring; computer scoring via telephone and fax; scoring service available

Cost: Contact publisher

Applicant Productivity Profile (APP™)

Date not provided	NCS Pearson Reid London House

Population: Adults

Purpose: Assesses attitudes toward counterproductive behaviors in individuals with low reading ability

Description: These dimensions can help evaluate trustworthiness and productivity: honesty, drug avoidance, employee relations, work values, supervision attitudes, safety, tenure, validity/candidness, and validity/accuracy. Results in an Employability Index.

Format: Self-administered; computer administered; untimed: 15 minutes

Scoring: Telephone and fax scoring; software scoring available; scannable forms

Cost: Contact publisher

Attentional and Interpersonal Style (TAIS) Inventory
Robert M. Nideffer

| 1976 | Enhanced Performance Systems, Inc. |

Population: Ages 13 years and older

Purpose: Assesses performance under pressure (attention and interpersonal factors); used for business, sports, and military performance

Description: Using 144 items, this is a performance-based self-report inventory. Provides a direct link between the concentration and personality characteristics measured and performance. This test is also available in English, French, French Canadian, Dutch, Spanish, and German.

Format: Self-administered; untimed: 20 to 30 minutes

Scoring: Computer scored; test scoring available

Cost: Contact publisher

Campbell Organizational Survey (COS)
David P. Campbell

| 1995 | NCS Pearson |

Population: Adults

Purpose: Assesses employee attitudes regarding organizations

Description: Paper-pencil 67-item test with 17 scales plus an overall index. A sixth-grade reading level is required. Examiner must have taken psychology courses. Available also in Spanish and French.

Format: Self-administered; untimed

Scoring: Computer scored; test scoring service available from publisher

Cost: Contact publisher

Career Attitudes and Strategies Inventory (CASI™)
John L. Holland, Gary D. Gottfredson

| 1994 | Psychological Assessment Resources, Inc. |

Population: Adults

Purpose: Assesses an employee's current work situation, including common attitudes as well as strategies for coping with job, family, coworkers, and supervisors; used for career counseling

Description: Multiple-choice and true-false test with 130 items on nine scales: geographical barriers, job satisfaction, work involvement, skill development, dominant style, career worries, interpersonal abuse, family commitment, and risk-taking style. Materials used include a manual, inventory booklet, hand-scorable answer sheet, and interpretive summary booklet.

Format: Self-administered; untimed

Scoring: Hand key; self-scored

Cost: Introductory Kit $95.00

Career Survival: Strategic Job and Role Planning
Edgar H. Schein

| 1993 | Jossey-Bass/Pfeiffer |

Population: Adults

Purpose: Identifies the key elements of an individual's job now and in the future and helps to set appropriate priorities

Description: Helps managers, employers, and human resource specialists answer questions such as these: What does the job currently involve? How will the job itself change over the next few years? How will the environment around the job change? Do these changes mean that the job may require a different person? Career Survival helps organizations more accurately forecast their needs, and individual employees effectively structure their priorities and future plans.

Format: Self-administered; untimed

Scoring: Self-scored

Cost: $14.95

Career Values Card Sort
Richard L. Knowdell

| 2001 | Career Research & Testing, Inc. |

Population: Adults

Purpose: Prioritizes career values to assist in career planning

Description: A simple tool that allows clients to prioritize their values. Lists and describes 41 variables of work satisfaction, such as time freedom, precision work, power, technical competence, and public contact. The individual sorts these variables based on a 5-point Likert scale (*always, often, sometimes, seldom, never*). An effective tool for job seekers and people fine-tuning their present jobs. The kit includes guidelines for counselors and group facilitators, an overview of values and their role in career decision making, explicit instructions for the individual user, and supplementary activities for further clarification of career values.

Format: Examiner required; individual or group administration; untimed: 15 to 20 minutes

Scoring: Examiner evaluated

Cost: Cards and Manual $8.00

Change Readiness Assessment

2001	Performance Programs, Inc.

Population: Adults

Purpose: Measures employees' willingness to change

Description: How quickly and thoroughly an enterprise can respond to change in the fast-paced environment has an impact on people and their working relationships. This 41-question paper-pencil or on-line survey features 36 standardized questionnaire items, up to 5 customized questions, up to 5 demographic categories for reporting, and 3 open-ended questions.

Format: Self-administered; untimed

Scoring: Scoring service available

Cost: Contact publisher

Creativity Questionnaire
Allan Cameron

1994	Selby MillSmith Ltd.

Population: All ages

Purpose: Assesses innovation, creativity, and rule conformity

Description: Computer-administered or paper-pencil 48-item multiple-choice test. The categories are originality, rule consciousness, openness to change, assertiveness, and independence. An 11-year old reading level is required.

Format: Self-administered; untimed: 10 minutes

Scoring: Computer scored; test scoring service

Cost: Specimen Set $60.00

Cross-Cultural Adaptability Inventory™ (CCAI™)
Colleen Kelley, Judith Meyers

1995	NCS Pearson

Population: Adults

Purpose: A culture-general test used to assess an individual's ability to adapt to other cultures

Description: Paper–pencil 50-item test measures an individual's cultural adaptability.

Format: Self-administered; untimed

Scoring: Self-scored

Cost: Contact publisher

Diagnosing Organizational Culture
Roger Harrison, Herb Stakes

1993	Jossey-Bass/Pfeiffer

Population: Adults

Purpose: Designed to help identify the shared values and beliefs that constitute an organization's culture

Description: Organizations can use this instrument for team building, organizational development, productivity improvement, and human resources development. It defines four cultures basic to most organizations: Power, Role, Achievement, and Support.

Format: Self-administered; untimed

Scoring: Self-scored

Cost: $9.95

Dimensions of Self-Concept/ Adult Workers (DOSC–W)
William B. Michael, Betty Crowder

Date not provided	EdITS/Educational and Industrial Testing Service

Population: Adults

Purpose: Measures motivational characteristics central to job performance and achievement for adults in employment settings

Description: The dimensions measured are Level of Aspiration, Level of Anxiety, Job Interest and Satisfaction, Leadership and Initiative, Identification vs. Alienation, and Level of Job Stress.

Format: Examiner required; suitable for group use; untimed: 20 to 40 minutes

Scoring: Hand or machine scoring

Cost: Specimen Set $8.25; 25 Test Forms $14.00; 25 Profile Sheets $5.00

Diversity Awareness Profile (DAP)
K. Stinson

1992	Jossey-Bass/Pfeiffer

Population: Adults

Purpose: Helps people become more aware of their behaviors, evaluate their own behaviors, and modify behaviors to be empowering and respectful to all people

Description: The DAP is based on the belief that if people discriminate, judge, or isolate others, the behavior is unintentional. These self-scoring instruments are based on information gathered in a series of focus groups and one-on-one interviews. The groups included older workers, women, people with disabilities, African Americans, Native Americans, Hispanics, and other groups that experience discrimination.

Format: Self-administered; untimed

Scoring: Self-scored

Cost: $5.00

Empathy Test
Willard A. Kerr, B. J. Speroff

1993	Psychometric Affiliates

Population: Adolescents, adults

Purpose: Measures empathic ability; used to select managerial and supervisory personnel and graduate students

Description: Multiple-item paper–pencil test measuring the ability to put oneself in another person's position, establish rapport, and anticipate another person's reactions, feelings, and behavior. Empathy is measured as a variable unrelated to intelligence and most other attitudes. Three forms—Form A, blue-collar emphasis; Form B, white-collar emphasis; and Form C, Canadian emphasis—are available.

Format: Examiner required; suitable for group use; timed: 15 minutes

Scoring: Examiner evaluated

Cost: Specimen Set $4.00; 25 Tests (specify form) $3.50

Employee Safety Inventory (ESI®)

1988	NCS Pearson Reid London House

Population: Adults

Purpose: Assesses attitudes toward on-the-job safety; used for screening, placement, and training of job applicants and current employees

Description: Paper–pencil multiple-choice and short-answer test yielding scores in four areas: Risk Avoidance, Stress Tolerance, Safety Control, and Validity. Scores on a supplemental scale (Driver Attitudes) and a composite are also available. Materials include test booklet, interpretation guide, and administrator's guide. Must purchase a minimum of 25 booklets.

Format: Examiner required; suitable for group use; untimed

Scoring: Computer scored; test scoring service available from publisher

Cost: Contact publisher

Employment Inventory (EI)
George Paajanen

1986	Personnel Decisions International

Population: Ages 15 years and older

Purpose: Assesses job applicants' probability of productive and counterproductive job behavior

Description: Paper–pencil 97-item multiple-choice and true–false test assessing job applicants' probability of engaging in counterproductive behavior in an hourly job and probability of voluntarily remaining on the job for at least 3 months. Questions are directed toward the applicant's opinions, attitudes, and background. The test yields a Performance score and a Tenure score. The Performance score indicates the likelihood the employee will be reliable, follow rules, have a good attendance record, and be strongly motivated. The Tenure score indicates the likelihood of premature turnover, another aspect of counterproductive job behavior.

Format: Examiner required; computer administration available; on-line administration available; suitable for group use; untimed: 15 to 20 minutes

Scoring: Computer scored; telephone and fax scoring; on-line scoring

Cost: Contact publisher

Employment Values Inventory (EVI)
Adrian Savage

1990	Selby MillSmith Ltd.

Population: Adolescents, adults

Purpose: Used in education and employment applications to assess work and educational values

Description: Computer-administered (DOS) or paper–pencil 168-item multiple-choice criterion-referenced test with 14 work-related factors. An 11-year-old reading level is required.

Format: Self-administered; untimed: 20 minutes

Scoring: Computer scored; test scoring service

Cost: Specimen Set $50.00

Feedback Edition of the Strength Deployment Inventory
Elias H. Porter

1996	Personal Strengths Publishing

Population: Adults

Purpose: Elicits feedback to describe how a person uses his or her personal strengths in relationships

Description: Used in team building, organizational development, career development, and relationship counseling. There are 20 items: 10 measure a significant other's perceptions of an individual's strength deployment when things are going well, and 10 measure strength deployment in the face of conflict. Uses self-ratings and ratings of a significant other. For use in conjunction with the Strength Deployment Inventory.

Format: Requires facilitation; individual or group administration; untimed: 20 to 40 minutes

Scoring: Self-scored; examiner evaluated

Cost: $4.50

Feedback Portrait of Overdone Strengths

1997	Personal Strengths Publishing

Population: Adults

Purpose: Elicits feedback to describe how a person may overdo or misapply his or her personal strengths; used in leadership development, career development, and relationship counseling

Description: A Q-sort of 40 overdone personal strengths provides a profile of top and least overdone per feedback giver. Used with Strength Deployment Inventory, Portrait of Personal Strengths, and Portrait of Overdone Strengths.

Format: Requires facilitation; individual or group administration; untimed: 20 to 40 minutes

Scoring: Examiner evaluated

Cost: $5.50

Feedback Portrait of Personal Strengths

1997	Personal Strengths Publishing

Population: Adults

Purpose: Elicits feedback to describe how a person uses his or her personal strengths in relationships; used in team building, leadership training, career development, and relationship counseling

Description: A Q-sort of 40 personal strengths provides a profile of a significant other's perceptions of an individual's use of personal strengths. Used with Portrait of Personal Strengths and Strength Deployment Inventory.

Format: Requires facilitation; individual or group administration; untimed: 20 to 40 minutes

Scoring: Examiner evaluated

Cost: $5.50

Job Descriptive Index, Revised (JDI REV)
Patricia C. Smith, Lorne M. Kendall, Charles L. Hulin

1997	Bowling Green State University

Population: Ages 17 to 100 years

Purpose: Assesses an individual's job satisfaction

Description: Paper–pencil 72-item test consisting of five scales: Satisfaction with Work (18 items), Pay (9 items), Promotions (9 items), Supervision (18 items), and Co-Workers (18 items). Items are answered in yes–no format. The test yields five scores, one per scale. A scoring service is available by special arrangement with the publisher. A second-grade reading level is required. The Job in General (JIG) test may be administered as a follow-up. Suitable for use with individuals with hearing and physical impairments. Also available in French, Spanish, Chinese, and other languages.

Format: Self-administered; untimed: 5 minutes

Scoring: Hand key; may be computer or machine scored

Cost: 100 Test Booklets (includes Job in General) $42.00

Job in General (JIG)
Gail H. Ironson, Patricia C. Smith, Michael T. Brannick

1985	Bowling Green State University

Population: Adults

Purpose: Assesses overall job satisfaction

Description: Paper–pencil 18-item yes–no test assessing workers' job satisfaction. The test is to be administered following the Job Descriptive Index, which measures five specific areas of job satisfaction. A scoring service is available by special arrangement with the publisher. A second-grade reading level is required. Suitable for use with individuals with hearing and physical impairments

Format: Self-administered; untimed: 1 minute

Scoring: Hand key; may be computer or machine scored

Cost: 100 Questionnaires $20.00; Job Descriptive Index included at no charge

Job Interactions Inventory (JII)
Elias H. Porter

1996	Personal Strengths Publishing

Population: Adolescents, adults

Purpose: Measures how well a person's style of relating fits with the demands of a given job; used for organizational development, team building, career development, and outplacement services

Description: A total of 10 items: 5 measure demands and rewards of a given job when things are going well, and 5 measure the sequence of responses demanded when things are not going well and there is conflict. Seven scores are obtained reflecting demands and rewards and 13 reflecting sequential responses. For use in conjunction with Strength Deployment Inventory. Not to be used as a selection tool.

Format: Requires facilitation; individual or group administration; untimed: 20 to 40 minutes

Scoring: Self-scored; examiner evaluated

Cost: Inventory $4.50; Manual $30.00

Job Stress Survey (JSS)
Charles D. Spielberger, Peter R. Vagg

1999, 2000	Psychological Assessment Resources, Inc.

Population: Adults

Purpose: Identifies major sources of stress in the workplace

Description: Thirty job-related stressor events are presented in three scales (Job Stress Index, Job Stress Severity, and Job Stress Frequency) and the following subscales: Job Pressure Index, Job Pressure Severity, Job Pressure Frequency, Lack of Organizational Support Index, and Lack of Organizational Support Frequency. Sixth-grade reading level is required.

Format: Self-administered; untimed: 10 to 15 minutes

Scoring: Hand key; computer scoring available

Cost: Kit (manual, 25 test booklets, 25 profile forms, 3.5-inch program disk with 5 bonus uses of Windows Scoring Program) $99.00

Listener Preference Profile (LPP)
Kittie W. Watson, Larry L. Barker,
James B. Weaver

Date not provided	SPECTRA, Inc.

Population: Adults

Purpose: Identifies listening responses

Description: The 20-item self-contained format measures four habitual listening responses: people, action, content, and time oriented. The trainer manual helps trainers, consultants, and individuals facilitate, administer, and interpret the instrument. It provides details about the development of, research with, and guidelines for use of the test.

Format: Self-administered; untimed

Scoring: Self-scored

Cost: Guide and Sample Instrument $24.95

Management Inventory on Leadership, Motivation, and Decision-Making (MILMD)
Donald L. Kirkpatrick

1993	Donald L. Kirkpatrick, PhD

Population: Adults

Purpose: Assesses attitudes and knowledge; used as a training tool to determine training needed, to stimulate classroom discussion, and to evaluate training programs

Description: Paper–pencil agree–disagree test.

Format: Self-administered; untimed: 15 to 20 minutes

Scoring: Self-scored

Cost: Kit (20 tests, 20 answer booklets, manual) $40.00

Miner Sentence Completion Scale: Form H
John B. Miner

1989	Organizational Measurement Systems Press

Population: Adults

Purpose: Measures an individual's hierarchic (bureaucratic) motivation; used for employee counseling and development and organizational assessment

Description: Multiple-item paper–pencil free-response or multiple-choice sentence completion test measuring an individual's motivation in terms of motivational patterns that fit the hierarchic (bureaucratic) organizational form. Both forms (free-response version or multiple-choice version offering six alternatives for each stem) measure the following subscales: authority figures, competitive games, competitive situations, assertive role, imposing wishes, standing out from the group, and routine administrative functions. The basic scoring guide (for use with the free-response version) discusses categorizing the responses, the subscales, supervisory jobs, total scores, and the sample scoring sheet.

Format: Examiner required; suitable for group use; untimed

Scoring: Examiner evaluated

Cost: 50 Scales (specify free-response or multiple-choice version) $30.00; Basic Scoring Guide (includes supplementary scoring guides) $10.00

Miner Sentence Completion Scale: Form P
John B. Miner

1981	Organizational Measurement Systems Press

Population: Adults

Purpose: Measures an individual's professional (specialized) motivation; used for employee counseling and development and organizational assessment

Description: Multiple-item paper–pencil free-response sentence-completion test measuring motivation in terms of motivational patterns that fit the professional (specialized) organizational form. The test measures the following subscales: acquiring knowledge, independent action, accepting status, providing help, and professional commitment. Each item consists of a sentence stem that individuals complete in their own words. The scoring guide discusses categorizing the responses, the subscales, actual scoring, reliability, normative data, use of Form P, and bibliographic notes.

Format: Examiner required; suitable for group use; untimed

Scoring: Examiner evaluated

Cost: 50 Scales $30.00; Scoring Guide $10.00

Miner Sentence Completion Scale: Form T
John B. Miner

1984	Organizational Measurement Systems Press

Population: Adults

Purpose: Measures an individual's task (entrepreneurial) motivation; used for employee counseling and development and organizational assessment

Description: Multiple-item paper–pencil free-response sentence-completion test measuring an individual's motivation in terms of patterns that fit the task (entrepreneurial) organizational form. The test measures the following subscales: self-achievement, avoiding risks, feedback of results, personal innovation, and planning for the future. These subscales are generally parallel to the five aspects of David McClelland's achievement situation. Each test item consists of a sentence stem that individuals complete in their own words. The scoring guide discusses categorizing the responses, the subscales, actual scoring, reliability, normative data, use of the Form T, and bibliographic notes.

Format: Examiner required; suitable for group use; untimed

Scoring: Examiner evaluated

Cost: 50 Scales $30.00; Scoring Guide $10.00

Minnesota Satisfactoriness Scales (MSS)

Date not provided	Vocational Psychology Research

Population: Supervisors

Purpose: Measures an employee's satisfactoriness on a job

Description: The MSS is usually completed by the employee's supervisor, who evaluates the employee on 28 items describing the employee's behavior on the job. The MSS provides scores on five scales: Performance, Conformance, Dependability, Personal Adjustment, and General Satisfactoriness. The MSS can be used to evaluate the effectiveness of job placement or the success of specific training programs.

Format: Self-administered; untimed: 5 minutes

Scoring: Hand scored; computer scoring service available

Cost: Sample Set (manual, one copy of scale) $3.75

Mirror Edition of the Personal Values Inventory
Elias H. Porter

1997	Personal Strengths Publishing

Population: Adolescents, adults

Purpose: Elicits feedback to describe how a person uses his or her personal strengths in relationships; used in team building, career development, and relationship counseling

Description: Of the 20 items, 10 measure a significant other's perception of an individual's use of his or her strengths and 10 measure the individual's response to conflict. For use in conjunction with the Personal Values Inventory. Requires a sixth-grade reading level.

Format: Requires facilitation; individual or group administration; untimed: 20 to 40 minutes

Scoring: Self-scored; examiner evaluated

Cost: $4.50

Motivated Skills Card Sort
Richard L. Knowdell

| 2001 | Career Research & Testing, Inc. |

Population: Adults

Purpose: Measures transferable skills for career planning

Description: Based on experience, feedback, and instinct, the client uses the cards to assess proficiency and motivation in 48 transferable skill areas. Complete instructional manual includes counselor guidelines, as well as an overview of achievement and its role in career decision making.

Format: Examiner required; individual or group administration; untimed: 30 to 45 minutes

Scoring: Examiner evaluated

Cost: Complete Kit (cards, category cards, blank cards, summary sheet, manual) $12.00

Motivation Questionnaire (MQ)

| 1992 | SHL Canada |

Population: Adult professionals

Purpose: Selection and development of staff motivation

Description: Measures 18 dimensions of motivation with 144 items in four categories: energy and dynamism, synergy, intrinsic, and extrinsic. Also available in French.

Format: Examiner required; individual administration; computer and on-line administration available; untimed: 35 minutes

Scoring: Hand key; machine scored; scoring service available; on-line scoring

Cost: Contact publisher

My BEST Communication Style

| 1989 | Associated Consultants in Education |

Population: Adults

Purpose: Improves communication skills

Description: An easy-to-administer, easy-to-follow instrument that helps participants understand the impact of their style on the communication process. Four major styles are identified: Bold, Expressive, Sympathetic, and Technical. In addition

to the clarifications for each style, brief suggestions for personal development are provided.

Format: Self-administered; untimed: 15 to 20 minutes

Scoring: Hand key

Cost: $2.95

Observational Assessments of Temperament
Melany E. Baehr

| 1979 | NCS Pearson Reid London House |

Population: Adults

Purpose: Provides self-assessment or observational assessments of behavior that can be used in either counseling or assessment center settings

Description: Paper–pencil test assessing three behavior factors that have been shown to be the most effective in predicting significant aspects of performance in higher level positions: introversive/cautious vs. extroversive/impulsive, emotional/responsive vs. nonemotional/controlled, and dependent/group oriented vs. self-reliant/self-oriented. When used in conjunction with the Temperament Comparator, the instrument provides a measure of insight through comparison of disguised and undisguised assessments of the same three behavior factors.

Format: Examiner required; suitable for group use; untimed: 10 minutes

Scoring: Hand key

Cost: Contact publisher

Occupational Interests Card Sort
Richard L. Knowdell

| 2001 | Career Research & Testing, Inc. |

Population: Adults

Purpose: Measures occupational and career interests

Description: Clarifies the high-appeal jobs and fields; the degree of readiness, skills, and knowledge needed; and competency-building steps for entry or progress. There are 110 occupational cards that the examinee rank orders as *definitely interested, probably interested, indifferent, probably disinterested,* or *definitely disinterested.*

Format: Examiner required; individual or group administration; untimed: 15 to 20 minutes

Scoring: Examiner evaluated

Cost: Complete Kit (cards, category cards, summary sheet, manual) $18.00

Occupational Stress Inventory Revised™ (OSI-R™)
Samuel H. Osipow, Arnold Spokane

1998	Psychological Assessment Resources, Inc.

Population: Adults

Purpose: Measures dimensions of occupational adjustment of individuals employed primarily in technical, professional, and managerial positions in school, service, and manufacturing settings

Description: Paper–pencil 140-item test measuring three dimensions of occupational adjustment: occupational stress, psychological strain, and coping resources. The instrument consists of three separate questionnaires. The Occupational Roles Questionnaire (ORQ; six scales with 10 items each) analyzes stress due to occupational roles. The Personal Strain Questionnaire (PSQ; four scales with 10 items each) measures psychological strain as reflected in behaviors and attitudes. The Personal Resources Questionnaire (PRQ; four scales with 10 items each) analyzes effective coping via personal resources. The profile form is used to convert raw scores to *T*-scores. The questionnaires may be administered together or separately.

Format: Self-administered; untimed: 20 to 40 minutes

Scoring: Self-scored

Cost: Kit $135.00

Organizational Assessment Survey
Larry A. Braskamp, Martin L. Maehr

1985	MetriTech, Inc.

Population: Adults

Purpose: Assesses organizational culture and employee commitment, assesses worker motivation by determining personal values and incentives, and evaluates the opportunities for fulfillment that individuals perceive in their present jobs

Description: A total of 200 Likert-scale items measuring four aspects of the worker, job, and organization: accomplishment, recognition, power, and affiliation. Both group and individual reports are available. Individual reports provide employees feedback about their incentives, personal values, and job opportunities. A second type of individual report provides supervisors with insights into their own management style and the impact their styles have on the people they supervise. The group report provides feedback on organizational culture, degree of employee commitment, and areas of job satisfaction.

Format: Examiner or self-administered; suitable for group use; untimed: 1 hour

Scoring: Computer scored through publisher

Cost: Introductory Kit (test materials, manual, processing of 2 reports) $49.50

Organizational Survey System (OSS™)
Melany E. Baehr

Date not provided	NCS Pearson Reid London House

Population: Adults

Purpose: Provides feedback on the functioning of an organization

Description: Helps gather information about an organization from employees working in health care or business/industry settings. Nine occupation-specific versions are available. Surveys are completed anonymously on work premises or at home and returned for processing. The survey can be modified to meet the workplace requirements.

Format: Self-administered; untimed: 45 minutes

Scoring: Scoring service

Cost: Contact publisher

Personal Outlook Inventory (POI)

1987	NCS Pearson Reid London House

Population: Adults

Purpose: Assesses the likelihood that a potential employee will try to steal cash, merchandise, or other company assets; designed to reduce employee theft

Description: This 37-item multiple-choice test has two scales: V-scale score indicates whether the instrument is valid for the examinee; S-scale score indicates the probability that the examinee will be fired for stealing.

Format: Examiner required; suitable for group use; untimed: 30 minutes

Scoring: Hand key

Cost: Contact publisher

Personal Values Inventory (PVI)
Elias H. Porter

1997	Personal Strengths Publishing

Population: Adolescents, adults

Purpose: Measures personal style of approaching tasks, conflicts, decision making, and relationships; used in team building, career development, and relationship counseling

Description: There are 20 items, 10 measuring motivational values when things are going well and 10 measuring predictable progressive responses to conflict. Requires a sixth-grade reading level.

Format: Requires facilitation; individual or group administration; untimed: 20 to 40 minutes

Scoring: Self-scored; examiner evaluated

Cost: Inventory $10.00; Manual $30.00

Personal Values Questionnaire (PVQ)

1993	Hay Group

Population: Adults

Purpose: Provides an analysis of personal values versus job requirements

Description: A total of 36 items measure the degree to which a person values Achievement, Affiliation, and Power—the three social motives that drive human behavior.

Format: Self-administered; on-line administration available; untimed: 20 minutes

Scoring: Self-scored

Cost: 10 Booklets $65.00; $10.00 each on-line

Personnel Reaction Blank (PRB)
Harrison G. Gough

Date not provided	Consulting Psychologists Press, Inc.

Population: Ages 15 years and older

Purpose: Measures a dependability-conscientiousness factor among rank-and-file workers; used by personnel officers for selecting new employees

Description: Paper–pencil 70-item test assessing interests and attitudes related to dependability and conscientiousness. The test is used with rank-and-file workers and is not recommended for management personnel. A manual explains the meaning of high and low scores. The test is restricted, and scoring keys are sold only to registered users.

Format: Self-administered; untimed: 10 to 15 minutes

Scoring: Hand key

Cost: Preview Kit (booklet, scoring keys, manual) $56.50

Portrait of Overdone Strengths
Elias H. Porter

1996	Personal Strengths Publishing

Population: Adults

Purpose: Demonstrates how a person may overdo or misapply personal strengths, thereby contributing to unwarranted conflict in relationships; used in team building, leadership training, and relationship counseling

Description: A Q-sort of 40 overdone personal strengths. A profile provides most and least overdone strengths. For use in conjunction with the Strength Deployment Inventory.

Format: Requires facilitation; individual or group administration; untimed: 20 to 40 minutes

Scoring: Self-scored; examiner evaluated

Cost: $5.50

Portrait of Personal Strengths
Elias H. Porter

1996	Personal Strengths Publishing

Population: Adults

Purpose: Designed to help a person see how well he or she uses his or her strengths when things are going well in a relationship; used for team building, leadership training, and relationship counseling

Description: This Q-sort of 40 personal strengths provides a profile of top six strengths and six least deployed strengths. A feedback edition is available. For use in conjunction with the Strength Deployment Inventory.

Format: Requires facilitation; individual or group administration; untimed: 20 to 40 minutes

Scoring: Self-scored; examiner evaluated

Cost: $5.50

Retirement Activities Kit
Richard L. Knowdell

2001	Career Research & Testing, Inc.

Population: Adults

Purpose: Measures activities of interest for people approaching retirement

Description: An easy-to-use and approachable tool to aid in the transition from formal employment to a meaningful retirement lifestyle. Forty-eight common pastimes—from cultural events to meditation, from entertaining to group leadership—are listed and described. Cards can be used to determine current frequency as well as preferred activity patterns. The manual provides explicit instructions for using the card sort, an overview of the concepts and issues of retiring, and activities for dealing with aging and retirement.

Format: Examiner required; individual or group administration; untimed: 15 to 20 minutes

Scoring: Examiner evaluated

Cost: Complete Kit (cards, category cards, blank cards, summary sheet, manual) $12.00

Retirement Descriptive Index (RDI)
Patricia C. Smith, Lorne M. Kendall, Charles L. Hulin

1975	Bowling Green State University

Population: Adults

Purpose: Assesses satisfaction with activities, finances, people, and health; used with retired persons and other nonworking adults

Description: Paper-pencil 63-item test consisting of four scales measuring satisfaction: Activities (18 items), Income (9 items), Persons (18 items), and Health (18 items). The items follow a yes-no format. The instrument yields scores for each of the four scales. A scoring service is available by special arrangement with the publisher. A second-grade reading level is required.

Format: Self-administered; untimed: 10 minutes

Scoring: Hand key; may be computer or machine scored

Cost: 100 Booklets $34.00

Stanton Profile®

Date not provided	Pinkerton Services Group

Population: Adults

Purpose: Evaluates a job candidate's qualifications for a specific position

Description: The paper-pencil scale measures trustworthiness, service orientation, work motivation, and adaptability.

Format: Individual administration; untimed

Scoring: Telephone and fax scoring; computer-generated results

Cost: Contact publisher

Stanton Survey®

Date not provided	Pinkerton Services Group

Population: Adults

Purpose: Screens job applicants about attitudes

Description: Applicants who score high are responsible, self-disciplined, conscientious, self-

controlled, and compliant. Applicants who score low are easily distracted, unpredictable, impulsive, unable to delay gratification, rebellious, and nonconforming. Attitudes about work-related theft, theft outside the workplace, and company policy violations are measured.

Format: Self-administered; untimed

Scoring: Telephone and fax scoring; computer-generated results

Cost: Contact publisher

Strength Deployment Inventory (SDI)
Elias H. Porter

2000	Personal Strengths Publishing

Population: Adults

Purpose: Assesses personal strengths when things are going well and when there is conflict

Description: In a total of 20 items, 10 measure motivational values when things are going well and 10 measure conflict sequence. Seven motivational values and 13 conflict sequences are the result. The motivational values are Altruistic–Nurturing, Assertive–Directing, Analytic–Autonomizing, Flexible–Cohering, Assertive–Nurturing, Judicious–Competing, and Cautious–Supporting. The items are written at a high-school reading level.

Format: Requires facilitation; individual or group administration; untimed: 20 to 40 minutes

Scoring: Self-scored; examiner evaluated

Cost: Inventory $10.00; Manual $30.00

Stress in General (SIG)
Jeffrey M. Stanton, William K. Balzer, Patricia C. Smith, Luis F. Parra

2000	Bowling Green State University

Population: Ages 15 years and older

Purpose: Self-report measure of work-related stress

Description: There are 15 items in two categories: Pressure Scale and Threat Scale.

Format: Self-administered; untimed: 10 minutes

Scoring: Hand key; may be computer or machine scored

Cost: $.50 per scale

SureHire
S. W. Stang, M. L. Holcom, W. W. Ruch

1997	Psychological Services, Inc.

Population: Adults

Purpose: Measures problem-solving abilities and

work attitudes; used to select personnel for convenience store, fast food, and retail industries

Description: Multiple-choice 50-item test, divided into two sections: Problem Solving (math and reading questions) and Work Orientation (questions about work situations and preferences). With Problem Solving the examinee must read a statement and choose the answer he or she believes is correct. With Work Orientation the examinee chooses the answer that most closely describes his or her views.

Format: Examiner required; suitable for group use; untimed: 25 minutes

Scoring: Self-scoring carbon form; fax-back scoring available

Cost: 25 Tests $175.00

Survey of Work Values (SWV)
Steven Wollack, James G. Goodale,
Jan P. Wijting, Patricia C. Smith

1976	Bowling Green State University

Population: Adults

Purpose: Assesses an individual's work values

Description: Paper–pencil 72-item test in which examinees use a 5-point scale (*strongly agree* to *strongly disagree*) to rate statements. The test contains six scales consisting of nine items each: Pride in Work, Social Status of Job, Attitude Toward Earnings, Activity Preference, Upward Striving, and Job Involvement. The test can be scored to measure two factors, Intrinsic Values and Extrinsic Values. The test yields scores for each of the scales and factors. A scoring service is available by special arrangement with the publisher. A fifth-grade reading level is required. Suitable for use with individuals with hearing and physical impairments.

Format: Self-administered; untimed: 10 minutes

Scoring: Hand key; may be computer or machine scored

Cost: 100 Booklets $21.00; 100 Answer Sheets $5.00; 100 Scoring Sheets $5.00

Time Problems Inventory
Albert A. Canfield

1987	Western Psychological Services

Population: Adults

Purpose: Evaluates an individual's time-use problems; identifies personal and internal causes of time-use problems; used for group discussions and to assess organizational time-use problems

Description: Multiple-item paper–pencil inventory measuring the comparative level of an individual's time-use problems in four areas: priority setting, planning, task clarification, and self-discipline. Questions are largely work related, representing time problems in all aspects of daily living. Interpretation focuses on internal causes of time-use problems and may be used to identify time-use problems common to members of any organization. Scoring provides information for the discussion of internal and external factors related to ineffective time use.

Format: Self-administered; untimed: 20 to 25 minutes

Scoring: Self-scored

Cost: Kit (10 inventories, manual) $38.50

Time Use Analyzer
Albert A. Canfield

1981	Western Psychological Services

Population: Adults

Purpose: Evaluates a person's time-use habits; provides a basis for discussions of time quality versus time quantity

Description: Multiple-item paper–pencil test assessing how individuals feel about how their time is being spent in eight aspects of life: at work, asleep, on personal hygiene, taking care of personal/family business, in community and church activities, with family or home members, in education and development, and on recreational and hobby activities. Test booklets contain a discussion of the implications of the results and the general findings. The test produces an awareness of common areas in which most people express some level of dissatisfaction with their time use and helps individuals differentiate between time efficiency and time effectiveness and stimulates concerns for improvement in both areas.

Format: Self-administered; untimed: 20 minutes

Scoring: Self-scored

Cost: Kit (10 inventories, manual) $38.50

Values Preference Indicator (VPI)
Everett T. Robinson

1990	Consulting Resource Group International, Inc.

Population: Adults

Purpose: Ascertains the most important values

Description: Forced-choice 21-item test to help

users gain a deeper understanding of which values are most important to them.

Format: Examiner required; individual administration; suitable for group use; untimed

Scoring: Self-scored

Cost: $10.95

ViewPoint
Wade M. Gibson, Melvin L. Holcom, Susan W. Stang, William W. Ruch

1998	Psychological Services, Inc.

Population: Adults

Purpose: Assesses work dimensions that are of concern to most employers

Description: Applications include job candidate preemployment screening. The ViewPoint has seven primary scales: Conscientiousness, Trustworthiness, Managing Work Pressure, Getting Along with Others, Drug/Alcohol Avoidance, Safety Orientation, and Service Orientation. The ViewPoint scales are published in five different combinations, providing employers the flexibility to focus on core work attitudes. Each of the five forms also include the Carelessness and Faking scales.

Format: Examiner required; individual or group administration; untimed: 10 to 30 minutes

Scoring: Hand key; may be computer scored; scoring software available from publisher

Cost: Price varies, depending on quantity and form ordered: $7.00 to $18.00 per test

Whisler Strategy Test
Lawrence Whisler

1973	Psychometric Affiliates

Population: Adults

Purpose: Assesses strategy used in approaching problems; used to evaluate applicants for employment

Description: Multiple-item paper–pencil measure of six aspects of strategy: solutions, speed, boldness, caution, hypercaution, and net strategy. The test detects both risk takers and risk avoiders and evaluates the subject with respect to the wisdom of his or her strategy.

Format: Examiner required; suitable for group use; timed: 25 minutes

Scoring: Hand key

Cost: Specimen Set $5.00; 25 Tests $5.00; 25 Answer Sheets $5.00

Work Aspect Preference Scale (WAPS)
R. Pryor

1983	Australian Council for Educational Research Limited

Population: Grades 10 and above

Purpose: Measures work qualities that individuals consider important; used in career counseling, vocational rehabilitation, the study of personal and work values, and research on career development and worker satisfaction

Description: Paper–pencil or computer-administered 52-item inventory assessing an individual's work values along 13 scales: altruism, coworkers, creativity, detachment, independence, lifestyle, management, money, physical activity, prestige, security, self-development, and surroundings. Computer scoring converts raw scores on each scale to percentiles and ranks the scales in order of raw score and percentile. The computer-administered and scored version requires an Apple II+, IIe, or IIc computer with 48K, an 80-column printer, and a disk drive.

Format: Examiner required; suitable for group use; untimed: 10 to 20 minutes

Scoring: Hand key; may be machine or computer scored

Cost: Contact publisher

Work Motivation Inventory
Larry A. Braskamp, Martin L. Maehr

1986	MetriTech, Inc.

Population: Adults

Purpose: Measures individual work motivation factors; used for employee selection and promotion, and career counseling

Description: Paper–pencil or computer-administered 77-item multiple-choice test measuring four basic work motivation factors: accomplishment, recognition, power, and affiliation. The information obtained from the test helps predict job success and aids in understanding burnout and stress. Responses to the paper–pencil version may be entered into a computer for scoring and analysis. The computer version, which operates on IBM PC systems, administers and scores the test and generates reports. This test is an adaptation of the Organizational Assessment Survey.

Format: Examiner/self-administered; suitable for group use; untimed: 15 minutes

Scoring: Computer scored

Cost: Introductory Kit (test materials, manual, processing of 5 reports) $49.00

Work Orientation Survey for Firefighters

| 1997 | Psychological Services, Inc. |

Population: Adults

Purpose: Measures work attitudes reflecting the degree to which an examinee can be expected to be reliable, dependable, and conscientious; used to select applicants for entry-level firefighter positions or training programs

Description: Multiple-choice 87-item survey questions; examinee selects the answer that most closely describes his or her views. The survey measures six work dimensions: Conscientiousness, Trustworthiness, Managing Work Pressure, Getting Along with Others, Drug/Alcohol Avoidance, and Safety Orientation. May be used in conjunction with Firefighter Selection Test or Firefighter Learning Simulation.

Format: Examiner required; suitable for group use; untimed: 15 to 20 minutes

Scoring: Scoring service available from publisher

Cost: $395.00 Base Fee; 10 tests per package (includes scoring service): 1 to 10 packages $82.50; 11 to 50 packages $77.50; 51 to 100 packages $72.50; 101 to 200 packages $70.00; 201 or more packages $67.50

Work Potential Profile (WPP)
Helga Rowe

| 1997 | Australian Council for Educational Research Limited |

Population: Adolescents, adults

Purpose: Describes psychological barriers to gaining employment

Description: Criterion-referenced tool for the initial assessment of long-term unemployed persons and persons having difficulty finding employment. Intended for collection and management of information in areas of support needs, strengths and weaknesses for employment, occupational planning, and the individual's developmental and current intervention or training needs. The WPP Questionnaire contains 171 items and can be self-administered.

Format: Examiner required; individual and group administration; untimed

Scoring: Hand key

Cost: Contact publisher

Work Styles Questionnaire (WSQ or WSQn)

| 1988 | SHL Canada |

Population: Adults in production and operations jobs

Purpose: Measures 17 dimensions of work styles

Description: Intended for individuals in manufacturing, retail, service, and similar jobs. A total of 162 items in four categories: relationships with people, thinking style, emotions, and energies. Also available in French and Indonesian.

Format: Examiner required; individual administration; untimed: 30 minutes

Scoring: Hand key; machine scored; scoring service available

Cost: Contact publisher

General Aptitude

ACER Advanced Tests AL-AQ and BL-BQ

| 1982 | Australian Council for Educational Research Limited |

Population: Adults

Purpose: Measures verbal and numerical intelligence

Description: Individual demonstrates the ability to see relationships and solve problems in verbal and numerical material.

Format: Examiner required; individual administration; untimed: 10 to 20 minutes

Scoring: Hand key; scoring service available

Cost: Contact publisher

ACER Test of Reasoning Ability (TORA)
Marion M. de Lemos

| 1990 | Australian Council for Educational Research Limited |

Population: Ages 15 years and older

Purpose: Assesses general intellectual ability

Description: A predominantly verbal test of general ability, based on the ACER Test of Cognitive Ability, which has been converted to a multiple-choice format. The 70 items include content that involves numerical and verbal reasoning. Examples of the types of items are analogies, word meanings, numerically based problems, number series, and number matrixes.

Format: Examiner required; individual and group administration; untimed: 45 minutes

Scoring: Hand key; scoring service available

Cost: Contact publisher

ACER Word Knowledge Test: Form F
Marion de Lemos

| 1990 | Australian Council for Educational Research Limited |

Population: Adults

Purpose: Measures verbal skills and general reasoning ability

Description: Tests of word knowledge have been found to correlate highly with other measures of verbal skills and general reasoning ability. Because they are relatively quick and easy to administer, they have been widely used as screening tests. This test enables the user to assess quickly student knowledge of word meanings. Students are required to select, from a list of five alternatives, the word or phrase that most closely approximates the meaning of each of 72 items.

Format: Examiner required; group administration; untimed: 10 minutes

Scoring: Hand key; scoring service available

Cost: Contact publisher

Adaptability Test
Joseph Tiffin, C. H. Lawshe

| 1942 | NCS Pearson Reid London House |

Population: Adults

Purpose: Measures mental adaptability and alertness; distinguishes between people who should be placed in jobs requiring more learning ability and those who should be in more simple or routine jobs

Description: Paper–pencil 35-item test consisting primarily of verbal items. The test predicts success in a variety of business and industrial situations. The test is available in two forms.

Format: Examiner required; suitable for group use; timed: 15 minutes

Scoring: Hand key

Cost: Contact publisher

Adaptive Ability Test–Language
Colin D. Selby

| 1989 | Selby MillSmith Ltd. |

Population: Ages 11 years and older

Purpose: Used in educational and industrial applications to assess verbal critical reasoning

Description: Computer-administered 30-item multiple-choice test. An 11-year-old reading level is required. A computer version using PC DOS is available.

Format: Examiner required; suitable for groups; timed: 15 minutes

Scoring: Computer scored

Cost: Specimen Set $50.00

Adaptive Ability Test–Numeracy
Colin Selby

| 1989 | Selby MillSmith Ltd. |

Population: Adolescents, adults

Purpose: Used in education and employment applications to assess numerical critical reasoning

Description: Computer-administered 30-item multiple-choice test. A computer version using PC DOS computers is available. An 11-year-old reading level is required.

Format: Examiner required; suitable for groups; timed: 15 minutes

Scoring: Computer scored

Cost: Specimen Set $50.00

Applied Technology Series (ATS) Diagrammatic Thinking (DTS6)

| 1988 | SHL Canada |

Population: Adults

Purpose: Looks at the person's ability to follow a sequence of interdependent symbols arranged in a logical order

Description: This 36-item test is arranged in the form of simple flowcharts and involves keeping track of changes in shape, size, and color of objects. This aptitude to apply checks and follow sequences is likely to be relevant in following process control systems, in debugging software, and in systems design. Also available in French.

Format: Examiner required; individual administration; untimed: 20 minutes

Scoring: Hand key; machine scored; scoring service available

Cost: Contact publisher

Applied Technology Series (ATS) Fault Finding (FTS4)

1988	SHL Canada

Population: Adults

Purpose: Assesses the ability to identify faults in logical systems

Description: This 36-item test requires no specialized knowledge of fault finding, but rather the ability to locate what element in an arrangement of color-coded symbols is not working as specified. This ability is appropriate in many applications, including electronics fault finding, debugging software, process control systems, and systems design. Also available in French.

Format: Examiner required; individual administration; untimed: 20 minutes

Scoring: Hand key; machine scored; scoring service available

Cost: Contact publisher

Applied Technology Series (ATS) Spatial Checking (STS5)

1988	SHL Canada

Population: Adults

Purpose: Measures the ability to locate differences between complex designs rotated and reversed in two or three dimensions

Description: This 40-item test measures the ability to locate differences between complex designs rotated and reversed in two or three dimensions. This ability is important in the checking and design of electronic systems, engineering components, and some applications of computer-aided design. Each item in this test involves identifying mismatches between master and copy designs. Also available in French.

Format: Examiner required; individual administration; untimed: 15 minutes

Scoring: Hand key; machine scored; scoring service available

Cost: Contact publisher

Bennett Mechanical Comprehension Test™ (BMCT™)
G. K. Bennett

1968 (Manual 1994)	The Psychological Corporation

Population: Adults

Purpose: Measures ability to understand mechanical relationships and physical laws in practical situations; used to screen job applicants for positions requiring practical application

Description: Multiple-item paper–pencil multiple-choice test assessing understanding of mechanical relationships. Materials include two equivalent forms. Tape recordings of the test questions read aloud are available for applicants with limited reading skills.

Format: Examiner required; suitable for group use; timed: 30 minutes

Scoring: Hand key; may be machine scored

Cost: Examination Kit (booklets, answer documents for both forms, manual) $43.00; Keys $39.00 each form

Closure Flexibility (Concealed Figures)
L. L. Thurstone, T. E. Jeffrey

1984	NCS Pearson Reid London House

Population: Adolescents, adults

Purpose: Measures the ability to hold a configuration in mind despite distracting irrelevancies as indicated by identification of a given figure "hidden" or embedded in a larger more complex drawing; used for vocational counseling and selection of personnel

Description: Paper–pencil 49-item test measuring visual and spatial perception skills. Each item consists of a figure, presented on the left of the page, followed by a row of four more complex drawings. The subject must indicate whether the figure appears or does not appear in each of the drawings.

Format: Examiner required; suitable for group use; timed: 10 minutes

Scoring: Hand key

Cost: Contact publisher

Creativity Measure—The SRT Scale
William C. Kosinar

1960	Psychometric Affiliates

Population: Grade 10 to adult

Purpose: Assesses level of creativity; used for

career guidance with youths and to select research and scientific personnel

Description: Multiple-item forced-choice paper-pencil test of creativity. The manual provides norms on scientific personnel, National Science Talent Search winners, college students, and high school students.

Format: Examiner required; suitable for group use; untimed: 5 minutes

Scoring: Examiner evaluated

Cost: Specimen Set 44.00; 25 Tests $4.50

Cree Questionnaire
Thelma Gwinn, Thurstone J. Mellinger

1995	NCS Pearson Reid London House

Population: Adults

Purpose: Evaluates an individual's overall creative potential and the extent to which his or her behavior resembles that of identified creative individuals; used for selection and placement of managerial and professional personnel and for career counseling

Description: Paper-pencil 58-item test measuring the 10 factorially determined dimensions of the creative personality: dominance vs. submission, independence vs. conformity, autonomous vs. structured work environment, pressured vs. relaxed situation, high vs. low energy level, fast vs. slow reaction time, high vs. low ideational spontaneity, high vs. low theoretical interests, high vs. low artistic interests, and high vs. low mechanical interests.

Format: Self-administered; untimed: 15 minutes

Scoring: Hand key

Cost: Contact publisher

Critical Reasoning Test Battery (CRTB) Diagrammatic Series (DC3.1)

1991	SHL Canada

Population: Ages 16 years to adult

Purpose: Measures critical reasoning ability for thinking sequentially

Description: Paper-pencil 40-item test assessing the logical or analytical ability to follow a sequence of diagrams and select the next one in a series from five alternatives. The test is appropriate where logical or analytical reasoning is required, such as technical research or computer programming positions. Also available in French.

Format: Examiner required; individual administration; untimed: 20 minutes

Scoring: Hand key; machine scored; scoring service available

Cost: Contact publisher

Differential Aptitude Tests® for Personnel and Career Assessment
George K. Bennett, Harold G. Seashore, Alexander G. Wesman

Date not provided	The Psychological Corporation

Population: Adults

Purpose: Identifies strengths and weaknesses

Description: Applicants are tested in eight key areas: verbal reasoning, numerical ability, abstract reasoning, mechanical reasoning, space relations, spelling, language usage, and clerical speed and accuracy. Each area is in a separate booklet.

Format: Examiner required; suitable for group use; can be taken on-line; untimed: 6 to 20 minutes per subtest

Scoring: Examiner evaluated

Cost: Examination Kit (manual, 1 of each subtest, directions) $58.00; Scoring Keys $18.00 per subtest

Employee Aptitude Survey Test #1— Verbal Comprehension (EAS#1)
G. Grimsley, F. L. Ruch, N. D. Warren, J. S. Ford

1984	Psychological Services, Inc.

Population: Adults

Purpose: Measures ability to use and understand the relationships between words; used for selection and placement of executives, secretaries, professional personnel, and high-level office workers; also used in career counseling

Description: Paper-pencil 30-item multiple-choice test measuring word-relationship recognition, reading speed, and ability to understand instructions. Each item consists of a word followed by a list of four other words from which the examinee must select the one meaning the same or about the same as the first word. The test is available in two equivalent forms. Also available in German.

Format: Examiner required; suitable for group use; timed: 5 minutes

Scoring: Hand key; may be computer scored; scan scoring software available

Cost: Contact publisher

Employee Aptitude Survey Test #2— Numerical Ability (EAS#2)

G. Grimsley, F. L. Ruch, N. D. Warren

1980   Psychological Services, Inc.

Population: Adults

Purpose: Measures basic mathematical skill; used for selection and placement of executives, supervisors, engineers, accountants, and sales and clerical workers; also used in career counseling

Description: Paper–pencil 75-item multiple-choice test arranged in three 25-item parts assessing addition, subtraction, multiplication, and division skills. Part I covers whole numbers, Part II decimal fractions, and Part III common fractions. The test is available in two equivalent forms. Also available in Spanish and German. Parts may be administered and timed separately.

Format: Examiner required; suitable for group use; timed: 10 minutes

Scoring: Hand key; may be computer scored; scan scoring software available

Cost: Contact publisher

Employee Aptitude Survey Test #3— Visual Pursuit (EAS#3)

G. Grimsley, F. L. Ruch, N. D. Warren, J. S. Ford

1984   Psychological Services, Inc.

Population: Adults

Purpose: Measures speed and accuracy in visually tracing lines through complex designs; used for selection and placement of drafters, design engineers, technicians, and other technical and production positions; also used in career counseling

Description: Paper–pencil 30-item multiple-choice test consisting of a maze of lines that weave from their starting points (numbered 1 to 30) on the right side of the page to a column of boxes on the left. The task is to identify for each starting point the box on the left at which the line ends. Examinees are encouraged to trace with their eyes, not their pencils. The test is available in two equivalent forms. Also available in Spanish and French.

Format: Examiner required; suitable for group use; timed: 5 minutes

Scoring: Hand key; may be computer scored; scan scoring software available

Cost: Contact publisher

Employee Aptitude Survey Test #4— Visual Speed and Accuracy (EAS#4)

G. Grimsley, F. L. Ruch, N. D. Warren

1980   Psychological Services, Inc.

Population: Adults

Purpose: Measures ability to see details quickly and accurately; used to select bookkeepers, accountants, clerical and administrative personnel, and supervisors; also used in career planning

Description: Paper–pencil 150-item multiple-choice test in which each item consists of two series of numbers and symbols that the subject must compare to determine whether they are the same or different. The test may be administered to applicants for sales, supervisory, and executive positions with the expectation that their scores will be above average. The test is available in two equivalent forms. On-line form is under development. Also available in Spanish.

Format: Examiner required; suitable for group use; timed: 5 minutes

Scoring: Hand key; may be computer scored; scan scoring software available

Cost: Contact publisher

Employee Aptitude Survey Test #5— Space Visualization (EAS#5)

G. Grimsley, F. L. Ruch, N. D. Warren, J. S. Ford

1985   Psychological Services, Inc.

Population: Adults

Purpose: Measures ability to visualize and manipulate objects in three dimensions by viewing a two-dimensional drawing; used to select employees for jobs requiring mechanical aptitude, such as drafters, engineers, and personnel in technical and production positions

Description: Paper–pencil 50-item multiple-choice test consisting of 10 perspective line drawings of stacks of blocks. The blocks are all the same size and rectangular in shape so that they appear to stack neatly and distinctly. Five of the blocks in each stack are lettered. The subjects must determine how many other blocks in the stack each lettered block touches. The test is available in two equivalent forms. Also available in Spanish.

Format: Examiner required; suitable for group use; timed: 5 minutes

Scoring: Hand key; may be computer scored; scan scoring software available

Cost: Contact publisher

Employee Aptitude Survey Test #6—Numerical Reasoning (EAS#6)
G. Grimsley, F. L. Ruch, N. D. Warren, J. S. Ford

1985   Psychological Services, Inc.

Population: Adults

Purpose: Measures the ability to analyze logical relationships and discover principles underlying such relationships, an important ingredient of "general intelligence"; used to select employees for professional, managerial, supervisory, and technical jobs

Description: Paper-pencil 20-item multiple-choice test in which each item consists of a series of seven numbers followed by a question mark to indicate the unknown next number of the series. Examinees must determine the pattern of each series and select (from five choices) the number that correctly follows. Logic and deduction, rather than computation, are emphasized. The test is available in two equivalent forms. On-line form is under development. Also available in Spanish, German, and French.

Format: Examiner required; suitable for group use; timed: 5 minutes

Scoring: Hand key; may be computer scored; scan scoring software available

Cost: Contact publisher

Employee Aptitude Survey Test #7—Verbal Reasoning (EAS#7)
G. Grimsley, F. L. Ruch, N. D. Warren, J. S. Ford

1985   Psychological Services, Inc.

Population: Adults

Purpose: Measures ability to analyze information and make valid judgments about that information; also measures the ability to decide whether the available facts provide sufficient information to support a definite conclusion; used for employee selection

Description: Paper-pencil 30-item multiple-choice test consisting of six lists of facts (one-sentence statements) with five possible conclusions for each list. The subject reads each list of facts and then looks at each conclusion and decides whether it is definitely true, definitely false, or unknown from the given facts. The test is available in two equivalent forms. On-line form under development. Also available in Spanish and French.

Format: Examiner required; suitable for group use; timed: 5 minutes

Scoring: Hand key; may be computer scored; scan scoring software available

Cost: Contact publisher

Employee Aptitude Survey Test #8—Word Fluency (EAS#8)
G. Grimsley, F. L. Ruch, N. D. Warren, J. S. Ford

1981   Psychological Services, Inc.

Population: Adults

Purpose: Measures flexibility and ease in verbal communication; used to select sales representatives, journalists, field representatives, technical writers, receptionists, secretaries, and executives; also used in career counseling

Description: Open-ended paper-pencil test measuring word fluency by determining how many words beginning with one specific letter, given at the beginning of the test, a person can produce in a 5-minute test period (75 answer spaces are provided).

Format: Examiner required; suitable for group use; timed: 5 minutes

Scoring: Hand scored

Cost: Contact publisher

Employee Aptitude Survey Test #9—Manual Speed and Accuracy (EAS#9)
G. Grimsley, F. L. Ruch, N. D. Warren, J. S. Ford

1984   Psychological Services, Inc.

Population: Adults

Purpose: Measures ability to make fine-finger movements rapidly and accurately; used to select clerical workers, office machine operators, electronics and small parts assemblers, and employees for similar precision jobs involving repetitive tasks

Description: Multiple-item paper-pencil test consisting of a straightforward array of evenly spaced lines of 750 small circles. The applicant must place a pencil dot in as many of the circles as possible in 5 minutes. Also available in Spanish.

Format: Examiner required; suitable for group use; timed: 5 minutes

Scoring: Hand scored

Cost: Contact publisher

Employee Aptitude Survey Test #10—Symbolic Reasoning (EAS#10)
G. Grimsley, F. L. Ruch, N. D. Warren, J. S. Ford

1985   **Psychological Services, Inc.**

Population: Adults

Purpose: Measures ability to manipulate abstract symbols and use them to make valid decisions; used to evaluate candidates for positions requiring a high level of reasoning ability, such as troubleshooters, computer programmers, accountants, and engineers

Description: Thirty-item multiple-choice test consisting of a list of abstract symbols (and their coded meanings) used to establish relationships in the pattern of "A" to "B" to "C." Given the statement, the examinee must decide whether a proposed relationship between "A" and "C" is true, false, or unknown. The test is available in two equivalent forms. Paper–pencil form; on-line form under development. Also available in Spanish, German, and French.

Format: Examiner required; suitable for group use; timed: 5 minutes

Scoring: Hand key; may be computer scored; scan scoring software available

Cost: Contact publisher

IPI Employee Aptitude Series: Blocks

1986   **Industrial Psychology International Ltd.**

Population: Adults

Purpose: Measures aptitude to visualize objects on the basis of three-dimensional cues; used to screen applicants for mechanical and technical jobs

Description: Paper–pencil 32-item test of spatial relations and quantitative ability. The test does not require the ability to read. Also available in French and Spanish.

Format: Examiner required; suitable for group use; timed: 6 minutes

Scoring: Hand key

Cost: Introductory Kit (20 test booklets, manual) $30.00

IPI Employee Aptitude Series: Dexterity

1986   **Industrial Psychology International Ltd.**

Population: Adults

Purpose: Determines ability to rapidly perform routine motor tasks involving eye–hand coordi-

nation; used to screen applicants for mechanical and technical jobs

Description: Three 1-minute paper–pencil subtests (maze, checks, dots) assess one's ability to perform routine motor tasks. The test does not require the ability to read or write. Also available in French and Spanish.

Format: Examiner required; suitable for group use; timed: 3 minutes

Scoring: No key required

Cost: Introductory Kit (20 test booklets, manual) $30.00

IPI Employee Aptitude Series: Dimension

1986   **Industrial Psychology International Ltd.**

Population: Adults

Purpose: Evaluates ability to visualize objects drawn in their exact reverse; used to screen applicants for mechanical and technical jobs

Description: Paper–pencil 48-item test measuring spatial relations at a high level. The test does not require the ability to read or write. Also available in French and Spanish.

Format: Examiner required; suitable for group use; timed: 6 minutes

Scoring: Hand key

Cost: Introductory Kit (20 test booklets, scoring key, manual) $30.00

IPI Employee Aptitude Series: Fluency

1981   **Industrial Psychology International Ltd.**

Population: Adults

Purpose: Assesses aptitude to think of words rapidly and easily; used to screen applicants for clerical, sales, and supervisory jobs

Description: Three 2-minute paper–pencil subtests measuring the ability to write or talk without mentally blocking or searching for the right word. Also available in French and Spanish.

Format: Examiner required; suitable for group use; timed: 6 minutes

Scoring: No key required

Cost: Introductory Kit (20 test booklets, manual) $30.00

IPI Employee Aptitude Series: Judgment

1981   **Industrial Psychology International Ltd.**

Population: Adults

Purpose: Evaluates an individual's ability to think logically and to deduce solutions to abstract problems; used to screen applicants for clerical, sales, and supervisory positions

Description: Paper-pencil 54-item test measuring aptitude to think logically, plan, and deal with abstract relations. Also available in French and Spanish.

Format: Examiner required; suitable for group use; timed: 6 minutes

Scoring: Hand key

Cost: Introductory Kit (20 test booklets, scoring key, manual) $30.00

IPI Employee Aptitude Series: Motor

1986	Industrial Psychology International Ltd.

Population: Adults

Purpose: Measures ability to coordinate eye and hand movements in a specific motor task; used to screen applicants for mechanical and technical jobs

Description: Three 2-minute trials of the same task that demonstrate manual dexterity and eye-hand coordination. The test requires a special motor apparatus for administration. Also available in French and Spanish.

Format: Examiner required; suitable for group use only if more than one apparatus is available; timed: 6 minutes

Scoring: No key required

Cost: Introductory Kit (20 test booklets, manual) $30.00; Motor Board $150.00

IPI Employee Aptitude Series: Numbers

1981	Industrial Psychology International Ltd.

Population: Adults

Purpose: Measures ability to perform numerical computations rapidly and accurately; used to screen applicants for clerical, administrative, mechanical, sales, technical, and supervisory positions

Description: Paper-pencil 54-item test measuring the ability to perform numerical computations and to understand mathematical concepts. This test is highly related to record keeping, typing, work planning, computational skills, and coding.

Format: Examiner required; suitable for group use; timed: 6 minutes

Scoring: Hand key

Cost: Introductory Kit (20 test booklets, scoring key, manual) $30.00

Learning Ability Profile (LAP)
Margarita Henning

1989	Walden Personnel Testing and Consulting, Inc.

Population: Adults

Purpose: Assesses a person's ability to learn; may be used to determine the potential for job success

Description: Paper-pencil 80-item test measuring overall learning ability, flexibility, frustration level, problem-solving ability, and decisiveness. Also available in French.

Format: Examiner required; suitable for group use; untimed: 1 hour

Scoring: Hand key; examiner evaluated

Cost: Complete Set (1 test booklet, answer sheet, manual) $79.00

Listening Practices Feedback Report–360 (LPFR–360)
Richard C. Brandt, Janice D. Brandt

1999	Brandt Management Group

Population: Adults

Purpose: Measures awareness of listening skills to provide a plan for increased use

Description: Twenty-eight listening practices are divided into Listening Categories of Attention, Empathy, Respect, Response, Memory, and Open Mind. The listener's ratings and the observer's ratings of the listener are computer compiled for raw averages that are presented side by side on the Listener's confidential feedback report. The averages are derived from a 10-increment Likert scale. Averages for each Listening Category and the total Listening Practices are given. The LPFR-360 does not measure listening ability; it measures perceptions regarding listening behaviors that are used by good listeners to encourage communication.

Format: Examiner required; individually computer administered; untimed: 10 minutes

Scoring: Computer scoring

Cost: Contact publisher

MD5 (Mental Ability Test)
D. Mackenzie Davey

Date not provided	Test Agency, Ltd.

Population: Adults

Purpose: Assesses a wide range of educational and ability levels

Description: Paper–pencil 57-item test used with adults, including supervisors and managers, for measuring mental ability. The test involves finding missing letters, numbers, or words. Norms exist for several managerial groups, and the test is correlated with other mental ability tests.

Format: Examiner required; individual or group administration; can be computer administered; timed: 15 minutes

Scoring: Self-scored; computer scored; test scoring service available from publisher

Cost: Contact publisher

Nonverbal Form
Robert N. McMurry, Joseph E. King
| 1986 | NCS Pearson Reid London House |

Population: Adults

Purpose: Assesses general learning ability; measures learning potential of individuals who have difficulty reading or understanding the English language; used with adults with a high school education or less and for employee selection and placement

Description: Paper–pencil 60-item test consisting of five drawings, each measuring recognition of differences.

Format: Examiner required; suitable for group use; timed: 10 minutes

Scoring: Hand key

Cost: Contact publisher

Nonverbal Reasoning
Raymond J. Corsini
| 1985 | NCS Pearson Reid London House |

Population: Adults

Purpose: Assesses capacity to reason logically as indicated by solutions to pictorial problems; used for job screening and selection and for vocational counseling

Description: Paper–pencil 44-item pictorial test. The subject studies one picture and then selects from among four others the one that best complements the first picture.

Format: Examiner required; suitable for group use; untimed: 20 minutes

Scoring: Hand key

Cost: Contact publisher

Occupational Preference Inventory
Robert C. Mecham
| 1999 | PAQ Services, Inc. |

Population: Adolescents, adults

Purpose: Assesses work preferences, job selection, and career planning for job seekers working with human resource departments

Description: Total of 150 items yield job matches based on preferences, perceptions, and aptitude.

Format: Self-administered on computer; untimed

Scoring: Computer scored; test scoring service available

Cost: Contact publisher

Omnia 720 Composite®
| Date not provided | Omnia Group, Incorporated |

Population: Adults

Purpose: Measures job applicants' abilities

Description: A customized database is created using a site's top performers. Candidates are compared to this sample, showing each applicant's compatibility with the job. Also useful for promotions and department transfers.

Format: Self-administered; on-line administration; untimed: 10 minutes

Scoring: Examiner evaluated; computer scored; scoring service

Cost: Contact publisher

Omnia Profile®
J. B. Caswell, H. F. Livingstone
| 1985 | Omnia Group, Incorporated |

Population: Adults

Purpose: Measures preferred workplace behavior

Description: A simple, easy-to-complete adjective checklist includes two active behaviors and two passive behaviors. An eight-column graph indicates the subject's level of assertiveness, risk avoidance, persuasion, analytical mindset, pace, patience, independence, and attention to detail. The report also notes energy, common sense, intensity, and stress measurements, as related to workplace behavior and career development.

Format: Self-administration; on-line administration available; untimed: 15 minutes

Scoring: Examiner evaluated; computer scored; scoring service by fax or mail

Cost: Contact publisher

Personnel Tests for Industry (PTI)
A. G. Wesman, J. E. Doppelt

| 1969 | The Psychological Corporation |

Population: Adults

Purpose: Assesses general ability; used to select workers for skilled positions in industrial settings

Description: Multiple-item paper–pencil multiple-choice tests covering two dimensions of general ability: verbal and numerical competence. Some items involve problem solving. Two equivalent forms and tapes for administering the test are available.

Format: Examiner required; suitable for group use; timed: verbal 5 minutes; numerical 20 minutes

Scoring: Hand key

Cost: Examination Kit (2 forms of each dimension, manual) $41.00

Personnel Tests for Industry— Oral Directions Test (PTI-ODT™)
C. R. Langmuir

| 1974; Manual updated in 1995 | The Psychological Corporation |

Population: Adults

Purpose: Assesses general mental ability and the ability to understand oral directions

Description: Recorded-format test measuring general mental ability of individuals with low education levels or who speak English as a second language. Scores reflect minimal proficiency in conversational English and the ability to comprehend oral directions. May be used to determine whether individuals can benefit from basic skills training, vocational training, training in conversational English, or educational remediation programs. Two alternate forms.

Format: Examiner required; suitable for group use; untimed: approximately 15 minutes

Scoring: Hand key

Cost: Examination Kit (scripts, answer documents, manual) $40.00

Pictorial Reasoning Test (PRT)
Robert N. McMurry, Phyllis D. Arnold

| 1966 | NCS Pearson Reid London House |

Population: Adolescents, adults

Purpose: Measures general reasoning ability of students, especially older nonreaders; used with individuals with a high school education or less,

for predicting job success, and as a basic screening test for entry-level jobs

Description: Paper–pencil 80-item pictorial test measuring aspects of learning ability. The test is culturally unbiased and does not require previously learned reading skills.

Format: Examiner required; suitable for group use; timed: 15 minutes (may also be given untimed)

Scoring: Hand key

Cost: Contact publisher

Professional Employment Test

| 1986 | Psychological Services, Inc. |

Population: Adults

Purpose: Measures three cognitive abilities— verbal comprehension, quantitative problem solving, and reasoning—important for successful performance in many professional occupations; used to select professional, technical, and managerial personnel

Description: Paper–pencil multiple-choice test measuring the ability to understand and interpret complex information, determine the appropriate mathematical procedures to solve problems, and analyze and evaluate information to arrive at correct conclusions. The test includes 40 items of four types: reading comprehension, quantitative problem solving, data interpretation, and reasoning. The test is available in two alternate forms and in a short form (20 questions). On-line form is under development.

Format: Examiner required; suitable for group use; timed: regular form 80 minutes; short form 40 minutes

Scoring: Hand key; may be computer scored; scoring software available from publisher

Cost: 10 Tests $75.00

Security Aptitude Fitness Evaluation–Resistance (SAFE–R)
John R. Taccarino

| 1987 | Stoelting Company |

Population: Adults

Purpose: Measures honesty, dependability, socialization, substance, credibility, and language and numerical skills for employee selection

Description: Has 130 multiple-choice items to assess numerical abilities, language abilities, and attitudes. Spanish version is also available.

Format: Examiner required; suitable for group use; timed: 15 minutes and untimed: 20 minutes

Scoring: Computer scored; scoring service available

Cost: Depending on report format $225.00 to $375.00

Space Relations (Paper Puzzles)
L. L. Thurstone, T. E. Jeffrey

| 1984 | NCS Pearson Reid London House |

Population: Adolescents, adults

Purpose: Assesses facility in visual-perceptual skills; used in vocational counseling or for selection for positions requiring mechanical ability and experience

Description: Paper-pencil 30-item test of the ability to visually select a combination of flat pieces that, together, cover a given two-dimensional space.

Format: Examiner required; suitable for group use; timed: 9 minutes

Scoring: Hand key

Cost: Contact publisher

Space Thinking (Flags)
L. L. Thurstone, T. E. Jeffrey

| 1984 | NCS Pearson Reid London House |

Population: Adolescents, adults

Purpose: Assesses the ability to visualize a rigid configuration (a stable figure, drawing, or diagram) when it is moved into different positions; used for vocational counseling or selection for positions requiring mechanical ability or experience

Description: Paper-pencil 21-item test in which a solid object (flag) is pictured on the left and pictures of six positions into which the object has been moved are on the right. The examinee must identify whether each position represents the same or the opposite side of the object.

Format: Examiner required; suitable for group use; timed: 5 minutes

Scoring: Hand key

Cost: Contact publisher

Strategic Assessment of Readiness for Training (START)
Claire E. Weinstein, David R. Palmer

| 1994 | H & H Publishing Co., Inc. |

Population: Adults

Purpose: Diagnoses learning strengths and

weaknesses in a work setting; used to increase a trainee's experience of the training experience; suitable for new employees and employees entering training programs

Description: Computer-administered or paper-pencil multiple-choice test with 56 items on eight scales measuring anxiety, attitude, motivation, concentration, identifying important information, knowledge acquisition strategies, monitoring learning, and time management. A chart yielding total scale scores and average item scores is used, as is a self-scored form or a computerized version. A Macintosh version is available.

Format: Self-administered; untimed: 20 to 30 minutes

Scoring: Computer scored; self-scored; also available on the Web

Cost: $5.95 each for 1 to 99

Technical Test Battery (TTB) Spatial Recognition (ST8.1)

| 1988 | SHL Canada |

Population: Adults

Purpose: Measures basic spatial ability

Description: Test with 36 items measures the ability to recognize shapes in two dimensions.

Format: Examiner required; individual administration; untimed: 10 minutes

Scoring: Hand key; machine scored; scoring service available

Cost: Contact publisher

Technical Test Battery (TTB) Visual Estimation (ET3.1)

| 1992 | SHL Canada |

Population: Adults

Purpose: Measures important elements of spatial perception

Description: Multiple-choice 36-item test involving the estimation of lengths, angles, and shapes. In each item, the respondent must select the two figures from a set of five that are identical in form, although in many cases they are rotated on the page.

Format: Examiner required; individual administration; untimed: 10 minutes

Scoring: Hand key; machine scored; scoring service available

Cost: Contact publisher

Verbal Form
L. L. Thurstone, Thelma Gwinn Thurstone

1955	NCS Pearson Reid London House

Population: Adults

Purpose: Measures an individual's overall adaptability and flexibility in comprehending and following instructions and in adjusting to alternating types of problems on the job; used in both school and industry for selection and placement

Description: Paper–pencil or computerized test of general mental abilities. The test measures both linguistic (vocabulary) and quantitative (arithmetic) factors. Items of both types are interspersed with a time limit. The test is similar to the Thurstone Test of Mental Alertness but has a time limit of 15 rather than 20 minutes. The test is available in two forms.

Format: Examiner required; suitable for group use; timed: 15 minutes

Scoring: Hand key; computer scored

Cost: Contact publisher

Verbal Proficiency Assessment/ Numeric Proficiency Assessment (VPA/NPA)

1997	Industrial Psychology International Ltd.

Population: Adults

Purpose: Assesses high-level verbal and math skills; used in preemployment and promotional screening

Description: The VPA has 20 items ranging from sentence completion to word analogies. The VPA uses series of vocabulary items to measure logical thinking and problem-solving ability. The NPA has 16 graphs, tables, and algebra word problems. The NPA measures the ability to evaluate and understand advanced mathematical concepts. Stanine scores available for verbal and numeric assessments on one report.

Format: Examiner required; individual administration (computer administered); timed: 20 minutes each

Scoring: Computer scored

Cost: Three-Report Demo Disk and Manual $63.00

Verbal Reasoning
Raymond J. Corsini, Richard Renck

1958	NCS Pearson Reid London House

Population: Adults

Purpose: Assesses individual capacity to reason

logically as indicated by solutions to verbal problems; used for job selection and vocational counseling

Description: Paper–pencil 36-item test of mental reasoning consists of 12 statements with three questions each.

Format: Examiner required; suitable for group use; timed: 15 minutes

Scoring: Hand key

Cost: Contact publisher

Watson-Glaser Critical Thinking Appraisal®-Forms A and B
Goodwin Watson, Edward M. Glaser

Date not provided	The Psychological Corporation

Population: Adults

Purpose: Predicts an employee's career path based on critical thinking skills

Description: The 80-item test assesses five content areas: Inference, Recognition of Assumptions, Deduction, Interpretation, and Evaluation of Arguments. The manual offers percentile ranks corresponding to total scores for groups, including students, teachers, police officers, sales representatives, and state trooper applicants.

Format: Examiner required; suitable for group use; untimed: 40 to 60 minutes

Scoring: Examiner evaluated

Cost: Examination Kit (1 of each form, manual) $55.00; Scoring Key $25.50 per form

Wesman Personnel Classification Test (PCT)
A. G. Wesman

1965	The Psychological Corporation

Population: Adults

Purpose: Assesses general mental ability; used for selection of employees for sales, supervisory, and managerial positions

Description: Multiple-item paper–pencil test of two major aspects of mental ability: verbal and numerical. The verbal items are analogies. The numerical items test basic math skills and understanding of quantitative relationships. Three forms, A, B, and C, are available. The verbal part of Form C is somewhat more difficult than the verbal parts of Forms A and B.

Format: Examiner required; suitable for group use; timed: Verbal 18 minutes; Numerical 10 minutes

Scoring: Hand key

Cost: Examination Kit (one booklet for each form, manual) $33.00

Wonderlic Personnel Test
E. F. Wonderlic

1988	Wonderlic Personnel Test, Inc.

Population: Adults

Purpose: Measures level of mental ability in business and industrial situations; used for selection and placement of business personnel and for vocational guidance

Description: Paper–pencil or computerized test with 50 items measuring general learning ability in verbal, spatial, and numerical reasoning. The test is used to predict an individual's ability to adjust to complex and rapidly changing job requirements and to complete complex job train-ing. Test items include analogies, analysis of geometric figures, arithmetic problems, disarranged sentences, sentence parallelism with proverbs, similarities, logic definitions, judgment, direction following, and others. Also available in Spanish (Mexican, Cuban, Puerto Rican), French, French Canadian, Chinese, German, Japanese, Korean, Portuguese, Russian, Tagalog, and Vietnamese.

Format: Examiner required; suitable for group use; timed: 12 minutes; may also be administered untimed

Scoring: Hand key; test scoring available from publisher

Cost: Paper–pencil Version: 25 Tests $75.00, 100 Tests $155.00, ADA Kit $155.00 (includes large print, audio and scoring key); PC Version: 25 Tests $75.00, 100 Tests $155.00

General Skills

ACER Applied Reading Test (ART)

1990	Australian Council for Educational Research Limited

Population: Ages 15 years and older

Purpose: Measures ability to read and understand technical reading material

Description: The instrument was designed for selection of apprentices, trainees, technical/trade personnel, and others who need to read and understand text. Six prose passages are presented in a reusable test booklet with four multiple-choice response alternatives for each of the items associated with each passage. The content of the passages deals with such topics as industrial safety and machine operation/maintenance, but attempts to avoid areas for which knowledge rather than reading ability is rewarded. Two alternate forms of the ART are available; both have 32 questions.

Format: Examiner required; individual and group administration; timed: 30 minutes

Scoring: Hand key; scoring service available

Cost: Contact publisher

ACER Test of Employment Entry Mathematics (TEEM)
John Izard, Ian Woff, Brian Doig

1992	Australian Council for Educational Research Limited

Population: Ages 15 years and older

Purpose: Assesses basic mathematical ability

Description: Questions cover basic mathematical problems of a type that might be encountered in a technical or trade training course or on the job in technical or trade positions. The test contains 32 items and is presented in a reusable multiple-choice test booklet with four response alternatives.

Format: Examiner required; individual and group administration; timed: 30 minutes

Scoring: Hand key; scoring service available

Cost: Contact publisher

Adaptive Ability Test– Detailed Checking
Colin Selby

1989	Selby MillSmith Ltd.

Population: Ages 11 years and older

Purpose: Used in educational and industrial applications to assess accuracy with detailed work under pressure

Description: Computer-administered 40-item multiple-choice test. Three subtests assess speed and accuracy of perception and checking ability. An 11-year-old reading level is required.

Format: Examiner required; suitable for groups; timed: 20 minutes

Scoring: Computer scored

Cost: Specimen Set $50.00

Applied Technology Series (ATS) Following Instructions (VTS1)

1988   **SHL Canada**

Population: Adults

Purpose: Assesses the ability to follow simple technical instructions

Description: Test with 36 items measures the ability to follow written instructions. The topics covered are designed to be relevant in a technical environment and draw on the kind of materials often associated with equipment manuals or operating instructions. No prior knowledge of technical words is assumed. Also available in French.

Format: Examiner required; individual administration; untimed: 20 minutes

Scoring: Hand key; machine scored; scoring service available

Cost: Contact publisher

Applied Technology Series (ATS) Numerical Estimation (NTS2)

1988   **SHL Canada**

Population: Adults

Purpose: Estimates answers to numerical calculations

Description: Test with 40 items measures the ability to estimate quickly the answers to numerical calculations. Fractions and percentages are included, as well as basic arithmetic. The task involves selecting an answer of an appropriate order of magnitude from a number of possible answers. Also available in French.

Format: Examiner required; individual administration; untimed: 10 minutes

Scoring: Hand key; machine scored; scoring service available

Cost: Contact publisher

Arithmetic Test–Form A
Roland T. Ramsay

1991   **Ramsay Corporation**

Population: Adults

Purpose: Measures the ability of industrial workers to perform basic computations

Description: Paper–pencil 24-item multiple-choice test assessing the ability to perform computations involving addition, subtraction, multiplication, and division of whole numbers and fractions.

Format: Examiner required; suitable for group use; timed: 20 minutes

Scoring: Hand key

Cost: Test Booklets $5.95 (minimum of 20); Manual with Scoring Key $24.95

Automated Office Battery (AOB) Numerical Estimation (NE1)

1988   **SHL Canada**

Population: Ages 16 years to adult

Purpose: Measures the ability to estimate the answers to a variety of numerical calculations

Description: Multiple-choice test assessing the ability to quickly estimate the answers to calculations. Candidates are presented with 50 items requiring addition, subtraction, multiplication, division, and percentages. Candidates are required to estimate the order of magnitude of the solution and choose the correct one from five alternatives. Candidates are discouraged from making precise calculations, and the time constraint encourages estimation.

Format: Examiner required; individual administration; untimed: 10 minutes

Scoring: Hand key; machine scored; scoring service available

Cost: Contact publisher

Behavioral Interviews

1991   **Personnel Decisions International**

Population: Adults

Purpose: Enables informed hiring decisions

Description: Helps the interviewer perform these critical tasks: focus the interview on relevant past achievements that predict future performance, establish proper control, ask appropriate questions, and consistently score candidates' answers. Interviews are available for the following positions: administrative; call center; customer service; front-line management; information technology developer, project leader, systems analyst, and manager; production; professional/technical; and sales.

Format: Examiner required; suitable for groups; untimed: 10 to 15 minutes

Scoring: Computer scored; test scoring service

Cost: Contact publisher

Biographical Index
Willard A. Kerr

| 1983 | Psychometric Affiliates |

Population: Adults

Purpose: Quantifies background data; used for predicting success in managerial and sales positions and in recruitment programs for general business

Description: Multiple-item paper-pencil measure of personal background information. The instrument yields five scores: stability, drive to excel, human relations, financial status, and personal adjustment. Three middle scores provide an estimate of basic energy level. The instrument predicts the annual salary increment of executives.

Format: Examiner required; suitable for group use; untimed: 30 minutes

Scoring: Hand key

Cost: Specimen Set $5.00; 25 Indexes $8.75; 25 Answer Sheets $5.00

Bruce Vocabulary Inventory
Martin M. Bruce

| 1974 | Martin M. Bruce, PhD |

Population: Adults

Purpose: Determines how a subject's vocabulary compares to the vocabulary of individuals employed in various business occupations

Description: Paper-pencil 100-item multiple-choice test in which the subject matches one of four alternative words with a key vocabulary word. Measures the ability to recognize and comprehend words. The subject's score can be compared to the scores of executives, middle managers, white-collar workers, engineers, blue-collar workers, and the total employed population. Suitable for individuals with physical, hearing, and visual impairments.

Format: Self-administered; untimed: 15 to 20 minutes

Scoring: Hand key

Cost: Specimen Set $37.50

Critical Reasoning Test Battery (CRTB) Interpreting Data (NC2.1)

| 1993 | SHL Canada |

Population: Ages 16 years to adult

Purpose: Measures ability to make correct decisions or inferences from numerical data

Description: Paper-pencil 40-item test assessing the ability to interpret statistical and other numerical data, presented as tables or diagrams. Candidates must select the correct answer to a question from five alternatives. The test is appropriate for jobs involving analysis or decision making based on numerical facts. Also available in French.

Format: Examiner required; individual administration; untimed: 30 minutes

Scoring: Hand key; machine scored; scoring service available

Cost: Contact publisher

Critical Reasoning Test Battery (CRTB) Verbal Evaluation (VC1.1)

| 1993 | SHL Canada |

Population: Ages 16 years to adult

Purpose: Measures ability to understand and evaluate the logic of arguments

Description: Sixty-item test measuring the ability to understand and evaluate the logic of various types of arguments. The candidate must decide if a statement is true or untrue, or whether there is insufficient information to judge. Also available in French.

Format: Examiner required; individual administration; untimed: 30 minutes

Scoring: Hand key; machine scored; scoring service available

Cost: Contact publisher

Customer Service Skills Inventory (CSSI™)
Juan Sanchez, Scott Frazer

| 1995 | NCS Pearson Reid London House |

Population: Adults

Purpose: Determines whether an individual has critical customer service skills; used for selection and placement

Description: Multiple-choice 63-item inventory assesses skills, behaviors, and traits indicative of success in service-oriented positions. The individual responds to situational-type questions to determine whether applicant shows a desire to help customers, understands and satisfies customers' needs, takes responsibility for assisting customers, cooperates with coworkers, puts forth extra job efforts, and keeps a reasonable balance between customer requests and company interests.

Format: Examiner required; individual administration; untimed: 30 minutes

Scoring: Hand key; computer scored

Cost: Contact publisher

Customer Service Skills Test

Date not provided	Walden Personnel Testing and Consulting, Inc.

Population: Adults

Purpose: Measures clerical, intellectual, administrative, and specific skills required in a customer service environment

Description: Provides a five-page report to the client. Measures the following: verbal communication skills, numerical skills, attention to detail, problem-solving ability, customer service skills, customer service problem solving, and customer service logic.

Format: Examiner required; suitable for group use; timed: 1 hour

Scoring: Scoring service available from publisher; on-line administration available

Cost: Booklet $299.00; On-line $49.00

Employee Application Resume Rating and Categorizing Scale
Thomas J. Rundquist

1995	NCS Pearson

Population: Adolescents, adults

Purpose: Allows an employer to rate and categorize employment applications using resumes or applications in a simple and organized fashion

Description: This product can review thousands of applicants' resumes or applications in short order, which saves time and effort and provides the best qualified employee applicants for interviews. Also, the database can be programmed to give the Human Resources Department data for researching their employees, present, past, and future, using the company's own criteria. Criteria include Job Categories from a list of 75 selections for three choices: Salary Requirements, Geographic Preferences, and Work Experience. Industries Categories are divided into 10 major headings.

Format: Computer administered; untimed: 5 minutes

Scoring: Computer scored

Cost: Contact publisher

ESSI In-Depth Interpretations
Terry D. Anderson, Howard L. Shenson

1988	Consulting Resource Group International, Inc.

Population: Adults

Purpose: Assesses entrepreneurial style preferences and success indicators

Description: Forced-choice test with 21 items measuring behavioral, cognitive, interpersonal, affective, and undifferentiated patterns. A 10th-grade reading level is required.

Format: Examiner required; individual administration; suitable for group use; untimed

Scoring: Self-scored

Cost: $9.95

Experienced Worker Assessments

Date not provided	National Occupational Competency Testing Institute

Population: Adults

Purpose: Measures knowledge of higher level concepts, theories, and applications in related occupations

Description: These tests are intended for evaluating individuals with a combination of education, training, and work experience. They can be used for both education and business and industry applications. Tests are available in the following categories: business, computer, construction, consumer economics, culinary arts, drafting, electrical/electronics, heating/air conditioning, and machine trades. Core competencies for each measure are available through a Web site. Customized assessments can be developed. Experienced worker assessments are designed for individuals who have 3 or more years of work experience in addition to training in the occupation.

Format: Examiner required; group administration; untimed

Scoring: Scoring service

Cost: Contact publisher

Flanagan Aptitude Classification Tests (FACT™)
John C. Flanagan

1953	NCS Pearson Reid London House

Population: Adolescents, adults

Purpose: Assesses skills necessary for the successful completion of particular occupational tasks; used for vocational counseling, curriculum planning, and selection and placement of employees

Description: Battery of 16 multiple-item paper–pencil aptitude tests designed to help the subject understand his or her abilities relative to others in the total population and in specific occupations. Each test is printed as a separate non-reusable booklet and may be administered individually or in combination. The FACT battery differs from the Flanagan Industrial Tests battery in that the tests are generally of a lower level and have longer time limits.

Format: Self-administered; untimed: 2 to 40 minutes per test

Scoring: Hand key

Cost: Contact publisher

Flanagan Industrial Tests (FIT™)
John C. Flanagan

1960	NCS Pearson Reid London House

Population: Adults

Purpose: Predicts success for given job elements in adults; used for employee screening, hiring, and placement in a wide variety of jobs

Description: Battery of 18 paper–pencil tests designed for use with adults in personnel selection programs. Each test is printed as a separate booklet and may be administered individually or in combination.

Format: Examiner required; suitable for group use; timed: 5 to 15 minutes per test

Scoring: Hand key

Cost: Contact publisher

General Aptitude Test Battery

1986	Nelson Thomson Learning

Population: Grade 9 to adult

Purpose: Measures aptitudes for career counseling and employee selection

Description: Developed by the U.S. Department of Labor and Human Resources Development of Canada, this test measures nine different aptitudes. Includes 12 subtests. Uses print, manual, and finger dexterity boards. Also available in French.

Format: Examiner required; group or individual administration; 50 minutes

Scoring: Hand key; examiner evaluated; machine

scored or computer scored; scoring service available from publisher

Cost: Contact publisher

Hay Aptitude Test Battery: Warm-Up
Edward N. Hay

1984	Wonderlic Personnel Test, Inc.

Population: Adults

Purpose: Introduces job applicants to the testing procedures of the Hay Aptitude Test Battery

Description: Unscored 20-item paper–pencil test provides a warm-up for the Hay Aptitude tests. The exercise is intended to quiet nervous applicants and to familiarize applicants with the format of the other tests. Also available in French and Spanish.

Format: Examiner required; suitable for group use; timed: 1 minute

Scoring: Hand key

Cost: 25 Forms $41.25; 100 Forms $80.00

IPI Aptitude–Reading Comprehension

2000	Industrial Psychology International Ltd.

Population: Adults

Purpose: Assesses literacy from functional to early college level

Description: Paper–pencil 25-item preemployment screening yielding grade-equivalent norms.

Format: Examiner required; group or individual administration; timed: 12 minutes

Scoring: Hand key; no scoring service available

Cost: Introductory Kit $38.00; 20 Answer/Score Sheets $28.00; 10 Test Booklets $18.00

IPI Employee Aptitude Series: Applied Math

1995	Industrial Psychology International Ltd.

Population: Adolescents, adults

Purpose: Measures the ability to solve one- and two-step algebra problems; used for employee selection, promotion, and training

Description: Paper–pencil 18-item multiple-choice test. A fourth-grade reading level is required. Scores predict abstract and numeric estimation skills.

Format: Examiner required; suitable for group use; timed: 12 minutes

Scoring: Hand key

Cost: Introductory Kit (20 test booklets, scoring key, manual) $30.00

IPI Employee Aptitude Series: Memory
1984   Industrial Psychology International Ltd.

Population: Adults

Purpose: Determines ability to remember visual, verbal, and numerical information; used to screen applicants for clerical, sales, and supervisory jobs

Description: Three 2-minute paper–pencil subtests demonstrating aptitude to recognize and recall associations with names, faces, words, and numbers. Also available in French and Spanish.

Format: Examiner required; suitable for group use; timed: 6 minutes

Scoring: Hand key

Cost: Introductory Kit (20 test booklets, scoring key, manual) $44.00

IPI Employee Aptitude Series: Office Terms
1981   Industrial Psychology International Ltd.

Population: Adults

Purpose: Measures ability to understand special terminology used in business and industry; used to screen applicants for clerical, sales, and supervisory jobs

Description: Paper–pencil 54-item test measuring comprehension of information of an office or business nature. It also indicates overqualification for routine, repetitive assignments. Also available in French.

Format: Examiner required; suitable for group use; timed: 6 minutes

Scoring: Hand key

Cost: Introductory Kit (20 test booklets, scoring key, manual) $30.00

IPI Employee Aptitude Series: Parts
1984   Industrial Psychology International Ltd.

Population: Adults

Purpose: Assesses ability to see the whole in relation to its parts; used to screen applicants for clerical, mechanical, technical, sales, and supervisory positions

Description: Paper–pencil 48-item test measuring aptitude for visualizing size, shape, and spatial relations of objects in two and three dimensions.

The test reveals one's sense of layout and organization. Also available in French and Spanish.

Format: Examiner required; suitable for group use; timed: 6 minutes

Scoring: Hand key

Cost: Introductory Kit (20 test booklets, scoring key, manual) $30.00

IPI Employee Aptitude Series: Perception
1981   Industrial Psychology International Ltd.

Population: Adults

Purpose: Measures ability to perceive differences in written words and numbers; used to screen applicants for clerical, sales, and supervisory jobs

Description: Paper–pencil 54-item test measuring the ability to rapidly scan and locate details in words and numbers and to recognize likenesses and differences. Also available in French and Spanish.

Format: Examiner required; suitable for group use; timed: 6 minutes

Scoring: Hand key

Cost: Introductory Kit (20 test booklets, scoring key, manual) $30.00

IPI Employee Aptitude Series: Precision
1986   Industrial Psychology International Ltd.

Population: Adults

Purpose: Determines ability to perceive details in objects; used to screen applicants for technical and mechanical jobs requiring visual accuracy, such as inspector-related jobs

Description: Paper–pencil 48-item test using pictures to test the ability to perceive details in objects and rapidly recognize differences and likenesses. The test does not require the ability to read or write. Also available in French and Spanish.

Format: Examiner required; suitable for group use; timed: 6 minutes

Scoring: Hand key

Cost: Introductory Kit (20 test booklets, scoring key, manual) $30.00

IS Manager Consultant Skills Evaluation
1990   Walden Personnel Testing and Consulting, Inc.

Population: Adults

Purpose: Measures technical, intellectual, and supervisory skills required for a senior-level information systems consultant, manager, or trainer

Description: Measures aptitude, proficiency, and knowledge of job applicants. Available in English and French.

Format: Self-administered; timed: 3 hours 5 minutes

Scoring: Scoring service available from publisher

Cost: $319.00

IS Project Leader Skills Evaluation

1988	Walden Personnel Testing and Consulting, Inc.

Population: Adults

Purpose: Evaluates all essential skills for the project leader position

Description: Measures procedural and analytical ability, and knowledge of project organization, control, scheduling, and planning concepts. Available in English and French.

Format: Self-administered; timed: 3 hours

Scoring: Scoring service available from publisher

Cost: Test Booklet and Detailed Report on each candidate; Basic $319.00, Comprehensive $699.00

Job Ready Assessments

Date not provided	National Occupational Competency Testing Institute

Population: Adolescents, adults

Purpose: Measures individual's knowledge of basic processes, including the identification and use of terminology and tools

Description: The tests can be used in an educational setting to measure curriculum effectiveness, improve instructional methods, successfully link the world of education with the world of work, and enhance the transition between school and work. In the workplace they can be used to assist in candidate selection. Tests are available in the following categories: agriculture, business, computer, construction, consumer economics, culinary arts, drafting, electrical/electronics, health related, machine trades, and maintenance services. Job-ready assessments are designed to test individuals who have completed training or education in the occupation.

Format: Examiner required; group administration; untimed

Scoring: Scoring service

Cost: Contact publisher

Job Style Indicator (JSI)
Terry D. Anderson, Everett T. Robinson

1988	Consulting Resource Group International, Inc.

Population: Adults

Purpose: Assesses work style behaviors; used in job placement and evaluation

Description: Forced-choice test with 16 items. A 10th-grade reading level is required.

Format: Examiner required; individual administration; suitable for group use; untimed

Scoring: Self-scored

Cost: $5.95

MainTest–Forms NL-1, B, and C
Roland T. Ramsay

1999	Ramsay Corporation

Population: Adults

Purpose: Assesses maintenance ability for trade and craft jobs; used for hiring and promotion

Description: Paper–pencil 153-item multiple-choice test. Use Form NL-1 or alternate Forms B and C.

Format: Examiner required; suitable for group use; untimed: 2 hours 30 minutes

Scoring: Scoring service

Cost: Kit (10 booklets, 10 answer sheets, manual) $500.00

Measurement, Reading, and Arithmetic–Form OE
Roland T. Ramsay

2001	Ramsay Corporation

Population: Adults

Purpose: Measures reading, arithmetic, and measurement skills for preemployment

Description: Paper–pencil 101-item multiple-choice test with three subtests: Reading, Measurement, and Arithmetic. One composite score and three subscores are yielded.

Format: Examiner required; suitable for group use; timed: 85 minutes

Scoring: Self-scored

Cost: Test Booklet $15.00 (minimum of 20); Administration Manual $24.95

Minnesota Job Description Questionnaire (MJDQ)

1986   Vocational Psychology Research

Population: Adults

Purpose: Measures the reinforcer (need-satisfier) characteristics of jobs along 21 reinforcer dimensions

Description: In typical applications, multiple raters are asked to rate a specific job. Composite scaling of the MJDQs completed by all raters results in an Occupational Reinforcer Pattern (ORP), which is the pattern of rated reinforcers or need satisfiers on a given job. The MJDQ is the instrument used to create the ORPs in Occupational Reinforcer Patterns (1986), and can be used to create ORPs locally. The MJDQ can also be used to obtain an individual's perception of jobs. The MJDQ comes in two forms: Form E for employees and Form S for supervisors.

Format: Self-administered; untimed: 20 minutes

Scoring: Scoring service

Cost: Sample Set (manual, Form S, Form E) $7.50

My Presentation Style

James H. Brewer

1989   Associated Consultants in Education

Population: Adults

Purpose: Used to assist individuals in making more effective presentations

Description: Used by trainers, conference leaders, and sales consultants to improve their own presentations. The instrument shows how personality type can dictate an individual's presentation style, outlines techniques for more effective presentations, explores strengths and weaknesses of each style of presentation, and promotes cross-type understanding.

Format: Self-administered; untimed: 15 to 20 minutes

Scoring: Hand key

Cost: $4.95 each

My Timestyle

James H. Brewer

1990   Associated Consultants in Education

Population: Adults

Purpose: Used to develop more productive time usage

Description: Sixteen items yield accurate information about an individual's time awareness.

Four time styles are identified by the instrument: Road Runner (high-velocity person who does not waste words or time), Race Horse (time-conscious team worker), New Pup (believes people are more important than time), and Tom Cat (independent worker with a low awareness of time and people). The instrument determines one's time usage style, describes how each style behaves, explores more positive time use, and promotes a better understanding of others.

Format: Self-administered; untimed: 15 to 20 minutes

Scoring: Hand key

Cost: $2.95 each

Personnel Test Battery (PTB) Numerical Computation (NP2.1)

1993   SHL Canada

Population: Adults

Purpose: Measures basic number skills

Description: Thirty-item multiple-choice test measuring the understanding of relationships between numbers and operations, as well as quick and accurate calculations. In each item, one number has been omitted from an equation. The examinee must select (from five choices) the number that will correctly complete the equation. Simple fractions and decimals are used, and some problems are expressed in numbers, but more complex notation or operations are deliberately omitted. The test is suitable for individuals with minimal educational qualifications. Also available in French.

Format: Examiner required; individual administration; untimed: 7 minutes

Scoring: Hand key; machine scored; scoring service available

Cost: Contact publisher

Personnel Test Battery (PTB) Numerical Reasoning (NP6.1, NP6.2)

1993   SHL Canada

Population: Adults

Purpose: Assesses simple numerical reasoning skills

Description: Both tests have short written problems that involve using decimals, fractions, or graphs. Test content includes items based on subjects relevant to sales, clerical, and general staff. NP6.2 (24 items) allows candidates to use a calculator. NP6.1 (30 items) is completed without a calculator. Also available in French.

Format: Examiner required; individual administration; untimed: 15 minutes

Scoring: Hand key; machine scored; scoring service available

Cost: Contact publisher

Personnel Test Battery (PTB) Verbal Comprehension (VP5.1)
1993 SHL Canada

Population: Adults

Purpose: Assesses an individual's knowledge of the meanings of words and the relationships between them; used for jobs in which verbal communication skills are important

Description: Forty-item multiple-choice test requires the candidate to identify the relationship (same or opposite) between one pair of words and to select (from five choices) the word that relates in the same way to a third given word. The vocabulary used is nonspecialist, everyday language. VP5.1 is more difficult than VP1.1 of the same battery. Also available in French.

Format: Examiner required; individual administration; untimed: 18 minutes

Scoring: Hand key; machine scored; scoring service available

Cost: Contact publisher

Position Analysis Questionnaire (PAQ)
Ernest J. McCormick, P. R. Jeanneret, Robert C. Meacham
1989 PAQ Services, Inc.

Population: Adults

Purpose: Analyzes jobs in terms of job elements that reflect directly or infer the basic human behaviors involved, regardless of their specific technological areas or functions; used with jobs at all levels

Description: Paper–pencil 187-item job analysis rating scale in which the examiner indicates the degree of involvement of each element listed using appropriate rating scales, such as importance or frequency. The job elements are organized so that they provide a logical analysis of the job's structure. Six broad areas are assessed: information input, mental processes, work output, relationships with other persons, job context, and other job characteristics. Examples of specific job elements are the use of written materials, the level of decision making, the use of me-

chanical devices, working in a hazardous environment, and working at a specified pace. Analysis of the questionnaire is in terms of job dimensions.

Format: Self-administered; on-line administration; untimed

Scoring: Computer scored; scoring service

Cost: Contact publisher

Position Classification Inventory (PCI)
Gary Gottfredson, John L. Holland
1991 Psychological Assessment Resources, Inc.

Population: Adults

Purpose: Used by human resources development and career counselors to classify positions or job classes

Description: Paper–pencil 84-item three-point scale inventory. A Self-Directed Search summary code is produced. Materials used include a manual, reusable item booklet, and answer/profile form.

Format: Self-administered; untimed: 10 minutes

Scoring: Computer scored; scoring service available

Cost: Intro Kit $73.00

Power and Performance Measures (PPM)
James Barrett
1996 Test Agency, Ltd.

Population: Adults

Purpose: Measures general abilities required by employees

Description: Total of 314 items within nine subtests: Applied Power, Processing Speed, Mechanical Understanding, Numerical Computation, Numerical Reasoning, Perceptual Reasoning, Spatial Ability, Verbal Comprehension, and Verbal Reasoning.

Format: Examiner required; individual or group administration; can be computer administered; timed

Scoring: Self-scored; computer scored; scoring service available

Cost: Contact publisher

Press Test
Melany E. Baehr, Raymond J. Corsini
1985 NCS Pearson Reid London House

Population: Adults

Purpose: Assesses adults' ability to work under pressure by comparing objective measures of reaction time under normal and high-pressure conditions; used for selection, career counseling, and placement of high-level personnel, where efficiency must be maintained

Description: Multiple-item paper-pencil test measuring speed of reaction to verbal stimuli, color stimuli, and color stimuli under distraction caused by interfering verbal stimuli. For valid results, stopwatch time limits and strict monitoring must be employed in the administration of the test, which is not designed to be completed in the allotted time. The test has been used to select high-level managers, professionals, and airline pilots.

Format: Examiner required; suitable for group use; timed: 10 to 12 minutes

Scoring: Hand key

Cost: Contact publisher

Problem-Solving Skills Questionnaire (PSSQ)
Dennis C. Kinlaw

| 1989 | Jossey-Bass/Pfeiffer |

Population: Managers and supervisors

Purpose: Measures conversational skills

Description: Self-scoring instrument used to assess participants' understanding and use of specific conversational skills.

Format: Self-administered; untimed: 2 to 4 hours

Scoring: Self-scored

Cost: $7.95

Purdue Pegboard Test

| 1992 | NCS Pearson Reid London House |

Population: Adults

Purpose: Measures hand–finger–arm dexterity required for certain types of manual work; used in the selection of business and industrial personnel

Description: Multiple-operation manual test of gross- and fine-motor movements of hands, fingers, arms, and tips of fingers. The test measures the dexterity needed in assembly work, electronic production work, and similarly related jobs. Materials consist of a test board with two vertical rows of holes and four storage wells holding pegs, washers, and collars. The subject must complete as many assemblies as possible in the allotted time.

Format: Examiner required; suitable for group use; timed: 3 to 9 minutes

Scoring: Hand key

Cost: Contact publisher

Quality Service Audit for Employees
James H. Brewer

| 1992 | Associated Consultants in Education |

Population: Adults

Purpose: Used to give employees an opportunity to evaluate how they rate in quality customer service

Description: The instrument measures employees' beliefs, knowledge, commitment to, and performance in quality customer service; promotes more positive attitudes toward quality customer service; uses self-assessment as a tool for change; and shows how each employee is vital to quality customer service.

Format: Self-administered; untimed: 15 to 20 minutes

Scoring: Hand key

Cost: $5.95 each

Reading Test–Form A
Roland T. Ramsay

| 1991 | Ramsay Corporation |

Population: Adults

Purpose: Assesses the ability to read, comprehend, and answer written questions

Description: Paper–pencil 40-item multiple-choice test designed to measure an individual's ability to read, comprehend, and answer questions based on a printed passage. The topics of the passages are Plant Safety, Hydraulic Systems, Industrial Machines, Lubrication, and Operating a Computer Terminal.

Format: Examiner required; suitable for group use; timed: 35 minutes

Scoring: Self-scored

Cost: Test Booklet $10.00 (minimum of 20); Administration Manual $24.95

Reading–Arithmetic Index (RAI™)

| 1995 | NCS Pearson Reid London House |

Population: Adults

Purpose: Assesses proficiency levels through Grade 12

Description: The Reading Index contains 60 items that test applicants' ability to read and understand basic materials through Grade 9 level. The Arithmetic Index contains 54 items that test ability to add, subtract, multiply, divide, and use fractions, decimals, and percentages through Grade 8 level.

Format: Examiner required; suitable for group use; untimed: 35 minutes

Scoring: Hand key; computer scored

Cost: Contact publisher

Self-Employment Questionnaire (SEQ)
Frank W. D. Thaxton

1995	Selby MillSmith Ltd.

Population: Adults

Purpose: Used in employment counseling to measure skill and readiness for self-employment

Description: Multiple-choice computer-administered projective test with a narrative text. An 11-year-old reading level is required.

Format: Self-administered; timed: 90 minutes

Scoring: Computer scored

Cost: $47.00

Skills and Attributes Inventory
Melany E. Baehr

1976	NCS Pearson Reid London House

Population: Adults

Purpose: Assesses the relative importance of 13 skill and attribute factors necessary for successful job performance and the degree to which the incumbent possesses the skills and attributes; used for systematic job analysis, test validation, and selection

Description: Paper–pencil 96-item test measuring general functioning, intelligence, visual activity, visual and coordination skills, physical coordination, mechanical skills, graphic and clerical skills, general clerical skills, leadership ability, tolerance in interpersonal relations, organization identification, conscientiousness and reliability, efficiency under stress, and solitary work. Each item is rated on importance to the job, using a 4-point, equal-interval scale ranging from *little or none* to *outstanding*. An ability form also may be used to assess the incumbent's strength in the relative skills and attributes.

Format: Examiner required; suitable for group use; untimed: 45 minutes

Scoring: Hand key; may be computer scored

Cost: Contact publisher

TABE™ Work-Related Foundation Skills (TABE–WF)

1994	CTB/McGraw-Hill

Population: Adults

Purpose: Assesses adults' foundation skills in reading, mathematics, and language

Description: Multiple-item paper–pencil multiple-choice test that evaluates basic reading, math, and language skills. There are three forms, each presenting questions and situations within the context of a specific workplace environment: Health, Business/Office, and Trade/Technical. In addition, there is a General Form that covers a variety of work contexts. The test produces a variety of results, including norm-referenced scores useful for growth measurement and student placement for reading, language, mathematics computation, applied mathematics, total mathematics, and total battery. Computer version available.

Format: Examiner required; suitable for group use; untimed: 120 minutes

Scoring: Machine scored; hand key; computer scored

Cost: 25 Test Books and Examiner's Manual $59.25

TABE™ Work-Related Problem Solving (TABE–PS)

1994	CTB/McGraw-Hill

Population: Adults

Purpose: Measures a wide range of problem-solving competencies in a variety of work-related applications

Description: Multiple-item paper–pencil essay, short answer, and verbal performance assessment that helps employers, educators, and training professionals diagnose how an examinee deals with various aspects of problem solving: defining the problem, examining the problem, suggesting possible solutions, evaluating solutions, and extending the meaning of the solution. Tasks are based on realistic workplace situations and measure problem-solving skills. Computer version available.

Format: Examiner required; suitable for group use; untimed: 60 minutes

Scoring: Machine scored; hand key; computer scored

Cost: 25 Test Books and Examiner's Manual/Scoring Guide $34.75

Technical Test Battery (TTB) Numerical Computation (NT2.1)

1995	SHL Canada

Population: Adults

Purpose: Measures basic ability to work with numbers in a technical setting

Description: Multiple-choice test assessing the understanding of mathematical relationships and operations and the ability to calculate quickly and accurately. In each of 36 items, one number or operation has been omitted from an equation. The examinee must select the missing element from five possible answers. Fractions, decimals, and percentages are included, but more complex notations or operations are omitted deliberately. The range extends from minimal educational qualifications to high school graduate level. Available in French.

Format: Examiner required; individual administration; untimed: 18 minutes

Scoring: Hand key; machine scored; scoring service available

Cost: Contact publisher

Test of English for International Communication (TOEIC)

Date not provided	Educational Testing Service

Population: Adult nonnative speakers of English

Purpose: Measures English language proficiency required in business; used as a basis for employee selection and placement, for decisions concerning assignment, and to measure achievement in company-sponsored English-language programs

Description: Paper–pencil 200-item multiple-choice test of English language skills. Section I contains 100 listening comprehension items administered via audiocassette. Section II contains 100 reading items. Total test scale scores range from 10 to 990; scale subscores for Sections I and II range from 5 to 495. The scores are correlated to direct measures of listening, speaking, reading, and writing, as well as to indirect measures. The test is used by multinational corporations, language schools, government agencies,

and public and private organizations for hiring, assignment to overseas posts, and assignment to or promotion within departments where English is desirable. Application to take the test is made through national regional offices. A cassette player is required.

Format: Examiner required; suitable for group use; timed: 2 hours 30 minutes

Scoring: Hand key; may be computer scored

Cost: Contact publisher

Test of Practical Judgment–Revised
Alfred J. Cardall

1999	Institute of Psychological Research, Inc.

Population: Adults

Purpose: Determines employees' ability to use practical judgment in solving problems; used to screen for management and sales positions

Description: Multiple-item paper–pencil multiple-choice test of judgment factors that may be used in conjunction with intelligence testing. The test also may be used for screening and for selection and placement of individuals whose work involves thinking, planning, or getting along with people. The test examines such factors as empathy, drive, and social maturity. Materials include five tests, a key, and a manual. Also available in French.

Format: Examiner required; suitable for group use; untimed: 30 minutes

Scoring: Hand key

Cost: Contact publisher

Test of Work Competency and Stability
A. Gaston Leblanc

Date not provided	Institute of Psychological Research, Inc.

Population: Ages 21 to 67 years

Purpose: Measures stress levels in motor coordination and mental concentration; used to evaluate psychological capacity for work performance

Description: Multiple-item paper–pencil interview and manual dexterity test of six factors related to work competency in industry, including work stability, assertiveness, persistence and concentration, psychomotor steadiness, capacity, and stress tolerance. Scores screen workers and provide information for rehabilitation. The materials include a manual, interview questionnaire sheets, mirror tracing patterns, tapping patterns, and record blanks. Also available in French.

Format: Examiner required; individual administration; untimed

Scoring: Hand key

Cost: Contact publisher

Thurstone Test of Mental Alertness (TMA™)

L. L. Thurstone, Thelma Gwinn Thurstone

| 1959 | NCS Pearson Reid London House |

Population: Adults

Purpose: Measures an individual's capacity to acquire new knowledge and skills and to use what has been learned to solve problems; measures individual differences in ability to learn and perform mental tasks of varying types and complexity

Description: Test with 126 items measuring linguistic (vocabulary) and quantitative (arithmetic) factors. This test is available in two forms.

Format: Examiner required; suitable for group use; timed: 20 minutes

Scoring: Hand key; computer scored

Cost: Contact publisher

Understanding Communication

Thelma Gwinn Thurstone

| 1984 | NCS Pearson Reid London House |

Population: Adults

Purpose: Measures comprehension of verbal material in short sentences and phrases; used for industrial screening and selection of clerical, first-line supervisors, or other employees that need to understand written material and communications

Description: Paper–pencil 40-item single-score test measuring verbal comprehension through the ability to identify the one of four words that will complete a given sentence.

Format: Examiner required; suitable for group use; timed: 15 minutes

Scoring: Hand key

Cost: Contact publisher

VCWS 3—Numerical Sorting

| 1993 | Valpar International Corporation |

Population: Adults

Purpose: Measures an individual's ability to perform work tasks requiring sequential sorting of a combined numerical/alphabetical problem; provides insight into spatial and form perception, accuracy, and attention to detail in transferring data

Description: Manual test measuring the ability to sort, file, and categorize objects using a numerical code. The individual must transfer 42 of 56 numerically ordered white plastic chips inserted into correspondingly marked slots in Board I to the appropriate slots in Board II. After the chip placements on Board II are scored, the individual transfers the chips back to Board I. Work activities related to the test include examining, grading, and sorting; keeping records and receipts; recording or transmitting verbal or coded information; and posting verbal or numerical data on stock lists. The test should not be used with individuals with severe impairment of the upper extremities.

Format: Examiner required; individual administration; timed

Scoring: Examiner evaluated

Cost: $1,555.00

VCWS 6—Independent Problem Solving

| 1993 | Valpar International Corporation |

Population: Adults

Purpose: Measures the ability to perform work tasks requiring visual comparison and proper selection of abstract designs; may be used with individuals with mental retardation and hearing impairment

Description: Manual test measuring a person's ability to perform work tasks requiring a visual comparison of colored shapes. Work activities relating to the test are characterized by emphasis on decision-making and instruction-following abilities. The test should not be used with individuals with severe impairment of the upper extremities or severe visual impairment.

Format: Examiner required; individual administration; timed

Scoring: Examiner evaluated

Cost: $1,555.00

Wonderlic Basic Skills Test (WBST)

Eliot R. Long, Winifred L. Clonts, Victor S. Artese

| 1994 | Wonderlic Personnel Test, Inc. |

Population: Ages 15 years and older

Purpose: Used in employment and job training to measure job-related math and verbal skills and for vocational guidance

Description: Multiple-choice paper–pencil test with two subtests: Test of Verbal Skills (50 questions, 20 minutes) and Test of Quantitative Skills (45 questions, 20 minutes). JRT scale scores, scores by job requirements, and scores by grade level are yielded. Verbal forms VS1 and VS2 and Quantitative forms QS1 and QS2 are available. A sixth-grade reading level is required.

Format: Examiner required; individual administration; timed: 40 minutes

Scoring: Computer scored; test scoring service available from publisher

Cost: Composite of both tests: 25 Tests $110.00, 100 Tests $245.00; Verbal Skills: 25 Tests $80.00, 100 Tests $165.00; Quantitative: 25 Tests $80.00, 100 Tests $165.00

Word Fluency

1961   NCS Pearson Reid London House

Population: Adults

Purpose: Determines the speed of relevant verbal associations and individual's ability to produce appropriate words rapidly; used for vocational counseling and personnel selection in fields requiring communication skills, such as supervision, management, and sales

Description: Paper–pencil 80-item test measuring verbal fluency.

Format: Examiner required; suitable for group use; timed: 10 minutes

Scoring: Hand key

Cost: Contact publisher

Work Keys Applied Mathematics Test

2001   ACT, Inc.

Population: Adolescents, adults

Purpose: Assesses mathematical problem solving

Description: Thirty-item multiple-choice criterion-referenced test across five levels. A test form, formula sheet, answer folder, administrator's manual, and videotaped administrator's manual are used.

Format: Examiner required; individual or group administration; computer-administered version available; timed: 45 minutes

Scoring: Machine scored; scoring service available; computer scored

Cost: Contact publisher

Work Keys Applied Technology Test

2001   ACT, Inc.

Population: Adolescents, adults

Purpose: Used for program evaluation, skills profile, and selection to assess technological problem solving

Description: Multiple-choice criterion-referenced test with 32 items across four levels. Measures skills in applying the principles of mechanics, electricity, fluid dynamics, and thermodynamics to workplace problems. A test booklet, answer folder, administrator's manual, and videotaped administrator's manual are used.

Format: Examiner required; individual or group administration; computer-administered version available; timed: 45 minutes

Scoring: Machine scored; scoring service available; computer scored

Cost: Contact publisher

Work Keys Listening Test

1992   ACT, Inc.

Population: Adolescents, adults

Purpose: Used in program evaluation, skills profiling, and selection to assess listening skills

Description: Six-prompt criterion-referenced test across five levels. An audiocassette, answer folder, administrator's manual, and videotaped administrator's manual are used.

Format: Examiner required; individual or group administration; timed: 45 minutes

Scoring: Holistic scoring by publisher only

Cost: Contact publisher

Work Keys Locating Information Test

2001   ACT, Inc.

Population: Adolescents, adults

Purpose: Used in program evaluation, skills profiling, and selection to assess locating information in business graphics and other materials

Description: Multiple-choice criterion-referenced test with 32-item across four levels. A test booklet, answer folder, administrator's manual, and videotaped administrator's manual are used.

Format: Examiner required; individual or group administration; computer-administered available; timed: 45 minutes

Scoring: Machine scored; scoring service available; computer scored

Cost: Contact publisher

Work Keys Observation Test

2001   **ACT, Inc.**

Population: Adolescents, adults

Purpose: Assesses observation skills in the workplace

Description: Multiple-choice criterion-referenced test with 36 items across four levels. A test video, answer folder, administrator's manual, and videotaped administrator's manual are used.

Format: Examiner required; individual or group administration; timed: 60 minutes

Scoring: Machine scored; scoring service available

Cost: Contact publisher

Work Keys Reading for Information Test

2001   **ACT, Inc.**

Population: Adolescents, adults

Purpose: Used to assess reading skills for program evaluation, skills profiling, and selection

Description: Multiple-choice criterion-referenced test with 30 items across five levels. A test booklet, answer folder, administrator's manual, and videotaped administrator's manual are used.

Format: Examiner required; individual or group administration; computer-administered version available; timed: 60 minutes

Scoring: Machine scored; scoring service available; computer scored

Cost: Contact publisher

Work Keys Teamwork Test

2001   **ACT, Inc.**

Population: Adolescents, adults

Purpose: Assesses teamwork skills

Description: Multiple-choice criterion-referenced test with 36 items across four levels. A video, answer folder, administrator's manual, and videotaped administrator's manual are used.

Format: Examiner required; individual administration; suitable for group use; timed: 60 minutes

Scoring: Machine scored; scoring service available

Cost: Contact publisher

Work Keys Writing Test

1992   **ACT, Inc.**

Population: Adolescents, adults

Purpose: Used for program evaluation, skills profiling, and selection to assess business writing skills

Description: Six-prompt essay test across five levels. An audiocassette, answer folder, administrator's manual, and videotaped administrator's manual are used.

Format: Examiner required; individual administration; suitable for group use; timed: 40 minutes

Scoring: Holistic scoring by publisher only

Cost: Contact publisher

Work Readiness Profile (WRP)
Helga A. Rowe

1995   **Australian Council for Educational Research Limited**

Population: Adolescents, adults

Purpose: Assesses individuals with major disabilities and rates their adaptive functioning

Description: Criterion-referenced tool designed to assist in the initial assessment of individuals with disabilities. This measure focuses on abilities, supports, and empowerment, rather than on the level of disability. The multidimensional profile obtained focuses on the whole person and how he or she functions within the environment. It seeks to identify what people can do rather than what they cannot do. Ratings are completed on 12 factors: health, hearing, vision, travel, movement, fine motor skills, gross motor skills and strength, social and interpersonal skills, work adjustment, communication effectiveness, abilities and skills, and literacy and numeracy.

Format: Examiner required; individual and group administration; untimed

Scoring: Examiner evaluated

Cost: Contact publisher

Work Skills Series (WSS) Understanding Instructions (VWP1)

1988   **SHL Canada**

Population: Adults

Purpose: Assesses the ability to follow and understand simple written instructions

Description: Test with 39 items measuring the ability to follow and apply instructions in practical and work-related situations. Candidates read a series of paragraphs outlining particular work procedures and are then tested on their understanding of these procedures. The contents have been designed to look like those typically found in many technical, production, or manufacturing environments.

Format: Examiner required; individual administration; untimed: 12 minutes

Scoring: Hand key; machine scored; scoring service available

Cost: Contact publisher

Work Skills Series (WSS) Visual Checking (CWP3)

1990	SHL Canada

Population: Adults

Purpose: Assesses the ability to check that one set of visual indicators corresponds with another

Description: Thirty-item test measuring the ability to check that one set of indicators corresponds to another set of indicators according to a number of simple rules. This skill is important whenever production or control equipment is used by semiskilled operators. Also available in French.

Format: Examiner required; individual administration; untimed: 7 minutes

Scoring: Hand key; machine scored; scoring service available

Cost: Contact publisher

Work Skills Series (WSS) Working with Numbers (NWP2)

1988	SHL Canada

Population: Adults

Purpose: Assesses the ability to perform simple numerical computations, such as in stock control

Description: Test with 36 items measuring the ability to apply the basic rules of arithmetic to practical and work-related situations. The test content involves dealing quickly with stock levels and use of various types of mechanical components. This test is relevant to any job in industry or manufacturing where the appropriate application of basic arithmetic skills is important. Also available in French.

Format: Examiner required; individual administration; untimed: 10 minutes

Scoring: Hand key; machine scored; scoring service available

Cost: Contact publisher

Worker Rehabilitation Questionnaire (WRQ)
David D. Robinson

2001	PAQ Services, Inc.

Population: Adults with disabilities

Purpose: Matches capabilities and tolerances of individuals with disabilities with characteristics of jobs in a database; supports or prevents litigation

Description: This questionnaire can benefit people in human resource departments, vocational rehabilitation counselors, health service providers, and so on. This questionnaire rates individuals on 150 work behaviors and compares ratings with characteristics of 2,500 jobs. Assesses capabilities and tolerances regarding stimulus input; cognitive processes; work output; and social, environmental, and other characteristics of jobs. Generates a list of jobs potentially appropriate for individuals with disabilities.

Format: Examiner required; individual or computer administration; untimed: approximately 1.5 hours

Scoring: Computer scored

Cost: Contact publisher

Working: Assessing Skills, Habits, and Style
Curtis Miles, Phyllis Grummon

Date not provided	H & H Publishing Company, Inc.

Population: Adults

Purpose: Assesses workplace competencies

Description: A self-scoring instrument designed to assess proficiency in nine competencies that go beyond academic and technical skills and knowledge. It provides information to the individual being assessed and gives teachers, trainers, and others a framework within which they can develop instructional activities.

Format: Self-administered; untimed: 20 to 30 minutes

Scoring: Computer scored; self-scored; also available on the Web

Cost: 1 to 99 Tests $4.00 each

Workplace Skills Survey (WSS)

1998	Industrial Psychology International, Ltd.

Population: Ages 16 years and older

Purpose: Assesses nontechnical employability skills

Description: Preemployment and promotional screening. Contains 48 items within six skill areas: teamwork, communication, adaptation to change, problem solving, work ethics, and technological literacy. Yields stanine scores and T-scores.

Format: Examiner required; individual or group administration; timed: 20 minutes

Scoring: Hand key

Cost: Introductory Kit $40.00; Answer/Score Sheets $30.00; 10 Test Booklets $18.00

Aptitude and Skills

Banking

Basic Banking Skills Battery (BBSB®)

1987	NCS Pearson Reid London House

Population: Ages 16 years and older

Purpose: Measures potential for successful performance as a bank teller and customer service representative; used for employee selection and promotion

Description: Paper–pencil 317-item multiple-choice battery measuring potential in several key areas related to an applicant's ability to perform as a teller or customer service representative. Scores are provided for 13 scales: Drive, School Achievement, Arithmetic Computation, Interpersonal Relations, Cognitive Skills, Error Recognition, Motor Ability, Math Ability, Name Comparison, Self-Discipline, Leadership, Number Comparison, and Perceptual Skills. The battery yields a single score, the Potential Estimate, for the bank teller and customer service positions. Form A combines the timed and untimed tests. A Short Form is composed of the timed tests only.

Format: Examiner required; suitable for group use; timed

Scoring: Computer scored

Cost: Contact publisher

Personnel Selection Inventory for Banking (PSI-B)

1987	NCS Pearson Reid London House

Population: Job applicants

Purpose: Identifies banking job applicants who might engage in theft or counterproductive behavior in the workplace; designed to help banks select quality employees and reduce losses

Description: Multiple-item paper-pencil survey designed to enable employers to screen job applicants. Four versions of the inventory, PSI-B1, PSI-B3, PSI-B7, and PSI-B77, are available. Each version contains one or more of the following scales: Honesty, Drug-Avoidance, Non-Violence, Customer/Employee Relations, Work Values, Supervision Attitudes, Tenure, and Employability. Significant Behavioral Indicators and follow-up interview questions are available for the PSI-B7 and PSI-B77. Banking industry norms are available for all three versions. All versions contain a distortion and an accuracy scale. Scoring options include Operator-Assisted scoring, Touch-Test telephone, microcomputer, and mail-in service.

Format: Self-administered; untimed: 30 to 45 minutes

Scoring: Computer scored; scoring service available from publisher

Cost: Contact publisher

Clerical

ACER Short Clerical Test (Forms C, D, and E)

1984	Australian Council for Educational Research Limited

Population: Ages 15 years and older

Purpose: Measures speed and accuracy in checking names and numbers and in basic arithmetic; used as a test of clerical aptitude in selecting employees for routine clerical jobs

Description: Multiple-item paper-pencil test measuring an individual's ability to perceive, remember, and check written or printed material (both verbal and numerical) and to perform arithmetic operations. The test is available in three

forms: Forms C and D are used for personnel selection and Form E for guidance and counseling
in business training colleges.
Format: Examiner required; suitable for group
use; timed: 5 minutes per part
Scoring: Hand key
Cost: Contact publisher

ACER Speed and Accuracy Test–Form A

1963	Australian Council for Educational Research Limited

Population: Ages 13 years 6 months and older
Purpose: Measures individuals' checking skills;
useful in the selection of clerical personnel
Description: Multiple-item paper–pencil test
measuring the ability to perceive, retain, and
check relatively familiar material in the form of
printed numbers and names while working in a
limited amount of time. The test contains two
sections: name checking and number checking.
Australian norms are available for school, university, adult, and some occupational groups.
Format: Examiner required; suitable for group
use; timed: 6 minutes per part
Scoring: Hand key
Cost: Contact publisher

Automated Office Battery (AOB) Computer Checking (CC-2)

1990	SHL Canada

Population: Adults in administrative and clerical
jobs
Purpose: Selection and development of staff using automated equipment
Description: Forty-item test to check input
against printout. For selection and development
of staff using automated equipment. Also available in French, Chinese, Japanese, and Korean.
Format: Examiner required; individual administration; untimed: 12 minutes
Scoring: Hand key; machine scored; scoring
service available
Cost: Contact publisher

Automated Skills Assessment Program (ASAP)
Wallace Judd

1992	Wonderlic Personnel Test, Inc.

Population: Ages 18 years and older

Purpose: Measures clerical skills; used in
preemployment selection
Description: Computer-administered test with
five subtests: typing, 10 key, data entry, spelling,
and filing.
Format: Self-administered; timed and untimed
Scoring: Computer scored
Cost: 25 Forms $65.00; 100 Forms $135.00

Clerical Abilities Battery (CAB)

1987	The Psychological Corporation

Population: Adults
Purpose: Assesses clerical skills
Description: Contains seven subtests that measure clerical tasks of filing, copying information,
comparing information, using tables, proofreading, addition and subtraction, and reasoning
with numbers.
Format: Examiner required; suitable for group
use; timed: 5 to 20 minutes
Scoring: Hand key
Cost: Examination Kit (one booklet for each subtest, manual) $55.00

Clerical Aptitude Tests
*Andrew Kobal, J. Wayne Wrightstone,
Andrew J. MacElroy*

1961	Psychometric Affiliates

Population: Grade 7 to adult
Purpose: Assesses aptitude for clerical work;
used for screening job applicants
Description: Three-part paper–pencil test measuring clerical aptitudes, including business practice; number checking; and date, name, and address checking. Scores correlate with job success.
Format: Examiner required; suitable for group
use; timed: 40 minutes
Scoring: Hand key
Cost: Specimen Set $4.00; 25 Tests $8.75

Clerical Aptitudes

1947	NCS Pearson Reid London House

Population: Adults
Purpose: Assesses general aptitudes necessary
for clerical work; used in employee screening
and placing
Description: Three-part paper–pencil test measuring office vocabulary, office arithmetic, and office checking. The tests indicate the ability to

learn tasks usually performed in various clerical jobs. The office vocabulary test (48 items) measures command of basic vocabulary and verbal relations. The arithmetic test (24 items) requires application of basic math processes to the solution of practical problems. The checking test (144 items) measures the ability to perceive details easily and rapidly.

Format: Examiner required; suitable for group use; timed: 25 minutes

Scoring: Hand key

Cost: Contact publisher

Clerical Series Tests

Date not provided	International Personnel Management Association

Population: Adults

Purpose: Measures entry-level skills

Description: The Clerical Series 1-A includes grammar, punctuation, vocabulary, spelling, and basic filing skills. The Clerical Series 1-B includes reasoning, basic math calculations, and following written instructions.

Format: Examiner required; individual administration; 40 minutes

Scoring: Examiner evaluated; machine scoring

Cost: Combined Clerical Module Test Booklets $12.50

Clerical Skills Series, Revised
Martin M. Bruce

1990	Martin M. Bruce, PhD

Population: Adults

Purpose: Assesses the language, physical coordination, and mathematical abilities necessary for various clerical jobs; used for screening prospective employees, measuring student skills, and evaluating current employees

Description: Ten-category paper–pencil test series covering alphabetizing, filing, arithmetic, clerical speed and accuracy, coding, eye–hand accuracy, grammar and punctuation, spelling, vocabulary, and word fluency. The series consists of 10 short tests, six of which are timed. Suitable for individuals with physical, hearing, or visual impairments.

Format: Examiner required for timed items; suitable for group use; timed: 2 to 8 minutes per section

Scoring: Hand key

Cost: Specimen Set (total series) $64.35

Clerical Skills Test Series

1990	Walden Personnel Testing and Consulting, Inc.

Population: Adults

Purpose: Used for measuring clerical skills

Description: Series of tests that measure attention to detail, problem solving, numerical skills, spelling, alphabetizing and filing, grammar and punctuation, vocabulary, reading comprehension, receptionist skills, keyboard skills, 10-key calculator, bookkeeping, PC graphics, coding, manual dexterity, electronics knowledge, mechanical comprehension, and spatial perception.

Format: Examiner required; suitable for group use; timed: 1 hour, 45 minutes

Scoring: Hand key; on-line administration available for some tests

Cost: 20 Tests $260.00

Clerical Staff Selector

1984	Walden Personnel Testing and Consulting, Inc.

Population: Adults

Purpose: Evaluates candidates of all levels of experience for clerical positions

Description: Multiple-item tests measuring skills required for various clerical positions, including accounting, inventory, secretarial, and factory. Skills measured are problem solving, coding, attention to detail, manual dexterity, alphabetizing and filing, spelling, grammar and punctuation, and numerical facility. Also available in French.

Format: Examiner required; suitable for group use; timed: 30 minutes; untimed: 30 minutes

Scoring: Hand key; scoring service provided

Cost: $45.00 per person

CRT Skills Test

1995	NCS Pearson Reid London House

Population: Adults

Purpose: Measures individual's ability to enter alpha and numeric data and retrieve and interpret files; used to measure skills for selection and placement decisions for data-entry operators and customer service representatives

Description: Computerized test consists of three parts. The first part assesses speed and accuracy in entering both alpha and numeric data. The second part assesses speed and accuracy in entering numeric data only. The third part assesses the ability to retrieve customer files and identify the correct answers to assorted customer questions.

Format: Examiner required; individual administration; timed: 5 to 10 minutes

Scoring: Computer scored

Cost: Contact publisher

Curtis Verbal-Clerical Skills Tests
James W. Curtis

1964	Psychometric Affiliates

Population: Ages 16 to adult

Purpose: Assesses clerical and verbal abilities; used to evaluate job applicants

Description: Four multiple-item paper–pencil tests of clerical abilities. The tests are Computation, measuring practical arithmetic; Checking, measuring perceptual speed and accuracy; Comprehension, measuring reading vocabulary; and Capacity, measuring logical reasoning ability.

Format: Examiner required; suitable for group use; timed: 2 minutes per test

Scoring: Hand key

Cost: Specimen Set $5.00; 25 Tests (specify form) $4.00

General Clerical Test–Revised

Date not provided	The Psychological Corporation

Population: Adults

Purpose: Assesses clerical aptitude; used for selecting applicants and evaluating clerical employees for promotion

Description: Multiple-item paper–pencil test of three types of abilities needed for clerical jobs: clerical speed and accuracy, numerical ability, and verbal ability. The clerical subtest involves finding errors by comparing copy with the original and using an alphabetical file. The numerical subtest requires the applicant to solve arithmetic problems, find numerical errors, and solve numerical word problems. The verbal subtest involves correcting spelling errors, answering questions about reading passages, understanding word meanings, and correcting grammatical errors. Separate booklets for the clerical and numerical subtests combined and the verbal subtest only are available for use where one ability is of consideration.

Format: Self-administered; timed: 46 minutes

Scoring: Hand key

Cost: Examination Kit (1 copy of each test booklet, manual, answer key) $50.00

Hay Aptitude Test Battery
Edward N. Hay

1984	Wonderlic Personnel Test, Inc.

Population: Adults

Purpose: Identifies job applicants with the greatest aptitude for handling alphabetical and numerical clerical detail; used to select personnel for office and clerical positions, and trainee positions requiring innate perceptual skills

Description: Four paper–pencil tests assessing clerical and numerical aptitude: Warm-Up, Number Perception Test, Name Finding Test, and Number Series Completion Test. The Warm-Up Test, which is not scored, is designed to prepare the examinee for testing. The Number Perception Test (4 minutes) assesses numerical accuracy. Applicants must identify exact pairs of numbers from groups of similar pairs. Results do not necessarily indicate general mental ability. The Name Finding Test (4 minutes) screens the applicant's short-term memory and word accuracy. The examinee must read words and retain them long enough to verify them. The Number Series Completion Test (4 minutes) assesses numerical reasoning abilities. Also available in Spanish and French.

Format: Examiner required; suitable for group use; timed: 13 minutes total

Scoring: Hand key

Cost: 25 sets of Forms $130.00; 100 Sets $300.00

Hay Aptitude Test Battery: Name Finding
Edward N. Hay

1984	Wonderlic Personnel Test, Inc.

Population: Adults

Purpose: Measures ability to check and verify names quickly and accurately; used to select office and clerical personnel

Description: Paper–pencil 32-item multiple-choice test assessing the ability to read names and hold them in memory long enough to accurately identify them from four similarly spelled names on the back of the same sheet. The task is similar to many clerical tasks, including making bookkeeping entries or typing invoices or checks. Also available in French and Spanish.

Format: Examiner required; suitable for group use; timed: 4 minutes

Scoring: Hand key

Cost: 25 Forms $52.50; 100 Forms $105.00

Hay Aptitude Test Battery: Number Perception
Edward N. Hay

1984   Wonderlic Personnel Test, Inc.

Population: Adult

Purpose: Measures ability to check pairs of numbers and identify those that are the same; used to select office and clerical personnel

Description: Paper-pencil 200-item test measuring speed and accuracy of numerical checking. Each test item consists of a pair of numbers and the applicant decides whether they are the same or different. Items are designed to include the most common clerical errors.

Format: Examiner required; suitable for group use; timed: 4 minutes

Scoring: Hand key

Cost: 25 Forms $52.50; 100 Forms $105.00

Hay Aptitude Test Battery: Number Series Completion
Edward N. Hay

1984   Wonderlic Personnel Test, Inc.

Population: Adults

Purpose: Measures the ability to deduce the pattern in a series of six numbers and provide the seventh and eighth numbers in the series; used to select office and clerical personnel

Description: Paper-pencil 30-item test assessing numerical reasoning abilities. Each item presents a series of six numbers (1 to 3 digits) related by an unknown pattern. Applicants must provide the next two numbers in the series. Good clerks can find the additional numbers more readily than poor ones. Also available in French and Spanish.

Format: Examiner required; suitable for group use

Scoring: Hand key

Cost: 25 Forms $52.50; 100 Forms $105.00

IPI Job-Field Series: Clerical Staff

1997   Industrial Psychology International Ltd.

Population: Ages 16 years and older

Purpose: Assesses skills and personality of applicants for supervisory positions in an office setting; used to screen for the positions of administrator, controller, department head, and vice president

Description: Multiple-item paper-pencil battery

of seven aptitude and two personality tests. The tests are Judgment, Parts, Fluency, Office Terms, Numbers, Neurotic Personality Factor, Contact Personality Factor, Perception, and Memory. For individual test descriptions, see the IPI Employee Aptitude Series. Also available in French and Spanish.

Format: Examiner required; suitable for group use; timed: 82 minutes

Scoring: Hand keys

Cost: Starter Kit (test materials for 5 applicants, scoring keys, manuals) $80.00; Test Package $12.00 per applicant

Minnesota Clerical Assessment Battery (MCAB)

1995   Assessment Systems Corporation

Population: Adults

Purpose: Assesses six job-relevant clerical skills (typing, proofreading, filing, business math, business vocabulary, and clerical knowledge)

Description: Created through an extensive research and development effort, including a detailed job analysis of clerical jobs and the kinds of tasks that are performed on those jobs, as well as the knowledge, skills and abilities that are required to perform those jobs successfully. Based on results of the job analysis, test questions were constructed to assess those skills that are essential to clerical employees. The development of the tests and questions was a lengthy process culminating in six tests that are reliable measures of the essential skills for clerical employees.

Format: Self-administered; untimed: 90 minutes

Scoring: Computer scored

Cost: Contact publisher

Minnesota Clerical Test (MCT)
D. M. Andrew, D. G. Peterson, H. P. Longstaff

1979   The Psychological Corporation

Population: Adults

Purpose: Measures ability to see differences or errors in pairs of names and pairs of numbers; used to select clerical applicants

Description: Multiple-item paper-pencil test of speed and accuracy of visual perception. Items are pairs of names and numbers. The applicant checks each pair that is identical. The test predicts performance in numerous jobs, including adding machine operators, clerical employees, key machine operators, and filing and cataloging personnel. Materials include optional tapes for test administration.

Format: Examiner required; suitable for group use; timed: 15 minutes

Scoring: Hand key

Cost: Examination Kit (test booklet, manual) $32.00; Scoring Key $25.00

Office Arithmetic Test–Form CA
Roland T. Ramsay

1990	Ramsay Corporation

Population: Adults

Purpose: Assesses math skills necessary for the position of office clerk; used for hiring

Description: Paper-pencil 40-item multiple-choice test assessing addition and subtraction of 1-, 2-, and 3-digit whole numbers and decimals; multiplication and division of 1- and 2-digit whole numbers and decimals; and reading of simple charts and tables. Materials include reusable booklet, answer sheet, and manual with key.

Format: Examiner required; suitable for group use; untimed: 30 minutes

Scoring: Hand key

Cost: Kit (10 test booklets, 100 answer sheets, scoring key, 1 test manual) $200.00

Office Proficiency Assessment & Certification® (OPAC®)

Date not provided	NCS Pearson Reid London House

Population: Adults

Purpose: Assesses general office and basic software skills

Description: Consists of four modules: keyboarding and word processing, language arts and records management, financial record keeping and applications, and 10 key and data entry. The modules may be used independently of each other.

Format: Computer administered; time set by administrator

Scoring: Computer scored

Cost: Contact publisher

Office Reading Test–Form G
Roland T. Ramsay

1990	Ramsay Corporation

Population: Adults

Purpose: Assesses reading skills necessary for office workers; used for hiring

Description: Paper-pencil 40-item multiple-choice test based on five written passages: Operating the Copier, Travel Arrangements, Operating a Computer, The Business Letter, and Telephone Procedures. Materials include reusable booklet, answer sheet, and manual with key.

Format: Examiner required; suitable for group use; untimed: 30 minutes

Scoring: Hand key

Cost: Kit (10 test booklets, 100 answer sheets, scoring key, test manual) $200.00

Office Skills Achievement Test
Paul L. Mellenbruch

1970	Psychometric Affiliates

Population: Grades 10 to adult

Purpose: Assesses clerical skills; used for educational and vocational guidance and for screening applicant for employment

Description: Multiple-item paper-pencil test measuring several important office and clerical skills, including business letter writing, English usage, checking, filing, simple arithmetic, and following written instructions. The test was developed in office work situations, using clerical employees.

Format: Examiner required; suitable for group use; timed: 20 minutes

Scoring: Hand key

Cost: Specimen Set (test, manual, key) $5.00; 25 Tests $8.75

Office Skills Assessment Battery (OSAB®)

Date not provided	NCS Pearson Reid London House

Population: Adults

Purpose: Assesses the attitudes and skills needed to be productive, dependable office employees

Description: A brief, yet comprehensive questionnaire. One section, the Attitudes Inventory, addresses interest, motivation, and knowledge related to office work; a second section, the Skills Inventory, measures clerical and language skills.

Format: Self- or computer administered; untimed: 15 minutes

Scoring: Telephone scoring available; computer scoring; scannable form

Cost: Contact publisher

Office Skills Tests (OST ™)

| 1977 | NCS Pearson Reid London House |

Population: Adults

Purpose: Assesses clerical ability of job applicants; used for employee selection and placement

Description: Twelve tests suitable for screening clerks, accounting clerks, typists, secretaries/stenographers, library assistants, and other office personnel. The tests are Checking, Coding, Filing, Forms Completion, Grammar, Numerical Skills, Oral Directions, Punctuation, Reading Comprehension, Spelling, Typing, and Vocabulary. Each test is available in two forms. Norms are provided for timed and untimed administration.

Format: Examiner required; suitable for group use; untimed: 3 to 10 minutes per test

Scoring: Hand key; computer scored

Cost: Contact publisher

Perceptual Speed (Identical Forms)

L. L. Thurstone, T. E. Jeffrey

| 1984 | NCS Pearson Reid London House |

Population: Adults

Purpose: Measures ability to identify rapidly the similarities and differences in visual configurations; used to select clerical personnel or workers in occupations that require rapid perception of inaccuracies in written materials and diagrams

Description: Paper–pencil 140-item test of perceptual skill. The subject selects the figure among five choices that appears to be most similar to the illustration.

Format: Examiner required; suitable for group use; timed: 5 minutes

Scoring: Hand key

Cost: Contact publisher

Personnel Test Battery (PTB) Audio Checking (CP8.1)

| 1991 | SHL Canada |

Population: Adults

Purpose: Assesses an individual's ability to receive and check information that is presented orally; used to select clerical staff who must process information presented orally as in telesales or airline and hotel bookings

Description: Multiple-choice 60-item test in which the task is to listen to a string of numbers or letters presented on an audiocassette and select the identical string from the five choices presented in the question booklet. Three subtests cover letters, numbers, and mixed letters and numbers. The test is suitable for individuals with minimal educational qualifications. Also available in French.

Format: Examiner required; individual administration; untimed: 10 minutes

Scoring: Hand key; machine scored; scoring service available

Cost: Contact publisher

Personnel Test Battery (PTB) Basic Checking (CP7.1)

| 1991 | SHL Canada |

Population: Adults

Purpose: Measures speed and accuracy in checking a variety of materials at a very basic level; used for selection of clerical and general staff concerned with simple routine checking

Description: Forty-item multiple-choice test consisting of two subtests. One involves checking a list of numbers and the other involves checking a list of letters. In each subtest, strings of numbers or letters are presented. These are compared with another page from which the identical string must be selected (from five choices). The test is suitable for individuals with minimal educational qualifications. Also available in French.

Format: Examiner required; individual administration; untimed: 5 minutes

Scoring: Hand key; machine scored; scoring service available

Cost: Contact publisher

Personnel Test Battery (PTB) Classification (CP4.1)

| 1993 | SHL Canada |

Population: Adults

Purpose: Measures the ability to perceive and classify material in accordance with a set of instructions; appropriate when data handling, filing, and following instructions are important skills

Description: Sixty-item test representing a clerical task in which a number of sales order forms must be filed. The candidate classifies each order and then records the order in coded form. Some orders ("account sales") must be filed alphabetically and others ("cash sales") must be classified under seven categories of goods purchased. Also available in French.

Format: Examiner required; individual administration; untimed: 7 minutes

Scoring: Hand key; machine scored; scoring service available

Cost: Contact publisher

Personnel Test Battery (PTB) Clerical Checking (CP3.1)

1993   SHL Canada

Population: Adults

Purpose: Measures ability to perceive and check a variety of materials quickly and accurately

Description: Forty-item proofreading test in which two lists of information about hotels are presented; one list is handwritten and the other is printed. The material contained in the lists includes names, numbers, and symbols. The candidates must compare the two lists and note any errors in accordance with a given code (designed to represent an actual clerical task). Also available in French.

Format: Examiner required; individual administration; untimed: 7 minutes

Scoring: Hand key; machine scored; scoring service available

Cost: Contact publisher

Personnel Test Battery (PTB) Text Checking (CP9.1)

1993   SHL Canada

Population: Adults

Purpose: Measures proofreading speed and accuracy

Description: Fifty-item test that assesses speed and accuracy in proofreading, an important skill in the production of all kinds of documents. The test requires detailed proofreading from one text to another, with candidates required to specify the exact nature of errors identified. Also available in French.

Format: Examiner required; individual administration; untimed: 10 minutes

Scoring: Hand key; machine scored; scoring service available

Cost: Contact publisher

PSI Basic Skills Tests for Business, Industry, and Government: Classifying (BST #11)

W. W. Ruch, A. N. Shub, S. M. Moinat, D. A. Dye

1981   Psychological Services, Inc.

Population: Adults

Purpose: Measures ability to place information into appropriate categories; used to select customer service, clerical, and administrative personnel

Description: Multiple-choice 48-item test presenting four sets of data. Each set contains 12 items that must be properly categorized. The test is available in two equivalent paper–pencil forms and in computerized form. Transported validity study is available.

Format: Examiner required for paper–pencil forms; suitable for group use; timed: 5 minutes

Scoring: Hand key; may be computer scored; scoring software available

Cost: Contact publisher

PSI Basic Skills Tests for Business, Industry, and Government: Coding (BST #12)

W. W. Ruch, A. N. Shub, S. M. Moinat, D. A. Dye

1981   Psychological Services, Inc.

Population: Adults

Purpose: Measures ability to code information according to a prescribed system; used to select customer service, clerical, and administrative personnel

Description: Multiple-choice 72-item test in which the subjects are given systems for coding information (each system codes four categories of related information). For each test item, the subject must code the given information into categories. The test is available in two equivalent paper–pencil forms and in computerized form. Transported validity study is available.

Format: Examiner required for paper-pencil forms; suitable for group use; timed: 5 minutes

Scoring: Hand key; may be computer scored; scoring software available

Cost: Contact publisher

PSI Basic Skills Tests for Business, Industry, and Government: Computation (BST #4)
W. W. Ruch, A. N. Shub, S. M. Moinat, D. A. Dye

1981   Psychological Services, Inc.

Population: Adults

Purpose: Measures ability to solve arithmetic problems; used to select customer service, clerical, and administrative personnel

Description: Forty-item multiple-choice test measuring the ability to add, subtract, multiply, and divide, using whole numbers, fractions, and decimals. The test is available in two equivalent paper-pencil forms and in computerized form. Transported validity study is available.

Format: Examiner required for paper-pencil forms; suitable for group use; timed: 5 minutes

Scoring: Hand key; may be computer scored; scoring software available

Cost: Contact publisher

PSI Basic Skills Tests for Business, Industry, and Government: Decision Making (BST #6)
W. W. Ruch, A. N. Shub, S. M. Moinat, D. A. Dye

1981   Psychological Services, Inc.

Population: Adults

Purpose: Measures ability to read a set of procedures and apply them to new situations by determining the appropriate action; used to select customer service, clerical, and administrative personnel

Description: Paper-pencil 20-item multiple-choice test in which sets of procedures (related to clerical or office duties) and a set of action codes for implementing the procedures are described. The examinee is presented with a number of problems and must decide the course of action for each item and mark the appropriate action code. The test is available in two equiva-

lent paper-pencil forms. Transported validity study is available.

Format: Examiner required; suitable for group use; timed: 5 minutes

Scoring: Hand key; may be computer scored; scoring software available

Cost: Contact publisher

PSI Basic Skills Tests for Business, Industry, and Government: Filing Names (BST #13)
W. W. Ruch, A. N. Shub, S. M. Moinat, D. A. Dye

1981   Psychological Services, Inc.

Population: Adults

Purpose: Measures ability to file simple entries alphabetically; used to select customer service, clerical, and administrative personnel

Description: Fifty-item multiple-choice test in which the subject is presented with a name, followed by a list of four other names (arranged alphabetically). The subject "files" the given name at the beginning, between two of the names, or at the end of the list. The test is available in two equivalent paper-pencil forms and in computerized form. Transported validity study is available.

Format: Examiner required for paper-pencil forms; suitable for group use; timed: 90 seconds

Scoring: Hand key; may be computer scored; scoring software available

Cost: Contact publisher

PSI Basic Skills Tests for Business, Industry, and Government: Filing Numbers (BST #14)
W. W. Ruch, A. N. Shub, S. M. Moinat, D. A. Dye

1981   Psychological Services, Inc.

Population: Adults

Purpose: Measures ability to file numbers in numerical order; used to select customer service, clerical, and administrative personnel

Description: Multiple-choice test in which each of 75 test items consists of a 6-digit number to be filed numerically in a list of four other 6-digit numbers (already arranged in numerical order). The test is available in two equivalent paper-pencil forms and in computerized form. Transported validity study is available.

Format: Examiner required for paper–pencil forms; suitable for group use; timed: 2 minutes

Scoring: Hand key; may be computer scored; scoring software available

Cost: Contact publisher

PSI Basic Skills Tests for Business, Industry, and Government: Following Oral Directions (BST #7)

W. W. Ruch, A. N. Shub, S. M. Moinat, D. A. Dye

1981   Psychological Services, Inc.

Population: Adults

Purpose: Measures ability to listen to information and instructions presented orally and answer questions about what is heard; used to select customer service, clerical, and administrative personnel

Description: Paper–pencil 24-item multiple-choice test in which the subjects listen to a 6½ minute prerecorded cassette tape and then answer questions about the content of the tape. The tape is played only once (no rewinding or stopping of the tape is allowed), and subjects are encouraged to take written notes during the playing of the tape. The tape is a recording of conversations that take place in an employment setting.

Format: Examiner required; suitable for group use; timed: 5 minutes

Scoring: Hand key; may be computer scored; scoring software available

Cost: Contact publisher

PSI Basic Skills Tests for Business, Industry, and Government: Following Written Directions (BST #8)

W. W. Ruch, A. N. Shub, S. M. Moinat, D. A. Dye

1981   Psychological Services, Inc.

Population: Adults

Purpose: Measures ability to read, understand, and apply sets of written instructions; used to select customer service, clerical, and administrative personnel

Description: Multiple-choice 36-item test requir-

ing examinees to read sets of rules and apply them to a number of case examples. The test is available in two equivalent paper–pencil forms and in computerized form. Transported validity study is available.

Format: Examiner required for paper–pencil forms; suitable for group use; timed: 5 minutes

Scoring: Hand key; may be computer scored; scoring software available

Cost: Contact publisher

PSI Basic Skills Tests for Business, Industry, and Government: Forms Checking (BST #9)

W. W. Ruch, A. N. Shub, S. M. Moinat, D. A. Dye

1981   Psychological Services, Inc.

Population: Adults

Purpose: Measures ability to verify the accuracy of completed forms; used to select customer service, clerical, and administrative personnel

Description: True–false 42-item test in which the examinee verifies the accuracy of information in clerical forms filled out using information in written paragraphs. The examinee must check a number of the entries on each form against the information in the paragraphs to determine whether the entries are correct or incorrect. The test is available in two equivalent paper–pencil forms and in computerized form. Transported validity study is available.

Format: Examiner required for paper–pencil forms; suitable for group use; timed: 5 minutes

Scoring: Hand key; may be computer scored; scoring software available

Cost: Contact publisher

PSI Basic Skills Tests for Business, Industry, and Government: Language Skills (BST #1)

W. W. Ruch, A. N. Shub, S. M. Moinat, D. A. Dye

1981   Psychological Services, Inc.

Population: Adults

Purpose: Measures language skills used in proofing written material

Description: Multiple-choice 25-item test in which examinee reads a sentence, part of which is underlined, and determines whether the underlined portion contains errors in spelling, punctuation, capitalization, grammar, or usage. The test is available in two equivalent paper-pencil forms and in computerized form. Transported validity study is available.

Format: Examiner required for paper-pencil forms; suitable for group use; timed: 10 minutes

Scoring: Hand key; may be computer scored; scoring software available

Cost: Contact publisher

PSI Basic Skills Tests for Business, Industry, and Government: Problem Solving (BST #5)
W. W. Ruch, A. N. Shub, S. M. Moinat, D. A. Dye

1981	Psychological Services, Inc.

Population: Adults

Purpose: Measures ability to solve written math problems

Description: Multiple-choice 25-item test in which examinee reads a word problem and applies the appropriate arithmetic operations to solve the problem. The test is available in two equivalent paper-pencil forms and in computerized form. Transported validity study is available.

Format: Examiner required for paper-pencil forms; suitable for group use; timed: 5 minutes

Scoring: Hand key; may be computer scored; scoring software available

Cost: Contact publisher

PSI Basic Skills Tests for Business, Industry, and Government: Reading Comprehension (BST #2)
W. W. Ruch, A. N. Shub, S. M. Moinat, D. A. Dye

1981	Psychological Services, Inc.

Population: Adults

Purpose: Measures basic reading comprehension; used to select clerical and administrative personnel

Description: Paper-pencil 23-item multiple-choice test measuring the ability to read short passages and answer literal and inferential questions about them.

Format: Examiner required; suitable for group use; timed: 10 minutes

Scoring: Hand key; may be computer scored; scoring software available

Cost: Contact publisher

PSI Basic Skills Tests for Business, Industry, and Government: Reasoning (BST #10)
W. W. Ruch, A. N. Shub, S. M. Moinat, D. A. Dye

1981	Psychological Services, Inc.

Population: Adults

Purpose: Measures ability to analyze a list of facts and draw valid and logical conclusions from that information; used to select clerical and administrative personnel

Description: Multiple-choice 30-item test consisting of six lists of facts (one-sentence statements), with five possible conclusions for each list of facts. The examinee must read each list of facts and decide whether each conclusion is definitely true, definitely false, or unknown based on the given facts. The test is available in two equivalent paper-pencil forms and in computerized form. Transported validity study is available.

Format: Examiner required for paper-pencil forms; suitable for group use; timed: 5 minutes

Scoring: Hand key; may be computer scored; scoring software available

Cost: Contact publisher

PSI Basic Skills Tests for Business, Industry, and Government: Visual Speed and Accuracy (BST #15)
W. W. Ruch, A. N. Shub, S. M. Moinat, D. A. Dye

1981	Psychological Services, Inc.

Population: Adults

Purpose: Measures ability to see details quickly and accurately; used to select clerical and administrative personnel

Description: Multiple-choice 150-item test in which each test item consists of two series of numbers and symbols. The examinee compares the numbers or symbols and determines whether they are the same or different. The test is available in two equivalent paper-pencil forms and in computerized form. Transported validity study is available.

Format: Examiner required for paper-pencil forms; suitable for group use; timed: 5 minutes

Scoring: Hand key; may be computer scored; scoring software available

Cost: Contact publisher

PSI Basic Skills Tests for Business, Industry, and Government: Vocabulary (BST #3)
W. W. Ruch, A. N. Shub, S. M. Moinat, D. A. Dye

1981	Psychological Services, Inc.

Population: Adults

Purpose: Measures the ability to identify the correct synonym for the word underlined in each sentence; used to select clerical and office workers

Description: Multiple-choice 45-item test in which each item consists of a sentence with one word underlined, followed by four words. The examinee must select the word meaning the same or about the same as the word that is underlined in the sentence. The test is available in two equivalent paper–pencil forms and in computerized form. Transported validity study is available.

Format: Examiner required for paper–pencil forms; suitable for group use; timed: 5 minutes

Scoring: Hand key; may be computer scored; scoring software available

Cost: Contact publisher

Secretarial Staff Selector

1984	Walden Personnel Testing and Consulting, Inc.

Population: Adults

Purpose: Evaluates candidates of all levels of experience for secretarial positions

Description: Multiple-item paper–pencil set of seven timed subtests and two optional subtests available in three formats for assessing attention to detail, alphabetizing and filing skills, grammar and punctuation, spelling and vocabulary, manual dexterity, logical and problem-solving abilities, numerical skills, desire for people contact (optional), and emotional stability (optional). The tests are used for selecting senior clerks, secretaries, and administrative assistants. Also available in French.

Format: Examiner required; suitable for group use; timed: 75 minutes

Scoring: Scoring service available

Cost: $299.00 each

Short Employment Tests® (SET®)
G. K. Bennett, Marjorie Gelink

1951; Manual updated in 1993	The Psychological Corporation

Population: Adults

Purpose: Measures verbal, numerical, and clerical skills; used to select qualified individuals for a variety of administrative and entry-level positions

Description: Three 5-minute subtests: verbal, numerical, and clerical aptitude. May be used as a complete battery to produce a total score or as individual tests. Available in four forms.

Format: Examiner required; suitable for group use; timed: 5 minutes per subtest

Scoring: Hand key

Cost: Examination Kit (booklet for each of three tests and manual) Form 1 $43.00; Forms 2, 3, and 4 $47.00

Short Tests of Clerical Ability (STCA™)

1959	NCS Pearson Reid London House

Population: Adults

Purpose: Assesses aptitudes and abilities important to the successful completion of typical office tasks; used for selection and placement of office personnel

Description: Multiple-item paper–pencil battery consisting of seven subtests: arithmetic skills, business vocabulary, checking accuracy, coding, oral and written directions, filing, and language (grammar and mechanics).

Format: Examiner required; suitable for group use; untimed: 3 to 6 minutes per subtest

Scoring: Hand key

Cost: Contact publisher

SkillCheck® Professional Plus

Date not provided	NCS Pearson Reid London House

Population: Adults

Purpose: Assesses software knowledge or keyboard skills

Description: Measures competency on a variety of Windows-based software programs. This unique program offers more than 100 interactive questions covering all levels and functions of a software program. Organizations may choose the basic, standard, or advanced tests or create their own instrument.

Format: Computer administered; time set by administrator

Scoring: Computer scoring

Cost: Contact publisher

TapDance® Skills Testing Software

Date not provided	NCS Pearson Reid London House

Population: Adults

Purpose: Assesses software knowledge or keyboard skills

Description: The comprehensive information provided is designed to help in hiring and placement decisions and also for training needs assessment.

Format: Computer administered; time set by administrator

Scoring: Computer scoring

Cost: Contact publisher

Typing 5

1975	NCS Pearson Reid London House

Population: Adults

Purpose: Measures a person's ability to type a particular kind of assignment; used with a variety of typing positions requiring different skills

Description: Task assessment consisting of three forms measuring typing speed and accuracy. Typing Speed, Form A, consists of a letter with approximately 215 words measuring keystroking speed and accuracy. Business Letter, Form B, for the more experienced typist, measures the ability to set up a business letter and type it quickly and accurately. Numerical, Form C, containing approximately 115 words and 40 numbers, measures speed and accuracy in typing complex material containing words, symbols, and numbers in columns with headings.

Format: Examiner required; suitable for group use; timed: 5 minutes per test (after practice time)

Scoring: Hand key

Cost: Contact publisher

VCWS 5—Clerical Comprehension and Aptitude

1993	Valpar International Corporation

Population: Adults

Purpose: Measures basic clerical aptitude and ability to communicate effectively both verbally and in writing

Description: Manual test features three separate work samples measuring an individual's ability

to perform a variety of clerical tasks and ability to learn the tasks. The test begins with mail sorting and simultaneous phone answering. A tape plays a series of phone conversations at prerecorded intervals, requiring the individual to stop the mail sorting in order to take the phone message. The individual also must complete an alphabetical filing task. In the second section of the test, the individual must use a 10-key adding machine to perform three exercises emphasizing accurate recording of numerical data and basic math skills. In the typing section, the typewriter has been modified to measure a person's typing coordination skills.

Format: Examiner required; individual administration; timed

Scoring: Examiner evaluated

Cost: $2,680.00

Computer

Automated Office Battery (AOB) Coded Instructions (CI3)

1988	SHL Canada

Population: Ages 16 years to adult

Purpose: Measures the ability to understand and follow instructions coded into machine-oriented language

Description: Forty-item test assessing the ability to understand and follow coded instructions. Candidates are presented with instructions on how to enter and retrieve information from a machine. They must understand the instruction in the text and decide on the appropriate course of action for each question. The content is office based and related to technology within the office environment, particularly to the kinds of instructions that an individual must follow when operating computer systems and word processors.

Format: Examiner required; individual administration; untimed: 18 minutes

Scoring: Hand key; machine scored; scoring service available

Cost: Contact publisher

Business Analyst Skills Evaluation (BUSAN)

1984	Walden Personnel Testing and Consulting, Inc.

Population: Adults

Purpose: Evaluates aptitude and potential for positions in business systems analysis, procedures analysis, and user department–information systems department interface

Description: Multiple-item paper–pencil test with two groups of subtests. Section 1 subtests measure analytical ability, flow charting, deductive reasoning, procedures and systems analysis, and development of departmental user reports and subsystems. Section 2 subtests measure horizontal interpersonal relationship abilities, people contact desired, emotional stability, stress tolerance, group participation skills, consistency, dominance, adventurousness, maturity, enthusiasm, tough-mindedness, practicality, sophistication, self-sufficiency, and leadership potential.

Format: Examiner required; on-line administration available; suitable for group use; timed: 1 hour 45 minutes

Scoring: Scoring service

Cost: $350.00

Computer Operator Aptitude Battery (COAB)

1973	NCS Pearson Reid London House

Population: Adults

Purpose: Helps predict job performance of computer operators; used by data processing managers and personnel directors to select applicants for computer operator positions

Description: Paper–pencil test predicting success as a computer operator. The test consists of three separately timed subtests: Sequence Recognition, Format Checking, and Logical Thinking.

Format: Examiner required; suitable for group use; timed: 45 minutes

Scoring: Hand key

Cost: Contact publisher

Computer Programmer Aptitude Battery (CPAB™)

1964	NCS Pearson Reid London House

Population: Adults

Purpose: Measures potential for success in the computer programming field; used by data processing managers and personnel directors to identify people with the aptitude for computer programming

Description: Five separately timed paper–pencil subtests measuring verbal meaning, reasoning, letter series, number ability, and diagramming (problem analysis and logical solution). The test is available in a short version, which includes reasoning and diagramming.

Format: Examiner required; suitable for group use; timed: 1 hour 19 minutes

Scoring: Hand key

Cost: Contact publisher

Database Analyst Staff Selector

Date not provided	Walden Personnel Testing and Consulting, Inc.

Population: Adults

Purpose: Measures analytical reasoning and detail skills necessary for the position of Database Analyst or Database Programmer

Description: Multiple-item tests measuring skills.

Format: Self-administered; untimed: 85 minutes

Scoring: Scoring service

Cost: $319.00

Information Technology Test Series (ITTS) Diagramming (DIT5)

1988	SHL Canada

Population: Adults

Purpose: Measures logical analysis through the ability to follow complex instructions; appropriate for technical occupations and jobs involving systems design, flow charting, and similar skills

Description: Fifty-item multiple-choice test consisting of a series of abstract designs in logical sequences. Respondents must select, from five choices, the design that completes the logical sequence. Candidates must think logically and flexibly. Also available in French.

Format: Examiner required; individual administration; untimed: 20 minutes

Scoring: Hand key; machine scored; scoring service available

Cost: Contact publisher

Information Technology Test Series (ITTS) Spatial Reasoning (SIT7)

1988	SHL Canada

Population: Adults

Purpose: Measures ability to visualize and manipulate shapes in three dimensions when given a two-dimensional drawing

Description: Forty-item multiple-choice test consisting of a series of folded-out cubes and perspective drawings of assembled cubes. The respondents must identify the assembled cubes that could be made from the folded-out cube, each face of which has a different pattern. The test discriminates at a high level and would be relevant for engineers, designers, architects, and information technology staff. Also available in French.

Format: Examiner required; individual administration; untimed: 20 minutes

Scoring: Hand key; machine scored; scoring service available

Cost: Contact publisher

Language-Free Programmer/ Analyst Aptitude Test (LPAT)

| 1999 | Applied Personnel Research |

Population: Adults

Purpose: Measures the aptitude to be a computer programmer/analyst; can be given to a person with no computer training or background; designed for use in personnel selection for trainee and entry-level positions

Description: Objective multiple-item paper–pencil test to measure aptitude and potential rather than knowledge of specific computer language syntax or commands. A "miniature training and evaluation" approach is used for several questions in which the candidates are given information and then asked to apply that information. The test questions resemble tasks done by applications and database programmers. There are three main test areas: reasoning and problem solving, numerical and logical analysis, and understanding and analyzing written documentation. There are nine question types providing nine diagnostic scores and an overall score.

Format: Self-administered; 2 hours

Scoring: Scoring service provided; 1-day turnaround

Cost: Specimen Set (test, sample test report, test manual) $100.00

Microcomputer User Aptitude Test
Richard Label

| 1986 | Walden Personnel Testing and Consulting, Inc. |

Population: Adults

Purpose: Measures aptitude and potential for work with a microcomputer

Description: Multiple-item test measuring the following abilities necessary for working with a microcomputer: logical ability; ability to work with spreadsheets, databases, and operating systems; and vendor manual interpretation. The test consists of five problems that simulate the use of the most commonly used microcomputer applications. Skills are assessed independent of any specific hardware or software.

Format: Examiner required; individual administration; timed: 1 hour

Scoring: Scoring service provided

Cost: $139.00

Network Analyst Staff Selector

| Date not provided | Walden Personnel Testing and Consulting, Inc. |

Population: Adults

Purpose: Measures basic knowledge of data communication systems components and evaluates the candidate's problem-solving ability relevant to common network problems

Description: Multiple-item test measuring the abilities necessary for working with a microcomputer.

Format: Self-administered; untimed: 1 hour 45 minutes

Scoring: Scoring service provided

Cost: Test Booklet and Detailed Report on each candidate $319.00

Network Technician Staff Selector

| Date not provided | Walden Personnel Testing and Consulting, Inc. |

Population: Adults

Purpose: Measures basic knowledge of data communication systems components and evaluates the candidate's problem-solving ability relevant to common network problems

Description: Multiple-item test measuring the abilities necessary for working with a microcomputer.

Format: Self-administered; untimed: 1 hour 45 minutes

Scoring: Scoring service provided

Cost: Test Booklet and Detailed Report on each candidate $319.00

Object-Oriented Programmer Analyst Staff Selector

Date not provided	Walden Personnel Testing and Consulting, Inc.

Population: Adults

Purpose: Measures object-oriented programming ability and specific knowledge of C++

Description: Multiple-item test measuring the abilities necessary for working with a microcomputer.

Format: Self-administered; untimed: 2 hours

Scoring: Scoring service provided

Cost: Test Booklet and Detailed Report on each candidate $319.00

Programmer Analyst Aptitude Test (PAAT)

1984	Walden Personnel Testing and Consulting, Inc.

Population: Adults

Purpose: Evaluates aptitude and potential for computer programming and business analysis positions

Description: Paper–pencil 6-item test assessing logical ability, skill in interpreting business specifications, potential for translating business problems into symbolic logic, and ability to follow complex business procedures and analyze them to supply specific requirements. Available with interpersonal measures. One-hour version available on-line. Also available in French.

Format: Examiner required; suitable for group use; timed: 1 or 2 hours

Scoring: Scoring service provided

Cost: $230.00 (1 hour); $310.00 (2 hour)

Software Knowledge Series

1994	Walden Personnel Testing and Consulting, Inc.

Population: Adults

Purpose: Measures knowledge of software for microcomputers

Description: Additions to the 5-minute knowledge test series: Mac, OS/2, WordPerfect, Novell Netware, Excel, dBASE, Harvard Graphics, Windows, Windows 95, DOS, Word for Windows, UNIX, Lotus, Sybase, and C.

Format: Examiner required; suitable for group use; timed: 75 minutes

Scoring: Scoring service available from publisher

Cost: 20 Tests $219.00

Technical Support Staff Selector

Date not provided	Walden Personnel Testing and Consulting, Inc.

Population: Adults

Purpose: Evaluates knowledge and ability to work in client–server and help desk environments; generally for candidates who provide technical user support for those who must interface with information systems departments

Description: Multiple-item tests measuring skills.

Format: Self-administered; untimed: 1 hour 45 minutes

Scoring: Scoring service available from publisher

Cost: Test Booklet and Detailed Report on each candidate $319.00

Technology and Internet Assessment (TIA)
Michael R. Ealy

Date not provided	H & H Publishing Co., Inc.

Population: Adolescents, adults

Purpose: Designed to determine strengths and weaknesses related to a basic understanding of computer, Internet, and information technology skills

Description: Focuses on eight areas that present barriers for individuals seeking employment and for those striving to succeed in the educational system. The results can be used to provide baseline information for academic instructors and counselors, workplace trainers, and social service professionals. The TIA is administered via the Web. Immediately upon completion, a two-page report is displayed listing the percentile scores for each scale along with suggestions for improving each area.

Format: Self-administered; untimed: 20 to 30 minutes

Scoring: Scored on the Web

Cost: Contact publisher

Wolfe-Winrow CICS/VS Command Level Proficiency Test (WWCICS)
B. W. Winrow

1982	Walden Personnel Testing and Consulting, Inc.

Population: Adults

Purpose: Measures a person's knowledge of IBM CICS/VS Command Level; used for hiring, training, and promoting applications programmers and software specialists

Description: Five-part paper–pencil test measuring general knowledge of CICS/VS concepts, facilities and commands, and the ability to code CICS/VS commands from specifications and debug and test in a CICS/VS environment. The test also includes an optional measure of specific knowledge of Basic Mapping Support and related commands.

Format: Examiner required; suitable for group use; timed: 30 minutes

Scoring: Scoring service provided

Cost: Test and Detailed Report for each candidate $109.00

Wolfe-Winrow DOS/VS JCL Proficiency Test
B. W. Winrow

1982	Walden Personnel Testing and Consulting, Inc.

Population: Adults

Purpose: Measures a person's knowledge of DOS, DOS/VS, or DOS/VSE JSL language; may be used for hiring, training, and promoting purposes

Description: Five-part paper–pencil test measuring the ability to identify common JCL errors, code, overwrite catalogued procedures, and specific knowledge of JCL parameters. Suitable for examining computer operators, DOS JCL analysts, and applications programmers at all experience levels.

Format: Examiner required; suitable for group use; timed: 30 minutes

Scoring: Scoring service provided

Cost: Test and Computer Report for each candidate $109.00

Wolfe-Winrow OS JCL Proficiency Test
B. W. Winrow

1982	Walden Personnel Testing and Consulting, Inc.

Population: Adults

Purpose: Measures a person's knowledge of IBM OS/JCL language; used for hiring, promoting, and training computer operators, analysts, and programmers

Description: Five-part paper–pencil test measuring general knowledge of JCL statements and parameters and understanding of JCL parameters, catalogued procedures, symbolic parameters, GDGs, and overriding JCL. The test also assesses the ability to identify OS/JCL errors and code OS/JCL.

Format: Examiner required; suitable for group use; timed: 30 minutes

Scoring: Scoring service provided

Cost: Test and Computer Report $109.00 per person

Wolfe-Winrow Structured COBOL
B. W. Winrow

1982	Walden Personnel Testing and Consulting, Inc.

Population: Adults

Purpose: Assesses a person's knowledge of structured COBOL; used for hiring, evaluating existing staff, evaluating training needs and effectiveness, and promotion

Description: Five-question paper–pencil test measuring the ability to identify structured programming tools for COBOL, use concepts such as table look-up and debugging aids, define storage attributes and code PICTURE clauses for COBOL, code from specifications, and understand arithmetic operations and programming efficiencies.

Format: Examiner required; suitable for group use; timed: 30 minutes

Scoring: Scoring service provided

Cost: Test and Report $109.00 per person

Wolfe-Winrow TSO/SPF Proficiency Test (WWTSO)
B. W. Winrow

1982	Walden Personnel Testing and Consulting, Inc.

Population: Adults

Purpose: Assesses a person's knowledge of IBM TSO/SPF; used for hiring, training, and promoting programmers and software specialists

Description: Five-part paper–pencil test evaluating an applicant's knowledge of TSO/SPF features and commands.

Format: Examiner required; suitable for group use; timed: 30 minutes

Scoring: Scoring service provided

Cost: Test and Detailed Report $109.00 per person

Customer Service

Assessment of Service Readiness (ASR)

| 1993 | Life Office Management Association |

Population: Adults

Purpose: Assesses entry-level customer service skills; used for selection and development of employees in insurance/financial services

Description: The system has two parts. The first consists of videotaped situations that present job candidates with difficult customer service scenarios. Candidates indicate how they would handle or resolve the situations by responding to a series of paper-pencil questions. The second part is a background information inventory that asks questions about experiences, interests, and activities that lead to the development of customer service skills.

Format: Examiner required; individual and group administration; timed: 90 minutes

Scoring: Computer scored

Cost: Contact publisher

Customer Service Applicant Inventory (CSAI™)

| Date not provided | NCS Pearson Reid London House |

Population: Adults

Purpose: Evaluates skills and attitudes considered necessary for service-oriented employees

Description: Measures customer service, teamwork, communication, stress tolerance, honesty, drug avoidance, safety, training readiness, applied math, employability index, validity/candidness, and validity/accuracy to identify people who can effectively handle concerns, establish rapport with other employees, and work effectively in group or individual situations.

Format: Self-administered; untimed: 50 minutes

Scoring: Computer scored

Cost: Contact publisher

Customer Service Profile (CSP™)

| Date not provided | NCS Pearson Reid London House |

Population: Adults

Purpose: Evaluates applicants' attitudes

Description: The CSP dimensions help identify people who can effectively establish rapport with customers, sell promotional items, and display pride and enthusiasm on the job. Significant Behavioral Indicators are included in a report that provides narrative evaluation of details on an individual's strengths and weaknesses.

Format: Self-administration; untimed: 20 minutes

Scoring: Computer scored; telephone scoring available

Cost: Contact publisher

Electrical

ElecTest Form A-C
Roland T. Ramsay

| 1997 | Ramsay Corporation |

Population: Adults

Purpose: Assesses the ability to answer electrical and electronics questions; used for hiring and promotion for trade and craft jobs

Description: Paper–pencil 60-item multiple-choice test. The categories are Power Dist., Construction and Installation, Tools, Motors, Digital and Analog Electronics, Schematics, Print Reading and Control Circuits, AC/DC Theory and Elec. Maint., Computers/PLC, Power Supplies, and Mechanical and Hand and Power Tools.

Format: Examiner required; suitable for group use; untimed: 60 minutes

Scoring: Self-scored

Cost: Test Booklet $15.00 (minimum of 20); Administration Manual $24.95

Electrical & Electronics Test (EET)
John D. Morgan

| Date not provided | Test Agency, Limited |

Population: Adolescents, adults

Purpose: Assesses knowledge and ability in electrical and electronics fields

Description: Thirty-item paper–pencil test for determining knowledge of fundamental laws, symbols, and definitions related to electricity and electronics. The test emphasizes the ability to use knowledge in practical situations.

Format: Examiner required; suitable for group use; timed: 15 minutes

Scoring: Hand key; scoring service available
Cost: Contact publisher

Electrical Maintenance Trainee—Form UKE-IC
Roland T. Ramsay

1998	Ramsay Corporation

Population: Adults
Purpose: Measures electrical knowledge and skills
Description: Sixty items assess skills in these 11 areas: motors; digital and analog electronics; schematics and electrical print reading; control; power supplies; basic AC/DC theory; construction, installation, and distribution; test instruments; computers and PLC; mechanical, equipment operation, and hand and power tools; and electrical maintenance.
Format: Examiner required; suitable for group use; untimed: approximately 60 minutes
Scoring: Self-scored
Cost: Test booklet $15.00 (minimum of 20); Administration Manual $24.95

Electrical Repair Apprentice Battery—Form CEB
Roland T. Ramsay

1996	Ramsay Corporation

Population: Adults
Purpose: Measures basic electrical skills and knowledge
Description: A basic skills test battery assessing the following: Reading, Arithmetic, Electrical Print Reading, Troubleshooting and Problem Solving, and Basic Electricity. These five subtests are more demanding of job knowledge than a basic skills battery, but less demanding than the Electrical Maintenance Trainee test.
Format: Examiner required; suitable for group use; untimed: ranges from 25 to 45 minutes per subtest
Scoring: Self-scored
Cost: $200.00 per subtest (10 reusable test booklets, 100 answer sheets, manual, key)

Electrical Sophistication Test
Stanley Ciesla

1989	Psychometric Affiliates

Population: Adult

Purpose: Assesses electrical knowledge; used to evaluate job applicants
Description: Multiple-item paper-pencil test of sophistication of electrical knowledge. The test discriminates between persons with electrical know-how and those with none and between electrical engineers and other types of engineers.
Format: Examiner required; suitable for group use; untimed: 10 minutes
Scoring: Hand key
Cost: Specimen Set $4.00; 25 Tests $4.00

ElectronTest Form H-C
Roland T. Ramsay

1998	Ramsay Corporation

Population: Adults
Purpose: Measures knowledge and skill in the area of electronics
Description: Paper-pencil 60-item multiple-choice test assessing AC/DC theory, digital and analog electronics, print reading, power supplies, regulators, test instruments, motors, electronic equipment, radio theory, power distribution, computers and PLC, and mechanical.
Format: Examiner required; suitable for group use; untimed: 60 minutes
Scoring: Self-scored
Cost: Test Booklet $15.00 (minimum of 20); Administration Manual $24.95

Instrument Technician Test—Form IPO
Roland T. Ramsay

1989	Ramsay Corporation

Population: Adults
Purpose: Measures technical knowledge of instrumentation
Description: The test for Level 1 has 100 items in 11 categories: mathematics, digital electronics, analog electronics, electrical print reading, process control, power supplies, basic AC/DC theory, test instruments, mechanical, computers and PLC, and chemical processes. The more advanced Level II has 122 items in the same categories.
Format: Examiner required; suitable for group use; untimed: 120 minutes
Scoring: Hand key
Cost: $498.00 per level (10 reusable test booklets, 100 answer sheets, manual, key)

VCWS 12—Soldering and Inspection (Electronic)

| 1993 | Valpar International Corporation |

Population: Adults

Purpose: Measures an individual's ability to acquire and apply basic soldering techniques to tasks requiring varying degrees of precision; provides insight into the ability to follow sequential instructions and acquire new tool use skills

Description: The examinee uses wire cutters, wire strippers, needlenose pliers, a soldering iron, and a solder to perform exercises involving the use of the tools in precision solder tasks. Exercises include work with both wires and circuit board assemblies. Performance indicates the individual's degree of ability to become a successful worker in jobs related to electronic assembly and soldering.

Format: Examiner required; individual administration; timed

Scoring: Examiner evaluated

Cost: $1,765.00

VCWS 15—Electrical Circuitry and Print Reading

| 1993 | Valpar International Corporation |

Population: Adults

Purpose: Measures the ability to understand, comprehend, and apply the principles and functions of electrical circuitry through the modality of electronic components; provides insight into potential without basing performance exclusively on prior knowledge

Description: The examinee performs various exercises in three areas: testing for circuit continuity using probes; testing and repairing circuits using probes, wires, and pliers; and reading an electrical schematic print and inserting wires, diodes, and two types of resisters as specified by the print. The examinee is given trays containing various electrical components and appropriate tools. The various electrical circuits to be tested range from very simple to complex. The examinee tests each circuit, records malfunctions, and, if necessary, repairs nonfunctioning circuits. No previous experience with electrical or electronic principles is required.

Format: Examiner required; individual administration; timed

Scoring: Examiner evaluated

Cost: $1,765.00

Factory

Industrial Assessments

| Date not provided | National Occupational Competency Testing Institute |

Population: Adults

Purpose: Measures knowledge of competencies related specifically to industrial occupations

Description: Intended for evaluating individuals with a combination of education, training, and work experience. Tests are available in a variety of job titles.

Format: Examiner required; group administration; untimed

Scoring: Scoring service

Cost: Contact publisher

VCWS 8—Simulated Assembly

| 1993 | Valpar International Corporation |

Population: Adults

Purpose: Measures an individual's ability to work at an assembly task requiring repetitive physical manipulation and evaluates bilateral use of the upper extremities; determines standing and sitting tolerance

Description: Manual test measuring an individual's ability to work at conveyor-assembly jobs. The individual stands or sits in front of two parts bins, one containing metal pins and the other containing a black washer and white cap. The individual must place the pin, then the washer, and then the cap on the assembly board, which rotates automatically at a constant speed. Correct assemblies are counted automatically, and all assemblies are recycled to the parts bins automatically. Work activities relating to the test include placing materials in or on automatic machines; following simple instructions; and starting, stopping, and observing the functions of machines and equipment.

Format: Examiner required; individual administration; timed

Scoring: Examiner evaluated

Cost: $2,700.00

VCWS 9—Whole Body Range of Motion

| 1993 | Valpar International Corporation |

Population: Adults

Purpose: Assesses the ability to perform successfully gross- and fine-finger dexterity tasks while in kneeling, crouching, stooping, bending, and stretching positions

Description: Nonmedical measurement of gross body movements of the trunk, hands, arms, legs, and fingers as they relate to an individual's functional ability to perform job tasks. The individual stands in front of the work sample, with the frame adjusted to 6 inches above his or her head. The individual takes three colored shapes, one at a time, and transfers them from shoulder height to overhead. The individual then transfers the shapes to waist level, which requires bending forward at the waist; to knee level, which requires crouching or kneeling; and then back to shoulder height. In each transfer, the individual must remove a total of 22 nuts and then replace them, using one hand, onto each of the three colored shapes. May be used with individuals with hearing or visual impairments.

Format: Examiner required; individual administration; timed

Scoring: Examiner evaluated

Cost: $2,185.00

VCWS 10—Tri-Level Measurement
1993   Valpar International Corporation

Population: Adults

Purpose: Measures an individual's ability to perform inspecting and measuring tasks ranging from the very simple to the very precise; measures ability to use independent judgment in following sequences of operations and selecting proper instruments

Description: Manual test measuring a person's ability to perform very simple to very precise inspection and measurement tasks. The individual must sort 61 incorrectly or correctly machined parts into nine inspection bins. The seven inspection tasks involved are visual and size discrimination, comparison (using jigs), and measurement with a ruler, micrometer, and vernier caliper. Performance indicates the ability to succeed in jobs requiring varying degrees of measurement and inspection skills and decision-making abilities. The test should not be administered to individuals with severe impairment of the upper extremities.

Format: Examiner required; individual administration; untimed

Scoring: Examiner evaluated

Cost: $2,075.00

VCWS 14—Integrated Peer Performance
1977   Valpar International Corporation

Population: Adults

Purpose: Measures an individual's instruction-following ability and color discrimination skills; stimulates interaction among workers

Description: Manual test measuring an individual's ability to follow instructions and discriminate between colors. The test emphasizes the ability to interact effectively with both peers and supervisors and the ability to work as a team member in order to complete a task. Three or four examinees are seated and given colored assembly pieces and an assembly pattern booklet. The examiner places assembly boards on the table and moves them from worker to worker every 20 seconds. Each examinee performs his or her portion of assembly and then waits for the next assembly board. As each assembly board is completed, the examiner inspects each board and informs the appropriate examinee of any errors made.

Format: Examiner required; suitable for group use; timed

Scoring: Examiner evaluated

Cost: $3,295.00

VCWS 19—Dynamic Physical Capacities
1993   Valpar International Corporation

Population: Adults

Purpose: Measures the Physical Demands factor of the Worker Qualifications Profile of the *Dictionary of Occupational Titles;* evaluates an individual's endurance and strength; may be used in post-injury cases

Description: Objective measure of functional capacity in terms of strength. The exercise measures each of the strength levels represented in the Physical Demands factor: sedentary, light, medium, heavy, and very heavy. The examinee, who assumes the role of a shipping and receiving clerk, handles materials varying in weight from 5 pounds to 115 pounds. The examinee begins with exercises on the sedentary level and gradually moves through the range of strengths until his or her capacity is reached. The test may be discontinued at any time. The test should be administered only to individuals who are able to walk, are free of visual handicaps, and have use of their upper extremities.

Format: Examiner required; individual administration; timed

Scoring: Examiner evaluated
Cost: $4,475.00

Health Services

Healthcare Employee Productivity Report™

Date not provided	NCS Pearson Reid London House

Population: Adults
Purpose: Identifies those applicants who have the potential to become highly productive staff members
Description: Helps measure five dimensions correlated with workplace productivity: Conscientiousness, Reliability, Punctuality, Responsibility, and Consistency. Designed and statistically validated to assist employers in documenting compliance with applicable employment laws.
Format: Examiner required; suitable for group use; timed: 15 minutes
Scoring: Hand key; scoring service available
Cost: Contact publisher

Healthcare Numerical Skills Profile™

Date not provided	NCS Pearson Reid London House

Population: Adults
Purpose: Measures the mathematical aptitude of a job applicant in medical settings
Description: Measures healthcare mathematical aptitude and identifies individuals who are likely to have strong numerical skills and thus to reduce errors associated with dosages and treatment levels.
Format: Examiner required; suitable for group use; timed: 15 minutes
Scoring: Hand key; scoring service available
Cost: Contact publisher

Healthcare Risk Avoidance Profile™

Date not provided	NCS Pearson Reid London House

Population: Adults
Purpose: Identifies employees likely to abstain from illegal drug use or intoxication on the job
Description: Helps measure applicant opinions

with regard to acceptability of illegal use in the workplace.
Format: Examiner required; suitable for group use; timed: 15 minutes
Scoring: Hand key; scoring service available
Cost: Contact publisher

Healthcare Safety Profile™

Date not provided	NCS Pearson Reid London House

Population: Adults
Purpose: Measures key applicant attitudes toward safety policies and procedures
Description: Helps to create a potentially safer workplace by eliminating from consideration candidates who exhibit risky attitudes or behaviors.
Format: Examiner required; suitable for group use; timed: 15 minutes
Scoring: Hand key; scoring service available
Cost: Contact publisher

Healthcare Service Relations Profile™

Date not provided	NCS Pearson Reid London House

Population: Adults
Purpose: Identifies candidates who are likely to exhibit strong interpersonal skills
Description: Helps measure job candidates across key dimensions correlated with strong service relations: valuing of interpersonal relationships, self-restraint, enjoyment of helping others, and optimism.
Format: Examiner required; suitable for group use; timed: 15 minutes
Scoring: Hand key; scoring service available
Cost: Contact publisher

IPI Job-Field Series: Medical Office Assistant

1997	Industrial Psychology International, Ltd.

Population: Ages 16 years and older
Purpose: Assesses skills and personality of applicants for medical assistant positions
Description: Used to screen individuals who will act as a support person for physicians, work with the practitioner and patients, and perform reception and secretarial duties. Multiple-item paper-pencil battery of five aptitude and two personality tests. The tests are Numbers, NPF, CPF, Office

Terms, Judgment, Perception, and Fluency. For individual test descriptions, see the IPI Employee Aptitude Series. Also available in French and Spanish.

Format: Examiner required; suitable for group use; timed: 50 minutes

Scoring: Hand key

Cost: Starter Kit (test materials for five applicants, scoring keys, manuals) $80.00; Test Package $12.00 per applicant

Quality Healthcare Employee Inventory (QHEI™)

Date not provided	NCS Pearson Reid London House

Population: Adults

Purpose: Helps to select applicants who exhibit favorable attitudes necessary for quality patient care

Description: The assessment provides Healthcare Service Index and healthcare-specific norms, and covers virtually all healthcare employees.

Format: Self-administration; computer administration; untimed: 40 minutes

Scoring: Telephone and fax scoring; software scoring available; scannable forms

Cost: Contact publisher

Insurance

Insurance Selection Inventory (ISI)

1986	NCS Pearson Reid London House

Population: Ages 16 years and older

Purpose: Evaluates potential for success as a claims examiner, customer service representative, and correspondence representative; used for employee selection and promotion

Description: Paper–pencil 275-item multiple-choice test measuring 11 basic functions necessary to succeed in key insurance positions: Number Comparison, Verbal Reasoning, Applied Arithmetic, Arithmetic Computation, Error Recognition, Drive, Interpersonal Skills, Cognitive Skills, Self-Discipline, Writing Skills, and Work Preference. Potential estimate scores for the positions of claims examiner, customer service representative, and correspondence representative are yielded. Standard scores for each of the 11 measures are profiled.

Format: Examiner required; suitable for group use; timed

Scoring: Computer scored

Cost: Contact publisher

LOMA's Employee Assessment Program for Nonmanagement

2000	Life Office Management Association

Population: Adults

Purpose: Preemployment testing, to assess general abilities and soft personal attributes

Description: This preemployment screening can be used by any business in the insurance and financial services industry. Seven tests yield background information inventory and situational judgment inventory. The seven tests are Reading Comprehension, Language Usage, Following Policies, Procedures, Quantitative Reasoning, Proofing, and Checking. Forms available are support and professional. This test is PC or Web based. The system provides information on key developmental needs and strengths.

Format: Computer administered; on-line administration available; untimed

Scoring: Computer scored

Cost: Contact publisher

Mechanical

ACER Mechanical Comprehension Test

1989	Australian Council for Educational Research Limited

Population: Ages 13 years 6 months and older

Purpose: Measures mechanical aptitude; used for employee selection and placement for positions requiring some degree of mechanical aptitude

Description: Paper–pencil 45-item multiple-choice test consisting of problems in the form of diagrams that illustrate various mechanical principles and mechanisms. Australian norms are provided for various age groups, university and technical college groups, and national service trainees and applicants for apprenticeships. Materials include a reusable booklet, separate answer sheet, scoring key, manual, and specimen set.

Format: Examiner required; suitable for group use; timed: 30 minutes

Scoring: Hand key; may be computer scored

Cost: Contact publisher

ACER Mechanical Reasoning Test (Revised Edition)

1989	Australian Council for Educational Research Limited

Population: Ages 15 years and older

Purpose: Measures basic mechanical reasoning abilities; used for employee selection and placement for positions requiring some degree of mechanical aptitude

Description: Multiple-item paper–pencil multiple-choice test consisting of problems in the form of diagrams that illustrate various mechanical principles and mechanisms. This test is a shortened version of the ACER Mechanical Comprehension Test and contains some different items and less verbal content. Australian norms are provided for apprenticeship applicants for a variety of trades and for apprentices beginning training. Materials include a reusable booklet, answer sheet, score key, manual, and specimen set.

Format: Examiner required; suitable for group use; timed: 20 minutes

Scoring: Hand key; may be machine scored

Cost: Contact publisher

Applied Technology Series (ATS) Mechanical Comprehension (MTS3)

1988	SHL Canada

Population: Adults

Purpose: Assesses the understanding of basic mechanical principles

Description: Test with 36-items assesses the understanding of basic mechanical principles and their application to such devices as pulleys, gears, and simple structures. The task involves selecting the answer to a short written question from a number of alternatives, which is supported by a realistic technical drawing. Also available in French.

Format: Examiner required; individual administration; untimed: 15 minutes

Scoring: Hand key; machine scored; scoring service available

Cost: Contact publisher

Bennett Hand-Tool Dexterity Test

George K. Bennett

Date not provided	The Psychological Corporation

Population: Adults

Purpose: Measures basic hand-tool skills required for a job

Description: The test measures key skills by having the examinee disassemble 12 fasteners in a directed order; reassemble the nuts, washers, and bolts on the opposite side; and use wrenches, screwdrivers, and other tools. Score is determined by speed. No reading is required. Included in the manual are percentile ranks for maintenance mechanics, technical trainees, physically injured workers, special education and vocational training students, and trainees with mental or emotional disabilities.

Format: Examiner required; individual administration; timed: 10 minutes

Scoring: Examiner evaluated

Cost: Complete Set (all equipment, manual) $331.00

BldgTest—Form MBI-C

Roland T. Ramsay

1998	Ramsay Corporation

Population: Adults

Purpose: Measures building maintenance knowledge and skill

Description: Uses 60 items to measure the following nine areas: electrical, print reading, plumbing, HVAC, general repairs, carpentry, painting, masonry, and clerical records.

Format: Examiner required; suitable for group use; timed: approximately 60 minutes

Scoring: Self-scored

Cost: Test Booklets $15.00 (minimum of 20); Administration Manual $24.95

CB and A Maintenance Mechanics— Forms CI-C, BI-C, and AI-C

Roland T. Ramsay

1999	Ramsay Corporation

Population: Adults

Purpose: Measures mechanical knowledge and skills

Description: There are three forms of the instrument, each containing 60 items. Each version measures four to five categories of the following skills: welding, plumbing, HVAC, electrical, pneumatics, lubrication, shop, tools, machines, rigging, mechanical, and print reading. Each version has a differing number of items for each skill measured.

Format: Examiner required; suitable for group use; untimed: 60 minutes
Scoring: Self-scored
Cost: Test Booklets $15.00 (minimum of 20); Administration Manual $24.95

Closure Speed (Gestalt Completion)
L. L. Thurstone, T. E. Jeffrey

1984	NCS Pearson Reid London House

Population: Adolescents, adults

Purpose: Measures the ability to hold a configuration in mind despite distracting irrelevancies as indicated by identification of a given figure "hidden" or embedded in a larger more complex drawing; used for vocational counseling and selection of personnel

Description: Paper–pencil 24-item test in which each item consists of an incomplete picture drawn in black on a white background. The examinee must identify and briefly describe the subject of the picture.

Format: Examiner required; suitable for group use; timed: 3 minutes
Scoring: Hand key
Cost: Contact publisher

CNC Operator—Form CNC-2
Roland T. Ramsay

2000	Ramsay Corporation

Population: Adults

Purpose: Measures knowledge and skill in CNC operation

Description: Has 101 multiple-choice items in seven categories: general knowledge, coordinate systems, interpolation, program structure, tool compensation, M-codes, and operations.

Format: Examiner required; suitable for group use; untimed: 2 hours
Scoring: Hand key
Cost: $498.00 (10 reusable test booklets, 100 answer sheets, manual, key)

Combined Basic Skills—Form LCS-C
Roland T. Ramsay

1998	Ramsay Corporation

Population: Adults

Purpose: Measures basic manufacturing and processing skills

Description: Enables a quick evaluation of literacy and performance skills. A total of 52 multi-

ple-choice items measure reading, arithmetic, inspection and measurement, and process monitoring and problem solving. Spanish version also available.

Format: Examiner required; suitable for group use; untimed: approximately 120 minutes; on-line administration available
Scoring: Self-scored
Cost: Test Booklet $10.00 (minimum of 20); Administration Manual $24.95

Crawford Small Parts Dexterity Test (CSPDT)
John Crawford

1981	The Psychological Corporation

Population: Adolescents, adults

Purpose: Measures fine-motor dexterity and eye–hand coordination; used for selecting applicants for such jobs as engravers, watch repairers, and telephone installers

Description: Two-part performance measure of dexterity. Part 1 measures dexterity in using tweezers to assemble pins and collars. Part 2 measures dexterity in screwing small screws with a screwdriver after placing them in threaded holes. The test may be administered in two ways. In the work-limit method, the subject completes the task and the total time is the score. Using the time-limit procedure, the score is the amount of work completed during a specified time. Materials include an assembly plate, pins, collars, and screws.

Format: Examiner required; suitable for group use; timed: 10 to 15 minutes
Scoring: Examiner evaluated
Cost: Complete Set (manual, board and plate, tools, spare parts) $446.00

Curtis Spatial Tests: Object Completion Test and Space–Form Test
James W. Curtis

1961	Psychometric Affiliates

Population: Adults

Purpose: Assesses perceptual efficiency; used for screening applicants for jobs requiring manual skills

Description: Two paper–pencil tests of perceptual efficiency. One test is two-dimensional and one is three-dimensional.

Format: Examiner required; suitable for group use; timed: 1 minute per test

Scoring: Hand key

Cost: Specimen Set $4.00; 25 Tests (specify form) $3.50

Intuitive Mechanics (Weights and Pulleys)
L. L. Thurstone, T. E. Jeffrey

| 1984 | NCS Pearson Reid London House |

Population: Ages 16 years and older

Purpose: Measures ability to understand mechanical relationships and to visualize internal movement in a mechanical system; used for vocational counseling or for selection in positions requiring mechanical interest and experience

Description: Paper-pencil 32-item test in which each item is a drawing that represents a system of weights and pulleys. For each system, the examinee must determine whether the system is stable (will not produce movement) or unstable (will produce movement).

Format: Examiner required; suitable for group use; timed: 3 minutes

Scoring: Hand key

Cost: Contact publisher

IPI Employee Aptitude Series: Tools

| 1986 | Industrial Psychology International Ltd. |

Population: Adults

Purpose: Measures ability to recognize simple tools and mechanical equipment; used to screen applicants for mechanical and technical jobs

Description: Paper-pencil 48-item test measuring the ability to recognize pictures of common tools, equipment, and machines used in factory and mechanical areas. The test does not require the ability to read or write. Also available in French and Spanish.

Format: Examiner required; suitable for group use; timed: 6 minutes

Scoring: Hand key

Cost: Introductory Kit (20 test booklets, scoring key, manual) $30.00

Machinist Test—Forms AC and AC-SF
Roland T. Ramsay

| 1998, 2000 | Ramsay Corporation |

Population: Adults

Purpose: Assesses knowledge and skill in machine shop practices

Description: Form AC contains 60 items meas-uring knowledge in the following areas: heat treating; layout; cutting and assembly; print reading; steel, metals, and materials; rigging; mechanical principles and repair; machine tools; tools, material, and equipment; and machine shop lubrication. Form AC-SF contains 45 items measuring layout, cutting, and assembly; print reading; mechanical principles and repair; machine tools; tools, material, and equipment; and rigging.

Format: Examiner required; suitable for group use; untimed: 60 minutes for Form AC, 45 minutes for Form AC-SF

Scoring: Self-scored

Cost: Test Booklet $15.00 (minimum of 20); Administration Manual $24.95

Maintenance Electrician— Forms BTA-C and BTB-C
Roland T. Ramsay

| 2000 | Ramsay Corporation |

Population: Adults

Purpose: Measures electrical knowledge and skills

Description: Forms A and B have 60 items in seven categories: motors; digital and analog electronics; schematics; print reading, control circuits; power supplies, power distribution, construction, and installation; basic AC/DC theory, electrical maintenance, and troubleshooting; test instruments, computers, and PLC; and mechanical maintenance.

Format: Examiner required; suitable for group use; untimed: 60 minutes

Scoring: Self-scored

Cost: Test Booklet $15.00 (minimum of 20); Administration Manual $24.95

Measurement Test—Form A-C
Roland T. Ramsay

| 1999 | Ramsay Corporation |

Population: Adults

Purpose: Assesses an individual's ability to measure accurately with a ruler; used to predict job performance in areas such as maintenance, machine operation, and quality control

Description: Paper-pencil 20-item multiple-choice test designed to assess an individual's ability to measure accurately with a scale in rule dimensions of wholes, halves, quarters, eighths, and sixteenths.

Format: Examiner required; suitable for group use; timed: 15 minutes

Scoring: Self-scored

Cost: Test Booklet $10.00 (minimum of 20); Administration Manual $24.95

Mechanical Aptitudes
1947   NCS Pearson Reid London House

Population: Grades 10 and above

Purpose: Evaluates an individual's mechanical aptitude; used for employee selection and placement

Description: Three-part paper–pencil aptitude test measuring mechanical knowledge, space relations, and shop arithmetic. The Mechanical Knowledge subtest consists of 46 pictures of common tools and measures general mechanical background. The Space Relations subtest (40 items) measures the ability to visualize and mentally manipulate objects in space. The Shop Arithmetic subtest (24 problems) measures application of quantitative reasoning and fundamental math operations.

Format: Examiner required; suitable for group use; timed: 35 minutes

Scoring: Hand key

Cost: Contact publisher

Mechanical Maintenance Trainee—Form UKM-IC
Roland T. Ramsay
1998   Ramsay Corporation

Population: Adults

Purpose: Measures mechanical knowledge and skills

Description: Sixty-item test assessing skills in these 12 areas: hydraulics; pneumatics; print reading; welding; power transmission; lubrication; pumps; piping; rigging; maintenance; shop machines; and tools, material, and equipment.

Format: Examiner required; suitable for group use; untimed: 60 minutes

Scoring: Self-scored

Cost: Test Booklet $15.00 (minimum of 20); Administration Manual $24.95

Mechanical Movements
L. L. Thurstone, T. E. Jeffrey
1984   NCS Pearson Reid London House

Population: Adolescents, adults

Purpose: Determines degree of mechanical interest and experience; used for vocational counseling and to select persons for mechanical occupations in industry

Description: Paper–pencil 37-item multiple-choice measure of mechanical comprehension indicating the ability to visualize a mechanical system in which there is internal movement or displacement of the parts.

Format: Examiner required; suitable for group use; timed: 14 minutes

Scoring: Hand key

Cost: Contact publisher

Mechanical Repair Apprentice Battery—Form CMB
Roland T. Ramsay
1996   Ramsay Corporation

Population: Adults

Purpose: Measures basic mechanical skills and knowledge

Description: A basic skills test battery measuring five different areas: reading, arithmetic, measurement, reading prints and drawings, and basic mechanical knowledge. The reading items are directly related to mechanical repair. These tests, in multiple-choice format, are more demanding of job knowledge than a basic skills battery, but less demanding than the Mechanical Maintenance Trainee test.

Format: Examiner required; suitable for group use; untimed: 15 to 20 minutes per subtest

Scoring: Self-scored

Cost: $200.00 per subtest (10 reusable test booklets, 100 answer sheets, manual, key)

MecTest—Form AU-C
Roland T. Ramsay
1998   Ramsay Corporation

Population: Adults

Purpose: Assesses mechanical ability for trade and craft jobs; used for hiring and promotion

Description: Sixty-item multiple-choice test. Assesses skills in eight areas: hydraulics and pneumatics; print reading; welding and rigging; power transmission; lubrication; pumps and piping; mechanical maintenance; and shop machines, tools, and equipment.

Format: Examiner required; suitable for group use; untimed: 60 minutes

Scoring: Self-scored

Cost: Test Booklet $15.00 (minimum of 20); Administration Manual $24.95

Millwright Test—Form MWB-1C
Roland T. Ramsay

| 2000 | Ramsay Corporation |

Population: Adults

Purpose: Measures millwright knowledge and skill

Description: Contains 60 items in seven categories: hydraulics and pneumatics; burning and fabrication and print reading; power transmission and lubrication; pumps and piping; rigging; mechanical/maintenance; and shop equipment and tools, materials, and equipment.

Format: Examiner required; suitable for group use; untimed: 60 minutes

Scoring: Self-scored

Cost: Test Booklet $15.00 (minimum of 20); Administration Manual $24.95

Minnesota Paper Form Board Test—Revised
Rensis Likert, W. H. Quasha

| 1941; Manual updated in 1995 | The Psychological Corporation |

Population: Adolescents, adults

Purpose: Measures ability to visualize and manipulate objects in space; used to select applicants for jobs requiring mechanical-spatial ability

Description: Multiple-item paper–pencil test of spatial perception. The applicant is required to visualize the assembly of two-dimensional geometric shapes into a whole design. The test is related to both mechanical and artistic ability. Two equivalent forms, AA and BB (hand scoring) and MA and MB (machine scoring), are available. Also available in French Canadian.

Format: Examiner required; suitable for group use; timed: 20 minutes

Scoring: Hand key; may be machine scored locally

Cost: Examination Kit (manual, test booklets for each form) $49.00

Minnesota Rate of Manipulation Tests

| 1969 | American Guidance Service |

Population: Adults

Purpose: Measures finger–hand–arm dexterity; used for employee selection for jobs requiring manual dexterity and in vocational and rehabilitation training programs

Description: Five-test battery measuring manual

dexterity. The five tests are the Placing Test, Turning Test, Displacing Test, One-Hand Turning and Placing Test, and Two-Hand Turning and Placing Test. Materials consist of two test boards with holes and blocks. Each block is painted orange on the upper half and yellow on the lower half. The blocks are manipulated in prescribed ways. Specific tests assess movements with the preferred hand and with both hands. The five tests may be administered separately. All tests are repeated for four complete trials. The Displacing and Turning tests are suitable for use with individuals who are blind.

Format: Individual administration; 10 minutes for each test

Scoring: Examiner interpreted

Cost: Complete Kit (manual, protocols, test boards, blocks, carrying case) $353.95

Multi-Craf Test—Form MC-C
Roland T. Ramsay

| 2000 | Ramsay Corporation |

Population: Adults

Purpose: Measures maintenance knowledge and skill

Description: Test with 60 items in seven categories: hydraulics and pneumatics; welding and rigging; power transmission, lubrication, mechanical/maintenance, shop machines, and tools and equipment; pumps, piping, and combustion; motors, control circuits, schematics, and print reading; digital electronics, power supplies, computers and PLC, and test instruments; and basic AC/DC theory, power distribution, and electrical maintenance.

Format: Examiner required; suitable for group use; untimed: 60 minutes

Scoring: Self-scored

Cost: Test Booklet $15.00 (minimum of 20); Administration Manual $24.95

Pennsylvania Bi-Manual Worksample
John R. Roberts

| 1969 | American Guidance Service |

Population: Age 16 years to adult

Purpose: Measures manual dexterity and eye-hand coordination; used for employee placement

Description: Multiple-operation manual dexterity test using an 8 × 24 inch board containing 100 holes arranged in 10 rows and a set of nuts and bolts to test finger dexterity of both hands, whole movement of both arms, eye–hand coordination, and bimanual coordination. The employee grasps a nut between the thumb and index finger of the other hand, turns the bolt into the nut, and places both in a hole in the board. Twenty practice motions are allowed, and 80 motions are timed. Disassembly reverses the process and involves timing 100 motions. A special supplement contains directions for administration to blind employees.

Format: Individual and small (4) group administration; 12 minutes

Scoring: Examiner interpreted

Cost: Complete Kit (manual, protocols, board, bolts, nuts, carrying case) $199.95

PipeTest—BJP-IC
Roland T. Ramsay

1998	Ramsay Corporation

Population: Adults

Purpose: Measures pipe fitting knowledge and skills

Description: The test contains 60 multiple-choice items in 10 categories: piping, plumbing, and combustion; pumps; hydraulics; pneumatics; burning, soldering, and fabrication; print reading; rigging; mathematics and layout; mechanical maintenance; and tools, materials, and equipment.

Format: Examiner required; suitable for group use; untimed: 60 minutes

Scoring: Self-scored

Cost: Kit (10 test booklets, 100 answer sheets, scoring key, test manual) $200.00

PrinTest—Form A-C or B-C
Roland T. Ramsay

1998	Ramsay Corporation

Population: Adults

Purpose: Assesses ability to read mechanical prints and drawings; used for hiring and promotion

Description: Paper–pencil 33-item multiple-choice test assessing ability to read mechanical prints and drawings. Form A-C (functions) and Form B-C (decimals) both measure skills in views and surfaces, simple drawings, intermediate drawings, and complex drawings.

Format: Examiner required; suitable for group use; timed: 35 minutes

Scoring: Self-scored

Cost: Test Booklet $15.00 (minimum of 20); Administration Manual $24.95

Stromberg Dexterity Test (SDT)
E. L. Stromberg

1981	The Psychological Corporation

Population: Adults

Purpose: Measures manipulative skill in sorting by color and sequence; used to select applicants for jobs requiring manual speed and accuracy; also used for assessing manual dexterity of individuals with disabilities in vocational training programs

Description: Two-trial performance test of manual dexterity in which the applicant is asked to discriminate and sort biscuit-sized discs and to move and place them as fast as possible. The score is the number of seconds required to complete the two trials. Materials include assembly board and discs.

Format: Examiner required; individual administration; timed: 5 to 10 minutes

Scoring: Score obtained by timing

Cost: Complete Set (all necessary equipment, manual, case) $614.00

Technical Test Battery (TTB) Mechanical Comprehension (MT4.1)

1992	SHL Canada

Population: Adults

Purpose: Measures understanding of basic mechanical principles

Description: Multiple-choice test with 36 items measuring knowledge of the classic mechanical elements, such as gears, pulleys, and levers, and a wide range of domestic and leisure applications of physics and mechanics, from electric ovens to billiard balls. Each item consists of a three-choice question about a technical drawing. The drawings are presented in technical workshop style without demanding any specific preknowledge to interpret them.

Format: Examiner required; individual administration; untimed: 18 minutes

Scoring: Hand key; machine scored; scoring service available

Cost: Contact publisher

Test of Mechanical Concepts

1975	NCS Pearson Reid London House

Population: Adults

Purpose: Measures an individual's ability to visualize and understand basic mechanical and spatial interrelationships; used for employee selection and screening for such jobs as assembler, maintenance mechanic, machinist, and factory production worker

Description: Paper-pencil 78-item test consisting of three subtests measuring separate skills or abilities necessary for jobs requiring mechanical ability. The Mechanical Interrelationships subtest consists of 24 drawings depicting mechanical movements and interrelationships. The Mechanical Tools and Devices subtest consists of 30 items measuring knowledge of common mechanical tools and devices. The Spatial Relations subtest consists of 24 items measuring the ability to visualize and manipulate objects in space. The test is available in two forms.

Format: Examiner required; suitable for group use; untimed: 35 to 45 minutes

Scoring: Hand key

Cost: Contact publisher

Tool Knowledge and Use Test— Form JLR
Roland T. Ramsay

1994	Ramsay Corporation

Population: Adults

Purpose: Assesses knowledge of tools and their uses; used for hiring for trade and craft jobs

Description: Paper-pencil 70-item multiple-choice test. Materials used include paper, pencil, and a separate answer sheet.

Format: Examiner required; suitable for group use; untimed: 60 minutes

Scoring: Hand key

Cost: Kit (10 reusable tests, 100 answer sheets, manual, key) $498.00

VCWS 1—Small Tools (Mechanical)

1993	Valpar International Corporation

Population: Adults

Purpose: Measures an individual's understanding of small tools and ability to work with them

Description: Manual test measuring understanding of small tools and the ability to work with them. The design of the test challenges the individual to demonstrate skill in working in small, confined spaces while using the fingers and hands to manipulate tools to perform the assigned task. The individual works through a

small hole in the work sample to simulate working conditions in which an individual is unable to view the work he or she is doing. The individual completes five panels. In each panel, the individual uses a different set of tools to insert fasteners such as screws, bolts, and hitch pin clips. Performance indicates the ability to complete successfully jobs requiring various degrees of ability in using small tools. May be used with individuals with mental retardation, visual impairment, and hearing impairment.

Format: Examiner required; individual administration; timed: 90 minutes

Scoring: Examiner evaluated

Cost: $1,765.00

VCWS 2—Size Discrimination

1993	Valpar International Corporation

Population: Adults

Purpose: Measures an individual's ability to perform tasks requiring visual size discrimination; provides insight into problem-solving abilities, work organization, ability to follow directions, and psychomotor coordination

Description: Manual test measuring an individual's ability to visually discriminate sizes. The individual must use his or her dominant hand to screw 49 hex nuts onto 32 bolt threads of various sizes. Both hands may be used to remove the nuts during disassembly. Performance indicates the ability to work successfully in occupations requiring visual size discrimination, eye–hand coordination, and bilateral dexterity. Work activities related to the test include examining and measuring for purposes of grading and sorting; tools; and working within prescribed tolerances or standards. The test should not be used with individuals with severe impairment of the upper extremities.

Format: Examiner required; individual administration; timed

Scoring: Examiner evaluated

Cost: $1,450.00

VCWS 4—Upper Extremity Range of Motion

1993	Valpar International Corporation

Population: Adults

Purpose: Measures an individual's upper extremity range of motion, including the shoulders, upper arms, forearms, elbows, wrists, and hands; provides insight into factors such as neck and back fatigue, finger dexterity, and finger tactile sense

Description: Manual test measuring the range of motion and work tolerances of an individual in relation to his or her upper torso. The individual works through an opening in front of the work sample, the inside of which is half red and half blue. Using opposite hands for each color, the individual fastens two sizes of nuts to bolts on each of five panels. The design of the work sample allows the examiner to view muscle action in the individual's wrist and fingers. Performance indicates coordination, spatial, and perceptual skills, susceptibility to fatigue, and the ability to succeed in jobs requiring reaching, handling, fingering, feeling, and seeing. The test should not be used with individuals with severe impairment of the upper extremities.

Format: Examiner required; individual administration; timed

Scoring: Examiner evaluated

Cost: $1,660.00

VCWS 7—Multi-Level Sorting

1993 | Valpar International Corporation

Population: Adults

Purpose: Measures an individual's decision-making ability while performing tasks requiring physical manipulation and visual discrimination

Description: Manual test measuring an individual's ability to make decisions while performing work tasks requiring physical manipulation and visual discrimination. The individual sorts 168 coded chips into 48 sorting slots showing on a board. Each chip is coded in one of the following ways: color; color and letter; color and number; or color, letter, and number. The test allows the examiner to observe the individual's orientation, approach, and organization in regard to the task, color, and letter; number discrimination skills; simple decision making; and physical manipulation. A time/error score relating directly to the level of supervision the individual will need while performing a particular job is derived.

Format: Examiner required; individual administration; timed

Scoring: Examiner evaluated

Cost: $1,765.00

VCWS 11—Eye-Hand-Foot Coordination

1993 | Valpar International Corporation

Population: Adults

Purpose: Measures eye, hand, and foot coordination; provides insight into individual concentration, learning, planning, spatial discrimination, and reaction to immediate positive and negative feedback

Description: Manual test measuring an individual's ability to use his eyes, hands, and feet simultaneously in a coordinated manner. The examinee sits in front of the work sample and maneuvers nine steel balls, one at a time, through a maze containing 13 holes into which the steel balls may drop, thus ending the examinee's attempt to make it to the end of the maze with that particular ball. To move the ball, the examinee tilts the maze left and right with his hands, forward and backward with his feet, and traces the track of the ball with his eyes.

Format: Examiner required; individual administration; timed

Scoring: Examiner evaluated

Cost: $1,765.00

WeldTest—Form AC
Roland T. Ramsay

1998 | Ramsay Corporation

Population: Adults

Purpose: Assesses welding ability for trade and craft jobs; used for hiring and promotion

Description: Multiple-choice 60-item test that measures skills in six areas: print reading; welding, cutting torch and arc air cutting; welder maintenance operations; tools, machines, materials, and equipment; mobile equipment and rigging; and production welding calculations.

Format: Examiner required; suitable for group use; untimed: 60 minutes

Scoring: Self-scored

Cost: Test Booklet $15.00 (minimum of 20); Administration Manual $24.95

Wiesen Test of Mechanical Aptitude (WTMA)–PAR Edition
Joel P. Wiesen

1999 | Psychological Assessment Resources, Inc.

Population: Ages 18 years and older

Purpose: Measures mechanical aptitudes for employment

Description: Sixty items, consisting of eight mechanical/physical principles classified into three types. Sixth-grade reading level is required.

Format: Self-administered; timed: 30 minutes

Scoring: Hand key

Cost: Intro Kit (manual, 10 reusable item booklets, 25 answer sheets, scoring key) $189.00

Work Skills Series (WSS) Findex

1991	SHL Canada

Population: Adults

Purpose: Measures the ability to manipulate small objects requiring fine finger dexterity

Description: The candidate is required to insert thin steel rods into small holes and secure them with the aid of a screwdriver. The working area is restricted and both hands need to be used to complete the task.

Format: Examiner required; individual administration; untimed: 10 minutes

Scoring: Hand score

Cost: Contact publisher

Work Skills Series (WSS) Mandex

1991	SHL Canada

Population: Adults

Purpose: Measures ability to manipulate and construct components using medium finger and hand dexterity

Description: The candidate is presented with a preassembled structure (mounted on one end of a wood base) consisting of six steel plates joined together by an assortment of nuts, bolts, washers, and spacers. Using this as a model, the task is to build an identical structure on the other end of the base using a set of plates and related materials provided. No tools are necessary. Scoring is achieved by awarding points for the correct selection and positioning of plates. The number of nuts, bolts, washers, and spacers used are also taken into account.

Format: Examiner required; individual administration; untimed: 15 minutes

Scoring: Hand score

Cost: Contact publisher

Municipal Services

A-3 Police Officer Series

Date not provided	International Personnel Management Association

Population: Adults

Purpose: Used as a preemployment evaluation

Description: No prior training or experience in the job of police officer is assumed of candidates taking this test. The test is supported by criterion-related validity and psychometric analysis. There are 100 items on three alternate forms measuring the following job dimensions: Ability To Learn and Apply Police Information, Ability to Remember Details, Verbal Ability, Ability To Follow Directions, and Ability To Use Judgment and Logic. Includes a Study Guide designed to be used immediately before the test.

Format: Examiner required; individual administration; 2 hours 10 minutes

Scoring: Examiner evaluated; machine scoring

Cost: Service Charge $45.00; Test Booklets $11.00 each

A-4 Police Officer Video Test

Date not provided	International Personnel Management Association

Population: Adults

Purpose: Used as a preemployment evaluation

Description: No prior training or experience in the job of police officer is assumed of candidates taking this test. The test is supported by criterion-related validity and psychometric analysis. Developed as an alternative to traditional paper-pencil entry-level police officer tests. The same abilities are measured while reducing the possibility of adverse impact on minority group candidates. There are 90 questions measuring ability to observe, listen to, and remember information; ability to make situational judgments; interpersonal ability; and ability to learn and apply police information.

Format: Examiner required; individual administration; 2 hours 30 minutes

Scoring: Examiner evaluated; machine scoring

Cost: $17.50 (video and booklet)

Correctional Officers' Interest Blank (COIB)

Harrison G. Gough

1982	Mind Garden, Inc.

Population: Adults

Purpose: Recommended for research in the development of selection techniques for correctional officers

Description: Forty questions about interests and attitudes that have been found to have good potential for predicting performance of correctional officers. Scoring information is only by special license.

Format: Self-administered; untimed: 10 minutes

Scoring: Hand key through special permission; test scoring service available

Cost: Sampler Set $25.00

D-1 and D-2 Police Officer Tests

Date not provided	International Personnel Management Association

Population: Adults

Purpose: Used as a preemployment evaluation

Description: Designed to assess a wide range of characteristics. In addition to evaluating basic skills, the D-1 and D-2 contain a noncognitive component that assesses motivation for police work, attitude toward people, and sense of responsibility. The tests are closely attuned to the community policing philosophy.

Format: Examiner required; individual administration; 1 hour 45 minutes

Scoring: Examiner evaluated; machine scoring

Cost: Service Charge $45.00; Test Booklets $11.00 each

Fire Candidate Background Self-Report (FCBS)

2001	Applied Personnel Research

Population: Firefighter candidates

Purpose: Provides system for collection of background information from job candidates; can improve and simplify the work of the background investigator

Description: Collects background information to be used in assessment of appropriateness of hire. Paper–pencil multiple-item fill-in-the-blank test. Collects both factual data and opinions. The subjects covered include basic identification information, military experience, work experience, education, illegal behaviors, weapon ownership and use, finances, hobbies/interests, group memberships, self-evaluation, illegal drug use, alcohol use, work-style preferences, interpersonal behavior, and family. Test yields scores in 10 areas. First of two score reports consists of a listing of red flags. Second score report provides scores on each of the 10 areas (reported as high, medium, or low).

Format: May be given on a take-home basis; suitable for group use; untimed: 2 hours

Scoring: Scoring service provided; turnaround about 1 week

Cost: Specimen Set (test, sample test reports, test manual) $75.00

Firefighter Learning Simulation (FLS)

1998	Psychological Services, Inc.

Population: Adults

Purpose: Measures the ability to learn information similar to material presented in the fire academy; used to select applicants for entry-level firefighter positions or training programs

Description: Multiple-choice 65-item test based on material presented in a Firefighter Learning Simulation Training Manual that is distributed to examinees in advance of the testing session. Examinee must answer the questions only on the basis of information contained in the training manual. May be used in conjunction with Firefighter Selection Test, Work Orientation Survey for Firefighters, or both.

Format: Examiner required; suitable for group use; untimed: 90 minutes

Scoring: Hand key; may be computer scored; scoring service available

Cost: $195.00 Base Fee; 10 tests per package: 10 packages $72.50; 11 to 50 packages $67.50; 51 to 100 packages $62.50; 101 to 200 packages $60.00; 201+ packages $57.50

Firefighter Selection Test

1983	Psychological Services, Inc.

Population: Adults

Purpose: Measures three abilities important for learning and performing the job of firefighter: mechanical comprehension, reading comprehension, and report interpretation; used to select applicants for entry-level firefighter positions or training programs

Description: Paper–pencil 100-item multiple-choice test measuring the understanding of mechanical principles relevant to the firefighting job (39 items), the ability to read and interpret a passage (51 items), and the ability to read and interpret charts and reports (10 items). The items consist of drawings and passages based on firefighter training materials and sample charts and reports presenting fire department data. May be used with the Firefighter Learning Simulation, Work Orientation Survey for Firefighters, or both.

Format: Examiner required; suitable for group use; timed: 2 hours 30 minutes

Scoring: Hand key; may be computer scored; scoring service available

Cost: $195.00 Base Fee; 10 tests per package: 10 packages $62.50; 11 to 50 packages $57.50; 51 to 100 packages $52.50; 101 to 200 packages $50.00; 201+ packages $47.50

Firefighter Service Tests

Date not provided	International Personnel Management Association

Population: Adults

Purpose: Used as a preemployment evaluation

Description: Four forms of the test are available measuring reading comprehension, interpreting tables, situational judgment, logical reasoning, reading gauges, applying basic math rules, mechanical aptitude, spatial sense, map reading, and vocabulary. No prior training or experience in the job of firefighter is assumed of candidates taking these tests. A nationwide analysis of the job resulted in development of examinations designed to assess abilities.

Format: Examiner required; individual administration; 1 hour 45 minutes

Scoring: Examiner evaluated; machine scoring

Cost: Service Charge $45.00; Test Booklets $11.00 each

Hilson Background Investigation Inventory (HBI)
Robin E. Inwald

1998	Hilson Research, Inc.

Population: Adults

Purpose: Screens public safety and security applicants

Description: Total of 300 items to screen applicants dealing with public safety, security screening, and background investigations. Also available in Spanish.

Format: Examiner required; suitable for groups; untimed: 45 minutes

Scoring: Computer scored; scoring service available

Cost: Contact publisher

Inwald Personality Inventory (IPI)
Robin E. Inwald

1980	Hilson Research, Inc.

Population: Adults

Purpose: Assesses behavior patterns and characteristics of police, security, firefighter, and correction officer candidates; used for preemployment screening

Description: Paper-pencil 310-item true-false instrument consisting of a validity measure and multiple scales assessing specific external behavior, attitudes and temperament, internalized conflict measures, and interpersonal conflict measures: Guardedness, Alcohol, Drugs, Driving Violations, Job Difficulties, Trouble with the Law and Society, Absence Abuse, Substance Abuse, Antisocial Attitudes, Hyperactivity, Rigid Type, Type "A," Illness Concerns, Treatment Programs, Anxiety, Phobic Personality, Obsessive Personality, Depression, Loner Type, Unusual Experience/Thoughts, Lack of Assertiveness, Interpersonal Difficulties, Undue Suspiciousness, Family Conflicts, Sexual Concerns, and Spouse/Mate Conflicts. The test yields raw scores and t-scores.

Format: Self-administered; untimed: 30 to 45 minutes

Scoring: Computer scored

Cost: Contact publisher

Inwald Survey 5-Revised (IS5-R)
Robin E. Inwald

2001	Hilson Research, Inc.

Population: Adults

Purpose: Used for preemployment screening

Description: Total of 192 items for police applicants. Screens for work ethic, domestic violence, social initiative, work adjustment, and frustration/anger.

Format: Examiner required; suitable for group use; untimed: 20 minutes

Scoring: Computer scored; scoring service available

Cost: Contact publisher

National Firefighter Selection Test (NFST)

1994	Stanard & Associates, Inc.

Population: Adults

Purpose: Assesses basic cognitive skills; used for preemployment screening

Description: Paper-pencil 70-item multiple-choice test with three subtests: Reading Comprehension (25 items, 25 minutes), Mathematics (25

items, 30 minutes), and Listening (20 items, 20 minutes). Scores are provided for each subtest. Forms A and B are available.

Format: Examiner required; individual administration; suitable for group use; timed

Scoring: Machine/self-scored

Cost: Contact publisher

National Police Officer Selection Test (POST)

| 1991 | Stanard & Associates, Inc. |

Population: Adults

Purpose: Assesses basic cognitive skills; used for preemployment screening

Description: Paper–pencil 75-item multiple-choice short-answer true–false test with four subtests: Reading Comprehension (20 items, 20 minutes), Mathematics (20 items, 20 minutes), Grammar (25 items, 25 minutes), and Writing (10 items, 20 minutes). Forms A, B, and C are available.

Format: Examiner required; individual administration; suitable for group use; timed

Scoring: Machine/self-scored

Cost: Contact publisher

New Municipal Fire Fighter Examination

| 1992 | Applied Personnel Research |

Population: Adults

Purpose: Measures the knowledge and cognitive ability required for successful job performance; designed for use in personnel selection

Description: Paper–pencil multiple-choice test based on a nationwide study of the job of firefighter. The test covers five areas: mechanical aptitude, reasoning and problem solving, reading ability, mathematical ability, and spatial ability. Other versions offer two additional areas: emergency medical service and basic algebra. Test services include candidate orientation booklets, written test booklets, on-site test administration, computerized scoring, and computerized score reporting.

Format: Self-administered; untimed: 2 hours

Scoring: Scoring service provided; 1-week turnaround

Cost: Base price for one-time use for 50 candidates $950.00

Police Candidate Background Self-Report (PCBS)

| 2001 | Applied Personnel Research |

Population: Police officer candidates

Purpose: Provides system for collection of background information from job candidates; can improve and simplify the work of the background investigator

Description: Collects background information to be used in assessment of appropriateness of hire. Paper–pencil multiple-item fill-in-the-blank test for collecting both factual data and opinions. The subjects covered include basic identification information, military experience, work experience, education, illegal behaviors, weapon ownership and use, finances, hobbies/interests, group memberships, self-evaluation, illegal drug use, alcohol use, work-style preferences, interpersonal behavior, and family. Provides two score reports: one consists of a listing of red flags, and the other lists scores on each of 10 areas (reported as high, medium, or low).

Format: May be given on a take-home basis; suitable for group use; untimed: 2 hours

Scoring: Scoring service provided; turnaround about 1 week

Cost: Specimen Set (test, sample test reports, test manual) $75.00

Police Selection Test

| 1995 | Psychological Services, Inc. |

Population: Adults

Purpose: Measures five abilities important in learning and performing the job of police officer: reading comprehension, quantitative problem solving, data interpretation, writing skills, and reasoning; used to select applicants for entry-level police positions

Description: Paper–pencil 100-item multiple-choice test measuring the ability to read and interpret a passage (19 items), the ability to analyze logical numerical relationships (20 items), the ability to interpret data and other information (23 items), the ability to express information in writing (15 items), and the ability to analyze information and make valid judgments based on available facts (23 items). The test consists of passages, tables, forms, and maps based on police officer training material. Scoring service available. Study guide available.

Format: Examiner required; suitable for group use; timed: 2 hours

Scoring: Hand key; may be computer scored
Cost: Contact publisher

Police Supervisor (Corporal/Sergeant)

Date not provided	International Personnel Management Association

Population: Adults
Purpose: Measures skills suitable for promotion
Description: Five alternate forms that are supported by content validity study and psychometric analysis. The examinations are not psychometrically equivalent and should not be used interchangeably. Content: Basic Police Procedures, Investigation Procedures, Laws Related to Police Work, Supervisory Principles, Administrative Principles, and Reports.
Format: Examiner required; individual administration; 1 hour 45 minutes
Scoring: Examiner evaluated; machine scoring
Cost: Service Charge $45.00; Test Booklets $11.00 each

Public Safety Telecommunicator Test

Date not provided	International Personnel Management Association

Population: Adults
Purpose: Used as a preemployment evaluation
Description: No prior training or experience in the job is assumed of candidates taking the test. The two forms of the test (one with 100 items and the other with 80 items) measure listening skills, reading comprehension, ability to learn and apply information, reasoning ability, and ability to use situational judgment. The 80-item test does not measure listening comprehension.
Format: Examiner required; individual administration; timed: 2 hours 24 minutes (100-item test) or 2 hours (80-item test)
Scoring: Examiner evaluated; machine scoring
Cost: Service Charge $45.00; Test Booklets $11.00 each

Sales

Canadian Personnel Selection Inventory (PSI™) and Sales PSI™

Date not provided	NCS Pearson Reid London House

Population: Adults

Purpose: Measures a candidate's job-related attitudes and behaviors
Description: These assessments help businesses make more confident hiring decisions and improve their chances for success.
Format: Self-administration; untimed: 30 to 75 minutes depending on the version
Scoring: Software scoring; computer scoring via telephone and fax; scoring service available
Cost: Contact publisher

Career Profile+ (CP+)

1992	LIMRA International

Population: Adults
Purpose: Evaluates the career experience and expectations of individuals considering an insurance or financial services sales career; used for employee screening and selection
Description: Multiple-choice on-line or paper-pencil questionnaire assessing career information related to future success as an insurance salesperson. Each candidate is rated on four key personality characteristics: persuasiveness, energy, achievement drive, and initiative and persistence. Validated for use in the United States, Canada, and the Caribbean.
Format: Suitable for group use; on-line administration; untimed
Scoring: Computer scored; on-line scoring
Cost: Contact publisher

Client Relations

1998	Clark Wilson Group

Population: Consultants and client service representatives
Purpose: Measures the strengths and soft spots of the internal or external consultant or representative in responding to client's needs
Description: Contains 55 questions with three open-ended questions. Available in two languages.
Format: Self-administered; untimed
Scoring: Scoring service
Cost: $260 for up to 15 surveys

Customer Contact Aptitude Series (CCAS) Numerical Evaluation (NCC4)

1996	SHL Canada

Population: Customer-facing staff

Purpose: Assesses the numerical information skills of sales, customer service, and call center staff

Description: Forty-item test measuring the ability to make correct decisions or inferences from numerical data. More demanding than NCC2, this test allows candidates to use a calculator to analyze the statistical information presented. The nature of the data presented simulates a sales or customer service environment.

Format: Examiner required; individual administration; untimed: 30 minutes

Scoring: Hand key; machine scored; scoring service available

Cost: Contact publisher

Customer Contact Aptitude Series (CCAS) Numerical Interpretation (NCC2)

1996   SHL Canada

Population: Customer-facing staff

Purpose: Assesses the numerical interpretation skills of sales, customer service, and call center staff

Description: Test with 35 items measuring the ability to understand numerical data to answer questions. The task involves using tables provided to solve numerical problems, including addition, subtraction, multiplication, division, and percentages. Calculators may be used. The data and questions simulate numerical information that may be featured in sales and customer service roles.

Format: Examiner required; individual administration; untimed: 20 minutes

Scoring: Hand key; machine scored; scoring service available

Cost: Contact publisher

Customer Contact Aptitude Series (CCAS) Verbal Evaluation (VCC3)

1996   SHL Canada

Population: Customer-facing staff

Purpose: Assesses the verbal information skills of sales, customer service, and call center staff

Description: Test with 60 items measuring the ability to understand and evaluate the logic of various written passages. More demanding than VCC1, it includes a variety of relevant topics.

Format: Examiner required; individual administration; untimed: 30 minutes

Scoring: Hand key; machine scored; scoring service available

Cost: Contact publisher

Customer Contact Aptitude Series (CCAS) Verbal Interpretation (VCC1)

1996   SHL Canada

Population: Customer-facing staff

Purpose: Assesses the verbal interpretation skills of sales, customer service, and call center staff

Description: Test with 36 items measuring the ability to understand written information to arrive at reasoned conclusions. Performance on the test depends on extracting relevant information from a paragraph of text simulating product and market information or customer communication.

Format: Examiner required; individual administration; untimed: 12 minutes

Scoring: Hand key; machine scored; scoring service available

Cost: Contact publisher

Customer Contact Styles Questionnaire (CCSQ5.2 or CCSQ7.2)

1998   SHL Canada

Population: Front-line staff

Purpose: Selection and development of sales, customer service, and call center staff

Description: Assesses 16 dimensions of workstyle. There are 136 items in three categories: relationships with people, thinking styles, and emotions and drives. Also available in French.

Format: Examiner required; individual administration; untimed: 25 minutes

Scoring: Hand key; machine scored; scoring service available

Cost: Contact publisher

Diplomacy Test of Empathy
Willard A. Kerr

1984   Psychometric Affiliates

Population: Adults

Purpose: Measures empathic ability; used for selecting applicants for sales positions

Description: Multiple-item paper–pencil test measuring the ability to sell and to be persuasive, tactful, and diplomatic. Items correlate with the mean salary increases of executives but have little or no relationship with intelligence. Norms are available for general adults, management, sales, and sales management.

Format: Examiner required; suitable for group use; untimed: 20 minutes

Scoring: Hand key

Cost: Specimen Set $5.00; 25 Tests $5.00; 25 Answer Sheets $5.00

Drug Store Applicant Inventory (DSAI™)

1989	NCS Pearson Reid London House

Population: Adults

Purpose: Assesses potential for successful employment; used in selection and screening of drug store cashier and clerk applicants

Description: Paper–pencil 144-item multiple-choice test with eight diagnostic scales yielding scores in Background and Work Experience, Applied Arithmetic, Customer Service, Job Stability, Honesty, Interpersonal Cooperation, Drug Avoidance, and Risk Avoidance. Two validity scales, Distortion and Accuracy, are also included. A composite Employability Index based on the eight diagnostics is provided for decision-making purposes. In addition to scores, the DSAI generates behavioral indicators and training needs based on examinee responses to individual items.

Format: Examiner required; suitable for group use; untimed: 45 minutes

Scoring: Computer scored; test scoring service available

Cost: Contact publisher

Field Sales Skills Test

1990	Walden Personnel Testing and Consulting, Inc.

Population: Adults

Purpose: Measures aptitude for work as a field sales representative, including general sales knowledge and understanding of sales principles

Description: Provides a five-page report to the client. Measures the following: verbal communication skills, numerical skills, attention to detail, problem-solving ability, customer service skills, customer service problem solving, and customer service logic.

Format: Self-administered; untimed: 51 minutes

Scoring: Scoring service available

Cost: $319.00

Hilson Personnel Profile/Success Quotient–Sales Version (HPP/SQ–S)
Robin E. Inwald

1995	Hilson Research, Inc.

Population: Adults

Purpose: Screens job applicants in sales positions

Description: Paper–pencil 160-item true–false test used for prescreening job applicants for sales positions. Assesses Achievement History, Social Ability, and Sales Interest. Materials used are a test booklet, answer sheets, and scoring program. Also available in Spanish.

Format: Examiner required; suitable for groups; untimed: 30 minutes

Scoring: Computer scored; scoring service available

Cost: Contact publisher

IPI Employee Aptitude Series: Sales Terms

1984	Industrial Psychology International Ltd.

Population: Adults

Purpose: Measures ability to understand information of a sales or contract nature; used to assist employers in the selection, placement, promotion, and training of different levels of sales personnel

Description: Paper–pencil 54-item test measuring comprehension of sales-related information. The test also indicates whether a person is over-qualified for routine or repetitive assignments. French and Spanish versions are a combination of sales terms and office terms.

Format: Examiner required; suitable for group use; timed: 5 minutes

Scoring: Hand key

Cost: Introductory Kit (20 test booklets, scoring key, manual) $30.00

IS Sales Assessment Battery

1988	Walden Personnel Testing and Consulting, Inc.

Population: Adults

Purpose: Measures logic and reasoning ability,

as well as understanding of sales and problem solving in a sales environment

Description: Available in English and French.

Format: Self-administered; timed: 1 hour 40 minutes

Scoring: Scoring service available

Cost: Test Booklet and Detailed Report on each candidate $319.00

Retail Sales Skills Test

Date not provided	Walden Personnel Testing and Consulting, Inc.

Population: Adults

Purpose: Tests for retail sales knowledge, problem-solving ability in a retail environment, and sales logic

Description: Multiple-item test measuring skills.

Format: Self-administered: untimed: 45 minutes

Scoring: Scoring service provided

Cost: Test Booklet and Detailed Report on each candidate $199.00

Sales Achievement Predictor (SalesAP)
Jotham Friedland, Sander Marcus, Harvey Mandel

Date not provided	Western Psychological Services

Population: Ages 14 years and older

Purpose: Measures traits that are critical to success in sales and related fields

Description: Composed of 140 items, the on-line or paper-pencil test can be scored on the computer or via fax or mail. An interpretive report is received that gives the applicant one of three clear-cut ratings: highly recommended for sales, recommended with areas that could be improved, or not recommended for sales. Validity scales identify applicants who are exaggerating strengths or minimizing weaknesses, and the scores of those applicants are automatically adjusted. In addition, the report includes recommendations for training and motivation.

Format: Self-administered; untimed

Scoring: Computer scored; scoring service available

Cost: Complete Kit $180.00

Sales Attitude Checklist
Erwin K. Taylor

1992	NCS Pearson Reid London House

Population: Adults

Purpose: Measures attitudes and behaviors involved in sales and selling; used for sales selection programs

Description: Paper–pencil 31-item test assessing basic attitudes toward selling and habits in the selling situation.

Format: Examiner required; suitable for group use; untimed: 10 to 15 minutes

Scoring: Hand key

Cost: Contact publisher

Sales Comprehension Test
Martin M. Bruce

1988	Martin M Bruce, PhD.

Population: Adults

Purpose: Measures sales ability and potential based on the understanding of the principles of selling; used for evaluating prospective sales people, vocational counseling, and training projects for salespersons

Description: Paper–pencil 30-item multiple-choice test. Also available in French, Spanish, Italian, Dutch, and German.

Format: Self-administered; untimed: 15 to 20 minutes

Scoring: Hand key

Cost: Specimen Set $55.95

Sales Motivation Inventory, Revised
Martin M. Bruce

1985	Martin M. Bruce, PhD.

Population: Adults

Purpose: Assesses interest in and motivation for sales work, both commission and wholesale–retail

Description: Paper–pencil 75-item test measuring sales motivation and drive. Consists of multiple-choice triads. Available also in French. Suitable for individuals with physical, hearing, and visual impairments.

Format: Self-administered; untimed: 20 to 30 minutes

Scoring: Hand key

Cost: Specimen Set $55.95

Sales Professional Assessment Inventory (SPAI™)

1989	NCS Pearson Reid London House

Population: Adults

Purpose: Assesses potential for success in sales positions; used for selection and screening of candidates for direct sales to business and retail sales of consumer durable goods or special services

Description: Paper–pencil 210-item multiple-choice test with 12 diagnostic scales yielding scores in Sales and Work Experience, Sales Interest, Sales Responsibility, Sales Orientation, Energy Level, Self-Development, Sales Skills, Sales Understanding, Customer Service, Business Ethics, and Job Stability. Two validity scales, Candidness and Accuracy, are provided. A sales Potential Index that is a composite of the 12 diagnostic scales is provided for decision-making purposes. In addition to scores, the SPAI generates positive indicators, training needs, and follow-up interview questions, based on examinee responses to individual items.

Format: Examiner required; suitable for group use; untimed: 60 minutes

Scoring: Computer scored; scoring service available

Cost: Contact publisher

Sales Relations

1994	Clark Wilson Group

Population: Internal and external sales representatives

Purpose: Measures skills necessary for carrying out the responsibilities of sales

Description: Feedback is obtained using 50 questions with three open-ended questions from individuals who perceive the needed skills on a daily basis. Measures the strengths and soft spots.

Format: Self-administered; untimed

Scoring: Scoring service

Cost: $260 for up to 15 surveys

Sales Sentence Completion Blank, Revised
Martin M. Bruce

1982	Martin M. Bruce, PhD

Population: Adults

Purpose: Aids in evaluating and selecting sales personnel by providing insight into how the applicant thinks and his or her social attitudes and general personality

Description: Paper–pencil 40-item test consisting of sentence fragments to be completed by the subject. The examiner assesses the responses by scoring them on a 7-point scale. Responses

are a projection of the subject's attitudes about life, self, and others. Suitable for individuals with physical, hearing, or visual impairments.

Format: Self-administered; untimed: 20 to 35 minutes

Scoring: Hand key

Cost: Specimen Set $28.05

Sales Series "360" Feedback
Clark L. Wilson

Updated yearly	Clark Wilson Group

Population: Adults

Purpose: Measures interpersonal skills that influence internal organizations

Description: Two scales are available: Improving Your Sales Skills and Managing a Sales Force. Confidential raters are selected who know the individual's work best: peers, supervisors, prospects, and customers. They anonymously complete surveys regarding key sales practices.

Format: Survey; untimed

Scoring: Self-scored; computer scored; scoring service available; surveys available on-line

Cost: Contact publisher

Sales Skills—Form A-C
Roland T. Ramsay

2000	Ramsay Corporation

Population: Adults

Purpose: Measures sales knowledge

Description: The test contains 48 multiple-choice items in 12 categories: prospecting skills, interpersonal skills, communication/expressiveness skills, persistence, product knowledge, confidence, listening skills, closing skills, follow-up skills, negotiating skills, honesty, and motivation.

Format: Examiner required; suitable for group use; untimed: 60 minutes

Scoring: Self-scored

Cost: Test Booklet $10.00 (minimum of 20); Administration Manual $24.95

Sales Style
James H. Brewer

1990	Associated Consultants in Education

Population: Adults

Purpose: Used to sharpen sales skills

Description: Identifies four general patterns: Quick-Sell, Talkative-Sell, Persistent-Sell, and Precise-Sell types. The instrument relates personality type to sales style, identifies strengths and weaknesses of each personality type, helps sales people develop new approaches, and explores other styles.

Format: Self-administered; untimed: 15 to 20 minutes

Scoring: Hand key

Cost: $2.95 each

Sales Style Indicator (SSI)
Terry D. Anderson, Bruce R. Wares

1991	Consulting Resource Group International, Inc.

Population: Adults

Purpose: Assesses sales style preferences; used in sales training

Description: Forced-choice test with 16 items. A 10th-grade reading level is required.

Format: Examiner required; individual administration; suitable for group use; untimed

Scoring: Self-scored

Cost: $14.95

Selling Judgment Test
Martin M. Bruce

1959	Martin M. Bruce, PhD

Population: Adolescents, adults

Purpose: Measures sales comprehension; used by sales trainers to develop discussion topics

Description: Paper–pencil five-item multiple-choice test assessing sales competence in the retail and wholesale fields. The items in this test are taken from the Sales Comprehension Test and were chosen by the Associated Merchandising Corporation as particularly pertinent to the department retail store field. The test is used primarily for training and discussion purposes. The Sales Comprehension Test is more appropriate for assessment purposes. Suitable for individuals with physical, hearing, or visual impairments.

Format: Self-administered; untimed: 3 minutes

Scoring: Examiner evaluated

Cost: 20 Forms $17.50

SSI In-Depth Interpretation
Terry D. Anderson, Bruce R. Wares

1991	Consulting Resource Group International, Inc.

Population: Adults

Purpose: Assesses sales style preferences; used in sales training

Description: Test with 21 items. A 10th-grade reading level is required.

Format: Individual administration; suitable for group use; untimed

Scoring: Self-scored

Cost: $9.95

Station Employee Applicant Inventory (SEAI®)

1986	NCS Pearson Reid London House

Population: Adults

Purpose: Assesses on-the-job attitudes and behaviors of gas station and convenience store cashier applicants; used to predict which applicants will have low rates of tardiness and absenteeism, safeguard funds, and handle cash and charge transactions accurately

Description: Paper–pencil 144-item multiple-choice test that evaluates characteristics in five major areas measured by the following scales: Honesty, Interpersonal Cooperation, Drug Avoidance, Arithmetic Skills, and Job-Specific Skills and Abilities. An Applicant Employee Index and a validity scale are included also. Optional scales include safety attitudes and a tenure scale that predicts turnover. Standard and percentile scores are available in each of the five major areas. Three scoring options are available: operator-assisted telephone, Touch-Test, and PC based. Results are available immediately and written confirmation is mailed the next day.

Format: Examiner required; suitable for group use; untimed: 45 minutes

Scoring: Operator-assisted telephone; computer scored

Cost: Contact publisher

Telemarketing Applicant Inventory (TMAI®)

Date not provided	NCS Pearson Reid London House

Population: Adults

Purpose: Measures an applicant's potential for success in telephone sales and service positions

Description: The TMAI helps measure sales interest and skills, sales responsibility, productivity, confidence and influence, interpersonal orientation, stress tolerance, job stability, job simulation rating, communicator competence, applied verbal reasoning, validity/candidness, and validity/accuracy.

Format: Self-administration; untimed

Scoring: Computer scored; telephone and fax scoring available

Cost: Contact publisher

Test of Sales Aptitude, Revised
Martin M. Bruce

1983	Martin M. Bruce, PhD

Population: Adults

Purpose: Evaluates an individual's aptitude for selling; used as an aid in vocational guidance and in the selection and training of sales personnel

Description: Paper–pencil 50-item test measuring the subject's knowledge and understanding of the principles of selling a wide variety of goods ranging from heavy industrial capital items to door-to-door housewares. Norms are available to compare the subject's score with salespeople, men, women, and selected special sales groups. The subject reads the directions and completes the test. Suitable for individuals with physical, hearing, or visual impairments.

Format: Self-administered; untimed: 20 to 30 minutes

Scoring: Hand key

Cost: Specimen Set $52.20

Technical

VCWS 16—Drafting

1993	Valpar International Corporation

Population: Adults

Purpose: Measures potential to compete in an entry-level position requiring basic drafting and print reading skills; provides insight into the ability to visualize abstract problems and to acquire new tool use skills

Description: Manual test measuring an individual's potential to compete in an entry-level position requiring basic drafting skills. The examinee performs a series of exercises measuring his or her ability to measure objects accurately in inches and centimeters; learn the use of drafting tools such as a T square, compass, circle template, and triangles; and read blueprints. The examinee must produce three view drawings of three wooden blocks. Each subtest screens the examinee in terms of ability to cope successfully with the next subtest. The test is designed to accommodate a range of needs within the drafting industry from minimal expertise to sophisticated high-level performance.

Format: Examiner required; individual administration; timed

Scoring: Examiner evaluated

Cost: $1,660.00

Interests

Canadian Occupational Interest Inventory (COII)
G. Booth, Luc Begin

1982	NCS Pearson

Population: High school students, adults

Purpose: Identifies an individual's interest in occupationally related activities

Description: Paper–pencil 70-item measure of attitudes as they relate occupationally to activities. Interests and activities are measured by the following bipolar factors: things vs. people, business contact vs. scientific, routine vs. creative, social vs. solitary, and prestige vs. production. The test relates to the Canadian computer guid-ance programs DISCOVER and CHOICES. An IBM microcomputer program, Profile, which accesses over 6,000 occupations, is available for administration and scoring. Available also in French.

Format: Examiner required; suitable for group use; untimed: 40 minutes

Scoring: Hand key; computer scored

Cost: Contact publisher

Curtis Interest Scale
James W. Curtis

1964	Psychometric Affiliates

Population: Grade 10 to adult

Purpose: Assesses individual vocational interest

patterns; used for vocational guidance, screening, and selection

Description: Paper–pencil 55-item test of vocational interests in 10 occupational areas: applied arts, business, computation, direct sales, entertainment, farming, interpersonal, mechanics, production, and science. The test yields an estimate of "level of responsibility."

Format: Self-administered; suitable for group use; untimed: 10 minutes

Scoring: Examiner evaluated; scoring service available

Cost: Specimen Set (test, manual, profile sheet) $4.00; 25 Scales $7.00; 25 Profiles $4.00

World of Work Inventory (WOWI)
Robert E. Ripley, Karen Hudson,
Gregory P. M. Neidert, Nancy L. Ortman

2001   World of Work, Inc.

Population: Ages 13 to 65+ years

Purpose: Measures work-related temperaments, interests, and aptitudes; used for career counseling, vocational rehabilitation, employee selection

and development, and adult/career education classes

Description: The short form is administered as a 330-item on-line or paper–pencil inventory. The 98 multiple-choice items assess verbal, numerical, abstractions, spatial-form, mechanical–electrical, and clerical areas. The 232 rating items (3-point Likert) assess 12 job-related temperament factors and career interests in activities related to 17 professional and industrial career areas. The WOWI paper–pencil long form has 516 items. Results for all forms are provided in profile, summary, and interpretive report formats. Available in a variety of reading levels. Keyed to *Dictionary of Occupational Titles* career families and the *O*NET Dictionary of Occupational Titles.*

Format: Self-administered; untimed: on-line 1 hour, short form $1\frac{1}{2}$ hours, long form $2\frac{1}{2}$ hours

Scoring: On-line scoring instantly; machine scored; computer scored; test scoring service available

Cost: On-line Site License $189.00; Reusable Test Booklet $7.00; Interpretation Manual $19.95; each report priced separately

Management

Advanced Managerial Tests (AMT) Numerical Analysis (NMT4)

1995   SHL Canada

Population: Adults

Purpose: Assesses numerical skills of managers, professional staff, and work-experienced graduates across a range of functions

Description: Thirty-item test measuring the ability to interpret and use complex business-related numerical information. The test consists of a number of charts, tables, and graphs relating to one business organization. Candidates are required to interpret the data and combine the information from different sources to answer the questions. Calculators may be used. This test would be used in assessing a manager's ability to identify trends across a wide range of data or combine statistics from different departments to establish new information.

Format: Examiner required; individual administration; untimed: 35 minutes

Scoring: Hand key; machine scored; scoring service available

Cost: Contact publisher

Advanced Managerial Tests (AMT) Numerical Reasoning (NMT2)

1995   SHL Canada

Population: Adults

Purpose: Assesses verbal skills of managers, professional staff, and work-experienced graduates across a range of functions

Description: Test with 35 items measuring the ability to understand the relationship between pieces of numerical information and to complete the relevant operations needed to solve specific problems. The test consists of a series of short problems set in a range of business contexts. Candidates are required to use the information given and, with the aid of a calculator, reach appropriate solutions. Problem types range from arithmetic to proportions, ratios, and probabilities. The main use of this test is to establish a manager's competence in handling basic business data.

Format: Examiner required; individual administration; untimed: 20 minutes

Scoring: Hand key; machine scored; scoring service available

Cost: Contact publisher

Advanced Managerial Tests (AMT) Verbal Analysis (VMT3)

1995 — SHL Canada

Population: Adults

Purpose: Assesses numerical skills of managers, professional staff, and work-experienced graduates across a range of functions

Description: Test with 35 items measuring the ability to interpret high-level written information in a variety of ways. The test consists of a series of passages of complex information. The questions asked address a broad range of verbal analysis skills, such as summarizing, drawing appropriate inferences, and logical reasoning. This test assesses a manager's ability to interpret complex reports and documents.

Format: Examiner required; individual administration; untimed: 35 minutes

Scoring: Hand key; machine scored; scoring service available

Cost: Contact publisher

Advanced Managerial Tests (AMT) Verbal Application (VMT1)

1995 — SHL Canada

Population: Adults

Purpose: Assesses verbal skills of managers, professional staff, and work-experienced graduates across a range of functions

Description: Test with 35 items measuring the ability to understand the meaning of words, logic within sentences, and the use of grammar. The test consists of short sentences from which two or three words have been omitted. Candidates are required to select the correct combination of words to complete the sentences. One use of this test would be to assess a candidate's ability to understand, complete, or correct high-level written text.

Format: Examiner required; individual administration; untimed: 20 minutes

Scoring: Hand key; machine scored; scoring service available

Cost: Contact publisher

Assessment Inventory for Management (AIM)

1991 — LIMRA International

Population: Adults

Purpose: Identifies candidates with the greatest potential for success at all levels of field sales management for the insurance and financial services industry

Description: The AIM identifies strengths and developmental opportunities for 12 key behavioral competencies that are essential prerequisites for performing management tasks, including interpersonal, leadership, and organizational. The AIM provides each candidate with a list of training exercises, training courses, and other developmental ideas to groom promising candidates for field management. Copies of the Management Selection Interview Guide (one for inexperienced candidates and one for experienced candidates) are included with every AIM feedback report. The guides help the interviewer understand the candidate's background and match the candidate's experiences to the job requirements.

Format: Self-administered on-line; untimed

Scoring: On-line scoring

Cost: Contact publisher

ASSET: A Supervisory Selection and Development Tool

1990 — Life Office Management Association

Population: Adults

Purpose: Provides a valid selection system to identify supervisory potential for the insurance and financial services industry

Description: The system consists of two paper-pencil test batteries. Battery 1 provides developmental data in addition to selection information. Battery 2 provides selection information only. A three-test supplement, which can be used with either battery, tests for basic skills. Training is available for individuals planning to implement the ASSET tests.

Format: Examiner required; individual and group administration; timed

Scoring: Hand key

Cost: Contact publisher

BEST Leaderstyle Match (Computer Software)
James H. Brewer

1989	Associated Consultants in Education

Population: Adults

Purpose: Used to improve leadership skills

Description: This computer program calculates the leader's personality type, the leadership role characteristics in the leader's current position, and the compatibility between the two. With this information, the leader can modify his or her behavior to match the organization's needs.

Format: Self-administered; untimed: 15 to 20 minutes

Scoring: Hand key

Cost: $99.95 each

Campbell-Hallam™ Team Leader Profile (TLP™)

Date not provided	NCS Pearson Reid London House

Population: Adults

Purpose: Provides multisource feedback on group leadership skills

Description: The TLP survey helps provide objective information on the team leader's strengths and weaknesses based on the perceptions of the leader and selected observers such as direct reports, peers, and managers. The normative sample includes 2,500 team members who rated 500 team leaders in more than 100 different organizations.

Format: Self-administered; untimed: 20 minutes

Scoring: Scoring service

Cost: Contact publisher

Coaching Practices

1993	Clark Wilson Group

Population: Managers and supervisors

Purpose: Provides information to strengthen basic managerial skills that support an organization's appraisal programs

Description: Contains 77 questions with three open-ended questions to provide feedback to managers on their skills at coaching, appraising, and counseling for performance management.

Format: Self-administered; untimed

Scoring: Scoring service

Cost: $260 up to 15 surveys

Coaching Skills Inventory (CSI): Observer
Dennis C. Kinlaw

1990	Jossey-Bass/Pfeiffer

Population: Adults

Purpose: Helps managers develop skills in counseling, mentoring, tutoring, and confronting

Description: Measures participants' coaching skills and helps them create action plans for improvement. They measure the coaching skills used by superior leaders: Contact and Core Skills, Counseling, Mentoring, Tutoring, Confronting, and Challenging.

Format: Self-administered; untimed

Scoring: Peer scored

Cost: $4.95

Coaching Skills Inventory (CSI): Self
Dennis C. Kinlaw

1990	Jossey-Bass/Pfeiffer

Population: Adults

Purpose: Helps managers develop skills in counseling, mentoring, tutoring, and confronting

Description: Measures participants' coaching skills and helps them create action plans for improvement. Measures the coaching skills used by superior leaders: Contact and Core Skills, Counseling, Mentoring, Tutoring, and Confronting and Challenging.

Format: Self-administered; untimed

Scoring: Self-scored

Cost: $9.95

Critical Thinking Test (CTT) Numerical Critical Reasoning (NCT1)

1988	SHL Canada

Population: Adults

Purpose: Assesses numerical critical reasoning skills in managers

Description: Forty-item multiple-choice test measuring understanding and reasoning of numerical data, rather than pure computation. Candidates are required to make decisions or inferences from numerical data presented in a variety of formats. The use of calculators is permitted. The format has clear relevance to management decision making based on numerical and statistical data. Also available in French.

Format: Examiner required; individual administration; untimed: 35 minutes

Scoring: Hand key; machine scored; scoring service available

Cost: Contact publisher

Critical Thinking Test (CTT) Verbal Critical Reasoning (VCT1)

1988	SHL Canada

Population: Adults

Purpose: Assesses verbal critical reasoning skills in managers

Description: Multiple-choice 52-item test measuring the ability to evaluate the logic of various kinds of argument within a realistic context. Candidates are given passages of information followed by series of statements. The candidates must decide whether a given statement is true or untrue, or whether there is insufficient information to make the judgment. The test clearly relates to a key element in managerial or senior specialist jobs in which decisions or inferences must be made or evaluated either on paper or in meetings. Also available in French.

Format: Examiner required; individual administration; untimed: 25 minutes

Scoring: Hand key; machine scored; scoring service available

Cost: Contact publisher

Decision Making Strategies
Herbert S. Kindler

Updated yearly	Center for Management Effectiveness, Inc.

Population: Ages 17 and older

Purpose: Selection of best decision-making strategy

Description: Applications include training, development, and coaching. Intended for working and nonworking adults. A multiple-choice paper–pencil test with 12 items. Also available in Spanish.

Format: Individually self-administered; untimed: 15 minutes

Scoring: Self-scored

Cost: $8.95, with a minimum purchase of 20

Developing the Leader Within (DLW)
Linda Phillips-Jones

1995	Mind Garden, Inc.

Population: Adults

Purpose: Assesses leadership skills levels; used in psychology and leadership development

Description: Likert scale test with 45 items covering Developing Within, Helping Others Excel, Improving Critical Processes, and Showing Commitment to the Team. Uses 360-degree feedback.

Format: Individual administration; untimed: 15 minutes

Scoring: Computer scored

Cost: Multi-rater $80.00; Single Version $20.00

Diversity Awareness Profile: Manager's Version
K. Stinson

1992	Jossey-Bass/Pfeiffer

Population: Adults

Purpose: Helps managers to be aware of their actions or inactions that inhibit the success of others; reveals areas where managers could be proactive in eliminating biases

Description: Questions are based on those in the Diversity Awareness Profile, but are stated in ways that are relevant to managers. These questions help managers to be aware of their actions or inactions that inhibit the success of others. The profile also reveals areas where managers could be proactive in eliminating biases. Trainer's Notes include an overview, discussion questions, and instructions for administering and helping participants create action plans. Use these instruments as stand-alone interventions or as part of a program on improving working relationships.

Format: Self-administered; untimed

Scoring: Self-scored

Cost: $5.00

Executive Leadership

1998	Clark Wilson Group

Population: Senior executive staff

Purpose: Measures the skills and attributes that contribute to the success of leadership

Description: Provides feedback from multiple levels on key executive competencies including vision, organizational and marketplace awareness, and executive energy. Contains 84 questions and three open-ended questions. Available in 10 languages and on-line.

Format: Self-administered; untimed

Scoring: Scoring service

Cost: $425 up to 15 surveys

Executive Profile Survey (EPS)
Virgil R. Lang

| 1978 | Institute for Personality and Ability Testing, Inc. |

Population: Adults

Purpose: Measures executive potential; facilitates the identification of individuals likely to succeed; used for employee evaluation and placement, screening applicants, and professional development

Description: Eighty-one items plus 13 short paragraphs are rated on a 7-point scale to measure self-attitudes, values, and beliefs of individuals in comparison with over 2,000 top-level executives. Based on a 15-year study of the "executive personality," the EPS measures the 11 personality-profile dimensions most important in business, management, and executive settings: ambitious, assertive, enthusiastic, creative, spontaneous, self-focused, considerate, open-minded, relaxed, practical, and systematic. The survey also provides two validity scales. Norms, reliability, validity, and developmental background are explained.

Format: Self-administered; untimed: 1 hour

Scoring: Computer scored; scoring service available

Cost: Introductory Kit $28.00

Executive Series "360" Feedback
Clark L. Wilson

| Updated yearly | Clark Wilson Group |

Population: Adults

Purpose: Identifies the skills and talents needed to manage the complexities of fast-paced change

Description: Peers and board members are selected to complete written surveys. They anonymously answer questions in areas such as communicating strategic vision, reading internal and external environments, handling complexities, and developing an effective management team. Complete confidentiality is assured. Scores are benchmarked against more than 3,500 other senior managers.

Format: Survey; untimed

Scoring: Self-scored; computer scored; test scoring service available; surveys available on-line

Cost: Contact publisher

Experience and Background Inventory (EBI)
Melany E. Baehr, Ernest C. Froemel

| 1996 | NCS Pearson Reid London House |

Population: Adults

Purpose: Evaluates an individual's past performance and experience on nine factorially determined dimensions of quantified personal background data; used for selection, promotion, and career counseling of higher level managerial and professional personnel

Description: Paper–pencil 55-item multiple-choice inventory assessing the following background areas: school achievement, choice of a college major, aspiration level, drive/career progress, leadership and group participation, vocational satisfaction, financial responsibility, general responsibility, and relaxation pursuits. Different combinations of factors have been validated for selection and evaluation of potential for successful performance in higher level managerial and professional positions.

Format: Self-administered; untimed: 20 minutes

Scoring: Hand key

Cost: Contact publisher

Hilson Job Analysis Questionnaire (HJAQ)
Robin E. Inwald

| 1997 | Hilson Research, Inc. |

Population: Adults

Purpose: Assesses job-related qualities

Description: Total of 134 items used in analysis of administrators and supervisors to determine job-related qualities needed for a specific position.

Format: Examiner required; suitable for groups; untimed: 30 minutes

Scoring: Computer scored; scoring service

Cost: Contact publisher

Hilson Management Inventory (HMI)
Robin E. Inwald

| 1997 | Hilson Research, Inc. |

Population: Adults

Purpose: Screens individuals for managerial and executive positions

Description: Measures leadership, work ethic, drive, social skills, and so forth. Used for preemployment screening or promotion of job candidates. A 263-item true–false test.

Format: Examiner required; suitable for groups; untimed: 30 minutes

Scoring: Computer scored; scoring service available

Cost: Contact publisher

Hilson Management Survey (HMS)
Robin E. Inwald

1995   Hilson Research, Inc.

Population: Adults

Purpose: Assesses work-related behavioral characteristics

Description: Paper–pencil 103-item true–false test with a profile graph within a computer-generated report. A test book and scannable answer sheets are used. A fifth-grade reading level is required.

Format: Examiner required; suitable for groups; untimed: 30 minutes

Scoring: Computer scored; scoring service available

Cost: Contact publisher

Influence Strategies Exercise (ISE)

1993   Hay Group

Population: Adults

Purpose: Assesses influence techniques

Description: Consists of 54 items dealing with nine influence strategies: empowerment, interpersonal awareness, bargaining, relationship building, organizational awareness, common vision, impact management, logical persuasion, and coercion. At least three people provide feedback per participant. There are no right or wrong styles; all nine influence techniques can make communication more efficient and effective. Used at all levels within organizations.

Format: Self-administration; untimed: 30 minutes

Scoring: Self-scored

Cost: 10 Participant Questionnaires and Interpretive Notes $65.00; 10 Employee Questionnaires $25.00

Inventory of Management Competencies (IMC)

1994   SHL Canada

Population: Managers (all levels)

Purpose: Measures managerial competencies

Description: Assesses 16 generic management competencies using 40 questions. One test is for self-assessment; two to six tests are for 360-degree feedback. A two-page color profile and optional expert narrative report are provided. Also available in French.

Format: Examiner required; individual administration; computer and on-line administration available; untimed: 20 minutes

Scoring: Hand key; machine scored; scoring service available; on-line scoring

Cost: Contact publisher

IPI Job-Field Series: Production/Mechanical

1997   Industrial Psychology International Ltd.

Population: Adults

Purpose: Assesses skills and personality for supervisory positions in a factory setting; used to evaluate the achievement and personality of maintenance and production people, foremen, and superintendents

Description: Multiple-item paper–pencil battery of seven aptitude and two personality tests. The tests are Motor, Precision, Blocks, Dexterity, Dimension, Parts, Numbers, Neurotic Personality Factor, and Contact Personality Factor. For individual test descriptions, see the IPI Employee Aptitude Series. Also available in French and Spanish.

Format: Examiner required; suitable for group use; timed: 128 minutes

Scoring: Hand key

Cost: Starter Kit (test materials for five applicants, scoring keys, manuals) $80.00; Test Package $12.00 per applicant

IPI Job-Field Series: Sales Personnel

1997   Industrial Psychology International Ltd.

Population: Adults

Purpose: Assesses skills and personality of applicants for supervisory positions in various sales fields; used to screen for advertising, credit, merchandise, service, and store sales supervisor positions

Description: Multiple-item paper–pencil battery of seven aptitude and two personality tests. The tests are Fluency, Sales Terms, Memory, Judgment, Parts, Numbers, Perception, Contact Personality Factor, and Neurotic Personality Factor. For individual test descriptions, see the IPI Employee Aptitude Series. Also available in French and Spanish.

Format: Self-administered; timed: 82 minutes

Scoring: Hand key

Cost: Starter Kit (test materials for five applicants, scoring keys, manuals) $80.00; Test Package $12.00 per applicant

Job Analysis Kit (JAK)
Sandra A. McIntire, Mary Ann Bucklan, Deonda R. Scott

1995	Psychological Assessment Resources, Inc.

Population: Adults

Purpose: Used as a step-by-step method for conducting job analysis by human resource management and industrial psychologists; intended for supervisors

Description: Oral-response short-answer verbal measure of knowledge, skills, abilities, and other characteristics.

Format: Examiner required; individual administration; untimed

Scoring: Examiner evaluated

Cost: Kit $185.00

Leadership Competencies for Managers

1998	Clark Wilson Group

Population: Middle to senior level managers

Purpose: Measures the skills essential to both management and leadership roles

Description: A multiple-rater assessment that provides feedback on management skills. Contains 92 questions with three open-ended questions. Also available in Spanish and Portuguese.

Format: Self-administered; untimed

Scoring: Scoring service

Cost: $260 up to 15 surveys

Leadership in Health Services

2000	Clark Wilson Group

Population: Managers in health care industry

Purpose: Measures leadership skills needed to lead the organization in competing successfully in the changing health care environment

Description: A multiple-rater assessment that provides the health services executive with feedback about his or her management and leadership skills. Contains 106 questions with three open-ended questions. Also available in Spanish.

Format: Self-administered; untimed

Scoring: Scoring service

Cost: $260 up to 15 surveys

Leadership Inventories

Date not provided	Personnel Decisions International

Population: Adults

Purpose: Assesses potential and current leaders

Description: Measure of leadership potential of entry- and mid-level leaders. Developed as screening tools, they measure the basic abilities, traits, values, interests, and motivations that are critical to becoming an effective leader. They identify the building blocks upon which leadership knowledge, experiences, and skills are developed.

Format: Examiner required; suitable for groups; untimed: 10 to 15 minutes

Scoring: Computer scored; telephone and fax scoring; on-line scoring

Cost: Contact publisher

Leadership Opinion Questionnaire (LOQ)
Edwin A. Fleishman

1989	NCS Pearson Reid London House

Population: Adults

Purpose: Measures leadership style; used in a variety of industrial and organizational settings for selection, appraisal, counseling, and training of employees

Description: Paper–pencil or computerized 40-item test measuring two aspects of leadership: consideration (how likely an individual's job relationship with subordinates is to be characterized by mutual trust, respect, and consideration) and structure (how likely an individual is to define and structure personal and subordinates' roles toward goal attainment).

Format: Self-administered; untimed: 10 to 15 minutes

Scoring: Hand key; computer scored

Cost: Contact publisher

Leadership Practices

1996	Clark Wilson Group

Population: Senior executive staff

Purpose: Measures the skills and personal attributes that will move the organization toward positive change

Description: A multiple-rater assessment that provides the organizational leader with feedback on his or her leadership skills. Contains 77 questions with eight additional questions on sources of influence and three open-ended questions. Also available in Spanish, Portuguese, and Arabic, and on-line.

Format: Self-administered; untimed

Scoring: Scoring service

Cost: $260 up to 15 surveys

Leadership Practices Inventory–Second Edition, Revised (LPI)
James M. Kouzes, Barry Z. Posner

Date not provided	Jossey-Bass/Pfeiffer

Population: Managers and supervisors

Purpose: Helps managers set goals, create solid action plans, cultivate innovative thinking, improve interpersonal skills, and take other positive steps to develop essential leadership traits

Description: Revised edition includes 10-point Likert scale, scoring software, participant workbooks, tools needed to obtain complete 360-degree feedback, and 3-month follow-up program to track progress. The self-inventory evaluates performance and effectiveness as a leader. The observer inventory provides a balanced picture of how others perceive leadership traits and allows for constructive discussion of ways to improve.

Format: Self-administered; untimed: 2 to 4 hours

Scoring: Self-scored; computer scored

Cost: Deluxe Facilitator's Package (1 each of guide and book) $59.95; Self $12.95; Observer $3.95

Leadership Skills Inventory–Other's (LSI)
Terry D. Anderson

1992	Consulting Resource Group International, Inc.

Population: Adults

Purpose: Assesses others' leadership skills; used in leadership development

Description: Ranking test with 56 items to provide feedback to guide individual to skills that need developing. A 10th-grade reading level is required. Also available in Swedish.

Format: Examiner required; individual administration; suitable for group use; untimed

Scoring: Self-scored

Cost: $7.95

Leadership Skills Inventory–Self (LSI)
Terry D. Anderson

1992	Consulting Resource Group International, Inc.

Population: Adults

Purpose: Measures leadership skills; used in leadership development

Description: Rating test with 56 items to provide insight and formulate a training plan. A 10th-grade reading level is required.

Format: Examiner required; individual administration; suitable for group use; untimed

Scoring: Self-scored

Cost: $12.95

Leatherman Leadership Questionnaire (LLQ)
Richard W. Leatherman

1992	International Training Consultants, Inc.

Population: Adults

Purpose: Used in career counseling and training needs assessment to determine the organization's needs and to provide the individual with specific career development "prescriptions" based on objective information of strengths and areas of needed improvement

Description: Multiple-choice 339-item test with one most correct answer and three distractors, with 27 scales. A summary report, two transparency bar charts, training needs analysis, and individual report are available. A 129-page administrator's manual, 143-page questionnaire (Parts 1 and 2), two answer sheets, 109-page research report, and a 346-page development manual for each test taker are used. A high school reading level is required. Also available in German.

Format: Examiner required; individual and group administration; untimed: $4\frac{1}{2}$ hours

Scoring: Machine scored

Cost: Complete Testing Kit for 10 people $1,500.00; Additional Testing Service $95.00 per person

London House™ System for Testing and Evaluation of Potential (LH-STEP™)

Date not provided	NCS Pearson Reid London House

Population: Adults

Purpose: Helps add insight to hiring, training, and promotion decisions to enhance the quality of management teams

Description: First, members of a staff complete a questionnaire to create a profile of the job functions most critical to the position needing to be filled. This description is matched to a national data bank of job profiles to develop a clear definition of the skills, abilities, and attitudes of job applicants. The second phase consists of administering candidates a battery measuring up to 50 skills, abilities, and attributes for six key areas. The third step compares an individual with the critical job functions defined in the first step. Helps to reduce turnover.

Format: Self-administration; untimed: 2 hours 30 minutes

Scoring: Scoring service

Cost: Contact publisher

Management and Supervisory Skills—Form A-C
Roland T. Ramsay

2000	Ramsay Corporation

Population: Adults

Purpose: Measures knowledge of management and supervisory skills

Description: In 40 items, the following five skills are measured: planning, organizing, communicating, motivating, and managing.

Format: Examiner required; suitable for group use; untimed: 60 minutes

Scoring: Self-scored

Cost: Test Booklet $10.00 (minimum of 20); Administration Manual $24.95

Management Aptitude Test™ (MAT)

Date not provided	NCS Pearson Reid London House

Population: Adults

Purpose: Assesses a leadership candidate's critical thinking ability and business knowledge

Description: Measures problem solving, planning and organizing, communication, supervi-

sory skills, administrative skills, and business control to provide a Manager Potential Index. Candidates are asked to respond to situational questions.

Format: Self-administration; untimed: 90 minutes

Scoring: Software scoring; computer scoring via telephone

Cost: Contact publisher

Management Development Questionnaire (MDQ)
Allan Cameron

1996	Test Agency, Ltd.

Population: Adults

Purpose: Assists managers and supervisors to identify strengths and weaknesses in their management style

Description: The MDQ can be used as a candidate self-perception inventory in a recruitment environment alongside personality assessment instruments to provide a candidate's perception of his or her managerial ability. The MDQ provides tailored reports of candidate profiles. It works by applying a set of decision rules to the candidate's sten scores. Depending on the sten scores, certain statements give the meaning and potential implications of the scores.

Format: Examiner required; individual or group administration; can be computer administered; untimed

Scoring: Self-scored; computer scored; machine scored; test scoring service available from publisher

Cost: Contact publisher

Management Inventory on Managing Change (MIMC)
Donald L. Kirkpatrick

1994	Donald L. Kirkpatrick, PhD

Population: Adults

Purpose: Measures a manager's attitudes and knowledge in regard to managing change within an organization; used in conjunction with training programs aimed at teaching all levels of managers how to deal with change

Description: Paper–pencil 65-item inventory measuring attitudes, knowledge, and opinions regarding principles and approaches for managing change. Items 1 through 50 are statements of beliefs or attitudes concerning organizational change and various ways of implementing such change. Individuals indicate whether they agree or disagree with each statement. Items 51 through 60 are free-response questions asking for a list of reasons why people might accept or resist change. Items 61 through 65 are multiple-choice items calling for an assessment of a situation involving change within an organization. Item content is intended to help managers understand their role in managing change.

Format: Self-administered; untimed: 20 minutes

Scoring: Self-scored

Cost: 20 Tests and Answer Booklets, Instructor's Manual $40.00

Management Inventory on Modern Management (MIMM)
Donald L. Kirkpatrick

1992	Donald L. Kirkpatrick, PhD

Population: Adults

Purpose: Measures philosophy, principles, and approaches related to the effective performance of middle- and upper-level managers; used to determine need for training, as a tool for conference discussions, and to evaluate effectiveness of a training program

Description: Paper–pencil 80-item agree–disagree test of eight topics important to managers: leadership styles, selection and training, communicating, motivating, managing change, delegating, decision making, and managing time. Other available materials include an explanatory audiocassette, a book on communication, and a communication training kit.

Format: Self-administered; untimed: 20 minutes

Scoring: Self-scored

Cost: 20 Tests and Answer Booklets, Instructor's Manual $40.00

Management Inventory on Performance Appraisal and Coaching (MIPAC)
Donald L. Kirkpatrick

1992	Donald L. Kirkpatrick, PhD

Population: Adults

Purpose: Measures knowledge and agreement with principles and techniques in performance appraisal and coaching; used in conjunction with management training programs

Description: Paper–pencil 45-item two-choice test measuring the extent to which supervisors

understand and accept the principles, facts, and techniques of performance appraisal and coaching. Individuals indicate whether they agree or disagree with each statement about beliefs or behaviors presented in each test item. The answer booklet provides a rationale for each correct answer. Test results identify topics that should be emphasized in training programs and provide information for on-the-job coaching.

Format: Self-administered; untimed: 15 minutes

Scoring: Self-scored

Cost: 20 Tests and Answer Booklets, Instructor's Manual $40.00

Management Inventory on Time Management (MITM)
Donald L. Kirkpatrick

1994	Donald L. Kirkpatrick, PhD

Population: Adults

Purpose: Measures a manager's knowledge and attitudes regarding effective management of time and delegation; used in conjunction with training programs on time management

Description: Paper–pencil 60-item two-choice test assessing managers' knowledge of the principles and practices concerning the effective management of time. Test items are statements about time use within an organization. Individuals indicate for each item whether they agree or disagree with the statement. The answer booklet includes the rationale for all correct answers. Test results identify topics that should be emphasized in training programs, serve as a tool for conference discussions, measure the effectiveness of training programs, and provide information for on-the-job coaching. A list of books and films for use in time management training programs is included.

Format: Self-administered; untimed: 15 minutes

Scoring: Self-scored

Cost: 20 Tests and Answer Booklets, Instructor's Manual $40.00

Management of Differences Inventory
Herbert S. Kindler

Updated yearly	Center for Management Effectiveness, Inc.

Population: Ages 17 years and older

Purpose: Assesses ways to manage differences and conflict

Description: Nine approaches to managing

differences and conflicts, with 36 items. Applications include training, development, and coaching. Intended for working and nonworking adults. A paper–pencil multiple-choice instrument with self and feedback forms. Also available in Spanish.

Format: Self-administered

Scoring: Self-scored

Cost: $8.95 each (minimum purchase of 20)

Management Practices

1995	Clark Wilson Group

Population: Managers and supervisors at all levels

Purpose: Provides feedback for managers to enhance their management skills

Description: A multiple-rater assessment that provides managers with feedback on their management skills and practices. Contains 100 or 145 questions with three open-ended questions. Also available in Spanish, French, Portuguese, German, Polish, and Arabic, and on-line.

Format: Self-administered; untimed

Scoring: Scoring service

Cost: $260 up to 15 surveys

Management Readiness Profile (MRP™)

1988	NCS Pearson Reid London House

Population: Adults

Purpose: Evaluates job applicants or employees for managerial interests and basic management orientation

Description: Paper–pencil 188-item multiple-choice test with seven subtests: Management Interests, Leadership, Energy and Drive, Practical Thinking, Management Responsibility, Sociability, and Candidates. Subscale scores and a composite Management Readiness Index are generated.

Format: Self-administered; untimed: 20 minutes

Scoring: Computer scored

Cost: Contact publisher

Management Series "360" Feedback
Clark L. Wilson

Updated yearly	Clark Wilson Group

Population: Adults

Purpose: Measures strengths and weaknesses on key behaviors

Description: To perform "360" assessments, the individual selects confidential raters who know his or her work best: peers, supervisors, and customers. These individuals anonymously complete surveys about management and leadership skills. The results are reviewed with a trained human resources coach.

Format: Survey; untimed

Scoring: Self-scored or computer scored; scoring service available; surveys available on-line

Cost: Contact publisher

Management Success Profile (MSP™)

Date not provided	NCS Pearson Reid London House

Population: Adults

Purpose: Evaluates skills and attitudes that are critical to management success

Description: Identifies those candidates who will follow company procedures and make ethical business decisions. The following areas are assessed: work background, leadership, coaching, adaptability, management responsibility, practical thinking, customer service orientation, productivity, job commitment, business ethics, validity/accuracy, and validity/candidness.

Format: Self-administered; untimed: 45 minutes

Scoring: Software scoring; computer scoring via telephone and fax

Cost: Contact publisher

Manager/Supervisor Staff Selector

1984	Walden Personnel Testing and Consulting, Inc.

Population: Adults

Purpose: Measures intellectual and personality characteristics of candidates for manager and supervisor positions

Description: Multiple-item paper–pencil set of seven subtests assessing logic, problem-solving, planning, and conceptualizing skills; numerical skills and reasoning; verbal fluency and communication skills; business judgment and ability to deal with peers; supervisory practices and practical leadership; emotional stability; and people contact skills. The test is used for selecting first- and second-line supervisors for all positions and as a screening test for middle and senior management candidates. Three subtests are timed. Available in Basic, Screening, or Comprehensive versions depending on depth of assessment required. Also available in French.

Format: Examiner required; suitable for group use; timed/untimed: 120 minutes

Scoring: Scoring service provided

Cost: $499.00 each

Managerial and Professional Job Functions Inventory (MP-JFI)
Melany E. Baehr, Wallace G. Lonergan, Bruce A. Hunt

1978	NCS Pearson Reid London House

Population: Adults

Purpose: Assesses the relative importance of functions performed in higher level managerial and professional positions and the incumbent's ability to perform them; used to clarify job positions and organizational structure, and to diagnose training needs

Description: Multiple-item paper–pencil inventory assessing the relative importance of job functions in the following 16 categories: setting organizational objectives, financial planning and review, improving work procedures and practices, interdepartmental coordination, developing and implementing technical ideas, judgment and decision making, developing teamwork, coping with difficulties and emergencies, promoting safety attitudes and practices, communications, developing employee potential, supervisory practices, self-development and improvement, personnel practices, promoting community–organization relations, and handling outside contacts. Items are rated by incumbent employees for each position. The test may be used for self or supervisory ratings.

Format: Examiner required; suitable for group use; untimed: 40 to 60 minutes

Scoring: Hand key

Cost: Contact publisher

Managerial Style Questionnaire (MSQ)

1994	Hay Group

Population: Adults

Purpose: Identifies a manager's style and the impact of managerial style on performance, productivity, and profits

Description: This questionnaire consists of 36 items that measure six different managerial styles: Coercive, Democratic, Authoritative, Coaching, Pacesetting, and Affiliative. Identifies which style or styles a manager relies on most

and when those styles are most and least effective. Also available in Spanish and French.

Format: Self-administered; untimed: 30 minutes

Scoring: Self-scored

Cost: 10 Participant Questionnaires and Interpretive Notes $65.00; 10 Employee Questionnaires $25.00

Multi-Factor Leadership Questionnaire for Research (MLQ)
Bernard M. Bass, Bruce J. Avolio

1995	Mind Garden, Inc.

Population: Adults

Purpose: Assesses leadership and management abilities

Description: The MLQ provides the best relationship of survey data to organizational outcome. The multirater report brings home the relationship between the leader's perceptions and those of the raters. The new report shows how best to use the MLQ data, explains Full Range Leadership, and provides tips for improving leadership. The 45-item MLQ contains 12 scales: Idealized Attributes, Idealized Behaviors, Inspirational Motivation, Intellectual Stimulation, Individualized Consideration, Contingent Reward, Management-by-Exception (Active), Management-by-Exception (Passive), Laissez-faire, Extra Effort, Effectiveness, and Satisfaction. The narrative report is available both with and without group data.

Format: Self-administered, suitable for group use; untimed

Scoring: Examiner evaluated; computer scored; scoring service available

Cost: Multi-Rater Report (leader and 8 rater forms) $120.00; Group Data $125.00

My BEST Leadership Style
James H. Brewer

1994	Associated Consultants in Education

Population: Adults

Purpose: Used to improve leadership skills

Description: Using My BEST Leadership Style, human resource developers can help supervisors, managers, executives, and others understand how to modify their behaviors to deal more effectively with subordinates. The test gives examples of how personality types affect leadership styles, suggests modification techniques for more successful leadership, describes how to lead different personality types, and discusses organization needs versus personal leadership style.

Format: Self-administered; untimed: 15 to 20 minutes

Scoring: Hand key

Cost: $4.95 each

Negotiating Style
James H. Brewer

| 1991 | Associated Consultants in Education |

Population: Adults

Purpose: Used to build productive negotiating strategies

Description: The instrument identifies negotiating style, describes how styles behave in negotiating sessions, suggests ways to improve each style, and promotes more productive negotiating techniques.

Format: Self-administered; untimed: 15 to 20 minutes

Scoring: Hand key

Cost: $2.95 each

Occupational Personality Questionnaire (OPQ32)

| 1999 | SHL Canada |

Population: Managers and other professionals

Purpose: Used for assessment and development of behavior at work

Description: A total of 230 items in three categories: relationships with people, thinking style, and feelings and emotions. Describes 32 dimensions of preferred/typical style of behavior at work. Provides variety of expert reports on assessment and development. Also available in French.

Format: Examiner required; individual administration; computer and on-line administration available; untimed: 35 minutes

Scoring: Hand key; machine scored; scoring service available; on-line scoring

Cost: Contact publisher

Organizational Description Questionnaire (ODQ)
Bernard M. Bass, Bruce J. Avolio

| 1992 | Mind Garden, Inc. |

Population: Adults

Purpose: Explores the relationship between leaders of an organization

Description: Brief paper–pencil 28-item ques-

tionnaire and resulting report. Measures how often each member of the organization perceives the culture of his or her unit, department, or organization to be using a full range of specific leadership factors. The ODQ places the organization on a nine-point scale spanning cultures such as Bureaucratic, Coasting, and Highly Developed.

Format: Self-administered; untimed

Scoring: Examiner evaluated; computer scored; scoring service available from publisher

Cost: 100 Forms $200.00

Peer Relations

| 1994 | Clark Wilson Group |

Population: Adults

Purpose: Measures management skills with the focus on the horizontal relationship between professional or technical specialists and their internal clients

Description: Looks at the skills needed to work with others as an independent contributor. Evaluates the specialist's management expertise, which is as important as technical expertise on the job. Contains 80 questions with three open-ended questions. Also available in Spanish and on-line.

Format: Self-administered; untimed

Scoring: Scoring service

Cost: $260 up to 15 surveys

Personnel Performance Problems Inventory (PPPI)
Albert A. Canfield

| 1987 | Western Psychological Services |

Population: Adults

Purpose: Assesses the use of delegation skills at all levels of management; identifies specific elements in the delegation process that are creating problems; used for manager and supervisor training and development

Description: Paper–pencil 30-item test assessing the effectiveness of a supervisor's delegation relationships in the following areas: mutual understanding of job responsibilities, authority, accountability, results expected, and employment conditions. Each test item describes a common performance problem of subordinates. The supervisor or manager must indicate the extent to which each is a problem with a present employee or group of employees. Test booklets contain complete descriptions of areas for improvement.

Norms are provided for supervisors and managers to identify key areas for improvement. A bibliography for additional reading also is included.

Format: Self-administered; untimed: 30 minutes

Scoring: Self-scored

Cost: Kit (10 inventories, manual) $38.50

Perspectives on Management Competencies

1998   **SHL Canada**

Population: Managers (all levels)

Purpose: An in-depth assessment of management competencies

Description: A total of 144 items. One test is for self-assessment; two to six tests provide 360-degree assessment. Thirty-six key management competencies are viewed from multiple perspectives. Multiple reports and detailed behavioral feedback are available. Also available in French.

Format: Examiner required; individual administration; untimed: 18 minutes

Scoring: Hand key; machine scored; scoring service available

Cost: Contact publisher

Professional and Managerial Position Questionnaire (PMPQ)
J. L. Mitchell, E. J. McCormick

1990   **PAQ Services, Inc.**

Population: Adults

Purpose: Job analysis used by human resource administrators

Description: Measures job functions, personal requirements, and other information. Includes questionnaire booklet, answer sheet, and job analysis manual.

Format: Examiner required; suitable for groups; untimed

Scoring: Computer scored; scoring service available

Cost: Contact publisher

Quality Improvement Audit for Leaders
James H. Brewer

1990   **Associated Consultants in Education**

Population: Adults

Purpose: Assesses the leader's knowledge and behaviors during quality improvement implementation as compared to leading Japanese and American firms

Description: Serves as a guide for implementing basic quality improvement behaviors while helping the leader take a personal assessment of his or her quality improvement knowledge and behaviors. The instrument assesses personal leadership factors in quality implementation, compares achievement to accepted Total Quality Management models, and increases leadership skills.

Format: Self-administered; untimed: 15 to 20 minutes

Scoring: Hand key

Cost: $6.95 each

Retail Management Assessment Inventory (RMAI®)

1989   **NCS Pearson Reid London House**

Population: Adults

Purpose: Selects and screens applicants for the position of unit manager in retail or restaurant outlets

Description: Multiple-item multiple-choice paper–pen test composed of 10 subtests: Background and Work Experience, Management and Leadership Interests, Management Responsibility, Understanding Management Procedures and Practices, Customer Service, Applied Management Computations, Energy Level, Job Stability, Business Ethics, and Management Orientation. Scores are provided for each subtest and for an overall Management Potential Index. In addition to scores, the RMAI generates positive indicators, training needs, and follow-up interview questions.

Format: Examiner required; suitable for group use; untimed: 75 minutes

Scoring: Computer scored

Cost: Contact publisher

Sales Management Practices

1994   **Clark Wilson Group**

Population: Managers and supervisors

Purpose: Provides feedback on management skills and practices

Description: Contains 145 questions with three open-ended questions completed by multiple raters.

Format: Self-administered; untimed

Scoring: Scoring service

Cost: $260 up to 15 surveys

Station Manager Applicant Inventory (SMAI™)

1987	NCS Pearson Reid London House

Population: Adults

Purpose: Screens gas station dealers and managers for operating a gas station; also used for franchise screening for gas stations

Description: Paper–pencil 218-item multiple-choice test used for screening station manager applicants. The test contains eight subtests: Background, Managerial Arithmetic, Honesty, Interpersonal Cooperation, Drug Avoidance, Temperament, Understanding Organizational Policies and Practices, and Distortion. Eight subtest scores and a composite Manager Potential Index are generated.

Format: Examiner required; suitable for group use; untimed: 1 hour, 30 minutes

Scoring: Computer scored; scoring service available from publisher

Cost: Contact publisher

Supervisory Behavior Description (SBD) Questionnaire
Edwin A. Fleishman

1989	NCS Pearson Reid London House

Population: Adults

Purpose: Measures leadership style as perceived by supervisors, peers, and subordinates; used in a variety of industrial and organizational settings for selection, appraisal, counseling, and training of employees

Description: Multiple-choice 48-item test measuring two aspects of leadership: consideration (how likely an individual's job relationship with subordinates is to be characterized by mutual trust, respect, and consideration) and structure (how likely an individual is to define and structure personal and subordinates' roles toward goal attainment).

Format: Examiner required; suitable for group use; untimed: 20 minutes

Scoring: Hand key; computer

Cost: Contact publisher

Supervisory Inventory on Communication (SIC)
Donald L. Kirkpatrick

2000	Donald L. Kirkpatrick, PhD

Population: Adults

Purpose: Measures knowledge of proper supervisory use of communication procedures within an organization; used in conjunction with training programs aimed at improving the communication effectiveness of supervisors

Description: Paper–pencil 80-item two-choice test assessing knowledge and understanding of communication philosophy, principles, and methods for supervisors. Each item describes an action or belief concerned with on-the-job communication. Individuals indicate whether they agree or disagree with each statement. Test results identify topics that should be emphasized in training programs, serve as a tool for conference discussions, measure the effectiveness of training programs, provide information for on-the-job coaching, and assist in the selection of supervisory personnel. The instructor's manual includes a discussion of the inventory's development, normative data, research data, and interpretive guidelines.

Format: Self-administered; untimed: 20 minutes

Scoring: Self-scored

Cost: 20 Tests and Answer Booklets, Instructor's Manual $40.00; No-Nonsense Communication Book $5.50 (discount for multiple orders)

Supervisory Inventory on Human Relations (SIHR)
Donald L. Kirkpatrick

1994	Donald L. Kirkpatrick, PhD

Population: Adults

Purpose: Measures knowledge of basic human relations principles involved in effective supervisory job performance; used in conjunction with management training programs aimed at increasing knowledge and improving attitudes in dealing with people

Description: Paper–pencil 80-item two-choice test measuring the extent to which supervisors understand and accept the principles, facts, and techniques of human relations in management. Test items cover human relations issues in the following areas; the supervisor's role in management, understanding and motivating employees, developing positive employee attitudes, problem-solving techniques, and principles of learning and training. Individuals indicate whether they agree or disagree with the statement about beliefs or behaviors presented in each test item. The answer booklet provides a rationale for each correct answer. Test results identify topics that should be emphasized in training programs and provide information for on-the-job coaching.

Format: Self-administered; untimed: 15 minutes

Scoring: Self-scored

Cost: 20 Tests and Answer Booklets, Instructor's Manual $40.00

Supervisory Practices Inventory (SPI)
Judith S. Canfield, Albert A. Canfield

1981	Western Psychological Services

Population: Adults

Purpose: Evaluates how an individual prefers to be supervised, how the individual's supervisor actually functions, and the difference between preferred and actual supervisory behaviors

Description: Paper–pencil 20-item inventory assessing a subordinate's view of 10 areas of supervisory behavior: setting objectives, planning, organization, delegation, problem identification, decision making, performance evaluation, subordinate development, team building, and conflict resolution. The inventory items consist of a list of supervisory behaviors, which the subordinate must rank first in order of personal preference and second to indicate how his or her supervisor actually functions. Questions measure supervisory behavior rather than trait or personality characteristics. Dissonance scores are developed from the difference between preferred and actual rankings. Test booklets include explanations for the scales and possible interpretations.

Format: Self-administered; untimed: 20 to 40 minutes

Scoring: Self-scored

Cost: Kit (10 inventories, manual) $39.50

Supervisory Practices Test, Revised
Martin M. Bruce

1994	Martin M. Bruce, PhD

Population: Adults

Purpose: Evaluates supervisory ability and potential in a business-world setting; used for personnel selection, evaluation, and training

Description: Paper–pencil 50-item multiple-choice test indicating the extent to which the subject is able to choose a desirable course of action (as compared with the perceptions and attitudes of managers and subordinates) when presented with a business decision. Minority group data are available. Suitable for individuals with physical, hearing, and visual impairments. Also available in French, Spanish, and German.

Format: Self-administered; untimed: 20 minutes

Scoring: Hand key

Cost: Specimen Set $55.95

Watson-Glaser Critical Thinking Appraisal®–Short Form
Goodwin Watson, Edward M. Glaser

Date not provided	The Psychological Corporation

Population: Adults

Purpose: Used for placing applicants in a variety of supervisory and managerial jobs

Description: Presents the applicant with questions that include reading passages. These passages present problems, statements, arguments, and interpretations. Each question is accompanied by challenging items. The answers provide a single score that represents an individual's ability in the same five areas as Watson-Glaser Critical Thinking Appraisal–Forms A and B. The manual offers percentile ranks corresponding to raw scores from lower, middle, and upper management normative groups in a wide variety of occupations.

Format: Examiner required; can be taken on-line; untimed: 30 to 45 minutes

Scoring: Examiner evaluated

Cost: Examination Kit (1 of each form, manual) $55.00; Scoring Key $25.50

Working with Others

2000	Clark Wilson Group

Population: Candidates for supervisory roles

Purpose: Screens to identify candidates for promotion, or to coach and counsel those who have recently been promoted

Description: Multilevel survey of organizational skills for people entering supervisory positions. Contains 60 questions with three open-ended questions. Also available in Spanish.

Format: Self-administered; untimed

Scoring: Scoring service

Cost: $260 up to 15 surveys

Personality

Adult Personality Inventory
Samuel E. Krug

1982   MetriTech, Inc.

Population: Adults

Purpose: Assesses personality characteristics, interpersonal style, and career preferences for personnel evaluation, career planning, rehabilitation counseling, and family therapy

Description: Series of computer-administered multiple-item multiple-choice paper–pencil subtests yielding scores in three areas: Personality Characteristics (extroverted, adjusted, tough minded, independent, disciplined, creative, enterprising), Interpersonal Style (caring, adapting, withdrawn, submissive, hostile, rebellious, sociable, assertive), and Career Orientation (practical, scientific, aesthetic, social, competitive, structured). Four validity scales (Good Impression, Bad Impression, Infrequency, Uncertainty) complete the test profile. Reports available through mail-in service or three on-site software programs (MS/PC DOS on IBM systems).

Format: Self-administered; untimed: 30 to 60 minutes

Scoring: Computer scored

Cost: Introductory Kit (test material, manual, processing of 5 reports) $49.00 to $59.00

Adult Personality Inventory (API)

Date not provided   Pinkerton Services Group

Population: Adults

Purpose: Measures a variety of personality traits for job applicants and current employees

Description: Paper–pencil inventory can be used for selection, promotion, or training. Seven personal characteristic scales are used to measure an individual's basic personality: extroverted, disciplined, adjusted, creative, tough minded, enterprising, and independent. Eight interpersonal scales are assessed: caring, hostile, adapting, rebellious, withdrawn, sociable, submissive, and assertive. The API also examines six career scales to help assess in what type of work setting an individual will feel comfortable and productive: practical, social, scientific, competitive, aesthetic, and structured.

Format: Individual administration; untimed

Scoring: Telephone and fax scoring; computer-generated results

Cost: Contact publisher

Assessment and Development Profile (ADP)

Date not provided   Winslow Research Institute

Population: Adults

Purpose: Measures personality, behavior, and attitudes

Description: This comprehensive assessment program measures 33 personality traits of coaching program participants. Presents suggestions for self-improvement. The reports enhance the probability that clients will achieve and maintain optimum career performance and personal happiness. The characteristics are measured in 726 questions and grouped by the following: interpersonal, organizational, dedication, and self-control.

Format: Self-administered; untimed: 3 hours

Scoring: Completed on-line; scoring service available

Cost: Contact publisher

BarOn Emotional Quotient 360™ Assessment (BarOn EQ-360™)
Reuven Bar-On

2002   Multi-Health Systems, Inc.

Population: Ages 16 years and older

Purpose: Measures emotional intelligence from a multirater perspective

Description: Independent observer ratings are compared with the results of a self-assessment that is completed by the subject of focus. What emerges is a more complete 360-degree profile in which external impressions of a person's emotional quotient are combined with the person's self-rating. The EQ-360 is ideal for use in corporate environments, where the nature of human interactions relating to leadership, team, and organizational development is a key component.

Format: Self- administered; untimed: 20 minutes

Scoring: Scoring service available

Cost: Contact publisher

Behavioral Profiles: Observer Assessment
Tony Alessandra

| 1995 | Jossey-Bass/Pfeiffer |

Population: Adults

Purpose: Helps people define their own styles; provides a picture of how others perceive an individual's interactions

Description: Used together with the Behavioral Profiles: Self Assessment, these instruments provide valuable information for personal growth. Participants can recognize differences between the way they think they are and the way they are actually perceived by others. This evaluation provides tangible goals for improving versatility and enhancing relationships.

Format: Self-administration; untimed

Scoring: Self-scoring

Cost: $5.00

Behavioral Profiles: Self Assessment
Tony Alessandra

| 1995 | Jossey-Bass/Pfeiffer |

Population: Adults

Purpose: Helps people define their own styles; determines how a person believes he or she interacts with others

Description: Used together with the Behavioral Profiles: Observer Assessment, these instruments provide valuable information for personal growth. Participants can recognize differences between the way they think they are and the way they are actually perceived by others. This evaluation provides tangible goals for improving versatility and enhancing relationships.

Format: Self-administration; untimed

Scoring: Self-scoring

Cost: $5.00

Benchmarking Organizational Emotional Intelligence (BOEI)

| 2002 | Multi-Health Systems, Inc. |

Population: Ages 18 years and older

Purpose: Measures the level of emotional intelligence in an organization as a whole and its parts

Description: Items are categorized into one of the following 20 subscales: Teamwork, Work Environment, Balancing Work/Life, Leveraging Diversity, Employee Empowerment, Pay, Job Satisfaction, Attitude, Organizational Courage, Supervisory Leadership, Coworker Relationships, Changes of Work, Diversity Climate, Workplace Tension, Training and Innovation, Benefits, Organizational Climate, Problem Solving/Decision Making, Change Management, and Senior Management Leadership.

Format: Self-administered; untimed

Scoring: Scoring service

Cost: Contact publisher

Business Judgment Test, Revised
Martin M. Bruce

| 1999 | Martin M. Bruce, PhD |

Population: Adults

Purpose: Evaluates the subject's sense of "social intelligence" in business-related situations; used for employee selection and training

Description: Paper–pencil 25-item multiple-choice test in which the subject selects one of four ways to complete a stem statement, allowing the examiner to gauge the subject's sense of socially accepted and desirable ways to behave in business relationships. The score suggests the degree to which the subject agrees with the general opinion of businesspeople as to the proper way to handle various relationships. Also available in French.

Format: Self-administered; untimed: 10 to 15 minutes

Scoring: Hand key

Cost: Specimen Set $51.80

C&RT (Creativity and Risk Taking)
Richard E. Byrd

| 1986 | Jossey-Bass/Pfeiffer |

Population: Adults

Purpose: Assesses an individual's creativity and risk-taking orientations, the implications of these orientations on management styles, what contributions a person with this style is likely to make, and how this person might hinder organizational progress

Description: Participants respond to a series of questions and are able to calculate their own score to see immediate results. The instrument includes a section on the possibility of changing styles, a background of the inventory, a bibliography, and trainer's guidelines.

Format: Self-administered; untimed

Scoring: Self-scoring

Cost: $10.00

Career Anchors: Discovering Your Real Values
Edgar H. Schein

| 1990 | Jossey-Bass/Pfeiffer |

Population: Adults

Purpose: Helps people define dominant themes and patterns in their lives, understand their own approach to work and a career, find reasons for choices they make, and take steps to fulfill their self-image

Description: Helps people uncover their real values and use them to make better career choices. The instrument includes the orientations inventory, the career anchor interview, and conceptual material. The trainer's manual provides facilitation instructions for a 2-hour workshop and an extended workshop of 4 hours or more. A lecturette on the concept of career anchors is included.

Format: Self-administered; untimed

Scoring: Self-scoring

Cost: Career Anchors Package $28.00; Instrument $9.95

Comprehensive Personality Profile
Larry L. Craft

| 1980 | Wonderlic Personnel Test, Inc. |

Population: Ages 18 years and older

Purpose: Used in preemployment selection to measure personality and assess job compatibility

Description: Paper–pencil 88-item test with seven primary scales, 10 secondary scales, and sales training reports. A ninth-grade reading level is required. Also available in Spanish and French.

Format: Self-administered; untimed

Scoring: Computer scored; scoring service available

Cost: 5 Tests $25.00; 25 Tests $500.00

Comprehensive Personnel System (CPS)
Terry D. Anderson, Brian Zeiner

| 1989 | Consulting Resource Group International, Inc. |

Population: Adults

Purpose: Screens for selection and development of exceptional employees; used for employee selection

Description: Projective test with 14 items. A 10th-grade reading level is required.

Format: Examiner required; individual administration; suitable for group use; untimed

Scoring: Self-scored

Cost: $19.95

Curtis Completion Form
James W. Curtis

| 1971 | Western Psychological Services |

Population: Adolescents, adults

Purpose: Evaluates the emotional adjustment of older adolescents and adults; used in employment situations to screen individuals whose emotional adjustment makes them poor employment risks; also used in educational and industrial counseling

Description: Multiple-item paper–pencil free-response sentence-completion test measuring emotional adjustment. It is similar to a projective test, but is scored using relatively objective, standardized criteria.

Format: Examiner required; individual and group administration; untimed: 30 minutes

Scoring: Examiner evaluated

Cost: Kit (25 forms, manual) $42.50

Emo Questionnaire
George O. Baehr, Melany E. Baehr

| 1995 | NCS Pearson Reid London House |

Population: Adults

Purpose: Determines an individual's personal-emotional adjustment; used to evaluate the potential of sales, managerial, and professional personnel and to screen applicants for jobs requiring efficient performance under pressure

Description: Paper–pencil 140-item examination measuring 10 traditional psychodiagnostic categories (rationalization, inferiority feelings, hostility, depression, fear and anxiety, organic reaction, projection, unreality, sex problems, withdrawal) and three composite adjustment factors (internal, external, somatic). The results reflect both the individual's internal psychodynamics and his or her relationship with the external environment. In combination with other instruments, the test has been validated for selection of salespersons, police and security guards, and transit operators. In hospital settings, it is useful as a diagnosis of emotional health and to chart the course of psychotherapy. Basic reading skills are required.

Format: Examiner required; suitable for group use; untimed: 20 minutes

Scoring: Hand key

Cost: Contact publisher

Emotional Competence Inventory (ECI)
Daniel Goleman, Richard Boyatzis

1999	Hay Group

Population: Adults

Purpose: Measures emotional intelligence for organizational improvement and management development

Description: This 110-item multirater assessment provides individual feedback reports. Workforce composites are available. Requires that the examiner be accredited through the Hay Group. Also available in Spanish, Italian, German, Japanese, and Portuguese.

Format: Examiner required; individual or group administration; timed: 45 to 60 minutes

Scoring: Examiner evaluated; computer scored

Cost: Accreditation Fee $3,000.00; Test $135.00 for on-line or $200.00 for paper-based per participant

Employment Productivity Index (EPI)

Date not provided	NCS Pearson Reid London House

Population: Job applicants

Purpose: Assesses personality trait combinations that lead to productive and responsible work behavior; used to identify applicants who will remain on the job, have low absentee rates, and obey company rules, particularly those prohibiting alcohol and drugs

Description: Multiple-item paper–pencil survey consisting of four scales measuring personality traits that lead to productive employment: Dependability, Interpersonal Cooperation, Drug Avoidance, and Validity. A Composite Productivity Index is provided. In addition, a test analysis report includes a Significant Behavioral Indicators section highlighting specific responses that may be useful in making decisions about borderline candidates. The EPI-3S version includes a safety scale measuring safety consciousness and identifying applicants at risk for on-the-job accidents.

Format: Self-administered; untimed: 30 minutes

Scoring: Operator-assisted telephone; computer scored

Cost: Contact publisher

Entrepreneurial Quotient (EQ)
Edward J. Fasiska

1984	Wonderlic Personnel Test, Inc.

Population: Adults

Purpose: Assesses adaptability, management, and personality traits to measure entrepreneurial potential

Description: Paper–pencil 100-item multiple-choice test. The following reports are yielded: four summary scales, adaptability, managerial traits, personality traits, and EQ index.

Format: Self-administered; untimed

Scoring: Computer scored

Cost: 5 Tests $125.00; 25 Tests $500.00

Gordon Personal Profile–Inventory (GPP–I™)
Leonard V. Gordon

1978 (Manual 1993)	The Psychological Corporation

Population: Adults

Purpose: Provides measurement of factors in the personality domain

Description: Eight factors provide coverage of five personality traits (extroversion, agreeableness, conscientiousness, emotional stability, and openness). Respondents select one item in each group of four as being most like themselves and one as being least like themselves.

Format: Examiner required; suitable for group use; untimed: 20 to 30 minutes

Scoring: Hand key or machine scorable

Cost: Examination Kit (booklets, answer document, manual) $66.00

Hilson Life Adjustment Profile (HLAP)
Robin E. Inwald

1993	Hilson Research, Inc.

Population: Ages 18 years and older

Purpose: Measures emotional adjustment

Description: Total of 144 items for preemployment screening of high-risk occupations. Screens for emotional adjustment, functioning level, and psychopathology. Also available in Spanish.

Format: Examiner required; suitable for group administration; untimed: 15 minutes

Scoring: Computer scored; scoring service available

Cost: Contact publisher

Hilson Personnel Profile/Success Quotient (HPP/SQ)
Robin E. Inwald

| 1988 | Hilson Research, Inc. |

Population: Ages 15 years and older

Purpose: Assesses behavioral patterns and characteristics related to success in the working world; measures individual strengths and positive features; used for preemployment screening and in-house staff training programs

Description: Paper–pencil 15-item behaviorally oriented true–false instrument consisting of one validity measure and five scales: Candor, Achievement History, Social Ability (SA), "Winner's" Image (WI), Initiative (IN), and Family Achievement Expectations. Content areas for the SA scale include Extroversion, Popularity, and Sensitivity. Areas covered by the WI scale include Competitive Drive and Self-Worth. For the IN scale, four content areas are included: Drive, Preparation Style, Goal Orientation, and Anxiety About Organization. A narrative report and two profile graphs of six scales and nine scale content areas are provided with raw scores and *t*-scores. Local/specific job category norms are also available. A fifth-grade reading level is required.

Format: Self-administered; untimed: 20 minutes

Scoring: Computer scored

Cost: Contact publisher

Hogan Development Survey (HDS)
Robert Hogan, Joyce Hogan

| 1997 | Hogan Assessment Systems, Inc. |

Population: Working adults

Purpose: Assesses common dysfunctional dispositions

Description: Applications include leadership coaching, counseling, and development. Total of 168 items, with 11 scales: Excitable, Skeptical, Cautious, Reserved, Leisurely, Bold, Mischievous, Colorful, Imaginative, Diligent, and Dutiful. Each scale has 14 items. The HDS yields an Interpretive Report, Graphic Report, Data File, and Leadership Challenge Report. Also available in Spanish.

Format: Individual or group administration; untimed: 20 minutes

Scoring: Computer scored; scoring service available

Cost: Test Booklet and Answer Sheet $2.50 each

Hogan Personality Inventory (HPI)
Robert Hogan

| 1995 | Hogan Assessment Systems, Inc. |

Population: Adults

Purpose: Measures normal personality for personnel selection and assessment

Description: True–false 206-item test with seven primary scales: Adjustment, Ambition, Sociability, Likeability, Prudence, Intelligence, and School Success. There are also six occupational scales. Together these scales provide a comprehensive evaluation of a person's strengths and shortcomings with regard to his or her social and occupational goals. The HPI also provides an interpretive report that includes an easy-to-read graph and a scale-by-scale interpretation of the test results. The report provides a detailed examination of a person's strengths and shortcomings in the pursuit of his or her social and occupational goals.

Format: Examiner required; suitable for group use; untimed: 20 minutes

Scoring: Computer scored; scoring service available

Cost: Contact publisher

INQ-Your Thinking Profile
Allen Harrison, Robert Bramson, Susan Bramson, Nicholas Parlette

| 1994 | InQ Educational Materials |

Population: Adults

Purpose: Identifies one's preferred mode of thinking; used in training, team building, and sales

Description: Multiple-choice 18-item test yielding scores in five categories: Analyst, Synthesist, Pragmatist, Idealist, and Realist. Also available in Spanish and French.

Format: Suitable for group use; untimed: 15 to 20 minutes

Scoring: Self-scored

Cost: 10 Tests $59.95

Inwald Survey 2 (IS2)
Robin E. Inwald

| 1994 | Hilson Research, Inc. |

Population: Adults

Purpose: Assesses violence-related behavior characteristics; used for preemployment and promotional screening for job applicants

Description: Paper-pencil 110-item true-false test with a profile graph and computer-generated report. A test book and scannable answer sheets are used. Scales include denial of shortcomings—validity scale, risk-taking tendencies, lack of temper control, reckless driving/safety patterns, firearms interest, work difficulties, lack of social sensitivity, lack of leadership interest, attitudes—antisocial behaviors; and behavior patterns—integrity concerns. A fifth-grade reading level is required. A computer version is available using software for IBM compatibles. Also available in Spanish.

Format: Examiner required; suitable for group use; untimed: 15 minutes

Scoring: Computer scored; scoring service available

Cost: Contact publisher

IPI Employee Aptitude Series CPF Contact Personality Factor

1992	Industrial Psychology International Ltd.

Population: Adults

Purpose: Measures extroversion versus introversion; used for screening, placement, and promotion of employees

Description: Paper-pencil 40-item personality test determines contact versus noncontact factor to determine Contact Personality Factor. Also available in French and Spanish.

Format: Examiner required; suitable for group use; untimed: 5 to 10 minutes

Scoring: Hand key

Cost: Introductory Kit (20 test booklets, scoring key, manual) $30.00

IPI Employee Aptitude Series NPF Neurotic Personality Factor

1992	Industrial Psychology International Ltd.

Population: Adults

Purpose: Measures emotional balance, stability, and stress tolerance; used to screen applicants for a variety of positions and to place and promote employees

Description: Paper-pencil 40-item test measuring an individual's general stability and emotional balance to determine Neurotic Personality Factor. Also available in French and Spanish.

Format: Examiner required; suitable for group use; untimed: 5 to 10 minutes

Scoring: Hand key

Cost: Introductory Kit (20 test booklets, scoring key, manual) $30.00

Kirton Adaption-Innovation Inventory (KAI)
Michael J. Kirton

1985	Occupational Research Centre

Population: Adolescents, adults

Purpose: Evaluates an individual's cognitive style preference in creativity, problem solving, and decision making; used in personality and occupational psychology and in business management for training and team building

Description: Paper-pencil 33-item test containing three subtests: Sufficiency, Efficiency Preference, and Rule/Group Conformity Preference. Scores are yielded for each subtest. The preferred cognitive style measured is unrelated to an individual's capacity; however, it is strongly related to a critical cluster of personality traits. Also available in Italian, Dutch, French, and Slovak/Czech.

Format: Examiner required; group administration; untimed: 10 to 15 minutes

Scoring: Examiner evaluated

Cost: 50 Inventories $275.00

Leadership/Personality Compatibility Inventory (L/PCI)
James H. Brewer

1994	Associated Consultants in Education

Population: Adults

Purpose: Used to promote more productive leadership in organizations

Description: Helps respondents determine and understand three major factors affecting their leadership: basic personality style, present leadership role, and the compatibility between the two. The instrument consists of two inventories: a personality inventory and a leadership role inventory. The respondents first learn about their dominant personality using the Brewer framework: Bold, Expressive, Sympathetic, or Technical. Their leadership role characteristics are determined by their organizational environment: Active/Competitive, Persuasive/Interactive, Precise/Systematic, and Willing/Steady. A full interpretation is included.

Format: Self-administered; untimed: 15 to 20 minutes
Scoring: Hand key
Cost: $6.95 each

Meyer–Kendall Assessment Survey (MKAS)
Henry D. Meyer, Edward L. Kendall

| 1991 | Western Psychological Services |

Population: Adults

Purpose: Surveys work-related personality and interpersonal functioning for use in personnel assessment

Description: Paper-pencil test with 105 dichotomous items assessing 10 aspects of personal functioning relevant to performance at work. The scales are dominance, attention to detail, psychosomatic tendencies, independence, extroversion, anxiety, determination, people concern, stability, and achievement motivation. Scores are also obtained for two broad-band scales: Assertive Drive and Self-Assurance. An optional feature of the MKAS is the Pre-Assessment Worksheet, which determines the profile of an "ideal" applicant for a position. Computer scoring is achieved using the WPS Test Report mail-in service.

Format: Self-administered; untimed: 15 minutes
Scoring: Computer scored
Cost: Kit (2 WPS Test Report assessment sheets, 2 WPS Test Report preassessment sheets, 1 manual) $92.50

Minnesota Importance Questionnaire (MIQ)

| Date not provided | Vocational Psychology Research |

Population: Adults

Purpose: Measures an individual's vocational needs and values, which are important aspects of the work personality

Description: The MIQ is designed to measure the following six vocational values (and the 20 vocational needs from which the values derive): Achievement, Altruism, Comfort, Safety, Status, and Autonomy. The MIQ currently permits the comparison of the vocational needs of individuals with estimates of reinforcers present in 185 occupations representative of the major fields and levels of the world of work. There are two equivalent forms of the MIQ: the Paired form and the Ranked form. The Paired form is more suitable for individual clients. The Ranked form may be more suitable in group settings. Also available in Spanish.

Format: Self-administered; untimed: Paired form 30 to 40 minutes, Ranked form 15 to 25 minutes
Scoring: Scoring service
Cost: Sample Set (manual, 1 booklet, 1 answer sheet for both Paired and Ranked forms) $11.00

Minnesota Satisfaction Questionnaire (MSQ)

| 1963, 1967, 1977 | Vocational Psychology Research |

Population: Adults

Purpose: Measures an employee's satisfaction with his or her job

Description: Three forms are available: two long forms (1977 and 1967 version) and a short form. The MSQ provides more specific information on the aspects of a job that an individual finds rewarding than do more general measures of job satisfaction. The MSQ is useful in exploring client vocational needs, in counseling follow-up studies, and in generating information about the reinforcers in jobs. All three forms are gender neutral. Instructions for the administration of the MSQ are given in the booklet. It is strongly recommended that the long form be used, because it provides much more information. The long form has 20 scales, with five items each.

Format: Self-administered; untimed; long form 15 to 20 minutes, short form 5 minutes
Scoring: Hand scored; computer scoring service available
Cost: Sample Set (manual, both versions of long form, and one short form) $6.60

Motives, Values, Preferences Inventory
Joyce Hogan, Robert Hogan

| 1996 | Hogan Assessment Systems, Inc. |

Population: Adults

Purpose: Assesses individual values, interests, and preferences

Description: Applications include employment decisions and determining organizational fit. Total of 200 items, with 10 scales: Aesthetic, Affiliation, Altruistic, Commercial, Hedonistic, Power, Recognition, Scientific, Security, and Tradition. Yields Interpretive Report, Graphic Report, Data File, and Leadership Values Report. Also available in Spanish and Portuguese.

Format: Individual administration; untimed: 20 minutes

Scoring: Computer scored; scoring service available

Cost: Test Booklet and Answer Sheet $2.50 each

MPQ 14.2
Allan Cameron

| 1997 | Test Agency, Limited |

Population: Adults

Purpose: Identifies key personality traits likely to have a high impact on behavior and success at work, and to highlight individual strengths, weaknesses, and competence

Description: Multiple-choice questionnaire available in three forms. MPQ Factor Version 14.2 is the full questionnaire covering all the factors and dimensions measured by the instrument. MPQ Factor Version 5 is a shorter questionnaire that looks at the Big Five factors only. It has been specially designed for those who do not need the full set of information, but who need a simple, cost-effective global measure. MPQ 7 is an unique questionnaire variant that looks carefully at creativity. MPQ questionnaires are all untimed. The longest of the questionnaires is MPQ 14.2, which contains 120 multiple-choice items. It is, however, generally completed in under 25 minutes. The other questionnaires require less time.

Format: Examiner required; individual or group administration; can be computer administered; untimed

Scoring: Self-scored; computer scored; machine scored; scoring service available

Cost: Contact publisher

My BEST Profile
James H. Brewer

| 1989 | Associated Consultants in Education |

Population: Adults

Purpose: Used to improve self-understanding and interpersonal relations

Description: Profile with 32 items determines personality types, fosters positive interpersonal relations, creates self-awareness, and promotes greater productivity. Paper–pencil format is easily completed and scored using pressure-sensitive paper. Two sections are included: word association and situation analysis.

Format: Self-administered; untimed: 15 to 20 minutes

Scoring: Hand key; computer software available

Cost: Paper–Pencil Version $4.95; Computer Version $99.95

Occupational Personality Questionnaire (OPQ Concept)

| 1987 | SHL Canada |

Population: Adults

Purpose: Assesses personality traits used in personnel selection, placement, counseling, and development

Description: Paper–pencil or computer-administered 248-item multiple-choice questionnaire measuring 30 work-related personality traits covering relationships with people (persuasive, outgoing, democratic), thinking style (practical, conceptual, conscientious), and feelings and emotions (worrying, critical, competitive), along with others. Application is expanded by using in conjunction with Hurmis EXPERT Software to produce a 25-page interpretive report.

Format: Examiner required; individual administration; computer and on-line administration available; untimed: 35 minutes

Scoring: Hand key; machine scored; scoring service available; on-line scoring

Cost: Contact publisher

Occupational Relationships Profile (ORP)
Colin D. Selby

| 1998 | Selby MillSmith Ltd. |

Population: Adolescents, adults

Purpose: Used in employment counseling to assess social behavior at work

Description: Computer-administered or paper–pencil 102-item multiple-choice criterion-referenced projective test. The categories are sociability, power, teamwork, and warmth. Narrative reports are available. A computer version using DOS is available. An 11-year-old reading level is required. Also available in French.

Format: Self-administered; untimed: 20 minutes

Scoring: Computer scored; scoring service available

Cost: Specimen Set $60.00

Occupational Type Profile (OTP)
Colin D. Selby

| 1998 | Selby MillSmith Ltd. |

Population: Adolescents, adults

Purpose: Used in employment counseling to assess Jungian types in the workplace

Description: Computer-administered or paper-pencil 88-item multiple-choice criterion-referenced projective test. Psychological type profile norms, an uncertainty index, and narrative reports are available. A computer version using PC DOS computers is available. Also available in French.

Format: Self-administered; untimed: 20 minutes

Scoring: Computer scored; scoring service available

Cost: Specimen Set $60.00

PASAT 2000
Steven Poppleton, Peter Jones

1998	Test Agency Ltd.

Population: Adults

Purpose: Measures those personality attributes that have a direct bearing on success in a sales environment

Description: The PASAT 2000 has eight main scales: Social Adjustment, Motivational Adjustment, Emotional Adjustment, Adaptability, Conscientiousness, Social Control, Emotional Stability, and Self-Assurance. In addition, the PASAT 2000 has three further scales designed to detect attempts to present false impressions: Attentive Distortion, Adaptive Distortion, and Social Distortion. Respondents use a 5-point scale to indicate the degree to which they have or have not used the behaviors described by each questionnaire item. The value of each item response is cumulated for each of the instrument's scales to produce a scale score, which is then converted into a stanine score.

Format: Examiner required; individual or group administration; can be computer administered; untimed

Scoring: Self-scored; computer scored; scoring service available

Cost: Contact publisher

PEP/Pre-Evaluation Profile
James H. Brewer

1989	Associated Consultants in Education

Population: Adults

Purpose: Prepares supervisors for performance evaluation of employees without personality type bias

Description: Provides a profile of the supervisor

and the employee being evaluated, leads supervisor to understand how personality may affect employee evaluation, explores methods of fair employee evaluations, and describes how to interpret personality factors in the evaluation process. The taker must know the other person well enough to make valid observations.

Format: Self-administered; untimed: 15 to 20 minutes

Scoring: Hand key

Cost: $4.95 each

Personal Audit
Clifford R. Edams, William M. Lepley

Date not provided	NCS Pearson / Reid London House

Population: Grade 7 to adult

Purpose: Assesses an individual's personality as a factor of how well that person will perform in school or industry; also used for clinical diagnosis of maladjustment

Description: Paper-pencil 450-item personality test. Nine scales of 50 items each measure relatively independent components of personality: seriousness-impulsiveness, firmness-indecision, tranquility-irritability, frankness-evasion, stability-instability, tolerance-intolerance, steadiness-emotionality, persistence-fluctuation, and contentment-worry. The test acquaints teachers with personality characteristics of students, is an aid to vocational and educational counseling, and provides an index of employees' job satisfaction and success in terms of their personal adjustment. Two forms are available.

Format: Self-administered; untimed: Form LL 40 to 50 minutes, Form SS 30 to 40 minutes

Scoring: Hand key

Cost: Contact publisher

Personal Drive Alert (PDA)
Debra L. Jacobs

Date not provided	SPECTRA, Inc.

Population: Adults

Purpose: Helps individuals learn which of five primary psychological motivators are preferred when focusing on task attainment

Description: This instrument can be completed in minutes and is both self-scorable and easily interpreted through the use of an extensive interpretive guide. Group composite scores help teams identify norms that may impede effectiveness. Style differences are quickly and easily understood and better appreciated as people become familiar with PDA types and the reasons for individual differences.

Format: Self-administered; untimed
Scoring: Self-scored
Cost: $10.00

Personal Dynamics Profile (PDP)

Date not provided	Winslow Research Institute

Population: Adults
Purpose: Measures behavioral characteristics relevant to career success and personal contentment
Description: The information provides objective feedback to enable participants in Personal Coaching to attain a maximum return on their investment. The characteristics are divided into interpersonal organization, dedication, and self-control. There are 260 questions.
Format: Self-administered; untimed: less than 1 hour
Scoring: Completed on-line; scoring service
Cost: Contact publisher

Personal Stress Assessment Inventory
Herbert S. Kindler

Updated yearly	Center for Management Effectiveness, Inc.

Population: Age 17 to adult
Purpose: Predisposition, resilience, and sources of stress
Description: Applications include training, coaching, and counseling. This inventory has eight subtests with 177 items (multiple choice). Examples: Predisposition to Stress, Resilience, Occasional Stress Sources, Ongoing Stress Sources, and Health Symptoms. Also available in Spanish.
Format: Self-administered; untimed: 40 minutes
Scoring: Self-scored
Cost: $8.95 each (minimum purchase of 20)

Personal Style Indicator (PSI)
Terry D. Anderson, Everett T. Robinson

1988	Consulting Resource Group International, Inc.

Population: Adults
Purpose: Assesses personal style preferences; used for marital counseling, conflict resolutions, leadership and personal development, and team building

Description: Forced-choice test with 16 items. An 11th-grade reading level is required. Also available in Japanese, French, and Dutch. Individuals with special needs will need assistance.
Format: Self-administered; untimed
Scoring: Examiner evaluated; self- or computer scored
Cost: $12.95

Personal Success Profile (PSP)

Date not provided	Winslow Research Institute

Population: Adults
Purpose: Measures behavioral characteristics relevant to career success and personal contentment
Description: Innovative assessment program designed for individuals new to the personality assessment process, and for those experiencing time or financial constraints. This assessment is easy to understand, and all individuals can benefit, regardless of education, sophistication, or experience. The 11 characteristics measured in 130 questions are grouped by competitiveness, self-control, and dedication.
Format: Self-administered; untimed: less than 30 minutes
Scoring: Completed on-line; scoring service
Cost: Contact publisher

Personal Values Index (PVI)
Lynn Ellsworth Taylor

1999	First2Learn

Population: Ages 10 years and older
Purpose: Identifies an individual's "core values"
Description: A one-page assessment with 144 values loaded into 36 boxes with forced preference of two in each box. Each of nine subtests uses the same 144 values in a different fashion. Results are reported for Personal Values Index, Ideal Profile, Core Values Business Optimization Protocol, Conflict Resolution Protocol, Mentoring Protocol, and 720 Degree Review. A tool for personal and professional development, business reorganization, productivity optimization, reduction in employee turnover, prescreening for employment, and matching Ideal Profile with individual profiles to create best job fit.
Format: Self-administered on-line; timed: participant is unaware of timing
Scoring: On-line scoring; results sent by e-mail
Cost: Contact publisher

Personnel Selection Inventory (PSI™)

1988	NCS Pearson Reid London House

Population: Job applicants

Purpose: Assesses personality trait combinations that lead to honest, productive, and service-oriented employees; designed to reduce absenteeism, shrinkage, turnover, on-the-job accidents, and substance abuse; meets both human resource and loss-prevention needs

Description: Multiple-item paper–pencil test survey. Eight versions of the PSI are available to meet various companies' screening needs. The forms range from PSI-1, which assesses honesty only, to PSI-7ST, which assesses a wide range of attributes. The various forms contain combinations of the following scales: Honesty, Supervision Attitudes, Employee/Customer Relations, Drug Avoidance, Work Values, Safety, Emotional Stability, Nonviolence, and Tenure. Distortion and accuracy scales are included. Some versions contain a detailed personal and behavioral history section that aids in making decisions about borderline candidates. Industry-specific norms are available for some PSI versions. A seventh-grade reading level is required.

Format: Self-administered; untimed: 30 to 40 minutes

Scoring: Computer scored

Cost: Contact publisher

Power Management
James H. Brewer

1987	Associated Consultants in Education

Population: Adults

Purpose: Provides a systematic approach to improving leadership through an understanding of the forces of power

Description: The three-in-one package can be used as a text, as a workbook, or for the fullest comprehension—a "worktext" complete with personality profiles. It provides complete flexibility for group training or independent study. A video supplement and computer software are also available.

Format: Self-administered; untimed: 15 to 20 minutes

Scoring: Hand key

Cost: Complete Package (worktext, video, computer program) $149.95

Power Selling
James H. Brewer

1995	Associated Consultants in Education

Population: Adults

Purpose: Enables an individual to understand how to behave in each new selling situation and how to communicate with prospects of different personality types

Description: The model identifies critical elements of your personality that will help or hurt your selling, and helps you analyze your prospects' personality types so that you can "speak their language" and plan the best sales approach based on each prospect's personality and situation.

Format: Self-administered; untimed: 15 to 20 minutes

Scoring: Hand key

Cost: Power Selling (test only) $19.95; My BEST Presentation Style $4.95; Sales Style $2.95; Complete Set $22.95

PSI In-Depth Interpretations
Terry D. Anderson, Everett T. Robinson

1988	Consulting Resource Group International, Inc.

Population: Adults

Purpose: Assesses personal style preferences; used for personal development

Description: The 21-item test provides specific feedback to apply to work and everyday life situations. Also available in Japanese, French, and Dutch. A 10th-grade reading level is required.

Format: Examiner required; individual administration; suitable for group use

Scoring: Self-scored

Cost: $9.95

Rahim Organizational Conflict Inventories (ROCI)
Afzalur Rahim

Date not provided	Consulting Psychologists Press, Inc.

Population: Adults

Purpose: Measures conflict experienced within an organization and assesses varying styles of handling the conflict

Description: Paper–pencil 105-item self-report inventory in two parts assessing the types of conflict and the various styles of handling conflict found within an organization. The ROCI I contains 21 items assessing three dimensions or types of organizational conflict: intrapersonal, intergroup, and intragroup. The ROCI II consists of three 28-item forms assessing conflict with one's boss (Form A), with one's subordinates (Form B), and with one's peers (Form C). Five styles of handling interpersonal conflict are identified: integrating, obliging, dominating, avoiding, and compromising. Both parts use a 5-point Likert scale. Limited norms are provided for college students and managerial groups.

Format: Examiner required; suitable for group use; untimed: 10 to 12 minutes

Scoring: Examiner evaluated

Cost: Preview Kit (Inventories I and II, answer sheets, manual) $42.40

Risk Taking Inventory and Guide
Herbert S. Kindler

| 1997-2001 | Center for Management Effectiveness, Inc. |

Population: Ages 17 years and older

Purpose: Assesses propensity to take risks

Description: Applications include training, development, and coaching. The Guide is a multiple-choice paper–pencil test with 18 items, and is also available in Spanish.

Format: Self-administered; untimed: 15 minutes

Scoring: Self-scored

Cost: $8.95 each (minimum purchase of 20)

Sales Aptitude Test

| 1993 | NCS Pearson Reid London House |

Population: Adults

Purpose: Measures behavioral and personality characteristics indicative of success in sales positions; used for sales selection programs

Description: Multiple-choice 86-item test measures eight traits important to sales success: ego strength, persuasiveness, sociability, entrepreneurship, achievement motivation, energy, self-confidence, and empathy.

Format: Examiner required; suitable for group use; untimed: 30 minutes

Scoring: Hand key; computer scored

Cost: Contact publisher

Self Worth Inventory (SWI)
Everett T. Robinson

| 1990 | Consulting Resource Group International, Inc. |

Population: Adults

Purpose: Identifies self-worth

Description: Forced-choice test with 40 items that help individuals understand what self-worth is, how it is developed, and how to increase it. A 10th-grade reading level is required.

Format: Examiner required; individual administration; suitable for group use; untimed

Scoring: Self-scored

Cost: $10.95

Stress Indicator and Health Planner (SHIP)
Gwen Faulkner, Terry D. Anderson

| 1990 | Consulting Resource Group International, Inc. |

Population: Adults

Purpose: Assesses personal distress, interpersonal stress, wellness, time-stress, and occupational stress

Description: Forced-choice test with five items to help develop a plan to increase overall level of well-being. A 10th-grade reading level is required.

Format: Self-administered; untimed

Scoring: Self-scored

Cost: $12.95

Sup'r Star Profiles
James H. Brewer

| 1994 | Associated Consultants in Education |

Population: Adults

Purpose: Used for a more advanced and in-depth study of personality types

Description: Updates personality assessment by using color and integrating additional research findings for a more complete study of personality types. The four types of personality are Self-Reliant, Upbeat, Patient, and Reasoning.

Format: Self-administered; untimed: 15 to 20 minutes

Scoring: Hand key

Cost: $5.95 each

Survey of Interpersonal Values (SIV)
Leonard V. Gordon

| 1960 | NCS Pearson Reid London House |

Population: Grades 10 and above

Purpose: Measures individuals' values by assessing what they consider important in relationships with others; used to measure values associated with adjustment and performance for selection, placement, employment counseling, and research purposes

Description: Paper-pencil 30-item inventory assessing interpersonal values. Each item consists of a triad of value statements. For each triad, examinees must indicate most and least important values. Six values are measured: support, conformity, recognition, independence, benevolence, and leadership.

Format: Self-administered; untimed: 15 minutes

Scoring: Hand key

Cost: Contact publisher

Survey of Personal Values
Leonard V. Gordon

1965	NCS Pearson Reid London House

Population: Grades 10 and above

Purpose: Measures the critical values that help an individual determine coping ability with everyday problems; used for employee screening and placement, vocational guidance, and counseling

Description: Paper-pencil 30-item inventory assessing personal values. Each item consists of a triad of value statements. For each triad, examinees must indicate most and least important values. Six values are measured: practical mindedness, achievement, variety, decisiveness, orderliness, and goal orientation.

Format: Self-administered; untimed: 15 minutes

Scoring: Hand key

Cost: Contact publisher

Temperament Comparator (TC)
Melany E. Baehr

1985	NCS Pearson Reid London House

Population: Adults

Purpose: Determines the strength of relatively permanent temperament traits characteristic of an individual's behavior; used to evaluate the potential of sales and of higher level managerial and professional personnel and for job screening and vocational counseling

Description: Paper-pencil 66-item test consisting of trait pairs derived from the application of a paired comparison technique to 12 individual traits. Emphasis is on individual variations in significant dimensions within the "normal" range of behavior. The factors measured are the 12 individual traits and three factorially determined behavior factors: extroversive/impulsive vs. introversive/cautious, emotional/responsive vs. nonemotional/controlled, self-reliant/self-oriented vs. dependent/group oriented. The test provides a measure of internal consistency of response.

Format: Examiner required; suitable for group use; untimed: 15 minutes

Scoring: Hand key

Cost: Contact publisher

Thurstone Temperament Schedule (TTS™)
L. L. Thurstone, Thelma Gwinn Thurstone

1991	NCS Pearson Reid London House

Population: Adults

Purpose: Evaluates permanent aspects of personality and how normal, well-adjusted people differ from one another; used by managers to determine employee suitability for particular jobs

Description: Paper-pencil or computerized 120-item inventory assessing seven areas of temperament: active, vigorous, impulsive, dominant, stable, sociable, and reflective. The inventory is limited to use by individuals with advanced training in personality instruments.

Format: Self-administered; untimed: 15 to 20 minutes

Scoring: Hand key; computer scored

Cost: Contact publisher

Time Perception Inventory
Albert A. Canfield

1987	Western Psychological Services

Population: Adults

Purpose: Measures the difference between physical and mental presence; helps employees understand how much of their time is wasted due to mental preoccupations

Description: Multiple-item paper-pencil inventory measuring an individual's tendencies to focus attention on the past, future, or present. Percentile comparison on perceived time effectiveness (typically related to an individual's motivation to improve) is provided. All scales provide opportunities to consider positive and negative aspects of thinking in a particular time reference. Group patterns can be identified through a simple show of hands. The test booklet provides interpretations of scales and implications of scores

on scales. Recommendations for additional reading are included. Normative data are available.
Format: Self-administered; untimed: 10 minutes
Scoring: Self-scored
Cost: Kit (10 inventories, manual) $39.50

Trait Evaluation Index
Alan R. Nelson

| 1967 | Martin M. Bruce, PhD |

Population: Adults
Purpose: Assesses adult personality traits; used for job placement and career counseling
Description: Paper–pencil 125-item two-choice test measuring 24 personality dimensions, including social orientation, elation, self-control, sincerity, compliance, ambition, dynamism, caution, propriety, and intellectual orientation. Available also in German.
Format: Self-administered; untimed: 30 to 40 minutes
Scoring: Hand key
Cost: Specimen Set (manual, answer keys, answer sheets, profile sheets) $74.25

Values Scale—Second Edition
Donald E. Super, Dorothy D. Nevill

| Date not provided | Consulting Psychologists Press, Inc. |

Population: Adults
Purpose: Measures intrinsic and extrinsic life-career values
Description: Paper–pencil 106-item inventory measuring intrinsic and extrinsic life-career values and many cultural perspectives of adults. Items are rated on a 4-point scale ranging from *little or no importance* to *very important*. The scales are Ability Utilization, Achievement, Advancement, Aesthetics, Altruism, Authority, Autonomy, Creativity, Economic Rewards, Lifestyle, Personal Development, Physical Activity, Prestige, Risk, Social Interaction, Social Relations, Variety, Working Conditions, Cultural Identity, Physical Prowess, and Economic Security. The scale was developed as part of the international Work Importance Study and has international norms. The profile available through the computer scoring service plots 21 subscales and provides local percentiles and group summary data.
Format: Examiner required; suitable for group use; untimed: 30 to 45 minutes

Scoring: Hand scored; computer scoring service available
Cost: Preview Kit (booklet, answer sheet, manual) $62.00

Work Profile Questionnaire (WPQ)
Allan Cameron

| 1998 | Test Agency, Ltd. |

Population: Adults
Purpose: Measures work preferences and identifies situations in which the individual is most likely to flourish and be effective
Description: The profile report looks at the individual's strengths and preferences and reports them under five broad headings: Communication Style, Emotions, Drive and Determination, Relationships with People, and Thinking Style. The main section of the WPQ report is written in the second person so that, if required, the report can be presented to and discussed with an applicant as part of the interview process. For each of the five domains analyzed by the WPQ, four probing questions are given: two designed to examine personality strengths associated with that trait, and two to assist the interviewer to probe the extent of any weaknesses. Report gives information for two areas: Relationships and Accomplishing Tasks.
Format: Examiner required; individual or group administration; can be computer administered; untimed
Scoring: Self-scored; computer scored; test scoring service available from publisher
Cost: Contact publisher

Working With My Boss

| 1989 | Associated Consultants in Education |

Population: Adults
Purpose: Used to improve the productive relationship between employee and supervisor
Description: Uses BEST personality dimensions to help people understand the personality of their bosses and what they need to do to work successfully with them. Assesses both employee and employer personality types, explores consequences of similarities and differences, suggests how to develop a more productive relationship, and identifies more productive approaches to boss.
Format: Self-administered; untimed: 15 to 20 minutes

Scoring: Hand key

Cost: $4.95 each

WPQei
Allan Cameron

1998   Test Agency, Ltd.

Population: Adults

Purpose: Designed to measure emotional intelligence

Description: This measure, which incorporates much of the latest thinking on the measurement of personality, is based on a conceptual model of emotional intelligence that has seven components: Self-Awareness, Empathy, Intuition, Emo-

tions, Motivation, Innovation, and Social Skills. The WPQei gives a score on each of seven competencies together with an overall score for emotional intelligence. A PC-generated narrative report provides more detail on each of these areas. Where necessary, the report advises on areas for development and identifies respondents' preferred team role using the Belbin model.

Format: Examiner required; individual or group administration; can be computer administered; untimed

Scoring: Self-scored; computer scored; scoring service available

Cost: Contact publisher

Team Skills

Assessing Your Team:
7 Measures of Team Success
Dick Richards, Susan Smyth

1995   Jossey-Bass/Pfeiffer

Population: Intact work group or new team

Purpose: Helps secure high-quality team performance, enhances productivity, increases involvement, and clarifies roles and procedures

Description: This instrument focuses on team interaction and creates a group profile based on each member's perceptions of overall group functioning. It can be administered by the team leader or an outside facilitator and scored in-house. The Team Leader's Manual provides guidance to follow-up actions.

Format: Examiner required; group administration; untimed

Scoring: Scored by team leader or facilitator

Cost: Team Leader's Package $27.00; Team Member's Manual $9.95

Campbell-Hallam Team Development Survey (TDS™)
David P. Campbell, Glenn Hallam

1994   NCS Pearson

Population: Adults

Purpose: Assesses perceptions of team effectiveness; used for identifying team strengths and weaknesses

Description: Paper–pencil 72-item test with 18 dimensions, plus an overall index. A sixth-grade reading level is required. Examiner must have taken psychology coursework.

Format: Self-administered; untimed

Scoring: Computer scored; scoring service available

Cost: Contact publisher

Coaching Practices Inventory (CPI)
Debra L. Jacobs

Date not provided   SPECTRA, Inc.

Population: Adults

Purpose: Measures leadership competencies

Description: Supervisors, managers, or team leaders can be assessed as coaches. Direct-report employees and the individual being assessed respond to statements about coaching behavior. The CPI produces detailed individual feedback reports to identify coaching strengths, suggest developmental opportunities, and give a complete analysis of both quantitative and qualitative input. A Coaching Practices journal is also available to guide recipients in the development of their coaching skills.

Format: Self-administered; untimed

Scoring: Self-scored

Cost: $25.00

Executive Team

1996	Clark Wilson Group

Population: Teams with strategic responsibility

Purpose: Assesses how well the team develops a vision for the organization, how well the team functions as a unit, and how well it has developed team processes

Description: This multiple-rater survey provides feedback for the team and its members on the crucial elements of team management. Contains 77 questions with three open-ended questions.

Format: Self-administered; untimed

Scoring: Scoring service available

Cost: $425 up to 15 surveys

Lake St. Clair Incident
Albert A. Canfield

1988	Western Psychological Services

Population: Adults

Purpose: Examines individual and group decision-making processes; used to improve decision making, communication skills, and teamwork

Description: Multiple-item paper–pencil test requiring a team of three to seven individuals to work together to solve a hypothetical problem situation involving cold weather and cold water survival. Participants are provided with considerable information on the subject, maps, charts, drawings, and a list of 15 items available for them to use in their struggle for survival. The team must reach a decision on what action to take and the relative importance of the 15 items. Three different decision-making processes are required: independent, consultive, and participative/consensual. Scoring procedure uses Coast Guard officer decisions and rankings as "expert" opinions. Scores are provided for three types of decision-making processes.

Format: Self-administered (teams must cooperate to get team performance scores); suitable for group use; untimed: $1\frac{1}{2}$ to 2 hours

Scoring: Self-scored

Cost: Kit (10 booklets, manual) $39.95

Mentoring Skills Assessment
Linda Phillips-Jones

Date not provided	Mind Garden, Inc.

Population: Adults

Purpose: Assessment feedback report designed to improve mentoring and mentee skills

Description: The mentor version, for managers and leaders, includes a survey for the mentor and three for colleagues to rate skills in the areas of Quality and Frequency of mentoring skills. The profile provides an objective assessment of the mentor in nine areas and includes personalized tips to improve mentoring skills. The mentee version includes a survey for the mentee and three for colleagues to rate skills in the areas of Quality and Frequency of skills. The profile provides an objective assessment of nine areas and includes personalized tips.

Format: Individual administration; untimed

Scoring: Computer scored; scoring service available

Cost: Mentor or Mentee Version $100.00

MTR-i
Steve Myers

2000	Test Agency, Ltd.

Population: Adults

Purpose: Measures the contribution being made by an individual to the team and profiles an individual's work persona

Description: The test measures how Jungian function-attitudes are currently being used, by trying to measure how people see themselves affecting the inner or outer worlds. MTR-i team roles change from situation to situation, in accord with the demands of the environment. By using the MTR-i with the Myers Briggs Type Indicator, individuals can derive a comparison between innate preference and how the Jungian function-attitudes are being used in daily work life. The MTR-i can be applied in guidance, development, and training. MTR-i reports eight distinct team roles.

Format: Examiner required; individual or group administration; can be computer administered; untimed

Scoring: Self-scored

Cost: Contact publisher

Multi-Factor Leadership Questionnaire for Teams
Bernard M. Bass, Bruce J. Avolio

1996	Mind Garden, Inc.

Population: Adults

Purpose: Assesses the leadership style of the team

Description: Paper–pencil full-range assessment of the leadership style of the team. The report shows how best to use the data, explains full-range leadership, and provides tips for improving team leadership. The questionnaire contains 53 items on 12 scales: Idealized Attributes, Idealized Behaviors, Inspirational Leadership, Intellectual Stimulation, Individualized Consideration, Contingent Reward, Management-by-Exception (Active), Management-by-Exception (Passive), Laissez-faire, Extra Effort, Effectiveness, and Satisfaction.

Format: Self-administered; untimed

Scoring: Examiner evaluated; computer scored; scoring service available

Cost: Team Report (for up to 10 team members) $150.00

My Team Mates

1998	Clark Wilson Group

Population: Work groups and intact teams

Purpose: Shows the aggregate evaluation of the team by all members

Description: One's own evaluation of the team may be compared to the group norm to assess where one is in step with the rest of the team. Contains 58 questions with three open-ended questions. Also available in Spanish and on-line.

Format: Self-administered; untimed

Scoring: Scoring service

Cost: $260 for up to 15 surveys

Our BEST Team
James H. Brewer

1989	Associated Consultants in Education

Population: Adults

Purpose: Used to build more productive teaming

Description: The instrument identifies team members' personality types, determines the mix of types in a team, explores decisions made by different types of personality mixes, helps teams overcome poor decision making caused by personality conflicts, and suggests kinds of tasks each team member should be assigned based on personality.

Format: Self-administered; untimed: 15 to 20 minutes

Scoring: Hand key

Cost: $6.95 each

Our Team

1993	Clark Wilson Group

Population: Work groups and intact teams

Purpose: Measures how closely the member's individual evaluation agrees with the average of the other members' evaluations

Description: Using 71 questions with three open-ended questions, assesses the self-management processes of the team as a unit. Also available in Spanish and Portuguese, and on-line.

Format: Self-administered; untimed

Scoring: Scoring service

Cost: $260 up to 15 surveys

Project Leadership Practices

1995	Clark Wilson Group

Population: Project manager, project leaders

Purpose: Identifies the skills that are important for overall project effectiveness

Description: Contains 90 questions with three open-ended questions that will help the project leader be more effective in directing team efforts. Available on-line.

Format: Self-administered; untimed

Scoring: Scoring service

Cost: $260 up to 15 surveys

Team & Workgroup Series "360" Feedback
Clark L. Wilson

Updated yearly	Clark Wilson Group

Population: Adults

Purpose: Measures effectiveness and visibility

Description: The key skills measured include Moving Toward Self Management, Your Value as a Team Member, Staying Focused on Strategy, and Maintaining the Commitment to Quality. Team and workgroup members confidentially rate the group's performance. Members also invite ratings from other groups and individuals who know their work. Results are compared to a national database and reviewed with the group by a trained human resources professional who helps the group plan positive changes.

Format: Survey; untimed

Scoring: Self-scored; computer scored; scoring service available; surveys available on-line

Cost: Contact publisher

Team Leadership Practices Inventory
James M. Kouzes, Barry Z. Posner

1992	Jossey-Bass/Pfeiffer

Population: All types of work teams

Purpose: Helps identify leadership practices currently used within the team, helps identify areas for enhancing and improving leadership practices within the team, and creates action plans for becoming a more effective team through enhanced leadership

Description: Thirty-item questionnaire designed to be used by every team member. The accompanying guidebook includes instructions for scoring, comparing scores from each team member, and interpreting scores, as well as worksheets for creating team action plans and keeping commitments.

Format: Self-administered; untimed: 2 to 4 hours

Scoring: Facilitator scored

Cost: Facilitators' Guide $24.95; Workbook $5.95

Team Skills—Form A-C
Roland T. Ramsay

1998	Ramsay Corporation

Population: Adults

Purpose: Measures team building knowledge and skills

Description: This 35-item multiple-choice test measures seven categories, including conflict resolution, group dynamics, team decision making, productivity and motivation, communication skills, leader and member skills, and interpersonal skills. Written at an eighth-grade reading level.

Format: Examiner required; suitable for group use; untimed: 60 minutes

Scoring: Self-scored

Cost: Test Booklet $10.00 (minimum of 20); Administration Manual $24.95

Teamwork-KSA Test
Michael J. Stevens, Michael A. Campion

1995	NCS Pearson Reid London House

Population: Adults

Purpose: Assesses individuals who work well in a team-oriented work environment

Description: Multiple-choice 35-item test measures the essential knowledge skills and abilities that individuals must have to work effectively in teams. Three interpersonal skill areas (conflict resolution skills, collaborative problem-solving skills, and interpersonal communicative skills) and two self-management areas (team goal setting and performance management, and team planning and task coordination) are measured.

Format: Examiner required; suitable for group use; untimed: 30 to 40 minutes

Scoring: Hand key; computer scored

Cost: Contact publisher

Work Environment

Business Culture and Climate Survey

2000	Performance Programs, Inc.

Population: Adults

Purpose: Measures how employees feel about the practices and values of an organization

Description: This 75-question survey reflects the topics requested most since 1987. The first 70 questionnaire items are standardized. The site chooses the last five questions. Up to five categories may be selected for reporting.

Format: Paper–pencil; on-line administration

Scoring: Scoring service available

Cost: Contact publisher

Employee Opinion Survey

2000	Performance Programs, Inc.

Population: Adults

Purpose: Measures a broad range of employee-organizational issues

Description: With 65 standardized questionnaire items, the following topics are measured: commitment, satisfaction, communications, jobs, organization's culture, and organizational leadership. In addition, up to five customized questions and two open-ended questions can be added.

Format: Paper–pencil; on-line administration

Scoring: Scoring service available

Cost: Contact publisher

Employee-Management Relations Survey

| 2001 | Performance Programs, Inc. |

Population: Adults

Purpose: Measures overall opinions and feelings toward management at a company

Description: This survey helps diagnose improvement opportunities so they can be addressed through training, structure, communications, and other interventions. The 45 questions reflect the topics most requested. The first 40 questionnaire items are standardized, and the last 5 are chosen by the site.

Format: Paper-pencil; on-line administration

Scoring: Scoring service available

Cost: Contact publisher

Innovation at the Workplace Inventory (IWI)
Debra L. Jacobs

| Date not provided | SPECTRA Inc. |

Population: Adults

Purpose: Identifies helps and detriments to innovation

Description: This survey can be used by any population to identify the kinds of behaviors, symbols, reinforcers, and practices that promote or detract from innovative outcomes. Useful in prioritizing changes in human resource programs, training content, and continuous improvement initiatives.

Format: Self-administered; untimed

Scoring: Self-scored

Cost: $250.00 (bundles of 50)

Oliver Organization Description Questionnaire (OODQ)
John E. Oliver

| 1981 | Organizational Measurement Systems Press |

Population: Adults

Purpose: Evaluates the organizational form of a particular organization

Description: Multiple-item paper-pencil questionnaire measuring the extent to which four organizational forms exist within a particular organization. The forms are hierarchic (bureaucratic), professional (specialized), task (entrepreneurial), and group (sociotechnical). The scoring guide discusses the form of the instrument, the four domains, scoring, potential uses of the scores, development of the instrument, interpretation of individual scores, and interpretation of organization scores.

Format: Examiner required; suitable for group use; untimed

Scoring: Examiner evaluated

Cost: 50 Questionnaires $30.00; Scoring Guide $5.00

Productivity Environmental Preference Survey (PEPS)
Rita Dunn, Kenneth Dunn, Gary E. Price

| 1995 | Price Systems, Inc. |

Population: Adults

Purpose: Assesses the manner in which adults prefer to function, learn, concentrate, and perform in their occupational or educational activities; used for employee placement, counseling, and office design and layout

Description: Paper-pencil or computer-administered 100-item Likert-scale inventory measuring the following environmental factors related to educational or occupational activities: immediate environment (sound, temperature, light, and design), emotionality (motivation, responsibility, persistence, and structure), sociological needs (self-oriented, peer-oriented, authority-oriented, and combined ways), and physical needs (perceptual preferences, time of day, intake, and mobility). Test items consist of statements about the ways people like to work or study. Respondents are asked to indicate whether they agree or disagree with each statement.

Format: Self-administered; untimed: 20 to 30 minutes

Scoring: Computer scored

Cost: Specimen Set (manual, answer sheet) $11.00; Diskette (100 administrations per licensing agreement) $295.00; each 100 additional administrations $60.00; NCS Scanner Program $395.00; 100 Answer Sheets for NCS Scanner Program $60.00

Work Environment Scale (WES)
Rudolf H. Moos

| Date not provided | Consulting Psychologists Press, Inc. |

Population: Adults

Purpose: Evaluates the social climate of work units; used to assess correlates of productivity, worker satisfaction, quality assurance programs, work stressors, individual adaptation, and supervisory methods

Description: Paper-pencil 90-item measure of 10 dimensions of work social environments: involvement, peer cohesion, supervisor support, autonomy, task orientation, work pressure, clarity, control, innovation, and physical comfort. These dimensions are grouped into three sets: relationships, personal growth, and system maintenance and change. Three forms are available: the Real Form (Form R), which measures perceptions of existing work environments; the Ideal Form (Form I), which measures conceptions of ideal work environments; and the Expectations Form (Form E), which measures expectations about work settings. Forms I and E are not published, although items and instructions will be provided upon request.

Format: Examiner required; suitable for group use; untimed: 20 minutes

Scoring: Hand key; computer scoring service available

Cost: Preview Kit $63.00; Self-Scored Preview Kit $13.20

Indexes

Index of Publishers

Ablin Press Distributors
700 John Ringling Boulevard #1603
Sarasota, FL 34236-1504
941/361-7521; FAX 941/361-7521

Academic Communication Associates
4149 Avenida de la Plata
Oceanside, CA 92052-4279
760/758-1604; FAX 760/758-9593
www.acadom.com

Academic Therapy Publications
20 Commercial Boulevard
Novato, CA 94949-6191
800/422-7249; FAX 415/883-3720
www.ATP-HIGHNOONBOOKS.com

Accrediting Association of Bible Colleges
PO Box 780339
Orlando, FL 32878
407/207-0808; FAX 407/207-0840
www.aabc.org

ACT, Inc.
PO Box 168
2255 North Dubuque Road
Iowa City, IA 52243-0168
800/498-6065; FAX 319/337-1598
www.act.org

ADECCA Educational Alternatives
1217 Ironwood Drive
Fairborn, OH 45324
937/754-0139; FAX 937/829-2729

American Association for Active Lifestyles and Fitness
1900 Association Drive
Reston, VA 22091
800/321-0789; FAX 301/567-9553
www.aahperd.org/aaalf/aaaf.htm

American Association of Teachers of German
112 Haddontowne Court #104
Cherry Hill, NJ 08034
856/795-5553; FAX 856/795-9398
www.aatg.org

American Dental Association
211 East Chicago Avenue
Chicago, IL 60611
312/440-7465
www.ada.org/prof/ed/testing/dat.asp

American Guidance Service
4201 Woodland Road
Circle Pines, MN 55014-1796
800/328-2560; FAX 800/471-8457
www.agsnet.com

American Occupational Therapy Association, Inc.
4720 Montgomery Lane
Bethesda, MD 20814-3425
888/466-8878; FAX 301/652-7711
www.aota.org

Andrews University Press
213 Information Services Building
Berrien Springs, MI 49104-1700
616/471-3435; FAX 616/471-6224
www.andrewsuniversitypress.com

Applied Personnel Research
27 Judith Road
Newton, MA 02459-1715
617/244-8859; FAX 617/244-8904
www.personnelselection.com

Assessment-Intervention Resources
6 North Mount Vernon Drive
Iowa City, IA 52245
www.assessment-intervention.com

Assessment Resource Center
University of Missouri
100 Townsend Hall
Columbia, MO 65211
314/882-4694; FAX 314/882-8937
www.arc.missouri.edu

Assessment Systems Corporation
2233 University Avenue, Suite 200
St. Paul, MN 55114-1629
651/647-9220; FAX 651/647-0412
www.assess.com

Associated Consultants in Education
124 East Amite Street
Jackson, MS 39201
800/748-9073; FAX 601/924-6378
www.msmall.com/best

ASVAB Career Exploration
800/323-0513
www.dmdc.osd.mil/asvab/CareerExploration
Program/signup.html

Australian Council for Educational Research Limited
19 Prospect Hill Road
Private Bag 55
Camberwell, Victoria 3124 Australia
3 9835 7441; FAX 3 9835 7499
www.acerpress.com.au

Ball Foundation
800 Roosevelt Road C-120
Glen Ellyn, IL 60137
630/469-6270; FAX 630/469-6279
www.ballfoundation.org

Donna Bardis
2533 Orkney Drive
Toledo, OH 43606
419/535-6146; FAX 419/535-6146

James Battle and Associates, Ltd.
10240 124th Street #500
Edmonton, Alberta T5N 3W6 Canada
780/488-1362; FAX 780/482-3332
www.jamesbattle.com

Behavior Data Systems, Ltd.
PO Box 44256
Phoenix, AZ 85064-4256
602/234-2888; FAX 602/266-8227
www.bdsltd.com

Behavior Science Systems, Inc.
PO Box 580274
Minneapolis, MN 55458
612/929-6220; FAX 612/920-4925

Behavioral–Developmental Initiatives
14636 North 55th Street
Scottsdale, AZ 85254
800/405-2313; FAX 602/494-2688
www.b-di.com

Ber-Sil Company
3412 Seaglen Drive
Rancho Palos Verdes, CA 90275
310/541-1074

Bowling Green State University
Department of Psychology
Bowling Green, OH 43403
419/372-8247; FAX 419/372-6013
www.bgs.edu/departments/psych/JDI

Brain Train
727 Twin Ridge Lane
Richmond, VA 23235
804/320-0105; FAX 804/320-0242
www.braintrain.com

Brandt Management Group
5909F Willow Oaks Drive
Richmond, VA 23225
804/232-6121
www.vcu.org

Brigham Young University
Foreign Language Testing
3060 JKHB
Provo, UT 84602
801/378-3511; FAX 801/378-4649

Paul H. Brookes Publishing Company, Inc.
PO Box 10624
Baltimore, MD 21285-0624
800/638-3775; FAX 410/337-8539
www.brookespublishing.com

Brougham Press
PO Box 2702
Olathe, KS 66063-0702
913/782-5179; FAX 913/782-1116
www.workingmagic.com

Martin M. Bruce, PhD
22516 Caravelle Circle
Boca Raton, FL 33433
561/393-2428; FAX 561/362-6185

Arnold R. Bruhn, Publisher
7910 Woodmont Avenue, Suite 1300
Bethesda, MD 20814
301/654-2255; FAX 301/718-4945
www.arbruhn.com

C.P.S., Inc.
PO Box 83
Larchmont, NY 10538
914/833-1633; FAX 914/833-1633

California Academic Press
217 La Cruz Avenue
Milbrae, CA 94030
650/697-5628; FAX 650/697-5628
www.calpress.com

Camelot Unlimited
5757 North Sheridan Road, Suite 13B
Chicago, IL 60660
773/506-6285; FAX 508/519-8187

Canadian Test Centre
Educational Assessment Services
85 Citizen Court, Suites 7 & 8
Markham, Ontario L6G 1A8 Canada
800/668-1006; FAX 905/513-6639
www.canadiantestcentre.com

Career Research & Testing, Inc.
2081-F Bering Drive
San Jose, CA 95131
408/441-9100; FAX 408/441-9101
www.careertrainer.com

Carousel House
212 Aguello Boulevard
San Francisco, CA 94118
800/526-4824; FAX 415/777-9832
www.carousehouse.com

Center for Applied Linguistics
4646 40th Street NW
Washington, DC 20016-1859
202/362-0700; FAX 202/362-3740
www.cal.org

Center for Management Effectiveness
PO Box 1202
Pacific Palisades, CA 90272
310/459-6052; FAX 310/459-9307
www.tools4trainers.com

Center for Rehabilitation Effectiveness
Trustees of Boston University
635 Commonwealth Avenue
Boston, MA 02215
617/358-1593; FAX 617/358-1355
www.bu.edu/cre/index.html

Center for the Study of Aging and Human Development
Duke University Medical Center
PO Box 3203
Durham, NC 27710
919/660-7530; FAX 919/684-8569
www.geri.duke.edu

Center for the Study of Ethical Development
206 A Burton Hall
178 Pillsbury Drive SE
Minneapolis, MN 55455
612/624-0876; FAX 612/624-824
www.education.umn.edu/csed/

Center for the Study of Higher Education
The University of Memphis
Memphis, TN 38152
901/678-2775; FAX 901/678-4291
www.memphis.edu/~coe_cshe/CCSEQ_main.htm

Central Institute for the Deaf Publications
4560 Clayton Avenue
St. Louis, MO 63110
877/444-4574; FAX 314/977-0016
www.cid.wustl.edu

Central Wisconsin Center for
the Developmentally Disabled
317 Knuston Drive
Madison, WI 53704
608/243-2232; FAX 608/243-2115

CFKR Career Materials
11860 Kemper Road, Unit 7
Auburn, CA 95603
800/525-5626; FAX 800/770-0433
www.CFKR.com

Checkmate Plus, Ltd.
PO Box 696
Stony Brook, NY 11790-0696
800/779-4292; FAX 516/360-3432
www.checkmateplus.com

Chronicle Guidance Publications, Inc.
66 Aurora Street
Moravia, NY 13118-3576
800/622-7284; FAX 315/497-3359
www.ChronicleGuidance.com

Clark Wilson Group Performance Programs, Inc.
20 Research Parkway
Old Saybrook, CT 06475
800/565-4223; FAX 860/388-6862
www.PerformancePrograms.com

CogniSyst, Inc.
3937 Nottaway Road
Durham, NC 27707
800/799-4654; FAX 919/489-0607
www.cognisyst.com

College Board
45 Columbus Avenue
New York, NY 10023-6992
212/713-8193; FAX 212/713-8063
www.collegeboard.com

Comprehensive Adult Student
Assessment System (CASAS)
5151 Murphy Canyon Road, Suite 220
San Diego, CA 92123
800/255-1036; FAX 858/292-2910
www.casas.org

Consulting Psychologists Press, Inc.
PO Box 10096
3803 East Bayshore Road
Palo Alto, CA 94303
800/624-1765; FAX 415/969-8608
www.cpp-db.com

Consulting Resource Group International, Inc.
200 West Third Street #386
Sumas, WA 98295-8000
604/852-0566; FAX 604/850-3003
www.crgleader.com

Creative Learning Press, Inc.
PO Box 320
Mansfield Center, CT 06250
888/518-8004; FAX 860/429-7783
www.creativelearningpress.com

Critical Thinking Books & Software
PO Box 448
Pacific Grove, CA 93950
800/458-4849; FAX 831/393-3277
www.criticalthinking.com

CTB/McGraw-Hill
20 Ryan Ranch Road
Monterey, CA 93940
800/538-9547; FAX 800/282-0266
www.ctb.com

Curriculum Associates, Inc.
PO Box 2001
North Billerica, MA 01862-0901
800/225-0248; FAX 800/366-1158
www.curriculumassociates.com

Dallas Educational Services
PO Box 833114
Richardson, TX 75083-3114
281/234-6371; FAX 281/498-6531

Dansk psykologisk Forlag
Stockholmsgade 29DK-2100
Copenhagen 0 Denmark
45 3538 1655; FAX 45 3538 1665
www.dpf.dk

Denver Developmental Materials, Inc.
PO Box 371075
Denver, CO 80237-5075
800/419-4729; FAX 303/355-5622

Development Associates, Inc.
1730 North Lynn Street
Arlington, VA 22209-2023
703/276-0677; FAX 703/276-0432
www.devassocl.com

Developmental Therapy Institute, Inc.
PO Box 5153
Athens, GA 30604-5153
706/543-6281; FAX 706/548-5795
www.uga.edu/dttp

Ed & Psych Associates
2071 South Atherton Street, PMB 900
State College, PA 16801
814/235-9115; FAX 814/235-9115

EdITS/Educational and Industrial Testing Service
PO Box 7234
San Diego, CA 92107
800/416-1666; FAX 619/226-1666
www.edits.net

Education Associates, Inc.
8 Crab Orchard Road
Frankfort, KY 40601
502/227-4783; FAX 502/227-8608
www.educationassociates.com

Educational Activities, Inc.
1937 Grand Avenue
Baldwin, NY 11520
800/645-3739; FAX 516/623-9282
www.edact.com

Educational Assessment Service, Inc.
W6050 Apple Road
Watertown, WI 53098
800/795-7466; FAX 414/261-6622
www.sylviarimm.com

Educational Testing Service
PO Box 6736
Rosedale Road
Princeton, NJ 08541-6736
609/921-9000; FAX 609/734-5410
www.ets.org

Educators Publishing Service, Inc.
31 Smith Place
Cambridge, MA 02138-1000
800/435-7728; FAX 617/547-0412
www.epsbooks.com

Elbern Publications
PO Box 09497
Columbus, OH 43209
614/235-2643; FAX 614/237-2637

Ellsworth & Vandermeer Press, Ltd.
PO Box 68164
Nashville, TN 37206
615/226-4460; FAX 615/227-0411
www.pedstest.com

Meryl E. Englander
3508 William Court
Bloomington, IN 47401
812/336-2746

English Language Institute Test Publications
University of Michigan
3020 North University Building
Ann Arbor, MI 48109-1057
734/764-2416 ext. 3; FAX 734/763-0369
www.lsa.umich.edu/eli

Enhanced Performance Systems, Inc.
1010 University Avenue, Suite 265
San Diego, CA 92103
619/497-0516; FAX 619/497-0820
www.enhanced-performance.com

First2Learn
3131 Elliott Avenue, Suite 740
Seattle, WA 98121
206/283-8144; FAX 206/283-0844
www.first2learn.com

GIA Publications, Inc.
7404 South Mason Avenue
Chicago, IL 60638
708/496-3800; FAX 708/496-3828
www.giamusic.com

Gordon Systems, Inc.
PO Box 746
DeWitt, NY 13214
800/550-2343; FAX 315/446-2010
www.gsi-add.com

Guilford Publications, Inc.
Department 5X
72 Spring Street
New York, NY 10012
800/365-7006; FAX 212/966-6708
www.GUILFORD.com

H & H Publishing Company
1231 Kapp Drive
Clearwater, FL 33765
800/366-4079; FAX 727/442-2195
www.hhpublishing.com

Harcourt Brace Educational Measurement
19500 Bulverde Road
San Antonio, TX 78259
800/211-8378; FAX 800/232-1223
www.hemweb.com

Hawthorne Educational Services, Inc.
800 Gray Oak Drive
Columbia, MO 65201
800/542-1673; FAX 800/442-9509

Hay Group
116 Huntington Avenue
Boston, MA 02116
800/729-8074; FAX 617/927-5060
www.trgmcber.haygroup.com

Heinemann
PO Box 5007
Westport, CT 06881-5007
800/541-2086; FAX 800/847-0938
www.heinemann.com

High/Scope Educational Research Foundation
600 North River Street
Ypsilanti, MI 48198-2898
734/485-2000; FAX 734/485-4467
www.highscope.org

Hilson Research, Inc.
PO Box 150239
82-28 Abingdon Road
Kew Gardens, NY 11415-0239
800/926-2258; FAX 718/849-6238
www.HilsonResearch.com

Joseph A. Hirsch, PhD, PsyD
55 Perry Street #4D
New York, NY 10014-3278
212/807-6530

Hogan Assessment Systems, Inc.
PO Box 521176
2622 East 21st Street, Suite 14
Tulsa, OK 74152
800/756-0632; FAX 918/749-2337
www.hoganassessments.com

Hogrefe & Huber Publishers
PO Box 2487
Kirkland, WA 98083
800/228-3749; FAX 425/823-8324
www.hhpub.com

Industrial Psychology International Ltd.
4106 Fieldstone Road
Champaign, IL 61821
217/398-1437; FAX 217/398-5798
www.metritech.com

InQ Educational Materials, Inc.
640 Davis Street, Suite 28
San Francisco, CA 94111-1949
800/338-2462; FAX 415/434-8602
www.iNQ-hpa.com

Institute for Personality and Ability Testing, Inc.
PO Box 1188
Champaign, IL 61824-1188
217/352-4739; FAX 217/352-9674
www.IPAT.com

Institute of Psychological Research, Inc.
34 Fleury Street West
Montreal, Quebec H3L 1S9 Canada
514/382-3000; FAX 514/382-3007

International Personnel Management Association
1617 Duke Street
Alexandria, VA 22314
800/381-8378; FAX 703/684-0948
www.ipma-hr.org

International Society for General Semantics
PO Box 728
Concord, CA 94522
925/798-0311; FAX 925/798-0312
www.generalsemantics.org

International Training Consultants, Inc.
PO Box 35613
9400 Midlothian Turnpike
Richmond, VA 23235
804/320-2415; FAX 804/320-4108
www.trainingitc.com

Janelle Publications, Inc.
PO Box 811
1189 Twombley Road
DeKalb, IL 60115-0811
800/888-8834; FAX 719/685-1999
www.janellepublications.com

JIST Publishing
8902 Otis Avenue
Indianapolis, IN 46216-1033
800/648-5478; FAX 317/264-3709
www.jist.com

Jossey-Bass/Pfeiffer
989 Market Street, 5th Floor
San Francisco, CA 94104
800/569-0443
www.pfeiffer.com

Kaplan Press
1310 Lewisville-Clemmons Road
Lewisville, NC 27023
800/334-2014; FAX 800/452-7526
www.kaplanco.com

Key Education, Inc.
229 Newman Springs Road
Tinton Falls, NJ 07724
800/255-3827; FAX 732/747-1130
www.kevas.com

Kindergarten Interventions and Diagnostic Services, Inc.
825 Sandpiper Street
Denton, TX 76205
800/594-4649
www.kindinc.com

Donald L. Kirkpatrick, PhD
3137 Citadel Court
Indianapolis, IN 46268
317/334-9652; FAX 414/797-3276
www.management-inventories.com

Life Advance, Inc.
81 Front Street
Nyack, NY 10960
845/353-2020; FAX 845/358-2651

Life Innovations, Inc.
PO Box 190
St. Paul, MN 55440-0190
651/635-0511; FAX 651/635-0716
www.lifeinnovation.com

Life Office Management Association
2300 Windy Ridge Parkway #600
Atlanta, GA 30339
770/984-6450; FAX 770/984-3758
www.loma.org

LIMRA International
PO Box 208
300 Day Hill Road
Windsor, CT 06095
860/298-3901; FAX 860/298-9555
www.limra.com

LinguiSystems, Inc.
PO Box 747
East Moline, IL 61244
800/255-8463; FAX 309/755-2377
www.linguisystems.com

Lippincott Williams & Wilkins
351 West Camden Street
Baltimore, MD 21201
410/528-4036; FAX 410/528-5897

Massachusetts School of Professional Psychology
221 Rivermoor Street
Boston, MA 02132-4905
617/327-6777; FAX 617/327-4447
www.mspp.edu

Kenneth M. Matthews, EdD
355 University Circle
Athens, GA 30605
706/353-7090; FAX 706/353-2737

McCarron-Dial Systems
PO Box 45628
Dallas, TX 75245
214/634-2863; FAX 214/634-9970
www.mccarrondial.com

McGraw-Hill Companies, Educational
& Professional Publishing Group
860 Taylor Station Road
Bluelick, OH 43004
800/338-3987; FAX 614/755-5654
www.mhhe.com

Albert Mehrabian, PhD
1130 Alta Mesa Road
Monterey, CA 93940
831/649-5710
www.kaaj.com/psych/scales/

MetriTech, Inc.
4106 Fieldstone Road
Champaign, IL 61821
217/398-4868; FAX 217/398-5798
www.metritech.com

Miller & Tyler, Ltd.
Psychological Assessment and Counseling
96 Greenway
London N20 8EJ UK
20-8445-7463; FAX 20-8445-0143

Mind Garden, Inc.
1690 Woodside Road, Suite 202
Redwood City, CA 94061
650/261-3500; FAX 650/261-3505
www.mindgarden.com

Model of Human Occupation Clearinghouse
University of Illinois–Chicago
312/413-7469; FAX 312/413-0256
www.uic.edu/ahs/OT/MOHOC

Modern Learning Press, Inc.
PO Box 167
Rosemont, NJ 08556
800/627-5867; FAX 888/558-7350
www.modlearn.com

Moreno Educational Company
PO Box 19329
San Diego, CA 92159
619/461-0565; FAX 619/469-1073
www.members.home.net/stevemoreno

James H. Morrison
10932 Rosehill
Overland Park, KS 66210
913/339-6670

Moving Boundaries
1375 Southwest Blaine Court
Gresham, OR 97080
888/661-4433; FAX 503/661-5304
www.movingboundaries.com

Multi-Health Systems, Inc.
PO Box 950
North Tonawanda, NY 14120-0950
800/456-3003; FAX 888/540-4487
www.mhs.com

National Occupational Competency Testing Institute
500 North Bronson
Big Rapids, MI 49307
800/334-6283; FAX 231/796-4699
www.nocti.org

National Reading Styles Institute, Inc.
PO Box 737
179 Lafayette Drive
Syosset, NY 11791
800/331-3117; FAX 516/921-5591
www.nrsi.com

National Spanish Exam
2051 Mount Zion Drive
Golden, CO 80401-1737
303/278-1021; FAX 303/278-6400
www.aatsp.org

National Study of School Evaluation
1699 East Woodfield Road #406
Schaumburg, IL 60173
847/995-9080; FAX 847/995-9088
www.nsse.org

NCS Pearson
5605 Green Circle Drive
Minnetonka, MN 55343
952/939-5000; FAX 952/939-5099
www.ncspearson.com

NCS Pearson Reid London House
9701 West Higgins Road
Rosemont, IL 60018-4720
800/221-8378; FAX 847/292-3400
www.ncspearson.com

Nelson Thomson Learning
1120 Birchmount Road
Scarborough, Ontario M1K 5G4 Canada
800/914-7776; FAX 416/752-9646
www.assess.nelson.com

New Zealand Council for Educational Research
Education House West
178-182 Willis Street, Box 3237
Wellington 6000 New Zealand
64-4-802-1448; FAX 64-4-384-7933
www.nzcer.org.nz

Nichols and Molinder Assessments
437 Bowes Drive
Tacoma, WA 98466-7047
253/565-4539; FAX 253/565-0164
www.nicholsandmolinder.com

Norland Software
PO Box 84499
Los Angeles, CA 90073-0499
310/825-9689; FAX 310/202-9431
www.calcaprt.com

Northwest Publications
710 Watson Drive
Natchitoches, LA 71457
318/352-5313

Nova Media, Inc.
1724 North State
Big Rapids, MI 49307
231/796-7539; FAX 231/796-0486
www.nov.com

Occupational Research Centre
Highlands
Gravel Path
Berkhamsted, Hertfordshire HP4 2PQ UK
44 1442-871 200; FAX 44 1442-871 200
www.kaicentre.com

Omnia Group, Incorporated
601 South Boulevard, 4th Floor
Tampa, FL 33606-2629
800/525-7117; FAX 813/254-8558
www.omniagroup.com

Organizational Measurement Systems Press
PO Box 70586
34199 Country View Drive
Eugene, OR 97401
541/484-2715; FAX 541/465-1602

Pain Assessment Resources
3312 South McCarran Boulevard #309
Reno, NV 89502
800/782-1501; FAX 775/857-4344
www.painassessmentresources.com

Pain Resource Center
PO Box 2836
1314 Broad Street
Durham, NC 27715
800/542-7246; FAX 919/286-4506

PAQ Services, Inc.
Data Processing Division
1625 North 1000 East
Logan, UT 84321
435/752-5698; FAX 435/752-5712
www.paq.com

Pearson Learning/Modern Curriculum Press
4350 Equity Drive
Columbus, OH 43216
800/876-5507; FAX 877/940-2300
www.pearsonlearning.com

Penn State Gerontology Center
College of Health and Human Development
105 Henderson Building South
University Park, PA 16802-6500
814/865-1710; FAX 814/863-9423
http://geron.psu.edu

Performance Programs, Inc.
Clark Wilson Group
PO Box 630
Old Saybrook, CT 06475
860/388-9777; FAX 860/388-6862
www.performanceprograms.com

Personal Strengths Publishing
PO Box 2605
Carlsbad, CA 92018-2605
800/624-7347; FAX 760/730-7368
www.PersonalStrengths.com

Personnel Decisions International
2000 Plaza VII Tower
45 South Seventh Street
Minneapolis, MN 55402-1608
800/633-4410; FAX 612/339-8292
www.personneldecisions.com

PESCO International
21 Paulding Street
Pleasantville, NY 10570
800/431-2016; FAX 914/769-2970
www.pesco.org

I. Pilowsky
University of Adelaide
Department of Psychiatry
Royal Adelaide Hospital
Adelaide 0001 South Australia

Piney Mountain Press, Inc.
PO Box 333
Cleveland, GA 30528
800/255-3127; FAX 800/905-3127
www.pineymountain.com

Pinkerton Services Group
6100 Fairview Road, Suite 900
Charlotte, NC 28210-3277
800/528-5745; FAX 704/554-1806
www.psg-pinkerton.com

Price Systems, Inc.
1714 East 700 Road
Lawrence, KS 66049
913/843-7892; FAX 913/843-0101
www.learningstyle.com

PRO-ED, Inc.
8700 Shoal Creek Boulevard
Austin, TX 78757
800/897-3202; FAX 512/451-8542
www.proedinc.com

Program Development Associates
PO Box 2038
Syracuse, NY 13220-2038
800/543-2119; FAX 315/452-0710
www.PDAssoc.com

Prufrock Press, Inc.
PO Box 8813
Waco, TX 76714-8813
800/998-2208; FAX 800/240-0333
www.prufrock.com

Psychological and Educational Publications, Inc.
PO Box 520
Hydesville, CA 95547-0520
800/523-5775; FAX 800/447-0907

Psychological Assessment Resources, Inc.
PO Box 998
Odessa, FL 33556
800/331-8378; FAX 800/727-9329
www.parinc.com

Psychological Corporation, The
555 Academic Court
San Antonio, TX 78204
800/211-8378; FAX 800/232-1223
www.PsychCorp.com

Psychological Growth Associates, Inc.
Products Division
3813 Tiffany Drive
Lawrence, KS 66049
785/841-1141; FAX 785/749-2190
www.nvo.com/tcs

Psychological Publications, Inc.
PO Box 3577
Thousand Oaks, CA 91359-0577
805/373-7360; FAX 805/373-1573
www.TJTA.com

Psychological Services Bureau, Inc.
PO Box 327
8918 Fort McCord Road
St. Thomas, PA 17252
888/828-9772; FAX 717/369-4222
www.psbtests.com

Psychological Services, Inc.
Test Publication Division
100 West Broadway, Suite 1100
Glendale, CA 91210
800/367-1565; FAX 818/247-3055
www.PSIonline.com

Psychological Test Specialists
PO Box 9229
Missoula, MT 59807
406/728-1702

Psychology Press
Taylor & Francis
325 Chestnut Street, Suite 800
Philadelphia, PA 19106
800/634-7064; FAX 215/625-2940
www.taylorandfrancis.com

Psychology Press, Inc.
PO Box 328
Brandon, VT 05733-0328
800/639-4122; FAX 802/247-8312
www.great-ideas.org

Psychometric Affiliates
PO Box 807
1805 Lexington Trace
Murfreesboro, TN 37133-0807
615/898-2565

Psychometric Software, Inc.
PO Box 1677
2210 South Front Street, Suite 208
Melbourne, FL 32901
800/882-9811; FAX 407/951-9508
www.psipsych.com

Donald K. Pumroy
4006 Oliver Street
Hyattsville, MD 20782-3036
FAX 301/864-8935

Ramsay Corporation
Boyce Station Offices
1050 Boyce Road
Pittsburgh, PA 15241-3907
412/257-0732; FAX 412/257-0732
www.ramsaycorp.com

Rebus, Inc.
PO Box 4479
Ann Arbor, MI 48106-4479
800/435-3085; FAX 734/665-4728
www.rebusinc.com

Research Center for Children, Youth, and Families
University of Vermont
One South Prospect Street
Burlington, VT 05401-3456
802/656-8313; FAX 802/656-2602
www.ASEBA.org

Richmond Products, Inc.
1021 South Rogers Circle, Suite #6
Boca Raton, FL 33487-2894
561/994-2112; FAX 561/994-2235
www.richmondproducts.com

Risk & Needs Assessment, Inc.
  PO Box 32818
  Phoenix, AZ 85064-2818
  800/231-2401; FAX 602/266-8227
  www.riskandneeds.com
Riverside Publishing Company
  435 Spring Lake Drive
  Itasca, IL 60143-2079
  800/323-9540; FAX 630/693-0325
  www.riversidepublishing.com
Rocky Mountain Behavioral Science Institute, Inc.
  419 Canyon Avenue, Suite 316
  Fort Collins, CO 80521
  800/447-6354; FAX 970/221-0595
  www.rmbsi.com
Rohner Research
  255 Codfish Falls Road
  Storrs, CT 06268-1425
  860/429-6217; FAX 860/486-3452
  www.home.earthlink.net/~rohneresearch

SAGE Publications, Inc.
  2455 Teller Road
  Thousand Oaks, CA 09320
  805/499-0721; FAX 805/499-0871
  www.sagepub.com
SASSI Institute
  Route 2, Box 134
  Springville, IN 47462
  800/726-0526; FAX 800/697-2774
  www.sassi.com
Nina G. Schneider, PhD
Nicotine Research Unit
  11301 Wilshire Boulevard, Building 210, 2nd Floor
  Mail Code: 691/B151D
  Los Angeles, CA 90073
  310/312-0564; FAX 310/478-6349
Scholastic Testing Service, Inc.
  480 Meyer Road
  Bensenville, IL 60106-1617
  630/766-7150; FAX 630/766-8054
  www.ststesting.com
SEFA (Publications) Ltd.
  The Globe
  4 Great William Street
  Stratford-upon-Avon, Warwickshire CV37 6RY UK
  43-676-3560142; FAX 43-2236-29554
  www.bjdd.org
Selby MillSmith Ltd.
  30 Circus MewsBath
  Avon BA1 2PW UK
  44-1225-446655; FAX 44-1225-446643
  www.selbymillsmith.com
SELF Research Centre
Faculty of Education
University of Western Sydney
  MacArthur
  PO Box 555
  Campbell Town NSW 2560 Australia
  61-2-9772-6428; FAX 61-2-9772-6432
  http://edweb.uws.edu.au/self/

Sensonics, Inc.
  PO Box 112
  Haddon Heights, NJ 08035
  856/547-7702; FAX 856/547-5665
  www.smelltest.com
SHL Canada
  10 Bay Street, Suite 600
  Toronto, Ontario M5J 2N8 Canada
  416/361-3454; FAX 416/361-1114
Sidran Foundation
  200 East Joppa Road, Suite 207
  Twoson, MD 21286-3107
  410/825-8888; FAX 410/337-0747
  www.sidran.org
Sigma Assessment Systems, Inc.
  PO Box 610984
  1110 Military Street
  Port Huron, MI 48061-0984
  800/265-1285; FAX 800/361-9411
  www.sigmaassessmentsystems.com
Slosson Educational Publications, Inc.
  PO Box 280
  East Aurora, NY 14052
  888/756-7766; FAX 800/655-3840
  www.slosson.com
Sopris West Educational Services
  PO Box 1809
  Longmont, CO 80502-1809
  800/547-6747; FAX 303/776-5934
  www.sopriswest.com
SPECTRA, Inc.
  PO Box 13591
  New Orleans, LA 70185-3591
  504/831-4440; FAX 504/831-0631
  www.spectraweb.com
Stanard & Associates, Inc.
  309 West Washington Street, Suite 1000
  Chicago, IL 60606
  800/367-6919; FAX 312/573-0218
  www.stanard.com
Stoelting Company
  620 Wheat Lane
  Wood Dale, IL 60191
  630/860-9700; FAX 630/860-9775
  www.stoeltingco.com/tests
Student Development Associates, Inc.
  PMB500
  2351 College Station Road
  Athens, GA 30605-3664
  706/542-1812; FAX 706/542-4130
  www.geocities.com/CollegePark/classroom/3022/
    SDTLA.html

Teachers College Press
Teachers College
Columbia University
  1234 Amsterdam Avenue
  New York, NY 10027
  800/575-6566; FAX 212/678-4149
  www.teacherscollegepress.com

Test Agency, Ltd.
Cray House
Woodlands Road
Henley Oxon RG9 4AE UK
01491-413413; FAX 01491-572249
www.testagency.com

Test Analysis and Development Corporation
2400 Park Lake Drive
Boulder, CO 80301
303/666-8651

Thames Valley Test Company, Ltd.
7-9 The Green
Flempton
Bury St. Edmunds Suffolk IP28 6EL UK
44-1284-728608; FAX 44-1284-728166
www.tvte.com

Touchstone Applied Science Associates, Inc.
PO Box 382
4 Hardscrabble Heights
Brewster, NY 10509
800/800-2598; FAX 914/277-3548
www.tasaliteracy.com

TRT Associates, Inc.
1579 Monroe Drive #F510
Atlanta, GA 30324
404/406-8781
www.mindspring.com/~trtbasis

Trust Tutoring
912 Thayer Avenue, Suite #205
Silver Spring, MD 20910
800/301-3131; FAX 301/589-0733
www.wdn.com/trust

Universal Attention Disorders, Inc.
4281 Katella Avenue #215
Los Alamitos, CA 90720
800/729-2886; FAX 714/229-8782
www.tovatest.com

University of Maryland
3404 Benjamin
College Park, MD 20742
301/405-2801

Valpar International Corporation
PO Box 5767
2450 West Ruthrauff Road, Suite 180
Tucson, AZ 85705
800/633-3321; FAX 262/797-8488
www.Valparint.com

Variety Child Learning Center
47 Humphrey Drive
Syosset, NY 11791
800/933-8779; FAX 516/921-8130
www.vpsw.org

Village Publishing
73 Valley Drive
Furlong, PA 18925
215/794-0202; FAX 215/794-3386
www.custody-vp.com

Vocational Psychology Research
University of Minnesota
N620 Elliot Hall
Minneapolis, MN 55455-0344
612/625-1367; FAX 612/626-0345
www.psych.umn.edu/psylabs/vpr

Vocational Research Institute
1528 Walnut Street, Suite 1502
Philadelphia, PA 19102
800/874-5387; FAX 215/875-0198
www.vri.org

VORT Corporation
PO Box 60132
Palo Alto, CA 94306
888/757-8678; FAX 650/327-0747
www.vort.com

Walden Personnel Testing and Consulting, Inc.
1000-4115 Sherbrooke West
Montreal, Quebec H3Z 1K9 Canada
800/361-4908; FAX 514/989-9934
www.waldentesting.com

Arthur Weider, PhD
552 LaGuardia Place
New York, NY 10012
212/777-7303
www.realsolutions.org/weider.htm

Otto Weininger
Ontario Institute for Studies in Education
University of Toronto
1033 Bay Street, Suite 204
Toronto, Ontario M5S 3A5 Canada
416/929-2348; FAX 416/929-3440

Western Psychological Services
12031 Wilshire Boulevard
Los Angeles, CA 90025-1251
310/478-2061; FAX 310/478-7838
www.wpspublish.com

Wide Range, Inc.
15 Ashley Place, Suite 1A
PO Box 3410
Wilmington, DE 19804-0250
800/221-9728; FAX 302/652-1644
www.widerange.com

Winslow Research Institute
1933 Windward Point
Discovery Bay, CA 94514
925/516-8686; FAX 925/516-7015
www.WinslowResearch.com

Wonderlic Personnel Test, Inc.
1795 North Butterfield Road
Libertyville, IL 60048
800/963-7542; FAX 847/680-9492

World of Work, Inc.
64 East Broadway Road
Tempe, AZ 85282
800/272-9694; FAX 480/966-6200
www.wowi.com

Index of Publishers Not in the Fifth Edition

Addiction Research Foundation; no response

American College Testing; now ACT, Inc. (included)

Bay State Psychological Associates, Inc.; no response

Behaviordyne, Inc.; returned

Brandon House, Inc.; no response

Brink, T. L.; no response

Cambridge Stratford, Ltd.; no response

Centec Learning; no longer in business

Center for Leadership Studies, Inc.; no response

Center for Talented Youth; returned

Center for the Study of Parental Acceptance and Rejection; now Rohner Research (included)

CHECpoint Systems, Inc.; returned

CHES; no response

Clinical Psychometric Research, Inc.; no response

Communication Skill Builders; now published by The Psychological Corporation (included)

DBM Publishing; returned

Defense Manpower Data Center; now ASVAB Career Exploration (included)

Developmental Reading Distributors; returned

Devereux Foundation; now published by Kaplan Press (included)

Dragon Press; no response

Educational & Psychological Consultants, Inc.; returned

Educational Evaluation Enterprises; asked to be deleted

Educational Records Bureau, Inc.; returned

Educators'/Employers' Tests & Services Associates; no response

Exceptional Education; returned

Faculty of Education, Memorial University of Newfoundland; no updated information

Four Oaks Institute; no response

Gough, Harrison G.; now published by C.P.S. and Mind Garden (included)

Harter, Susan; no response

Herrmann International; no response

Human Sciences Center; no response

Human Sciences Research Council; no response

Humanics Psychological Test Corporation; no response

Imaginart International, Inc.; no longer publishing

Institute for the Advancement of Philosophy for Children; no response

Institute of Foundational Training and Development; no response

J-K Screening, no updated information

Kent Developmental Metrics, Inc.; now published by Western Psychological Services (included)

Leach, Glenn C., EdD; no longer publishing

Learnco, Inc.; no updated information

Life Science Associates; no response

Madison VA Geriatric Research, Education, and Clinical Center; no response

Management Strategies, Inc.; returned

Marathon Consulting and Press; no response

McBer and Company, Inc.; now Hay Group (included)

Mentoring Institute, Inc.; no response

Modern Curriculum Press; now Pearson Learning (included)

National League for Nursing; returned

New Standards, Inc.; returned

Optometry Admission Testing Program; no response

Organizational Tests Ltd.; no updated information

Owens, Ned, MEd, Inc.; returned

Phylmar Associates; no response

Predictive Surveys Corporation; no response

Preventive Measures, Inc.; returned

Psychologists and Educators, Inc.; no response

Reid Psychological Systems; returned

Richardson, Bellows, Henry and Company, Inc.; returned

Saville & Holdsworth Ltd.; now SHL Canada (included)

Schmeck, Ronald R., PhD; no response

Search Institute; no response

Select Press; returned

Steck-Vaughn/Berrent Publishing Co.; no response

Swets Test Services; no updated information

Teleometrics International; no updated information

Timao Foundation for Research & Development; no response

Index of Tests Not in the Fifth Edition

Index of Authors

Index of Test Titles

About the Editor

Taddy Maddox joined PRO-ED in 1994 after completing her doctorate in special education at the University of Texas at Austin. Previously she worked as an educational diagnostician in Texas public schools for 15 years. Prior to that, Dr. Maddox was a special education teacher in self-contained and resource settings.

Since joining PRO-ED, Dr. Maddox has worked on the development of many test instruments and is co-author on the *Basic School Skills Instrument* and *Developmental Assessment of Young Children*. She was also the editor of the Fourth Edition of *Tests*. In addition, she has been active in professional organizations as officer and committee member.